QUANTITATIVE HISTORY AND UNCHARTED PEOPLE

QUANTITATIVE HISTORY AND UNCHARTED PEOPLE

CASE STUDIES FROM THE SOUTH AFRICAN PAST

Edited by Johan Fourie

BLOOMSBURY ACADEMIC
LONDON · NEW YORK · OXFORD · NEW DELHI · SYDNEY

BLOOMSBURY ACADEMIC
Bloomsbury Publishing Plc
50 Bedford Square, London, WC1B 3DP, UK
1385 Broadway, New York, NY 10018, USA
29 Earlsfort Terrace, Dublin 2, Ireland

BLOOMSBURY, BLOOMSBURY ACADEMIC and the Diana logo are trademarks of Bloomsbury Publishing Plc

First published in Great Britain 2023

Copyright © Johan Fourie, 2023

Johan Fourie has asserted his right under the Copyright, Designs and Patents Act, 1988, to be identified as Editor of this work.

Cover image: Vulindlela Nyoni, eNdabeni, 2021, Lithograph, 1/5.
Cover design: Graham Robert Ward.

All rights reserved. No part of this publication may be reproduced or transmitted in any form or by any means, electronic or mechanical, including photocopying, recording, or any information storage or retrieval system, without prior permission in writing from the publishers.

Bloomsbury Publishing Plc does not have any control over, or responsibility for, any third-party websites referred to or in this book. All internet addresses given in this book were correct at the time of going to press. The author and publisher regret any inconvenience caused if addresses have changed or sites have ceased to exist, but can accept no responsibility for any such changes.

A catalogue record for this book is available from the British Library.

A catalog record for this book is available from the Library of Congress.

ISBN:	HB:	978-1-3503-3115-0
	PB:	978-1-3503-3114-3
	ePDF:	978-1-3503-3117-4
	eBook:	978-1-3503-3116-7

Typeset by Integra Software Services Pvt. Ltd.

To find out more about our authors and books visit www.bloomsbury.com and sign up for our newsletters.

CONTENTS

List of Figures		vi
List of Tables		ix
Foreword		xi
Preface		xii
Terminology		xiv
1	Quantitative history and uncharted people *Johan Fourie*	1
2	Bridal pregnancy in the Mother City, 1900–60 *Laura Richardson and Jan Kok*	33
3	Sex ratios and girl preference in the Cape, 1894–2011 *Johan Fourie and Francisco Marco-Gracia*	63
4	Khoe households in Swellendam, 1825 *Calumet Links*	91
5	Race reclassification in Cape Town, 1950–84 *Brittany Chalmers, Johan Fourie and Kris Inwood*	117
6	Advertising the enslaved for sale: A quantitative approach to the *Zuid-Afrikaan*, 1830–4 *Wouter Raaijmakers and Kate Ekama*	139
7	Domestic service in Cape Town before the Second World War *Amy Rommelspacher*	169
8	Female investors at the Cape, 1892–1902 *Lloyd Maphosa and Edward Kerby*	195
9	Black Africans in Cape Town, 1890–1939 *Nobungcwele Mbem and Michiel de Haas*	219
10	Political innovation in African Nationalist Organisations, 1880–90 *Jonathan Schoots*	249
11	Petitions to the Cape Parliament, 1854–1909 *Kara Dimitruk and Kelsey Lemon*	285
12	Death during the influenza of 1918 *Jonathan Jayes and Johan Fourie*	317
13	Quantitative history in practice *Johan Fourie*	353
Index		363

FIGURES

1.1	Total publications in four history journals, by year (1956–2019)	19
1.2	Average number of tables per paper, by journal and decade	21
1.3	Proportion of papers with a single author, two authors or three or more authors, by year	23
2.1	Map of the transcribed parishes with circle size indicating the total number of baptisms in the dataset for each parish	40
2.2	Density plot of the number of days elapsed between marriage and the birth of a couple's first child	41
2.3	Pregnancy type by profession of primary breadwinner in absolute numbers	46
3.1	Evolution of under-five sex ratios in South Africa according to race, 1894–2011	67
3.2	Evolution of under-five sex ratios in the Cape according to race, 1894–1960	68
3.3	Country level distribution of under-five sex ratios, 1950 (A), 1980 (B) and 2010 (C).	70
3.4	Under-five sex ratios by ethnic group, 1951–91	78
3.5	Under-five sex ratios for Niger-Congo language countries	81
4.1	Swellendam Khoe population 1825	100
4.2	Swellendam Khoe labour on settler farms 1825	101
4.3	Swellendam Khoe livestock numbers 1825	102
4.4	Khoe crop yields Swellendam 1825	103
4.5	Household structure 1	106
4.6	Household structure 2	107
5.1	The marriage certificate of Mr Barsby and Mrs Barsby (maiden name Moller); first names masked for privacy	125
5.2	Duration of marriage before reclassification, arranged by year of reclassification	126
5.3	Literacy as measured by signatures on marriage certificates	128
6.1	The nameplate of *De Zuid-Afrikaan*	142
6.2	Course of advertisements in *De Zuid-Afrikaan*, Apr. 1830–Nov. 1834, per monthly average, with linear trends	147
6.3	Course of advertisements per category in *De Zuid-Afrikaan*, Apr. 1830–Nov. 1834, per monthly average, with linear trends	147
6.4	Course of advertisements for additional categories in *De Zuid-Afrikaan*, Apr. 1830–Nov. 1834, per monthly average, with linear trends	148

Figures

6.5	Seasonality of advertisements in *De Zuid-Afrikaan*, Dec. 1830–Nov. 1834, per monthly average	152
6.6	Seasonality of advertisements per category in *De Zuid-Afrikaan*, Dec. 1830–Nov. 1834, per monthly average	152
6.7	Seasonality of advertisements in *De Zuid-Afrikaan*, Dec. 1830–Nov. 1834, per monthly average	153
6.8	Occurrences of variables in slave-specific sale advertisements in *De Zuid-Afrikaan*, Apr. 1830–Nov. 1834, per gender	158
7.1	Monthly incomes of white households that did and did not employ domestic workers (n = 498)	179
7.2	Share of different types of white households according to domestic worker employment (n = 153)	180
7.3	Birthplaces of white household heads with and without a domestic worker, that is the employment of domestic workers according to birthplace of white household head	182
7.4	Share of different types of coloured households according to domestic worker employment	183
7.5	Birthplaces of coloured household heads comparing households that did and did not have someone working as a domestic.	190
8.1	Cumulative number of women investors in the Cape capital market, 1892–1902	204
8.2	Annual distribution of women investors at the Cape, 1892–1902	205
8.3	Profile of Cape female investors, 1892–1902	206
8.4	Kin-dependency among Cape women investors in the capital market, 1892–1902	211
8.5	The influence of kin-dependency on the distribution of women's capital value, 1892–1902	213
8.6	Industries financed by women, 1892–1902	214
8.7	Women investors per region at the Cape, 1892–1902	218
8.8	Capital value of women's investments in the Cape capital market broken down in regions, 1892–1902	218
9.1	Location of surveyed households	230
9.2	Migration histories of migrant household heads and wives	233
9.3	Year of migration relative to marriage (sorted by male year of migration relative to marriage), years of separation during marriage (if any) indicated	236
9.4	Occupations observed in the Batson survey and their frequency	240
9.5	Earnings per occupation: average and by gender	241
9.6	Distribution of rent as percentage of household income	242
10.1a	Whole network overview – organisations and members	258
10.1b	Whole network overview – organisations only	259
10.2a	Community detection – organisations and members	261
10.2b	Community detection – organisations only	262

Figures

10.3	Map of the Eastern Frontier of the Cape Colony and adjacent territories	264
10.4	IOTT with members who linked to other organisations	268
10.5	*Imbumba* with members who linked to other organisations	271
10.6	Thembu Association (left) and South African Native Association (right) with members who linked to other organisations	276
11.1	Petitions submitted to the Cape Parliament, 1854–1909	291
11.2a	Social and Economic Petitions, 1854–1909	298
11.2b	Transport and Government Petitions, 1854–1909	298
11.3a	Number of Petition-Issues	299
11.3b	Social Petitions	299
11.3c	Economic Petitions	300
11.4	British Cape Colony, 1879 District Borders	306
12.1	Form of information of the death of Liza Goxo	321
12.2	Map of 1918 flu mortality across South Africa	324
12.3	Heatmap of deaths per week across fifteen districts, 1915–1920	326
12.4	Number of deaths in district by day during pandemic peak, Sep-Dec 1918	327
12.5	Density plot comparing causes of death during the pandemic in Cradock and Paarl	328
12.6	Mortality by week across districts, excluding 1918	330
12.7	Excess mortality based on methodology by Acuña-Soto et al.	333
12.8	Linear trend for predicted and excess mortality	334
12.9	Excess mortality based on ensembled regression methods	335
12.10	Bump chart of district ranking across our three methods or calculating excess morality	336
12.11	Correlation between terms used in cause of death	338
12.12	Comparison of excess mortality estimates, respiratory deaths and government estimates	339
12.13	Infant mortality per 1000 children, with confidence band	340
12.14	Scatterplot and linear fit of infant and pandemic mortality by district	341
12.15	Child mortality per 1000 children by race	342
12.16	Scatterplot and linear fit of pneumonia mortality and pandemic mortality by district	345
12.17	Sketch of local government policies adopted during 'outbreak' week, 14 October to 18 October 1918	348
12.18	Sketch of local government policies removed towards the end of the epidemic, 1 November to 9 November 1918	349

TABLES

1.1	Descriptive statistics of journal papers	20
2.1	Characteristics and general demographic makeup of the transcribed parishes	40
2.2	Pregnancy type by parish, 1900–60, measured in absolute numbers and as a proportion of total number of first births after marriage	41
2.3	Age at marriage by interval between marriage and the birth of the first child for the complete matched dataset	44
2.4	Regression measuring the likelihood of a premarital conception at first marriage of matched Cape Town couples, with a first child baptised between 1900 and 1960	47
2.5	Regression measuring the likelihood of a Sunday baptism of matched Cape Town couples, with a first child baptised between 1900 and 1960	50
3.1	Average sex ratios at birth according to world region and year	69
3.2	OLS regression models on the determinants of under-five sex ratios, 1894–1960	72
3.3	OLS regression models on the determinants of under-five sex ratios, 1890, 1904, 1936, 1946 and 1960 censuses	75
3.4	Simple linear regression relating under-five sex ratios to ethnicity for black South Africans in the 1951, 1960, 1970 and 1991 censuses	77
3.5	Percentage of unmarried men and women at age forty-five by race in the 1911, 1951 and 1991 censuses	82
4.1	Per household wealth levels for Swellendam and frontier districts (in rixdollars)	104
4.2	Settler and Khoe livestock holdings in 1825	104
4.3	Khoe and settler crops planted in 1825	104
4.4	OLS regression Swellendam on wealth per capita	109
4.5	Percentage share of wealth, all households	110
4.6	Percentage share of wealth, with polygamous households	111
5.1	Race reclassification from white to coloured	127
5.2	Changes in occupation	130
5.3	Changes in location	131
6.1	An exhaustive list of adjectives slave owners used to describe slaves and their labour in the *De Zuid-Afrikaan* advertisements, Apr. 1830–Nov. 1834	162
7.1	Types of domestic employees in white households	178
8.1	Descriptive statistics of the capital value contributions for women investors at the Cape, 1892–1902. Values in British Pounds	209

Tables

8.2	The financial contribution of women in the middle-class category, 1892–1902	215
9.1	Black African population of Cape Town, 1865–1939	222
9.2	Categories of household members, sorted by frequency	231
9.3	Duration of current residence in Cape Town at time of survey, by age cohort	234
10.1	Organisations and members included in the analysis	253
11.1	Types of Petitions, 1854–1909	296
11.2	Types of Petitioners	301
11.3	Correlation between Labour Laws, Temperance Laws and Petitions	302
11.4	Language, Number of Signatures and Format	305
11.5	Examples from the First Page of Signatures in Four Petitions	307
12.1	Descriptive statistics of sample from fifteen districts	323
12.2	Comparison of common causes of death in Cradock and Paarl during the pandemic	329
12.3	Excess mortality based on SAMRC method	331
12.4	Excess mortality based on Acuña-Soto, Viboud and Chowell method	332
12.5	Excess mortality based on ensembled regression methods	335
12.6	Association between infant mortality and pandemic mortality	343
12.7	Association between child mortality and pandemic mortality by district	344
12.8	Association between pneumonia and influenza mortality prior to the pandemic and pandemic mortality	346
13.1	First-year history grades by high-school mathematics grade, 2018–21	356

FOREWORD

Historians of South Africa, over the past half-century (and no doubt longer), have been notoriously non-numerate. There are probably no more than a couple of statistics which all of us would be able to produce without hesitation: such as the proportion of the land allotted to black Africans under segregation and apartheid (13 per cent), or the position of South Africa in a global ranking of income inequality as expressed by the Gini coefficient (first). This state of affairs is, to say the least, unfortunate.

There is also a notorious bias in the historical record against black South Africans, in contrast to their white fellow countrymen and -women. It is often very difficult to discover directly what black South Africans thought of the various acts of government or other important matters of social debate. Although the amount of direct testimony that has been discovered is greater than often thought, and continually increasing, almost invariably these statements are only preserved because of the intervention of some white-run institution – editorial policy (for newspapers, mission journals, publishers and so forth), the judicial process (statements in numerous court cases) or something similar. As a result, there is necessarily a filter, or a distorting lens, through which the thought of black South Africans had to pass before it reached the historian of the twenty-first century. Historians have learned, and have been trained, to deal with this problem as best they can. Nevertheless, it remains the case that virtually all the expressions of black South African opinion have to be viewed with a degree of caution, as they have almost all survived because of the intervention of some once white-run institution (which includes the State Archives). And on occasion, black South Africans and others from among the oppressed were quite rationally too afraid to open their mouths. The enslaved of the Cape Colony before emancipation is only the most obvious such group, but there are many others.

There is a way to overcome this difficulty, at least to some extent. Very often, what people in the past thought of the situation in which they found themselves can be deduced from what they did, rather than from what we know of what they said. And what they did only becomes clear when a large enough group is taken into account. Far from being 'dry', which is the way they are stereotypically presented, both by some economists and by some non-quantitative historians, statistics can be evidence of a true expression of the collective consciousness of those whose voices are unheard but whose actions to a large extent created South Africa. The essentially quantitative approaches and research presented in this book make possible an understanding of the past which is, at bottom, profoundly humanistic.

Robert Ross
Professor of African History (emeritus)
Leiden University
The Netherlands

PREFACE

Quantitative sources and methods can add value to history writing. This should be uncontroversial, even to those who question historians' claim to scientific rigour. The particular value that we demonstrate in this book is how these sources and methods can be used to recover the histories of people excluded from conventional archives. Advances in the digitisation, transcription and analyses of large historical datasets can, and must, be used to chart uncharted people, to write new histories from below.

The book is the culmination of a five-year project in the History department at Stellenbosch University. The Biography of an Uncharted People project, generously funded by the Andrew W. Mellon Foundation between 2018 and 2022, had two objectives: to transcribe large quantities of individual or household information, and to give a new generation of history students the tools to analyse and interpret this material. The aim was to use these sources and methods to tell more inclusive stories. South Africa is an ideal testing ground for this approach, firstly because of its history of exclusion and secondly because of its generally excellent preservation of records. The eleven case studies in this edited collection display the diversity of research questions we asked and the sources and methods we used. They show how the authors discovered (and recovered) a richer South African past.

An edited volume is of course a team effort. I want to thank each of the authors who wrote a chapter. Some have had to wait three years to see their work in print; others have had to push against the clock to get it ready in time. But we, the authors, could have done nothing without our foundation of solid support. I thank our transcribers Elizabeth Baldwin, Kudzai Chidamwoyo, Chris de Wit, Martie du Toit, Anneen Fourie, Abel Gwaindepi, Hans Heese, Gustav Hendrich and Helena Liebenberg of the Tracing History Trust, for their countless hours of painstaking work that helped to open up the archives. I thank the scholars Jonathan Jayes, Claire Lemercier, Auke Rijpma and Willem Wilken for their time and effort in providing training workshops for our students. I thank Mike Cruywagen of Nudge Studio for providing superb web support and Philip du Plessis of Blindspot Films for creating documentaries that captured various parts of the project, including an art exhibition that can be viewed at our website www.unchartedpeople.org, along with all the supporting material for this volume. Vulindlela Nyoni, associate professor at Nelson Mandela University, created one of the images for the exhibition. eNdabeni (2021, Lithograph, 1/5) is the result of a collaborative conversation with Nobungcwele Mbem (Chapter 9), depicting the historical migration and displacement of black communities in the Western Cape. I am grateful to Vuli who agreed that eNdabeni could be used as cover artwork.

Preface

In the production of this book, I have relied heavily on my former students Amy Rommelspacher and Kelsey Lemon. Robert Ross has been an avid supporter of the project and provided a thoughtful foreword. Di Kilpert has, as always, made invaluable editorial contributions. In Bloomsbury we found an eager and engaged publisher, and Maddie Holder, Abigail Lane and Megan Harris in particular made thoughtful contributions.

The project has also benefited from the support of several colleagues in other Stellenbosch departments, notably my colleagues in Economics. Local and international scholars, other than the authors of the chapters, contributed as either supervisors or advisors: Emmanuel Akyeampong (Harvard), Keith Breckenridge (Wits), Jeanne Cilliers (Lund), Dan de Kadt (UC Merced), Wayne Dooling (SOAS), Erik Green (Lund), Lindie Koorts (UFS), Claire Lemercier (Sciences Po), Dries Lyna (Nijmegen), Koenraad Matthys (KU Leuven), Anne McCants (MIT), Laura Mitchell (UC Irvine), Khumisho Moguerane (UJ), Tinashe Nyamunda (UP), Laura Phillips (NWU), Auke Rijpma (Utrecht), Hilary Sapire (Birkbeck), Michelle Sikes (Penn State), Christie Swanepoel (UWC), Rebecca Swartz (UFS), Charles van Onselen (UP), Gustav Venter (Stellenbosch) and Joachim Wehner (LSE).

I thank our donors, who enable us to do the things we do, and in particular the Andrew W. Mellon Foundation, who funded the Biography project, and Celia Bradley, our Mellon Foundation liaison in New York.

Finally, I am most indebted to Anton Ehlers, Head of the History department until his retirement in 2021. I thank Anton for motivating me to apply for Mellon funding in 2016 and for championing the project in the History department. Without him, there would have been no project, and no book. We dedicate this book to him.

Dedication:
To Anton Ehlers

TERMINOLOGY

On race terms:

A book about South African history inevitably involves racial classification. An unfortunate reality of the South African archive is its history of racial discrimination. It is well known that successive governments prior to democracy categorised people according to race and applied their conception of race to all areas of a person's life – a fact that the chapters in this collection inevitably reflect. Although race labels can be inflammatory, they are nonetheless part of South Africa's past. We are thus obliged to retain the use of the terms 'black' (or 'African'), 'white' and 'coloured', which remain in common parlance today, and are used in official statistics for consistency with past classification and to measure the progress of change and redress. Some chapters provide more extensive contextualisation of race terminology.

CHAPTER 1
QUANTITATIVE HISTORY AND UNCHARTED PEOPLE
*Johan Fourie**

No archive, and therefore no history, is ever complete. Records of the powerful and privileged are preserved, while documents reflecting the lives of ordinary men and women, particularly the illiterate, the poor and the subjugated, are often missing, lost through dereliction, disaster or decree, or never saved at all. Such omissions in our recorded histories have consequences. Records inform our current identities and ideologies and shape our future. By distorting the past – and our place in it – an incomplete history can be a misleading guide for the future.

Historians have found creative ways to overcome the biases of the conventional archive. Sometimes they use oral testimonies to view history 'from below', the stories of how ordinary men and women shaped and were shaped by history. This can reveal the hidden histories of minority or marginalised groups. But such sources have their pitfalls.

This chapter, and indeed the whole book, makes the case for a different way to remedy the omissions of the archive. The method we use is quantitative history, the application of statistical data to the study of history. New quantitative tools and techniques now enable scholars to analyse information from administrative sources at a fraction of the cost and effort of a few decades ago. While administrative records are often of little interest individually, when combined with hundreds or sometimes even hundreds of thousands of similar records, they become a powerful means to test existing hypotheses and find new avenues to explore.

Quantitative history, I argue, can be especially powerful in South Africa, where large quantities of historical records are preserved but questions of bias and prejudice persist. With statistical tools we can extract information from historical documents and make it tell us far more than could have been imagined by those who collected and preserved it. This allows us to mitigate or condition for the bias. In some cases, it might even allow us to measure the extent of bias.

In this book's eleven research chapters, written by scholars associated with the *Biography of an Uncharted People* project at Stellenbosch University, we hope to

---

*Fourie: Department of Economics, Stellenbosch University, South Africa. I am grateful to Keith Breckenridge, Michiel de Haas, Jan Kok, Robert Ross and Charles van Onselen for their extensive comments on earlier versions of this chapter.

illuminate the ways in which the new tools and techniques can help us question what are taken to be historical truths and reveal new insights. The book is aimed at broadly two audiences: first, a younger generation of historians – from senior undergraduate students to PhDs and postdocs – interested in the opportunities (and pitfalls) that quantitative sources and tools offer. It is for that reason that we have created slides and tutorials for each of the chapters in the book.[1] A second audience is established academic historians (of South Africa) who are interested in finding new digital tools that can help to uncover sources perhaps previously ignored, new research questions to ask from their existing source material, or new techniques for writing histories from below.

We hope not to suffer from the overconfidence of an earlier generation of quantitative historians: we do not say that quantification should displace other methods of historical inquiry. It is, at best, a complementary approach to writing good history. There is much that quantitative sources and tools cannot do. Yet as long as archives have gaps, as long as some people are uncharted, the quantitative approach will be valuable in the quest for completeness of the historical record. And for shaping our identities, ideologies and future.

The rise of quantitative history

We are, of course, not the first to make use of quantitative techniques to study the past, nor the first to make the case for it. With its roots in the *Annales* school, a twentieth-century movement of predominantly French historians, quantitative history flourished from around 1950 to 1980. Peter Burke identifies three phases in the evolution of its interests: first, economic history (investigating prices in France, with the economist Francois Simiand and the historian Ernest Labrousse being the two main proponents), then social history, notably population studies and demography, and finally cultural history.[2]

It was its adoption by economists in the United States that propelled quantitative history forward. They made three telling contributions: the use of quantitative tools, and an enlargement of scale and scope. Although economic historians had long used statistics as supporting evidence, what was new, as explained by Douglas North, who in 1993 shared the Nobel Prize in Economics with Robert Fogel, was the use of quantitative tools to test hypotheses.[3] Rather than just calculating annual price fluctuations, as Simiand, Labrousse and many others had done, Harvard economists Conrad and Meyer used prices – slave prices, to be precise – applied to economic theory to make a causal claim, with counterfactual implications: that US slavery was more profitable than previously

---

[1] See the final chapter for more information.

[2] P. Burke, *The French Historical Revolution: The Annales School, 1929-2014* (Stanford: Stanford University Press, 2015): 60.

[3] D.C. North, 'The New Economic History after Twenty Years', *American Behavioural Scientist* 21, no. 2 (1977): 187–200.

thought, and that it was unlikely to have ended without the Civil War.[4] The objective was to use economic theory to find a general *causal* interpretation of historical events.[5]

Now known as 'cliometricians', the group increased the scale of their analysis.[6] They began to use information available at the individual (farm or household) level, rather than just regional or national averages. This is best exemplified by Fogel and Engerman's *Time on the Cross*, which relied on Parker and Gallman's 1860 Census of Agriculture sample of cotton-belt farms that was made accessible by being converted into machine-readable historical micro-data sets.[7]

Extending their scope, they made telling contributions to fields beyond economic history – even to the domain of policy. Reflecting on Fogel's *Railroads and American Economic Growth*,[8] another seminal contribution, economic historian Barry Eichengreen said that Fogel had argued that technical innovations that were thought indispensable, like the railroad, were not necessarily so, and generalised his findings to a rethinking of US economic policy and even the US space program.[9] The controversial findings of *Time on the Cross* caused a stir both within and far beyond the fields of economics and history.

Although it was the cliometricians who most enthusiastically adopted a more rigorous quantitative approach, quantification was not limited to the field of economic history. In fact, what defined quantitative history was its interdisciplinary nature. The need for history to move beyond the confines of mere narrative had already been apparent much earlier. In 1912 the American historian James Harvey Robinson extolled the virtues of interdisciplinary research, arguing that this 'New History', as he called it, 'will avail itself of all those discoveries that are being made about mankind by anthropologists, economists, psychologists and sociologists'.[10] But it was only in the 1950s, after Fernand Braudel's insistence that history and geography should march in lockstep over the *longue durée*, and in particular the 1960s and 1970s, that an enthusiasm for quantification with explanatory power took off.[11] One example of this was the launch in 1970 of the *Journal*

---

[4] A.H. Conrad, and J.R. Meyer, 'The Economics of Slavery in the Ante Bellum South', *Journal of Political Economy* 66, no. 2 (1958): 95–130.

[5] J.R. Meyer and A.H. Conrad, 'Economic Theory, Statistical Inference, and Economic History', *The Journal of Economic History* 17, no. 4 (1957): 524–44.

[6] 'Cliometrics' combines 'Clio', the muse of history, and 'metrics', as in 'econometrics'. See D.N. McCloskey, 'The Achievements of the Cliometric School', *The Journal of Economic History* 38, no. 1 (1978): 13–28; C. Goldin, 'Cliometrics and the Nobel', *Journal of Economic Perspectives* 9, no. 2 (1995): 191–208. For a more recent overview, see C. Diebolt and M. Haupert, 'Cliometrics: Past, Present, and Future', in *Oxford Research Encyclopedia of Economics and Finance* (Oxford: Oxford University Press, 2021): 19.

[7] R. Fogel and S. Engerman, *Time on the Cross: The Economics of American Negro Slavery* (Boston: Little, Brown and Co., 1974).

[8] R.W. Fogel, *Railroads and American Economic Growth* (Baltimore: Johns Hopkins Press, 1964).

[9] B. Eichengreen, 'The Contributions of Robert W. Fogel to Economics and Economic History', *The Scandinavian Journal of Economics* 96, no. 2 (1994): 167–79.

[10] J.H. Robinson, *The New History: Essays Illustrating the Modern Historical Outlook* (New York: The Macmillan Company, 1912): 24.

[11] F. Braudel, 'Histoire et sciences sociales: la longue durée', *Annales. Histoire, Sciences Sociales* 13, no. 4 (1958): 725–53.

of Interdisciplinary History. In its first issue, the editors announced that: 'Whole new fields, such as historical demography, and entirely new techniques, such as computer data processing, have appeared and have made a broad impact on many areas of research'. In a review of five decades of the journal, Ruggles and Magnuson note that 'quantification was the central defining element of the "new" histories – the new social history, new economic history, and new political theory – that transformed the landscape of historical research in the 1960s and 1970s'.[12]

Social historians began to use probate inventories and marriage and death records and often employed new methods from the social sciences. The Cambridge Group for the History of Population and Social Structure, for example, reconstructed families from vital records to show that English households were more nuclear, more geographically mobile and more likely to marry later.[13] Others used soldiers' heights reported on military attestation forms to measure living standards across time – a field that became known as anthropometric history – or used the signatures on documents (or lack thereof) as a way to measure literacy in the past.[14] Political historians in the United States, unhappy with the lack of empirical rigour in political theory, began to analyse voting patterns, correlating voting outcomes with characteristics like class or religion.[15] By the 1970s, the need to organise these disparate disciplines under one roof resulted in the establishment of the Social Science History Association[16] whose explicit aim was to bring together social scientists who were working with historical materials. Its journal, *Social Science History*, was first published in 1976.

Interdisciplinary work also meant collaboration. Articles or books were generally co-authored, often by three or more authors. This was in contrast to the single-authored publications that were common in the field of history. Research projects also grew in size and scope. Teams of research assistants were often required to process the large quantities of information, initially by hand but later, as computers became more accessible, on punch cards. One welcome advantage of using the methods of the hard sciences was that historians could now apply for grants not usually accessible to the humanities.[17]

---

[12]S. Ruggles and D.L. Magnuson, 'The History of Quantification in History: The JIH as a Case Study', *Journal of Interdisciplinary History* 50, no. 3 (2019): 363–81.

[13]P. Laslett, 'Size and Structure of the Household in England Over Three Centuries', *Population studies* 23, no. 2 (1969): 199–223; P. Laslett, 'Characteristics of the Western Family Considered Over Time', *Journal of Family History* 2, no. 2 (1977): 89–115.

[14]R. A. Margo, and R.H. Steckel, 'Heights of Native-born Whites During the Antebellum Period', *The Journal of Economic History* 43, no. 1 (1983): 167–74; R.W. Beales, 'Studying Literacy at the Community Level: A Research Note', *The Journal of Interdisciplinary History* 9, no. 1 (1978): 93–102.

[15]L. Benson, *The Concept of Jacksonian Democracy: New York as a Test Case* (Princeton: Princeton University Press, 1961); A.G. Bogue, 'The Quest for Numeracy: Data and Methods in American Political History', *Journal of Interdisciplinary History* 21 (1990): 89–116.

[16]There seems to be some disagreement about the date: the American Historical Association reports the founding of the SSHA as 1972, the SSHA's own website reports 1974 and Wikipedia reports 1976.

[17]C. Lemercier and C. Zalc, *Quantitative Methods in the Humanities: An Introduction* (Charlottesville: University of Virginia Press, 2019).

Yet despite all this excitement, by the early 1980s, quantitative history was on the decline. There were good reasons for this. Historians, who had dabbled in quantitative history during these early years became emboldened by the attention from economists whose own profession was becoming increasingly mathematical, often used their sources uncritically to make bold assertions about the universality or generalizability of their findings. The particular and the idiosyncratic were lost in their sometimes anachronistic classifications. Quantification became a synonym for the positivist approach – the antithesis of the postmodern, relativist approach that was becoming popular just as the merits of quantitative history were being questioned.

And there were practical concerns too: quantification required large investments of time and resources, yet the returns were not immediately obvious. Many of the early proponents of quantification became increasingly sceptical and began to ask whether it was all worth it.[18] What questions could quantification solve that other approaches could not? For some, using sophisticated techniques took precedence over asking a relevant research question. As historian Lawrence Stone put it, they 'used the most sophisticated techniques either to prove the obvious or to claim to prove the implausible ... The results sometimes combine the vices of unreadability and triviality'.[19] Historians Claire Lemercier and Claire Zalc put it plainly: 'Quantitative historians were often boring, and had themselves become bored.'[20]

For the next two decades at least, quantitative history took a back seat. It gave way to other approaches, from Marxism to postmodernism. E. P. Thompson's *The Making of the English Working Class*, published in 1963, stimulated new ways of viewing the past.[21] Gender history is one example of new subfields that flourished.[22] So, too, did earlier work by French philosophers like Michel Foucault and Jacques Derrida shift the historian's gaze. By the 1980s, objective truth was questionable and power relations explained all.

One thing these diverse schools had in common, however, was the desire to write 'history from below' or 'history from the bottom up'; that is, to focus explicitly on those who have not been accounted for, the marginalised, the inarticulate – whom we have called the 'uncharted' people.

The decline of quantitative history ended abruptly by the early 2000s. There are both demand- and supply-side reasons for this turnaround, or 'renaissance'.[23] On the demand side, the inability of postmodernism to explain (or even engage with) material progress – the rapid improvement in global living standards since the Industrial Revolution and

---

[18] L. Benson, 'The Mistransference Fallacy in Explanations of Human Behavior', *Historical Methods: A Journal of Quantitative and Interdisciplinary History* 17, no. 3 (1984): 118–31.

[19] L. Stone, 'The Revival of Narrative: Reflections on a New Old History', *Past & Present* 85 (1979): 11.

[20] Lemercier and Zalc, *Quantitative Methods*, 15.

[21] E.P. Thompson, *The Making of the English Working Class* (London: Gollancz, 1963).

[22] J.W. Scott, *Gender and the Politics of History* (New York: Columbia University Press, 1988).

[23] G. Austin and S. Broadberry, 'Introduction: The Renaissance of African Economic History', *The Economic History Review* 67, no. 4 (2014): 893–906.

particularly since the Second World War – necessitated a new approach. The new field of global history was interested in pinpointing the date when the gap between the West and the rest began to open up.[24] Economists and political scientists rediscovered institutions; history and its ability to explain persistent differences in living standards and political systems were suddenly top of the agenda.[25] And in economics a methodological revolution had begun: the credibility revolution, with empirical hypothesis-testing preferred to theoretical models.

On the supply side, the immense advances in computing power, the internet and the availability of statistical software packages lowered the costs of both statistical analysis and knowledge acquisition. As economic historian Steven Ruggles explains, a wealth of new data is now available with a few clicks: 'IPUMS has made freely available billions of cases of historical data from hundreds of censuses and surveys taken in more than 100 countries over the past 250 years.'[26] Instead of the large teams required to run quantitative history projects in the 1970s, individual historians, armed with a laptop and enough patience to watch a few online tutorials, can now construct their own artisanal datasets, create a pivot table and run a regression. As I explain in the final chapter, free software like R and its community of contributors further democratised (and continues to democratise) data discovery and coding. New user-generated packages give us new ways of documenting, describing and displaying data.

Despite this renewed interest in quantification, however, traditional historians remain largely sceptical. In fact, much of this revival has come not from historians but from other social scientists – economists, political scientists, demographers – just as the first wave of quantification also drew impetus from outside. What are the merits of quantification, then, and why is this time different? Will enthusiasm not inevitably be followed by disillusionment? In the next section, I explain why we can be optimistic that this is not simply history repeating itself.

A history from below

There have always been good reasons to count things. 'Many qualitative judgements or descriptions used by historians', said the economic historian Roderick Floud, 'have an implicit quantitative significance, which it is sometimes necessary to make explicit'. He added that 'many descriptions of the behaviour of individuals or groups have quantitative significance; such words as "usually," "normally," "often," "many," refer to quantitative

---

[24] K. Pomeranz, *The Great Divergence* (Princeton: Princeton University Press, 2021).

[25] D. Acemoglu, S. Johnson and J.A. Robinson, 'Reversal of Fortune: Geography and Institutions in the Making of the Modern World Income Distribution', *The Quarterly Journal of Economics* 117, no. 4 (2002): 1231–94.

[26] S. Ruggles, 'The Revival of Quantification: Reflections on Old New Histories', *Social Science History* 45, no. 1 (2021): 21.

concepts, and although we may often not wish to test them exactly, in principle their significance or truth can only be established by quantitative measurement'.[27]

The demographic historian Peter Laslett was somewhat more blunt:

> Writers of history in [the] established, conventional mode are perpetually proclaiming that such and such an individual was typical, such and such an event or a trait was characteristic. But they do so without apparently recognising that to decide on typicality requires that the whole class of the phenomena under examination has to be surveyed and that all possible individual events or all possible traits must be taken into account.[28]

Quantification helps us identify whether an observation or sample of observations is representative of the total. Imagine a distribution of per capita incomes in the year 1500, or a distribution of marriage ages in the year 1920, or a distribution of experiences at a recent festival. The income per capita of Spain in 1500, or the age of a bride in 1920 or the complaints of a festival attendee can only be analysed once we know where on the distribution that income level, or occupation or experience fell. If we want to know whether Spain was rich or poor in 1500, we need to know whether other countries were richer or poorer. If we want to know whether it was common for a wife to be the same age as her husband in 1920, we need to know the ages of all women that married in that year – or at least a large proportion. If we want to know whether the experience of the festival attendee is the exception rather than the rule, we need to know the experiences of others.

Naturally, some things are easier to quantify than others. Incomes and ages are, by definition, numerical. Festival experiences less so. That is a concern that historians have had for some time, at least since Arthur Schlesinger Jr claimed that 'almost all important questions are important precisely because they are not susceptible to quantitative answer'.[29] There are two responses to this, one old and one new. It is true that not all things can be quantified, but it is equally true that quantitative evidence helps us understand the qualitative. As Floud put it: 'Quantitative evidence will almost certainly not provide a complete answer, but it may well provide some of the answer, and to throw it away unseen is both wasteful and irresponsible.'[30]

The new response is that, in the past two decades, new tools and techniques have allowed us to investigate a broader array of issues than was available to historians in the 1970s. The information and communication revolution has shifted not only how

---

[27] R. Floud, *An Introduction to Quantitative Methods for Historians* (London: Methuen, 1973): 2.

[28] P. Laslett, 'Signifying Nothing: Traditional History, Local History, Statistics and Computing', *History and Computing* 11, nos. 1 & 2 (1999): 130.

[29] A. Schlesinger Jr, 'The Humanist Looks at Empirical Social Research', *American Sociological Review* 27, no. 6 (1962): 770.

[30] Floud, *Introduction to Quantitative Methods for Historians*, 3.

sources are preserved but also the questions we ask and the ways we attempt to answer them. The historian of technology Adam Crymble notes that 'in a field so quick to point out why it is important for us to have a deep knowledge of the past, historians have been slow to recognise how their work and their ideas have not been immune to the transformative rise of the computer, which has brought about the greatest social and cultural transformation the world has perhaps ever seen'.[31] Optical character recognition (OCR) tools allow us to rapidly transcribe large corpuses of text, increasingly even when handwritten. Geographic information systems (GIS) make accurate spatial analysis easy. Free statistical software packages are available to match observations and merge datasets, map and analyse networks of relationships, and even use machine learning tools to analyse historical photos, videos or soundbites. The computational toolkit has expanded to such an extent that even Schlesinger Jr would have to admit that *some* important questions are now within the purview of the quantitative.

Asking the important questions might indeed be what historians can bring to the table. Elsewhere, I have argued that historians, 'because of their ability to operate at the intersections of the different social sciences – and perhaps the natural sciences in some ways too – … should be well-positioned to ask the big research questions about human and societal behaviour'.[32] That implies, however, being open to the use of numbers. Historian Caitlin Rosenthal, one of the main proponents of a 'new history of capitalism' literature, warns her history colleagues that 'we ignore the data-driven work of economic historians at our peril'. She continues: 'Even if we do not need their questions, their data and methods can help us to discipline our inquiries – to rule out interpretations that are incorrect and to suggest new ways forward.'[33]

Such data need not be Big Data. True, large datasets with thousands or even hundreds of thousands of observations are now easy to create and curate, owing to cheaper digitisation and transcription techniques, from OCR to outsourcing, and an abundance of (open-source) software packages, with R and Python being the most popular. But one strand of quantitative history involves what I call 'artisanal' quantification. Increasingly, our databases can include 'messy' entries, with notes. Because file size is of no concern anymore (no more need to fit everything onto a punch card), and because packages like Microsoft Excel are accessible and easy to use, and because we have a variety of techniques for dealing with both numerical values and text, we can preserve original entries in datasets before the data is 'cleaned' to allow for analysis. In fact, in some cases, it is exactly the 'uncleaned' versions of the data that allow the researcher to uncover new facts.

I will use an example from this book, Chapter 5, on race reclassification in apartheid-era Cape Town, to show what I mean. This study's small sample of 100 cases, drawn from

---

[31] A. Crymble, *Technology and the Historian: Transformations in the Digital Age* (Urbana: University of Illinois Press, 2021): 2.

[32] J. Fourie, et al., 'Making South African Historians Count', *Historia* 66, no. 1 (2021): 4.

[33] C. Rosenthal, 'Seeking a Quantitative Middle Ground: Reflections on Methods and Opportunities in Economic History', *Journal of the Early Republic* 36, no. 4 (2016): 659–80.v

a population of more than 50,000 marriage records, was found by looking at notes in the marriage records indicating when a couple was reclassified. If a standardised, 'cleaned' dataset had been used, the reclassification details would have likely been ignored because they appeared on a very small percentage of records. This kind of study, say Lemercier and Zalc, 'can be part of an experimental practice of history that is playful, in the sense of not boring (yet attentive to ethics): numbers, when used as tools, not fetishes, allow familiarisation, comparison, and oblique readings of sources'.[34]

But there is another reason to use quantitative approaches, one that has not received the attention it deserves. Quantitative history can help to illuminate the experiences of people who have remained hidden in the conventional archive. Large administrative datasets include information about people who are absent from the archival sources generally used in narrative accounts, such as letters, diaries, newspapers and reports. Digitising, transcribing and analysing such administrative sources opens new opportunities to account for those people.

To date, ways of writing histories from below have had some successes and suffered from some shortcomings. To explain, it helps, again, to begin with the *Annales* school. Not only was the 'total history' promoted by *Annales* historians closely linked to quantification, often of the artisanal kind; their interest was explicitly less in the deeds of great men than in the experiences of ordinary people. While their focus was initially on compiling long-term series (of, say, prices and wages) and identifying trends and patterns of different duration, their emphasis had always been on incorporating the histories of those outside the domains of power and privilege. To do so, their national and regional focus increasingly shifted towards the local. One popular approach of later *Annalistes* was to write microstudies of villages, relying on detailed quantitative and qualitative information to bring to life the lives of women, children, peasants and other overlooked people.

These approaches can be seen as a prelude to the microhistory approach that would later develop in Italy; an approach, historian Giovanni Levi explains, that advocates for incorporating the research process into the narrative itself.[35] Microhistorians, says Lemercier and Zalc, 'allowed us to think of quantification in constructionist terms suited to the scales of interaction among individuals, and to approach it experimentally – open to non-standard procedures, including the idea that meaningful results can be obtained by studying a small, situated unit, such as a family or a village, systematically and even quantitatively'.[36] Not only did this kind of quantification help to identify the exceptional or outliers (rather than the mean or the median), it allowed data construction (and the source criticism associated with it) to become part of the text – 'not preliminary

---

[34]Lemercier and Zalc, *Quantitative Methods*, 27.

[35]G. Levi, 'On Microhistory', in *New Perspectives on Historical Writing*, ed. P. Burke (Cambridge: Polity Press, 1991): 93–113.

[36]C. Lemercier and C. Zalc, 'Back to the Sources: Practicing and Teaching Quantitative History in the 2020s', *Capitalism: A Journal of History and Economics* 2, no. 2 (2021): 480.

operations to be dispensed with or standardised'.[37] The focus on the exceptional or outliers, however, meant that these approaches had difficulty integrating the stories of those uncharted back into the larger narratives of history. Microhistories of this kind, apart from a few notable exceptions, had the unfortunate consequence that their impact was micro too.

The most popular 'histories from below', by contrast, did not rely on numbers. In fact, some historians feared that large datasets pushed them to write 'histories without people'. In Britain, an early initiative to write history from below, sometimes referred to as the 'Old History from Below', was by British Marxists. Starting in the 1940s, a group of historians that included E. P. Thompson, Eric Hobsbawm, Rodney Hilton, Christopher Hill, Raphael Samuel and George Rude combined their political activism in the Communist Party with a desire to write a new kind of social history, one of and for the working class.[38] In contrast to the more structural social histories of the time which, they believed, reduced the working class to a simple statistical artefact, theirs followed a humanist, narrative approach that explored the social and cultural dimensions of politics.[39] Thompson's widely popular *The Making of the English Working Class* is a classic example of this bottom-up view, emphasising the creation, by the late nineteenth century, of a working-class identity: 'The working class made itself as much as it was made'.[40] It was an argument that would prove immensely popular and powerful outside of England, notably in India, where Subaltern Studies would emerge as an energetic new approach to writing history from below.[41]

Subaltern Studies benefited from the popularity of postcolonial studies and critical theory, which had roots in postmodernism. By the 1970s, a group of French philosophers that included Michel Foucault, Jacques Derrida and Jean-François Lyotard began to offer a radical critique of objectivity, truth, reality and reason. Pointing to unequal power structures in the past and present, historians who adopted postmodernist approaches refused to prioritise one aspect of history over another, often preferring the trivial to the grand narrative and the symbolic to the real. In short, postmodern historians began to question not only the partialness of archival sources, but the archive itself.

In some cases, the belief that archival sources are more myth than material verged on the absurd: 'The idea of the historical past can … be considered as just one more example of the many imaginaries we have fabricated to help us make some sense of the apparent senselessness of existence', said the historian Keith Jenkins.[42] Not all historians,

---

[37]Ibid, 480.

[38]S. Scott-Brown, 'The Art of the Organiser: Raphael Samuel and the Origins of the History Workshop', *History of Education* 45, no. 3 (2016): 372–90.

[39]K. Gentry, 'Ruskin, Radicalism and Raphael Samuel: Politics, Pedagogy and the Origins of the History Workshop', *History Workshop Journal* 76, no. 1 (2013): 187–211.

[40]Thompson, *Making of the English Working Class*, 194.

[41]S. Bhattacharya, 'History from Below', *Social Scientist* 11, no. 4 (1983): 3–20; V. Chaturvedi, ed., *Mapping Subaltern Studies and the Postcolonial* (London: Verso, 2000).

[42]K. Jenkins, *Why History? Ethics and Postmodernity* (London: Routledge, 1999): 14.

fortunately, adopted such an extreme view. By the late 1990s, historian Richard J. Evans could declare that history 'is an empirical discipline, and it is concerned with the content of knowledge rather than its nature. Through the sources we use, and the methods with which we handle them, we can, if we are very careful and thorough, approach a reconstruction of past reality that may be partial and provisional, and certainly will not be objective, but is nevertheless true'.[43]

Another belief of postmodernist historians is that the authors' identity is inextricably bound up with their subject. Why and by whom history was written sometimes became more important than what was written. Although the idea that each group writes its own history is often unrealistic, it is true that people who write their own histories will bring their own concerns to bear on them. There is thus a justifiable concern that not only have some groups been systematically excluded from the archive, but those who should write their histories have been excluded from the academic profession. This is particularly true of quantitative history, a field that has not been very successful at attracting scholars from marginalised backgrounds. As I will argue in the conclusion, South Africa, with its history of racial discrimination, is a sad example of such inability and the reason why the Biography project, and the tools it will have created, is one small attempt at righting the imbalance.

Attracting a more diverse group of researchers is just one challenge in writing more complete histories from below. A more fundamental challenge, in the past and in the present, is the lack of sources. Some histories are missing because no evidence – of an event, a person, a thought – was ever recorded. One obvious example where this happens is an illiterate society. Oral history approaches have been of immense benefit. Just consider the excellent histories of African societies based on oral testimonies.[44]

But, as oral historians know only too well, such sources have shortcomings. Human memory is fickle. There are good reasons why humans remember poorly. Psychologists have shown that humans have a negativity bias: negative information and experiences are more likely to be remembered than equally extreme positive information and experiences.[45] People are more likely to search their memory for certain events if prompted to do so by other events. For example, patients who have been diagnosed with cancer are more likely to report previous minor illnesses than patients who have not been

---

[43]R.J. Evans, *In Defence of History* (London: Granta, 1997): 249.

[44]J.M. Vansina, *Oral Tradition as History* (Madison: University of Wisconsin Press, 1985). For South Africa, see B. Bozzoli and M. Nkotsoe, *Women of Phokeng: Consciousness Life Strategy and Migrancy in South Africa, 1900–1983* (Johannesburg: Ravan, 1991); I. Hofmeyr, *We Spend Our Years as a Tale that Is Told: Oral Historical Narrative in a South African Chiefdom* (Johannesburg: University of Witwatersrand Press, 1993). For more recent work in African history, see N. Achebe, *The Female King of Colonial Nigeria: Ahebi Ugbabe* (Bloomington: Indiana University Press, 2011); A. Wiemers, *Village Work: Development and Rural Statecraft in Twentieth-century Ghana* (Athens, US: Ohio University Press, 2021); E.L. Osborn, *Our New Husbands Are Here: Households, Gender, and Politics in a West African State from the Slave Trade to Colonial Rule* (Athens, US: Ohio University Press, 2011).

[45]C.J. Norris, 'The Negativity Bias, Revisited: Evidence from Neuroscience Measures and An Individual Differences Approach', *Social Neuroscience* 16, no. 1 (2021): 68–82.

diagnosed with cancer. Researchers need to avoid this 'recall bias'. Neuroscientists know that human evolution shaped story-telling into a useful tool for survival. But, argues the philosopher Alex Rosenberg, as narratives are almost always wrong, historians have turned this useful tool into a defective theory of human nature:

> If we humans are ever to move beyond our internecine histories, we will have to put historical 'understanding' behind us. We will have to recognise that even the best histories we can contrive are mostly wrong or, when right, are right by accident, that they fail to identify the real causal forces that drive events, that they obstruct efforts to really understand our past, and that they serve as harmful tools of the worse angels of our natures.[46]

The sociologist Zygmunt Bauman has argued that the need to reinvent the past also depends on our future outlook: 'Having lost all visions of an alternative – better – society of the future – associating the future, if not with "worse than the present" then with "more of the same"' – no wonder that, when seeking genuinely meaningful ideas, we turn, nostalgically, to the buried grand ideas of the past.'[47] In short, then, our recollections of the past are affected by our preference for the negative, the irrelevant and story-telling, and by our hopes for the future.

The problem is not only what gets remembered, but who is asked for their memories. Oral histories introduce concerns that are front-of-mind in survey design: How do we know we have a representative sample of views? Should we pay more attention to the average experience or the outlier? To what extent do we account for survivorship bias, the tendency to value the experiences of those who survived over the experiences of those who did not? What are the motives of the interviewer and interviewee? Not only are humans bad at remembering, but memory fades; testimonies become less reliable the further we go back in time, with serious implications for oral histories going back two or more generations.

Of course, oral testimonies are not the only method to have shortcomings. Where written records do remain, they invariably provide only a partial view of the past. The histories of the poor, the powerless and those on the periphery of society are often excluded because any evidence of their thoughts, feelings and experiences was lost or not preserved, either intentionally or unintentionally. British historian E. H. Carr observed in 1961 that historians are not impartial actors in the preservation of knowledge: prevailing preferences, politics and protocols shape what they preserve and protect, and the same can be said of archivists.[48]

---

[46] A. Rosenberg, *How History Gets Things Wrong: The Neuroscience of Our Addiction to Stories* (Cambridge, US: MIT Press, 2019).

[47] Z. Bauman, *Retrotopia* (Cambridge: Polity Press, 2017): 128.

[48] E.H. Carr, *What Is History?* (1961; repr. London: Penguin Random House, 2018).

Financial considerations also play a role in the creation and preservation of written records. For both supply and demand-side reasons, recordkeeping is expensive. In the late nineteenth-century Cape Colony, land surveys of African property, for example, were first simplified (in comparison to white landowners) to speed up the process and then, when the costs outweighed the benefits, abandoned completely.[49] In the past and present, the budgetary requirements of preserving large amounts of seemingly unimportant documentation in fiscally constrained environments have also meant the destruction of archival material. This is particularly true for poorer regions, those places where uncharted people most likely reside.

On the demand side, people may have had good reason to want to avoid being recorded, making it costly (or nigh impossible) for the state to record accurate information. Tax censuses are a classic example; in earlier work, I found that eighteenth-century Cape farmers substantially underreported their assets to avoid tax.[50] In addition, for economic, political or social reasons, the formerly oppressed may not want their histories to be known. Ally describes how the residents of the former Bantustan KaNgwane 'actively lay the past to waste', destroying the archive of the apartheid 'puppet' state that subjugated them.[51]

Where historical texts do remain, however, reading them against the grain is one way to remedy or, in the least, uncover biases. It can help to expose the unexamined beliefs and attitudes of the authors, and allow us to draw attention to the silences, contradictions and prejudices of the archive. In fact, as Stoler has shown, archives – and in particular colonial archives – themselves can and should be subjects of study, allowing the historian to not only work against but along the archival grain.[52] Quantitative history, I argue, can perform a similar function.

It can do this because of two recent technological advances: the digitisation and transcription of large quantities of archival material, and the availability of a statistical toolkit to analyse these at low cost. The digitisation of archival sources has opened up vast quantities of archival sources for analysis. The most common of these are the volumes of parliamentary papers, colonial reports, letters and other text-rich documents that historians have traditionally relied on. But another source – what I call administrative records – has the potential to illuminate parts of society that may have been hidden from view: birth records, death notices, probate inventories, voters' rolls and many more. These individual-level records are uninteresting on their own; other than, perhaps, for

---

[49] R.T. Ally, 'The Development of the System of Individual Tenure for Africans: With Special Reference to the Glen Grey Act, c. 1984–1922' (MA diss., Rhodes University, Makhanda, 1985).

[50] J. Fourie, 'The Remarkable Wealth of the Dutch Cape Colony: Measurements from Eighteenth-century Probate Inventories', *The Economic History Review* 66, no. 2 (2013): 419–48.

[51] S. Ally, 'Material Remains: Artifice Versus Artefact (s) in the Archive of Bantustan Rule', *Journal of Southern African Studies* 41, no. 5 (2015): 969–89.

[52] A.L. Stoler, *Along the Archival Grain: Epistemic Anxieties and Colonial Common Sense* (Princeton: Princeton University Press, 2009).

the individuals' immediate descendants, or for genealogists. But combining them into a large dataset and matching individuals across many such sources allows us to not only reconstruct trends in the previously uncharted groups – of their fertility, infant mortality, wealth, mobility and much more – but also to arrive at new causal insights that will provide a more nuanced and complete interpretation of historical change. This is especially applicable, as I argue elsewhere, in settings where conventional archival sources are limited.[53]

These methods are not without their detractors. As I mentioned earlier, the first wave of quantitative history, much of which was also based on large volumes of such administrative records, was criticised for its lack of definitive conclusions, inability to answer important questions, technical difficulty and high costs, among other things. The biggest concern now is undeniably ethical. Responding in a Broadstreet blog post to a January 2022 *New York Times* column by Jamelle Bouie on American slavery and quantification, political scientist Emily Sellars lists the ethical concerns when historians begin to quantify: 'the extent to which quantifying history can be "dehumanising", the practical and ethical consequences of relying on data generated by immoral historical processes like the slave trade, how our academic projects or datasets might be misused or misinterpreted, and, most importantly, what our ethical responsibilities are to those we study, to their descendants, and to society as a whole'.

These are all valid concerns, and are beginning to receive the attention they deserve.[54] There is no denying that working with numbers – rather than, say, an individual story – exacts less of an emotional toll. This has two consequences. First, it makes quantification less attractive for those hoping to effect change. As activists know all too well, statistics rarely make a good slogan: a picture is often worth a thousand numbers. Second, and perhaps more seriously, numbers that are abstracted from their context can indeed be misused and, in the extreme case, become dehumanising. At least since Foucault, historians have known that the data-generating process itself is often an exercise of power, usually by the state.

But as Sellars remarks in the same January 2022 post, the impersonality can also be an advantage: 'There are some ways in which quantitative research may be *less* exploitative than qualitative research. It may be easier to preserve the confidentiality of specific people, for example, which is an important consideration given that our research subjects can't usually consent to having their stories shared.'[55] Another advantage, already highlighted above, is that quantification helps to distinguish the average from the outlier. This is helpful when dealing with narratives, especially the narratives of those

---

[53] J. Fourie, 'The Data Revolution in African Economic History', *Journal of Interdisciplinary History* 47, no. 2 (2016): 193–212.

[54] A.M. Lerner, 'Quantifying the Archives: Leveraging the Norms and Tools of Data Science to Conduct Ethical Research on the Holocaust', *Holocaust Studies* 28, no. 3 (2021): 1–19.

[55] E. Sellars, 'What Are Our Ethical Responsibilities as HPE Scholars?', *Broadstreet*, 7 February 2022. Available online: https://broadstreet.blog/2022/02/07/what-are-our-ethical-responsibilities-as-hpe-scholars/.

who have been previously overlooked. If we find an example of a slave who did not want to be freed, does that mean that all slaves felt the same way? Says Sellars: 'One thing that quantitative research can contribute is to illustrate how distorted and misleading those narratives are'.[56] Quantification can also help us understand scale: 'quantifying the scope of processes like the slave trade makes it difficult to dismiss them as historical blips'.[57]

Finally, data generated by coercive systems can easily replicate the biases of those systems. This is, of course, true for both quantitative and qualitative data. But quantification has two properties that, I argue, have distinct advantages over qualitative approaches. Firstly, it can explicitly reveal the size of those biases. To give just one example: in work with Jonathan Jayes, I used a novel technique to calculate the extent of discrimination by white doctors when treating black patients during the Spanish flu.[58] (We found little evidence of such discrimination, which accords with the qualitative evidence of the time.) Secondly, quantification can help to answer questions orthogonal to the original purpose of data collection. Consider that anthropometric historians often make use of the heights of soldiers reported in attestation forms. Although the colonial recruits might have suffered from the prejudices of their superiors, it is unlikely that those prejudices would have manifested in biased measurements of a man's height.[59] But the standards of living that can be calculated using the height data have helped anthropometric historians to expose the ways in which colonial policies disadvantaged certain groups in society.

If we are to account for the people lost in the records or never recorded, we should do so in a way that is sensitive to the data-generating process, acknowledges the coercive nature of state bureaucracy, questions arbitrary classifications and categories and, in short, takes context seriously.

Quantitative history in South Africa

South Africa is a good place to show how quantification can help write 'histories from below'. That assertion might surprise many readers. According to historian Keith Breckenridge, civil registration in South Africa was a 'complete and prolonged failure'.[60] The proximate causes of such failure were obvious: a lack of state funding and the racist disparagement of African subjects by some white officials. A more basic problem, argues

---

[56] Ibid.

[57] Ibid.

[58] J. Fourie and J. Jayes, 'Health Inequality and the 1918 Influenza in South Africa', *World Development* 141 (2021): 105407.

[59] A. Moradi, 'Towards an Objective Account of Nutrition and Health in Colonial Kenya: A Study of Stature in African Army Recruits and Civilians, 1880-1980', *The Journal of Economic History* 69, no. 3 (2009): 719-54.

[60] K. Breckenridge, *Biometric State: The Global Politics of Identification and Surveillance in South Africa, 1850 to the Present* (Cambridge: Cambridge University Press, 2014): 136.

Breckenridge, was the absence of a political constituency demanding civil registration: 'Here the contrast with the many different forms of registration in other regions of the world is striking, because both elites and the poor – who, in other contexts, sought registration for many different ends – were silenced by the workings of customary law.'[61] The inertia of civil registration allowed the apartheid-era government to launch a project of universal fingerprint registration; a project that would, ironically and unintentionally, make possible the well-targeted social transfers programmes of democratic-era South Africa.[62]

Breckenridge's claim that civil registration in South Africa was a failure is only partially true. It is true for much of the region that became the Union of South Africa in 1910, but in the British Cape Colony (1806–1910) and for the Cape Province (1910–94), regions outside the scope of Breckenridge's study, civil registrations were widespread. This is true across population groups. It is true for those that would be classified under the later apartheid-era Population Registration Act as white as well as for those classified as coloured and black, although, as one would expect, there was likely to be some regional variation. As Chapter 12 on the Spanish flu shows, the criteria for registering a death were different in rural and urban areas.

The series on death registrations is just one of many sets of records that remain well preserved, in the Cape Archives and elsewhere. The British colonial authorities collected and preserved a copious amount of information on its subjects. Several censuses were undertaken, in 1865, 1875, 1891 and 1904, although, sadly, the original records, with a few exceptions, have been lost. The liberal franchise at the Cape meant that there was no legal reason to exclude certain groups. Except for the 1865 census, which includes only white and coloured inhabitants, the censuses made a full enumeration of the population in the territories annexed by the British. Chapter 3 uses these and the South African censuses to calculate and analyse under-five sex ratios by race.

The records go much further than census data. Huge numbers of probate inventories were preserved and these have now been made available online on FamilySearch.org.[63] More than 3 million civil records of the Cape Province are available on the same site, as well as 2.7 million civil marriage records for South Africa (which, presumably, would include the Cape Province). But it was not only the state that collected individual-level information. The two largest religious denominations, the Dutch Reformed Church and the Anglican Church, collected and preserved baptism and marriage records and membership lists. Chapter 2 matches Anglican baptism and marriage records to calculate bridal pregnancy, for example. Records of other denominations, like the Lutheran Church in Cape Town, remain well preserved too, although less accessible to the public. Churches collected not just vital statistics but financial statistics too: a series

---

[61] Ibid, 136.
[62] Ibid, 188–93.
[63] As of January 2022, the total number of probate records for the Cape Province (1834–1989) was 2,752,260.

of cashbook transactions across more than a century remains preserved in the Dutch Reformed Church Archive in Stellenbosch.

Why was recordkeeping so much better at the Cape than elsewhere in South Africa? Two reasons come to mind. Firstly, and most pertinently, Cape Town and colonial Cape society was founded by the first multinational company, the Dutch East India Company (*Vereenigde Oostindische Compagnie*), in the mid-seventeenth century. Because of the profit-maximising motive and for the purposes of reporting to shareholders, the VOC kept meticulous records of all its activities and subjects throughout the 143 years of its rule.[64] British rule (first from 1795 and then again from 1806) largely adopted the existing Dutch bureaucracy.

The VOC was remarkably meticulous in its recordkeeping. From the 1660s, an annual tax census was collected of all free households. The *opgaafrolle* include not only information about the settler family and the workforce (wage labourers, Khoe and slaves), but also a detailed breakdown of agricultural assets, inputs and outputs. It is a remarkable series, one that is currently being transcribed as part of the Cape of Good Hope Panel project.[65] The VOC-era records are not limited to farm production: the Master of the Orphan Chamber collected probate inventories, auction rolls and several other series. As Dutch economic historian Jan Luiten van Zanden remarked, the Cape Archive 'has a more complete record of eighteenth-century Cape Colony life than what is available in The Hague for economic historians of eighteenth-century Holland'.[66]

A second reason for the large difference in data quality between the Cape Province and the rest of South Africa can be found, perhaps, in the reasons for the Great Trek. One purported reason for frontier farmers in the 1830s to migrate into the interior was to escape British rule. The extent to which this explains the migration of more than 5,000 settler farmers is still debated, but it does explain why those who settled the interior were unwilling – quite literally – to be charted, or in other words, put on the map. This was especially true for those farmers who migrated into the territories that would become known as the Transvaal. Dimitruk, Du Plessis and Du Plessis have shown how the Transvaal's poor administrative capacity was reflected in less accurate maps, which hindered the provision of property rights.[67] It was only towards the second half of the twentieth century that more accurate maps became available. Poor state capacity for much of the late nineteenth and early twentieth century probably also explains the lack of good civil registration records.

---

[64] J. Fourie, 'The Quantitative Cape: A Review of the New Historiography of the Dutch Cape Colony', *South African Historical Journal* 66, no. 1 (2014): 142–68.

[65] J. Fourie and E. Green, 'Building the Cape of Good Hope Panel', *The History of the Family* 23, no. 3 (2018): 493–502; A. Rijpma, J. Cilliers and J. Fourie, 'Record Linkage in the Cape of Good Hope Panel', *Historical Methods: A Journal of Quantitative and Interdisciplinary History* 53, no. 2 (2020): 112–29.

[66] Quoted in J. Fourie and S. Schirmer, 'The Future of South African Economic History', *Economic History of Developing Regions* 27, no. 1 (2012): 114–24.

[67] K. Dimitruk, S. Du Plessis and S. Du Plessis, 'De jure Property Rights and State Capacity: Evidence from Land Specification in the Boer Republics', *Journal of Institutional Economics* 17, no. 5 (2021): 764–80.

Despite the larger quantity and better quality of administrative records for the Cape Colony and Cape Province, South African historians have largely neglected these sources. There have been exceptions. By the 1980s, just when historians elsewhere turned away from quantification, a new generation of South African historians (and historians interested in South Africa) turned to the study of Cape slavery. Inspired by the political changes that were afoot in the country, and an openness to counter-narratives of the colonial past, these scholars made extensive use of the abundance of VOC records to expose the centrality of slavery to the Cape economy.

Although historians had often used statistics to support their hypotheses, what was unique about this generation was their willingness to generate and analyse their own datasets. Nigel Worden calculated farm productivity.[68] Leonard Guelke reconstructed land grants to investigate inequality.[69] Robert Ross and Pieter van Duin used tax censuses to calculate population, production and export totals for the Dutch period.[70] Hans Heese used rich genealogical records meticulously reconstructed by amateur genealogists in the 1960s and 1970s to investigate the evolution of settler and slave families.[71] Many of these contributions appeared in *The Shaping of South African Society, 1652–1820*, an impressive collection edited by Richard Elphick and Hermann Giliomee.[72] Robert Shell's work deserves special mention. Studying for a master's degree at the University of Rochester in the late 1970s, Shell would certainly have been influenced by Stanley Engerman, co-author of *Time on the Cross*. He went on to do a PhD at Yale on 'Slavery at the Cape of Good Hope, 1680–1731' and continued to publish extensive series of statistics and visualisations on Cape slavery.[73] Before his untimely death in 2015, Shell was proud of being 'South Africa's only trained cliometrician'.[74]

Despite the work by Shell and others on slave statistics, the 1980s 'cultural turn' in history quickly stymied the possibility of further quantification.[75] I offer two further

---

[68] N. Worden, *Slavery in Dutch South Africa*, vol. 44 (Cambridge: Cambridge University Press, 1985).

[69] L. Guelke and R. Shell, 'An Early Colonial Landed Gentry: Land and Wealth in the Cape Colony 1682–1731', *Journal of Historical Geography* 9, no. 3 (1983): 265–86.

[70] J. Fourie, 'Subverting the Standard View of the Cape Economy: Robert Ross's Cliometric Contribution and the Work It Inspired', *Magnifying Perspectives: Contributions to History, a Festschrift for Robert Ross, ASC Occasional Publication* 26 (2014): 261–73.

[71] H.F. Heese, 'Slawegesinne in die Wes-Kaap, 1665–1795', *Kronos: Journal of Cape History* 4, no. 1 (1981): 38–48.

[72] R. Elphick and H. Giliomee, eds., *The Shaping of South African Society, 1652–1820* (Cape Town: Maskew Millar Longman, 1984).

[73] R. Shell, *Children of Bondage: A Social History of the Slave Society at the Cape of Good Hope, 1652–1838* (Hanover, US: Wesleyan and University Press of New England, 1995).

[74] In personal communication.

[75] Here, too, there were exceptions. A decade or more later, Susan Newton-King used probates to investigate the wealth of settler farmers and Wayne Dooling used land transactions to investigate social mobility. See S. Newton-King, *Masters and Servants on the Cape Eastern Frontier, 1760–1803*, vol. 97 (Cambridge: Cambridge University Press, 1999); W. Dooling, 'The Making of a Colonial Elite: Property, Family and Landed Stability in the Cape Colony, c. 1750–1834', *Journal of Southern African Studies* 31, no. 1 (2005): 147–62.

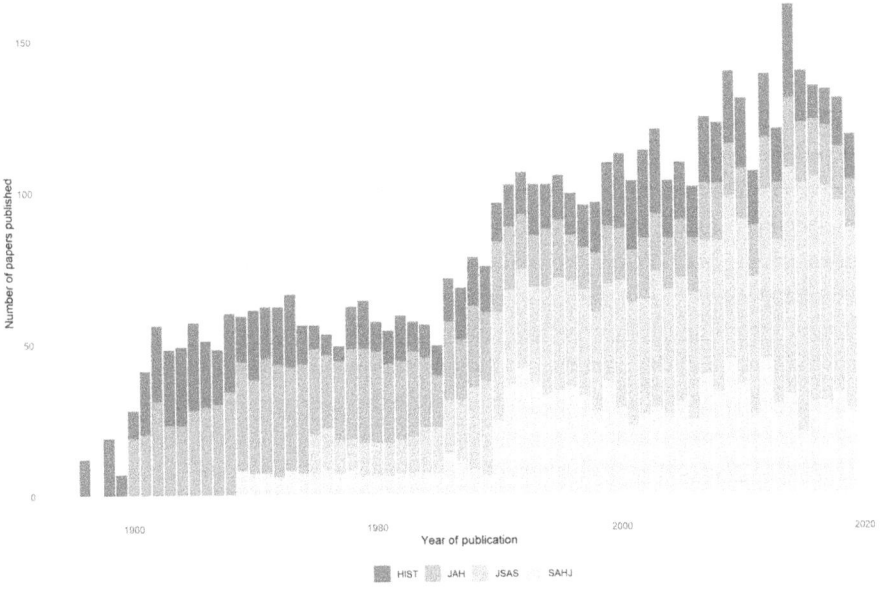

Figure 1.1 Total publications in four history journals, by year (1956–2019).

pieces of evidence, one qualitative and one quantitative. I recently asked Charles van Onselen, one of South Africa's leading historians, what role quantification played in South African historiography. He replied:

> Did quantification ever arise here in the sense that you are after? If it did then, as usual, I did not notice it. I think that there were some social scientists in the inter-war years who tried to quantify things on, say, poverty, and so on, but I am not sure that any historians attempted anything similar. I think that the historians tended to raid such findings to support their arguments, but I do not know they ever generated any primary data themselves.[76]

I found support for his opinion from a very different source. To quantify the extent of quantification in South African history, I analysed all the research papers published in four prominent history journals between 1956 and 2019: *Historia*, the *Journal of African History*, the *Journal of Southern African Studies* and the *South African Historical Journal*. A total of 5,217 papers were published over the period. Figure 1.1 shows the number of papers published by year between 1956 and 2019. The average is just over fifty for much

---

[76]Personal e-mail correspondence. 10 February 2020.

of the period until the 1980s, and then increases rapidly to a new equilibrium around 100. By the late 2000s, another shift occurs, although less obvious, rising to around 130 papers per year.

I wanted to know whether this increase in history output also resulted in more papers of a quantitative nature. To count such papers, I counted the number of tables, graphs, maps and images in each paper. I classified a paper that included a table as a quantitative history paper. This was of course a broad assumption – some papers that include tables might not be considered 'quantitative', while others that are quantitative might not include a table – but I believe it provides a useful proxy for research that uses numbers, to put it simply.

Besides recording these in-paper features, I also recorded whether a paper had one or more authors and the number of Google citations in 2020 for that paper. Table 1.1 provides an overview of the four journals, with the average for each of these features reported by journal.

The statistics reveal several noteworthy differences between the journals. The two more 'international' journals, the *Journal of Southern African Studies* and the *Journal of African History*, dedicated to publishing research beyond South Africa, have not only published a larger number of papers – a surprising finding, given that the *JSAS* was first published in 1975, almost two decades after *Historia* – but its papers also receive significantly more citations. Papers published in the *JAH* receive almost twenty times more Google citations than papers published in *Historia*. Another noteworthy difference is the number of single-authored papers. The *JAH* publishes very few co-authored papers, roughly one in sixteen. By contrast, one in seven papers in the *JSAS* has more than one author. This is probably due to the interdisciplinary nature of the *JSAS*. As we will see later, there is also a noticeable time trend associated with multi-authored papers.

A third noteworthy trend is the difference in the average number of tables, graphs, maps and images published per paper. Here, again, there are two groups. The *JSAS* and the *JAH* publish significantly more tables and graphs than do the two South Africa-specific journals: whereas the *JSAS* and *JAH* publish, on average, a table and a graph in every

Table 1.1 Descriptive statistics of journal papers.

Journal	Number	Citations	Author	Tables	Graphs	Maps	Images
SAHJ	1100	6.7	0.09	0.18	0.05	0.09	0.49
JSAS	1640	33.0	0.14	0.52	0.14	0.18	0.33
HIST	1091	2.0	0.07	0.24	0.03	0.14	0.61
JAH	1386	39.0	0.06	0.50	0.12	0.57	0.45

Notes: 'Number' refers to the number of observations (papers). 'Citations' refers to the average number of citations per paper. 'Author' reports the share of papers with more than one author. 'Tables', 'Graphs', 'Maps' and 'Images' count the number of tables, graphs, maps and images per paper, respectively.

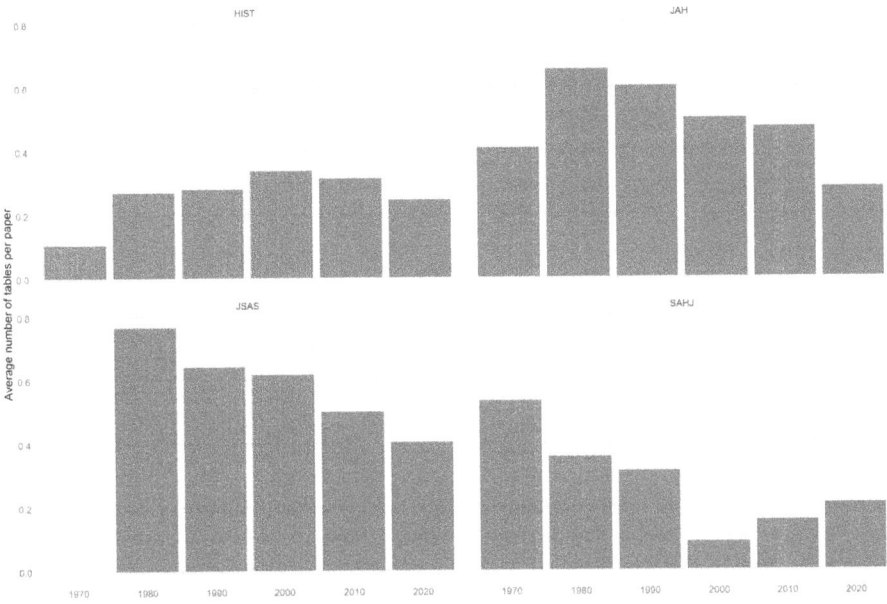

Figure 1.2 Average number of tables per paper, by journal and decade.

second paper, the *SAHJ* and *Historia* do so for one in every four and five, respectively.[77] I found a similar result for graphs. A different split occurs for maps. Here, the *JAH* is far more likely than the other three journals to publish maps, with one in every two papers having maps, compared to one in every five for the *JSAS* and one in every ten for the *SAHJ*. Of all four journals, *Historia* is the most likely to publish images.

I was, however, more interested in the trend over time. Has the number of tables, as a proxy for quantification, declined since the 1970s? Figure 1.2 shows the average number of tables per paper by decade for each of the four journals. Each decade reflects the previous ten years' papers; so, 1990 would include all papers published between 1981 and 1990.

The answer to the above question seems to be a resounding yes. The number of tables per paper declines sharply in the two journals that published the most tables, the *JAH* and *JSAS*. From a high of more than 0.7 tables per *JSAS* paper in the 1970s, the average falls to 0.4 by the 2010s. A steeper decline can be seen for the *JAH* (0.6 to less than 0.3) and *SAHJ* (above 0.5 to below 0.25). It is only *Historia* that, bar the pre-1970s period, maintains the same level, albeit at a very low rate of between 0.25 and 0.3.

---

[77]It is important to keep in mind that these are averages. It could be that one article includes several tables. Although I report it as one in every five to make it easily comparable, the average is pushed higher by one or two outlier articles. The reality is that the frequency of tables is, in fact, lower across the board.

My findings enabled me to test two hypotheses about the reasons for the decline. One hypothesis was that quantitative papers – defined as those with tables – received fewer citations, on average. Given that journals aim to attract citations, editors were thus less likely to accept those papers for publication. This hypothesis is easily refuted: I found that the 4,476 papers without a table had an average of twenty-one Google citations, while the 740 papers with at least one table had an average of thirty-five Google citations. The difference is statistically meaningful: it would suggest that papers with tables actually attract more citations. When I did an Ordinary Least Squares regression analysis with the number of Google citations as the dependent variable, and several factors, including the number of tables, the number of graphs, the number of maps and the number of images as independent variables, I found a statistically significant and positive coefficient for tables. On average, adding one additional table increases the number of Google citations by two.[78] Editors should prefer papers with tables because they attract more citations.

One interesting observation from the above regression is that multi-authored papers also attract more citations.[79] My second hypothesis was therefore that quantitative history papers are more likely to have more than one author. This would be because quantitative history, as explained above, is more likely to be interdisciplinary, requiring collaboration. The statistics support this conjecture. The 4,724 papers with a single author have, on average, 0.34 tables per paper. By contrast, the 493 papers with more than one author have, on average, 0.74 tables per paper.

Although historians still predominantly publish single-authored papers, there is evidence of more collaboration. Figure 1.3 shows the evolution of multi-authored papers over time. From almost universal single authorship in the early years, dual authorship increased somewhat during the 1990s and 2000s. It is only since the 2010s that papers with three or more authors have become common. Although the rise (albeit from a very low base) of multi-authored papers contrasts with the decline in the number of quantitative history papers, the fact that history journals are largely dominated by single-authored papers perhaps explains why interdisciplinary teams of scholars have looked elsewhere to publish their work.

This five-decade decline in quantification in South African history journals is mirrored by international trends, with one important exception. As Ruggles and Magnuson report, the number of papers per year published in the *Journal of Interdisciplinary History* by

---

[78]In the regression I also controlled for the number of pages, the issue number, and whether the paper has multiple authors. I also included journal and year dummies. Longer papers tend to attract more citations, the explanation for this probably being that the comments and editorials, that tend to be shorter, receive fewer citations. Articles with maps also tend to attract more citations, although the relationship is weak. The relationship between tables and citations is statistically significant with 99 per cent confidence. The regression output is available from the author on request.

[79]Moving from a single to two or more authors, conditional on all else staying constant, increases the number of citations by 4. This relationship is statistically significant with 90 per cent confidence.

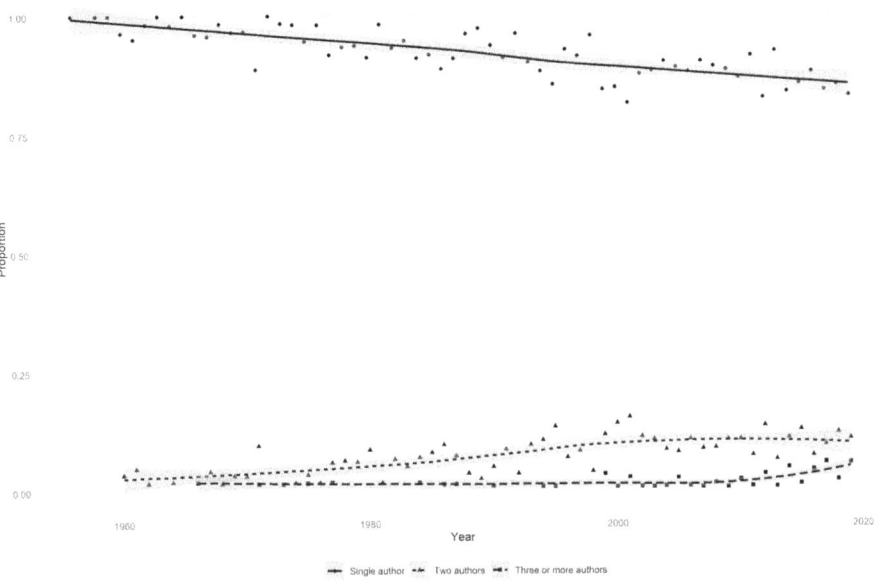

Figure 1.3 Proportion of papers with a single author, two authors or three or more authors, by year.

historians using quantitative methods fell by 72 per cent from the 1970s to the 2000s.[80] The parallel trend for papers in South African history journals is clear. Yet a major shift is currently underway in the leading history journals: the number of papers using quantitative techniques has increased in the past decade by 126 per cent. Although the magnitudes are smaller, this 'revival of quantification in historical research', as Ruggles and Magnuson have called it, is true also for the *American Historical Review*, the *Journal of American History*, the *Journal of Modern History* and *Past & Present*.[81] There is little evidence of this revival in South African history journals.

Look beyond history journals, however, and a more optimistic picture of quantitative history in South Africa emerges. As happened during the earlier wave of quantification, it was in economic history that the first green shoots began to appear. In the late 2000s, an economic history research cluster within the Department of Economics at Stellenbosch University, inspired by what later would be called the 'renaissance in African economic history', began to use historical datasets, notably of the Cape Colony, and analyse them using the economist's toolkit.[82] Several papers were published in some of the leading

---

[80] Ruggles and Magnuson, 'History of quantification in history'.

[81] Ibid, 379.

[82] This fledgling but dynamic group gained further momentum when Stellenbosch was announced as host of the 2012 World Economic History Congress.

international economic history journals.[83] In 2016, I published a paper in the *Journal of Interdisciplinary History*, reviewing the 'data revolution in African economic history'.[84] The team at Stellenbosch was very much part of that revolution.

By 2015, this research unit formalised into the Laboratory for the Economics of Africa's Past, with the aim of using quantitative methods to investigate the past. From the very beginning, LEAP encouraged interdisciplinary engagement, with historians, sociologists and even agriscientists with an interest in history often joining seminars. This meant that the research focus shifted to investigating questions beyond the confines of economic history – in social, gender, military, business and demographic history. A few examples convey the diversity of topic and audience. In 2018, Mpeta, Fourie and Inwood used the First World War and the Second World War attestation forms – and several other unconventional sources – to reconstruct the living standards of black South Africans over the twentieth century.[85] The paper was published in the *South African Journal of Science*. In 2019, Fourie and Inwood investigated interracial marriages in Cape Town using Anglican Marriage Records.[86] In 2020, Nyika and Fourie used nineteenth-century voters' rolls to investigate the effect of disenfranchisement on black voter registrations. In the same year, Fourie, Inwood and Mariotti published a paper in *Social Science History* which argued that changing military technology may account for the decline in the heights of recruits and, as a result, the apparent decline in living standards.[87] In 2021, Maphosa et al. used limited liability company records to describe the growth of the private capital market at the Cape at the turn of the twentieth century.[88] The paper was published in the *Economic History of Developing Regions*. In the same year, Cilliers and Mariotti used genealogical records to measure nineteenth-century birth spacing, building

---

[83] W.H. Boshoff and J. Fourie, 'The Significance of the Cape Trade Route to Economic Activity in the Cape Colony: A Medium-term Business Cycle Analysis', *European Review of Economic History* 14, no. 3 (2010): 469–503; J. Fourie and D. Von Fintel, 'The Dynamics of Inequality in a Newly Settled, Pre-industrial Society: The Case of the Cape Colony', *Cliometrica* 4, no. 3 (2010): 229–67; S. Du Plessis and S. Du Plessis, 'Happy in the Service of the Company: The Purchasing Power of VOC Salaries at the Cape in the 18th Century', *Economic History of Developing Regions* 27, no. 1 (2012): 125–49; J. Fourie and D. Von Fintel, 'A History with Evidence: Income Inequality in the Dutch Cape Colony', *Economic History of Developing Regions* 26, no. 1 (2011): 16–48; J. Fourie and D. von Fintel, 'Settler Skills and Colonial Development: The Huguenot Wine-makers in Eighteenth-century Dutch South Africa', *The Economic History Review* 67, no. 4 (2014): 932–63; D. Von Fintel, S. Du Plessis and A. Jansen, 'The Wealth of Cape Colony Widows: Inheritance Laws and Investment Responses Following Male Death in the 17th and 18th Centuries', *Economic History of Developing Regions* 28, no. 1 (2013): 87–108.

[84] Fourie, 'Data Revolution'.

[85] B. Mpeta, J. Fourie and K. Inwood, 'Black Living Standards in South Africa before Democracy: New Evidence from Height', *South African Journal of Science* 114, nos. 1–2 (2018): 1–8.

[86] Chapter 5 makes use of the same dataset to investigate race reclassification in Cape Town.

[87] J. Fourie, K. Inwood and M. Mariotti, 'Military Technology and Sample Selection Bias', *Social Science History* 44, no. 3 (2020): 485–500.

[88] L.M. Maphosa, et al., 'The Growth and Diversity of the Cape Private Capital Market, 1892–1902', *Economic History of Developing Regions* 36, no. 2 (2021): 149–74.

on earlier work that investigated South Africa's fertility transition.[89] Marco-Gracia and Fourie used census data to expose unbalanced sex ratios for infants in twentieth century South Africa.[90] And Ekama et al. published the first descriptive results of a large project that transcribed the full series of valuation rolls compiled during the period of emancipation in the 1830s.[91]

Two projects made possible by generous international funding deserve special attention. One is an ambitious attempt to fully transcribe a series of records of the Dutch and early-British colonial period, from the 1660s to the 1840s. In an attempt to account for the Khoesan in Cape economic history[92], the *Cape of Good Hope Panel* project intends to fully transcribe the Cape *opgaafrolle*, the annual tax censuses of all free households in the Colony.[93] The project, begun in 2015 and since 2021, funded by the Swedish Riksbankens Jubileumfonds, is ongoing.

The other is the *Biography of an Uncharted People* project. Generously funded by the Andrew W. Mellon Foundation, the project has two aims: to transcribe historical administrative records that have so far been largely ignored by historians and to encourage students to equip themselves with the quantitative tools to use these records in their research about marginalised, uncharted people. The choice of which source material to transcribe has been entirely up to the researcher. It has included baptism records, marriage records, voters' rolls, tax censuses, valuation rolls, death notices, company records, petitions to parliament, newspaper advertisements, civil service employee records, attestation forms, surveys, almanacs, probate inventories, auction rolls and mortgage records. Several of these sources form the basis for the chapters published in this volume. The transcribed sources have, where possible, been made available online to encourage wider usage.

This book

This edited collection brings together a selection of work on the *Biography of an Uncharted People* project. The purpose is to show the innovative ways in which quantitative tools and techniques can illuminate the past, shedding light on those that have often been

---

[89]J. Cilliers and M. Mariotti, 'Stop! Go! What Can We Learn about Family Planning from Birth Timing in Settler South Africa, 1835–1950?' *Demography* 58, no. 3 (2021): 901–25; J. Cilliers and M. Mariotti, 'The Shaping of a Settler Fertility Transition: Eighteenth-and Nineteenth-century South African Demographic History Reconsidered', *European Review of Economic History* 23, no. 4 (2019): 421–45.

[90]F. Marco-Gracia and J. Fourie, 'The Missing Boys: Understanding the Unbalanced Sex Ratio in South Africa, 1894–2011', *Economic History of Developing Regions* 37-2 (2022): 128–146.

[91]K. Ekama, et al., 'When Cape Slavery Ended: Introducing a New Slave Emancipation Dataset', *Explorations in Economic History* 81 (2021): 101390.

[92]J. Fourie and E. Green, 'The Missing People: Accounting for the Productivity of Indigenous Populations in Cape Colonial History', *The Journal of African History* 56, no. 2 (2015): 195–215.

[93]Fourie and Green, 'Building the Cape of Good Hope Panel'.

absent from the historical account. It is quantitative history in the service of those whom history has generally ignored, the uncharted.

Charting those who have been uncharted helps to inform several branches of history. One of the more surprising outcomes of the project has been the contribution of quantitative history to expanding women's history in South Africa.[94] Several of the chapters explicitly focus on women or gender. Richardson and Kok investigate bridal pregnancy in Chapter 2, studying popular attitudes towards premarital sexuality in Cape Town using matches of baptism and marriage records. Their results – of high variance between different Anglican parishes in Cape Town – offer a window into family economics of the time. They find, for example, that 'Cape Town working-class families were less concerned than other socio-economic groups with when and how their children married'.

Chapter 7 by Rommelspacher uses a representative survey to study domestic work in Cape Town. She shows that existing literature frequently makes assumptions that 'every white women was freed from domestic work by the employment of a domestic servant'. The survey reveals, however, that only 31 per cent of white households employed domestic workers, far less than previously thought.

In Chapter 8, Maphosa and Kerby use limited liability company records to expose the extent of participation of women in the Cape's private capital market. They find that female investors 'were diverse, and comprised of spinsters, widows, housewives and professionals'. Without the transcription of thousands of investor transactions, and the analysis of these transactions, we would not have been able to know the surprisingly large role women played as investors.

Just like during the 1960s, demographic history (or historical demography) profits from the renewed interest in quantitative history. Three chapters in this volume make explicit contributions to South African demographic history. Marco-Gracia and Fourie use census records in Chapter 3 to test the mechanisms that explain the surprisingly low infant sex ratios in South African (and African) history. In Chapter 4, Links uses tax censuses to study Khoe kinship networks, concluding that how households are defined has implications for the level of wealth inequality. Jayes and Fourie use death notices in Chapter 12 to calculate the extent of excess mortality during the Spanish flu in South Africa.

Our knowledge of South Africa's political history benefits, in particular, from Chapter 10 by Schoots on African nationalist organisations and from Chapter 11 by Dimitruk and Lemon on petitions to the Cape parliament. Schoots uses network analysis techniques to map the way proto-nationalist African organisations in the late nineteenth-century Eastern Cape were connected to each other through shared members. In doing so, he exposes how traditional leaders 'forged new alliances with mission-educated

---

[94] A. Rommelspacher, 'Restating the Case for Women's History in South Africa', *Economic History of Developing Regions* 36, no. 3 (2021): 445–50.

leaders, creating organisations which could both mobilise rural communities and make new demands on the colonial state'. It would be these innovations that would later guide the growing African Nationalist movement.

In Chapter 11, Dimitruk and Lemon transcribed petitions to the House of Assembly in Cape Town during the second half of the nineteenth century, documenting patterns in the types of petitions, types of petitioners and their geographic distribution. They then study the relationship between labour issues and temperance, noting the rich historiography of coercive labour laws and alcohol abuse. Dimitruk and Lemon find that both labour and temperance petitioners 'were concerned about the reliability of labour but suggested different legislative solutions to the problem'. They also find that petitioners increasingly formed part of Colony-wide campaigns involving organisations like the Afrikaner Bond and Women's Christian Temperance Union.

Migration remains a pressing issue in the developing world. Chapter 9 by Mbem and De Haas investigates the factors that affected black residents' move to Cape Town in the first half of the twentieth century. The chapter contributes not only to a broader understanding of South African migration history that has largely focused on migration to the mines, but also contributes to women's, demographic and political history.

Several chapters cross disciplinary boundaries too. Aside from its demographic history contribution, Links's study also adds to our understanding of the Cape Colony's economic history. So, too, does Chapter 8 by Maphosa and Kerby on female investors in the Cape. One chapter that makes a more direct contribution to economic history is Chapter 6 by Raaijmakers and Ekama on slave sale advertisements. They transcribed 1,180 newspaper ads published in *De Zuid-Afrikaan* between 1830 and 1834 to describe the reasons for sales being made in the period immediately preceding emancipation. They find, surprisingly, that advertisers increasingly referenced the wishes of the enslaved person to be sold. This, the authors argue, reveals 'not only a veiled agency on the part the enslaved (and responsiveness by slave owners) but also the role of the newspaper connecting town and countryside to facilitate that move'.

Several chapters broadly contribute to social history, although this is most evident in Chapter 5 where Chalmers, Fourie and Inwood investigate how social mobility was affected by race reclassification before and during apartheid. The one unifying theme of the book is, undeniably, the interdisciplinary contribution, in terms of both topics and methods, to writing a history from below.

The eleven chapters are not ordered chronologically. They are, instead, arranged as if following a person's life course: from conception to death. It is, indeed, a biography of an uncharted people. In the final chapter, I explore ways in which more quantitative history can be encouraged, in South Africa and elsewhere. The hope is that this book, and the teaching resources made available as a consequence of the *Biography of an Uncharted People* project, will help to equip a new generation of scholars to tell the stories of those who remain unaccounted for in South African history.

Bibliography

Acemoglu, D., S. Johnson and J.A. Robinson. 'Reversal of Fortune: Geography and Institutions in the Making of the Modern World Income Distribution'. *The Quarterly Journal of Economics* 117, no. 4 (2002): 1231–94.

Achebe, N. *The Female King of Colonial Nigeria: Ahebi Ugbabe*. Bloomington: Indiana University Press, 2011.

Ally, R.T. 'The Development of the System of Individual Tenure for Africans: With Special Reference to the Glen Grey Act, c. 1984–1922'. MA diss., Rhodes University, Makhanda, 1985.

Ally, S. 'Material Remains: Artifice Versus Artefact (s) in the Archive of Bantustan Rule'. *Journal of Southern African Studies* 41, no. 5 (2015): 969–89.

Austin, G. and S. Broadberry. 'Introduction: The Renaissance of African Economic History'. *The Economic History Review* 67, no. 4 (2014): 893–906.

Bhattacharya, S. '"History from Below"'. *Social Scientist* 11, no. 4 (1983): 3–20.

Bauman, Z. *Retrotopia*. Cambridge: Polity Press, 2017.

Beales, R.W. 'Studying Literacy at the Community Level: A Research Note'. *The Journal of Interdisciplinary History* 9, no. 1 (1978): 93–102.

Benson, L. *The Concept of Jacksonian Democracy: New York as a Test Case*. Princeton: Princeton University Press, 1961.

Benson, L. 'The Mistransference Fallacy in Explanations of Human Behavior'. *Historical Methods: A Journal of Quantitative and Interdisciplinary History* 17, no. 3 (1984): 118–31.

Bogue, A.G. 'The Quest for Numeracy: Data and Methods in American Political History'. *Journal of Interdisciplinary History* 21 (1990): 89–116.

Boshoff, W.H. and J. Fourie. 'The Significance of the Cape Trade Route to Economic Activity in the Cape Colony: A Medium-term Business Cycle Analysis'. *European Review of Economic History* 14, no. 3 (2010): 469–503.

Bozzoli B. and M. Nkotsoe. *Women of Phokeng: Consciousness Life Strategy and Migrancy in South Africa, 1900–1983*. Johannesburg: Ravan, 1991.

Braudel, F. 'Histoire et sciences sociales: la longue durée'. *Annales. Histoire, Sciences Sociales* 13, no. 4 (1958): 725–53.

Breckenridge, K. *Biometric State: The Global Politics of Identification and Surveillance in South Africa, 1850 to the Present*. Cambridge: Cambridge University Press, 2014.

Burke, P. *The French Historical Revolution: The Annales School, 1929–2014*. Stanford: Stanford University Press, 2015.

Carr, E.H. *What Is History?* 1961; repr. London: Penguin Random House, 2018.

Chaturvedi, V., ed. *Mapping Subaltern Studies and the Postcolonial*. London: Verso, 2000.

Cilliers, J. and M. Mariotti. 'The Shaping of a Settler Fertility Transition: Eighteenth-and Nineteenth-century South African Demographic History Reconsidered'. *European Review of Economic History* 23, no. 4 (2019): 421–45.

Cilliers, J. and M. Mariotti. 'Stop! Go! What Can We Learn about Family Planning from Birth Timing in Settler South Africa, 1835–1950?' *Demography* 58, no. 3 (2021): 901–25.

Conrad, A.H. and J.R. Meyer. 'The Economics of Slavery in the Ante Bellum South'. *Journal of Political Economy* 66, no. 2 (1958): 95–130.

Crymble, A. *Technology and the Historian: Transformations in the Digital Age*. Urbana: University of Illinois Press, 2021.

Diebolt, C. and M. Haupert. 'Cliometrics: Past, Present, and Future'. In *Oxford Research Encyclopedia of Economics and Finance*, edited by Dixit, Avinash, Edwards, Sebastian, and Judd, Kenneth. Oxford: Oxford University Press, 2021. Available online: https://doi.org/10.1093/acrefore/9780190625979.013.552.

Dimitruk, K., S. Du Plessis and S. Du Plessis. 'De jure Property Rights and State Capacity: Evidence from Land Specification in the Boer Republics'. *Journal of Institutional Economics* 17, no. 5 (2021): 764–80.

Dooling, W. 'The Making of a Colonial Elite: Property, Family and Landed Stability in the Cape Colony, c. 1750-1834'. *Journal of Southern African Studies* 31, no. 1 (2005): 147–62.

Du Plessis, S. and S. Du Plessis. 'Happy in the Service of the Company: The Purchasing Power of VOC Salaries at the Cape in the 18th Century'. *Economic History of Developing Regions* 27, no. 1 (2012): 125–49.

Eichengreen, B. 'The Contributions of Robert W. Fogel to Economics and Economic History'. *The Scandinavian Journal of Economics* 96, no. 2 (1994): 167–79.

Ekama, K., J. Fourie, H. Heese and L. Martin. 'When Cape Slavery Ended: Introducing a New Slave Emancipation Dataset'. *Explorations in Economic History* 81 (2021): 101390.

Evans, R.J. *In Defence of History*. London: Granta, 1997.

Floud, R. *An Introduction to Quantitative Methods for Historians*. London: Methuen, 1973.

Fogel, R. *Railroads and American Economic Growth*. Baltimore: Johns Hopkins Press, 1965.

Fogel, R. and S. Engerman. *Time on the Cross: The Economics of American Negro Slavery*. Boston: Little, Brown and Co., 1974.

Fourie, J. 'The Remarkable Wealth of the Dutch Cape Colony: Measurements from Eighteenth-century Probate Inventories'. *The Economic History Review* 66, no. 2 (2013): 419–48.

Fourie, J. 'Subverting the Standard View of the Cape Economy: Robert Ross's Cliometric Contribution and the Work It Inspired'. *Magnifying Perspectives: Contributions to History, a Festschrift for Robert Ross, ASC Occasional Publication* 26 (2014): 261–73.

Fourie, J. 'The Quantitative Cape: A Review of the New Historiography of the Dutch Cape Colony'. *South African Historical Journal* 66, no. 1 (2014): 142–68.

Fourie, J. 'The Data Revolution in African Economic History'. *Journal of Interdisciplinary History* 47, no. 2 (2016): 193–212.

Fourie, J. and D. Von Fintel. 'The Dynamics of Inequality in a Newly Settled, Pre-industrial Society: The Case of the Cape Colony'. *Cliometrica* 4, no. 3 (2010): 229–67.

Fourie, J. and D. Von Fintel. 'A History with Evidence: Income Inequality in the Dutch Cape Colony'. *Economic History of Developing Regions* 26, no. 1 (2011): 16–48.

Fourie, J. and D. von Fintel. 'Settler Skills and Colonial Development: The Huguenot Winemakers in Eighteenth-century Dutch South Africa'. *The Economic History Review* 67, no. 4 (2014): 932–63.

Fourie, J. and E. Green. 'The Missing People: Accounting for the Productivity of Indigenous Populations in Cape Colonial History'. *The Journal of African History* 56, no. 2 (2015): 195–215.

Fourie, J. and E. Green. 'Building the Cape of Good Hope Panel'. *The History of the Family* 23, no. 3 (2018): 493–502.

Fourie, J. and J. Jayes. 'Health Inequality and the 1918 influenza in South Africa'. *World Development* 141 (2021): 105407.

Fourie, J. and S. Schirmer. 'The Future of South African Economic History'. *Economic History of Developing Regions* 27, no. 1 (2012): 114–24.

Fourie, J., K. Inwood and M. Mariotti. 'Military Technology and Sample Selection Bias'. *Social Science History* 44, no. 3 (2020): 485–500.

Fourie, J., F. Ballim, G. Groenewald, J. Upton, T. Nyamunda and J. Parle. 'Making South African Historians Count'. *Historia* 66, no. 1 (2021): 2–38.

Gentry, K. 'Ruskin, Radicalism and Raphael Samuel: Politics, Pedagogy and the Origins of the History Workshop'. *History Workshop Journal* 76, no. 1 (2013): 187–211.

Goldin, C. 'Cliometrics and the Nobel'. *Journal of Economic Perspectives* 9, no. 2 (1995): 191–208.

Guelke, L. and R. Shell. 'An Early Colonial Landed Gentry: Land and Wealth in the Cape Colony 1682–1731'. *Journal of Historical Geography* 9, no. 3 (1983): 265–86.
Heese, H.F. 'Slawegesinne in die Wes-Kaap, 1665–1795'. *Kronos: Journal of Cape History* 4, no. 1 (1981): 38–48.
Hofmeyr, I. *We Spend Our Years as a Tale that Is Told: Oral Historical Narrative in a South African Chiefdom*. Johannesburg: University of Witwatersrand Press, 1993.
Jenkins, K. *Why History? Ethics and Postmodernity*. London: Routledge, 1999.
Laslett, P. 'Size and Structure of the Household in England over Three Centuries'. *Population Studies* 23, no. 2 (1969): 199–223.
Laslett, P. 'Characteristics of the Western Family Considered over Time'. *Journal of Family History* 2, no. 2 (1977): 89–115.
Laslett, P. 'Signifying Nothing: Traditional History, Local History, Statistics and Computing'. *History and Computing* 11, nos. 1 & 2 (1999): 129–33.
Lerner, A.M. 'Quantifying the Archives: Leveraging the Norms and Tools of Data Science to Conduct Ethical Research on the Holocaust'. *Holocaust Studies* 28, no. 3 (2021): 1–19.
Levi, G. 'On Microhistory'. In *New Perspectives on Historical Writing*, edited by P. Burke, 93–113. Cambridge: Polity Press, 1991.
Lemercier, C. and C. Zalc. *Quantitative Methods in the Humanities: An Introduction*. Charlottesville: University of Virginia Press, 2019.
Lemercier, C. and C. Zalc. 'Back to the Sources: Practicing and Teaching Quantitative History in the 2020s'. *Capitalism: A Journal of History and Economics* 2, no. 2 (2021): 473–508.
Marco-Gracia, F. and J. Fourie. 'The Missing Boys: Understanding the Unbalanced Sex Ratio in South Africa, 1894–2011'. *Economic History of Developing Regions* 37–2 (2022): 128–146.
Margo, R.A. and R.H. Steckel. 'Heights of Native-born Whites during the Antebellum Period'. *The Journal of Economic History* 43, no. 1 (1983): 167–74.
Maphosa, L.M., A. Ehlers, J. Fourie and E.M. Kerby. 'The Growth and Diversity of the Cape Private Capital Market, 1892–1902'. *Economic History of Developing Regions* 36, no. 2 (2021): 149–74.
McCloskey, D.N. 'The Achievements of the Cliometric School'. *The Journal of Economic History* 38, no. 1 (1978): 13–28.
Meyer, J.R. and A.H. Conrad. 'Economic Theory, Statistical Inference, and Economic History'. *The Journal of Economic History* 17, no. 4 (1957): 524–44.
Moradi, A. 'Towards an Objective Account of Nutrition and Health in Colonial Kenya: A Study of Stature in African Army Recruits and Civilians, 1880–1980'. *The Journal of Economic History* 69, no. 3 (2009): 719–54.
Mpeta, B., J. Fourie and K. Inwood. 'Black Living Standards in South Africa before Democracy: New Evidence from Height'. *South African Journal of Science* 114, nos. 1–2 (2018): 1–8.
Newton-King, S. *Masters and Servants on the Cape Eastern Frontier, 1760–1803*. Vol. 97. Cambridge: Cambridge University Press, 1999.
Norris, C.J. 'The Negativity Bias, Revisited: Evidence from Neuroscience Measures and an Individual Differences Approach'. *Social Neuroscience* 16, no. 1 (2021): 68–82.
North, D.C. 'The New Economic History after Twenty Years'. *American Behavioural Scientist* 21, no. 2 (1977): 187–200.
Osborn, E.L. *Our New Husbands Are Here: Households, Gender, and Politics in a West African State from the Slave Trade to Colonial Rule*. Athens, US: Ohio University Press, 2011.
Pomeranz, K. *The Great Divergence*. Princeton: Princeton University Press, 2021.
Rijpma, A., J. Cilliers and J. Fourie. 'Record Linkage in the Cape of Good Hope Panel'. *Historical Methods: A Journal of Quantitative and Interdisciplinary History* 53, no. 2 (2020): 112–29.
Robinson, J.H. *The New History: Essays Illustrating the Modern Historical Outlook*. New York: The Macmillan Company, 1912.

Rommelspacher, A. 'Restating the Case for Women's History in South Africa'. *Economic History of Developing Regions* 36, no. 3 (2021): 445–50.

Rosenberg, A. *How History Gets Things Wrong: The Neuroscience of Our Addiction to Stories*. Cambridge, US: MIT Press, 2019.

Rosenthal, C. 'Seeking a Quantitative Middle Ground: Reflections on Methods and Opportunities in Economic History'. *Journal of the Early Republic* 36, no. 4 (2016): 659–80.

Ruggles, S. 'The Revival of Quantification: Reflections on Old New Histories'. *Social Science History* 45, no. 1 (2021): 1–25.

Ruggles, S. and D.L. Magnuson. 'The History of Quantification in History: The JIH as a Case Study'. *Journal of Interdisciplinary History* 50, no. 3 (2019): 363–81.

Schlesinger Jr, A. 'The Humanist Looks at Empirical Social Research'. *American Sociological Review* 27, no. 6 (1962): 768–71.

Scott, J.W. *Gender and the Politics of History*. New York: Columbia University Press, 1988.

Scott-Brown, S. 'The Art of the Organiser: Raphael Samuel and the Origins of the History Workshop'. *History of Education* 45, no. 3 (2016): 372–90.

Sellars, E. 'What Are Our Ethical Responsibilities as HPE Scholars?'. *Broadstreet*, 7 February 2022. Available online: https://broadstreet.blog/2022/02/07/what-are-our-ethical-responsibilities-as-hpe-scholars/.

Shell, R. *Children of Bondage: A Social History of the Slave Society at the Cape of Good Hope, 1652–1838*. Hanover, US: Wesleyan/University Press of New England, 1995.

Stoler, A.L. *Along the Archival Grain: Epistemic Anxieties and Colonial Common Sense*. Princeton: Princeton University Press, 2009.

Stone, L. 'The Revival of Narrative: Reflections on a New Old History'. *Past & Present* 85 (1979): 3–24.

Thompson, E.P. *The Making of the English Working Class*. London: Gollancz, 1963.

Vansina, J.M. *Oral Tradition as History*. Madison: University of Wisconsin Press, 1985.

Von Fintel, D., S. Du Plessis and A. Jansen. 'The Wealth of Cape Colony Widows: Inheritance Laws and Investment Responses Following Male Death in the 17th and 18th Centuries'. *Economic History of Developing Regions* 28, no. 1 (2013): 87–108.

Worden, N. *Slavery in Dutch South Africa*. Vol. 44. Cambridge: Cambridge University Press, 1985.

CHAPTER 2
BRIDAL PREGNANCY IN THE MOTHER CITY, 1900–60
Laura Richardson* and Jan Kok**

Introduction

On the 7th of February 1932 two babies were baptised at St. Mark's Anglican Church in Athlone, Cape Town. The first infant, a boy named Eduard, was born to Stephen and Antoniette, a working-class coloured couple, a year and several months after they were married. The second infant, a girl by the name of Frances, was born to James and Emma, also a working-class coloured couple, three months after they were married. Although neither child was formerly classified as illegitimate, Francis was conceived outside of marriage whereas Eduard was not. Indeed, Emma would have been a visibly pregnant bride. That the wedding went ahead and that Francis was baptised is significant, though. It hints at the possibility that such a birth and the sexual behaviour which preceded it were perhaps more frequent than expected.

This chapter examines conception trends in early to mid- twentieth-century Cape Town. Specifically, it analyses the prevalence and social distribution of bridal pregnancy – defined as pregnancy where birth occurs within the first eight months of marriage. Research is based on newly linked, individual-level baptism and marriage records drawn from seven socio-economically diverse Anglican parishes. Data from these parishes span the years 1900 to 1960, with the greatest concentration of data in the period from 1920 to 1950. Examination of this data supports the idea that bridal pregnancy was fairly common in Anglican Cape Town; between a quarter and a third of all brides were pregnant on their wedding day. It also indicates large differences between parishes in the number of bridal pregnancies recorded. We argue that at least part of this variation can be accounted for by looking at backgrounds of the couples in each parish. In order to demonstrate this we test a number of hypotheses regarding bridal pregnancy and its correlates, looking particularly at factors like age, income, race, literacy and migration status. Our quantitative analysis enables an understanding of behavioural trends in society taken as a whole, as opposed to relying on individual accounts which are more likely exposed to subjectivity and social pressure.

---

*Richardson: Department of History, Stellenbosch University, South Africa and Faculty of History, University of Cambridge, UK.
**Kok: Department of History, Art History and Classics, Radboud University, Nijmegen, the Netherlands.

There is currently a rich body of literature on gender and sexuality in early twentieth-century South Africa. Key authors include Deborah Gaitskill, Philip Bonner, Linda Chisholm, Karen Jochelson, Catherine Burns, Peter Delius, Clive Glaser, Susanne Klausen, Rebecca Hodes and Sarah Duff.[1] However, these authors have tended to make use of conventional qualitative sources. As a result, they have generally commented more easily on the mechanisms employed by religious bodies, welfare organisations and the state to regulate sexual behaviour, than they have on how individuals and communities navigated these controls. For example, a dominant strand of the literature has explored the effect that mass urbanisation had on African sexuality and its management in urban Johannesburg. For evidence of individuals' ability to negotiate these controls historians have had to rely on a small corpus of anthropological work, dating back to the 1940s and 1950s, which considers, albeit obliquely, the intimate lives and sexual practices of men and women living in the city.[2] Yet, sources like these are scarce and, as Burns notes, embody complex problems of representation and representativeness.[3] In South Africa, sexual and family historians are limited in the archival material which they can mine. Letters and diaries survive irregularly, if at all, for the rural and urban working classes.[4] Court cases (abortion, infanticide, child maintenance suits, etc.), although revealing, are usually highly performative and tend to reflect society at its extremes.[5] Oral histories can be effectively analysed but remain time-sensitive.

Against this backdrop, we propose using basic family reconstitution techniques to contribute to the existing literature. Family reconstitution – which involves the linking and analysis of demographic events within and between individual lives – is

---

[1] For an indication of this broad field consult: C. Walker, ed., *Women and Gender in Southern Africa to 1945* (Cape Town: David Philip Publishers, 1990); K. Jochelson, *The Colour of Disease: Syphilis and Racism in South Africa, 1880–1950* (Oxford: Palgrave in association with St. Antony's Press, 2001); P. Delius and C. Glaser, 'Sexual Socialisation in South Africa: A Historical Perspective', *African Studies* 61, no. 1 (2002): 27–54; C. Burns, 'Controlling Birth: Johannesburg, 1920–1960', *South African Historical Journal* 50, no. 1 (2004): 170–98; C. Glaser, 'Managing the Sexuality of Urban Youth: Johannesburg, 1920s–1960s', *International Journal of African Historical Studies* 38, no. 2 (2005): 301–27; S. Klausen, *Race, Maternity, and the Politics of Birth Control, 1910–1939* (Basingstoke: Palgrave Macmillan, 2004); R. Hodes, 'Kink and the Colony: Sexual Deviance in the Medical History of South Africa, c. 1893–1939', *Journal of Southern African Studies* 41, no. 4 (2015): 715–33; S. Duff, 'Facts about Ourselves: Negotiating Sexual Knowledge in Early Twentieth-Century South Africa', *Kronos* 41, no. 1 (2015): 215–35.

[2] See for example: E. Hellmann, *Rooiyard: A Sociological Survey of an Urban Slum Yard* (Cape Town: Oxford University Press for the Rhodes-Livingston Institute, 1948); L. Longmore, *The Dispossessed: A Study of the Sex life of Bantu Women in Urban Areas in and around Johannesburg* (London: Jonathan Cape, 1959); T.D. Moodie (with V. Ndatshe and B. Sibuyi), 'Migrancy and Male Sexuality on the South African Gold Mines', *Journal of Southern African Studies* 14, no. 2 (1988): 228–56.

[3] Burns, 'Controlling Birth', 178.

[4] K. Breckinridge, 'Reasons for Writing: African Working-Class Letter-Writing in Early Twentieth Century South Africa', in *Africa's Hidden Histories: Everyday Literacy and Making the Self*, ed. K. Barber (Bloomington: Indiana University Press, 2006): 144.

[5] G. Frost, *Promises Broken: Courtship, Class, and Gender in Victorian England* (Charlottesville: University of Virginia Press, 1995): 11.

a methodology which has not been widely utilised in South Africa.[6] The limitations of family reconstitution are well-documented.[7] Nevertheless, family reconstitution is a valuable tool with which to investigate micro-level trends in sexual and marital behaviour, especially in contexts where civil and church records are one of relatively few written sources documenting the everyday lives of the non-elite classes.

Since the 1960s historical demographers have used family reconstitution to debate the oftentimes tenuous link between sexual prescription and practice.[8] Their research has shown that despite exhortations by both church and secular authorities to delay sexual intercourse until after marriage, general attitudes towards premarital sexuality tended to be more ambiguous and courtship experiences more diverse than official prescriptions imply. In Europe, for example, detailed analysis of rural and urban parish registers has revealed that, despite low illegitimacy rates, sexual activity in advance of marriage was surprisingly common throughout both the nineteenth and early twentieth centuries. Kok et al. show that between 1870 and 1950 roughly a quarter of Dutch brides were pregnant at marriage.[9] In his analysis of the agricultural parish of Gosforth, England, Williams found the bridal pregnancy rate to be as high as 40 per cent between 1920 and 1951.[10] A similar, if less marked, incidence of bridal pregnancy was observed in Australia and the United States throughout the first half of the twentieth century.[11] Recent scholarship has also examined the prevalence of bridal pregnancy in twentieth century Asia, although most studies have focused on data collected after the 1970s.[12]

---

[6]C. Campbell, 'Demographic Techniques: Family Reconstitution', in *International Encyclopaedia of the Social and Behavioural Sciences*, ed. J. Wright, 2nd edn. (Elsevier, 2015): 138. Available online: https://www.sciencedirect.com/science/article/pii/B9780080970868310121.

[7]E.A. Wrigley, 'Some Problems of Family Reconstitution using English Parish Register Material', *Proceedings of the 3rd International Economic History Conference, Munich, 1965. Section VII, demography and economy* (Paris: De Gruyter Mouton, 1972): 199–221; P. Thestrup, 'Methodological Problems of a Family Reconstitution Study in a Danish Rural Parish before 1800', *Scandinavian Economic History Review* 20, no. 1 (1972): 1–26; S. Åkerman, 'An Evaluation of the Family Reconstitution Technique', *Scandinavian Economic History Review* 25, no. 2 (1977): 160–70.

[8]Some of the earliest studies on bridal pregnancy were published by scholars associated with the Cambridge for the History of Population and Social Structure. which was established in 1964. See, for example: P. Laslett, *The World We Have Lost* (London: Methuen, 1965): chapter 5; P.E.H. Hair, 'Bridal Pregnancy in Rural England in Earlier Centuries', *Population Studies* 20 (1966): 233–43; P.E.H. Hair, 'Bridal Pregnancy in Earlier Rural England Further Examined', *Population Studies* 24, no. 1 (1970): 59–70.

[9]J. Kok, H. Bras and P. Rotering, 'Courtship and Bridal Pregnancy in the Netherlands, 1870–1950', *Annales De Démographie Historique* 2 (2016): 165–91.

[10]W.M. Williams, *The Sociology of an English Village: Gosforth* (London: Routledge & Kegan Paul, 1956): 64. For another English example see J. Robin, 'Prenuptial Pregnancy in a Rural Area of Devonshire in the Mid-nineteenth Century: Colyton, 1851–1881', *Continuity and Change* 1, no. 1 (1986): 113–24.

[11]Both of these countries had bridal pregnancy rates of roughly 10 per cent. D.S. Smith and M. Hindus, 'Premarital Pregnancy in America 1640–1971: An Overview and Interpretation', *Journal of Interdisciplinary History* 5, no. 4 (1975): 537–70; W. Refshauge, 'Non-Marital Pregnancy in Australia' (MA diss., Australian National University, Canberra, 1982).

[12]See, for example: J. Raymo and M. Iwasawa, 'Bridal Pregnancy and Spouse Pairing Patterns in Japan', *Journal of Marriage and Family* 70, no. 4 (2008): 847–60; Y. Kim & J. Lee, 'Bridal Pregnancy and Women's Educational Attainment in South Korea, 1970–2009', *History of the Family* 23, no. 3 (2018): 426–45.

Previous research has helped scholars to recognise that the history of conception is intertwined with many broader themes in the transition towards modern societies. Clearly, it involves questions of sexual behaviour and its determinants over time. But a range of other issues are also implicated, such as the position of women in society; the presence of racial, ethnic and class inequalities; the nature and influence of religion; parental authority and the transfer of wealth across generations as well as the geographical movement of people. Even in relatively homogeneous societies, historical demographers have found bridal pregnancy rates to be extremely diverse, not only in terms of social class, but also age, religious denomination, family structure, local community and migration status. Twentieth-century Cape Town is a useful addition to the literature because of its social and economic heterogeneity. To quote Burman and Naude, Cape Town, as a society divided by skin colour, class and, to a lesser extent, by both religion and language, 'never had only one set of community values but several'.[13] Yet, although scholars have commented on the prevalence of out-of-wedlock births among the city's poorer families, we still know little about premarital conception in Cape Town.[14] This is especially true for the city's large coloured population.

A city in flux

The first half of the twentieth century was a period of rapid economic and social transformation in Cape Town. The coming of the railways in the late 1800s led it to function as a commercial entrepôt, connecting the country's mineral rich hinterland to the world beyond Southern African shores.[15] Between 1899 and 1901 the South African war ravaged the country. In its aftermath, migrants, both local and global, flocked to the area, stimulating economic development. During the inter- and post- world war years Cape Town expanded from a medium-sized commercial port to a modern industrial city, specialising in food processing and textile manufacturing. Population growth was substantial. In 1911 Cape Town had 187,331 inhabitants.[16] By 1946 it had a population of just under half a million people.[17] White and coloured inhabitants accounted for

---

[13]S. Burman and M. Naude, 'Bearing a Bastard: The Social Consequences of Illegitimacy in Cape Town, 1896-1939', *Journal of Southern African Studies* 17, no. 3 (1991): 410.

[14]See, for example: V. Malherbe, 'Illegitimacy and Family Formation in Colonial Cape Town to c. 1850', *Journal of Social History* 39, no. 4 (2006): 1153; S. Burman and P. Van der Spuy, 'The Illegitimate and the Illegal in a South African City: The Effects of Apartheid on Births Out of Wedlock', *Journal of Social History* 29, no. 3 (1996): 615–17.

[15]J. Fourie and F. Herranz-Loncan, 'Growth (and Segregation) by Rail: How the Railways Shaped Colonial South Africa', *ERSA Working Paper*, no. 538 (2016)

[16]Bureau of Census and Statistics. *Union Statistics for Fifty Years* (Pretoria: Government Printers, 1961): A12.

[17]V. Bickford-Smith, E. van Heyningen and N. Worden, *Cape Town in the Twentieth Century* (Cape Town: David Philip, 1999): 118.

over 200,000 each. African and Asian inhabitants, combined, totalled slightly less than 50,000, although census figures probably underestimated the number of 'illegal' Africans living in the city.[18]

Economically, white English-speaking males dominated government, industry, the professions and many skilled trades. In addition, the city accommodated significant numbers of coloured semi-skilled and factory workers, even as 'civilised' labour policies narrowed employment opportunities for coloured males.[19] Portuguese, Greek (and later Indian) migrants established successful independent enterprises.[20] From the 1930s onwards a growing manufacturing and commercial sector also offered opportunities for white women to enter the labour market just at a time when this was becoming an economic imperative for many Afrikaans families.[21] Female participation in the work force rose steadily, with women constituting nearly a fifth of the total working population in the Cape by 1936.[22]

Socially, the city remained heavily stratified. Between 1920 and 1950, the dislocation of war, the depression and the invention of new technologies (including the motorcar and the cinema) stimulated social anxieties. Reflecting a gradual hardening of racial attitudes, the gap in living conditions between white and coloured families began to widen and racial segregation became further entrenched.[23] Concern was frequently expressed about the growth of urban slums, while attitudes towards rising female employment remained ambivalent. Such factors precipitated a more stringent discourse on the importance of 'respectability', with the dichotomy between deserving and undeserving poor being used to incentivise the wider absorption of middle-class values and domestic habits.[24] This discourse formed part of an international conversation about how and to what extent societies ought to regulate the moral practices of the poor.[25] In South Africa, as in Britain, churches and charitable institutions were at the forefront of this conversation.[26]

---

[18]Ibid, 118.

[19]Wits Historical Papers Archive, AD 1715, 24/2/4. 'The Coloured People: A Factual Survey', South African Institute of Race Relations, 1953.

[20]Bickford-Smith, van Heyningen and Worden, *Cape Town in the Twentieth Century*, 118.

[21]L. Vincent, 'Bread and Honour: White Working Class Women and Afrikaner Nationalism in the 1930s', *Journal of Southern African Studies* 26, no. 1 (2000): 61.

[22]At 4: 20 the Cape female to male worker ratio was better than the country's average of 4:64. For more information, see the 1936 Union of South Africa Census.

[23]Stellenbosch Special Collections, Batson Collection, Overcrowding Report, 24 March 1944.

[24]W. Dooling, 'Poverty and Respectability in Early Twentieth Century Cape Town', *Journal of African History* 59, no. 2 (2018): 411–35.

[25]Romano suggests that the 'nexus between morality, poverty and public policy is nothing new', but that the deserving/undeserving poor dichotomy became particularly stark during the late-Victorian period as fears surrounding the 'urban invasion of the dangerous poor' mounted, especially among the middle classes. S. Romano, *Moralising Poverty: The 'Undeserving' Poor in the Public Gaze* (London: Routledge, 2018): 15, 32.

[26]Burman and Naude, 'Bearing a Bastard', 410.

At the time, the Anglican Church was not only the largest but also one of fastest growing Christian denominations in Cape Town, incorporating 34.7 per cent and 39.2 per cent of white and coloured residents respectively in 1936.[27] Despite rapid population growth these percentages would remain more or less unchanged over the course of the next fifteen years, with the Dutch Reformed Church, the city's second biggest Christian denomination in Cape Town, continuing to lag behind the Anglican Church, particularly in its ability to attract a sizeable coloured membership. In 1946, for example, coloured members of the Anglican Church outnumbered coloured members of the Dutch Reformed Church in Cape Town by 2:1, while outnumbering the Methodist and Roman Catholic Churches by more than double that margin.

The Anglican Church promoted a vision of domestic respectability which presupposed that women and men would remain sexually pure until marriage. It played an important role in setting up organisations which intended, among other things, to impress upon a burgeoning urban youth the consequences of failing to respect the 'divine law of human fertility'.[28] The White Cross League, for example, established by the Anglican Church in England but operational in Cape Town throughout the early twentieth century, was specifically aimed at convincing young men to live sober and moral lives, with the deleterious effects of sex outside of marriage and adolescent masturbation being made known to them in a subtle but definitive manner.[29] The Church was also involved in the founding of the Marion Institute, an organisation which sought to protect young working-class girls from the 'temptations' of city life by providing them with access to religious networks and training in domestic arts, such as sewing, knitting, cooking and childrearing.[30]

Yet financial considerations, gender and generation, as well as different family and community structures complicated the way in which men and women responded to this ideal.[31] There were social and practical incentives to marry even for the city's poorer inhabitants. In most communities, marriage remained a necessary condition of social and moral respectability, particularly for women. It could also provide substantial material advantages. In many urban areas public housing was restricted to married couples.[32] However, premarital conception did not automatically negate the benefits of marriage.

---

[27] Republic of South Africa, *Bureau of Statistics: Population Census 1936, Volume VI: Religions* (Pretoria: Government Printers, 1938): 9, 96.

[28] 'The Bishop of Oxford on the Responsibility of Marriage', *The Anchor*, 15 August 1916.

[29] 'The White Cross League', *The Anchor*, 15 March 1916.

[30] 'The Marion Institute', *Cape Argus*, 18 May 1922.

[31] Burman and Naude, 'Bearing a Bastard', 410.

[32] D. Posel, 'Marriage at the Drop of a Hat: Housing and Partnership in South Africa's Urban African Townships, 1920s–1960s', *History Workshop Journal* 61 (2006): 58–63, 68; A. van Graan, 'The Influences on the two Inner City Housing Projects of the Bo Kaap and District Six in Cape Town that were built between 1938 and 1944' (MA diss., University of Cape Town, Cape Town, 2004): 30. Van Graan notes that in allocating the newly built residences the committee responsible for these projects always raised issues of morality: applicants had to be married to their partner and individuals of sober habits were given preference.

By the early twentieth century most of the more punitive measures employed by the church to deal with pregnancy outside of marriage had fallen away; in the Anglican Church there was nothing explicitly preventing premaritally pregnant women, especially once married, from receiving communion or having their children baptised.[33]

We discuss other local factors affecting the likelihood of a bridal pregnancy in the second half of the chapter. Anecdotally it seems that coloured or racially mixed, working-class suburbs such as District Six were the most tolerant of pre- and extramarital sexuality. In his autobiography, writer and academic Richard Rive describes how the women from a brothel close to where he grew up in District Six would all attend an Anglican Mass on Christmas Eve, and subsequently host a Christmas party at their house of ill-repute attended by the church minister (albeit briefly) and much of the neighbourhood.[34]

How to make parish records speak

From the latter half of the nineteenth century, clerics at the Cape compiled handwritten volumes in which they recorded baptisms and marriages in their parishes. The volumes dealing with marriage recorded each person's first name and surname, age, profession, birthplace, current place of residence, race, condition at marriage (bachelor, spinster, widow, widower, divorcé, divorcee) and 'race change', if any.[35] Chalmers, Fourie and Inwood, Chapter 5, use the latter entry, in combination with voters' roll data, to examine race reclassification in the mid- to late-twentieth century. The date of marriage was noted, as was the contract type (ante-nuptial or in community of property) and whether or not a couple was married by banns or by licence. Also included were the consent of a legal guardian (in the case of individuals under the age of twenty-one) and whether or not the bride and groom were able to sign the marriage register (a crude measure of literacy). The baptism volumes recorded a child's date of baptism, date of birth, first name, the father's name (blank if the child was illegitimate), the mother's first name (and surname if illegitimate), the father's occupation or rank and the parents' place of residence.

For the purposes of this chapter, we linked (Appendix A) the baptism and the marriage records of couples living in Langa, Athlone, Maitland, Mowbray, Sea Point, Kenilworth and Parow, seven Anglican parishes in Cape Town that were geographically and socio-economically diverse, as shown in Figure 2.1 and Table 2.1. Parishes located

---

[33]UCT Special Collections, BC 1557, *Church of the Province of South Africa Handbook of Instructions Regarding Marriages* (Cape Town: Routledge, 1914).

[34]R. Rive, *Writing Black* (Cape Town: David Philip, 1981): 3–6.

[35]The 1950 Population Registration Act classified South Africans as white, black, coloured or Indian. However, because the determination of a person's race fell primarily to census takers and other bureaucrats and was often decided using arbitrary physical markers, individuals could petition the state to have their racial classification changed legally. If such a change occurred after marriage it was usually recorded by the priest.

Quantitative History and Uncharted People

Figure 2.1 Map of the transcribed parishes with circle size indicating the total number of baptisms in the dataset for each parish.

Table 2.1 Characteristics and general demographic makeup of the transcribed parishes.

Parish	Predominant race	Predominant class	Predominant ethnicity	Dwelling type
Athlone	Coloured	Working class	Malay	Small properties of wood and iron
Mowbray	Mixed	Working class	Mixed	Small properties of brick, wood and iron
Langa	African	Working class	Xhosa	Hostels, informal shacks made of iron
Maitland	Coloured	Working class	Malay	Farm Cottages
Parow	White	Middle and working class	Afrikaans	Small properties of stone and brick
Sea Point	White	Upper and middle class	Mixed	Large properties of stone and brick
Kenilworth	White	Upper and middle class	English	Medium-size properties of stone and brick

Bridal Pregnancy in the Mother City, 1900–60

Table 2.2 Pregnancy type by parish, 1900–1960, measured in absolute numbers and as a proportion of total number of first births after marriage.

Parish	Premarital conception (subset 2)	Post-marital conception (subset 3)
Athlone	379 (46.2%)	441 (53.8%)
Mowbray	145 (34.7%)	273 (65.3%)
Langa	10 (18.9%)	43 (81.1%)
Maitland	63 (48.8%)	66 (51.2%)
Parow	13 (19.1%)	55 (80.9%)
Sea Point	33 (13.6%)	209 (86.4%)
Kenilworth	15 (6.6%)	213 (93.4%)
Total	**658 (33.6%)**	**1300 (66.4%)**

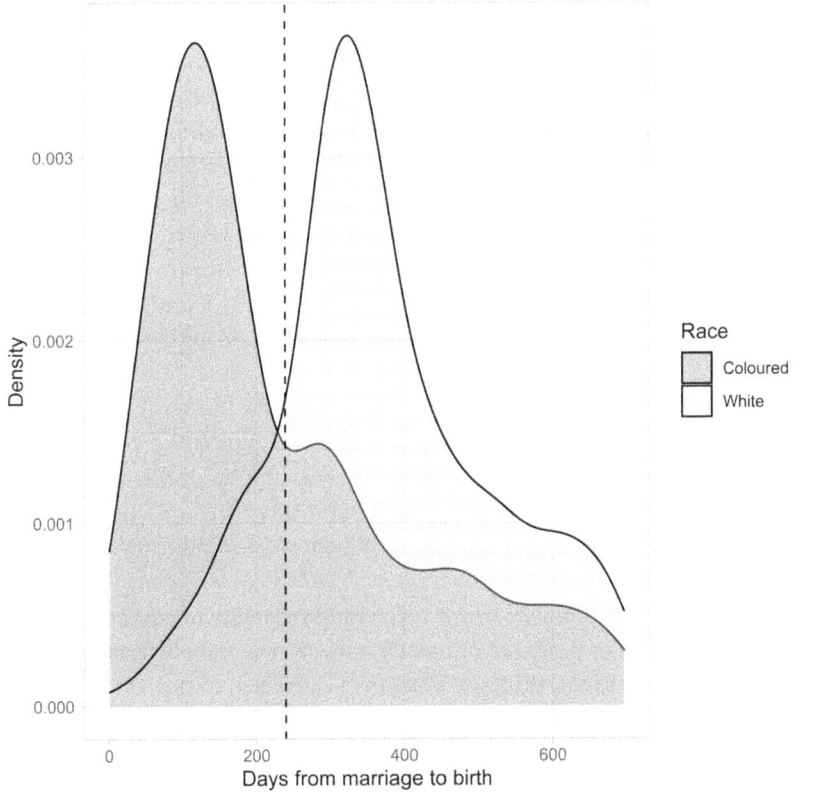

Figure 2.2 Density plot of the number of days elapsed between marriage and the birth of a couple's first child. Couples separated according to race. The vertical dashed line represents eight months from day of marriage.

in the heart of the inner-city (e.g. District Six, Woodstock) were not included because it was thought that slum clearances in the 1930s and 1940s might have lessened population stability, compromising the quality of the data.

This gave us a dataset of 2,308 couples, or 4,616 individuals, married in Cape Town and matched to at least one specific baptismal record between 1900 and 1960. Using the date of a couple's marriage and the date of birth of the first child registered as being born to them we split the dataset into three subsets: couples who gave birth to a child before getting married (i.e. legitimation by subsequent marriage), couples who conceived their first child outside of wedlock but who were able to marry before the child's birth, and couples who both conceived and produced their first child within marriage. In this chapter we consider only the second and third subsets.

Two things were immediately apparent: the average rate of bridal pregnancy in Cape Town was relatively high, but with significant variation between parishes and racial groups. For most of the period under investigation, 1900 to 1960, white and coloured congregants made up roughly equal parts of the Anglican population.[36] However, our dataset was biased in favour of the coloured population, who made up 71 per cent. This was because the largest of the parishes whose data we used, Athlone, served a predominantly coloured working-class area. The dataset is thus also slightly skewed towards the less affluent end of the socio-economic spectrum. To control for this discrepancy, it is possible to extrapolate what the figures might look like with a more accurately distributed population by calculating the likelihood of premarital birth or conception for each race group and then normalising this over the Anglican population as a whole. This puts the bridal pregnancy rate at just under 25 per cent.

For various reasons, this is only a lower bound estimate of the true proportion of men and women engaging in premarital sex in Anglican Cape Town during this time. As Jan van Bavel explains:

> It is common in quantitative historical research to use the incidence of extramarital pregnancy as an indicator for the sexual activity of unmarried people. Indeed, it is probably the best available indicator, but only the tip of the iceberg will be observed this way. We have to take into account that regular sexual intercourse yields a monthly probability of conception of between 15% and 50%.[37]

Conception was further impeded by the increased availability of contraceptive devices, although for much of the period of our study it was a criminal offence to advertise any 'means, methods, medicines, drugs or appliances calculated to prevent or intended for

---

[36] In 1936, for example, coloured membership of the Anglican Church was estimated at 60,086 and white membership at 57,591. See the 1936 Union Census for more details or the Bureau of Census and Statistics, *Union Statistics for Fifty Years Jubilee Issue: 1900–1910* (Pretoria, 1960): 12.

[37] J. van Bavel, 'Family Control, Bridal Pregnancy, and Illegitimacy: An Event History Analysis in Leuven, Belgium, 1846–1856', *Social Science History* 25, no. 3 (2001): 454.

the prevention of conception'.[38] In 1917 the South African Government considered passing legislation to curb access to these devices but could not come to an agreement with doctors about how to prevent birth control from being used for immoral purposes while still making it available in medically legitimate cases, such as for women who were too frail to bear another pregnancy.[39] So, despite information being limited, diaphragms, cervical caps, soluble pessaries and rubber sponges were all legally accessible contraceptive products.[40]

We also had to make allowance for brides whose premaritally conceived pregnancy ended in miscarriage or abortion (which was illegal).[41] It is difficult to find information about abortion during the period of our study, as it was often limited to closed networks of nurses, midwives, pharmaceutical travellers and a small body of independent clients, but court records indicate that a number of women at the Cape were able to make use of this option. Burman and Naude identify thirty-six individual cases of abortion or alleged abortion to reach the Cape Supreme Court between 1896 and 1940.[42] Despite the fact that procuring an abortion could cost upwards of £20 – a sum which would amount to several months' salary for a white domestic servant – it is likely that these cases provide only a glimpse into a far more widespread phenomenon. Indeed, as Bradford's work on abortifacients has shown, women were sometimes prepared to go to considerable lengths 'in the search for elusive control over their fertility'.[43]

The age difference between various groups of brides is commonly used to examine how far premarital sexuality constituted part of 'mainstream' behaviour in a particular setting. Where the difference is small it is likely that pregnant and non-pregnant brides went through similar courtships. Most pregnant brides would be at an age when, like most of their peers, they would be expected to marry soon or at least enter into a stable relationship with a man.

Table 2.3 shows that when brides in our dataset become pregnant just before marriage (with the child being born six to eight months later), the difference between their ages and those of non-pregnant brides (and between the ages of the grooms) was less than a year. Where a child was born very soon after marriage, however, the difference was much larger. Thus, the stage of the courtship process at which a woman fell pregnant seems to have been related to age at marriage.

---

[38] B. Goddefroy, 'Medical and Ethical Aspect of Abortion', *South African Medical Journal* 6 (July 1932): 472.

[39] Klausen, *Race, Maternity, and Politics of Birth Control*, 15.

[40] Ibid, 71.

[41] The likelihood of a pregnancy going to full term was probably lowest in the economic class with the highest concentration of premarital pregnancies, contributing to a downward bias in the data.

[42] Burman and Naude, 'Bearing a Bastard', 378.

[43] H. Bradford, 'Herbs, Knives and Plastic', in *Science, Medicine and Cultural Imperialism*, ed. T. Meade and M. Walker (London: Macmillan, 1991): 124–5.

Table 2.3 Age at marriage by interval between marriage and the birth of the first child for the complete matched dataset.

Birth status	Mean female age	Mean male age	Mean age difference	No. of observations
0–3 months after marriage	20.28	23.02	2.58	197
3–6 months after marriage	21.44	24.08	2.60	359
6–8 months after marriage	22.06	25.55	3.42	102
Post-marital conception	23.48	26.88	3.36	1300

The finding that, in the case of both pregnant and non-pregnant brides, marriages peaked between the ages of twenty-one and twenty-three years for women and twenty-four and twenty-six years for men implies a relatively long period of self-restraint. It also gives the impression that sexual intercourse in the time leading up to marriage was perhaps a more 'normal' behaviour than some accounts suggest, making premarital pregnancy, if not indistinguishable from, then at least fairly similar to 'conventional' pregnancy, particularly when a child was born between six and eight months after a marriage.

On average, coloured couples in the dataset were more than two years younger than white couples at marriage, and working-class men got married between two and three years earlier than their white-collar counterparts. This suggests that much of the variation in marriage age between the three groups is a product of group composition rather than of pregnancy type.

It is also relevant that, especially in the coloured population, the spousal age gap (the difference in age between bride and groom) did not vary significantly between the different conception groups. Historians working with marriage data often use age at first marriage and the spousal age gap as an indicator of female agency, arguing that a low female age at first marriage and a large difference in age between husband and wife diminished a woman's ability to decide the terms of a union and to exert influence within it.[44] A relatively similar spousal age gap and age at first marriage would thus seem to indicate that bridal pregnancy was not simply the result of older men taking advantage of much younger women.

Factors influencing the likelihood of a bridal pregnancy

In South Africa, as elsewhere, it is difficult to pin down exactly what led individuals to adopt, either deliberately or by force of circumstance, one avenue of family formation over another. Both the white and coloured communities claimed to conform to the

---

[44] For further information see S. Carmichael, 'Marriage and Power: Age at First Marriage and Spousal Age Gap in Lesser Developed Countries', *History of the Family* 16, no. 4 (2011): 416–32.

social ideals of European civilisation. The Coloured Joint Council demanded that coloured men and women throughout the Union be subject to the same marriage laws as 'other communities whose methods of life, whose outlook on marriage and its consequences, individual or social, [are] derived from the long established and widely recognised principles of Roman Law'.[45] At the same time, the state and the dominant bourgeoisie strove hard to ensure that respectability – an essential element of which was sexual restraint – became an important part of working-class identity regardless of race.[46] And yet bridal pregnancy remained prevalent, and not merely among the city's 'most wretched' or vulnerable.[47]

To make sense of this paradox, we examined our data to identify the circumstances in which bridal pregnancy occurred and the way ordinary people responded to it. In particular, we hypothesise that bridal pregnancy would have been more common within lower-income groups, for whom respectability was a more flexible concept and where the passage of wealth across generations was less of a concern. Taking into account the research of Burman and Van der Spuy, we also expect that bridal pregnancy would have been a more culturally acceptable and rational choice for the city's coloured inhabitants. During the period under discussion 'the legal and social provisions [around premarital pregnancy] were largely those imposed or provided by one group – the upper-class, white, community'.[48] The coloured population, with its unique cultural history, and its frequent exposure to racial discrimination and economic insecurity (both of which fuelled social immobility), had limited incentive to support these provisions.[49] Moreover, assuming that educated women generally had better access to contraceptive knowledge, we expect to see an inverse relationship between literacy (a crude measure of education) and bridal pregnancy.

The effect of migration on bridal pregnancy is more difficult to predict. Parental control was probably weaker among those who had moved away from their birth communities, meaning that migrants may have been freer to experiment sexually. However, another, potentially competing, hypothesis is that the greater the familiarity between two people, the more likely it was that they (and their parents) would acquiesce in 'risky' courtship behaviour. It is also possible that rural and urban migrants may have behaved differently. Those new to city life, perhaps less accustomed to its pace and anonymity, may have adopted an approach that was more conservative, but their lack of social connections and knowledge may also have increased their vulnerability within courtship.

---

[45]Wits Historical Papers Archive, AD 843, 52/3/6, 'Memorandum of the Marriage Law as It Affects the Cape Coloured Community', 1942.

[46]Dooling, 'Poverty and Respectability', 411.

[47]E. van Heyningen, 'The Social Evil in the Cape Colony 1868–1902: Prostitution and the Contagious Diseases Acts', *Journal of Southern African Studies* 10, no. 2 (1984): 171.

[48]Burman and Naude, 'Bearing a Bastard', 410.

[49]Burman and van der Spuy, 'The Illegitimate and the Illegal', 616–21.

Remarriage is another factor which might have affected the likelihood of a bridal pregnancy. Particularly for women, it makes sense that premarital chastity and the virginity it implied, both factors which might significantly influence one's chances at a first marriage, would be far less important in the courtship preceding a second or third marriage, at which point a loss of virginity would be assumed. It also seems probable that within this context parental control would have been limited; men and women remarrying were generally older, and thus more independent, than those marrying for the first time.

For these reasons, it might be assumed that bridal pregnancy would be a common feature of second or third marriages. Yet, couples entering second and third marriages (many of which were marriages of convenience) might also have had shorter engagements and focused more on practical matters, therein decreasing the possibility of a bridal pregnancy. Relatively older women also had lower fecundity.

To test what effect, if any, the above factors had on the likelihood of a bridal pregnancy we ran a logistic regression (Appendix B). Given a sample size of only seventy-seven black couples, it is difficult to draw statistically significant conclusions about premarital pregnancy and its frequency in this group. It is, however, immediately apparent from the data (see Figure 2.3) that coloured couples in Cape Town did experience significantly higher levels of bridal pregnancy than white couples. Explanations for why this is so are multi-faceted and will require further scholarly debate.

Until linked to census data, the parish registers cannot provide any information about the composition and family backgrounds of individual spouses. We thus could not test factors like father's occupation, the timing of father's or mother's death, the family size and sibling order against more general community attitudes and traits.

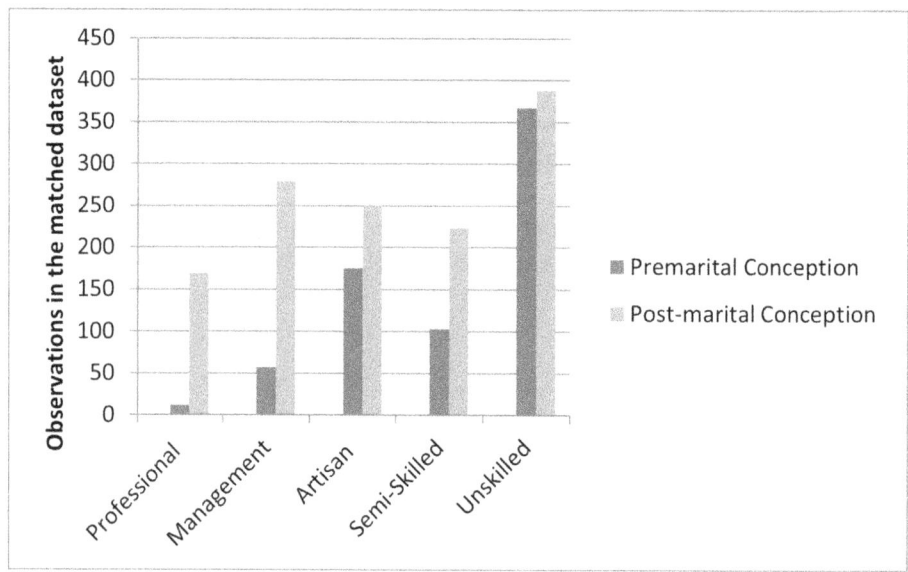

Figure 2.3 Pregnancy type by profession of primary breadwinner in absolute numbers.

Table 2.4 Regression measuring the likelihood of a premarital conception at first marriage of matched Cape Town couples, with a first child baptised between 1900 and 1960.

	Dependent variable: Bridal pregnancy					
	{1}	{2}	{3}	{4}	{5}	{6}
Race black/African (ref = coloured)	12.674	12.623	12.477	12.481	12.480	12.443
	(324.744)	(324.744)	(324.744)	(324.744)	(324.744)	(324.744)
Race white (ref = coloured)	−1.772***	−1.446***	−1.476***	−1.477***	−1.477***	−1.494***
	(0.233)	(0.244)	(0.243)	(0.247)	(0.247)	(0.248)
Occupation professional (ref = artisan)		−1.154**	−1.142**	−1.14**	−1.139**	−1.142**
		(0.453)	(0.453)	(0.457)	(0.456)	(0.457)
Occupation managerial (ref = artisan)		−0.635***	−0.637***	−0.586***	−0.586***	−0.589***
		(0.225)	(0.225)	(0.227)	(0.227)	(0.227)
Occupation semi-skilled (ref = artisan)		−0.132	−0.096	−0.105	−0.079	−0.087
		(0.178)	(0.179)	(0.181)	(0.181)	(0.182)
Occupation unskilled (ref = artisan)		0.021	0.077	0.085	0.091	0.088
		(0.145)	(0.148)	(0.149)	(0.149)	(0.149)
Male signed			0.469**	0.483**	0.465**	0.486**
			(0.218)	(0.219)	(0.219)	(0.220)
Female signed			0.664***	0.659***	0.654***	0.651***
			(0.233)	(0.234)	(0.234)	(0.234)
Male rural migrant (ref = native of Cape Town)				0.399	0.402	0.381
				(0.260)	(0.260)	(0.261)
Male urban migrant (ref = native of Cape Town)				0.088	0.076	0.054

Dependent variable:
Bridal pregnancy

	{1}	{2}	{3}	{4}	{5}	{6}
				(0.558)	(0.559)	(0.560)
Male international migrant (ref = native of Cape Town)				0.226	0.219	0.217
				(0.677)	(0.678)	(0.677)
Female rural migrant (ref = native of Cape Town)				−0.018	−0.032	−0.035
				(0.261)	(0.262)	(0.262)
female urban migrant (ref = native of Cape Town)				−0.703	−0.711	−0.703
				(0.640)	(0.641)	(0.641)
female international migrant (ref = native of Cape Town)				0.206	0.213	0.21
				(0.898)	(0.898)	(0.897)
migration status (common)				0.207	0.204	0.198
				(0.246)	(0.246)	(0.246)
Male migration status (missing)				−0.564	−0.558	−0.563
				(0.622)	(0.622)	(0.622)
Female migration status (missing)				0.311	0.320	0.317
				(0.611)	(0.612)	(0.612)
Male remarriage					−0.526	−0.648*
					(0.321)	(0.341)
Female remarriage					−0.092	−0.092
					(0.369)	(0.375)
Age difference						0.017
						(0.016)

Dependent variable:
Bridal pregnancy

	{1}	{2}	{3}	{4}	{5}	{6}
Parish, Kennilworth, Christ Church (ref = Athlone, St. Marks)	−0.759**	−0.479	−0.51	−0.500	0.508	−0.517
	(0.353)	(0.366)	(0.366)	(0.393)	(0.393)	(0.393)
Parish, Seapoint, St. James the Great	−0.134	0.007	−0.146	−1.21	−0.217	−0.235
	(0.413)	(0.419)	(0.421)	(0.422)	(0.423)	(0.423)
Parish, Mowbray, St Peters	0.335**	0.334**	0.290*	0.355**	0.353**	0.351**
	(0.157)	(0.158)	(0.159)	(0.164)	(0.165)	(0.165)
Parish, Parow, St. Margarets	−0.337	−0.413	−0.417	−0.247	−0.248	−0.255
	(0.358)	(0.358)	(0.359)	(0.381)	(0.381)	(0.381)
Parish, Maitland, Good Shepard	0.1	0.054	0.197	0.2	0.21	0.204
	(0.263)	(0.266)	(0.274)	(0.274)	(0.276)	(0.276)
Parish, Langa, St. Cyprian's	−14.086	−14.056	−13.92	−13.778	−13.723	−13.766
	(324.744)	(324.744)	(324.744)	(324.744)	(324.744)	(324.744)
Year baptised	0.004	0.005	0.001	−0.006	−0.006	−0.006
	(0.006)	(0.006)	(0.006)	(0.008)	(0.008)	(0.008)
Constant	−7.167	−9.62	−2.708	10.448	11.062	10.798
	(11.213)	(11.74)	(11.895)	(14.659)	(14.672)	(14.665)
Observations	1603	1589	1589	1589	1588	1588
Log likelihood	−928.623	−917.47	−908.538	−904.557	−902.858	−902.268
Akaike Inf. Crit.	1887.246	1862.939	1849.076	1859.115	1859.715	1860.536

*p<0.1; **p<0.05; ***p<0.01

Table 2.5 Regression measuring the likelihood of a Sunday baptism of matched Cape Town couples, with a first child baptised between 1900 and 1960.

	Dependent variable:		
	Baptism Sunday		
	{1}	{2}	{3}
Bridal pregnancy	−1.405***	−1.624***	−2.245***
	(0.145)	(0.155)	(0.194)
Race white (ref = coloured)		−1.783***	−2.802***
		(0.297)	(0.341)
Race black/African (ref = coloured)		12.336	10.615
		(324.744)	(324.746)
I (Race white × bridal pregnancy)			2.541***
			(0.433)
I (Race black/African × bridal pregnancy)			2.007*
			(1.204)
Constant	44.073	43.317	45.863
	(12.811)	(13.046)	(13.183)
Parish fixed effects	Yes	Yes	Yes
Year fixed effects	Yes	Yes	Yes
Month fixed effects	Yes	Yes	Yes
Observations	1528	1528	1525
Log likelihood	−746.051	−725.803	−705.56
Akaike Inf. Crit.	1532.102	1495.607	1459.119

Although difficult to prove unequivocally, it does appear that bridal pregnancy may have carried less stigma in the coloured community. This could explain (and be explained by) the prevalence of bridal pregnancy in this community.[50] To examine this hypothesis (namely that bridal pregnancy carried less stigma in the coloured community) we assume that the larger the stigma attached to premarital pregnancy within a particular community, the less likely parents would be to baptise their premaritally conceived children on a Sunday – a day on which baptisms typically took place in full view of the congregation. We tested this hypothesis by running a regression. The results, shown in Table 2.5, indicate that only when combined with race did the incidence of a bridal pregnancy affect the day on which a couple baptised

---

[50] The parish registers also provide no way for researchers to distinguish between children born of consensual and non-consensual premarital sex despite the fact that exploitative relationships (i.e. rape or incest) may account for some of the observed births.

their child. In other words, white couples were less likely than coloured couples to have their premaritally conceived child baptised on a Sunday. This suggests that for coloured couples the stigma associated with bridal pregnancy was not a significant deterrent to Sunday baptism.

However, stigma alone does not explain why premarital pregnancy was so much less likely among white Capetonians.[51] So what deterred young white couples from falling pregnant out of wedlock? Better access to birth control was probably one factor. Another may be that premarital pregnancy could thwart white women's aspirations.

During South Africa's industrial take-off, white South Africans experienced high levels of social mobility. For white men, upward mobility was primarily the product of intergenerational improvements in occupational attainment.[52] For white women it was mostly through marriage, but the possibility of 'marrying up' existed only for 'the right sort of women'.[53] These women thus had a strong incentive to be seen as respectable and to avoid behaviour, particularly extramarital sex, which would diminish their prospects on the marriage market.

Coloured women, by contrast, may have had lesser aspirations – or at least recognised that the kind of position available to white women was probably beyond their grasp. With segregation slowly replacing assimilation in liberal ideology and practice, opportunities for social and material advancement became increasingly slim for the coloured community, undermining the incentive to remain chaste.[54] This explanation, though, excludes the calculations of lighter-skinned coloured women for whom marriage to a man socially recognised as 'white' may have been a route to middle-class status.

Caution needs to be exercised, however, before concluding that race was in any way a driver of bridal pregnancy. The data enabled us to hold profession constant and make comparisons between race groups, but not to take into account the policies of racial discrimination that would have given white artisans, for example, or white teachers, a better income than their coloured counterparts. Furthermore, even if race did influence the attitudes and practices of certain parts of the coloured community, the term 'community' itself is problematic in that it suggests a level of social cohesion which is unlikely to have existed in reality. It may have been that a greater cosmopolitanism and tolerance of difference predominated in certain diverse, socially and economically

---

[51] This is obviously an imperfect assumption, although it does seem that, if not sexual practice, then at least sexual desire has been largely constant over time. E. Griffin, 'Sex, Illegitimacy and Social Change', *Social History* 38, no. 2 (2013): 141.

[52] J. Cilliers and J. Fourie, 'Occupational Mobility during South Africa's Industrial Take-Off', *South African Journal of Economics* 86, no. 1 (2018): 4.

[53] *Imperial Colonist*, (2) (4), April 1903 quoted in J. Bush, '"The Right Sort of Woman": Female Emigrators and Emigration to the British Empire, 1890–1910', *Women's History Review* 3, no. 3 (1994): 395.

[54] This was despite the continued existence of a non-racial franchise and the formal equality of all citizens before the law – both part of Cape Town's so-called 'special tradition'. V. Bickford-Smith, 'South African Urban History, Racial Segregation and the Unique Case of Cape Town?', *Journal of South African Studies* 21, no. 1 (1995): 68.

complex, lower-income and largely coloured or mixed residential areas than in white middle-class suburbs. However, in slightly more affluent coloured areas like Walmer Estate, formerly part of District Six, attitudes were probably far less flexible.

In foregrounding race it is also easy to overlook the extent to which bridal pregnancy was contingent on other factors such as changing class attitudes towards courtship, educational and economic opportunities, social cohesion and the effects of poverty and urbanisation on relationships between men and women in Cape Town. Our data indicate that in the Anglican community it was not just coloured women but working- and lower-class coloured women who were most likely to fall pregnant before marriage. This is logical for a number of reasons.

In an environment where bourgeois status and the accumulation of wealth across generations depended on legitimate children inheriting, bridal pregnancy was especially risky for the more affluent. The courtship of couples from wealthy backgrounds, whether white or coloured, was therefore likely to be very public and monitored by a chaperone. Engagements became longer and more ritualised as the century progressed but nevertheless did not entirely prevent such pregnancies from taking place. Indeed, a small number of pregnant brides in our dataset occupied semi-professional positions in teaching and clerical work. However, middle- and upper-class couples, whether because of better access to contraception or greater incentive to remain chaste, were far less likely to fall pregnant before marriage than their less affluent counterparts.

Yet bridal pregnancy, as well as the premarital sexual activity which it implied, was by no means a phenomenon specific to the poor.[55] Rather, as Figure 2.3 shows, it was relatively common, even among the 'respectable' working classes.

To understand why this was so, we need to recognise the ambivalent status of the young people in this group and the conflicting incentives that motivated them. In urban working-class communities, with fathers and mothers at work all day, youths were often less restricted in their courtship activities than their middle-class peers and spent more time unsupervised with members of the opposite sex. Cramped homes meant that they sought, and were perforce permitted, recreational possibilities beyond domestic surveillance.

From the 1930s and 1940s in District Six and other working-class communities in Cape Town, there were many ways that young people could mix with the opposite sex. There were beach outings and mountain picnics, cinema-going was particularly popular, and the number of dancehalls and cabaret clubs was growing.[56] In Sea Point from the

---

[55] An example of the prevailing discourse surrounding premarital sexuality is provided by R. Solinger, 'The Girl Nobody Loved: Psychological Explanations for White Single Pregnancy in the Pre-Roe v. Wade Era, 1945–1965', *Frontiers* 11, no. 2 (1990): 47. For a more South African interpretation see: A. Loots, 'Die Ongehude Moeder: Volgens 'n Studie in die Inrigtings vir Ongehude Moeders in Kaapstad' (MA diss., Stellenbosch University, Stellenbosch, 1951).

[56] B. Nasson, '"She preferred living in a cave with Harry the snake-catcher": Towards an Oral History of Popular Leisure and Class Expression in District Six, Cape Town, c. 1920s–1950s', paper presented at the Wits history workshop, 'The Making of Class', 9–14 February 1987.

1930s to the 1950s coloured youths would spend hours wandering together on Lion's Head, enjoying the relative privacy that the mountain allowed them. When not up the mountain they would escape the confinement of their homes to socialise in the street, often deliberately seeking out members of the opposite sex. An interviewee remembered that 'standing on Allie Parker's *stoep* [local shop front] was something. You could watch the girls'.[57]

As a result of these activities – some of which would have been discouraged in middle class families – working-class youths had more opportunity to experiment sexually. Despite this relative freedom, though, social integration and family pressure in these communities ensured that should a pregnancy occur a marriage usually followed.

A 1950 thesis on coloured factory workers in the late 1940s described how in middle-class coloured families it would hardly ever happen that a girl would fall pregnant and not get married. The only known case in three years 'was treated as an absolute disaster'. Among working-class families unmarried pregnancy was more common and the parents would 'not be quite so drastic'. The girl would 'most probably get a hiding' and the man would be made to marry her, but once they were married the incident would be forgotten.[58]

What is being described here is not a collapse of social control over the working-class youth but rather a process of value stretching in which working-class groups subscribed to middle-class values when and if circumstances allowed, but also developed their own alternative values. These values enabled them to uphold the mantle of respectability while acting in ways which accommodated their practical needs. In a society where working-class youths were often regarded as a source of additional income for their families and were expected to have the resources necessary to set up a home before marrying, there were genuine restrictions on marriage.[59] Still, the fact that extramarital pregnancies did usually end in marriage attests, if not to the centrality of marriage within this social stratum, then at least to its long-term desirability. In working-class communities the family played an important part in mediating courtship relations.

After controlling for socio-economic status and race, one of our most surprising findings was the positive association between bridal pregnancy and female literacy; in other words, the more educated a woman, the more likely she was to fall pregnant before marriage. Initially we assumed this was a selection effect of our study period starting in 1900. Illiterate women born in, say 1870, and marrying earlier because of pregnancy were missing from the dataset, whereas illiterates marrying after 1900, who were older and less likely to be pregnant at marriage, would have been included. In a separate

---

[57]M. Paulse, 'An Oral History of Tramway Road and Ilford Street, Sea Point, 1930s–2001: The Production of Place, by Race, Class and Gender' (PhD diss., University of Cape Town, Cape Town, 2002): 164, 172.
[58]A.G. Weiss, 'The Cape Coloured Woman: Within an Industrial Community and at Home' (MA diss., University of Cape Town, Cape Town, 1950): 44–5.
[59]Paulse, 'Oral History of Tramway Road and Ilford Street', 80–2. Paulse explains that for residents in her sample marriage during their early twenties permitted young adults to contribute economically to their parental households for a certain period of their adult lives before setting up their own independent households.

analysis (not shown here) we tested this assumption and controlled for age at marriage, as well as for any interaction between age and illiteracy, but the effect remained more or less the same. We were puzzled by this, since literacy could be supposed to reflect better knowledge of contraception. But in Cape Town other factors related to literacy may have been more important. Illiterate women may have been more likely than literate women to have jobs, for example as domestic servants, that came with stricter control or less opportunities to meet and spend time with men. Literate women may also have had greater bargaining power – because of higher social or cultural capital – in marriage negotiations, which enabled them to make sure that the progenitor of their child did not abandon them.

Women in our dataset were generally less likely to remarry than men.[60] Interestingly, it seems that women marrying a bachelor had a higher chance of bridal pregnancy than women marrying a widower. This may have been because widowers, possibly seeking a new wife to take care of the children and the household, took a more practical approach to marriage and were less likely to enter into protracted courtships. We did not find a strong correlation between female remarriage and bridal pregnancy, suggesting perhaps that spinsters and widows were subject to similar expectations and controls regarding their sexual behaviour prior to marriage.

As expected, age difference between spouses was not linked to the likelihood of a bridal pregnancy. Nor was migration status, but this may simply reflect the lack of data – only about a third of our dataset had this status recorded – so any conclusions on the basis of this information must be tentative.

Conclusion

While it is useful to keep in mind the sensitive nature of this kind of data, statistics on bridal pregnancy offer us a fascinating window through which it is possible to observe intimate life in the past. Analysing long-term trends in America, Smith and Hindus describe a cycle of increasing and decreasing bridal pregnancy levels.[61] They attribute this to the degree of incorporation of adolescents and young adults into broader society: the more they felt they had a 'stake in society', in the sense of job security, career prospects and political representation, the stronger was their adherence to and internalisation of dominant sexual norms. Church sanctions against bridal pregnancy (or 'fornication') had been fierce, especially in the seventeenth century in Scotland, the puritan colonies in North America and the Netherlands but weakened over time. In

---

[60] See for example F. van Poppel, 'Widows, Widowers and Remarriage in Nineteenth Century Netherlands', *Population Studies* 49, no. 3 (1995): 421–41.

[61] Smith and Hindus, 'Premarital Pregnancy in America', 550. Similar cycles have also been observed in Europe, see for example J. Kok, 'The Moral Nation: Illegitimacy and Bridal Pregnancy in the Netherlands from 1600 to the Present', *Economic and Social History in the Netherlands* II (1990): 7–35.

the Netherlands, for instance, the mainstream Dutch Reformed Church had abandoned punishment altogether by 1850. In Anglican Cape Town, there seem not to have been any official sanctions against premarital pregnancy, but white couples seem to have felt the congregation's reprobation more than coloured couples and avoided public baptisms on Sundays.[62]

Overall, our dataset shows that approximately a quarter of legitimate first-born children were conceived before marriage. This in itself already indicates a low level of conformity to Anglican sexual norms. The fact that pregnant and non-pregnant brides were all much the same age further suggests that intercourse in the final stages of courtship was common, albeit risky. It must be acknowledged, though, that the incidence of bridal pregnancy differed widely between parishes; our research suggests that this variation can be attributed, at least in part, to the unique racial and socio-economic composition of each parish. Coloured and/or working-class youths were far more likely to experience a premarital pregnancy. Explanations for why this is so are complex, although one possible reason for this finding might be that such youths generally had a lesser stake (i.e. limited career prospects, social mobility and political representation) in Cape Anglican society, and thus fewer incentives to comply with its social and religious dictates.

Statistics on bridal pregnancy can tell us something about the relative agency of the sexes. Various authors have commented on the 'double standard' in courtship.[63] In the Victorian era women were supposed to be chaste and ignorant in sexual matters, but by not giving in to male demands they ran the risk of being labelled prudish. They alone carried the risk of pregnancy with all the social, health and reputational consequences attached. It is probable that a woman in a strong bargaining position, with her own income, job and support network, would engage in sex only when she was sure that her partner would marry her if she fell pregnant. Possibly, this explains why in our Cape Town dataset more literate than illiterate brides were pregnant. The rules of the 'sexual game' changed with the arrival of reliable and cheap contraceptives. There is still much to be learned about who had knowledge of and access to condoms and pessaries and who was supposed to take the initiative to use them. This hidden history might still come to light if surviving members of our dataset could be interviewed. 'Ego documents' such as letters, diaries, memoirs and local newspapers, as well as oral history, can be used to put our analysis in its proper local context: the entertainment world, meeting places, the rituals and stages of courtship in each neighbourhood and social class, perceptions and memories of social control and stigma, and so on.

Bridal pregnancy also sheds light on family economics. Young people setting up a household needed not only their own savings and salary but also financial support from their parents. 'Untimely' marriages could be a drain on parental resources and

---

[62]K. McQuillan, 'When Does Religion Influence Fertility?' *Population and Development Review* 30, no. 1 (2004): 25–56.

[63]See for example G. Alter, *Family and the Female Life Course: The Women of Verviers, Belgium, 1849–1880* (Madison: University of Wisconsin Press, 1988).

could deprive parents of their child's contribution. Intergenerational economic relations thus played a large part in parental control and in adolescents' internalisation of norms. Children who expected to join or take over a family business were more likely to comply with parental advice to delay marriage until the right moment. Our dataset suggests that Cape Town working-class families were less concerned than other socio-economic groups with when and how their children married. In addition, many working-class youths had to hand over all or at least a sizable part of their wages to their parents. This might have been an incentive for them to start their own families. Some studies show that bridal pregnancy could be an intentional strategy to claim independence from parents.[64]

Finally, we would like to emphasise that studies like ours will yield more insights for social historians if bridal pregnancy is seen not as a single demographic 'event' but as part of male and female life courses. It can then be seen as a result of socialisation, family dynamics, education, work experience and migration. It may also be seen as the cause of later life outcomes. A forwarded marriage could set a couple back in financial terms relative to their later marrying peers. The 'forced' nature of such a marriage could increase the chance of a later separation or divorce. What is ideally needed to pursue such questions are birth cohorts representative of the different parts of the population. Life courses could be reconstituted and compared in terms of family background (socio-economic status, number, age and gender of siblings, parental survival), migration history, education and work, marriage and own family, time (and if possible) cause of death. Such standardised biographies are a vital heuristic tool to understand how individuals and their families responded to, and in turn shaped, societal forces and factors such as demographic patterns, economic structures and opportunities, and shifting sexual morals.[65] Creating a longitudinal micro-level database is extremely time-consuming, but this chapter shows it was feasible to link different life events documented in church records. A next step would be to link these records to the census and other extant sources. Record linkage projects are taking off worldwide, often making use of crowdsourcing and newly available computational techniques. Reconstructed life courses can be a powerful addition to the toolbox of social historians, helping us to compare the experiences of women and men of different races, born into different classes and at different periods.

---

[64] Kok, Bras and Rotering, 'Courtship and Bridal Pregnancy', 170; M. Oris, G. Alter and P. Servais, 'Prudence as Obstinate Resistance to Pressure: Marriage in Nineteenth-Century Rural Eastern Belgium', in *Similarity in Difference: Marriage in Europe and Asia, 1700–1900*, ed. C. Lundh and S. Kurosu (Cambridge, US: Harvard MIT Press, 2014).

[65] T.K. Hareven, *Families, History, and Social Change, Life-Course and Cross-Cultural Perspectives* (Boulder: Westview Press, 2000). For an overview of the scientific output of a database with life courses, see K. Mandemakers and J. Kok, 'Dutch Lives. The Historical Sample of the Netherlands (1987–): Development and Research', *Historical Life Course Studies* (2020). Available online: http://hdl.handle.net/10622/23526343-2020-0001?locatt=view:master.

Bibliography

Åkerman, S. 'An Evaluation of the Family Reconstitution Technique'. *Scandinavian Economic History Review* 25, no. 2 (1977): 160–70.

Alter, G. *Family and the Female Life Course: The Woman of Verviers, Belgium, 1849–1880.* Madison: University of Wisconsin Press, 1988.

Bickford-Smith, V. 'South African Urban History, Racial Segregation and the Unique Case of Cape Town?' *Journal of Southern African Studies* 21, no. 1 (1995): 63–78.

Bickford-Smith, V., E. van Heyningen and N. Worden. *Cape Town in the Twentieth Century.* Cape Town: David Philip, 1999.

Bradford, H. 'Herbs, Knives and Plastic'. In *Science, Medicine and Cultural Imperialism*, edited by T. Meade and M. Walker, 120–47. London: Macmillan, 1991.

Breckinridge, K. 'Reasons for Writing: African Working-Class Letter-Writing in Early Twentieth Century South Africa'. In *Africa's Hidden Histories: Everyday Literacy and Making the Self*, edited by K. Barber, 143–54. Bloomington: Indiana University Press, 2006.

Burman, S. and M. Naude. 'Bearing a Bastard: The Social Consequences of Illegitimacy in Cape Town, 1896–1939'. *Journal of Southern African Studies* 17, no. 3 (1991): 373–413.

Burman, S. and P. van der Spuy. 'The Illegitimate and the Illegal in a South African City: The Effects of Apartheid on Births out of Wedlock'. *Journal of Social History* 29, no. 3 (1996): 613–35.

Burns, C. 'Controlling Birth: Johannesburg, 1920–1960'. *South African Historical Journal* 50, no. 1 (2004): 170–98.

Bush, J. '"The Right Sort of Woman": Female Emigrators and Emigration to the British Empire, 1890–1910'. *Women's History Review* 3, no. 3 (1994): 358–409.

Campbell, C. 'Demographic Techniques: Family Reconstitution'. In *International Encyclopaedia of the Social and Behavioural Sciences*, edited by J. Wright, 2nd edn. Oxford: Elsevier, 2015. Available online: https://www.elsevier.com/books/international-encyclopedia-of-the-social-and-behavioral-sciences/wright/978-0-08-097086-8.

Carmichael, S. 'Marriage and Power: Age at First Marriage and Spousal Age Gap in Lesser Developed Countries'. *History of the Family* 16, no. 4 (2011): 416–36.

Cilliers, J. and J. Fourie. 'Occupational Mobility during South Africa's Industrial Take-Off'. *South African Journal of Economics* 86, no. 1 (2018): 3–22.

Delius, P. and C. Glaser. 'Sexual Socialisation in South Africa: A Historical Perspective'. *African Studies* 61, no. 1 (2002): 27–54.

Dooling, W. 'Poverty and Respectability in Early Twentieth Century Cape Town'. *Journal of African History* 59, no. 2 (2018): 411–35.

Duff, S.E. 'Facts about Ourselves: Negotiating Sexual Knowledge in Early Twentieth-Century South Africa'. *Kronos* 41, no. 1 (2015): 215–35.

Fourie, J. and F. Herranz-Loncan. 'Growth (and Segregation) by Rail: How the Railways shaped Colonial South Africa'. *ERSA Working Paper*, no. 538 (2016).

Fourie, J. and E. Green. 'Building the Cape of Good Hope Panel'. *The History of the Family* 23, no. 3 (2018): 493–502.

Frost, G. *Promises Broken: Courtship, Class, and Gender in Victorian England.* Charlottesville: University of Virginia Press, 1995.

Glaser, C. 'Managing the Sexuality of Urban Youth: Johannesburg, 1920s–1960s'. *International Journal of African Historical Studies* 38, no. 2 (2005): 301–27.

Griffin, E. 'Sex, Illegitimacy and Social Change'. *Social History* 38, no. 2 (2013): 139–61.

Hair, P.E.H. 'Bridal Pregnancy in Rural England in Earlier Centuries'. *Population Studies* 20 (1966): 233–43.

Hair, P.E.H. 'Bridal Pregnancy in Earlier Rural England Further Examined'. *Population Studies* 24, no. 1 (1970): 59–70.

Hareven, T.K. *Families, History, and Social Change, Life-Course and Cross-Cultural Perspectives*. Boulder: Westview Press, 2000.

Hellmann, E. *Rooiyard: A Sociological Survey of an Urban Slum Yard*. Cape Town: Oxford University Press, 1948.

Hodes, R. 'Kink and the Colony: Sexual Deviance in the Medical History of South Africa, c. 1893–1939'. *Journal of Southern African Studies* 41, no. 4 (2015): 715–33.

Jochelson, K. *The Colour of Disease: Syphilis and Racism in South Africa, 1880–1950*. Oxford: Palgrave, 2001.

Kim, Y. and J. Lee. 'Bridal Pregnancy and Women's Educational Attainment in South Korea, 1970–2009'. *History of the Family* 23, no. 3 (2018): 426–45.

Klausen, S. *Race, Maternity, and the Politics of Birth Control, 1910–1939*. Basingstoke: Palgrave Macmillan, 2004.

Kok, J. 'The Moral Nation: Illegitimacy and Bridal Pregnancy in the Netherlands from 1600 to the Present'. *Economic and Social History in the Netherlands II* 2 (1990): 7–35.

Kok, J., H. Bras and P. Rotering. 'Courtship and Bridal Pregnancy in the Netherlands, 1870–1950'. *Annales De Démographie Historique* 2 (2016): 165–91.

Laslett, P. *The World We Have Lost*. London: Methuen, 1965.

Longmore, L. *The Dispossessed: A Study of the Sex Life of Bantu Women in Urban Areas in and around Johannesburg*. London: Jonathan Cape, 1959.

Loots, A. 'Die Ongehude Moeder: Volgens 'n Studie in die Inrigtings vir Ongehude Moeders in Kaapstad'. MA diss., Stellenbosch University, Stellenbosch, 1951.

Malherbe, V. 'Illegitimacy and Family Formation in Colonial Cape Town to c. 1850'. *Journal of Social History* 39, no. 4 (2006): 1153–76.

Mandemakers, K. and J. Kok. 'Dutch Lives, the Historical Sample of the Netherlands (1987–): Development and Research'. *Historical Life Course Studies* (2020). Available online: http://hdl.handle.net/10622/23526343-2020-0001?locatt=view:master.

McQuillan, K. 'When Does Religion Influence Fertility?' *Population and Development Review* 30, no. 1 (2004): 25–56.

Moodie, T.D., V. Ndatshe and B. Sibuyi. 'Migrancy and Male Sexuality on the South African Gold Mines'. *Journal of Southern African Studies* 14, no. 2 (1988): 228–56.

Nasson, B. '"She preferred living in a cave with Harry the snake-catcher": Towards an Oral History of Popular Leisure and Class Expression in District Six, Cape Town, c. 1920s–1950s'. Paper presented at the Wits History Workshop: 'The Making of Class', 9–14 February 1987.

Oris, M., G. Alter and P. Servais. 'Prudence as Obstinate Resistance to Pressure: Marriage in Ninteenth-Century Rural Eastern Belgium'. In *Similarity in Difference: Marriage in Europe and Asia, 1700–1900*, edited by C. Lundh and S. Kurosu, 261–93. Cambridge, US: Harvard MIT Press, 2014.

Paulse, M. 'An Oral History of Tramway Road and Ilford Street, Sea Point, 1930s–2001: The Production of Place, by Race, Class and Gender'. PhD diss., University of Cape Town, Cape Town, 2002.

Posel, D. 'Marriage at the Drop of a Hat: Housing and Partnership in South Africa's Urban African Townships, 1920s–1960s'. *History Workshop Journal* 61 (2006): 57–76.

Raymo, J. and M. Iwasawa. 'Bridal Pregnancy and Spouse Pairing Patterns in Japan'. *Journal of Marriage and Family* 70, no. 4 (2008): 847–60.

Reay, B. 'The Context and Meaning of Popular Literacy: Some Evidence from Nineteenth-Century Rural England'. *Past & Present* 131 (1991): 89–129.

Refshauge, W. 'Non-Marital Pregnancy in Australia'. MA diss., Australian National University, Canberra, 1982.

Rijpma, A., J. Cilliers and J. Fourie. 'Record Linkage in the Cape of Good Hope Panel'. *Historical Methods: A Journal of Quantitative and Interdisciplinary History* 53, no. 2 (2020): 112–29.

Rive, R. *Writing Black*. Cape Town: David Philip, 1981.

Robin, J. 'Prenuptial Pregnancy in a Rural Area of Devonshire in the Mid-nineteenth Century: Colyton, 1851–1881'. *Continuity and Change* 1, no. 1 (1986): 113–24.

Romano, S. *Moralising Poverty: The 'Undeserving' Poor in the Public Gaze*. London: Routledge, 2018.

Smith, D.S. and M. Hindus. 'Premarital Pregnancy in America, 1640–1971: An Overview and Interpretation'. *Journal of Interdisciplinary History* 5, no. 4 (1975): 537–70.

Solinger, R. 'The Girl Nobody Loved: Psychological Explanations for White Single Pregnancy in the Pre-Roe v. Wade Era, 1945–1965'. *Frontiers* 11, no. 2 (1990): 45–54.

Thestrup, P. 'Methodological Problems of a Family Reconstitution Study in a Danish Rural Parish before 1800'. *Scandinavian Economic History Review* 20, no. 1 (1972): 1–26.

Van Bavel, J. 'Family Control, Bridal Pregnancy, and Illegitimacy: An Event History Analysis in Leuven, Belgium, 1846–1856'. *Social Science History* 25, no. 3 (2001): 449–79.

Van Graan, A. 'The Influences on the two Inner City Housing Projects of the Bo Kaap and District Six in Cape Town That Were Built between 1938 and 1944'. MA diss., University of Cape Town, Cape Town, 2004.

Van Heyningen, E. 'The Social Evil in the Cape Colony, 1868–1902: Prostitution and the Contagious Diseases Acts'. *Journal of Southern African Studies* 10, no. 2 (1984): 170–97.

Van Poppel, F. 'Widows, Widowers, and Remarriage in Nineteenth Century Netherlands'. *Population Studies* 49, no. 3 (2005): 421–41.

Vincent, L. 'Bread and Honour: White Working Class Women and Afrikaner Nationalism in the 1930s'. *Journal of Southern African Studies* 26, no. 1 (2000): 61–78.

Walker, C., ed. *Women and Gender in southern Africa to 1945*. Cape Town: David Philip, 1990.

Weiss, A.G. 'The Cape Coloured Woman: Within an Industrial Community and At Home'. MA diss., University of Cape Town, Cape Town, 1950.

Williams, W.M. *The Sociology of an English Village: Gosforth*. London: Routledge & Kegan Paul, 1956.

Wrigley, E.A. 'Some Problems of Family Reconstitution using English Parish Register Material'. *Proceedings of the 3rd International Economic History Conference, Munich 1965. Section VII, Demography and Economy*. Paris: De Gruyter Mouton, 1972.

Wrigley, E. 'Births and Baptisms: The Use of Anglican Baptism Registers as a Source of Information about the Numbers of Births in England before the Beginning of Civil Registration'. *Population Studies* 31, no. 2 (1977): 281–312.

Primary Sources

The Anchor. 'The Bishop of Oxford on the Responsibility of Marriage'. 15 August 1916.

The Anchor. 'The White Cross League'. 15 March 1916.

Bureau of Census and Statistics. *Union Statistics for Fifty Jubilee Issue: 1900–1910*. Pretoria: Government Printers, 1960.

Cape Argus. 'The Marion Institute'. 18 May 1922.

Republic of South Africa. Bureau of Statistics. *Population Census 1936, Vol. VI: Religions*. Pretoria: Government Printers, 1938.

UCT Special Collections. BC 1557. *Church of the Province of South Africa Handbook of Instructions Regarding Marriages*. Cape Town, 1914.

Wits Historical Papers Archive. AD 843, 52/3/6. 'Memorandum of the Marriage Law as it affects the Cape Coloured Community', 1942.

Wits Historical Papers Archive. AD 1715, 24/2/4. 'The Coloured People: A Factual Survey'. South African Institute of Race Relations, 1953.

Appendix A: Record Linkage

The method used to link the baptism and marriage records in this chapter owes much to the pioneering work of Stellenbosch University's Cape of Good Hope Panel project, which has developed a sophisticated procedure for linking households in the Cape Colony tax records over several generations.[66] We used a 'random forest' model to predict whether a couple in the marriage register could be successfully matched to a couple in the baptism records.[67] We first created a training dataset using manual observation. We then identified candidates for comparison using the Jaro-Winkler string distance (with the penalty for first mismatches in the first four characters set to 0.15) between the men's surnames as the main blocking variable.[68] Half of the available data was subsequently used to fit a statistical model where the distances predict for each candidate pair the true manual link. The final step was to apply this model to the complete dataset.

In our final analysis we excluded couples who registered a birth ten or more years after their marriage, as they might have left the parish temporarily or have had miscarriages or stillbirths, meaning that previous pregnancies may have gone unrecorded in a particular parish register. We found that the average interval between birth and baptism, excluding adult baptisms, was roughly three months (101 days). There may also have been a number of children who died before they were able to be baptised – a problem which demographic historians have been grappling with for some time.[69]

---

[66] A. Rijpma, J. Cilliers and J. Fourie, 'Record Linkage in the Cape of Good Hope Panel', *Historical Methods: A Journal of Quantitative and Interdisciplinary History* 53, no. 2 (2020): 112–29.

[67] The authors designed this model in collaboration with Auke Rijpma of Utrecht University, who also helped develop the linkage strategy used in the Cape of Good Hope Panel project. For more information on this project see J. Fourie and E. Green, 'Building the Cape of Good Hope Panel', *The History of the Family* 23, no. 3 (2018): 493–502.

[68] The Jaro-Winkler distance is a string metric which measures the degree of similarity between two sequences and which is often used in record linkage to compare names in different datasets. The metric is scaled from 0 (not similar at all) to 1 (exact match) and uses a prefix scale 'p' which gives a higher similarity score when two strings have a common prefix of a defined maximum length. The Jaro-Winkler distance was used in this chapter as a means of filtering the available data by identifying candidates with like surnames and then situating them in distinct blocks within which further comparisons could then made on the basis of other key variables (first names, home addresses, professional status, etc.).

[69] E. Wrigley, 'Births and Baptisms: The Use of Anglican Baptism Registers as a Source of Information about the Numbers of Births in England before the Beginning of Civil Registration', *Population Studies* 31, no. 2 (1977): 281–312.

Appendix B: Regressions

Regression 1: General

$$\log\left(\frac{p}{1-p}\right) = B_0 + B_{1(race)} + B_{2(occupation)} + B_{4(literacy)}$$
$$+ B_{3(migration)} + B_{5(remarriage)} + B_{4(agedifference)} + \theta + \gamma + mu_{(error)}$$

The dependent variable was 'bridal pregnancy'. The regression calculates the probability (p) of the answer to the question 'Was a child born less than eight months after the marriage date?' being yes or no in terms of odds ratios (i.e. the probability of a yes divided by the probability of a no) for a range of independent variables. Dummy variables, represented by the symbols θ and γ, control for time and parish respectively.

We confined our analysis to couples with the racial classification white (n = 457), coloured (n = 1096) and black (n = 51). Couples who did not state their race (n = 314), who were of different races to one another (n = 30) or whose racial classification was ambiguous (n = 8) were excluded. There were too few Indian couples in the dataset (n = 2) to add Indian as a racial category. As a proxy for class we used the occupation of the primary breadwinner (i.e. the partner with the highest occupational classification, usually the man), coded to reflect the following broad occupational categories: professional, managerial, artisanal, semi-skilled and unskilled. To determine a person's level of literacy we used a simple measure: ability to sign one's name.[70] Not all historians support this method but it does provide at least a partial indication of learning, especially in communities where we do not have comprehensive evidence regarding educational attainment. We included individuals' migration status by simply comparing place of residence at marriage with place of birth (while acknowledging that some may have migrated with their parents after their birth). We could thus label them either as native to Cape Town or as rural migrants, urban migrants or international migrants (a dummy variable was added to show when individuals shared the same migration status). We coded for marital status (e.g. bachelor, spinster, widow or widower), but we did not differentiate between second, third and fourth marriages, etc. as there was no way to tell this from our data. There were no divorcés or divorcées in our sample. We also included age differences between spouses, although this did not appear to be connected with bridal pregnancy.

---

[70] Barry Reay, for example, warns that there is a 'real danger that the complexities of popular literacy are being hidden by the quantifier's all-too-easy division into literate and illiterate'. B. Reay, 'The Context and Meaning of Popular Literacy: Some Evidence from Nineteenth-Century Rural England', *Past & Present* 131 (1991): 131.

Quantitative History and Uncharted People

Regression 2: Sunday Baptism

$$\log\left(\frac{p}{1-p}\right) = B_0 + B_{1(race)} + B_{2(bp)} + B_{3(race \times bp)} + \theta + \mu + \gamma + mu_{(error)}$$

where *bp* stands for bridal pregnancy and *p* represents the probability of the dependent variable (baptism on a Sunday) being a yes or no. Race is coded in the same way as in the previous model. Dummy variables have been added to control for the year (θ), month (μ) and parish (γ) in which the baptism took place.

CHAPTER 3
SEX RATIOS AND GIRL PREFERENCE IN THE CAPE, 1894–2011

Johan Fourie* and Francisco Marco-Gracia**

Introduction

Almost three decades ago, Amartya Sen called attention to the discrimination suffered by women around the world, especially in Asia. The number of missing women, Sen estimated, was in excess of 100 million. This astounding figure was cited in 'Missing women', still one of the most cited publications in the field of demography.[1] The article launched research projects that showed how the preference for males exposed girls born in Asia and Europe to high mortality rates.[2]

Little attention, however, has been paid to the opposite phenomenon: the preference for girls in sub-Saharan Africa and the male excess mortality that it entails. This is the motivation of this chapter and what we attempt to do here. We have done so before. In 'The missing boys' we documented, for the first time, the low South African sex ratios for under-fives and the evolution of these ratios over the twentieth century.[3] In this chapter we focus on the Cape Colony and the Cape Province, which gives us census data for a longer period, stretching back to 1894. Again we find evidence of low sex ratios with deep historical roots. Our aim was to find explanations for this understudied but important historical trend.

The sex ratio is the number of boys for every 100 girls in a population. This may be measured as the primary sex ratio, the ratio at conception (before birth), thus including miscarriages, abortions and stillbirths, or as the secondary sex ratio, the ratio at birth. We use the sex ratio at five years, that is, the number of boys under five years who are

---

*Fourie: Department of Economics, Stellenbosch University, South Africa.
**Marco-Gracia: Department of History, Stellenbosch University, South Africa; Department of Applied Economics, Universidad de Zaragoza and Instituto Agroalimentario de Aragón IA2 (UNIZAR-CITA), Spain.

[1] A. Sen, 'Missing Women', *British Medical Journal* 304, no. 6827 (1992): 587–8.

[2] M. das Gupta, et al., 'Why Is Son Preference So Persistent in East and South Asia? A Cross-Country Study of China, India and the Republic of Korea', *Journal of Development Studies* 40, no. 2 (2003): 153–87; F. Beltrán Tapia and D. Gállego-Martínez, 'Where Are the Missing Girls? Gender Discrimination in 19th-century Spain', *Explorations in Economic History* 66 (2017): 117–26.

[3] F.J. Marco-Gracia and J. Fourie, 'The Missing Boys: Understanding the Unbalanced Sex Ratio in South Africa, 1894–2011', *Economic History of Developing Regions* 37, no. 2 (2022): 128–46.

alive for every 100 girls under five years who are alive. The sex ratio of young children between the ages of zero and four is often used to measure gender discrimination. High sex ratios, meaning there are substantially more boys than girls, have been found in many regions and periods. Sub-Saharan Africa has received far less attention. The few studies that have reported low sex ratios (substantially more girls than boys) for several African populations, such as Ciocco and James, have generally ascribed this to genetic factors of the African populations.[4] More recently, Garenne attributed to Bantu genetic origins the low sex ratios at birth that he found were common in southern and eastern African populations.[5] The lower sex ratio at birth of African Americans in the United States and black residents of the UK and the Caribbean islands seemed to corroborate this genetic explanation.[6] But this alone does not explain the low, and changing, sex ratios under five years that we have found historically in the Cape (and that we believe is true, though largely unproven, of other sub-Saharan regions).

Our hypothesis is that sub-Saharan Africa's high land-to-labour ratio incentivised households to favour girls over boys. To test this, we turned to a familiar source: census data. The Cape Colony and South African censuses allow comparisons between race groups, ethnic groups and regions. We find evidence of sex preference mostly in groups classified as 'black' in the past. We show that this discrimination diminished over time, disappearing in recent generations. Our results contribute to debates in three literatures: on gender discrimination (sex preferences) in women's history, on child health in children's history, and on unbalanced sex ratios and their evolution in demographic history.

We also make a methodological contribution. This chapter focuses on the early stages of the life cycle: birth and early childhood up to the age of five. Like elsewhere in this book, we use techniques from quantitative research in history to deepen our understanding of gender preferences in children of different race groups in the historical Cape. Until now, historical studies on gender preferences and infant mortality in South Africa have predominantly used sources such as personal diaries and newspapers.[7] However, no attempts had been made to approximate this with data for large population groups.

Census data, despite their many inherent problems, allow us to work with almost the totality of children under five in the province every few years over the last century. We pay attention to the high childhood mortality rates that were still present in the Cape well into the twentieth century. Therefore, if we assume that mortality can be related to

---

[4]A. Ciocco, 'Variation in the Sex Ratio at Birth in the United States', *Human Biology* 10, no. 1 (1938): 36–64; W. James, 'The Sex Ratios of Black Births', *Annals of Human Biology* 11, no. 1 (1984): 39–44.

[5]M. Garenne, 'Sex Ratios at Birth in African Populations: A Review of Survey Data', *Human Biology* 74, no. 6 (2002): 889–900; M. Garenne, 'Sex Ratios at Birth in Populations of Eastern and Southern Africa', *Southern African Journal of Demography* 9, no. 1 (2004): 91–6.

[6]Ciocco, 'Variation in Sex Ratio'; Garenne, 'Sex Ratios at Birth in Populations of Eastern and Southern Africa'; James, 'Sex Ratios of Black Births'; P.M. Visaria, 'Sex Ratio at Birth in Territories with a Relative Complete Registration', *Eugenics Quarterly* 14, no. 2 (1967): 132–42.

[7]See, for example: P. Badassy, 'A Severed Umbilicus: Infanticide and the Concealment of Birth in Natal, 1860–1935' (PhD diss., University of KwaZulu-Natal, Durban, 2011).

gender preferences and the decisions made by parents regarding the care of their children, the perspective from quantitative history allows us to delve into the issue of gender preferences in early childhood from a new perspective that have not been addressed by the current historiography. The results obtained raise several new questions about family relationships that would not have been possible with standard archival sources. We hope that historians and social scientists will take up these questions in future work.

Data and methods

We use the Cape Colony censuses of 1894 and 1904, and the South African censuses of 1911, 1921, 1936, 1946, 1951, 1960, 1970, 1980, 1991, 1996, 2001 and 2011. They include the distribution of the population by age, race and sex. The detailed census material allows us to observe the evolution of under-five sex ratios in the Cape throughout the twentieth century.

Because the Cape is a melting pot of cultures and ethno-linguistic groups, it is difficult to classify its people consistently by race group.[8] Traditionally, four groups have been used: white/European, black/Native, coloured/mixed and Asian/Indian/Malay. The classifications white, black and coloured have remained relatively constant over time, with some exceptions, but those classified as Asian were not consistently recorded. At the end of the nineteenth century the censuses for the Cape Colony introduced the category 'Malay', referring to these people's origin in the Southeast Asian islands, but the most modern censuses tend to focus only on 'Indian', 'Malays' being included in the 'coloured' group. Most immigrants from India came to the Cape in the late nineteenth and early twentieth centuries. The changing classification of those regarded as 'Asian' reflects not only the changing physiognomy but also, in part, different patterns of behaviour, especially regarding their political positioning.[9] We include the Asian/Indian/Malay group in the study, while acknowledging possible bias (changes and inaccuracies) in this group over time.

The 1911 census, the first for what was now the Union of South Africa, is a milestone in South African documentary sources. Completed in only fourteen months, it collected a mass of individual data on demography, economy, religion and so on. Yet despite its breadth, it is not devoid of the errors we see in South African censuses throughout the twentieth century.[10] For example, the 1951 census records 1,226,982 black children in the whole country from zero to four years and the 1960 census, following this same cohort, 1,287,998 (with ages from nine to thirteen years in 1960). That is, according to

---

[8] A.J. Christopher, '"To Define the Indefinable": Population Classification and the Census in South Africa', *Area* 34, no. 4 (2002): 401–8.

[9] K.E. Ferree, 'Explaining South Africa's Racial Census', *Journal of Politics* 68, no. 4 (2006): 803–15.

[10] A.J. Christopher, 'A South African Domesday Book: the First Union Census of 1911', *South African Geographical Journal* 92, no. 1 (2010): 22–34; A. J. Christopher, 'The Union of South Africa Censuses 1911–1960: An Incomplete Record', *Historia* 56, no. 2 (2011): 1–18.

these data, not only had no children died, but also 61,016 new children had appeared. This is clear evidence of under-reporting in 1951. Obviously, some children must have died, which makes the under-reporting even greater. Official immigration data do not explain the discrepancy. Estimates of the population in some of the earlier censuses are also incoherent. It appears as if 24,484 black children aged from zero to four years in 1936 had died or gone missing by 1946, and 167,904 black children aged from zero to four years in 1946 had died or gone missing by 1951. The variation in numbers in such a short space of time raises serious concerns about the accuracy of the censuses. Yet we want to stress that these errors should not affect the sex ratios we analyse. We have found no reason to suggest that one sex was under- or over-registered; that is, the numbers of boys or girls do not seem to be a consequence of the voluntary or wilful under-registration by census officials. The nineteenth-century Cape Colony censuses are also not free from problems of under-reporting. One additional cause of errors is the changing borders of the then Colony. Although we only use the last two censuses of the Colony, which at that time included most of the territories that would become the Cape Province as part of the Union of South Africa, we kept in mind that the newly incorporated territories may have much poorer record-keeping and therefore much poorer data quality than the more established districts.

Despite their shortcomings, the censuses remain valuable sources of information.[11] To avoid possible idiosyncrasies in the censuses, we ignored short-term variations and instead focused on the long-term trend across the entire century. Our large samples, except for those classified as Asian, helped to mitigate the bias caused by outliers. We also undertook a separate analysis for each of South Africa's provinces, although for a shorter time span, and found similar results. There does not seem to be a geographical bias that could affect our results.

The analysis in this chapter is a combination of descriptive and Ordinary Least Squares regression analyses with heteroscedasticity-robust estimation using as dependent variable the sex ratios in the various census years. In this section, we are interested in understanding the correlates of Cape's low sex ratios.

The Cape's sex ratios

We know very little about how sex ratios in South Africa before the 1970s compare with those of other countries. Figure 3.1 shows the evolution of under-five sex ratios for South Africa according to race and compares these with the ratios for England and Wales and the Netherlands (the main countries of origin of the European immigrants who settled in South Africa in the seventeenth, eighteenth and nineteenth centuries). The trends are very different. White sex ratios present high values, always above 100, very close to those

---

[11]T.A. Moultrie and I.M. Timæus, 'The South African Fertility Decline: Evidence from Two Censuses and a Demographic Health Survey', *Population Studies* 57, no. 3 (2003): 265–83; Christopher, 'Union of South Africa Censuses'.

Figure 3.1 Evolution of under-five sex ratios in South Africa according to race, 1894–2011.
Source: South African censuses (1911, 1921, 1936, 1946, 1951, 1960, 1970, 1980, 1991, 1996, 2001 and 2011), Cape Colony censuses (1894 and 1904) and Mitchell (2013).

of England and Wales and the Netherlands.[12] Only in recent decades have white people had slightly lower ratios than those countries. In contrast, the black sex ratios remain below 100 for almost the entire period under study, dropping to figures close to ninety in the first decades of the twentieth century. In this section we look at possible reasons for this extraordinary situation.

The coloured sex ratios are intermediate between those of white and black sex ratios. During the twentieth century, and later in the twenty-first century, almost all countries seem to have experienced a general increase in sex ratios.[13] South Africa has not been an exception.

Figure 3.2 shows the evolution of sex ratios by race in the Cape Colony and subsequently in the Cape Province between 1894 and 1960 compared to South Africa as a whole. We have chosen this period because it shows the most extreme sex ratios and have omitted the Asian category because of the large variability of results due to the paucity of data.

Although earlier censuses for the Cape Colony are available, they have serious limitations owing to poor data quality. From the 1865 census we can see that the

---

[12] B.R. Mitchell, *International Historical Statistics* (London: Palgrave Macmillan, 2013).

[13] James, 'Sex Ratios of Black Births'. L. Ulizzi and L. Zonta, 'Factors Affecting the Sex Ratio in Humans: Multivariate Analysis of the Italian Population', *Human Biology* 67, no. 1 (1995): 59–67; Beltrán Tapia and Gállego-Martinez, 'Where Are the Missing Girls?'

Quantitative History and Uncharted People

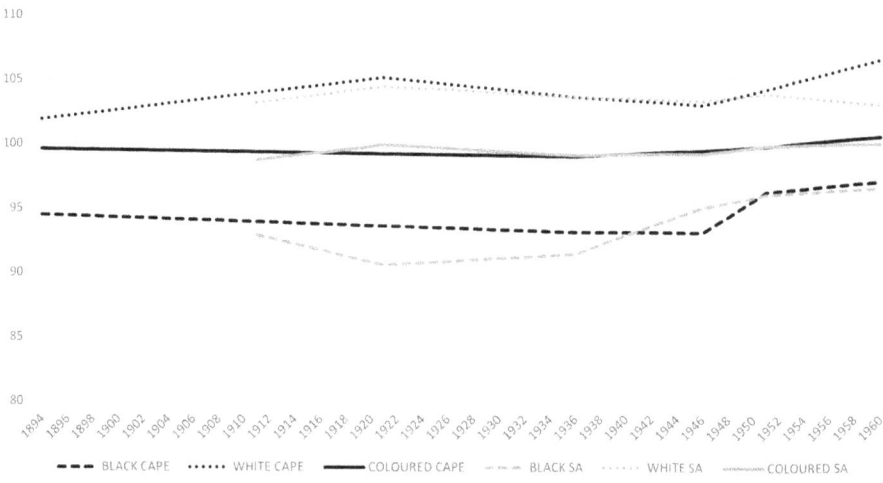

Figure 3.2 Evolution of under-five sex ratios in the Cape according to race, 1894–1960.
Source: Cape Colony censuses (1894 and 1904) and South African censuses (1911, 1921, 1936, 1946, 1951 and 1960).

under-five sex ratio for the Colony was 99.3, but this is only for white and coloured people. The 1875 census shows sex ratios by race, but only for the population aged zero to fourteen years (though for white people its data are more precise). In this age group we find a sex ratio of 103 for black people (though with notable differences between 101 for 'Fingo' and 104 for 'Hottentot'), ninety-five for 'Malay' and 100 for 'Mixed and others'). For white people, the under-five sex ratio is 102 and the under-fifteen sex ratio 99.4. Given our earlier mentioned concerns about changing territorial borders, we believe these figures are too unreliable to be included in a consistent time series.

The first census we include, therefore, is the 1894 Cape census. After 1911, when we compare the Cape Province to the rest of South Africa, we find that the Cape mirrors very closely the differences in the sex ratio for South Africa as a whole. The main difference is among the black population which seems to vary less in the case of the Cape. We were aware, however, that the 1921 census has only province level data for white people, which partly distorts our results. In summary, the available census data show us that the Cape was not an exception, but in our interpretation of the results we needed also to take into account the data for South Africa as a whole (and even sub-Saharan Africa as we shall see below) in order to contextualise the case of the Cape.

The Cape in the sub-Saharan context

The results we obtained for the Cape and South Africa are not exceptional but are similar to those obtained for most of sub-Saharan Africa. World Bank data, as reported in Table 3.1, shows that sub-Saharan African sex ratios at birth are lower than those of

Table 3.1 Average sex ratios at birth according to world region and year.

	1962	*1977*	*1992*	*2007*	*2016*
Sub-Saharan Africa	103.8	103.8	103.7	103.8	103.8
East Asia & Pacific	106.4	106.2	109.4	111.7	110.9
Europe & Central Asia	105.6	105.5	105.7	105.9	105.9
Latin America & Caribbean	104.9	104.9	104.9	104.9	104.9
Middle East & North Africa	105.3	105.2	105.3	105.5	105.4
North America	105.0	105.2	105.0	104.8	104.9
South Asia	105.9	105.9	108.1	109.7	109.6

Source: World Bank (https://data.worldbank.org/indicator/SP.POP.BRTH.MF).

many other regions of the world. The 1963 census in Northern Rhodesia noted that the main 'African' hospital in Southern Rhodesia (probably the hospital in Salisbury's, the then township of Harare, now the Harare Gomo Central Hospital) had registered the birth of 102 boys per 100 girls during the previous decade. Reports of the Medical Officer of Health of the City of Cape Town between 1989 and 1996 show a sex ratio at birth of 101 for Cape Town. In all cases, the sex ratios were lower than in other regions of the world. Nevertheless, while the sex ratio at birth is fairly low, boys still outnumber girls at birth.

In contrast, the sex ratios at five years, which we calculated from the available South African censuses and the United Nations population estimates, show very different ratios.[14] Figure 3.3 shows that the sex ratios at five years for most of sub-Saharan Africa were among the lowest in the world during the twentieth century and the first decade of the twenty-first century, below 100 for most of the period. The implication is that between zero and four years the boys in these countries were exposed to a higher mortality rate than girls. According to these UN estimates, South Africa would be an exception in having higher sex ratios than most African countries. But as we are demonstrating throughout this chapter using census data, South Africa actually had low sex ratios like most of the African continent. The UN estimates seem to be interpolated and not based on census data.

There are good reasons why most scholars have missed this remarkable pattern. As a result of improved health and nutrition, the trend is less dramatic today than it was in the mid-twentieth century. If we use the average sex ratio at birth calculated by the World Bank and the sex ratios at five years from the United Nations, we find that in 1960 there was an excess mortality of children born between 1956 and 1960 of around 800,000 boys. Between 1976 and 1980 this went up to 1,000,000 boys. If we had numbers for every year of the twentieth century, it is likely that tens of millions more boys than girls would have died in sub-Saharan Africa.

---

[14] Available online: https://population.un.org/wpp/.

Quantitative History and Uncharted People

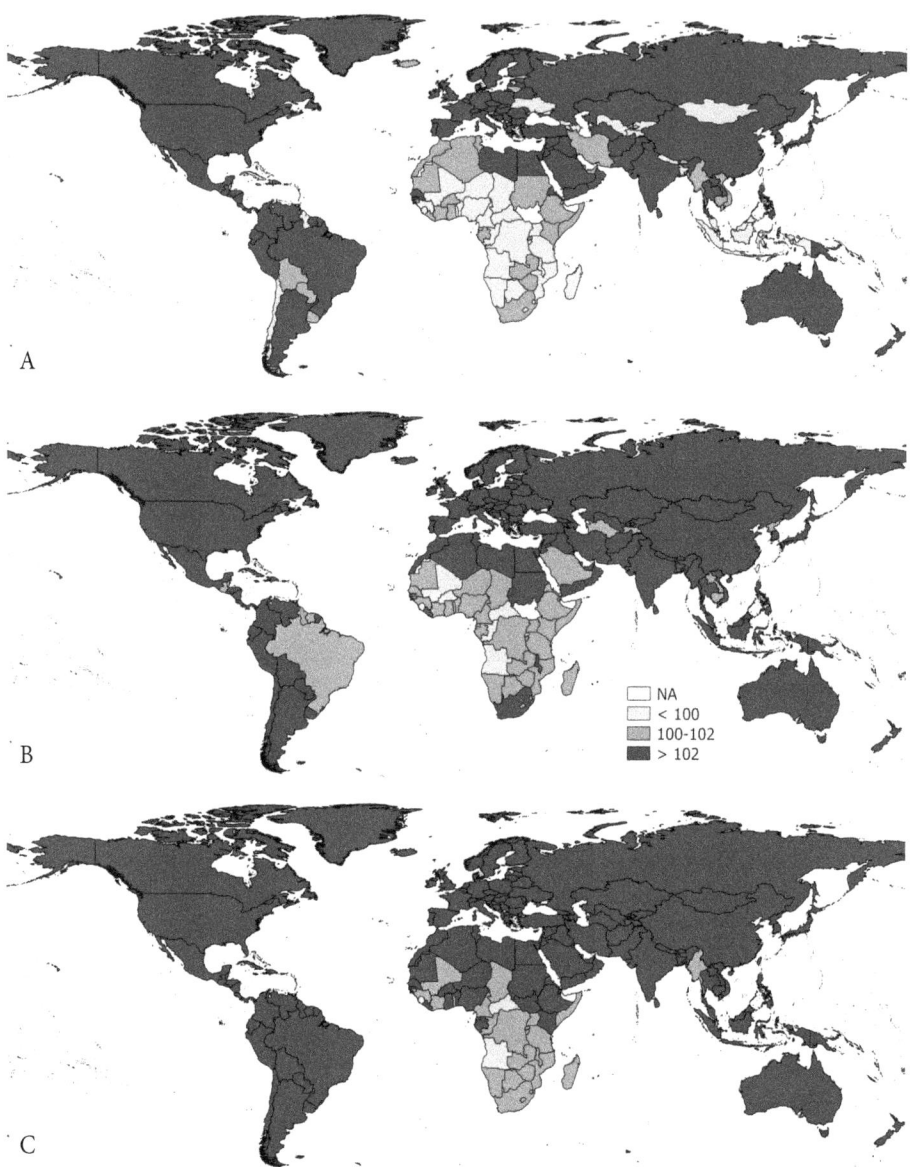

Figure 3.3 Country level distribution of under-five sex ratios, 1950 (A), 1980 (B) and 2010 (C).
Source: United Nations Population Data of 1950, 1980 and 2010.

The importance of this topic goes beyond its historical dimension. The problem of missing boys partly persists today. If there is discrimination against boys, especially in the more isolated and traditional areas with poor or non-existent medical services, we need to know about this so as to improve these boys' chance of survival and quality of life. Poor nutrition and care at a young age have large and irreversible consequences in adulthood. The excess mortality of boys has consequences beyond individual living standards: it can negatively affect the labour market and the marriage market.

Results

Using the data discussed above, in this section we perform several OLS regressions to investigate the correlates of under-five sex ratios. So far, we are aware that the sex ratios at birth of sub-Saharan Africans may be lower than those in other regions of the world. However, they are above 100 (more boys than girls), so we wanted to discover why the under-five sex ratios in South Africa and particularly in our specific area of study, the Cape, as revealed by the censuses, are much lower, and to follow the trend across the period of study.

We focused on the Cape for two reasons. First, we have the longest, uninterrupted series of censuses for the Cape Colony and subsequent Cape Province. This helps to mitigate our usual problem of poor data quality: using eleven censuses, across more than a century, reduces the likelihood that one or two poor-quality censuses will distort the results. Second, the Cape population had roughly equal shares of white, coloured and black inhabitants. Although these shares change considerably over the period, they are far more equal than those for South Africa as a whole, where black inhabitants make up the bulk of the population.

In Table 3.2 we show six models for the Cape data from 1890 to 1960, in all cases relating sex ratios to race. In model 1 we run a simple linear regression between sex ratio and race. We then add other variables: in model 2, the decade in which the census was taken, and in model 3, the percentage of urban dwellers in that race and census, the percentage of the population of that race in that census, the percentage over the age of sixty-five in that race, the percentage married by race and the percentages of numerate males and females (calculated using a Whipple's index). In model 4 we replicate model 3 for the period before 1930, before the period of intense racial segregation that followed the 1948 National Party victory. In model 5, we replicate model 3 for the 1930s, 1940s, 1950s and 1960s. In model 6, we replicate the model 3 for South Africa as a whole, for comparison with the results for the Cape.

The results in Table 3.1 show that Cape (and South African) under-five sex ratios were strongly conditioned by race during the twentieth century. In the basic model, black people have on average almost four points lower under-five sex ratios than coloured people. In fact, according to the R-squared measure, race alone explains almost 60 per cent of the variation in these sex ratios. Taking coloured people (who have average sex ratios below 100) as the reference category, we find that black people are associated with significantly lower sex ratios over the study period. In contrast, white people (and generally Asian people) have positive and generally significant coefficients. The OLS regressions thus indicate that under-five sex ratios were strongly related to race in the twentieth century Cape Province.

Table 3.2 OLS regression models on the determinants of under-five sex ratios, 1894–1960.

		Linear simple (1)	Basic model (2)	Complete model (3)	1890s–1920s (4)	1930s–1960s (5)	SA complete model (6)
Race	Coloured	Ref.					
	Black	−4.656***	−4.656***	−4.432***	−7.289***	−4.021	−5.846***
		(1.16)	(1.17)	(0.97)	(4.18)	(1.76)	(0.33)
	White	4.121***	4.121***	4.029***	1.348***	4.566	4.258***
		(1.16)	(1.17)	(0.97)	(1.29)	(3.02)	(0.33)
	Asian	0.726	0.726	0.663	−0.290	0.056	−0.600
		(1.16)	(1.17)	(0.99)	(1.54)	(2.04)	(0.39)
% urban population				0.233***	3.033***	0.225***	0.169***
				(0.01)	(1.11)	(0.01)	(0.01)
% population (by race)				0.074***	3.087***	0.077	0.106***
				(0.01)	(0.41)	(0.01)	(0.01)
% population over sixty-five				−5.955	−5.103	−5.915*	−0.741
				(1.24)	(1.14)	(1.12)	(1.01)
% married population				0.127	0.004	0.114***	0.011
				(0.02)	(0.04)	(0.02)	(0.11)
Male numeracy (Whipple's index)				0.022	10.607***	0.035	0.091***
				(0.02)	(1.43)	(0.02)	(0.01)

	Linear simple	Basic model	Complete model	1890s–1920s	1930s–1960s	SA complete model
	(1)	(2)	(3)	(4)	(5)	(6)
Female numeracy (Whipple's index)	98.821*** (0.82)					
Decade of the census			−0.037 (0.02)	−12.371*** (1.66)	−0.046* (0.02)	−0.122*** (0.01)
1890s		−2.039 (1.15)	−0.544 (0.30)	Ref.		−0.966* (0.39)
1900s		−1.004 (1.06)	0.354 (0.26)	0.898*** (0.25)		−0.067 (0.36)
1910s		−0.832 (1.01)	−0.451 (0.24)	0.207* (0.34)		−0.480 (0.35)
1920s		−2.202 (1.01)	−0.547* (0.24)	−0.482** (0.38)		−0.686* (0.35)
1930s	Ref.				Ref.	
1940s		0.974 (1.01)	0.888** (0.23)		0.897*** (0.20)	1.176* (0.35)
1950s		0.882 (1.01)	0.912** (0.24)		0.931* (0.26)	0.482 (0.34)
1960s		1.213 (1.21)	2.892* (0.56)		2.942* (0.48)	2.667*** (0.30=)
Intercept		98.202*** (1.01)	100.755*** (4.77)	234.666*** (9.14)	101.177*** (4.10)	94.818*** (4.15)
R-sq	0.572	0.583	0.933	0.945	0.947	0.923

Source: Cape Colony censuses (1894 and 1904) and South African censuses (1936, 1946, 1951 and 1960).
Notes: se denotes robust standard error. * Statistical significance at 10 per cent level, ** at 5 per cent level, *** at 1 per cent level.

Table 3.2 provides other results of interest. First, the passage of time seems to have played a major role. The under-five sex ratios increase gradually over the decades. This is partly to be expected, given that childhood mortality, which is the factor that can modulate sex ratios, declined over the twentieth century and especially in the last decades of that century. We must be careful not to over-interpret particular years, yet the negative impact on sex ratios in the 1920s is of particular interest. This was a decade when the South African economy performed poorly, which may help to explain this result.[15]

Another variable that is correlated with time is urban dwelling. Higher levels of urbanisation seem to have increased the sex ratios, possibly because urban children had better access to medical help and hygiene measures and thus lower mortality. It is also possible that cultural factors may be linked to urbanisation; if strong cultural beliefs and behaviours, as we'll surmise below, are likely to emerge and persist in rural settings, then these beliefs and behaviours will be less relevant in urban contexts.

The percentage of the population over sixty-five years of age does not seem to have played an important role in the under-five sex ratios. Nor does the percentage of the population married, which only seems to have had a positive impact in the period after the 1930s, when marriage patterns were changing and singleness was increasing among black and coloured people.

Finally, numeracy levels (as a proxy for education) seem to have played some kind of role in sex ratios, but only in the first decades of our study period. Several mechanisms may explain the link between numeracy and sex ratios. Numeracy could directly affect people's decisions about how many children to have. More numerate, and therefore more educated, households are likely to have fewer children, suppressing extreme sex ratios. But numeracy could also be a proxy for preference. Higher numeracy, for example, could signal a household preference for investment in education. If men are more numerate, meaning that parents prefer to invest in educating boys rather than girls, then the sex ratio is also likely to be higher. We find that a higher numeracy rate for men is correlated with a higher sex ratio and a higher numeracy rate for women with a lower sex ratio. This is consistent with both explanations.

Our regressions treat race as an independent variable. In order to delve deeper, Table 3.3 separates model 3 of Table 3.2 into four regressions, each for a different race group.

The results in Table 3.3 give us some additional clues to understanding the low sex ratios by race. One important caveat is that the low number of observations (conditioned by the number of censuses available and selected) restricts our ability to make stronger inferences.

One important result is that, for black children, a larger share of the population seems to increase its sex ratio. We suspect this is again because of its correlation with time: the numbers of black inhabitants of the Cape increased much more over the twentieth

---

[15] W. Boshoff and J. Fourie, 'The South African Economy in the Twentieth Century', in *Business Cycles and Structural Change in South Africa*, ed. W. Boshoff (Cham: Springer, 2020): 49–70.

Table 3.3 OLS regression models on the determinants of under-five sex ratios, 1890, 1904, 1936, 1946 and 1960 censuses.

		Black (1)	*White* (2)	*Coloured* (3)	*Asian* (4)
% urban population		0.016 (0.03)	0.188 (0.10)	0.004 (0.02)	0.040 (0.02)
% population (by race)		0.587** (0.21)	−2.243 (1.39)	0.05 (1.53)	−0.02 (3.21)
% population over sixty-five		−1.351 (0.98)	−0.316 (1.69)	−1.204 (0.74)	−7.861*** (1.72)
% married population		0.021* (0.01)	0.294* (0.13)	−0.038* (0.01)	0.048 (0.04)
Male numeracy (Whipple's index)		0.011 (0.03)	−0.352* (0.16)	−0.104 (0.06)	−0.143** (0.05)
Female numeracy (Whipple's index)		0.147 (0.12)	0.256* (0.12)	0.122 (0.08)	−0.345 (0.25)
Decade of the census	1890s	−0.335 (0.48)	0.441* (0.18)	−1.060*** (0.30)	3.677*** (0.61)
	1900s	−0.019 (0.47)	0.214 (0.17)	−0.655* (0.29)	0.258 (0.59)
	1910s	−1.554*** (0.31)	−0.177 (0.14)	−0.101 (0.19)	−0.640 (0.43)
	1920s	−2.700*** (0.29)	−0.309* (0.14)	−0.560** (0.19)	−1.301** (0.43)
	1930s	−2.057*** (0.25)	−0.123 (0.11)	−0.100 (0.15)	−2.041*** (0.36)
	1940s	−0.982* (0.43)	−0.233 (0.42)	−0.475 (0.25)	−1.741*** (0.42)
	1950s	Ref.			
	1960s	1.077 (0.77)	0.140 (0.88)	1.367 (0.82)	0.949 (11.63)
	Intercept	76.461*** (17.03)	227.833*** (91.27)	105.561*** (3.94)	174.699*** (32.22)
	R-sq	0.929	0.965	0.783	0.922

Source: Cape Colony censuses (1894 and 1904) and South African censuses (1936, 1946 and 1960).
Notes: *se* denotes robust standard error. * Statistical significance at 10 per cent level, ** at 5 per cent level, *** at 1 per cent level.

century than the numbers of white and coloured inhabitants. Another interpretation is that the increase in the likelihood of survival for black children, perhaps due to higher incomes, better nutrition or improved medical and other public services, explains both the population increase and the higher sex ratio. A micro-level study, with household information, would be required to tease out these effects.

The percentage of the population married seems to have had a positive effect on the under-five sex ratio for black and white people, but a negative effect for coloured people. This may be due to the evolution of the marriage market in South Africa. While at the beginning of the study period it was the black and coloured populations that had the lowest singleness rates, in the second half of the twentieth century these results reversed: the singleness rates were now very low for white people but increasingly high for coloured and black people.

These results point to some economic and social policies affecting sex ratios. Yet given the persistent low under-five sex ratio for black people, the question remains whether a genetic or cultural factor explains the results – one that cannot be observed with time series information. To investigate this, we compare black inhabitants of the Cape (predominantly Xhosa) with other black ethnic groups in South Africa. In Table 3.4 we run an OLS regression relating under-five sex ratios to the children's ethnic group, using the data available for the 1951, 1960, 1970 and 1991 censuses. We take the Xhosa as the reference category. The regression results show that only the Venda have a significant result. According to the 1960 census, the Venda population represented 2.26 per cent of black South Africans (just over 415,000 children under the age of five). Therefore, their sex ratios, while clearly low, should be taken with caution, as they may have been a response to temporary circumstances. In any case, from Table 3.4 we have evidence that the low sex ratios do not correspond to specific ethnic groups (beyond the anomalous case of the Venda, with a minimum sex ratio of eighty-four and a maximum of ninety-eight in the period analysed) but were common to all black South Africans although with small differences in intensity.

In Figure 3.4, we show the spatial distribution of sex ratios by ethnic group. Once again we find that ethnic differences do not explain the values obtained. The figure shows that all groups increased their under-five sex ratio over time. In general, and with slight variations, the sex ratios for some ethnic groups predominantly located in the west of South Africa (Xhosa, Tswana and Basotho) seem to be almost permanently slightly higher than those of the eastern ethnic groups (Zulu, Venda or Swazi). Therefore, lower values could be expected in the Cape than those we see in other regions of southern Africa (provinces and countries). This may be ascribable to differences in living standards, but more evidence is needed.[16] What we can confidently claim is that we do not observe differences between ethnic groups that are large enough to explain the evolution of the

---

[16] C.C. Sawyer, 'Child Mortality Estimation: Estimating Sex Differences in Childhood Mortality since the 1970s', *PLoS Medical* 9, no. 8 (2012); B. Mpeta, J. Fourie and K. Inwood, 'Black Living Standards in South Africa before Democracy: New Evidence from Height', *South African Journal of Science* 114, nos. 1–2 (2018): 1–8.

Table 3.4 Simple linear regression relating under-five sex ratios to ethnicity for black South Africans in the 1951, 1960, 1970 and 1991 censuses.

Dependent variable: Sex ratio		Coefficients and standard errors
Ethnicity	Xhosa	(ref.)
	Zulu	−1.757 (2.07)
	Swazi	−1.158 (2.07)
	Ndebele	−1.176 (2.07)
	Seshoeshe	−0.633 (2.07)
	Tswana	−0.834 (2.07)
	Sepedi	−1.385 (2.07)
	Shangaan	−1.202 (2.07)
	Venda	−6.241*** (2.07)
	Other	2.132 (2.07)
Intercept		99.134*** (1.46)
R-sq		0.377

Source: South African censuses of 1951, 1960, 1970, 1991.
Notes: *se* denotes robust standard error. * Statistical significance at 10 per cent level, ** at 5 per cent level, *** at 1 per cent level.

Cape's sex ratios during the twentieth century. Thus, black and coloured people in the Cape were not an exception but part of a much larger system, one that we explore in the next section.

Possible explanations

Historians and economists have not paid enough attention to the phenomenon of the low under-five sex ratios in Africa, what we have called elsewhere 'the missing boys'. This could be a question of considerable historical importance, comparable to the

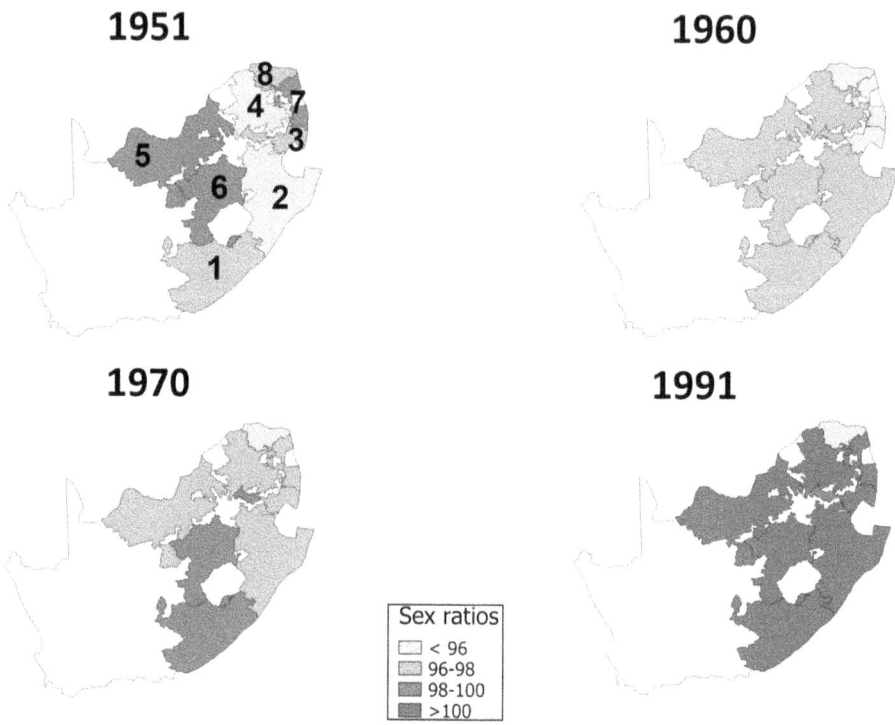

Figure 3.4 Under-five sex ratios by ethnic group, 1951–91.
Source: South African censuses of 1951, 1960, 1970, 1991.
Note: 1. Xhosa, 2. Zulu, 3. Swazi, 4. Sepedi, 5. Tswana, 6. Basotho, 7. Thonga, 8. Venda.

'missing women' phenomenon that has generated so much scholarship.[17] It could have serious implications: it could continue to affect African societies and economies today (although it would be necessary for new articles to know how the evolution of sex ratios had and has implications in the historical and today's life and economy). Its causes and consequences require further scholarly treatment. At this point we will tentatively look at possible causes, proposing some explanations.

Several theories have been put forward to explain Africa's low under-five sex ratios. We pay particular attention to those with deep historical roots, the genetic, biological and cultural theories. The most common explanation is biological. Scalone and Rettaroli point out that poor nutrition is linked to a higher rate of miscarriage, with males, who are weaker in the womb, more likely to be affected.[18] Given the difficulty of demonstrating this during the early stages of pregnancy, the theory of increased male intrauterine

---

[17] See, for example: S. Anderson and D. Ray, 'Excess Female Mortality in Africa' (WIDER: Working Paper 116, 2017): 1–22.

[18] F. Scalone and R. Rettaroli, 'Exploring the Variations of the Sex Ratio at Birth from an Historical Perspective', *Statistica* 75, no. 2 (2015): 213–26.

mortality is not universally accepted.[19] However, several research papers show evidence for the greater weakness of males in the womb.[20] This is because male embryos grow faster and have a more efficient placenta, but their smaller size would facilitate detachment in extreme cases such as malnutrition of the mother.[21] This could imply that female embryos are more likely to settle and to survive nine months of pregnancy, even in poor conditions. This theory is supported by several studies that have found low sex ratios in Europe at times of famine or war.[22]

However, none of these studies have found sex ratios as low as those we have found for black children at the Cape. In fact, as we have highlighted before, our results show a surprising difference between the sex ratio at birth and the under-five sex ratio: where evidence is available, there are always more boys than girls born at the Cape, yet within five years the ratio falls below 100. Our study thus focused on the steep decline in sex ratios between birth and under-five population data, especially in the older censuses. What happens in the womb – the biological explanation – cannot account for that.

These sex ratios at birth over 100 also imply that the low sex ratios for under-fives found cannot be the effect of sexual preferences (e.g. linked to polygamy), since these patterns would affect the sex ratio at birth (which in the available sources remains above 100) but would not explain the subsequent drop in sex ratios. There were, moreover, no efficient methods at the time to decide the sex of children before they were born.

Another explanation, very close to the previous ones, links higher sex ratios to the economic improvements that would lead to food improvements. Again, we find authors suggesting that better living standards are associated with higher sex ratios, as is the case in European countries.[23] Sex ratios tend to increase with economic growth, although it is generally difficult to disentangle this process from the many other mechanisms at work (such as urbanisation, which is usually also correlated with economic growth). Regardless of the mechanism, this explanation would be linked again to intrauterine mortality, in which male children would be the most affected. However, in no European country have sex ratios been found as low as those found for the twentieth-century Cape.[24]

To further substantiate this, we use death notices from the capital town of today's Northern Cape, Kimberley to show that in times of epidemic crises, black and coloured

---

[19] A. Chahnazarian, 'Determinants of the Sex Ratio at Birth: Review of Recent Literature', *Social Biology* 35, nos. 3–4 (1988): 214–35.

[20] C.E. Boklage, 'The Epigenetic Environment: Secondary Sex Ratio Depends on Differential Survival in Embryogenesis', *Human Reproduction* 20, no. 3 (2005): 583–87.

[21] J.G. Eriksson et al., 'Boys Live Dangerously in the Womb', *American Journal of Human Biology* 22, no. 3 (2010): 330–5.

[22] See, for example: K. Bromen and K.H. Jöckel, 'Change in Male Proportion among Newborn Infants', *Lancet* 349, no. 9054 (1997): 804–5.

[23] J. Fellman and A.W. Eriksson, 'Temporal Trends in the Secondary Sex Ratio in Nordic Countries', *Biodemography and Social Biology* 57, no. 2 (2011): 143–54; Beltrán Tapia and Gallego-Martínez, 'Where Are the Missing Girls?'

[24] Beltrán Tapia and Gallego-Martínez, 'Where Are the Missing Girls?'

boys suffered particularly high mortality rates.[25] Work by Fourie and Jayes in 2021 and in this volume, Chapter 12, further expands on the racial gaps in mortality that are observed during pandemics, also with the use of death notices.[26]

Another possible explanation is that family composition influenced sex ratios in Africa.[27] Low sex ratios would be associated with low fertility. But since black people in the Cape were likely to have larger families than other race groups, it seems unlikely that fertility explains the extremely low sex ratios at the Cape.

A common explanation is the genetic one. This theory says that the genetic component of Bantu-origin Africans explains the low sex ratios characteristic of many African populations.[28] Or, in reverse, that those genetic groups with lower sex ratios at birth would have the Bantu genes or, even further back, the genes of the Niger-Congo group. Although it would be difficult to entirely rebut genetics, one flaw we see in this theory is that gene make-up is unlikely to change within the four or five generations that our study covers. Yet we observe steadily increasing sex ratios across the twentieth century. If the genetic explanation was the only one, or even the dominant one, then the time variation would be minimal.

Yet genetics may be correlated to one factor we believe is at the root of the low sex ratios: culture. We hypothesise that a connection exists between Niger-Congo origin and particular kinds of cultural practices, which would include practices like brideprice (payment from the groom's family to the bride's family to contract a marriage), polygyny and even kinds of behaviour favourable to the survival of girls (who would be less valuable than boys in the marriage market). Economic historians studying Africa have argued that these traits spring from the factor endowments of the continent, namely a high land-to-labour ratio.[29] In a labour scarce setting, women's reproductivity ability is valued more so than in a setting where land is the scarce resource. Relative factor endowments may therefore explain the preference for women in sub-Saharan Africa compared to a preference for men in South Asia.

A strong possible explanation (related to the living standards explanation) for the evolution of sex ratios that we see in our data could be a combination of better nutrition and a preference for girls.[30] A preference for girls could explain why the mortality of boys has been so extreme in the sub-Saharan case during the twentieth century according

---

[25] Marco-Gracia and Fourie, 'Missing Boys'.

[26] J. Fourie and J. Jayes, 'Health Inequality and the 1918 Influenza in South Africa', *World Development* 141 (2021).

[27] M. Garenne, 'Sex Ratio at Birth and Family Composition in sub-Saharan Africa: Inter-couple Variations', *Journal of Biosocial Science* 41 (2009): 399–407.

[28] Ciocco, 'Variation in the Sex Ratio'; James, 'Sex Ratios of Black Births'.

[29] See, for example: G. Austin, 'Resources, Techniques, and Strategies South of the Sahara: Revising the Factor Endowments Perspective on African Economic Development, 1500–2000', *Economic History Review* 61, no. 3 (2008): 587–624.

[30] Marco-Gracia and Fourie, 'Missing Boys'.

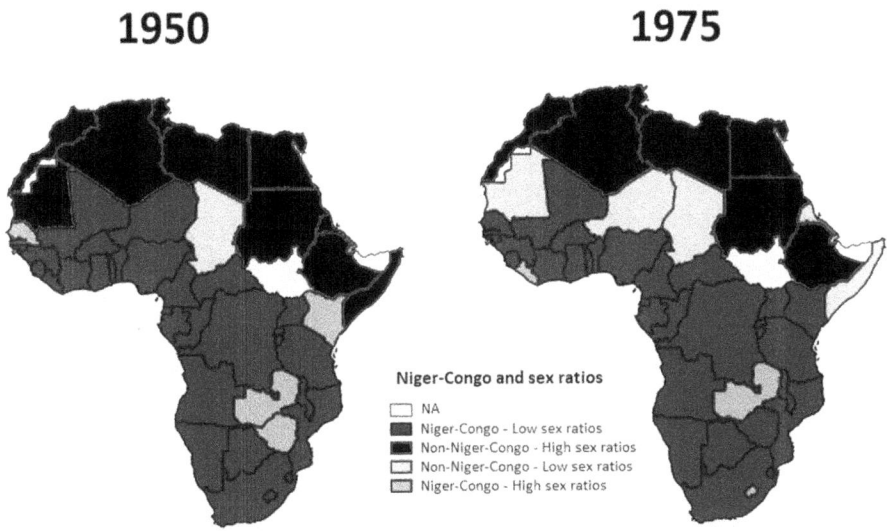

Figure 3.5 Under-five sex ratios for Niger-Congo language countries.
Source: UN Population Data 1950 and 1975, and South African censuses of 1946 and 1970.
Notes: To include a country in the Niger-Congo language area, if parts of the country belong to a different group, we take into account where the majority of the population is located. In the 1950 data, we rate the sex ratio as high if it was over 100, in the 1975 data we rate it as high if it was over 102 (because there was a worldwide increase in the sex ratios between those two dates). We have included all South West Africa (mainly Namibia and the western part of South Africa) as Niger-Congo language countries, although there were large areas of Khoekhoe native-speakers. Exceptionally, the case of Cape/South Africa has been adapted with the available census data.

to the censuses despite the absence of extreme infant mortality in black populations. For example, from 1945 in South Africa, infant mortality was around 180 per thousand for black people, 120 per thousand for coloured people and 38 per thousand for white people.[31] This is a very high mortality but no higher than in pre-industrial Western countries or other developing countries with much higher sex ratios.

Figure 3.5 shows the considerable similarities between the countries whose indigenous languages are of Niger-Congo origin (particularly the Bantu languages) and the countries that had low sex ratios in 1950 and 1975. The non-Niger-Congo countries in the north had high sex ratios, while those of southern and central Africa, with common origins linked to the Niger-Congo languages, had low sex ratios. There is a transition zone around the Sahara that includes countries with low sex ratios despite not having the Niger-Congo language origin. Nevertheless, it seems clear that factors common to communities of Niger-Congo origin have something to do with low sex

---

[31] N. Nattrass and J. Seekings, 'The Economy and Poverty in the Twentieth Century in South Africa', in *The Cambridge History of South Africa Vol. 2*, ed. R. Ross, A.K. Mager and B. Nasson (Cambridge: Cambridge University Press, 2010): 518–72.

Table 3.5 Percentage of unmarried men and women at age 45 by race in the 1911, 1951 and 1991 censuses.

	White		Black		Coloured		Non-white	
	Male	*Female*	*Male*	*Female*	*Male*	*Female*	*Male*	*Female*
1911 census	8.13	6.27					6.37	3.4
1951 census	6.48	8.45	5.82	2.73	13.23	10.77		
1991 census	3.73	3.86	8.29	8.94	9.83	10.09		

Source: South African censuses, 1911, 1951, 1991.

ratios. This could be related to a common ancestral culture that may have encouraged a preference for girls. This does not mean that families did not want to have at least one son, but they may have preferred not to have a large number of sons.[32]

A common ancestral culture would be associated with common traditions such as polygyny, a practice found in most of sub-Saharan Africa. To maintain a polygynous system with a very low singleness rate, as was characteristic of black South African populations historically, an excess of girls would be necessary (especially if, as among black people during the twentieth century, the mortality rate of adult males was not much higher than that of adult females). Table 3.5 shows the low levels of historical singleness in the South African population and especially among black people.

The low sex ratios could therefore be the consequence of the cultural beliefs and behaviour of Africans with Niger-Congo roots. Although South Africa's polygyny rates were not as high as those of other African countries, the earlier South African censuses nevertheless report large shares of polygynous marriages.[33] These decrease steadily over time. In the 1911 census, 29.5 per cent of married South African black women were in a polygynous marriage (there were 82.9 married men per 100 married women), but in the 1921 census, the figure was 27.8 per cent (and 84.1 married men per 100 married women), and in the 1998 Demographic and Health Survey of South Africa the figure was 16.3 per cent.[34] This decrease in polygynous marriages may be an explanation for the increase in the black sex ratio.

In addition to polygyny and the rate of singleness, we have mentioned brideprice as a factor associated with many of the Niger-Congo peoples. Anderson proposes that the brideprice is associated with traditional societies.[35] Ingalls describes how in classical

---

[32] D. Paulme, *Women of Tropical Africa* (London: Routledge & Kegan Paul, 2013).

[33] D. Budlender, N. Chobokoane and S. Simelane, 'Marriage Patterns in South Africa: Methodological and Substantive Issues', *Southern African Journal of Demography* 9, no. 1 (2004): 1–25.

[34] SA. Department of Health, *Demographic and Health Survey: Full Report* (Pretoria: Department of Health, 2008). Unfortunately, there no figures for polygynous marriages in the censuses after 1921.

[35] S. Anderson, 'The Economics of Dowry and Brideprice', *Journal of Economic Perspectives* 21, no. 4 (2007): 151–74.

Greece the brideprice tradition shifted to the dowry tradition (payment by the bride's family to the groom's, the opposite of the brideprice), which may then have been transmitted to the Roman empire and to other countries.[36] The brideprice has various names in southern Africa, such as *lobola* in Zulu, Xhosa and others, *bohali* in Sesotho, and *roora* in Shona.[37] Brideprice practices vary in nature, amount and the people involved. In South Africa it is the groom, his immediate family and sometimes his relatives who make a payment – in cattle or, increasingly, in cash – to the bride's family. In brideprice societies women are a source of family income. Zulu parents told Posel and Rudwick that a daughter's brideprice was economic compensation for the expenses involved in bringing her up. Some even said they wanted not just compensation but profit.[38]

Brideprice may have fostered a system in which girls were rewarded for their survival. Families with daughters received extra wealth through marriage, whereas those with more sons had to bear the expense. This may have encouraged a 'preference for girls', which may have materialised as poor nutrition or parental care or taken the more sinister form of infanticide, direct or indirect.[39] Infanticide has been a common practice among traditional societies around the world.[40]

Anthropologists who have studied African societies have known about this preference for girls. Case studies of the Herero in Botswana, the rural areas of southern Zambia or the Hausa in Nigeria all reveal a preference for girls.[41] Studies based on the Demographic and Health Surveys of the United Nations in Africa have also shown evidence of girls and women receiving better nutrition than boys and men.[42] This may be changing, though. Klasen, in a re-analysis of previous findings supplemented with new data, found a small but growing discrimination against girls.[43] This may be suggestive of a historical preference for girls that is being eroded, which fits our evidence of extremely low sex ratios that increased over time.

---

[36] W. Ingalls, 'Demography and Dowries: Perspectives on Female Infanticide in Classical Greece', *Phoenix* 56, nos. 3–4 (2002): 246–54.

[37] D. Posel and S. Rudwick, 'Marriage and Bridewealth (*ilobolo*) in Contemporary Zulu Society', *African Studies Review* 57, no. 2 (2014): 51–72.

[38] Ibid.

[39] G. Hanlon, 'Routine Infanticide in the West, 1500–1800', *History Compass* 14, no. 11 (2016): 535–48.

[40] A.A. Brewis, 'Anthropological Perspectives on Infanticide', *Arizona Anthropologist* 8 (1992): 103–19.

[41] H.C. Harpending and R. Pennington, 'Age Structure and Sex-biased Mortality among Herero Pastoralists', *Human Biology* 63, no. 3 (1991): 329–53; S. Clark, et al., 'Ten Thousand Tonga: A Longitudinal Anthropological Study from Southern Zambia, 1956–1991', *Population Studies* 49, no. 1 (1995): 91–109; N. Rehan, 'Sex Ratio of Live-born Hausa Infants', *BJOG: International Journal of Obstetrics & Gynaecology* 89, no. 2 (1982): 136–41.

[42] P. Svedberg, 'Undernutrition in Sub-Saharan Africa: Is There a Gender Bias?' *Journal of Development Studies* 26, no. 3 (1990): 469–86; D.E. Sahn and D.C. Stifel, 'Parental Preferences for Nutrition of Boys and Girls: Evidence from Africa', *Journal of Development Studies* 39, no. 1 (2002): 21–45; H. Wamani et al., 'Boys Are More Stunted than Girls in Sub-Saharan Africa: A Meta-Analysis of 16 Demographic and Health Surveys', *BMC Pediatrics* 7, no. 1 (2007): 1–10; A. Chakravarty, 'Gender Bias in Breastfeeding and Missing Girls in Africa: The Role of Fertility Choice', *Mimeo* (2012).

[43] S. Klasen, 'Nutrition, Health and Mortality in sub-Saharan Africa: Is There a Gender Bias?' *Journal of Development Studies* 32, no. 6 (1996): 913–32.

How might discrimination against boys manifest? Our evidence could suggest multiple mechanisms, from the intentional to the coincidental. We have already mentioned the possibility of girls being favoured in the allocation of food resources and parental care.[44] This could be connected with the matriarchal system and the greater importance accorded to women in Bantu society than in other areas of the world.[45] In matriarchal countries of sub-Saharan Africa, the women's greater power affected the sex-preference for children and thus also the care they were given.[46] But the transformation in the role of African women with the modernisation of society in recent decades makes it difficult to categorise social systems into single types and reach consensus.[47] For this reason, whether matriarchies predominated in Africa continues to be hotly debated.

The possibility of a cultural practice of infanticide, mentioned above, is controversial and difficult to prove. Clark et al. found that a preference for women in a rural community in Zambia in the second half of the twentieth century was reflected in higher male infant mortality.[48] This could have been due to better care and feeding of the girls. But discrimination in childhood went deeper when twins were born:

> Villagers reported that the male used to be killed in the case of different sex-twins, and the last born in the case of same-sex twins. We would, therefore, expect mortality to be lowest among single female infants and higher among male twins.[49]

Clark et al. reported a sex ratio of ninety-two in that community, similar to the figures in our data.[50] Some nineteenth-century sources confirm the existence of twin killing in South Africa or other infanticide practices.[51] These practices diminished or disappeared

---

[44]L. Cronk, 'Preferential Parental Investment in Daughters over Sons', *Human Nature* 2, no. 4 (1991): 387–417.

[45]See, for example: B. O'Laughlin, 'Missing Men? The Debate over Rural Poverty and Women-Headed Households in Southern Africa', *Journal of Peasant Studies* 25, no. 2 (1998): 1–48; E. Akyeampong and H. Fofack, 'The Contribution of African Women to Economic Growth and Development in the pre-Colonial and Colonial Periods: Historical Perspectives and Policy Implications', *Economic History of Developing Regions* 29, no. 1 (2014): 42–73.

[46]Chakravarty, 'Gender Bias in Breastfeeding'.

[47]D. Gaitskell, et al., 'Class, Race, and Gender: Domestic Workers in South Africa', *Review of African Political Economy* 10, nos. 27–8 (1983): 86–108; L. Manicom, 'Ruling Relations: Rethinking State and Gender in South African History', *Journal of African History* 33, no. 3 (1992): 441–65.

[48]Clark, et al., 'Ten Thousand Tonga'.

[49]Ibid, 106.

[50]Ibid.

[51]Badassy, 'A Severed Umbilicus'; P.J. Devlieger, 'The Logic of Killing Disabled Children: Infanticide, Songye Cosmology, and the Colonizer', in *Madness, Disability and Social Exclusion: The Archaeology and Anthropology of 'Difference'*, ed. J. Hubert (London: Routledge, 2000): 159–67.

during the last decades of the nineteenth century and the first decades of the twentieth century, continuing only in some small (rural) groups that maintained the tradition longer.[52] We may wonder whether infanticide could have played a part in the low under-five Cape sex ratios, but we can in no way confirm this. In fact, historical anthropologists who described infanticide practices in South Africa usually did not directly report sex preference practices, although with some exceptions.[53]

Finally, we note that several studies have shown that Cape (and South African) boys were generally in poorer health than girls throughout the twentieth century. But we have reliable information on the health of children under five years of age only since the last decades of the twentieth century (in fact, the first South Africa Demographic and Health Survey was conducted in 1998), when improvements in nutritional status had already taken place. Findings from the 1990s show that poor children (especially coloured and black children) were more likely to be stunted, and boys more than girls.[54] Poor black and coloured male children were therefore more likely to suffer problems related to poor nutrition.

In short, there are many factors that could have been responsible for the low under-five sex ratios in the black, and to some extent in the coloured, Cape populations. Many factors seem to indicate that the low levels of life of the black population led to a higher rate of male miscarriage (in situations of stress or poor nutritional conditions, a miscarriage of a boy is more likely than a miscarriage of a girl because of his/her growth strategy in the womb). But data on populations with Niger-Congo language origins show that black societies may have developed a preference for girls. The worst years in our study period economically speaking were around the 1920s, where we see the lowest under-five sex ratios. This could perhaps indicate a preference for girls in times of crisis (for considering that they could be a better investment) or a higher number of miscarriages of boys. In this section we have put forward various explanations that should be empirically tested with new data before confirming or rejecting each of the hypotheses. This study should serve to broaden the debate on under-five sex ratios in South Africa and the possible existence of gender-differentiated childcare behaviour in the twentieth and early twenty-first century, and whether it has receded today.

---

[52]Badassy, 'A Severed Umbilicus'.

[53]See, for example: H. A. Junod, *The Life of a South African Tribe – I. Social Life* (London: Macmillan, 1927); A.T. Bryant, *The Zulu People as They Were before the White Man Came*, 2nd edn. (Pietermaritzburg: Shuter and Shooter, 1967).

[54]Health Systems Trust, *South African Health Review 1998* (Durban: Health Systems Trust, 1999); M.S. Lesiapeto, et al., 'Risk Factors of Poor Anthropometric Status in Children under Five Years of Age Living in Rural Districts of the Eastern Cape and KwaZulu-Natal Provinces, South Africa', *South African Journal of Clinical Nutrition* 23, no. 4 (2010): 202–7; E. Zere and D. McIntyre, 'Inequities in Under-five Child Malnutrition in South Africa', *International Journal of Equity in Health* 2, no. 7 (2003): 1–10.

Conclusions

This chapter explored the under-five sex ratios in the Cape and South Africa by racial group since the late nineteenth century. Focusing on the Cape gave us the opportunity to explore sex ratios over a period of nearly 120 years, because we have good-quality census data by race for the Cape going back to 1894. This enabled us to delve deeper into the issue of sex ratios, childhood mortality and child sex preference from a case study of exceptional interest for sub-Saharan Africa.

Our results show an excess number of girls among black people and, to a lesser extent, among coloured people. This means low under-five sex ratios for most of our period of study. This is despite the fact that more boys were born than girls. Therefore, for the under-five sex ratios to vary so much, a higher mortality of boys than of girls would be necessary. Another possible explanation would be the under-reporting of girls, but we have no evidence that there was any voluntary under-reporting of boys at such a young age in the censuses. Therefore, we assume that excess mortality of boys was more likely.

In the traditional sub-Saharan African system, women were particularly active in family maintenance and household economic management and, in some ethnic groups, could even pass on their surnames and property. The brideprice system made girls especially valuable for maintaining family wealth. In the black populations of the Cape (and South Africa in general) very few men or women remained unmarried, so it is clear that almost all families were involved in this system. Families with more daughters than sons could obviously benefit. Traditional polygamy would also have boosted demand for women in the marriage market, so a low sex ratio (more women available than men) would have been an advantage. These factors may have been to the advantage of girls, ensuring that they received better food and care and thus had better survival chances than boys.

Bibliography

Akyeampong, E. and H. Fofack. 'The Contribution of African Women to Economic Growth and Development in the Pre-Colonial and Colonial Periods: Historical Perspectives and Policy Implications'. *Economic History of Developing Regions* 29, no. 1 (2014): 42–73.

Anderson, S. 'The Economics of Dowry and Brideprice'. *Journal of Economic Perspectives* 21, no. 4 (2007): 151–74.

Anderson, S. and D. Ray. 'Excess Female Mortality in Africa'. *WIDER Working Paper* 116 (2017): 1–22.

Austin, G. 'Resources, Techniques, and Strategies South of the Sahara: Revising the Factor Endowments Perspective on African Economic Development, 1500–2000'. *Economic History Review* 61, no. 3 (2008): 587–624.

Badassy, P. 'A Severed Umbilicus: Infanticide and the Concealment of Birth in Natal, 1860–1935'. PhD diss., University of KwaZulu-Natal, Durban, 2011.

Beltrán Tapia, F and D. Gallego-Martínez. 'Where Are the Missing Girls? Gender Discrimination in 19th-century Spain'. *Explorations in Economic History* 66 (2017): 117–26.

Boklage, C.E. 'The Epigenetic Environment: Secondary Sex Ratio Depends on Differential Survival in Embryogenesis'. *Human Reproduction* 20, no. 3 (2005): 583–87.
Boshoff, W. and J. Fourie. 'The South African Economy in the Twentieth Century'. In *Business Cycles and Structural Change in South Africa*, edited by W. Boshoff, 49–70. Cham: Springer, 2020.
Brewis, A.A. 'Anthropological Perspectives on Infanticide'. *Arizona Anthropologist* 8 (1992): 103–19.
Bromen, K. and K.H. Jöckel. 'Change in Male Proportion among Newborn Infants'. *Lancet* 349, no. 9054 (1997): 804–5.
Bryant, A.T. *The Zulu People as They Were before the White Man Came*, 2nd edn. Pietermaritzburg: Shuter and Shooter, 1967.
Budlender, D., N. Chobokoane and S. Simelane. 'Marriage Patterns in South Africa: Methodological and Substantive Issues'. *Southern African Journal of Demography* 9, no. 1 (2004): 1–25.
Chahnazarian, A. 'Determinants of the Sex Ratio at Birth: Review of Recent Literature'. *Social Biology* 35, nos. 3–4 (1988): 214–35.
Chakravarty, A. 'Gender Bias in Breastfeeding and Missing Girls in Africa: The Role of Fertility Choice'. *Mimeo* (2012).
Christopher, A.J. '"To Define the Indefinable": Population Classification and the Census in South Africa'. *AREA* 34, no. 4 (2002): 401–8.
Christopher, A.J. 'A South African Domesday Book: The First Union Census of 1911'. *South African Geographical Journal* 92, no. 1 (2010): 22–34.
Christopher, A.J. 'The Union of South Africa Censuses, 1911–1960: An Incomplete Record'. *Historia* 56, no. 2 (2011): 1–18.
Ciocco, A. 'Variation in the Sex Ratio at Birth in the United States'. *Human Biology* 10, no. 1 (1938): 36–64.
Clark, S., E. Colson, J. Lee and T. Scudder. 'Ten Thousand Tonga: A Longitudinal Anthropological Study from Southern Zambia, 1956–1991'. *Population Study* 49, no. 1 (1995): 91–109.
Cronk, L. 'Preferential Parental Investment in Daughters over Sons'. *Human Nature* 2, no. 4 (1991): 387–417.
Das Gupta, M., J. Zhenghua, L. Bohua, X. Zhenming, W. Chung and B. Hwa-Ok. 'Why Is Son Preference So Persistent in East and South Asia? A Cross-Country Study of China, India, and the Republic of Korea'. *Journal of Development Studies* 40, no. 2 (2003): 153–87.
Department of Health. *Demographic and Health Survey: Full Report*. Pretoria: Department of Health, 2008.
Devlieger, P.J. 'The Logic of Killing Disabled Children: Infanticide, Songye Cosmology, and the Colonizer'. In *Madness, Disability, and Social Exclusion: The Archaeology and Anthropology of 'Difference'*, edited by J. Hubert, 159–67. London: Routledge, 2000.
Eriksson, J.G., E. Kajantie, C. Osmond, K. Thornburg and D.J. Barker. 'Boys Live Dangerously in the Womb'. *American Journal of Human Biology* 22, no. 3 (2010): 330–5.
Fellman, J. and A.W. Eriksson. 'Temporal Trends in the Secondary Sex Ratio in Nordic Countries'. *Biodemography and Social Biology* 57, no. 2 (2011): 143–54.
Ferree, K.E. 'Explaining South Africa's Racial Census'. *Journal of Politics* 68, no. 4 (2006): 803–15.
Fourie, J. and J. Jayes. 'Health Inequality and the 1918 Influenza in South Africa'. *World Development* 141 (2021): 105407.
Gaitskell, D., J. Kimble, M. Maconachie and E. Unterhalter. 'Class, Race and Gender: Domestic Workers in South Africa'. *Review of African Political Economy* 10, nos. 27–28 (1983): 86–108.
Garenne, M. 'Sex Ratios at Birth in African Populations: A Review of Survey Data'. *Human Biology* 74, no. 6 (2002): 889–900.

Garenne, M. 'Sex Ratios at Birth in Populations of Eastern and Southern Africa'. *South African Journal of Demography* 9, no. 1 (2004): 91–6.

Garenne, M. 'Sex Ratio at Birth and Family Composition in sub-Saharan Africa: Inter-Couple Variations'. *Journal of Biosocial Science* 41 (2009): 399–407.

Hanlon, G. 'Routine Infanticide in the West, 1500–1800'. *History Compass* 14, no. 11 (2016): 535–48.

Harpending, H.C. and R. Pennington. 'Age Structure and Sex-Biased Mortality among Herero Pastoralists'. *Human Biology* 63, no. 3 (1991): 329–53.

Health Systems Trust. *South African Health Review 1998*. Durban: Health Systems Trust, 1999.

Ingalls, W. 'Demography and Dowries: Perspectives on Female Infanticide in Classical Greece'. *Phoenix* 56, nos. 3/4 (2002): 246–54.

James, W. 'The Sex Ratios of Black Births'. *Annals of Human Biology* 11, no. 1 (1984): 39–44.

Junod, H.A. *The Life of a South African Tribe – I. Social Life*. London: Macmillan, 1927.

Klasen, S. 'Nutrition, Health and Mortality in Sub-Saharan Africa: Is There a Gender Bias?' *Journal of Development Studies* 32, no. 6 (1996): 913–32.

Lesiapeto, M.S., C.M. Smuts, S.M. Hanekom, J. du Plessis and M. Faber. 'Risk Factors of Poor Anthropometric Status in Children under Five Years of Age Living in Rural Districts of the Eastern Cape and KwaZulu-Natal provinces, South Africa'. *South African Journal of Clinical Nutrition* 23, no. 4 (2010): 202–7.

Manicom, L. 'Ruling Relations: Rethinking State and Gender in South African History'. *Journal of African History* 33, no. 3 (1992): 441–65.

Marco-Gracia, F.J. and J. Fourie. 'The Missing Boys: Understanding the Unbalanced Sex Ratio in South Africa, 1894–2011'. *Economic History of Developing Regions* 37, no. 2 (2022): 128–46.

Mitchell, B.R. *International Historical Statistics*. London: Palgrave Macmillan, 2013.

Moultrie, T.A. and I.M. Timæus. 'The South African Fertility Decline: Evidence from two Censuses and a Demographic Health Survey'. *Population Studies* 57, no. 3 (2003): 265–83.

Mpeta, B., J. Fourie and K. Inwood. 'Black Living Standards in South Africa before Democracy: New Evidence from Height'. *South African Journal of Science* 114, nos. 1–2 (2018): 1–8.

Nattrass, N. and J. Seekings. 'The Economy and Poverty in the Twentieth Century in South Africa'. In *The Cambridge History of South Africa, vol. 2*, edited by R. Ross, A.K. Mager and B. Nasson, 518–72. Cambridge: Cambridge University Press, 2010.

O'Laughlin, B. 'Missing Men? The Debate Over Rural Poverty and Women-headed Households in Southern Africa'. *Journal of Peasant Studies* 25, no. 2 (1998): 1–48.

Paulme, D. *Women of Tropical Africa*. London: Routledge & Kegan Paul, 2013.

Posel, D. and S. Rudwick. 'Marriage and Bridewealth (*ilobolo*) in Contemporary Zulu Society'. *African Studies Review* 57, no. 2 (2014): 51–72.

Rehan, N. 'Sex Ratio of Live-born Hausa Infants'. *BJOG: International Journal of Obstetrics and Gynaecology* 89, no. 2 (1982): 136–41.

Sahn, D.E. and D.C. Stifel. 'Parental Preferences for Nutrition of Boys and Girls: Evidence from Africa'. *Journal of Development Studies* 39, no. 1 (2002): 21–45.

Sawyer, C.C. 'Child Mortality Estimation: Estimating Sex Differences in Childhood Mortality since the 1970s'. *Plos Med* 9, no. 8 (2012): e1001287.

Scalone, F. and R. Rettaroli. 'Exploring the Variations of the Sex Ratio at Birth from an Historical Perspective'. *Statistica* 75, no. 2 (2015): 213–26.

Sen, A. 'Missing Women'. *British Medical Journal* 304, no. 6827 (1992): 587–88.

Svedberg P. 'Undernutrition in Sub-Saharan Africa: Is There a Gender Bias?' *Journal of Development Studies* 26, no. 3 (1990): 469–86.

Ulizzi, L. and L. Zonta. 'Factors Affecting the Sex Ratio in Humans: Multivariate Analysis of the Italian Population'. *Human Biology* 67, no. 1 (1995): 59–67.

Visaria, P.M. 'Sex Ratio at Birth in Territories with a Relative Complete Registration'. *Eugenics Quarterly* 14, no. 2 (1967): 132–42.

Wamani, H., A. Åstrøm, S. Peterson, J. Tumwine and T. Tylleskär. 'Boys Are More Stunted than Girls in Sub-Saharan Africa: A Meta-analysis of 16 Demographic and Health Surveys'. *BMC Pediatrics* 7, no. 1 (2007): 1–10.

Zere, E. and D. McIntyre. 'Inequities in under-five Child Malnutrition in South Africa'. *International Journal of Equity in Health* 2, no. 7 (2003): 1–10.

Original sources

Cape Colony censuses of 1894 and 1904, published by Cape of Good Hope Census Office.

South African censuses of 1911, 1921, 1936, 1946, 1951, 1960, 1970, 1980, 1991, 1996, 2001 and 2011, published by Statistics South Africa.

CHAPTER 4
KHOE HOUSEHOLDS IN SWELLENDAM, 1825
*Calumet Links**

Introduction

Writing a history from the bottom up for uncharted people in South Africa would be incomplete without some reflection on Khoesan societies. Using quantitative household data in the form of British tax records and probate inventories for the Khoe of Swellendam in 1825, this chapter looks at independent Khoe communities that existed during the period of British colonial rule. The availability of the 1825 Swellendam household level tax data for the indigenous Khoe was not only rare but the manner in which the records where compiled were also perplexing. Upon closer inspection, Khoe household units were always recorded with an adult male and female marital pair; however, many households had numerous single adult females attached to them. This stood in contrast to the manner in which settler households were recorded at the Cape colony. Settler families were always recorded as a conjugal pair and their offspring. This difference in the way Khoe and settler households were recorded was particularly important since this quantitatively confirmed the fact that the organisation of the family worked differently for these two population groups. Resource distribution and inequality therefore also looked different between the Khoe and settlers.

Many have claimed that household structure and the life cycle of a family matter for the measurement of inequality in a given society.[1] Kuznets noted that in any analysis of inequality, whether based on wealth or income, the household serves as the basic unit of interest.[2] Estimates today of individual income or wealth often neglect to account for the contribution made by non-income-earning household members such as women and children. Economic historians who do take them into account seldom consider non-traditional household structures. Measures of inequality are also affected by when children leave the household, or whether the head of the household is a woman. In other words, if inequality estimates are to be meaningful, they must incorporate the nuances of different kinds of household structure.

---

*Links: Department of Economics, Stellenbosch University, South Africa.

[1] J. Muellbauer, 'Inequality Measures, Prices and Household Composition', *Review of Economic Studies* 41, no. 4 (1974): 493–504; R.I. Lerman, 'The Impact of the Changing US Family Structure on Child Poverty and Income Inequality', *Economica* S119-S139 (1996); B. Headey, G. Marks and M. Wooden, 'The Structure and Distribution of Household Wealth in Australia', *Australian Economic Review* 38, no. 2 (2005): 159–75.

[2] S. Kuznets, 'Demographic Aspects of the Size Distribution of Income: An Exploratory Essay', *Economic Development and Cultural Change* 25, no. 1 (1976): 1–94.

Investigations into economic inequality in pre-industrial societies have become popular recently, partly because new data sources have become available and partly because economic historians have become interested in the possibility of identifying the origins of inequality today.[3] In most of these income or wealth inequality studies they examine the relationship between historical inequality and long-run economic development – a strand of research initiated by Kuznets's seminal work.[4] But very few have noticed the impact that different household structures can have on observed inequality estimates. Very often they simply aggregate pre-industrial inequality or calculate it on a per capita basis, making very little or no adjustment for household or family structure.[5]

Much of the information about historical household structure is anecdotal, or it is classified, interpreted and encoded to suit the requirements of cognate disciplines such as anthropology or archaeology. As a result, the original income or wealth data required by studies in economics, particularly economic history, is already aggregated, and very little can be done to relate it to the micro-level household structures. One of the implications of this lack of micro-level data is that most pre-industrial inequality studies focus on inequality *between* rather than *within* groups. This is particularly worrying in studies of pre-industrial societies.[6]

Family structures across time and space have evolved. Today they look very different from their pre-industrial counterparts. 'Household' is a dynamic concept. Co-habitation patterns, fertility trends and marriage conventions have not remained static through the ages.[7] Skinner notes that family systems and household structures

---

[3] A. Booth, 'Living Standards and the Distribution of Income in Colonial Indonesia: A Review of the Evidence', *Journal of Southeast Asian Studies* 19, no. 2 (1988): 310–34; A. Berry, 'International Trade, Government, and Income Distribution in Peru since 1870', *Latin American Research Review* 25, no. 2 (1990): 31–59; B. Milanovic, 'An Estimate of Average of Income and Inequality in Byzantium around year 1000', *Review of Income and Wealth* 52, no. 3 (2006): 449–70; B. Milanovic, *Worlds Apart: Measuring International and Global Inequality* (2007; repr., Princeton: Princeton University Press, 2011); B. Milanovic, 'Towards an Explanation of Inequality in Premodern Societies: The Role of Colonies, Urbanization, and High Population Density', *Economic History Review* 71, no. 4 (2018): 1029–47; G. Alfani, 'Economic Inequality in Northwestern Italy: A Long-term View (Fourteenth to Eighteenth Centuries)', *Journal of Economic History* 75, no. 4 (2015): 1058–96; W. Ryckbosch, 'Economic Inequality and Growth before the Industrial Revolution: The Case of the Low Countries (Fourteenth to Nineteenth Centuries)', *European Review of Economic History* 20, no. 1 (2016): 1–22; T. Goda and A.T. García, 'The Rising Tide of Absolute Global Income Inequality during 1850–2010: Is It Driven by Inequality within or between Countries?' *Social Indicators Research* 130, no. 3 (2017): 1051–72.

[4] S. Kuznets, 'Economic Growth and Income Inequality', *American Economic Review* 45, no. 1 (1955): 1–28.

[5] P. H. Lindert and J.G. Williamson, 'Revising England's Social Tables, 1688–1812', *Explorations in Economic History* 19, no. 4 (1982): 385–408; Milanovic, *Worlds Apart*; J. Bolt and E. Hillbom, 'Long-term Trends in Economic Inequality: Lessons from Colonial Botswana, 1921–74', *Economic History Review* 69, no. 4 (2016): 1255–84; B. Milanovic, P.H. Lindert and J.G. Williamson, 'Pre-Industrial Inequality', *Economic Journal* 121, no. 551 (2011): 255–72.

[6] Kuznets, 'Demographic Aspects'.

[7] T.K. Burch and B.J. Matthews, 'Household Formation in Developed Societies', *Population and Development Review* 13, no. 3 (1987): 495–511; A.S. Alderson and S.K. Sanderson, 'Historic European Household Structures and the Capitalist World-Economy', *Journal of Family History* 16, no. 4 (1991): 419–32.

are constantly in flux, varying over time according to class, ethnicity and country.[8] This chapter argues that any study of inequality must take cognizance of these variations. Throughout this chapter the term family will refer to the conjugal pair and their offspring, whereas the term household can include co-habiting members that are not part of the immediate family.

The availability of micro-level household data in the form of British tax records for the Khoe of Swellendam in 1825 makes it possible to investigate the impact that household structures may have had on inequality estimates. That said, and even though individual-level data for the Khoe are available, we do not have much definitive information on the structure of Khoe households during the early nineteenth century. It also demonstrates that the Khoe society of the Swellendam region in 1825 was very unequal. Because of the lack of information on Khoe households for the period under study, I compare the levels of inequality that appear if I consider three kinds of household structure: a household consisting only of a nuclear family, and two types of extended households. An important result produced by this comparative exercise is that the level of inequality declines as the household structure is extended.

I argue that the Khoe's diminished economic status compelled them to devise coping strategies that would enable them to compensate for their increasing poverty. Before they came into contact with Europeans the Khoe moved around as small groups of nomadic pastoralists. Finding themselves now obliged to make their resources support more people, Khoe families in Swellendam extended their household structures – a common strategy for responding to adverse economic shocks throughout human history. This strategy of coping with hardship may also have been a remnant of pre-colonial contact society, which could have persisted into the present. Along with Chapter 9 by Mbem and De Haas who uncover the practice of multi-sited livelihood strategies among migrants living in Cape Town, this chapter contributes to our understanding of the forces which shaped household formation, albeit centuries apart.

Household structure and inequality

The failure to account for household structure in inequality calculations distorts both the within-group and the between-group economic differences observed.[9] One serious omission is the phenomenon of multiple-earner households. As more members of the household enter employment, so downward pressure is placed on both within-household

---

[8] G.W. Skinner, 'Family Systems and Demographic Processes', in *Anthropological Demography: Toward a New Synthesis*, ed. David I. Kertzer and Tom Fricke (Chicago: University of Chicago Press, 1997): 53–95.

[9] R. Angel and M. Tienda, 'Determinants of Extended Household Structure: Cultural Pattern or Economic Need?' *American Journal of Sociology* 87, no. 6 (1982): 1360–83.

inequality and overall inequality. This is especially true for households where spouses or non-nuclear members of the household enter the labour market.[10]

Another factor which may influence the structure of the household and thus the measure of inequality is a propensity to include non-nuclear family members in the household. These include any individuals other than the husband, wife and children who are the core of the household. Historically, this arrangement seems to have been more characteristic of marginalised or relatively impoverished communities that extended the household as a coping measure in times of hardship. Farley shows how African-Americans cushioned the shock of the economic downturn of the 1970s in the United States by making use of extended family networks of non-nuclear households, allowing more family members to maintain a decent standard of living.[11] Extended family systems are therefore an important way to reduce poverty and within-household inequality.[12] Such structures are not permanent but a response to adverse economic conditions.

Family structures have always been prone to change over time. The pre-industrial Basque family system was very different from French and Spanish household structures today. Similarly, Chinese family systems have changed over time: until as recently as 1946 more than 50 per cent of families had a grand family structure known as a *frérèche* (a French term for a household made up of sibling co-residents).[13] No region of the world has ever had a completely static family system. Family structures have been fluid in Africa, Asia, the Americas and Europe for millennia precisely in order to respond to economic challenges. The impermanence of family structures complicates measures of inequality

Households often combine temporarily in order to mitigate the effect of economic crises. Indonesian households did this in response to the economic crisis in Asia at the end of the 1990s.[14] Wealthier societies tend to have smaller family units or households since the trade-off between privacy and economic survival becomes less costly the richer

---

[10] J. Mincer, 'Labor Force Participation of Married Women: A Study of Labor Supply', in *Aspects of Labor Economics* (Princeton: NBER, Princeton University Press, 1962): 63–105; D. Hryshko, C. Juhn and K. McCue, 'Trends in Earnings Inequality and Earnings Instability among US Couples: How Important Is Assortative Matching?' *Labour Economics* 48 (2017): 168–82.

[11] R. Farley, 'Trends in Racial Inequalities: Have the Gains of the 1960s Disappeared in the 1970s?' *American Sociological Review* 42, no. 2 (1977): 189–208.

[12] Angel and Tienda, 'Determinants of Extended Household Structure'; R. Akresh, 'Flexibility of Household Structure Child Fostering Decisions in Burkina Faso', *Journal of Human Resources* 44, no. 4 (2009): 976–97; K. Abanokova and M. Lokshin, 'Changes in Household Composition as a Shock-Mitigating Strategy', *Economics of Transition* 23, no. 2 (2015): 371–88.

[13] Z. Zhao, 'Coresidential Patterns in Historical China: A Simulation Study', *Population and Development Review* 26, no. 2 (2000): 263–93.

[14] E. Frankenberg, B. Sikoki and W. Suriastini, 'Contraceptive Use in a Changing Service Environment: Evidence from Indonesia during the Economic Crisis', *Studies in Family Planning* 34, no. 2 (2003): 103–16.

a society becomes.[15] This form of coping with hardship is not culturally specific and seems to be characteristic of most societies across the globe.

A simple reason for change in household structure is the coming and going of children. Children leave and set up their own households, and parents may place children in the care of better resourced guardians. These changes obviously play a significant role in determining the structure of the household unit being observed.[16] In short, these variations and changes in family and household structures hugely complicate calculations of inequality. Omitting them places an upward bias on the inequality trends observed.

A further matter that complicates studies of pre-industrial inequality is intra-household resource distribution.[17] It is important to consider the stage of the household life cycle, since it determines how much of the resources available to the household is apportioned to each co-resident individual.[18] How domestic household units function matters for the ultimate inequality observed. Analysis of within-household resource allocation has largely been conducted in the fields of anthropology, sociology and history. But economic historians are hampered by the lack of historical data linked specifically to within-household resource distribution. This presents an almost insurmountable obstacle to approximating true inequality.

Income and wealth data are scarce for pre-industrial Western societies, but even more so for pre-industrial Africa, which makes the task of assessing historical inequality in African countries particularly difficult. One notable success is a ground-breaking study of inequality in the eighteenth-century Cape Colony by Fourie and Von Fintel.[19] Yet it fails to incorporate both household structures and the non-European people who were part of Cape Dutch society at the time. Other studies which have included non-European African groups have been limited to studying aggregate income levels (and therefore inequality) without incorporating household structures of the time. Examples are Bigsten, and Bolt and Hillbom, who studied inequality in twentieth-century Kenya and Botswana respectively.[20] The point of departure of this chapter, then, is that it is no longer acceptable to study inequality in Africa without paying due attention to household structures.

---

[15] Abanokova and Lokshin, 'Changes in Household Composition'.

[16] Akresh, 'Flexibility of Household Structure'.

[17] E.A. Hammel and P. Laslett, 'Comparing Household Structure Over Time and Between Cultures', *Comparative Studies in Society and History* 16, no. 1 (1974): 73–109.

[18] Kuznets, 'Demographic Aspects'.

[19] J. Fourie and D. von Fintel, 'The Dynamics of Inequality in a Newly Settled, Pre-Industrial Society: The Case of the Cape Colony', *Cliometrica* 4, no. 3 (2010): 229–67.

[20] A. Bigsten, 'Welfare and Economic Growth in Kenya, 1914–76', *World Development* 14, no. 9 (1986): 1151–60; Bolt and Hillbom, 'Long-term Trends in Economic Inequality'.

Swellendam

This background summary draws on work by Theal, Newton-King, Viljoen and Penn.[21] The Swellendam district of the Cape Colony lies approximately 218 km to the northeast of Cape Town, beyond the Hottentots-Holland Mountain range. Before Europeans settled in this area in the seventeenth century it was inhabited by Khoe tribes such as the Hessequa, Chainouqua and Gorouqua, a relatively prosperous pastoral people. But trade and barter with Europeans throughout the eighteenth century brought about a decline in their economic, political and social status, and they became impoverished as the settlers, or free burghers, moved further inland in search of grazing land for stock. Cattle and sheep farming became the cornerstone of the Cape frontier economy. Many of these settlers had failed as commercial crop farmers in and around Cape Town and a combination of poor weather conditions, lack of capital and persistent indebtedness drove them to the Swellendam district, where there was better water and grazing. By the 1770s there were about 600 independent European livestock farmers in the Swellendam district, and they of course came into contact with the Khoe, whose vast knowledge of livestock farming made their services invaluable to these farmers as they tried to establish themselves in the region.

This exploitative relationship would become one of the major causes of the Khoe's economic and social downfall. The Khoe social order, depending as it did on systems of patronage, made it easy for the Europeans to reduce them to a position of servitude. This clientelism, a system in which the poorer members of society entered the service of wealthier members, to receive payment in kind or work off their debts, was well established in Khoe society before the Europeans arrived. It was easy for the settler farmers to enter into informal labour agreements with the Khoe in order to take advantage of their pastoral knowledge and increase their numbers of sheep and cattle. Since the Khoe did not have the means to enforce these informal contractual relationships, instances of settler farmers not honouring these agreements became frequent throughout the late eighteenth century. These failed contractual relationships created opportunities for settlers to claim repayment for debts that did not exist, or to force the Khoe into service for periods that suited the farmers. This exploitative relationship led to systematic impoverishment of the Khoe in general and those of the Swellendam district in particular.[22]

---

[21]G.M. Theal, *History of South Africa, 1795–1834*, vol. 3 (London: Sonnenschein & Co., 1891); S. Newton-King, *Masters and Servants on the Cape Eastern Frontier, 1760–1803*, vol. 97 (Cambridge: Cambridge University Press, 1999); R. Viljoen, 'Aboriginal Khoikhoi Servants and Their Masters in Colonial Swellendam, South Africa, 1745–1795', *Agricultural History* 75, no. 1 (2001): 28–51; R. Viljoen, '"Sketching the Khoikhoi": George French Angas and His Depiction of the Genadendal Khoikhoi Characters at the Cape of Good Hope, c.1847', *South African Journal of Art History* 22, no. 2 (2007): 277–90; N. Penn, *The Forgotten Frontier: Colonist and Khoisan on the Cape's Northern Frontier in the 18th Century* (Athens, US: University of Ohio Press, 2005).

[22]Viljoen, 'Sketching the Khoikhoi'.

Throughout the eighteenth and early nineteenth century, the Khoe's nomadic pastoral existence gradually disintegrated as the competition for grazing and water resources in the Swellendam district increased. The settlers needed a cheap and efficient labour force for their various agricultural endeavours, the dispossession of Khoe was an obvious solution. As a result, throughout the eighteenth century the Swellendam Khoe were impoverished and politically disenfranchised so that by the start of the nineteenth century many had been reduced to indentured labourers. Those who remained free were also compelled by poor circumstances to work as seasonal or wandering labourers on settler farms. The result of this reduced social and economic position of the Khoe meant that they were soon much poorer than their settler counterparts.

A large proportion of Khoe families at Swellendam tended to reside on white settler farms although some independent communities continued to exist. Viljoen shows that where independent communities survived, married Khoe couples tended to work on different settler farms to diversify the risk of total income loss.[23] Independent Khoe clans were often quite poor, very few owned sheep and cattle and many had to work as migrant labour on settler farms during the harvesting season. Poorer boys and young men were forced to work as farm labour on white settler farms for meagre wages or in-kind payments.

Where Khoe families resided on white settler farms women were mostly responsible for kitchen duties, however; sex was also an important facet of the relationship between master and servant. Men would take care of herding, ploughing and gang labour to complete the harvests. In turn, boys between the ages of four and seven tended to fowl and small stock animals. The Khoe were thus a cheap source of labour who were relentlessly exploited to work on settler farms.

There was also inequality within the Khoe community, which necessitated survival strategies for those who had been left destitute. Since, before the arrival of the Europeans, the Khoe were nomadic pastoralists moving around in small tribes of kin, in order to survive they relied on extended family networks. Larger households or kinship units which extended beyond the conjugal pair and their offspring would have been an effective strategy to reduce inequality and hedge against the risk of starvation even prior to colonial contact. Viljoen confirms that the Khoe of Swellendam made use of extended household networks to survive in times of great strife.[24]

By 1825 Swellendam was no longer a frontier district. Its borders had been well established by the time Cape authorities conducted its 1825 tax census of the Khoe. Despite the closing of the frontier, however, independent Khoe communities continued to co-exist alongside the newly established settler farmers and began to cultivate barley and wheat since the climate and abundant fertile soil of the district made that possible. The Khoe probably used seeds supplied by the settlers to plant their barley and wheat crops since crop farming was not native to the Cape prior to contact with Europeans.

---

[23]Ibid.
[24]Ibid.

The data

For the analysis in this chapter, I transcribed the tax census or *opgaafrolle* compiled by the British colonial authorities for the indigenous population of the district of Swellendam in the Cape Colony of 1825. At the time, this was the only known detailed micro-level tax data for any Khoe. Unusually, and usefully for my purposes, it recorded micro-level information for each Khoe individual for any given year – in this instance, 1825. Khoe household information was recorded by listing the name of each adult member, their sex, the number of boys and girls attached to that particular family and their asset holdings. The asset holdings, in the form of livestock (the numbers of cattle, sheep, goats, horses, pigs and mules) were used to calculate the amount of tax the individual or household had to pay. In order to obtain the value of asset holdings I made use of the MOOC8-series probate inventory price data located in the Western Cape Archives and Records Services (WCARS).

But the critical detail, from the point of view of my study, *not* recorded in the dataset is the household structure. The large number of apparently single women and men recorded in the data, none of whom seem to have possessed any assets at all, is a strange and perplexing feature of the data. Although Viljoen gives us some reason to believe that the Khoe made use of extended household structures to cope with economic hardship, the lack of information on household structure may have been a result of bias on the part of the recording official – in this instance, a European *field cornet* – who could have encoded his own notions of what constitutes a household into the way in which the information was gathered.[25] For 1825, the dataset contains 1,266 Khoe households (a total of 3,341 individuals) across twenty-six sub-districts, with the sub-district of Swartrivier having the largest number of Khoe inhabitants (2,210). A point worth noting is that 866 individuals, particularly single females, did not report owning any assets at all.

To understand how household formation in general influences pre-industrial inequality estimates, I set out to examine the effect of changing household structures on inequality on the basis of data provided about the Khoe in the *opgaafrollen* for the Swellendam district for 1825. The strength of this study was the application of a flexible concept of household structure to inequality estimates. I assumed that familial structure was, to a large extent, dependent on exogenous shocks, such as impoverishment or indenturing, and I made informed guesses about the structure of households at the time on the basis of historical and anthropological literature. This simplifying assumption allowed for flexibility in selecting household structure.

Even if the family structure is assumed to have been determined by exogenous influences, the *size* of the hypothetical household still matters as far as income and health distribution within that specific household is concerned. At the most basic level, it is logical to assume that the larger the household (especially if it consisted of more

---

[25]Ibid.

than just the conjugal pair and their offspring), the more resources would have had to be stretched in order to meet the needs of all co-residents. Aside from the size of the specified household, it would also have been unrealistic to assume that household resources were shared equally.[26] Studies have shown that, in patriarchal societies, *within-household* distribution of resources generally favours children and men at the expense of women.[27] Findlay and Wright, and Becker have also demonstrated that an assumption that resources were shared equally among all household members can produce a distorted picture of poverty.[28] In other words, both the *size* and the *within-household distribution* of resources matter for determining the overall inequality observed. For the purposes of the analysis in this chapter, I made no assumptions about within-household distributions of resources, partly because I lacked information about the degree of access each Khoe household member had to the assets reported in the tax data. My analysis would not have stayed true to the imperative to move away from imposing today's biases on a past phenomenon such as household dynamics, if I allowed today's notion of resource distribution within households to influence the analysis.

The demographics of the Khoe in Swellendam, 1825

The Khoe people of the Cape Colony typically organised their lives in large residential kinship networks or *Kraals*. Much of our information about Khoe inheritance and family sharing practices in these networks stems from archaeological or anthropological studies of the way these networks functioned before the arrival of the settlers.[29] The study by Carstens offers an account of inheritance traditions practised by the Nama people during the early twentieth century, based mainly on information gleaned from the diary of South African anthropologist Mrs A.W. Hoernlé.[30] The following basic facts can be drawn from these journal entries: the woman who may also be described as the 'chief wife' typically inherited the homestead and was free to move it to wherever she chose; the eldest child usually inherited from the father and the youngest from the mother, regardless of the sex of the child; and resource sharing appears to have been very egalitarian regardless of the sex of those who stood to inherit. Despite the fact that these practices were recorded a century later, the Nama people were a sub-grouping of the

---

[26]D. Thomas, 'The Distribution of Income and Expenditure within the Household', *Annales d'Economie et de Statistique* 29 (1993): 109–35.

[27]J. Findlay and R.E. Wright, 'Gender, Poverty and the Intra-Household Distribution of Resources', *Review of Income and Wealth* 42, no. 3 (1996): 335–51.

[28]Ibid; G.S. Becker, *A Treatise on the Family* (Cambridge, US: Harvard University Press, 1991).

[29]A. Barnard, *Hunters and Herders of Southern Africa: A Comparative Ethnography of the Khoisan Peoples* (Cambridge: Cambridge University Press, 1992); P. Carstens, 'The Inheritance of Private Property among the Nama of Southern Africa Reconsidered', *Africa* 53, no. 2 (1983): 58–70; S. Kent, 'Sharing in an Egalitarian Kalahari Community', *Man* 28, no. 3 (1993): 479–514.

[30]Carstens, 'Inheritance of Private Property'.

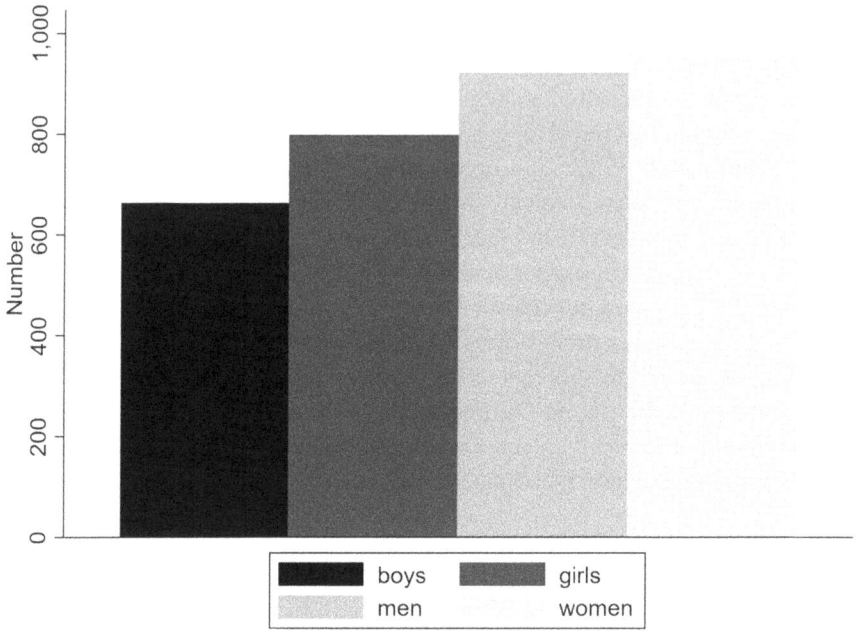

Figure 4.1 Swellendam Khoe population 1825.
Source: British tax census.

Khoe and shared similar customs. These facts alone serve as some justification for not making any assumptions about the within-household distribution of Khoe assets.

The shortage of solid evidence about Khoe household structures leaves much room to theorise what type of structure was dominant in 1825. What the British tax records do show is roughly how many Khoe were present in Swellendam district in that year. The tax records, by their very nature, of course may not offer a true or accurate reflection of the size of the Khoe population since many Khoe were still nomadic and many would have tended to evade taxation when and where possible. Theal argued that as much as two-thirds of assets were omitted from the tax data, as the records were dependent largely on self-reporting and whether or not individuals could be located.[31]

Figure 4.1 shows the Khoe numbers of Swellendam district for 1825. Women appear to have slightly outnumbered men. This is evident, for example, in the large number of single women who were linked to what was traditionally seen as the conjugal pair and their offspring. What is unclear from the data is whether these women should be considered part of the household, or the houseful.[32] Figure 4.1 also shows that Khoe

---

[31] Theal, *History of South Africa*.

[32] The houseful will refer to families living together outside of a conjugal pair and their offspring.

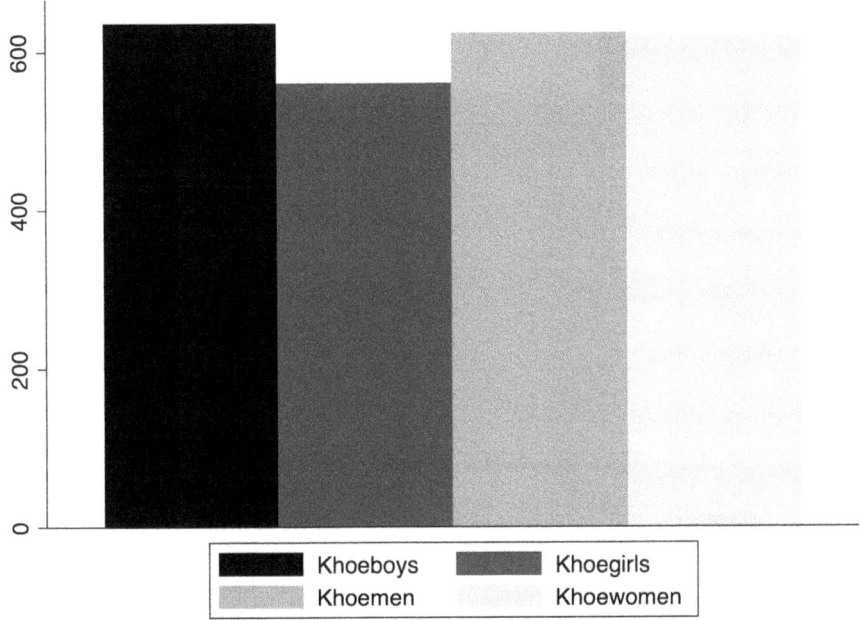

Figure 4.2 Swellendam Khoe labour on settler farms 1825.
Source: British Tax census.

children outnumbered Khoe adults in the Swellendam district. This is particularly interesting since high fertility rates were also prevalent during the nineteenth century for the settler population.[33] In Figure 4.2 it is also clear to see that less Khoe worked on settler farms than resided in independent communities. What is interesting is the fact that the largest number of Khoe farm labourers were boys. This confirms Viljoen's emphasis on the importance of Khoe boys for Swellendam settler agriculture.[34]

The tax census reveals that the Khoe of Swellendam district owned a variety of livestock, particularly horses, as shown in Figure 4.3.

Since they also grew crops, mainly wheat and barley, it is likely that the oxen were used for ploughing. Horses were not native to southern Africa and only arrived in the Cape Colony with the European settlers in 1652. Horse breeding therefore became part of Khoe livelihoods only after their contact with European settlers.[35] They may have bred horses for their own transport or for sale, perhaps to travellers passing through Swellendam

---

[33]J. Cilliers and E. Green, 'The Land-Labour Hypothesis in a Settler Economy: Wealth, Labour and Household Composition on the South African Frontier', *International Review of Social History* 63, no. 2 (2018): 239–71.

[34]Viljoen, 'Sketching the Khoikhoi'.

[35]S. Swart, 'Riding High: Horses, Power and Settler Society, c. 1654–1840', *Kronos* 28, no. 1 (2002): 47–63.

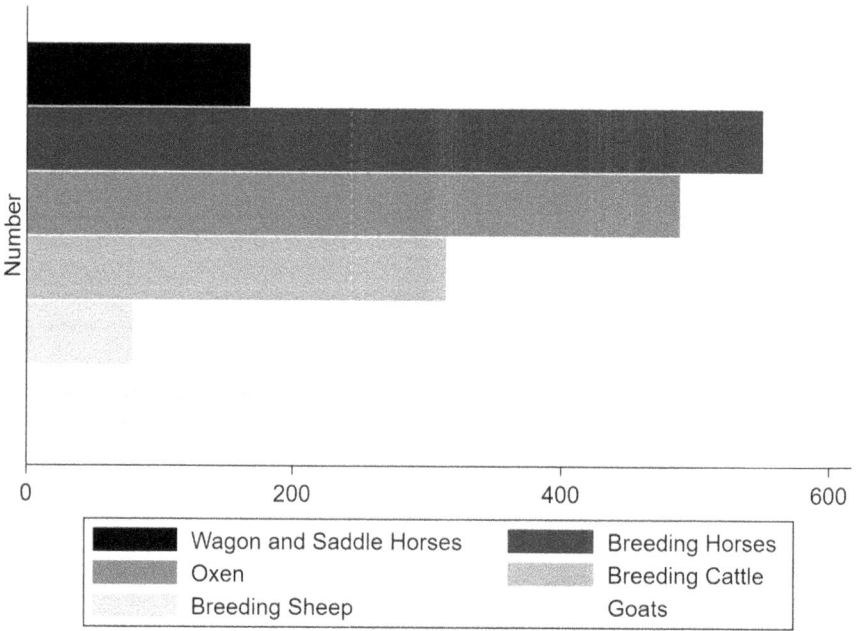

Figure 4.3 Swellendam Khoe livestock numbers 1825.
Source: British tax census.

from Graaff-Reinet. They would have been required for the arduous 219 km journey to Cape Town over the Hottentots-Holland mountains, sometimes driving livestock.[36] The Khoe adoption of horse breeding and crop farming after coming into contact with European settlers should be seen as part of a larger phenomenon of adaptive change after this contact.[37] Their lifestyle had changed in a fundamental way since the arrival of Europeans. This way of adapting in order to survive bears a striking resemblance to the adaptations by the Choctaw tribe of the Ohio basin in North America, who were eventually fully integrated into the cattle economy introduced by European settlers in the seventeenth century.[38] Figure 4.4 shows that in 1825 Swellendam the average crop yield for barley was much higher than that for wheat.

Tax data is primarily a wealth indicator and as such gives little or no indication of household income or within-household distribution of resources. That said, the data does offer plenty of scope to theorise household structure. In order to put the relative

---

[36] L. Guelke, 'Frontier Settlement in Early Dutch South Africa', *Annals of the Association of American Geographers* 66, no. 1 (1976): 25–42.

[37] Carstens, 'Inheritance of Private Property'; Penn, *Forgotten Frontier*.

[38] J.T. Carson, 'Native Americans, the Market Revolution, and Culture Change: The Choctaw Cattle Economy, 1690–1830', *Agricultural History* 71, no. 1 (1997): 1–18.

Khoe Households in Swellendam, 1825

Figure 4.4 Khoe crop yields Swellendam 1825
Source: British tax census.

poverty of the Khoe of Swellendam into perspective, I took the sheep and cattle stocks of the Khoe in the Swellendam district and the sheep and cattle stocks of settlers in the Swellendam, Graaff-Reinet and Tulbagh districts and for each case multiplied the number of animals by the average prices obtained from the MOOC-8 probate inventories. I obtained the average price of sheep and cattle for each district and multiplied by the number of animals. I then added the value of cattle and sheep together and divided by the number of farms or households per district.

Table 4.1 shows that the Khoe population of the Swellendam district were significantly poorer than their settler counterparts in all three districts. The average sheep and cattle wealth of the Khoe in Swellendam district was around 22.86 rixdollars, which was four times lower than that of Tulbagh, the poorest settler district. In 1825, the average settler in Swellendam district was thirty-eight times richer than the average Khoe. Although my estimates substantially underestimate wealth, given that other assets are excluded, they do illustrate the vast disparity in wealth between Khoe and settlers, and they support the historical accounts of severe poverty among the Khoe community at the time.[39] It is therefore theoretically sound to assume that the Khoe would have resorted to extended family households to mitigate the effects of severe poverty.

---

[39]See, for example: Penn, *Forgotten Frontier*.

When further details of the Swellendam settler *opgaaf* of 1825 is compared to that of the Khoe in Table 4.2, the stark differences in livestock holdings become even more striking. Where the entire Khoe population in the records owned a total of 160 breeding sheep, the settler community possessed 59,171. This roughly translates to ten sheep per settler included in the *opgaaf*, whereas the Khoe had less than one sheep per head.

Settler dominance also permeated through crop-based agriculture, with the varieties of planting activities including wheat, rye, barley, oats and vines being much greater than that of the Khoe. Table 4.3 confirms that settler agriculture dwarfed the Khoe planting

Table 4.1 Per household wealth levels for Swellendam and frontier districts (in rixdollars).

	(Khoe) Swellendam	(Settlers) Swellendam	(Settlers) Graaff-Reinet	(Settlers) Tulbagh
Wealth	22.86	875.23	294.10	96.16

Source: British tax census and MOOC-8 series.

Table 4.2 Settler and Khoe livestock holdings in 1825.

	Settler vs Khoe livestock	
Livestock	Settler Opgaaf	Khoe Opgaaf
Saddle horses	4,200	322
Draught oxen	9,741	980
Breeding oxen	12,317	858
Wether sheep	5,843	0
Breeding sheep	59,171	160
Spanish sheep	7,793	0
Donkeys	37	0
Goats	64,811	462
Pigs	1,488	20

Source: MOOC-8 series and British tax census.

Table 4.3 Khoe and settler crops planted in 1825.

	Settler vs Khoe agriculture	
Livestock	Settler Opgaaf	Khoe Opgaaf
Wheat sown (muiden)	26,915	1,910
Barley sown (muiden)	18,803	1,308
Rye sown (muiden)	12,943	0
Oats sown (muiden)	14,131	0
Vines (number)	1,468,660	0

Source: MOOC-8 Series and British tax census.

Household structure and the eighteenth-century Khoe of the Cape

Since we do not really know what the household structure of the Khoe of Swellendam district was like in 1825, I made some theoretical assumptions for the purpose of my study, using the anthropological schematic conventions designed by Hammel and Laslett as refined by Yanagisako and Brettell.[40] In their diagrammatic representations of the various theoretical households, a triangle represents males and a circle females. A solid line connecting males to females represents a married or other clearly defined conjugal unit. Their offspring are illustrated as originating from the original conjugal pair. Where the relationship between a pair is not clearly defined, the solid line is interrupted.

The first theoretical household structure I used, household structure 1, shown in Figure 4.5, consists of the typical conjugal pair and their offspring. I assume that in this theoretical household each member of the household receives an equal share of household resources.[41] Household structure 2, shown in Figure 4.6, is an extended family structure, a polygamous household unit consisting of a male head, his wives and the offspring of each male-female pair.

For the purpose of analysis, I again assumed that each member receives an equal share of the household resources. I acknowledge that the assumption of a 'polygamous household structure' is quite contentious, since many scholars would consider the household associated with each wife a separate household unit altogether.[42] However, I opted to consider the husband and all associated wives and children as one household for two reasons: firstly, the data for family units may have been recorded in specific groups that shared resources, which would imply that splitting these seemingly polygamous units into smaller sub-households would be incorrect; and secondly, since in this configuration the male head of the household is common to all women, it is reasonable and justifiable to assume that some level of resource sharing would have occurred between all individuals in this theoretical polygamous household.

Morton argues that a broad application of the polygamous household assumption may be incorrect since polygamy was often practised only by the elites or wealthy

---

[40] Hammel and Laslett, 'Comparing Household Structure'; S.J. Yanagisako, 'Family and Household: The Analysis of Domestic Groups', *Annual Review of Anthropology* 8, no. 1 (1979): 161–205; C.B. Brettell, 'Conceptualizing Migration and Mobility in Anthropology: An Historical Analysis', *Transitions: Journal of Transient Migration* 2, no. 1 (2018): 7–25.

[41] Becker, *Treatise on the Family*.

[42] B. Morton, 'The Hunting Trade and the Reconstruction of Northern Tswana Societies after the Difaqane, 1838–1880', *South African Historical Journal* 36, no. 1 (1997): 220–39.

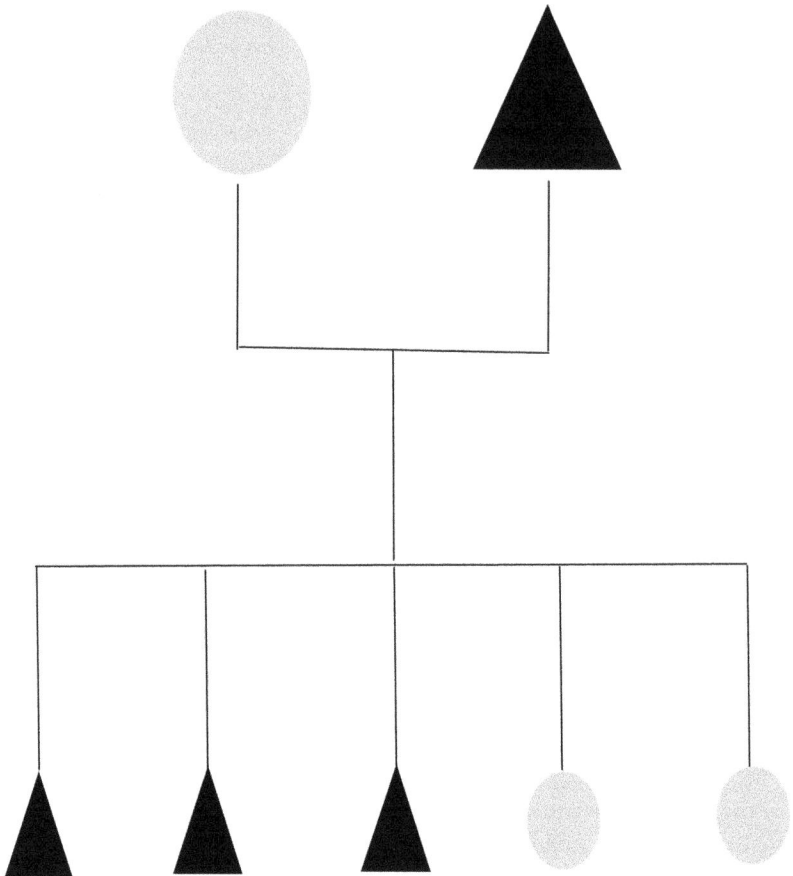

Figure 4.5 Household structure 1.
Source: Hammel and Laslett (1974).

members of a society.⁴³ However, others have observed that polygamous households tended to be poorer and more likely to be food insecure.⁴⁴ In this chapter I advance an alternative hypothesis regarding household formation which may explain why large numbers of single females appeared to have been attached to Khoe households in the Swellendam district. I suggest that wealthier Khoe men may have taken more wives, not only as a show of prestige, but also as a means of assisting other poor families in the Khoe community. I am not forwarding this hypothesis as a definitive explanation but as one

---

⁴³Morton, 'Hunting Trade'.

⁴⁴D.P. Hogan, B. Berhanu and A. Hailemariam, 'Household Organization, Women's Autonomy, and Contraceptive Behavior in Southern Ethiopia', *Studies in Family Planning* 30, no. 4 (1999): 302–14; C. Morrisson and J.R. de Laiglesia, 'Household Structures and Savings: Evidence from Household Surveys', *OECD Development Centre, Working Paper* (2008).

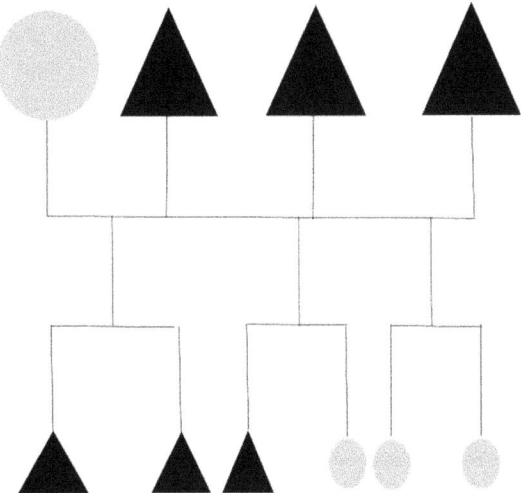

Figure 4.6 Household structure 2.
Source: Hammel and Laslett (1974).

of a number of alternative hypotheses; that is, a proposed explanation which, based on the available evidence, could help economic historians theorise the impact of changing household structure on inequality measurement.

Another possible explanation for the unusual household structure I observed in the data may be that a central household could have supported many connected but semi-dependent households which I refer to collectively as a 'houseful'. This explanation remains hypothetical. Read in conjunction with each other, my 'co-residential pair hypothesis' would explain why a large number of women are listed individually next to but as part of the same household as the traditional conjugal pair in the tax census. If the co-residential pair hypothesis that I put forward here is a true explanation of the data, many of these women may well have been the partners or mothers of Khoe seasonal workers on white settler farms in Swellendam district. The co-residential pairs would thus reside in the same homestead functioning as one household. Such an interpretation would to some extent be supported by the work of historians who have written on the history of Swellendam district and have specifically mentioned wandering Khoe farm workers.[45]

What makes this hypothesis difficult to prove is the fact that the Khoe located on white settler farms in the Swellendam district in 1825 had a 1:1 adult sex ratio. This does not indicate the presence of a large number of single male adults on white settler farms. A large presence of single Khoe male adults would at least partly support my hypothesis.

---

[45]Viljoen, 'Aboriginal Khoikhoi Servants'; Viljoen, 'Sketching the Khoikhoi'.

My contention is that the tax data do not accurately capture the activity or presence of seasonal Khoe workers since it is possible that they may not have been formally indentured to white settler farmers and would therefore not appear in any of the official records. However, assuming the co-residential pair hypothesis will not change the inequality estimate if I assume that all resources are divided equally between individuals, regardless of which of the two types I consider the household to be. It is only when I consider differences in *within-household* distribution of resources that the distinction between my two hypothetical household types becomes clear and meaningful.

To sum up: this section of the chapter has emphasised the fact that Khoe household formation would have been heavily dependent on their economic situation – which is, of course, not to suggest that other social norms, such as tribal customs, did not also influence the coping strategy or household structure they opted for. Despite the tentative and hypothetical nature of my speculation about the exact nature of Khoe households, I demonstrate in the following section how introducing varied household structures influences the inequality observed.

Empirical strategy

As the start to compiling the descriptive statistics, my first empirical strategy incorporated a simple OLS regression with wealth per capita for the Khoe as the dependent variable. The estimating equation is as follows:

$$Log(Y_i) = \beta_1 Khoewomen_i + \beta_2 married_i + \beta_3 Khoe-boys_i + \beta_3 Khoe-girls_i + \epsilon_i \quad (1)$$

In equation 1, $Log(Y)$ represents the log of per capita wealth for the Swellendam Khoe. The regressors which equation 1 focuses on are the number of Khoe women living in a homestead, whether there was a married couple present, and the impact of the number of Khoe boys and girls on per capita wealth.

Results

At this point I have already established that in 1825 the Khoe of Swellendam district were poorer than their settler counterparts. As a baseline comparison I took a standard wealth measure for each household and divided the total household wealth by the number of household members. I included in that calculation each asset owned by the household, whether head of livestock or a physical object such as a wagon. I treated each child as an adult. I obtained the wealth measure for each household by multiplying the number of assets by the average price of the asset obtained from the MOOC 8 probate inventory for Swellendam, 1825. I posited that Khoe families with more children would be richer in terms of assets owned. Table 4.4 shows the output of a simple cross-sectional OLS regression analysis on wealth per capita for Khoe farms, with controls for sub-districts.

Table 4.4 OLS regression Swellendam on wealth per capita.

VARIABLES	(1) OLS
Khoe women	−7.455***
	(2.671)
Married	8.663***
	(2.303)
Khoe boys	0.974
	(1.078)
Khoe girls	1.273
	(0.986)
Constant	2.877
	(3.354)
Sub-district controls	YES
Observations	1,266
R-squared	0.259

Standard errors in parentheses *** p<0.01, ** p<0.05, * p<0.1.
Source: British tax census and MOOC-8 series.

The results clearly show that when the number of Khoe boys and girls in the household is regressed on the wealth per capita, the effect is positive and significant (at a level of 1 per cent). When the sizes of the coefficients are considered, the number of Khoe girls appears to have been more beneficial to wealth per capita than the number of boys. According to the OLS regression, households with traditional marriage structures (one man and one woman) also tended to be wealthier. The regression results also confirm that the presence of adult Khoe women had a negative and significant effect on per capita wealth levels, which is probably because the dataset contains a large number of single Khoe women with no assets. This result does not distinguish between different household structures.

Table 4.5 shows that, after aggregating all asset wealth and dividing it by the entire population of 3,341 individuals, wealth inequality is quite high in the Swellendam Khoe population of 1825. About 84.1 per cent of its per capita wealth is concentrated in the wealthiest 20 per cent. The bottom 40 per cent of individuals held no wealth whatsoever. (As noted earlier, a significant proportion of the population, 866 individuals, particularly single females, had no assets to report.) Based on these figures, the Khoe Gini coefficient in 1825 would be 0.8. This may appear quite high but is comparable with inequality between adult males in the United States in the 1860s (0.83) and 1870s (0.81).[46] Piketty

---

[46] C. Shammas, 'A New Look at Long-Term Trends in Wealth Inequality in the United States', *American Historical Review* 98, no. 2 (1993): 412–31.

Table 4.5 Percentage share of wealth, all households.

Wealth quintile	Per capita	Household structure 1
1	0.00%	0.00%
2	0.00%	0.00%
3	1.82%	3.78%
4	14.08%	17.01%
5	84.10%	79.25%

Source: British tax census and MOOC-8 series.

notes that in Paris in 1827 the top 10 per cent of households owned around 98 per cent of the wealth.[47] Despite the wealth inequality being high for a largely stock farming community, it is similar to wealth inequalities in North America and France at roughly the same period.[48]

As a next level of analysis I considered the between-household wealth (between Structure 1 households) of the Khoe, as I would argue this is the most appropriate level of analysis for inequality. The household structure assumed here still resembles households today and may not truly reflect the situation of the Khoe of Swellendam in 1825. I assumed that all members of the household received or had access to an equal share of the household resources. Table 4.5 shows that when I analyse wealth inequality at the household level, it is still quite high but lower than the per capita estimate, with 79.25 per cent of the wealth concentrated in the hands of the top 20 per cent of the Khoe population. When I assume Household Structure 1, this reduces the inequality estimate from a Gini coefficient of 0.8 to 0.77. I included 1,266 households in the analysis and it shows that sub-dividing assets at the household level would have reduced the observed wealth inequality. What remains a matter of great concern is that 538 Khoe households still had no assets to report in 1825.

Using polygamous Household Structure 2, I assumed that all the single women became co-wives to a male, aside from the traditional conjugal pair. I also assumed that each single female name in the tax census which is listed below the male name refers to a co-wife, and that the offspring of that single female also formed part of the polygamous household. Only when the next male head name appears in the data did I assume that the next listed family unit began. I also continued to assume that each member of the household, including each child, received or had access to the same proportion of household resources.

---

[47] T. Piketty, *Capital in the Twenty-First Century* (Cambridge, US: Belknap Press of Harvard University Press, 2014).

[48] M. Borgerhoff Mulder, et al., 'Pastoralism and Wealth Inequality: Revisiting an Old Question', *Current Anthropology* 51, no. 1 (2010): 35–48.

Table 4.6 Percentage share of wealth, with polygamous households.

Wealth quintile	Per capita	Household structure 1	Household structure 2
1	0.00%	0.00%	0.00%
2	0.00%	0.00%	0.00%
3	1.82%	3.78%	6.44%
4	14.08%	17.01%	13.81%
5	84.10%	79.25%	79.75%

Source: British tax census and MOOC-8 series.

Table 4.6 shows the wealth distribution of these Khoe polygamous households. It shows that 79.75 per cent of the reported wealth was owned by the top 20 per cent of Khoe households. In this case, the only major change is that the third quintile increases in size – from 3.78 per cent of the population in the case of Household Structure 1, to 6.44 per cent in the case of Household Structure 2. This would suggest that at least some portion of the assets was reallocated to single women with no assets. The wealth Gini coefficient for Household Structure 2 is 0.77. These figures are only applicable for as long as I assume that each member of the Khoe household had equal access to family resources. The Gini coefficient remains virtually the same between the two different assumed household structures because of the high number of households which reported zero assets. Of the Structure 2 households, 532 reported owning no assets.

The next step in the analysis was to consider whether or not Household Structure 2 is an appropriate assumption to make with regard to Khoe families in the Swellendam district in 1825. I suspect that a number of co-residential families were grouped together to form a houseful which shared resources equally. In this dataset, such a household structure is very difficult to differentiate meaningfully from a polygamous household structure. If I were to assume that each of the single females in the tax census data represents a member of a separate conjugal pair within the houseful, it becomes quite difficult to determine the wealth or income levels of the missing male partner and vice versa. Since these male partners presumably belong to the group of migrant labourers not captured in the dataset, there is no way of knowing what they contributed to a houseful's wealth. Once we assume a scenario in which the main conjugal pair supported the survival of the females whose partners were absent, this houseful is reduced to a model that is similar to the one assumed for a polygamous household.

Historiography offers no indication that polygamy was widespread among the Khoe of southern Africa.[49] Assuming that the Khoe of Swellendam engaged in polygamous partnerships in 1825 would therefore be unrealistic. The probability of

---

[49]Carstens, 'Inheritance of Private Property'.

co-residential pairs residing in a *kraal* type of setup would probably be closer to the truth.[50] Many of these Khoe housefuls were probably dependent on wandering labourers for survival and it is likely that the absent men generated a large portion of their income. It is also very likely that these men did not appear in the settler tax records because they were not resident, indentured labourers. The resources of the main conjugal pair were also probably shared among the co-residential pairs. Another clue that the co-residential pairs may have had a familial link is to be found in the fact that many of the single women bore the same surname as the wife of the presumed head of the houseful.

Conclusion

Ignoring household structure in estimating inequality for a given society often distorts the picture of inequality in that society and may lead to incorrect inferences. Household structures are by no means a static concept since they change according to the customs and norms of a particular society and in response to adverse economic shocks. As a means of coping with shocks, households may come to include non-nuclear members who contribute additional resources. It therefore becomes important to incorporate household structure considerations in estimating Gini coefficients, Lorenz curves and other inequality metrics.

Many studies of pre-industrial inequality neglect to incorporate different household structures into their inequality calculations. One of the reasons for this is probably that the quality of available data often makes it difficult to obtain micro-level estimates for households and individuals. In the case of African societies, where information on household formation is scant and household level data even more so, this problem becomes more acute. In this study I tried to overcome this limitation by using British tax census data for the Khoe people of Swellendam in 1825 in conjunction with probate inventory estimates of asset values. This allowed me to demonstrate that household structure indeed plays a significant part in the inequality observed.

I found that in 1825 the Khoe of Swellendam were significantly poorer than their settler counterparts. Khoe households that had assets in the form of livestock or crops tended to have more children and fewer single adult females attached to them. I also found that wealth inequality among this Khoe population, although high, was not out of line with observed wealth inequality levels elsewhere in the world at the time. In the absence of specific knowledge about nineteenth-century Khoe household structures, I conducted my analysis on the basis of a number of simple but plausible assumptions about household structures for the Khoe. I conclude that extended household structures, be they polygamous or inclusive of other non-nuclear members, tended to exert downward pressure on inequality estimates, albeit to a modest degree.

---

[50]Carson, 'Native Americans'.

Bibliography

Abanokova, K. and M. Lokshin. 'Changes in Household Composition as a Shock-mitigating Strategy'. *Economics of Transition* 23, no. 2 (2015): 371–88.
Akresh, R. 'Flexibility of Household Structure Child Fostering Decisions in Burkina Faso'. *Journal of Human Resources* 44, no. 4 (2009): 976–97.
Alderson, A.S. and S.K. Sanderson. 'Historic European Household Structures and the Capitalist World-economy'. *Journal of Family History* 16, no. 4 (1991): 419–32.
Alfani, G. 'Economic Inequality in Northwestern Italy: A Long-term View (Fourteenth to Eighteenth Centuries)'. *Journal of Economic History* 75, no. 4 (2015): 1058–96.
Angel, R. and M. Tienda. 'Determinants of Extended Household Structure: Cultural Pattern or Economic Need?' *American Journal of Sociology* 87, no. 6 (1982): 1360–83.
Barnard, A. *Hunters and Herders of Southern Africa: A Comparative Ethnography of the Khoisan Peoples*. Cambridge: Cambridge University Press, 1992.
Becker, G.S. *A Treatise on the Family*. Cambridge, US: Harvard University Press, 1991.
Berry, A. 'International Trade, Government, and Income Distribution in Peru since 1870'. *Latin American Research Review* 25, no. 2 (1990): 31–59.
Bigsten, A. 'Welfare and Economic Growth in Kenya, 1914–76'. *World Development* 14, no. 9 (1986): 1151–60.
Bolt, J. and E. Hillbom. 'Long-term Trends in Economic Inequality: Lessons from Colonial Botswana, 1921–74'. *Economic History Review* 69, no. 4 (2016): 1255–84.
Booth, A. 'Living Standards and the Distribution of Income in Colonial Indonesia: A Review of the Evidence'. *Journal of Southeast Asian Studies* 19, no. 2 (1988): 310–34.
Borgerhoff Mulder, M., I. Fazzio, W. Irons, R.L. McElreath, S. Bowles, A. Bell, T. Hertz and L. Hazzah. 'Pastoralism and Wealth Inequality: Revisiting an Old Question'. *Current Anthropology* 51, no. 1 (2010): 35–48.
Brettell, C.B. 'Conceptualizing Migration and Mobility in Anthropology: An Historical Analysis'. *Transitions: Journal of Transient Migration* 2, no. 1 (2018): 7–25.
Burch, T.K. and B.J. Matthews. 'Household Formation in Developed Societies'. *Population and Development Review* (1987): 495–511.
Carson, J.T. 'Native Americans, the Market Revolution, and Culture Change: The Choctaw Cattle Economy, 1690–1830'. *Agricultural History* 71, no. 1 (1997): 1–18.
Carstens, P. 'The Inheritance of Private Property among the Nama of Southern Africa Reconsidered'. *Africa* 53, no. 2 (1983): 58–70.
Cilliers, J. and E. Green. 'The Land–labour Hypothesis in a Settler Economy: Wealth, Labour and Household Composition on the South African Frontier'. *International Review of Social History* 63, no. 2 (2018): 239–71.
Farley, R. 'Trends in Racial Inequalities: Have the Gains of the 1960s Disappeared in the 1970s?' *American Sociological Review* (1977): 189–208.
Findlay, J. and R.E. Wright. 'Gender, Poverty and the Intra-household Distribution of Resources'. *Review of Income and Wealth* 42, no. 3 (1996): 335–51.
Fourie, J. and D. von Fintel. 'The Dynamics of Inequality in a Newly Settled, Pre-industrial Society: The Case of the Cape Colony'. *Cliometrica* 4, no. 3 (2010): 229–67.
Frankenberg, E., B. Sikoki and W. Suriastini. 'Contraceptive Use in a Changing Service Environment: Evidence from Indonesia during the Economic Crisis'. *Studies in family planning* 34, no. 2 (2003): 103–16.
Goda, T. and A.T. García. 'The Rising Tide of Absolute Global Income Inequality during 1850–2010: Is It Driven by Inequality Within or Between Countries?' *Social Indicators Research* 130, no. 3 (2017): 1051–72.

Guelke, L. 'Frontier Settlement in Early Dutch South Africa'. *Annals of the Association of American Geographers* 66, no. 1 (1976): 25–42.

Hammel, E.A. and P. Laslett. 'Comparing Household Structure Over Time and Between Cultures'. *Comparative Studies in Society and History* 16, no. 1 (1974): 73–109.

Headey, B., G. Marks and M. Wooden. 'The Structure and Distribution of Household Wealth in Australia'. *Australian Economic Review* 38, no. 2 (2005): 159–75.

Hogan, D.P., B. Berhanu and A. Hailemariam. 'Household Organization, Women's Autonomy, and Contraceptive Behavior in Southern Ethiopia'. *Studies in Family Planning* 30, no. 4 (1999): 302–14.

Hryshko, D., C. Juhn and K. McCue. 'Trends in Earnings Inequality and Earnings Instability among US Couples: How Important is Assortative Matching?' *Labour Economics* 48 (2017): 168–82.

Kent, S. 'Sharing in an Egalitarian Kalahari Community'. *Man* 28, no. 3 (1993): 479–514.

Kuznets, S. 'Economic Growth and Income Inequality'. *American Economic Review* 45, no. 1 (1955): 1–28.

Kuznets, S. 'Demographic Aspects of the Size Distribution of Income: An Exploratory Essay'. *Economic Development and Cultural Change* 25, no. 1 (1976): 1–94.

Lerman, R.I. 'The Impact of the Changing US Family Structure on Child Poverty and Income Inequality'. *Economica* 63, no. 250 (1996): S119–S139.

Lindert, P.H. and J. G. Williamson (1982). 'Revising England's Social Tables 1688–1812'. *Explorations in Economic History* 19, no. 4 (1996): 385–408.

Milanovic, B. 'An Estimate of Average Income and Inequality in Byzantium around Year 1000'. *Review of Income and Wealth* 52, no. 3 (2006): 449–70.

Milanovic, B. *Worlds Apart: Measuring International and Global Inequality*. Princeton: Princeton University Press, 2011.

Milanovic, B. 'Towards an Explanation of Inequality in Premodern Societies: The Role of Colonies, Urbanization, and High Population Density'. *Economic History Review* 71, no. 4 (2018): 1029–47.

Milanovic, B., P.H. Lindert and J.G. Williamson. 'Pre-industrial Inequality'. *Economic Journal* 121, no. 551 (2011): 255–72.

Mincer, J. 'Labor Force Participation of Married Women: A Study of Labor Supply'. In *Aspects of Labor Economics*, 63–105. Princeton: NBER, Princeton University Press, 1962.

Morrisson, C. and J.R. de Laiglesia. 'Household Structures and Savings: Evidence from Household Surveys'. *OECD Development Centre*, Working Paper, 2008.

Morton, B. 'The Hunting Trade and the Reconstruction of Northern Tswana Societies after the Difaqane, 1838–1880'. *South African Historical Journal* 36, no. 1 (1997): 220–39.

Muellbauer, J. 'Inequality Measures, Prices and Household Composition'. *Review of Economic Studies* 41, no. 4 (1974): 493–504.

Newton-King, S. *Masters and Servants on the Cape Eastern Frontier, 1760–1803*. Cambridge: Cambridge University Press, 1999.

Penn, N. *The Forgotten Frontier: Colonist and Khoisan on the Cape's Northern Frontier in the 18th Century*. Athens, US: University of Ohio Press, 2005.

Piketty, T. *Capital in the Twenty-first Century*. Cambridge, US: The Belknap Press of Harvard University Press, 2014.

Ryckbosch, W. 'Economic Inequality and Growth before the Industrial Revolution: The Case of the Low Countries (Fourteenth to Nineteenth Centuries)'. *European Review of Economic History* 20, no. 1 (2016): 1–22.

Shammas, C. 'A New Look at Long-term Trends in Wealth Inequality in the United States'. *American Historical Review* 98, no. 2 (1993): 412–31.

Skinner, G.W. 'Family Systems and Demographic Processes'. *Anthropological Demography: Toward a New Synthesis* (1997): 53–95.

Swart, S. 'Riding High: Horses, Power and Settler Society, c. 1654–1840'. *Kronos* 28, no. 1 (2002): 47–63.

Theal, G.M. *History of South Africa, 1795–1834*. Vol. 3. London: Sonnenschein & Co., 1891.

Thomas, D. 'The Distribution of Income and Expenditure within the Household'. *Annales d'Economie et de Statistique* (1993): 109–35.

Viljoen, R. 'Aboriginal Khoikhoi Servants and Their Masters in Colonial Swellendam, South Africa, 1745–1795'. *Agricultural History* 75, no. 1 (2001): 28–51.

Viljoen, R. '"Sketching the Khoikhoi": George French Angas and His Depiction of the Genadendal Khoikhoi Characters at the Cape of Good Hope, c. 1847'. *South African Journal of Art History* 22, no. 2 (2007): 277–90.

Yanagisako, S.J. 'Family and Household: The Analysis of Domestic Groups'. *Annual Review of Anthropology* 8, no. 1 (1979): 161–205.

Zhao, Z. 'Coresidential Patterns in Historical China: A Simulation Study'. *Population and Development Review* 26, no. 2 (2000): 263–93.

CHAPTER 5
RACE RECLASSIFICATION IN CAPE TOWN, 1950–84

Brittany Chalmers*, Johan Fourie** and Kris Inwood***

Introduction

The Population Registration Act of 1950, which required every South African to be classified into one of four racial categories, plunged many couples into a long-running nightmare. Mr and Mrs Barsby, married as 'Europeans' in 1949, found themselves reclassified as 'Cape coloured' in 1954 and then again as 'white' in 1956.[1] Their story is just one example of the ramifications of attempted racial classification and the profound (and often chaotic) implications of reclassification. In this chapter we investigate a sample of couples married in Cape Town during three decades of apartheid, to see how many were affected and who these were likely to be.

We used recently transcribed marriage registers from the Anglican Diocese of Cape Town.[2] These registers identify at least 100 Cape Town couples whose race was reclassified after their marriage. Of these, eighty-three were reclassified from 'coloured' to 'white' and seventeen from 'white' to 'coloured'.[3] We wanted to know why this happened to these couples. We used the Anglican marriage registers and quantitative techniques to identify the characteristics most likely to lead to reclassification. Our findings call into question the belief that only those classified as coloured sought reclassification. The reasons for reclassification were neither singular nor obvious, but we did find that it was the more literate coloured couples who were likely to seek reclassification.

To investigate the implications of reclassification, we looked at the occupational and geographic mobility of eight of the couples from the Anglican marriage registers who had changed race between 1956 and 1963 that we subsequently found in the 1984 voters'

---

*Chalmers: Department of History, Stellenbosch University, South Africa.

**Fourie: Department of Economics, Stellenbosch University, South Africa.

***Inwood: Department of Economics and Department of History, University of Guelph, Canada.

[1] First names are excluded to protect the privacy of individuals who may be identifiable.

[2] South Africa, *Church of the Province of South Africa, Parish Registers, 1801-2004*. Database with images. FamilySearch. Available online: https://FamilySearch.org: 14 June 2016. Original series available in the William Cullen Library, Wits University, Johannesburg. Hereafter: Anglican marriage registers.

[3] We have used 'scare quotes' here to emphasise that the racial categories are arbitrary, but for simplicity we drop this convention in the rest of the chapter.

roll.[4] In our tiny sample, and without an obvious control group, we found that those people who reclassified to white were predictably likely to move to a neighbourhood classified as white, and women were likely to give up paid work and become housewives. We complemented this quantitative evidence of what Bowker and Star call these 'quieter, less visible aspects of the politics of classification' with a qualitative investigation into the reasons for reclassification.[5] Articles from the *Cape Herald*, the *Cape Times* and the *Rand Daily Mail* enabled us to piece together several stories, many with tragic consequences. They show that the costs of reclassification could be severe.

Before 1948, the formal reclassification of race was rare; legislation was applied loosely, if at all.[6] Many people lived and interacted in racially diverse areas and very few were even aware that there was such a process as reclassification. Suzman says 'the most striking feature of all this legislation was its variability and imprecision on the subject of race'. He observes that in most cases 'racial categories were used without any definition at all' and that 'where definitions were produced they typically excelled in vagueness'.[7] Race existed and carried weight, but because it was not yet mandatory to carry pass books stipulating race, many people enjoyed an ambiguous status.

In 1950, however, the Population Registration Act No. 30, which required everyone to carry a passbook confirming their race, precipitated a long period of confusion for the racially ambiguous. Families who did not align with what was regarded as white, coloured, Indian or black were faced with numerous difficulties, including possible separation. To avoid the risks, many turned to reclassification. Posel has written extensively on the Act, which was intended to eliminate racial ambiguity and secure racial separation.[8] It was this Act's universal application and all-encompassing scope, she notes, that 'made the apartheid system of racial classification notoriously distinctive'.[9] But the Act had many gaps that allowed untrained civil servants to make their own decisions.[10] The resulting inconsistent and unpredictable decision-making weighed heavily on the racially ambiguous. Erasmus and Ellison relate how one civil servant, inquiring as to how she should classify people, was told: 'Oh, you've got eyes.'[11] Authors such as Posel, Horrel, Erasmus and Ellison have extensively discussed the

---

[4]Access to the 1984 voters' roll data can be purchased through the website of the Genealogical Society of South Africa, see https://genza.org.za/index.php/en/gssa-products-services-main. Hereafter: Voters' Roll, 1984.

[5]G.C. Bowker and S.L. Star, *Sorting Things Out: Classification and Its Consequences* (Cambridge, US: MIT Press, 1999): 196.

[6]A. Suzman, *Race Classification and Definition in the Legislation of the Union of South Africa, 1910–1960* (Pretoria: Acta Juridica, 1960): 339–67.

[7]Ibid, 342.

[8]Ibid, 342.

[9]D. Posel, 'Race as Common Sense', *African Studies Review* 44, no. 2 (2001): 88.

[10]Y. Eramus and G.T.H. Ellison, 'What Can We Learn about the Meaning of Race from the Classification of Population Groups during Apartheid?' *South African Journal of Science* 104, nos. 11–12 (2008): 450–2.

[11]Ibid, 450–2.

process and implications of classification. Work on *re*classification, however, remains scant, in part because of limited sources.

Few case records of reclassification remain intact. Newspaper articles are instructive although of course subject to the usual biases in favour of the unusual or the extraordinary. While newspaper articles provide the chapter with human texture and experience, the Anglican marriage records paired with the voters' roll of 1984 allowed for a unique assessment. We were offered the possibility of identifying couples several decades after their marriage. By studying their address and occupation in the voter's roll, it was possible to determine geographic and occupational mobility. There were eight precise matches for couples in the Anglican marriage registers who reclassified from coloured persons to white persons, providing evidence of upward social mobility. Our findings from the marriage data and the voters' roll gave us new insight into the characteristics and mobility patterns of those who managed to reclassify, this would not have been possible by looking only at newspaper accounts.

We attempted to identify the general characteristics and tendencies of race reclassification by examining cases in the Anglican marriage registers. To do this we transcribed more than 55,000 marriage records. These records are obviously not a complete representation of reclassification in South Africa or even in Cape Town but they did reveal at least 100 cases of reclassification between 1950 and 1984. Anglican was the second most common Christian denomination for both white and coloured inhabitants of Cape Town.[12] Fortuitously, the Anglican marriage registers noted reclassification when a couple changed racial category after marrying. Artisanal quantification, which includes the 'messy' entries found in databases before they are cleaned, led to the discovery of this small but interesting aspect within the marriage records. As discussed in Chapter 1, this is the type of 'experimental' quantitative history approach that Lemercier and Zalc recommend.[13] The notes in the Anglican marriage registers revealed details about race reclassification that would otherwise have been ignored.

To our knowledge, we are the first to use marriage records and voters' roll data to investigate the changes in social mobility for reclassified individuals before and during apartheid. By investigating these and other sources, new insights and historical truths were illuminated from the bottom up.

This chapter relates a history of the fluidity of racial identity in Cape Town and the consequences for those who lived on the boundaries. We acknowledge that this is difficult terrain: how do we, as Martin puts it, 'define and recognise communities without perpetuating apartheid categories, attitudes and behaviours?'[14]

---

[12]South Africa Bureau of Census Statistics. *Population Census 8th May 1951, Volume VII, Marital Status, Religions and Birthplaces of Coloureds, Asiatics and Natives* (1960): 62. Over 20 per cent of the coloured population held Anglican membership during this period.

[13]C. Lemercier and C. Zalc, *Quantitative Methods in the Humanities: An Introduction* (Charlottesville: University of Virginia Press, 2019).

[14]D. Martin, *What's in the Name 'Coloured'* (Cape Town: Kwela Books & South African History Online, 2001): 262.

Racial classification and reclassification

In his Introduction to the Second Reading of the Population Registration Bill, 8 March 1950, Eben Dönges, Minister of the Interior, stated that:

> A population register is actually a book containing the life-story of every individual whose name is recorded on that register. It contains the most important facts relating to such a person ... All those important facts regarding the life of every individual will be combined in this book and recorded under the name of a specific person, *who can never change his identity* ... (Our emphasis)[15]

The Population Registration Act of 1950 formalised the definitions that would guide race classification in South Africa. Apartheid politicians saw the Act as the 'legislative lynchpin' of racial categorisation. Its goal was to separate and control people and reduce racial confusion.[16] The Act, however, did not define race precisely, and consequently failed to ensure that people could never change their identity. Instead, the Act made things more complicated and was full of loopholes that allowed some South Africans to switch race, that is, to reclassify.

The Act originally defined white, coloured, Indian and black people by how their communities accepted them, but in 1962, as the state began to realise the failures of their plan, the Population Registration Amendment Act, No. 61 was passed. This Act required that personal appearance and community acceptance be considered together.[17] The House of Assembly debated these issues and 'anomalies'. One member, Mr Oliver, in a rare admission, observed that the Minister of the Interior, Mr Le Roux, had failed in his attempts to produce a 'beautiful clean population register' that ensured people were in the 'watertight compartments' he wanted them in.[18] More commonly, of course, politicians clung to the 1950 line that 'we ... have never experienced any difficulties in distinguishing between Europeans and Non-Europeans'.[19] It was important that the state downplay the struggles to determine race, especially the race of those on the border between classifications, because racial fluidity or ambiguity undermined apartheid's racial separation argument.[20] To accept that it was possible for a person to change their race would be to accept that race was, in fact, not solely biological but to some extent socially constructed.

---

[15]*Hansard*, 8 March 1950, col. 2498, Population Registration Bill, Second Reading, cited in: K. Breckenridge, 'The Book of Life: The South African Population Register and the Invention of Racial Descent, 1950–1980', *Kronos* 40, no. 1 (2014): 225.

[16]D. Posel, 'What's in a Name? Racial Categorisations under Apartheid and Their Afterlife', *Transformation* 47, no. 1 (2001): 53.

[17]M. Horrell, *Legislation and Race Relations: A Summary of the Main South African Laws which Affect Race Relationships* (Johannesburg: South African Institute of Race Relations, 1963): 11.

[18]G. Oliver, 'Instant Race Bill Runs into Bitter Opposition', *Rand Daily Mail*, 8 March 1968, 5.

[19]Posel, 'Race as Common Sense', 95 for the comment by the Member of Parliament. She cites: House of Assembly Debates (HAD), 13 March 1950, col. 2782.

[20]Posel, 'Race as Common Sense', 95.

The real purpose of the first round of population registration, implemented via the 1951 National Census, was race classification. Officials assessed social and physical characteristics, from what people ate to the prominence of their cheekbones and the texture of their hair, and wrote down what they thought these characteristics implied, thus deciding the fate of thousands.[21] At first, race was shown subtly by the last digit of the personal identity number, but from the mid-1960s racial categories were stamped on identity cards in red ink.[22] In practice, however, it was never that simple. Many South Africans, especially those classified as coloured people, found ways to circumvent the Population Registration Act. They challenged it by appeals, by attempts to be reclassified and in many cases by playing a different race. In this way they found the agency to contest the Act and take back a degree of control over their racial classification and identity.

South Africans used the vagueness of the racial definitions and the flaws in the classification system to their advantage. The identity photograph, intended to help officials classify people, proved to be an unreliable racial identifier because South Africa was, as Rassool puts it, 'an uncertain and ambiguous visual economy' and inconsistencies in the categories made it possible to sidestep them. Appearance was one way for people to move between categories but not everyone could use it to their benefit and apply formally for reclassification. Another way to change race was to change location. People moved to another city or province, learnt new language skills and used other inventive measures to keep their jobs and their homes and keep loved ones together across racial lines.[23]

The coloured category in particular caused people problems because it was a catch-all for anyone who did not fit into the white or black categories. The classification process clumped people of many types into one general designation. Jeppie describes the confusion faced by members of the Malay and Muslim communities in the Western Cape as some were included in the coloured category and others not.[24] Reddy suggests that the Population Registration Act of 1950 was intended to politicise citizens' personal identity and is a significant reason why racial categories have persisted long into the new South Africa.[25]

Race reclassification is usually thought to be something that happened in a few unique cases. However, by May 1956, only six years after the Population Registration Act had been passed, officials had already handled 18,469 cases of reclassification. This indicates that it was far more frequent than what was intended or recognised.[26] The *Rand Daily Mail* confirmed the extent of reclassification ten years later in a short

---

[21] Erasmus and Ellison, 'What Can We Learn', 450.

[22] Breckenridge, 'Book of Life', 227.

[23] C. Rassool, 'The Politics of Nonracialism in South Africa', *Public Culture* 31, no. 2 (2019): 357–8.

[24] S. Jeppie, 'Re-classifications: Coloured, Malay, Muslim', in *Coloured by History, Shaped by Place: Perspectives on Coloured Identities in Cape Town*, ed. Z. Erasmus (Cape Town: Kwela, 2001): 80.

[25] T. Reddy, 'The Politics of Naming: The Constitution of Coloured Subjects in South Africa', in *Coloured by History, Shaped by Place: Perspectives on Coloured Identities in Cape Town*, ed. Z. Erasmus (Cape Town: Kwela, 2001): 77.

[26] Bowker and Star, *Sorting Things Out*, 207.

article entitled 'No End'.[27] It concerned the increase in requests to be reclassified, particularly from coloured to white. The Minister of the Interior, Mr. Le Roux, is quoted as saying that 'unless we do something we will never get to an end'. He said: 'The Race Reclassification Board started hearing appeals in 1951, almost 16 years ago. It is now 1966 and we haven't reached an end yet.' Another article in the same paper in 1967 said a further 356 people wanted to be reclassified.[28] Eleven years later, in 1978, the same paper recorded that 115 people had been reclassified the previous year.[29] The *Rand Daily Mail* was still recording reclassifications in 1981.[30] By 1980 over 100,000 people had applied for reclassification and the number continued to increase into the eighties.[31] Clearly, appeals to reclassify were sufficiently common to undermine the general belief that they were a few unique cases.

The full extent of race changing is unknown because of the state's attempt to suppress efforts to change or to 'pass' as a different race.[32] Many people reclassified in secret. They made subtle lifestyle changes in order to be assimilated into their new race and maintain personal privacy. They risked running into difficulties later in life when they needed to access state resources or send children to school.[33] Some did manage to change their legally defined racial identity in an often messy process involving 'documentary proof' of their identity. The application often included a letter of appeal to the Director of Census (sometimes also to the Director or Secretary of the Interior), who would then assess the case by calling for witnesses, reports and photographs, until a judgement was made.[34]

'People told: "Prove you are White"' was the title of an article in the *Rand Daily Mail* on 2 June 1960 describing one of the ways the state attempted to control reclassification.[35] The article records a Cape Town United Party spokesman's protests at a threat to remove people from the white voters' roll if they did not prove they were white. People were to be given only three weeks to verify their race or forfeit their identity. Many were unaware of alleged uncertainties about their classification until it was too late to offer proof or appeal the ruling.

An article in the *Rand Daily Mail* in 1969 described a case where Magistrate J. W. A. Van Wyk asked a coloured woman to stand and then to sit again swiftly. After this brief assessment of her appearance he told the court she was 'obviously White'.[36] This is an example of the rapid and capricious ways in which lives and futures were

---

[27]'No End', *Rand Daily Mail*, 13 December 1966, 1.

[28]'356 Want to Be Reclassified', *Rand Daily Mail*, 2 March 1967, 2.

[29]'115 Reclassified Last Year', *Rand Daily Mail*, 14 February 1978, 8.

[30]'Reclassified', *Rand Daily Mail*, 21 February 1980, 4.

[31]Bowker and Star, *Sorting Things Out,* 207.

[32]Posel, 'Race as Common Sense', 103.

[33]Bowker and Star, *Sorting Things Out,* 2010.

[34]R.E. van der Ross, *Myths and Attitudes: An Inside Look at the Coloured People* (Cape Town: Tafelberg, 1979): 7.

[35]'People Told: "Prove You Are White"', *Rand Daily Mail*, 2 June 1960, 3.

[36]E. Symons, '"This woman is White", Says Magistrate,' *Rand Daily Mail*, 20 September 1969, 1.

often determined with little regard for the repercussions. If she challenged the verdict, the woman in question would be subjected to further investigation and administrative burdens. She would have thirty days in which to submit an appeal and would live in limbo, unclassified, for an average waiting time of fourteen months, though many waited longer.[37] Some people waited years for a response to their requests.

By analysing letters and newspaper articles we pieced together what unfolded for at least some people who wanted to tick a different race box. We could see that many struggled to follow the necessary stipulations and rulings because both process and criteria were unclear and judges exercised considerable individual discretion. People attempting to reclassify were forced to undergo several tests and provide difficult-to-obtain documentation. Some were denied reclassification because of faulty processes or because of inconsistent criteria for racial identity. Others managed to forge documents and change their job or place of residence to pass as a different race in order to reclassify under false pretences.[38]

Two characteristics commonly invoked to determine racial status were appearance and community acceptance. A coloured person with a light complexion and straight hair or blue eyes had a good chance of being reclassified as white. Proof of membership to a specific white community and working and interacting with white people was also likely to bring success in reclassification applications. Community acceptance was linked to occupational class and class-specific behaviour as regards sexuality, dress and speech. If appearance was not enough to determine race, a person's place of residence and type of occupation might determine the outcome.[39] If an applicant for reclassification met neither the appearance nor the community acceptance criteria, the judge could reject the case with ease.

Applicants for reclassification came mostly from the coloured population, and it was this group, according to Bowker and Star, that accounted for the majority of borderline cases. Most would be people labelled as coloured and applying to be recognised as white or European.[40] Many of the applicants had the appearance of being white but lacked community acceptance because they lived in a coloured area or belonged to the coloured working class. Watson describes how those wishing to reclassify would steadily introduce themselves to 'members of the superordinate group', thus giving this group 'leeway' to make 'innumerable ad hoc decisions cumulatively favourable to the aspirant'.[41] The tricky process of moving into a different race group typically involved several steps. It started with finding a whites-only job where employers were not fussy about identity cards.

---

[37]Bowker and Star, *Sorting Things Out*, 206.

[38]Ibid, 216–17.

[39]P. Scully, 'Rape, Race, and Colonial Culture: The Sexual Politics of Identity in the Nineteenth-Century Cape Colony, South Africa', *American Historical Review* 100, no. 2 (1995): 341–7.

[40]Bowker and Star, *Sorting Things Out*, 206.

[41]G. Watson, *Passing for White: A Study of Racial Assimilation in a South African School* (London: Tavistock, 1970): 59.

The next step was to move into either a 'grey' suburb, that is, one where there was a mix of races, or, ideally, a whites-only suburb.[42] The couple would then attempt to ease into community life, and in this way gradually acquire sufficient grounds to make an appeal to the Race Reclassification Board. The fate of many applications hinged on sufficient evidence of community acceptance.

So far, our discussion has relied on official statistics and anecdotal accounts. These sources, while useful, can tell us only a little about the couples who reclassified, and they may be biased. Newspapers, for example, tend to focus on sensational cases that do not reflect the average reclassification experience. As we were interested in the typical rather than the exceptional, we turned to a hitherto unexamined source: the marriage registers.

The Anglican marriage registers

Cape Town's Anglican marriage registers are useful because they state the race of the individual. Race reclassification required that the original marriage record be altered. Figure 5.1 shows the entry in the marriage register for Mr and Mrs Barsby, mentioned in our introduction. Here, as in other cases, the presiding parish official simply crossed out the couple's former race and rewrote the new classification next to it. Some of the entries in the registers included letters indicating the processes to be followed. They show what the process of reclassification involved, and how administratively taxing this could be. Mr and Mrs Barsby were originally entered as European in 1949. There are two letters. One is from the Office of the Registrar of Births, Marriages and Deaths. Written in 1954, it states that:

> As the documentary proof has now been lodged, please amend the original register of this marriage in terms of the provisions of Regulation No. 13(5) framed under Act No. 17 of 1923 as amended by deleting the race description of wife and husband in the top portion of the original register and substituting therefore 'Cape Coloured'.[43]

The other letter, dated 1956, is from the parish official requesting that the couple be 're-reclassified' as white:

> With reference to my letter 754/120/150 of the 22nd July 1954, I have to inform you that as a result of an appeal to the Director of Census, the abovementioned parties have been re-classified as White persons, and I shall be glad if you will amend the race description of both parties accordingly.[44]

---

[42]Bowker and Star, *Sorting Things Out,* 2016.

[43]Anglican marriage registers, image 169.

[44]Anglican marriage registers.

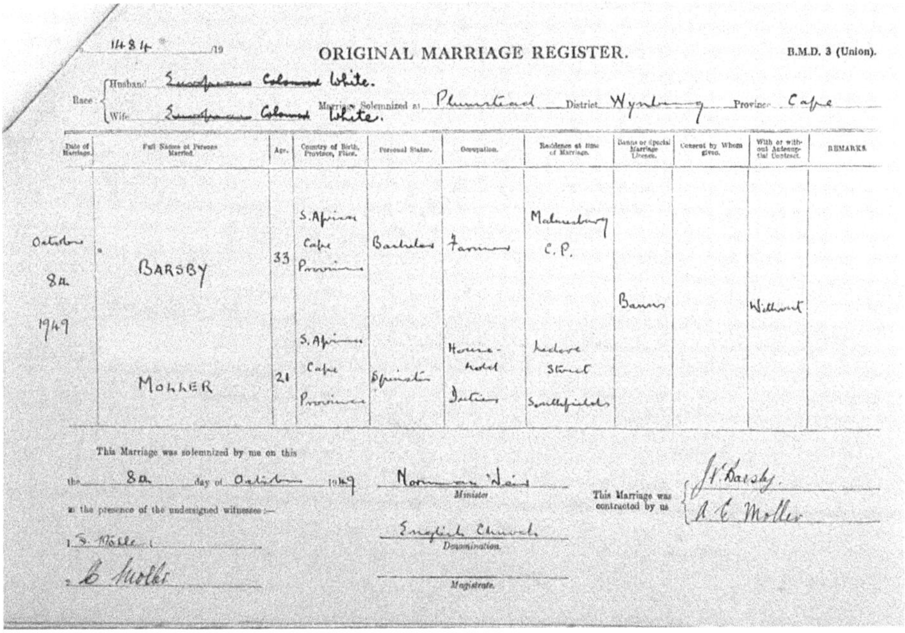
1484 19 ORIGINAL MARRIAGE REGISTER. B.M.D. 3 (Union).

Race: Husband European Coloured White. Wife European Coloured White. Marriage Solemnized at Plumstead District Wynberg Province Cape

Date of Marriage	Full Names of Persons Married	Age	Country of Birth, Province, Place	Personal Status	Occupation	Residence at time of Marriage	Banns or Special Marriage Licence	Consent by Whom given	With or without Antenuptial Contract	REMARKS
October 8th 1949	BARSBY	33	S. Africa Cape Province	Bachelor	Farmer	Malmesbury C.P.	Banns		Without	
	MOLLER	21	S. Africa Cape Province	Spinster	House-hold Duties	Street Southfields				

This Marriage was solemnized by me on this the 8th day of October 1949 Minister

in the presence of the undersigned witnesses:— 1. S. Moller 2. Moller

English Church Denomination

Magistrate

This Marriage was contracted by us Barsby, A. E. Moller

Figure 5.1 The marriage certificate of Mr Barsby and Mrs Barsby (maiden name Moller); first names masked for privacy.

Source: Marriages 1942–1972 (CT, Plumstead & Wynberg, All Saints Anglican Marriages), image 168: *Familysearch.org*.

Cases of reclassification are quite rare in the marriage registers. Of the 55,279 records we studied, only about 100 showed evidence of reclassification. Undoubtedly some reclassifications went unrecorded because the individual left the parish or ceased to attend the church. The reclassifications we found in the marriage registers were concentrated in the three parishes with the largest number of coloured households, Woodstock, Cape Town Central and Soutrivier.

Most reclassifications were from coloured to white (87 of the 100), but there were exceptions. One husband – Mr Pama, a thirty-five-year-old school teacher, who was classified as a coloured person when he married Miss Yoyo, a thirty-year-old domestic servant classified as coloured, in 1939 – was reclassified as a black person fifteen years later. It is unclear what this meant for the living arrangements of the Pama family, given that the Groups Areas Act designated separate neighbourhoods for black and coloured households.

The date of reclassification is specified in eighty-eight of the records. This enabled us to see how long the couple had been married before being reclassified. Figure 5.2 shows this information for the coloured marriages. There is no obvious trend over time. Six reclassifications, surprisingly, occurred before 1948, the year that the National Party came to power. These six couples had married in the previous decade. Some who

Quantitative History and Uncharted People

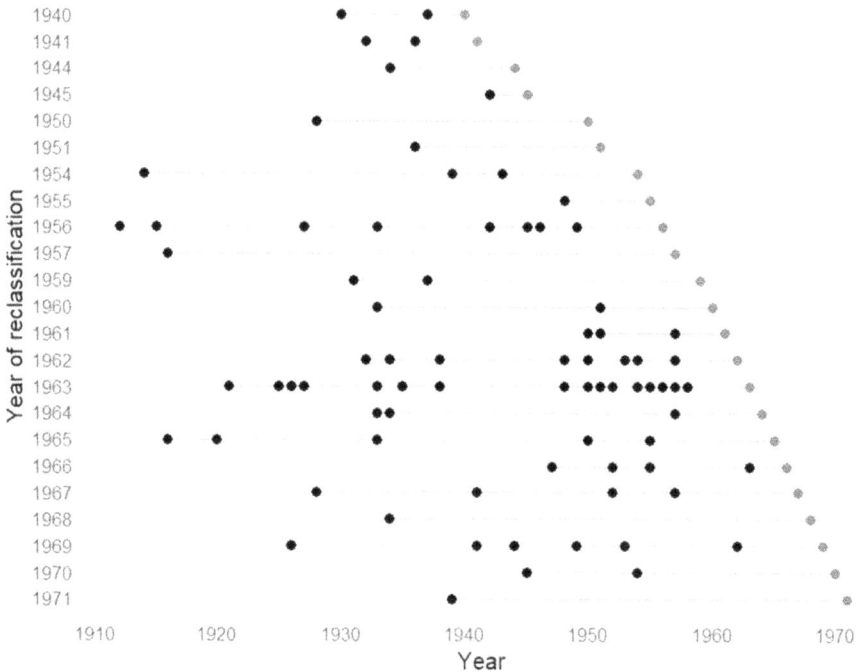

Figure 5.2 Duration of marriage before reclassification, arranged by year of reclassification.
Source: Anglican marriage registers. Author's own calculations.
Notes: The black dots indicate the year of marriage and the grey dots the year of reclassification.

reclassified after 1950, however, had been married for much longer. Mr Keet and Miss Kensley married on 12 June 1916. He is recorded as 'European' and she as 'Coloured'. In 1965, forty-nine years later, Mrs Keet was reclassified as 'white'. The average length of time between marriage and reclassification is twenty years and the median fifteen.

We wanted to identify the factors that best predict reclassification. One way to identify characteristics correlated with reclassification status is through regression analysis. When we ran a standard ordinary least squares regression with reclassification status as the dependent variable and demographic variables and other controls as independent variables, with a variety of specifications, we could find only one statistically significant predictor: literacy. Figure 5.3 shows the average literacy rate of marriage participants by year of marriage for those reclassified and those not reclassified. Only coloured marriage records are reported. Individuals who could not sign made a cross next to their name, which we interpreted as a sign of illiteracy. Four individuals signed a marriage register: the husband, the wife and two witnesses. The literacy associated with a marriage is the number of participants who could sign their name – a number ranging from 0 to 4.

Table 5.1 Race reclassification from white to coloured.

Surname	Change to coloured (year)
Mr Pearc	1940
Mr and Mrs Theyser	1954
Mrs Brown	1954
Mrs Wyeth	1954
Mr and Mrs Green	1955
Mr and Mrs Cook	1955
Mr Clarke	1965
Mr and Mrs Fowler	1956
Mr and Mrs Maasdorp	1956
Mrs Kloosman	1956
Mr and Mrs Collison	1959

Source: Anglican Marriage registers.

As Figure 5.3 shows, the literacy of the marriage participants increased from around 3.2 (meaning eight out of every ten individuals could sign their name) in 1910 to 4 (meaning ten out of ten individuals could sign their name) fifty years later. By contrast, among those who later reclassified, almost everyone was literate through the entire period. Literacy seems to have been a distinguishing characteristic of the people classed as coloured who were able to reclassify as white.

One of the most common reasons for reclassification was a desire for enhanced privilege. Privilege cannot, however, explain the seventeen people among our 100 couples who reclassified from white to coloured persons. Table 5.1 shows the dates when they did this. All except one of these cases occurred during the apartheid years, after the Population Registration Act of 1950 had been passed.

At a time of white political rule and domination, there had to be a compelling reason for a person to abandon their privileged white classification. Five of the seventeen in our sample changed race independently of their spouse. Arguably these changes were motivated by the 1949 Prohibition of Mixed Marriages Act.[45] Several white spouses conceivably changed their race in order to marry. '"Reclassify me" pleads Coloured's lover' reads the heading of an article in the *Rand Daily Mail*. This story was about Lynette Wilson, a white woman from Cape Town, who wanted to marry the father of her seven-month-old baby, Moegsien Solomon.[46] Marriage was impossible because

---

[45] J. Fourie and K. Inwood, 'Interracial Marriages in Twentieth-Century Cape Town: Evidence from Anglican Marriage Registers', *History of the Family* 24, no. 3 (2019): 629–30.
[46] '"Reclassify me" Pleads Coloured's Lover,' *Rand Daily Mail*, 3 June 1975, 5.

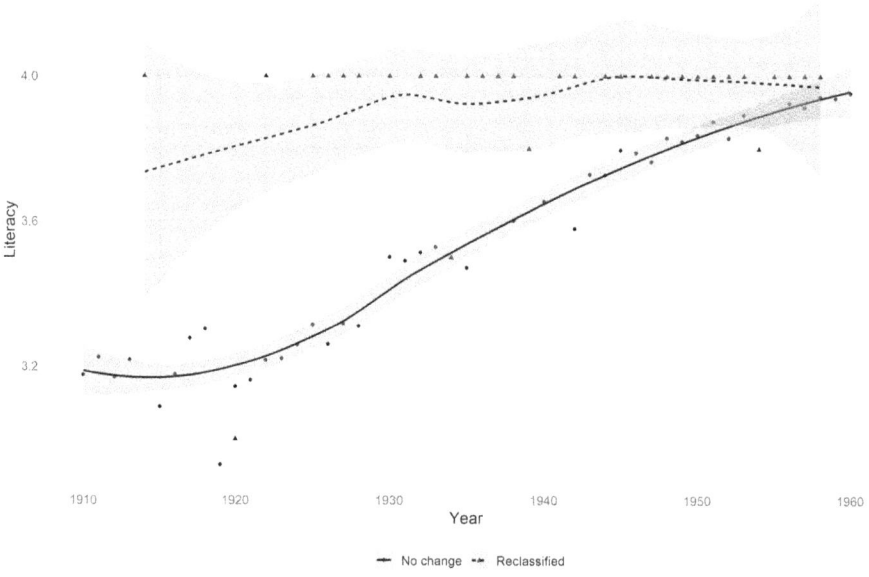

Figure 5.3 Literacy as measured by signatures on marriage certificates.
Source: Anglican marriage registers. Own calculations.

he belonged to a different racial group. The article said Lynette would apply to the Department of the Interior to be reclassified as a coloured person, choosing love over privilege.

Another motive for change was lack of acceptance within a race group. Andries du Toit requested to be reclassified as a coloured person after living his entire life as a white man. 'I've never found happiness as a White', is the title of the article in the *Rand Daily Mail*.[47] It reports that 'nothing will stop him in his fight to switch colour – not even the thought of his own flesh and blood remaining in the White zone'. It says that while Andries has a darker complexion than most white people, he is 'White all the way' but that, after living with coloured people in the Cape, he felt accepted and 'found happiness'. Because of his dark complexion he had been mocked in white areas and told he was a 'playwhite'. To this Andries replied, 'Let them have their way, I don't want to be White'. It was more important to belong than to be privileged.

Race reclassification from coloured to white was more common, but privilege was not the only reason for the change. An article from the *Rand Daily Mail* of 14 February 1980 tells the story of Mrs Green of Cape Town, a white woman fighting the reclassification as coloured of herself and six children. She threatened to commit suicide if they were not

---

[47] V. Prince, 'White Andries to Try for Coloured', *Rand Daily Mail*, 2 December 1975, 9.

classified as white people again as she had been on the verge of marrying her partner, Aubrey Jooste, who was classified as a white person. After her attempts to contact Cape Town's Department of the Interior failed, Mr Jooste wrote to the Minister of the Interior in Pretoria. Eventually, after weeks of back and forth, and the sending of colour photographs, her case was 'considered'.[48] Six months later an article in the *Rand Daily Mail* confirmed that she was reclassified as a white person and the marriage went ahead.[49] Some reclassifications, it appears, were done to reverse unexplained changes to racial status made by state officials acting on their own opinions.[50]

Sometimes reclassification was necessary because of a change in racial terminology. Before 1950, an Italian man could marry an English woman and register their child as mixed even though both they and the child had a fair complexion. However, in apartheid South Africa, being mixed meant being classified coloured.[51] To avoid this, such persons reclassified from mixed to white. In the Anglican Marriage registers, thirty-six couples were classified as mixed before they changed their race. Some of our reclassifications may reflect confusion between those who were mixed by nationality and those who were mixed racially according to the apartheid-era definition.

Clearly there could be many reasons for reclassifying. Most would have been to gain white privilege, but for some, love and belonging were reason enough.

Consequences of reclassification

The 1984 voters' roll offered us the possibility of identifying couples several decades after their marriage. We hoped their address and occupation in the voter's roll might provide evidence of geographic and occupational mobility. Of course, not everyone survived until 1984, and many people cannot be identified unambiguously. Table 5.2 shows the eight precise matches we did find for couples in the Anglican marriage registers who reclassified from coloured to white.[52] Their occupational changes are consistent with a broad pattern of upward social mobility. Admittedly, status in 1984 reflects more than the effect of reclassification. These people were younger at the time of their marriage, so life-cycle progression may account for some of the changes in 1984.[53] Nevertheless, reclassification unambiguously improved a couple's economic

---

[48] 'Marriage Law Victim Hopes for Reprieve', *Rand Daily Mail*, 14 February 1980, 1.

[49] 'Govt Allows a Mixed Marriage', *Rand Daily Mail*, 7 August 1980, 2.

[50] Posel, 'Race as Common Sense', 106.

[51] 'People Told: "Prove you are White,"' *Rand Daily Mail*, 21 June 1960, 3.

[52] Anglican marriage registers; Voters' roll, 1984.

[53] An ideal experiment would be to compare these couples who were reclassified from coloured to white with coloured couples who were not reclassified. But unfortunately we do not have a voters' roll for coloured individuals.

Table 5.2 Changes in occupation.

Surname	Occupation as a coloured person	Race changed to white	Occupation recorded in voters' roll of 1984
Mr Barsby	Farmer	1956	Supervisor
Mrs Barsby	Household duties	1956	Supervisor
Mr Jacobs	Presser	1961	Salesperson
Mrs Jacobs	Machinist	1961	Housewife
Mr Smith	Sailor	1963	Manager
Mrs Smith	Machinist	1963	Housewife
Mr Coskey	Labourer	1963	Foreman
Mrs Coskey	Ironer (zip factory)	1963	Housewife
Mr Echardt	Cutter	1966	Operator
Mrs Echardt	Shop assistant	1966	Housewife
Mr Canterbury	Wood machinist	1967	Supervisor
Mrs Canterbury	Domestic duties	1967	Housewife
Mr Muller	Plumber	1970	Civil servant
Mrs Muller	Printer's assistant	1970	Housewife
Mr Lomberg	'Working'	1970	Jeweller
Mrs Lomberg	Domestic duties	1970	Housewife

Sources: Anglican marriage registers. Voters' roll of 1984. Own calculations.

prospects. Coloured couples who reclassified to white would have had better opportunities for occupational advancement[54] and for salary increases.[55] The Industrial Colour Bar in 1956 and the Job Reservation Act of 1957 limited the opportunities for non-white people and ensured that coloured individuals would be retrenched before white persons, and that white immigrants would be prioritised for job security above coloured South Africans.[56]

Another pattern visible in Table 5.2 is a tendency for women to leave their jobs and become housewives. This may be because the husband now earned enough to support

---

[54] O. Crankshaw, 'Changes in the Racial Division of Labour during the Apartheid Era', *Journal of Southern African Studies* 22, no. 4 (1996): 634.

[55] G.J. van Deventer and S. van der Berg, *Socio-Economic Development of the Coloured Community since the Theron Commission* (Faculty of Economic Management Sciences, Stellenbosch University, 2000): 66–7; P.G. Moll, 'The Decline of Discrimination against Colored People in South Africa', *Journal of Development Economics* 37, nos. 1–2 (1991): 300.

[56] A. Hepple, 'Job Reservation – Cruel, Harmful and Unjust', *The Black Sash* (1963): 7.

Table 5.3 Changes in location.

Surname	Address as a coloured person	Race changed to white	Address recorded on voters' roll 1984 (race designation of area at that date)
Mr Barsby	Malmesbury	1956	Plumstead (*white*)
Mrs Barsby	Southfield	1956	Plumstead (*white*)
Mr Jacobs	Woodstock	1961	Observatory (*mixed*)
Mrs Jacobs	Woodstock	1961	Observatory (*mixed*)
Mr Smith	Athlone	1963	Tamboerskloof (*white*)
Mrs Smith	Athlone	1963	Tamboerskloof (*white*)
Mr Coskey	Hatfield	1963	Silverton, Pretoria
Mrs Coskey	Woodstock	1963	Silverton, Pretoria
Mr Echardt	Crawford	1966	Observatory (*mixed*)
Mrs Echardt	Salt River	1966	Observatory (*mixed*)
Mr Canterbury	Woodstock	1967	Maitland (*white*)
Mrs Canterbury	Somerset West	1967	Maitland (*white*)
Mr Muller	Wynberg	1970	Vredehoek (*white*)
Mrs Muller	Wynberg	1970	Vredehoek (*white*)
Mr Lomberg	Retreat	1970	Lansdowne (*white*)
Mrs Lomberg	Crawford	1970	Lansdowne (*white*)

Sources: Anglican marriage registers. Voters' roll of 1984. Own calculations.

the family on the male-breadwinner household model.[57] Another possibility is that previously coloured women became housewives to allay racial suspicions and facilitate community acceptance as white people. At the time, it was socially accepted that married white women did not need to work.[58]

Another dimension of reclassification was residential change. The Group Areas Act, which dictated residential areas according to race, made the location of the household an important element in reclassification.[59] Applicants could strengthen their case by moving from strictly coloured areas to mixed areas such as Observatory. Table 5.3 shows that most of our eight couples moved from predominantly coloured areas, such as Wynberg and Athlone, either to one of the few areas that were a mix of white and coloured people, such as Observatory and Woodstock, or to strictly white areas like Plumstead and

---

[57] A. Rommelspacher, 'Restating the Case for Women's History in South Africa', *Economic History of Developing Regions* 36, no. 3 (2021): 445–50.

[58] L. Clowes, 'Making It Work: Aspects of Marriage, Motherhood and Money-Earning among White South African Women, 1960–1990' (MA diss., University of Cape Town, 1994): 18.

[59] M. Adhikari, '"God Made the White Man, God Made the Black Man …" Popular Racial Stereotyping of Coloured People in Apartheid South Africa', *South African Historical Journal* 55, no. 1 (2006): 146.

Lansdowne.⁶⁰ Relocating to white areas diminished suspicions about race and enabled couples to stay below the state's radar.

Goldberg explains how race was specifically linked to address in a place like Observatory:

> At the top end of the road the families were clearly white. Some way down, in the language of the time, there were the 'three-eighths' (Coloured) people, followed by some homes with the 'halvies' and the 'five-eighths', followed by the houses of people who were undoubtedly Coloured. These differences were obvious to all and the gradations were quite strictly followed by the socially disadvantaged as well the advantaged. The attempt to pass for white, or to 'play white', was serious in terms of both income and social status.⁶¹

Goldberg's account shows how aware the public were of the various 'shades' of people and the significance of conforming to the designated areas in order to preserve community acceptance and to strengthen their racial case. The complexities of complexion within a single suburb suggest that much more complicated race classification was going on within the state's officially designated coloured category.

Personal experiences

Our findings from the Anglican marriage registers and the voters' roll gave us some idea of the characteristics and mobility patterns of those who managed to reclassify. Individual cases reported in newspapers and magazines and described in the literature added nuance and detail. In this section we look at the struggles of the 'playwhite' and the people who fell between racial groups, most of whom had one foot in the coloured community, the group most affected by reclassification.⁶²

Many coloured people believed they had been classified incorrectly. Reclassification gave light-complexioned people an opportunity to tick the coveted white box. Many had ancestral records and photographs of white family members to aid in their quest to be reclassified to what they believed was their rightful race. Valentine relates the case of a Lansdowne man who was fined in December 1971 for paying a sum of R300⁶³ to secure

---

⁶⁰'Cape Town the Segregated City', *South African History Online,* 27 August 2019. Available online: https://www.sahistory.org.za/article/cape-town-segregated-city (accessed 18 October 2022).

⁶¹D. Goldberg, *A Life of Freedom: The Mission to End Racial Injustice in South Africa* (Kentucky: University Press of Kentucky, 2016): 16.

⁶²Van der Ross, *Myths and Attitudes,* 6.

⁶³Roughly equivalent to R20,000 in 2019. Historic Inflation South Africa. CPI inflation. Available online: https://www.inflation.eu/inflation-rates/south-africa/historic-inflation/cpi-inflation-south-africa.aspx (accessed 4 October 2019).

a white identity card from a Department of the Interior official.[64] The desperation to be reclassified is manifest.

Adhikari cites an article from the *Cape Times* in which Nigerian writer Kole Omotoso describes the skin colour of coloured people as 'varying from charcoal black to breadcrust brown, sallow yellow and finally off-white cream that wants to pass for white'.[65] The considerable variation in skin colour made it difficult to classify people (even within the same family) as white or trying to pass for white.

Unable to remain ambiguous about race, many were forced to choose whether to be coloured people or white people, a tough choice when members of your own family looked different to you. Many felt they had to reclassify to avoid being separated or to gain access to a better life under the apartheid regime. The term 'playwhite' suggests the tension for the individual and the scrutiny that came from jealous darker-skinned neighbours or prying state officials. 'Playwhites' were often regarded as sell-outs, but they were just ordinary people trying to improve their situation.

Many people previously classified coloured attracted this derogatory label. Anthony Sampson, author and former editor of *Drum* magazine, said 'Whites scorned playwhites, playwhites scorned Coloureds, Coloureds scorned natives [and] light Coloureds scorned dark Coloureds'.[66] Differences of skin colour could undermine communities. Even family members might turn on each other when the Race Classification Board began asking questions.[67] This board was specifically created to handle 'borderline cases' and 'playwhites'. In 1961 an estimated 20,000 people were still uncertain whether they were officially coloured or white in Cape Town alone.[68] The Minister of the Interior admitted that the state had 'opened the gates too wide, making it possible for people to steal and ride on the backs of deserving cases'.[69] To stop this tendency the state exploited community tensions and jealousy to its advantage.[70]

A person who reclassified was immediately subject to a mass of legal and social difficulties and what the ANC bulletin *Mayibuye* called a 'witch hunt'.[71] They had to keep up a falsehood not only for the state but also for the people around them. Their friends or family could report them and appeal the reclassification.[72] This would kick-start a full investigation into their relationships and background, leading to family and community

---

[64] S. Valentine, 'An Appalling "science"', *Sunday Times Heritage Project*. Available online: http://sthp.saha.org.za/memorial/articles/an_appalling_science.htm (accessed 25 May 2019).

[65] *Cape Times*, 14 January 2002, cited in Adhikari 'God Made the White Man'.

[66] A. Sampson, *Drum: A Venture into the New Africa* (London: Collins, 1956): 210.

[67] Posel, 'Race as Common Sense', 108.

[68] Valentine, 'An Appalling "science"'.

[69] 'Minister Will Act to Curb Race Appeals', *Rand Daily Mail*, 13 December 1966, 1.

[70] Valentine, 'An Appalling "science"'.

[71] 'Mp'ayipele: Instant Race Classifications', *Mayibuye* 2, no. 20 (1968): 14.

[72] Valentine, 'An Appalling "science"'.

strife.[73] Richard Rive described how 'viciously a bewildered man can turn his suffering into an attack on his wife because of the shade of her skin' and because 'he is too dark to play white'.[74]

This picture of the darker consequences of reclassification gives us an idea of what may have been endured by the reclassified people we identified in the records, such as the Barsby couple, and the countless others who did what they deemed best under the state's oppression. Many coloured people denounced 'playing white' because they wished to stay loyal to their heritage and their identity and their own idea of colouredness.[75] Families lived with extreme anxiety trying to keep the secrets of reclassifying family members from the state.

Examples show the weight of anxiety and stress arising from reclassification. The headline of a 1962 article in the *Rand Daily Mail* reads: '"I'm White", says girl in "suicide" immorality case'.[76] The article explores the lives of Marie Dunstun and Andries Wihelmus Jacobus de Jager, a couple charged with contravening the Immorality Act. Dunstun, who was in a lengthy trial to reclassify herself from coloured to white, stood in court alone because her partner, de Jager, had taken his own life before they were set to appear. The article implies, although it does not say so explicitly, that the couple's racial struggles led to his suicide. A 1977 article in the same paper examines the suicide of the eldest son of a coloured couple who was trying to be reclassified as white. The man 'threw himself under a moving train at Maitland Station because he could not marry his pregnant white girlfriend'.[77]

Another distressing story is that of Dirk Brits, a young white man from Cape Town whose appeal to be reclassified so he could marry his coloured girlfriend was turned down. The *Rand Daily Mail* quotes him as saying, 'if they won't reclassify me Coloured, I will leave the country of my birth so that I can live legally with the woman I love and have children by her'.[78] Some people emigrated to escape South Africa's race laws. A spokesman for the Australian Department of Immigration in Canberra said that they would 'almost certainly allow' a coloured woman who was trying to be reclassified, to emigrate to Australia where she would be free to marry the white father of her child.[79]

Valentine mentions the case of Ronnie Van der Walt, a former Capetonian boxer, who also felt the effects of race reclassification. In 1967 a letter from the Minister of the Interior informed him that he had been reclassified as a coloured person. After living in

---

[73] Bowker and Star, *Sorting Things Out*, 208.

[74] R. Rive, *Emergency* (Cape Town: New Africa Books, 1988) cited in M.J. Daymond, 'Re-Emergency', *Reality* 21, no. 2 (1989): 19.

[75] Bowker and Star, *Sorting Things Out*, 216; Van der Ross, *Myths and Attitudes*, 21.

[76] '"I'm White" Says Girl in "suicide" Immorality Case', *Rand Daily Mail*, 11 May 1962, 3.

[77] 'Woman Must Remain a Coloured', *Rand Daily Mail*, 28 November 1977, 3.

[78] 'White Ready to Give Up All for Girl', *Rand Daily Mail*, 7 February 1975, 2.

[79] 'Reclassify Me Pleads Coloured's Lover', *Rand Daily Mail*, 3 June 1975, 5.

white areas and boxing as a white person all his life, Van der Walt was now prohibited from continuing his career. Van der Walt wanted to appeal but because his own wife had coloured heritage, he knew the risks that would come from a probe into their family. Consequently, he and his family, and his boxing talent, moved to Britain.[80]

Valentine also notes the family dissension that often accompanied race reclassification. She mentions a 1958 article in the *Star* about a man whose employer and family had recently found out he was 'mixed' and not white. He had to resign from his job on the railway and was completely cut off by his family. He said that when his white wife learned of his new classification she fell to the ground and cried profusely. In Afrikaans she told him, 'You have brought shame on me. Go away from me'. Shortly after this they were divorced, and he moved out of their home. His own family began to fear and despise him.[81]

An article from the *Weekend Argus* of 24 February 1979, entitled 'Looking inside the "Heartbreak File"', brings together in one place the many effects of reclassification. It describes a young Dr Frederick van Zyl Slabbert's 'bulging green-faced folder that contains the stories of frustration, heartache and suffering'. He was investigating the cases of victims of the racial laws, particularly the laws of classification and reclassification. The article refers to 'marriages threatened, families forced to flee the land' and people living together 'illegally', afraid that they would be exposed.[82] An article in the May 1980 edition of *Fair Lady* summarises the senselessness of reclassification. It observes that South Africa is 'a mixed society already and the laws which deny this fact of life attempt the impossible. The futility of the exercise only compounds the tragedy for people caught in natures cruellest trap'.[83]

Conclusion

This chapter combined evidence from marriage registers and voters' rolls with stories from newspaper articles to take a closer look at racial reclassification, one of the most depressing aspects of South Africa's apartheid period, and its consequences for individuals and communities. As far as we are aware, we are the first to use such records for this purpose.

The marriage registers show that, despite the relatively rare incidence of reclassification, certain characteristics were likely to predict those most likely to reclassify: living in a coloured neighbourhood (notably Woodstock, Cape Town Central and Soutrivier) and the literacy of the four individuals who signed the marriage register. Those who reclassified were more likely to be literate and have literate witnesses.

---

[80]Valentine, 'An Appalling "science"'.
[81]Ibid.
[82]'Looking inside the Heartbreak File', *Weekend Argus*, 24 February 1979, 10.
[83]'The Heartbreak behind the Headlines', *Fair Lady*, 28 May 1980, 43.

The voter's roll of 1984 enabled us to ascertain the geographic and social mobility of a few couples who reclassified from coloured to white. We found two trends: reclassification unambiguously improved a couple's economic prospects, and wives were likely to leave the labour market. We also found that people aiming to be reclassified as white moved into neighbourhoods designated white or mixed, although it is difficult to ascertain whether this move happened before or after reclassification.

More generally, our investigation has shed light on a phenomenon that merits further scholarly attention. Our approach complements existing oral histories and adds quantitative evidence drawn from archival records to counterbalance the newspaper sources, which tend to the exceptional or sensationalist. Much more can be done, though. Marriage registers of other denominations could support or question our findings. It should also be possible to match marriage registers to other individual-level records, like baptism registers (as is done in Chapter 2) or probate inventories. Observing the same individual across time would allow for a more precise assessment of the effect of racial reclassification – and not only for those who reclassified from coloured to white.

We recognise that this approach has its limits. It is likely that many reclassified couples were simply not recorded, either because they did not wish to be or simply through inertia. We are also limited in our analysis to the sparse information included in each marriage record in the register. Occupation, address and literacy are useful predictors, but other factors would also have influenced a person's desire and ability to reclassify. We offer our approach simply as a complementary method for exploring South Africa's past.

Our findings lead us to conclude by agreeing with a remark made by Muriel Horrell, Research Officer at the South African Institute of Race Relations from 1949 to 1977: 'How impracticable it is to try to classify human beings, for all time, into definite categories, and how much suffering has resulted from the efforts made to do this.'

Bibliography

Adhikari, M. '"God Made the White Man, God Made the Black Man…" Popular Racial Stereotyping of Coloured People in Apartheid South Africa'. *South African Historical Journal* 55, no. 1 (2006): 142–64.

Bowker, G.C. and S.L. Star *Sorting Things Out: Classification and Its Consequences* Cambridge, US: MIT Press, 1999.

Breckenridge, K. 'The Book of Life: The South African Population Register and the Invention of Racial Descent, 1950–1980'. *Kronos* 40, no. 1 (2014): 225–40.

'Cape Town the Segregated City'. *South African History Online*, 27 August 2019. Available online: https://www.sahistory.org.za/article/cape-town-segregated-city.

Clowes, L. 'Making It Work: Aspects of Marriage, Motherhood and Money-Earning among White South African Women, 1960–1990'. MA diss., University of Cape Town, 1994.

Crankshaw, O. 'Changes in the Racial Division of Labour during the Apartheid Era'. *Journal of Southern African Studies* 22, no. 4 (1996): 633–56.

Daymond, M.J. 'Re-Emergency'. *Reality* 21, no. 2 (1989): 19–20.

Erasmus, Y. and G.T.H. Ellison. 'What Can We Learn about the Meaning of Race from the Classification of Population Groups during Apartheid?' *South African Journal of Science* 104, nos. 11–12 (2008): 450–52.

Fourie, J. and K. Inwood. 'Interracial Marriages in Twentieth-Century Cape Town: Evidence from Anglican Marriage Registers'. *History of the Family* 24, no. 3 (2019): 629–52.

Goldberg, D. *A Life of Freedom: The Mission to End Racial Injustice in South Africa*. Kentucky: University of Kentucky, 2016.

Horrell, M. *Legislation and Race Relations: A Summary of the Main South African Laws which Affect Race Relationships*. Johannesburg: South African Institute of Race Relations, 1963.

Jeppie, S. 'Re-classifications: Coloured, Malay, Muslim'. In *Coloured by History, Shaped by Place: Perspectives on Coloured Identities in Cape Town*, edited by Z. Erasmus, 80–96. Cape Town: Kwela, 2001.

Lemercier, C. and C. Zalc. *Quantitative Methods in the Humanities: An Introduction*. Charlottesville: University of Virginia Press, 2019.

Martin, D. *What's in the Name 'Coloured'*. Cape Town: Kwela Books & South African History Online, 2001.

Moll, P.G. 'The Decline of Discrimination against Colored People in South Africa'. *Journal of Development Economics* 37, nos. 1–2 (1991): 289–307.

Posel, D. 'Race as Common Sense'. *African Studies Review* 44, no. 2 (2001): 87–114.

Posel, D. 'What's in a Name? Racial Categorisations under Apartheid and Their Afterlife'. *Transformation* 47, no. 1 (2001): 50–74.

Rassool, C. 'The Politics of Nonracialism in South Africa'. *Public Culture* 31, no. 2 (2019): 343–71.

Reddy, T. 'The Politics of Naming: The Constitution of Coloured Subjects in South Africa'. In *Coloured by History, Shaped by Place: Perspectives on Coloured Identities in Cape Town*, edited by Z. Erasmus, 64–79. Cape Town: Kwela, 2001.

Rive, R. *Emergency*. Cape Town: New Africa Books, 1988.

Rommelspacher, A. 'Restating the Case for Women's History in South Africa'. *Economic History of Developing Regions* 36, no. 3 (2021): 445–50.

Sampson, A. *Drum: A Venture into the New Africa*. London: Collins, 1956.

Scully, P. 'Rape, Race, and Colonial Culture: The Sexual Politics of Identity in the Nineteenth-Century Cape Colony, South Africa'. *American Historical Review* 100, no. 2 (1995): 335–59.

Suzman, A. *Race Classification and Definition in the Legislation of the Union of South Africa, 1910–1960*. Acta Juridica, 1960.

Valentine, S. 'An Appalling "Science"'. *Sunday Times Heritage Project*. Available online: https://sthp.saha.org.za/memorial/articles/an_appalling_science.htm.

Van der Ross, R.E. *Myths and Attitudes: An Inside Look at the Coloured People*. Cape Town: Tafelberg, 1979.

Van Deventer, G.J. and S. van der Berg. *Socio-Economic Development of the Coloured Community since the Theron Commission*. Faculty of Economic Management Sciences, Stellenbosch University, 2000.

Watson, G. *Passing for White: A Study of Racial Assimilation in a South African School*. London: Tavistock, 1970.

Primary Sources

Fair Lady. 'The Heartbreak behind the Headlines'. 28 May 1980, 43.

Hepple, A. 'Job Reservation – Cruel, Harmful and Unjust'. *The Black Sash*, 1963.

Historic Inflation South Africa. CPI inflation. Available online: https://www.inflation.eu/inflation-rates/south-africa/historic-inflation/cpi-inflation-south-africa.aspx (Accessed 4 October 2019).

Mayibuye. 'Mp'ayipele: Instant Race Classification'. No. 2, 1968, 14.
Oliver, G. 'Instant Race Bill Runs into Bitter Opposition'. *Rand Daily Mail*. 8 March 1968, 5.
Prince, V. 'White Andries to Try for Coloured', *Rand Daily Mail*. 2 December 1975, 9.
Rand Daily Mail. 'People Told: "Prove you are White"'. 2 June 1960, 3.
Rand Daily Mail. '"I'm White" Says Girl in "Suicide" Immorality Case'. 11 May 1962, 3.
Rand Daily Mail. 'No End'. 13 December 1966, 1.
Rand Daily Mail. 'Minister Will Act to Curb Race Appeals'. 13 December 1966, 1.
Rand Daily Mail. '356 Want to Be Reclassified'. 2 March 1967, 2.
Rand Daily Mail. 'White Ready to Give Up All for Girl'. 7 February 1975, 2.
Rand Daily Mail. '"Reclassify me" Pleads Coloured's Lover'. 3 June 1975, 5.
Rand Daily Mail. 'Woman Must Remain a Coloured'. 28 November 1977, 3.
Rand Daily Mail. '115 Reclassified Last Year'. 14 February 1978, 8.
Rand Daily Mail. 'Marriage Law Victim Hopes for Reprieve'. 14 February 1980, 1.
Rand Daily Mail. 'Reclassified'. 21 February 1980, 4.
Rand Daily Mail. 'Govt Allows a Mixed Marriage'. 7 August 1980, 2.
South Africa, Church of the Province of South Africa, Parish Registers, 1801–2004. Database with images. FamilySearch. Available online: https://FamilySearch.org: 14 June 2016. Original series available in the William Cullen Library, Wits University, Johannesburg.
South Africa. Bureau of Census Statistics. *Population Census 8th May 1951, Volume VII, Marital Status, Religions and Birthplaces of Coloureds, Asiatics and Natives*. Pretoria: Government Printers, 1960.
Symons, E. '"This woman is White", Says Magistrate'. *Rand Daily Mail*. 20 September 1969, 1.
Voters' Roll, 1984. Available for purchase online: https://genza.org.za/index.php/en/gssa-products-services-main.
Weekend Argus. 'Looking Inside the Heartbreak File'. 24 February 1979, 10.

CHAPTER 6
ADVERTISING THE ENSLAVED FOR SALE: A QUANTITATIVE APPROACH TO THE *ZUID-AFRIKAAN*, 1830–4

Wouter Raaijmakers* and Kate Ekama**

Introduction

On 2 December 1831 *De Zuid-Afrikaan* advertised an auction to be held at the house of auctioneer John Blore in Cape Town.[1] The enslaved man to be auctioned, named Fredrik, was described as forty-two years old, born in the Cape Colony and 'a complete coachman'. The newspaper ran many advertisements for upcoming slave sales at the time, but this one was unusual. Fredrik's former owner had instructed in her will that he should be sold at a public auction unless he purchased his freedom for 6,000 guilders. This was a high price for freedom.[2] Also unusually, the advertisement notes that 'Fredrik claims to be free', and that he was pursuing the matter before the Council of Justice.[3] The late owner's executors put Fredrik up for sale despite being unaware of the outcome of his proceedings, and regardless of whether Fredrik himself would be present or not.

By the 1830s, the international maritime slave trade had long been banned, but enslaved people continued to be bought and sold legally within the Cape Colony. What insights into this practice can be gleaned from newspaper advertisements? And what do they reveal about the views of both slave owner and enslaved who took part, willingly and unwillingly, in this trade? We use a quantitative approach to the advertisements placed in the *Zuid-Afrikaan* newspaper between the newspaper's founding in April 1830

---

†We are grateful to the Emancipation research group at Stellenbosch University, participants at the Economics of Cape Slavery Workshop (2022), Robert Ross, Dries Lyna, and peer reviewers for their comments and suggestions.

*Raaijmakers: Department of History, Stellenbosch University, South Africa and Department of Historical Studies, Radboud University, Nijmegen, the Netherlands.

**Ekama: Department of Economics, Stellenbosch University, South Africa.

[1] Stellenbosch University digital collections (SUNDigital), Zuid-Afrikaan (ZA), 2 December 1831.

[2] R.C.-H. Shell, *Children of Bondage: A Social History of the Slave Society at the Cape of Good Hope, 1652–1838* (Hanover: Wesleyan University Press published by University Press of New England, 1994): 33, 51. According to Shell, slave prices rose fourfold between 1807/8 and 1830, to over 1200 *Rijksdaalders* (Rds.). At a conversion rate of 3 *Guilders* =1 Rds., Fredrik was expected to pay 2000 Rds. for his freedom.

[3] ZA, 2 December 1831. All translations from Dutch to English are the first author's own, unless otherwise specified.

and *de jure* abolition of slavery in December 1834, focussing on the number and timing of advertisements, and the words used in them, to answer these questions.

Through a quantitative analysis of the newspaper advertisements, we show their growth over the years 1830–4. By dividing the advertisements according to type, we reveal the conjunctural movements of the different types of advertisements throughout the seasons and we find that while advertisements for general sales including enslaved people increased, advertisements for individual enslaved people were declining in the lead-up to emancipation. The second part of our analysis focuses on a selection of advertisements to reveal the characteristics of the enslaved people being sold. We find more men being advertised than women, the latter sometimes sold with their children. For men, we find that the majority of advertisements included skills or occupations; we find names used less frequently. An analysis of the advertisement texts reveals overlap between words used to describe enslaved people's character and labour, but a wider range of words and phrases used to describe the enslaved as person, not just labour. Advertisers' word choices reveal their ideals of the characteristics of a 'good slave'.

Our research is not the first to investigate slave sales at the Cape and elsewhere. In his 'taxonomy of transfers', Robert Shell identified three categories of slave sales in the domestic market with differing impacts on enslaved people's lives. Discretionary sales – in which the enslaved were sold for no apparent reason other than their owner no longer wanted or needed them, or needed to raise money more – likely meant a higher risk of the break-up of slave families than was the case with mandatory sales. In mandatory sales such as insolvent or deceased estate sales, enslaved people were more likely to be sold as a 'lot' and remain within the same family, and perhaps even on the same farm.[4] Both discretionary and mandatory sales were likely to be advertised in newspapers because they involved auctions while donation sales – an enslaved person was manumitted or sold to someone for the purpose of manumission – might not have been. Laura J. Mitchell, in her 2008 monograph *Belongings*, describes auctions in considerable detail, including the roles of enslaved people in these events. While some enslaved people were goods sold at these auctions, others performed the domestic labour necessary for the smooth running of these social and commercial events.[5] Turning to the newspapers where sales were advertised, Jaqueline L. Meltzer explores the public and private locations of these sales in the 1830s. She focuses on the 'Slave Tree' memorial in Cape Town. Meltzer's work highlights the continuity in the ways in which enslaved people were sold before *de jure* emancipation in 1834, and apprentices sold afterwards (until 1838).[6] While newspapers

---

[4]Shell, *Children of Bondage*, 104–23.

[5]L.J. Mitchell, *Belongings: Property, Family, and Identity in Colonial South Africa: An Exploration of Frontiers, 1725-c. 1830*, Gutenberg-e Series (New York: Columbia University Press, 2008): 151–5, 163–74.

[6]J.L. Meltzer, 'Slave Sales and Cape Town's Slave Tree Memorial', *Bulletin of the National Library of South Africa* 73, no. 1 (2019): 17–36, esp. 31–39. Also see: J.L. Meltzer, 'The Growth of Cape Town Commerce and the Role of John Fairbairn's Advertiser, 1835–1859' (Master's thesis, University of Cape Town, 1989).

advertised these sales, the role of the newspaper in the domestic trade was not Meltzer's focus. Jordan E. Taylor makes the point that newspapers and printers acted as 'mediators and brokers in the economy of slavery' in North America.[7] Taylor concludes that newspapers 'acted as crucial middlemen in the slave trade'.[8] We highlight this aspect of the *Zuid-Afrikaan*'s role at the Cape: as a print-medium connection between sellers and buyers in the domestic slave trade.

Throughout this chapter, we are acutely aware of the tension in these advertisements: the enslaved people who stand at the centre are presented as property for sale. The advertisements were placed by owners, executors of estates, auctioneers and others who described the enslaved for sale. In this way, the advertisements are more about the advertiser than the advertised. We treat the newspapers carefully in how far they can give insight into slave life, or experience; what the advertisements do offer is a window onto the domestic slave trade, from the vantage point of this print-media facilitator of sales.

De Zuid-Afrikaan

De Zuid-Afrikaan newspaper was first published in April 1830 under the editorship of French Capetonian Charles Etienne Boniface. It was printed in Cape Town on Friday mornings and dispatched to the country districts on Saturdays indicating that from the outset the newspaper intended to have both an urban and rural readership.[9] Furthermore, all editions were published in both Dutch and English. This includes the advertisements which appeared in Dutch at the beginning of each newspaper and then were repeated in English on the back pages.[10] Each edition comprised an editorial section, which includes reporting and discussion of news from across the colony and empire, and an advertising section.

When the paper was established in 1830, it was one of very few publications in the Cape Colony.[11] The previous year, 1829, marked an important change in the press

---

[7] J.E. Taylor, 'Newspaper-Brokered Slave Trade Advertisements in North America, 1704–1807', *Journal of Slavery and Data Preservation* 2, no. 2 (2021): 36–42. This is a non-peer-reviewed dataset article.

[8] Ibid.

[9] ZA, 9 April 1830. Later, the paper was dispatched to the country districts by post on the day of publication and the announcement was carried in Dutch and English on the nameplate. For example, ZA, 4 January 1833.

[10] The first pages of each edition were taken up with the Dutch content. This was followed by the English translations at the back of the paper. Each element of the Dutch content was translated for each edition. It is not clear from the way individual advertisements are published whether they were submitted to the newspaper in Dutch and then translated into English, or vice versa, nor who was doing the work of translation for the newspaper.

[11] The *South African Commercial Advertiser* was the first private newspaper, printed in 1824. There were other publications at the Cape before the 1830s, for instance the *Cape of Good Hope Literary Gazette*, but it was not a newspaper as such, and *De Verzamelaar*, which was short lived (1826–30, 1839–48). For an overview of activity in the newspaper world following 1829, see: T.E.G. Cutten, *A History of the Press in South Africa* (Cape Town: National Union of South African Students, 1935): 21–9.

Figure 6.1 The nameplate of *De Zuid-Afrikaan*.
Source: ZA, 30 April 1830. SUN Digital Collections.

landscape. Until then, press freedom was limited, with most newspapers being published under British authorities.[12] The government-run *Government Gazette* was published weekly, to communicate reports and regulations, and it carried news from across the colony and empire, and advertisements. It was not, however, a newspaper in the typical sense. It did not publish editorials; it was the government's vehicle for announcements, printed at the Castle.[13] *The South African Commercial Advertiser* was the first privately owned newspaper in the Colony. It was first published in 1824, and was suppressed by the government multiple times shortly after, only to reappear permanently from 1828 onwards. The legislative change of 1829 was brought about in no small part thanks to the continuous lobbying efforts by editors of the *Commercial Advertiser*.[14] Ordinance No. 60 of 1829, later dubbed the 'South African Magna Carta', granted the same press freedom within the British colonies as in Britain. This Ordinance was followed by an upsurge

---

[12] L. Rabe, *A Luta Continua: A History of Media Freedom in South Africa* (Stellenbosch: African Sun Media, 2020): 46–9; D. Wigston, 'A History of the South African Media', in *Media History, Media and Society*, ed. P.J. Fourie, 2nd ed., vol. 1, 3 vols., Media Studies (Cape Town: Juta Academic, 2008): 3–57, esp. 28–9. The *Commercial Advertiser* being the exception.

[13] Wigston, 'A History of the South African Media', 28–9; L.J. Picton, 'NICPRINT-50, Being Some Account of the History of the Printing, Packaging and Newspaper Industry of South Africa, and of the National Industrial Council for Printing, Prepared to Mark the Jubilee of the Council 1919–1969' (Cape Town: Cape & Transvaal Printers, 1969): 3; Rabe, *A Luta Continua*, 46–9.

[14] Ibid, 55–73. Rabe writes extensively on the six-year-long struggle for press freedom between the governor and colonial secretary on the one hand, and the editors and publisher of the *Commercial Advertiser* on the other, much of which was fought out in London.

in newspaper publishing in the Colony.[15] One of the newspapers that made use of this newly attained press freedom was the *Zuid-Afrikaan*.[16]

The general consensus on the two rival Cape newspapers has been that the *Zuid-Afrikaan* was the 'mouthpiece' of slave owners in the Colony and represented Cape Dutch interests in contrast to – and in conflict with – the more liberal *Commercial Advertiser*.[17] While no subscription records of the two papers have been found to date, that the *Zuid-Afrikaan* was published in both English and Dutch, and was sent to the country districts, would indicate a wide accessibility for readers. Dick's studies of reading cultures at the Cape point to a dispersed and diverse 'readership': Cape newspapers were not only read by individuals but were also read out loud: 'it was well known at the time that slaves hired people to read the newspapers to them and kept themselves informed of the latest developments.'[18] Scholars have concluded that in the early years of the *Zuid-Afrikaan*'s existence it was pro-slave owner in its sympathies, giving voice to their concerns regarding British intervention in the master-slave relationship and, importantly, on the consequences of emancipation. And some have suggested that the *Zuid-Afrikaan* was the first Dutch-language newspaper from Cape Town to voice an Afrikaner sentiment.[19]

During the 1830s, both the *Zuid-Afrikaan* and the *Commercial Advertiser* were occupied with slavery. This was reflected in the editorials, letters to the editor and advertisements. Whatever the nuances of editors' views on slavery, emancipation and compensation, both newspapers carried advertisements of slave sales as well as advertisements for the recapture of enslaved runaways.[20] What these advertisements

---

[15]Cutten, *A History of the Press*, 21–9; W. de Kock, *A Manner of Speaking: The Origins of the Press in South Africa* (Cape Town: Saayman & Weber, 1982): 5–10, 56–71; Rabe, *A Luta Continua*, 72–3. The *Graham's Town Journal* was first published in December 1831.

[16]De Kock, *A Manner of Speaking*, 5–12; P. Diedrichs, 'Newspapers: The Fourth Estate: A Cornerstone of Democracy', in *Mass Media for the Nineties: The South African Handbook for Mass Communication*, ed. A.S. de Beer (Pretoria: J. L. van Schaik, 1993): 71–100, esp. 73–6; H. Giliomee, *The Afrikaners: Biography of a People* (London: Hurst & Company, 2011): 112–14. Another example is the *Grahamstown Journal* which was first published in December 1831.

[17]Rick Watson refers to the Commercial Advertiser as the 'liberal newspaper' while the *Zuid-Afrikaan* he describes as the 'slaveholders' mouthpiece'. R.L. Watson, *Slave Emancipation and Racial Attitudes in nineteenth-century South Africa* (Cambridge: Cambridge University Press, 2012): 11, 18. See Wigston, 'A History of the South African Media' on the founding of the paper as a reaction against the English press, that is, the Commercial Advertiser. And on the *Zuid-Afrikaan* and Cape liberalism see G. Botma, 'De Zuid-Afrikaan en die teenstrydighede van 19de-eeuse Kaapse liberalisme', *Tydskrif vir Geesteswetenskappe* 62, no. 1 (2020): 92–111.

[18]A.L. Dick, 'Reading Authors of the Enlightenment at the Cape of Good Hope from the Late 1780s to the Mid 1830s', *Journal of Southern African Studies* 44, no. 3 (2018): 398.

[19]Cutten, *A History of the Press*, 22; De Kock, *A Manner of Speaking*, 8; Giliomee, *The Afrikaners*, 112; Picton, 'NICPRINT-50', 15–16; K. Roelofse, 'The History of the South African Press', in *Introduction to Communication*, ed. L.M. Oosthuizen (Kenwyn: Juta, 1996): 66–118, esp. 70–1; Wigston, 'A History of the South African Media', 34. In his recent article, Botma challenges the view of the *Zuid-Afrikaan* as a forerunner of the pro-Apartheid media of the twentieth century. See Botma, 'De Zuid-Afrikaan'.

[20]On the *Zuid-Afrikaan*'s advertisements for recapture of runaways see collaborative work by Karl Bergemann, Kathryn Smith and Pearl Mamathuba entitled 'Fugitives', most recently exhibited at The Castle, Cape Town, 6 June 2022.

cost slave owners/advertisers – and thereby contributed to the newspaper's financial survival – is, unfortunately, unknown. What is clear from the first edition of the *Zuid-Afrikaan* is that both subscriptions and advertisement costs had to be paid for in advance, likely to cover the printing costs of the paper. Payments could be made and advertisements received at the house of C.N. Neethling, 3 Shortmarket Street in Cape Town, at whose house the paper was also printed.[21] While we have not yet found an account of the price of placing an advertisement in the *Zuid-Afrikaan*, it is possible that revenue from advertising not subscriptions underpinned profits, as Law has shown was the case with Victorian periodicals. The balance between advertising space and other content is an important part of Law's investigation into revenue.[22] In the *Zuid-Afrikaan* advertising claimed the front page of the newspaper, preceding the editorial and news items. We interpret this prominent position as a signal of the importance of advertising.[23] In this vein, we also observed that the amount of space dedicated to advertising varied. It appears that the opinion section often had to cede some space to advertisements.

By placing their advertisements in the *Zuid-Afrikaan* we can assume that slave owners and advertisers were targeting a readership whom they considered to be a pool of potential purchasers. In this way then we consider the newspaper as the facilitator of a domestic trade in enslaved people.

Domestic trade in enslaved people

As a recent conquest and therefore part of the Empire, British legislation against the international maritime slave trade was in force at the Cape. The 1807 abolition of the trade shut off (legal) imports of enslaved people into the Colony. Ownership of enslaved people and the buying and selling of slave property continued within the Colony. It is this domestic trade that, in the 1830s, was facilitated by the newspapers. By that time, the British had introduced amelioration legislation and emancipatory legislation. The 1820s saw a 'reawakening', as Mason puts it, of the anti-slavery movement.[24] The 1822 British Parliament debate on the amelioration of slavery led in 1823 to the establishment of

---

[21] ZA, 9 April 1830. The costs of subscriptions were detailed on the nameplate in Dutch, and an insert in the English section of the paper announced the costs and other details in English, specifying that advertisements had to be paid in cash.

[22] Law delves into the balance of available space in periodicals during the Victorian Age: 'As a rule of thumb, periodicals […] would typically aim to fill around half of their available space with advertising copy. With the social character of the readership often counting as much as raw circulation, such a balance of content would generate income from advertising exceeding that from subscriptions, thus resulting in a clear profit.' G. Law. 'Distribution', in *The Routledge Handbook to Nineteenth-Century British Periodicals and Newspapers*, ed. A. King, A. Easley and J. Morton (Abingdon and New York: Routledge, 2016): 55.

[23] A. King, 'Periodical Economics', in *The Routledge Handbook to Nineteenth-Century British Periodicals and Newspapers*, ed. A. King, A. Easley and J. Morton (Abingdon and New York: Routledge, 2016): 60–74, esp. 60–4.

[24] J.E. Mason, *Social Death and Resurrection: Slavery and Emancipation in South Africa* (Charlottesville: University of Virginia Press, 2003): 46.

the abolitionist Anti-Slavery Society. At the Cape, Governor Somerset had implemented limited reforms which legalised marriage between Christian enslaved people and prohibited the sale of children away from their mothers, if Christian. The promulgation of Ordinance No. 19 in 1826 provided enslaved people with new rights to purchase their freedom – compulsory manumission – and an institutional outlet in the form of the office of the Guardian of Slaves. The prohibition of separating mothers and young children was extended to all enslaved people. Two years later, the British government implemented the emancipatory Ordinance No. 50 of 1828. In a reversal of earlier legislation, the ordinance gave Khoikhoi and San people, along with Free blacks, the same rights as white people.[25] Further changes to slavery regulations were introduced with the Consolidation Order of 1830 which reduced corporal punishment and was further revised in 1832 to close any loopholes in the legislation.[26]

In theory at least, these regulations limited the break-up of slave families by sale on the domestic market – we therefore expected to find advertisements in the newspapers for enslaved women to be sold with their young children. What we most often cannot recover is whether or not these families were being sold away from their husband/father.

The *Zuid-Afrikaan* offers a window onto the domestic market, but most likely not in its entirety. It is possible that slaveowners held particular ideas or beliefs about readership or stance which led them to choose to advertise in one or other of the Cape publications. If the costs of advertising differed between the *Commercial Advertiser*, *Government Gazette* and *Zuid-Afrikaan*, that likely played a role too. We are aware of these possible selection biases. A broad comparative study of advertisements across the Cape papers would show the differences between the papers, and offer a wider view of the market.

Furthermore, the advertisements we study here do not always mention the number of enslaved people being sold. Sale advertisements cannot, therefore, offer an overview of the number of people bought and sold on the domestic market. Bearing these limitations in mind, we now turn to analysing the advertisements which were placed in the *Zuid-Afrikaan* from its first edition in 1830 up to emancipation in December 1834.

Advertising enslaved people for hire and sale, 1830–4

Together, the 235 editions of the *Zuid-Afrikaan* which were printed between 1830 and 1834 carried 9,076 advertisements, 1,180 of which dealt with the sale or hire of enslaved people.[27] We divided the advertisements into four categories: general sale with slaves

---

[25] A.S. du Toit and H. Giliomee, *Afrikaner Political Thought: Analysis and Documents, 1780–1850*, vol. 1, Perspectives on Southern Africa 22 (Berkeley: University of California Press, 1983): 104–8.

[26] Mason, *Social Death and Resurrection*, 46–52; P. Scully, *Liberating the Family? Gender and British Slave Emancipation in the Rural Western Cape, South Africa, 1823-1853*, Social History of Africa (Portsmouth, N. H.: Heinemann, 1997): 38–45.

[27] See Appendix A for how we created the dataset.

(n=537), slave-specific sale (n=245), service hiring request (n=254) and service hiring offer (n=144).[28] We were interested not just in the type of sale (deceased versus insolvent estate; auction versus out-of-hand sale) but rather in the type of advertisement as it related to the enslaved who were advertised. Our categorisation gave us a starting point for exploring the role of the *Zuid-Afrikaan* in advertising and thus connecting sellers and buyers in the domestic market.

Conveniently, the 17 September 1830 edition of the *Zuid-Afrikaan* happened to contain typical examples of all four categories of advertisement. Auctioneers G. J. Joubert and J. C. Leewner advertised a general sale at Stellenbosch of goods belonging to J. C. Esterhuyze: 500 sheep, twenty oxen and three enslaved people, Saul from Mozambique, Aron from Mozambique and Eva from the Cape – advertised for sale 'not because of any insolence, but because their services are no longer required'.[29] A slave-specific sale was advertised by Michiel de Villiers for Dolphina of the Cape. She was twenty years of age, had served as a housemaid and would be sold 'at a fair price' because her services were no longer required.[30] A service hiring request was made by farmer J. R. Louw Jr. of Paarl. He advertised for field labourers, saying that those 'who can produce evidence of good conduct' would receive 'the highest daily wages'.[31] And in the fourth category, Izaak Rossouw of Paarl advertised a healthy, childless wetnurse for hire.[32]

Advertising trends, 1830–1834

The *Zuid-Afrikaan*'s popularity increased during its first four years. Although we cannot definitely attribute this to the programme that editor Charles Boniface laid out, we see in Figure 6.2 that during those years the paper attracted an increasing number of advertisements. The first edition carried ten advertisements; by 1834 the newspaper carried an average of forty-seven advertisements per edition. We interpret this increase in advertising as a marker of the Cape population's growing use of the newspaper and its concomitant embedding in the life of the Colony.

We find that the increase in advertising was not driven by an increase in advertisements for slave sales and hiring. During the first years of this formative period of the newspaper, the number of advertisements implicitly and explicitly referring to slaves remains remarkably stable. As Figure 6.2 shows, we see a period of higher

---

[28] For an elaboration on the categories, see Appendix B.

[29] ZA, 17 September 1830. '*Gemelde Slaven worden om geene onduegden verkocht, maar om dat de Eigenaar dezelve niet meer noodig heeft.*'

[30] ZA, 17 September 1830. '… *zoo wordt zy hierby te koop aangeboden, tegen eenen zeer billyken prys.*'

[31] ZA, 17 September 1830. '*Boeren werkslieden die bewyze van goed gedrag kunnen produceren zullen de hoogste Daglonen erlangen.*' Although this advertisement does not directly refer to slave labour, it doesn't exclude it either. For an elaboration of our selection process, see Appendix A.

[32] ZA, 17 September 1830. '*TE HUUR, eene gezonde MIN zonder Kind.*'

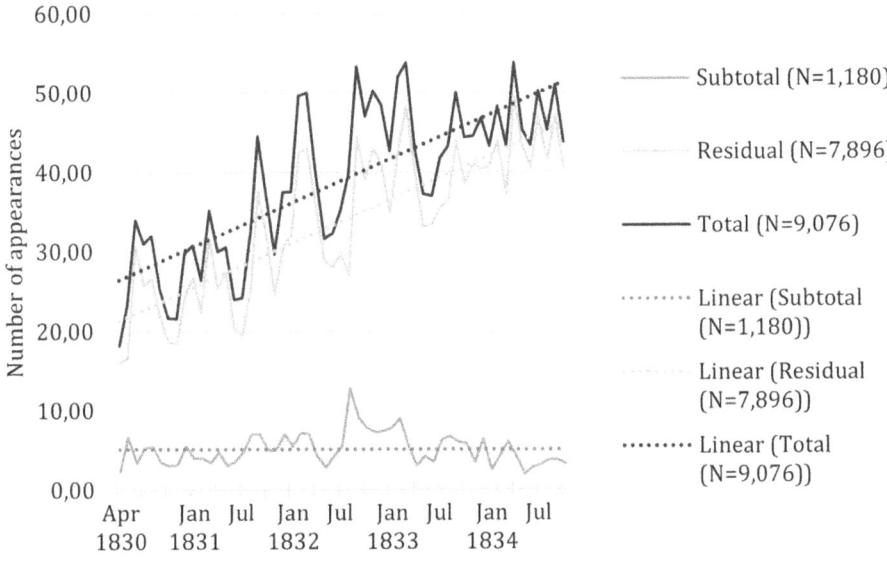

Figure 6.2 Course of advertisements in *De Zuid-Afrikaan*, Apr. 1830–Nov. 1834, per monthly average, with linear trends.
Source: ZA, Apr. 1830–Nov. 1834.

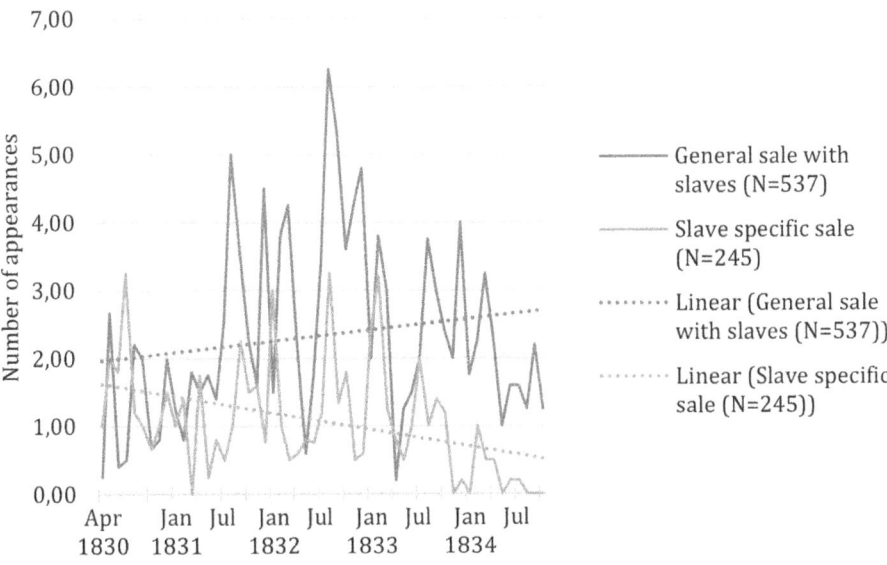

Figure 6.3 Course of advertisements per category in *De Zuid-Afrikaan*, Apr. 1830–Nov. 1834, per monthly average, with linear trends.
Source: ZA, Apr. 1830–Nov. 1834.

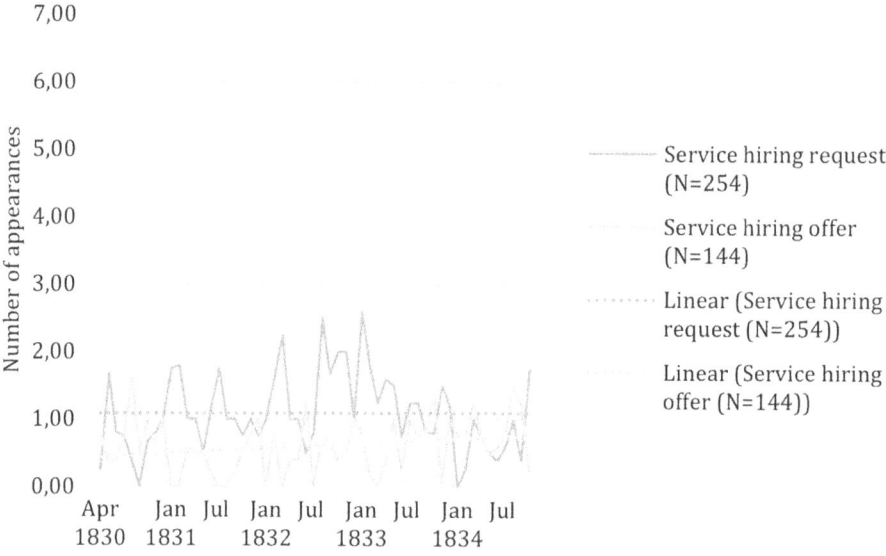

Figure 6.4 Course of advertisements for additional categories in *De Zuid-Afrikaan*, Apr. 1830–Nov. 1834, per monthly average, with linear trends.
Source: ZA, Apr. 1830–Nov. 1834.

numbers of slave-related advertisements in late 1832 and early 1833; but for the rest of the period, the advertising numbers remain stable. This indicates that as emancipation drew nearer, there was neither a quickening nor slackening of the domestic slave trade, as seen through the advertisements. We investigated trends within the categories to see how they changed over time and according to the seasons.

Trends over time

To find an explanation for the remarkably stable number of these advertisements over these four years (see Figure 6.2), we considered the demography of the Cape slave population after the abolition of the international slave trade in 1807, before which an increasing number of enslaved people were being imported under Dutch East India Company rule.[33] Andrew Bank noted three demographic shifts in the slave population at the Cape between the 1806 British occupation and 1834: a trend towards creolisation, due to foreign slave imports being cut off; a more balanced gender ratio, with men no longer vastly outnumbering women; and a change from a natural decrease to a natural

---

[33] J.C. Armstrong and N. Worden, 'The Slaves, 1652–1834', in *The Shaping of South African Society, 1652–1820*, ed. R. Elphick and H. Giliomee (Cape Town: Longman, 1979): 75–115, esp. 76–78; N. Worden, *Slavery in Dutch South Africa*, African Studies Series 44 (Cambridge: Cambridge University Press, 1985): 6–18.

increase, due to an increase in fertility rates.[34] The Cape slave population was thus increasing by reproduction, not imports, and decreasing as before through mortality and manumission. In this context of demographic change, the domestic trade was in theory the only trade in enslaved people taking place. The advertisements in the *Zuid-Afrikaan* provide a window into this market.

The number of slave advertisements begins to have meaning only when we realise that it in fact represents a decrease relative to the total number of advertisements in the paper. This relative decrease is difficult to interpret in relation to the demand for slave labour in the 1830s. We do know that it was a period of great uncertainty and consternation among slave owners regarding emancipation and compensation. Whether this would have led to more or fewer slaves being advertised for sale is unclear. But the labour market was changing in this period: Shell has pointed out that the 'capture and enserfment of the Khoi and also the San … became most apparent after the abolition of the slave trade in 1808' and it was a period of immigration of workers from Britain.[35] As a result, the demand for slave labour itself may simply have been in decline. A second and perhaps more important influence may have been what John Mason called 'a process of social resurrection' as a result of the amelioration of slavery through a process of emancipatory legislation since 1807.[36] The relative decrease in the number of slave advertisements in the *Zuid-Afrikaan* may indicate that slave owners and other advertisers were susceptible to these demographic and political developments. This argument is further supported by considering events during the period June 1832 to June 1833 that may account for the fluctuations we see in the number of slave sale advertisements at that time.

In Figure 6.2 we see a slight decrease in the number of advertisements and slave advertisements around June 1832. It is likely that this was caused by a paper shortage and consequent publishing constraints.[37] There is a clear recovery in the following months: in September 1832, the number of slave advertisements reached its highest peak, after which it plateaued until February 1833. The spike was probably caused by a combination of events.

---

[34]A. Bank, *The Decline of Urban Slavery at the Cape, 1806 to 1843*, Communications 22 (Rondebosch: Centre for African Studies, 1991): 6-7. These three shifts were derived from R.C.-H. Shell, 'The Family and Slavery at the Cape, 1680-1808', in *The Angry Divide: Social and Economic History of the Western Cape*, ed. W.G. James and M. Simons (Cape Town: David Philip, 1989): 20-30, and would later be incorporated in Shell, *Children of Bondage*. Also see: R. Ross, 'The Last Years of the Slave Trade to the Cape Colony', *Slavery & Abolition* 9, no. 3 (1988): 209-19, esp. 210, for a comparative perspective between the Cape and Batavia.

[35]Shell, *Children of Bondage*, 33; Giliomee, *The Afrikaners*, 193-4, 197-9; R. Ross, *Status and Respectability in the Cape Colony, 1750-1870: A Tragedy of Manners* (Cambridge: Cambridge University Press, 1999), 60-6.

[36]Mason, *Social Death and Resurrection*, 37-8; 46-52. For a negotiation on emancipation during the period of apprenticeship, see: W. Dooling, *Slavery, Emancipation and Colonial Rule in South Africa* (Scottsville, South Africa: University of KwaZulu-Natal Press, 2007): 112-58; Scully, *Liberating the Family?*, 38-45. Also see: A. Tewari, 'The Reform Bill (1832) and the Abolition of Slavery (1833): A Caribbean Link', *Proceedings of the Indian History Congress* 73 (2012): 1140-7.

[37]ZA, 15 June 1832. The paper shortage and its consequences for the *Zuid-Afrikaan* are discussed in this edition. Later editions sporadically comment on its printer's paper supply.

First, in July 1832 the Consolidation Order was revised, bringing in greater restrictions on the rights of slave owners. André du Toit and Hermann Giliomee note that in response, slave owners from Cape Town organised several protest meetings, the proceedings of which were later published in and spread with a brochure. These protest meetings were led by none other than P. A. Brand, the owner and then editor of the *Zuid-Afrikaan*.[38] Secondly, the *Zuid-Afrikaan* repeatedly reported on the slave revolts taking place in Mauritius in August 1832.[39] This likely contributed to slave owners' worries, already burdened as they were by their concerns around emancipation and how it would unfold with regard to the loss of their slave property. We thus expect that the peak of slave sale advertisements in September 1832 and the continued high level into early 1833 had much to do with slave owners' nervousness during this period of 'social resurrection' as Mason has called it.[40] In a context of uproar among slave owners in the colony regarding ameliorative legislation, reports of uprisings in Mauritius, and uncertainty about how much compensation they would receive, and where it would be paid, the spike might reflect a heightening of these worries which led to individuals selling off enslaved people rather than waiting for compensation in the future.

To consider this in more detail, Figure 6.3 shows the number of appearances and the trends for general sales with slaves and slave-specific sales. Besides the relative decrease in slave advertisements generally (Figure 6.2), the slave-specific sale advertisements even decreased in absolute numbers (Figure 6.3). This might be considered to confirm the explanations suggested above, but we might also wonder about the role of manumissions in reshaping the market. Andrew Bank's work on Cape Town shows that manumissions increased in the years leading up to emancipation.[41] Perhaps the decrease in slave-specific sale advertisements mirrors the increase in manumissions: following the ameliorative legislation which made self-purchase or 'compulsory manumission' a right (1826), it is possible that slave owners agreed to manumissions when previously they would have advertised their slave property for sale. Robert Shell identified the period 1809–34 as one characterised by the manumission of older enslaved people, both men and women.[42] We might also wonder about the extent of the market which falls outside the *Zuid-Afrikaan*'s view. Our study was of course limited to the *Zuid-Afrikaan* but slave sale advertisements were placed in other newspapers too. Future research on the advertisements in the *Commercial Advertiser* and the *Government Gazette* can shed more light on our reading of the *Zuid-Afrikaan*.

Interestingly, Figure 6.3 shows that the absolute number of advertisements for general sales with slaves increased over the period. These included deceased estate sales,

---

[38] Du Toit and Giliomee, *Afrikaner Political Thought*, 108–9.

[39] ZA, 27 July 1832; ZA, 3 August 1832; ZA, 17 August 1832.

[40] Mason, *Social Death and Resurrection*, 40–3.

[41] Bank, *Decline of Urban Slavery*, 24.

[42] Shell, *Children of Bondage*, 388. The earlier periods were 1658–85 during which sexual partners were manumitted and 1686–1808 during which wet nurses and their children were manumitted.

insolvent estate sales and general auctions. Wayne Dooling notes that because slave owners were heavily mortgaged in the years before emancipation, they did not receive the full compensation awarded to them.[43] It is possible that slave owners increasingly advertised enslaved people for sale in general auctions and insolvent estates in order to satisfy their creditors during a period of financial difficulty. One advertiser explicitly stated this in his reasons for sale, discussed below.[44]

Figure 6.4 shows that the service hiring requests and offers fluctuated over the course of the period, but generally opposed each other. Perhaps we can interpret this as the newspaper successfully connecting hirers and renters. Interestingly, the advertisements for hiring requests and offers are unclear as to whether enslaved people were involved. This might be an indication that employers were happy to hire irrespective of legal status. As Bank's and others' work shows, enslaved people in nineteenth-century Cape Town were involved in wage labour.[45] The *Zuid-Afrikaan* was clearly one of the channels through which that hiring process was organised, also outside of the town. Further research on the hiring of enslaved people in Cape Town and the country districts can illuminate what this meant for the enslaved: in particular, the extent to which hiring out, and thus earning a salary, was a means to accumulate enough money for self-purchase manumission prior to emancipation.

Seasonal trends

We next examined seasonal patterns in the advertisements. Considering the importance of seasonal patterns of labour demand in the agricultural regions of the colony (wine and wheat growing in the south-western Cape specifically) and the impact attributed to the changes in labour demand and intensity of desertion,[46] we plotted the advertisements according to the month in which each one was published, seen in Figures 6.5, 6.6 and 6.7.[47] Figure 6.5 shows that in general advertising peaked in April and October, as did the slave advertisements, though less noticeably. When we examine seasonality in the general sales with slaves and slave-specific sales, we see diverging patterns (Figure 6.6). The peaks we see in the slave advertisements in Figure 6.5 are surely driven by the peaks in the general sales with slaves depicted in Figure 6.6. The general sales with slaves peaked in January and September, with a lower peak in April. Perhaps this reflects the seasonality of auctions in the Cape.

---

[43] Dooling, *Slavery, Emancipation and Colonial Rule in South Africa*, 134–7. Their creditors received a portion of the compensation, and in some cases, the full amount. See also Kate Ekama, 'Bondsmen: Slave Collateral in the 19th-Century Cape Colony', *Journal of Southern African Studies* 47, no. 3 (2021): 437–53.

[44] ZA, 7 October 1831.

[45] Bank, *The Decline of Urban Slavery*, 20–5, 38–43.

[46] R. Ross, *Cape of Torments: Slavery and Resistance in South Africa* (London: Routledge & Kegan Paul, 1983): 29–37.

[47] In order not to produce peaks based on chronology and to provide each month with an equal sample size, we excluded all advertisements before December 1830.

Quantitative History and Uncharted People

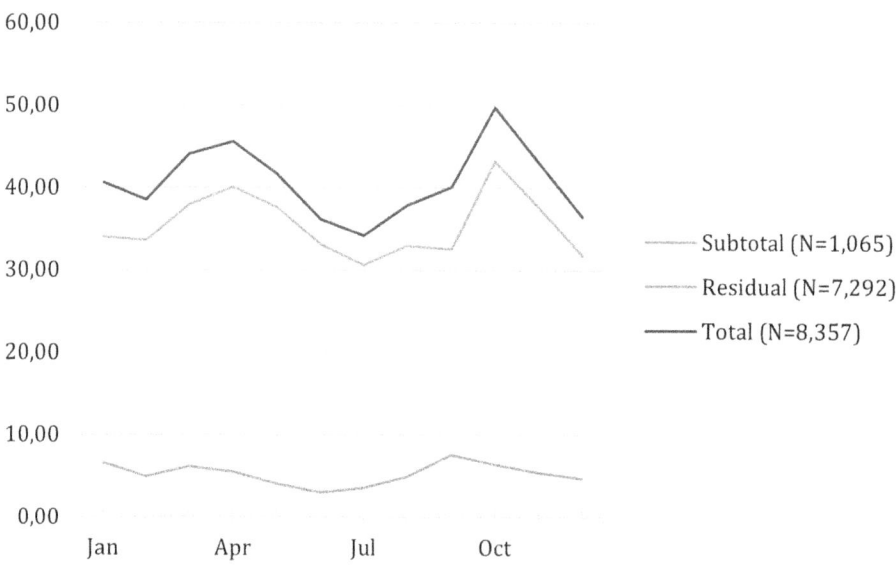

Figure 6.5 Seasonality of advertisements in *De Zuid-Afrikaan*, Dec. 1830–Nov. 1834, per monthly average.
Source: ZA, Dec. 1830–Nov. 1834.

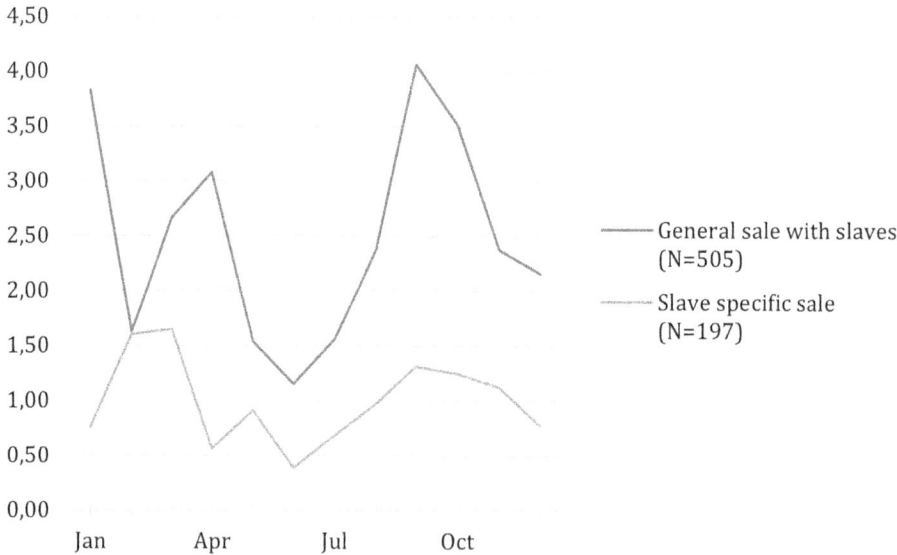

Figure 6.6 Seasonality of advertisements per category in *De Zuid-Afrikaan*, Dec. 1830–Nov. 1834, per monthly average.
Source: ZA, Dec. 1830–Nov. 1834.

Advertising the Enslaved for Sale

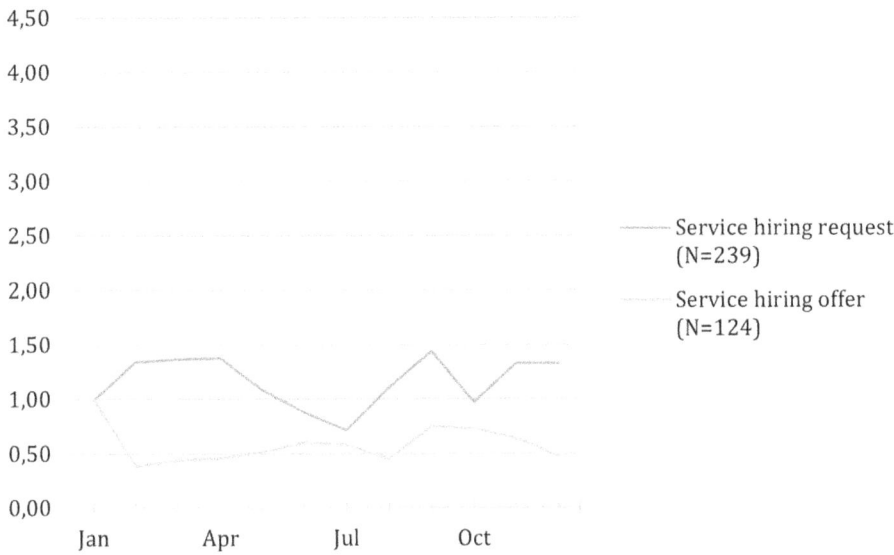

Figure 6.7 Seasonality of advertisements in *De Zuid-Afrikaan*, Dec. 1830–Nov. 1834, per monthly average.
Source: ZA, Dec. 1830–Nov. 1834.

When we examine the service hiring requests and offers (Figure 6.7) we see small changes between the months. Hiring requests, while few in number, do seem to follow the seasonal demands for labour in agriculture.[48] While it is not clear from the advertisements without matching them to other sources, it is possible that enslaved people were not only hired within rural, farming areas, but from urban to rural areas at times of higher demand such as harvest. After all, the *Zuid-Afrikaan* positioned itself at the crossroads of rural and urban readers: the newspaper was printed in Cape Town and posted to the country districts. Perhaps the seasonality reflects interactions between rural and urban labour markets.[49] Newton-King's analysis of the nineteenth-century Cape labour market shows that it operated in the context of shortage.[50]

From 1830, when the *Zuid-Afrikaan* was first published, until emancipation in 1834, the paper attracted more and more advertisements. However, over that same period, we found that the relative number of slave advertisements decreased. Understanding

---

[48]Ross, *Cape of Torments*, 25–7. Ross notes that the highpoints of wheat and wine farming dovetailed, with the grape harvest following the end of the wheat harvest. The period from December to the end of March was 'frenetic' (p. 25). Wine farmers rented out enslaved people to wheat farmers to assist with harvest, and additional Khoikhoi labour was also brought in, which strategies were also followed by the wine farmers until the pressing of the grapes was complete.

[49]Bank, *The Decline of Urban Slavery*, 26–35.

[50]S. Newton-King, 'The Labour Market of the Cape Colony, 1807–28', in *Economy and Society in Pre-Industrial South Africa*, ed. S. Marks and A. Atmore (London: Longman, 1980): 171–207, esp. 171–4.

the shifts, albeit small ones, within each category of advertisement, showed that general sales with slaves increased over time, while the slave-specific advertisements decreased. When broken down according to the month published, we also found a stronger seasonality in the advertisements for general sales with slaves which we suggest might be explained by patterns in holding auctions. The context of impending emancipation and dissatisfaction with compensation plans on the side of the slave owners, and new opportunities to purchase freedom on the parts of the enslaved, might also go some way to explaining the downward trend in slave-specific advertisements. Placing the slave advertisements in the context of all advertising in the *Zuid-Afrikaan* goes some way in contextualising the domestic market for enslaved people; future research can take this further by examining the advertisements placed in other Cape newspapers of the time.

Examining slave-specific sale advertisements

We now return to the case of the enslaved man Fredrik, put up for sale as a slave, although he considered himself free. Admittedly, this is a peculiar case. We do not present it as exemplifying the other 185 unique slave-specific sale advertisements that appeared between April 1830 and November 1834. Together, these advertisements announced the sale of 321 identifiable enslaved individuals.[51] We chose the advertisement for Fredrik as our example because it was particularly detailed and interesting, and it suggested that it would be fruitful to try to identify the core characteristics that reappeared in these advertisements and to examine the vocabulary that the advertisers used to describe the enslaved people they were selling.

Finding a buyer

Like the advertisement for Fredrik, 89 per cent of the advertisements for slave-specific sales were published only once. The rest were published twice, and a handful thrice, with an exception being an announcement of a group of enslaved people for sale placed five times in October and November 1831.[52] The fact that the majority appeared only once suggests that advertising in this paper was a good way of connecting sellers to potential buyers, and thus making a sale. Reading the advertisements along the grain, that is, from the point of view of making sales, we imagine that the success of the advertisements depended not just on how appealingly advertisers presented the enslaved, but on a variety of factors.

---

[51] In addition to these individuals, seven advertisements announced the sale of unnumbered groups of enslaved people.

[52] ZA, 14 October 1831, 21 October 1831, 28 October 1831, 4 November 1831, 11 November 1831. The auction was scheduled for 14 November 1831.

Payment was likely one such factor. Occasionally, advertisers offered credit.⁵³ Offering favourable terms might have widened the potential pool of buyers. Perhaps this showed a certain confidence between the buyer and seller, and in the social and legal frameworks to enforce the agreed sale terms. In the case of Fredrik, the price would be determined by auction, as in many cases described in the literature.⁵⁴ Whatever the payment method, we would have expected the price to be a determining factor and therefore a necessity in advertisements. Interestingly, the price was seldom mentioned, especially in advertisements for private sales.⁵⁵ This perhaps indicates room for negotiating the price of enslaved people, and there must have been a mutual understanding of value between the advertiser and the potential buyer. In twelve of the advertisements which announced the sale of enslaved people at auctions, it was specified that they were sold without reserve, perhaps in the hopes of enticing buyers with the possibility of low prices.⁵⁶

Another factor that might have contributed to making a sale was stating the reason for the sale but, surprisingly, only 30 per cent of the advertisements do this. This is understandable given that slave owners might have been motivated by what they considered negative characteristics or behaviours of the enslaved; running away, insolence, slow or poor work (or similar 'weapons of the weak') could have prompted sale. Few owners were transparent in advertising enslaved people for sale who had transgressed the boundaries of acceptable behaviour. Such transparency would render the enslaved person less desirable and possibly also less valuable. One of the very few examples is for a nameless enslaved man who 'has shown insolence towards his master'.⁵⁷ We look more closely at this case below. Generally, as would be expected, the reasons for sale tended not to draw attention to characteristics or events which would hamper sale.

The reasons that are stated are interesting, with Fredrik's legal struggle for freedom being one of the most striking. Services no longer required is a common one, such as the case of an unnamed man, who was described as 'generally recommended', a good labourer in the eyes of his owner, but also a competent baker. This versatile man was sold because he was no longer needed, and not, the advertisement stated, because of any deficiency or vice.⁵⁸ It is to be expected that slave owners and advertisers tried to reassure potential buyers by stating that the enslaved were not sold for negative reasons such as deficiency or vice. Occasionally, an advertiser said his reason for selling was to pay off his creditors.⁵⁹ One was even planning to leave the Colony altogether.⁶⁰

---

[53] For example, ZA, 20 May 1831; ZA, 26 August 1831.

[54] Mitchell, *Belongings*, 151–5, 163–74.

[55] The only two accounts of pricing in private sale advertisements are found in: ZA, 22 March 1833; ZA, 19 July 1833.

[56] For instance ZA, 13 January 1832 'ZONDER RESERVE'

[57] ZA, 25 November 1831. '*om dat hy eenige brutaliteit omtrent zynen Lyfheer heeft betoond.*'

[58] ZA, 18 May 1832. '*die algemeen kan worden geecommendeerd*', '*om gene gebreken verkocht of ondeugd*'.

[59] ZA, 7 October 1831.

[60] ZA, 13 January 1832. For information on insolvencies, see: Dooling, *Slavery, Emancipation and Colonial Rule in South Africa*.

Some enslaved people were advertised for sale because they wanted to move. Several nameless enslaved people sought a transfer from the town to the country or vice versa. W. C. Botha advertised a twenty-three-year-old man for sale or exchange because the enslaved man no longer wanted to remain in the city. The advertisement was addressed specifically to residents of the hinterland in order to fulfil the man's wish. One can only wonder why he wished to leave.[61] The opposite wish was expressed by Spatie, a fifty-one-year-old enslaved woman who had experience as a housemaid and nanny. She was sold 'only because she preferred city life to country life'.[62] In a different kind of case, an 'African Slave boy' between the ages of twenty and twenty-two is advertised who 'has no preference for staying longer with his master'.[63] The advertisement was put up anonymously: potential buyers were asked to address themselves to the office of the *Zuid-Afrikaan* for more information. On the surface, the stated reason indicates not only awareness but also responsiveness on the part of the owner and or advertiser to the enslaved man's wishes. But we are also left wondering what motivated his desire to leave.

Fredrik and these nameless cases point towards an element of agency among the enslaved that can be read in these advertisements. But they are the exception. Nevertheless, they are a glimpse into some of the dynamics of the master-slave relationship behind the advertisements.

Geographic location is another aspect that likely impacted the success or not of slave sale advertisements. Based on the dataset created, future research can investigate the locations of the sales, by district or town to shed light on the rural and urban contours of the market. One of the places that stands out in the slave sale advertisements is 7 Dorp Street Stellenbosch, the office of M. C. A. Neethling who was in the 1830s auction administrator. His name and address appear in numerous advertisements, as a place of sale as well as inquiry into the particulars of the enslaved whom he advertised.[64] Neethling's office likely functioned in much the same way the *Zuid-Afrikaan*'s own office did in Cape Town.

The newspaper's office in central Cape Town played an important role in the corner of the domestic market for slaves which was mediated by the paper. This is seen in twelve unique advertisements which mention 'the office of this paper' as the location at which interested buyers could request more information, whether about the enslaved

---

[61] ZA, 22 February 1833. It is possible that this enslaved man was in fact Andries, born in the Cape, and registered as W. C. Botha's property in 1830. At the time he was about nineteen years old which is reasonably close to his advertised age of about twenty-three in 1833. He was recorded as a 'housboy'. The register does not include any sale information which likely means that his desire to leave Cape Town was not fulfilled. Western Cape Archive and Records Service, Archives of the Registrar and Guardian of Slaves, Slave Office (SO) 6/8, Slave Registers, W. C. Botha.

[62] ZA, 3 May 1833. '*alleen om dat zy stads boven het buiten leven verkiest*'.

[63] ZA, 8 July 1831. '*geen verkiezing heeft langer by zynen heer te blyven.*'

[64] ZA, 18 March 1831; ZA, 21 October 1831; ZA, 16 March 1832; ZA, 29 June 1832; ZA, 24 August 1832; ZA, 14 September 1832; ZA, 21 September 1832; ZA, 15 March 1833; ZA, 26 April 1833; ZA, 19 July 1833.

Advertising the Enslaved for Sale

advertised, or the conditions of credit offered. For instance, when an enslaved woman was advertised for sale or hire in July 1832, the advertisement specified that she was African, twenty years old, and a 'good Housemaid' who could undertake washing and ironing, it concluded with the note that 'further details are available at the Office of this Paper'.[65] In this case, no details of the seller or advertiser were given; readers were directed only to the newspaper's office. Initially, it appears that the office was C. N. Neethling's house on Shortmarket Street, but by 1833 the Almanac listed the office of the *Zuid-Afrikaan* as Wale Street.[66] This is a strong link to Taylor's work, highlighting the role of the newspaper as a facilitator of slave sales, or at the least, locating the paper as the vehicle by which buyers and sellers of enslaved people were connected, to then later meet at auction or private sale to conclude their business.

Common characteristics

Figure 6.8 shows the gender distribution of four characteristics that are mentioned in some of the advertisements: origin, name, age and occupation. Given that 321 enslaved people were individually identifiable in the advertisements, it is remarkable that in only one instance the advertised person's gender was not mentioned or could not be inferred. This enslaved person was named February, but we know from other Cape Colony sources that this name was exclusively male.[67] Gender was thus undoubtedly an important factor for a buyer. The wording made it explicit, for example in terms like 'slave boy' or 'slave girl', or Dutch gendered forms like '*slavin*' (female slave) or '*slaaf*' (male slave), as in the advertisement for '*den Slaaf* Fredrik'.[68]

Considering the change in legislation in the 1820s which prevented separating by sale enslaved mothers from their young children, we expected to see some family units in the advertisements. And we do, both directly and indirectly. For instance, when Roset was advertised for sale in December 1831, her child Spaas was advertised for sale with her. The same edition carried an advertisement for the sale of Dina of the Cape, with her nine-year-old daughter, Nella.[69] Mothers and children are mentioned together; it is seldom that there was mention of a father or husband. The enslaved man August and

---

[65] ZA, 13 July 1832. '*SLAVIN TE KOOP. UIT de hand te Koop, of the Huur, eene Afrikaansche Slavin, 20 jaren oud, eene goede Huismeid, die het wasschen en stryken verstaat; verdere byzonderheden zyn te vernemen aan het Kantoor van dit Blad*.' For more references to the office see ZA, 8 July 1831; 15 July 1831; 21 October 1831; 1 June 1832; 24 August 1832; 2 November 1832; 7 September 1832; 22 March 1833; 5 July 1833; 20 September 1833.

[66] *The South African Alamac and Directory for the year 1833* (Cape Town: G. Grieg, 1833). The first edition of 1833 listed the place of publication as 4 Wale Street. ZA, 4 January 1833.

[67] ZA, 14 September 1832. All individuals by the name of February who were recorded in the Slave Registers for the Cape District and Cape Town (WCARS SO 6/8–35) were recorded as male.

[68] ZA, 2 December 1831.

[69] ZA, 16 December 1831.

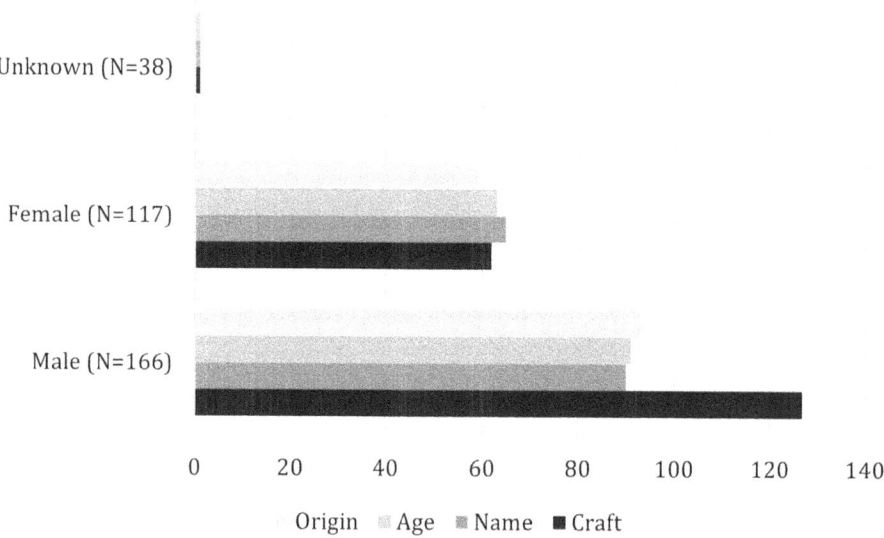

Figure 6.8 Occurrences of variables in slave-specific sale advertisements in *De Zuid-Afrikaan*, Apr. 1830–Nov. 1834, per gender.
Source: ZA, Apr. 1830–Nov. 1834.

his wife Maraar were advertised for sale along with their two daughters Sabina and Theresia in November 1831.[70] That Maraar and her daughters were advertised together is not unusual, what is unusual is the mention of August as a husband and father. We also have a glimpse into a purchase of a whole slave family which prompted the slave owner to sell another enslaved woman he owned at the time.[71] Advertisers did not use enslaved women's potential reproductive labour as a selling point. We found no traces in the advertisements of higher value attached to enslaved women for their childbearing potential, which is in line with Shell and Rama's conclusion that there was no price premium on enslaved women of childbearing age who were sold at auction after the abolition of the slave trade was enforced in 1808.[72] Figure 6.8 shows that the distribution

---

[70] ZA, 18 November 1831.

[71] ZA, 8 February 1833.

[72] R.C.-H. Shell and P. Rama, 'Breeders or Workers? The Structure of Slave Prices in the Cape Colony, 1823–1830', *Safundi* 8, no. 4 (2007): 413–33, 429. On family, see S. Newton-King, 'Family, Friendship and Survival among Freed Slaves', in *Cape Town between East and West: Social Identities in a Dutch Colonial Town*, ed. N. Worden (Auckland Park: Jacana Media, 2012): 153–75; Scully, *Liberating the Family*; Shell, *Children of Bondage*; Shell, 'The Family and Slavery at the Cape', 20–30. Also see: R.W. Fogel and S.L. Engerman, *Time on the Cross: The Economics of American Negro Slavery* (New York: Norton, 1995); H.G. Gutman, *The Black Family in Slavery and Freedom, 1750–1925* (New York: Vintage Books, 1977).

of men's and women's occupations matches the approximately two-to-one gender ratio (166 men to 117 women, excluding February).[73]

Age would probably be mentioned to indicate an enslaved person's general fitness to do his or her job. Origins were perhaps mentioned because buyers had preconceptions about different ethnicities. Origins of imported slaves at the Cape differed widely.[74] Malagasy, African and Indian descent, for example, are all mentioned in the advertisements, and buyers likely selected an enslaved person based on their preconceptions of character and skill being correlated to ethnicity or place of origin.[75] An enslaved person's suitability for a particular job would thus be gauged from more than just the job description.[76] Many of the advertisements use general terms like 'field labourer' or 'housemaid', but some describe the individual as having a specific skill. The thirty-five-year-old Cupido, for example, was advertised by M. C. A. Neethling on 21 October 1831 as 'a skilled cooper and cartwright', who 'also understands something of the blacksmith's craft'.[77] Figure 6.8 shows that a far higher number of enslaved men advertised for sale were described by craft or occupation (127, or 77 per cent) than enslaved women (62, or 53 per cent). Overall, between 50 per cent and 56 per cent of advertisements included descriptions of the enslaved for sale in terms of origin, age and name with enslaved men's occupations the outlier at 77 per cent. The wording of the advertisements attests to the care advertisers took in presenting appealing characteristics to increase the chance of a sale, an idea we find not only foreign but also repugnant now.

The names of enslaved people were mentioned in only 49 per cent of the advertisements. We should not be surprised at this. As Bank observes, 'slavery was, above all, a system of production, a means of labour extraction and exploitation. The rationale behind its establishment and functioning was primarily economic.'[78] Unlike gender, age and origin, a name would tell the buyer nothing about the enslaved person's ability to do a job. As a result, many advertisers may not have thought that including a name was necessary or would add much value. Adding such information would have increased the space needed for an advertisement, which might also have increased the cost to the advertiser. Where advertisers did include names we might speculate that the enslaved were known

---

[73] Notwithstanding thirty-seven individually identifiable enslaved persons who remained unnamed and were merely enumerated within their respective advertisements: ZA, 1 October 1830; ZA, 17 December 1830; ZA, 7 January 1831; 11 March 1831; ZA, 14 October 1831; ZA, 25 November 1831; 17 February 1832; ZA, 14 September 1832; ZA, 29 March 1833.

[74] Armstrong and Worden, 'The Slaves, 1652–1834'; N. Worden, 'Indian Ocean Slaves in Cape Town, 1695–1807', *Journal of Southern African Studies* 42, no. 3 (2016): 389–408.

[75] Shell, *Children of Bondage*, 51–4. What exactly African meant at this point is unclear – while it might be an indicator of Mozambiquan origin, it was likely used to indicate birth in the Cape Colony.

[76] For information on the categorization of labour, see Bank, *The Decline of Urban Slavery*, 20–38. Also see: G. Oostindie, 'Roosenburg en Mon Bijou. Twee Surinaamse plantages, 1720–1870' (Dordrecht, Foris Publications, 1989): 100–10.

[77] ZA, 21 October 1831. '*hy is een bekwame Kuiper, Wagendryver, en verstaat ook wat van het Smids ambacht.*'

[78] Bank, *The Decline of Urban Slavery*, 18.

to neighbours, near or far, and had a reputation, or perhaps some enslaved people in the slave-owning household were singled out for sale and the rest not, and thus naming added specificity.

An advertiser's vernacular

While we could identify common characteristics included in the slave-specific sale advertisements, the design and detail of the advertisements vary within the category. There is no standard layout or formulaic text, indicating that slaveowners and advertisers did not use pre-printed or standardised forms for their advertisements. However, there seems to have been something of a common understanding of how advertisements should be designed, either by the advertisers themselves or the paper's editor. Each advertisement generally started with something of a catchphrase, entirely in capital letters, that simultaneously clarified its purpose, such as 'slave for sale', 'sale of slaves' or just 'for sale'.[79] Capital letters were used to highlight names of advertisers, auctioneers, slave owners and testamentary executors. In contrast, names of enslaved people were often printed in italics.

In describing enslaved people for sale, advertisers seemed to rely on a common language with a limited vocabulary, as displayed in Table 6.1. They used some of the same words to describe enslaved people and their labour alike, but with different meanings according to the context. The adjective '*knap*', for example, which has the general meaning 'attractive', could refer to an enslaved person's physical well-being, as when auctioneers Jones & Cooke advertised a '*knappe*' slave girl,[80] or to the enslaved person's ability to do the job described, as when auctioneers Wolff & Bartman advertised Doortje as a '*knappe*' housekeeper and nanny.[81] Advertisers used '*goed*' regularly: it was used in combination with other phrases to denote good character which we see in 11 per cent of the advertisements; it was used slightly more often to describe labour or skill (14 per cent). There is a clear preference for the word '*kapitaal*' to describe character or person: advertisers used it to describe the person in 17 per cent of the advertisements but for labour/skill in only 1 per cent of the advertisements.

We find descriptions of person and labour occurred in very similar numbers. In some instances, a description is given of either their person, or their labour, and sometimes both are described by the advertiser. Perhaps surprisingly, we find a more varied vocabulary pertaining to the person or character of the enslaved for sale than for his or her labour. In a context where slave labour had formed the backbone of the economy for more than a century, we might expect more emphasis on labour.[82] Just two words – '*bekwaam*' and '*compleet*' – account for over 60 per cent of the labour descriptions.

---

[79] E.g. ZA, 21 May 1830; ZA, 4 June 1830; ZA, 11 June 1830; ZA, 2 July 1830; ZA, 9 July 1830; ZA, 16 July 1830; 23 July 1830, etc.

[80] ZA, 7 September 1832.

[81] ZA, 27 May 1831.

[82] Worden, *Slavery in Dutch South Africa*, 19–40.

The variation in person description is partly due to the varied ways of expressing the same thing: that the enslaved person for sale was well-behaved and of good character. This was expressed as *'deugdzaam'* (virtuous) in 25 per cent of the advertisements, and was the most common description of character. A very similar meaning is captured in *'goed van karakter'* and *'goed van humeur'* while *'goed van gedrag'* and *'onbesproken gedrag'* focus more on behaviour, using it as a marker of character.

Overall, the most common description used was *'bekwaam'* which appeared as a description of labour or skill in 35 per cent of the advertisements. Competence in a particular skill was sometimes emphasised with *'zeer'* (very, extremely) to communicate excellence, such as in the advertisement for the enslaved man Magloek who was described as an 'extremely competent' tailor.[83]

There are some remarkable advertisements that give us glimpses into the lives of the enslaved people who were advertised for sale, like that of Fredrik. Unexpectedly, we see evidence of enslaved people's reputations coming through the newspaper advertisements.[84] Some enslaved people even were 'too well-known to be recommended any further on paper'.[85] This striking reference to the reputation of the enslaved was included in the advertised sale of eleven men, women and children, who, as a group, were described as *'knappe slaven'*. This characteristic, it appears, was well-known in the area. In a similar vein, the enslaved man August, who was advertised alongside his wife and children, was described as 'well-known'.[86] We also found an exceptional advertisement which boasts of the reputation of the household, perhaps relying on the slave-owning family's good standing in the community to make a sale.[87] Broker and agent N. J. Lotz advertised a group of unnamed men, women and children for sale who were 'accustomed to good order', implying that they were used to discipline.

Conversely, bad behaviour is sometimes mentioned in these advertisements, evidence of the individual resistance that Ross describes in the atomised slave community at the Cape.[88] The offences mentioned are minor – clearly an advertiser would not want to mention desertion, theft or assault. We found only one reference to insolence, which we have mentioned earlier.[89] In this advertisement owner W. H. Theunissen offered for sale a nameless yet competent cartwright, born in the Colony and forty-three years of age, 'because he has shown insolence towards his master'. This man was to be sold in private and, most likely because of his alleged insolence, on favourable terms.

One description in the advertisements, of a woman 'in a pregnant condition', gives us another hint of the notion of family which we addressed earlier in the context of

---

[83]ZA, 26 August 1831.

[84]For example ZA, 18 November 1831; ZA, 3 February 1832; ZA, 7 September 1832.

[85]ZA, 27 May 1831. *'De bekwaamheid van deze Slaven is te wel bekend in eenige vordere aanpryzing te vereischen.'*

[86]ZA, 18 November 1831. *'zyn welbekende Slaaf August.'*

[87]ZA, 29 March 1833. *'aan goede orde gewoon zyn'.*

[88]Ross, *Cape of Torments*, 117–21.

[89]ZA, 25 November 1831. *'om dat hy eenige brutaliteit omtrent zynen Lyfheer heeft betoond'.*

Quantitative History and Uncharted People

Table 6.1 An exhaustive list of adjectives slave owners used to describe slaves and their labour in the *De Zuid-Afrikaan* advertisements, Apr. 1830–Nov. 1834.

	Person				*Labour*		
Adjective	Transl.	N	%	Adjective	Transl.	N	%
deugdzaam	virtuous	41	25%	bekwaam	competent	57	35%
kapitaal	capital	28	17%	compleet	complete	42	26%
knap	clever	25	15%	goed	Good	23	14%
gezond	healthy	17	10%	knap	handsome	22	13%
jong	young	16	10%	geschikt	Suitable	12	7%
sterk	strong	9	5%	proper	Good	2	1%
goed van gedrag	well-behaved	8	5%	sterk	Strong	2	1%
goed van karakter	good character	8	5%	volkomen	Utterly	2	1%
welbekend	well-known	4	2%	kapitaal	Capital	1	1%
gene gebreken	no defects	2	1%				
goed van humeur	good tempered	1	1%				
ondeugden	vices	1	1%				
van onbesproken gedrag	of irreproachable character	1	1%				
vrisch en gerond	graceful and rounded	1	1%				
wit	white	1	1%				
zwanger	pregnant	1	1%				
Total		164	100%	Total		163	100%

Source: ZA, Apr. 1830–Nov. 1834.

gender. The advertisement for a nameless young enslaved African girl stated that she was pregnant at the time, and would be sold publicly at auction on 25 April 1833. She and her unborn child could be bought on credit.[90] We might wonder who the father was; we cannot know from the advertisement. Emancipatory legislation increasingly protected (Christian) marriage and motherhood, although these laws were by no means all-encompassing, let alone well-observed.[91]

Our analysis of the timing and placement of the advertisements and the wording used in them reveals the role of the *Zuid-Afrikaan* in the domestic slave trade after the abolition of the international maritime trade. As Table 6.1 shows, newspaper advertisements were full of descriptions and adjectives of enslaved people themselves, not only of their

---

[90] ZA, 19 April 1833. '... *in eenen zwangeren staat*'.

[91] Mason, *Social Death and Resurrection*, 46–52; Scully, *Liberating the Family?* 38–45.

labour. In other words, newspapers not only created a space in which slave owners and advertisers communicated in a common language about renting and buying labour but also fashioned the enslaved themselves to make them, setting descriptions in print to be circulated, unsurprisingly without clear traces of self-determination from the enslaved.

Conclusion

After the abolition of the international maritime slave trade, a domestic market for enslaved people continued in the Cape Colony into the 1830s, with slave property bought and sold until Emancipation Day on 1 December 1834. We have used newspaper advertisements placed in the *Zuid-Afrikaan* as a window onto the final years of this trade, from the paper's first edition in April 1830 until the end of November 1834.

In total, we examined 1,180 advertisements across four categories which included different types of sale and hiring advertisements. We found that over the four-year period under study, the *Zuid-Afrikaan* published an increasing number of advertisements, but this was not driven by advertisements that either explicitly or implicitly included enslaved people for sale or hire. Rather, slave sale advertisements were decreasing relative to other advertisements in the lead-up to emancipation. Breaking this down by category, we found that while general sales with slaves increased, the number of slave-specific sales did not.

A particularly interesting point to come out of our close analysis of 185 slave-specific sale advertisements was the reasons for sale. While we might expect the somewhat formulaic statements that enslaved people were sold not because of insolence or vice but because they were no longer needed, that advertisers included references to the enslaved people's wishes was more surprising and revealed not only a veiled agency on the part the enslaved (and responsiveness by slave owners) but also the role of the newspaper connecting town and countryside to facilitate that move.

In line with Taylor's work, we consider the *Zuid-Afrikaan* as a facilitator of the domestic trade in enslaved people. From April 1830 to the end of November 1834 the newspaper accepted advertisements, paid in advance, in cash, for sales of enslaved people. In this way, the newspaper was the medium which connected the sellers to the pool of potential buyers of slave property. In a few of the advertisements we see the newspaper's office as an important location for information on these sales which then took place elsewhere.

While we cannot establish the extent of the paper's distribution or circulation, Boniface's choice to publish in both English and Dutch surely indicates his desire to reach as wide a readership as possible. Furthermore, the paper was made available to both urban and rural readers. Similarly, we cannot establish from this single newspaper the extent of the domestic market which is brought out in the advertisements. Whether or not *De Zuid-Afrikaan* includes all advertisements of slave sales remains to be seen in future work; it is possible that some advertisers chose to place advertisements in either the *Zuid-Afrikaan* or the *Commercial Advertiser*, not both.

Quantitative History and Uncharted People

Our investigation of the advertisements in the *Zuid-Afrikaan* opens the way for continued research on slave sales in Cape newspapers. Whether or not we see the same advertisements placed in the *South African Commercial Advertiser* will reveal some of the characteristics of the advertisers and the readership – as potential buyers – of each paper. In describing the enslaved for sale, advertisers in the *Zuid-Afrikaan* used a limited vocabulary, applied to both the enslaved person and his or her labour. Descriptions such as *knap* were common. Collecting advertisements from other newspapers to create a larger sample would provide the opportunity to analyse whether or not advertisers shared this vernacular, if and how it changed over time and whether or not there was continuity in the period of apprentice sales (1834–8).

Much more research connecting the newspaper advertisements to other 1830s records will reveal more of what it meant for the enslaved themselves. Auction records will reveal to whom they were finally sold, when, and whether or not families remained intact; slave registers will indicate the sorts of slave holdings from which individually identifiable enslaved were sold, and if and when they were later resold, or manumitted; and court records might highlight those exceptional cases where there was conflict over a sale, whether because of financial issues, or claims to freedom, made by enslaved people like Fredrik, which challenged the seller's right to sell him in the first place.

Bibliography

Armstrong, J.C. and N. Worden. 'The Slaves, 1652–1834'. In *The Shaping of South African Society, 1652–1820*, edited by R. Elphick and H. Giliomee, 75–115. Cape Town: Longman, 1979.

Bank, A. *The Decline of Urban Slavery at the Cape, 1806 to 1843*. Communications 22. Rondebosch: Centre for African Studies, 1991.

Botma, G. 'De Zuid-Afrikaan en die teenstrydighede van die 19de-eeuse Kaapse liberalisme'. *Tydskrif vir Geesteswetenskappe* 62, no. 1 (2022): 91–111.

Cutten, T.E.G. *A History of the Press in South Africa*. Cape Town: National Union of South African Students, 1935.

De Kock, W. *A Manner of Speaking: The Origins of the Press in South Africa*. Cape Town: Saayman & Weber, 1982.

Dick, A. 'Reading Authors of the Enlightenment at the Cape of Good Hope from the late 1780s to the mid 1830s'. *Journal of Southern African Studies* 44, no. 3 (2018): 383–400.

Diedrichs, P. 'Newspapers: The Fourth Estate: A Cornerstone of Democracy'. In *Mass Media for the Nineties: The South African Handbook for Mass Communication*, edited by A.S. de Beer, 71–100. Pretoria: J. L. van Schaik, 1993.

Dooling, W. *Slavery, Emancipation and Colonial Rule in South Africa*. Scottsville, South Africa: University of KwaZulu-Natal Press, 2007.

Du Toit, A.S. and H. Giliomee. *Afrikaner Political Thought: Analysis and Documents, 1780–1850*. Vol. 1. Perspectives on Southern Africa 22. Berkeley: University of California Press, 1983.

Ekama, Kate. 'Bondsmen: Slave Collateral in the 19th-Century Cape Colony'. *Journal of Southern African Studies* 47, no. 3 (2021): 437–53.

Fogel, R.W. and S.L. Engerman. *Time on the Cross: The Economics of American Negro Slavery*. New York: Norton, 1995.

Giliomee, H. *The Afrikaners: Biography of a People*. London: Hurst & Company, 2011.

Greig, George. *The South African Almanac and Directory for the Year 1833*. Cape Town: G. Grieg, 1833.
Gutman, H.G. *The Black Family in Slavery and Freedom, 1750–1925*. New York: Vintage Books, 1977.
King, A. 'Periodical Economics'. In *The Routledge Handbook to Nineteenth-Century British Periodicals and Newspapers*, edited by A. King, A. Easley and J. Morton, 60–74. Abingdon and New York: Routledge, 2016.
Law, G. 'Distribution'. In *The Routledge Handbook to Nineteenth-Century British Periodicals and Newspapers*, edited by A. King, A. Easley and J. Morton, 42–59. Abingdon and New York: Routledge, 2016.
Mason, J.E. *Social Death and Resurrection: Slavery and Emancipation in South Africa*. Charlottesville: University of Virginia Press, 2003.
Meltzer, J.L. 'Slave Sales and Cape Town's Slave Tree Memorial'. *Bulletin of the National Library of South Africa* 73, no. 1 (2019): 17–36.
Meltzer, J.L. 'The Growth of Cape Town Commerce and the Role of John Fairbairn's Advertiser, 1835–1859'. Master's thesis, University of Cape Town, 1989.
Mitchell, L.J. *Belongings: Property, Family, and Identity in Colonial South Africa: An Exploration of Frontiers, 1725–c. 1830*. Gutenberg-e Series. New York: Columbia University Press, 2008.
Newton-King, S. 'The Labour Market of the Cape Colony, 1807–28'. In *Economy and Society in Pre-Industrial South Africa*, edited by S. Marks and A. Atmore, 171–207. London: Longman, 1980.
Newton-King, S. 'Family, Friendship and Survival among Freed Slaves'. In *Cape Town between East and West: Social Identities in a Dutch Colonial Town*, edited by N. Worden, 153–75. Auckland Park: Jacana Media, 2012.
Oostindie, G. *Roosenburg en Mon Bijou: Twee Surinaamse plantages, 1720–1870*. Dordrecht: Foris, 1989.
Picton, L.J. 'NICPRINT-50, Being Some Account of the History of the Printing, Packaging and Newspaper Industry of South Africa, and of the National Industrial Council for Printing, Prepared to Mark the Jubilee of the Council 1919–1969'. Cape Town: Cape & Transvaal Printers, 1969.
Rabe, L. *A Luta Continua: A History of Media Freedom in South Africa*. Stellenbosch: African Sun Media, 2020.
Roelofse, K. 'The History of the South African Press'. In *Introduction to Communication*, edited by L.M. Oosthuizen, 66–118. Cape Town: Juta, 1996.
Ross, R. *Cape of Torments: Slavery and Resistance in South Africa*. London: Routledge & Kegan Paul, 1983.
Ross, R. 'The Last Years of the Slave Trade to the Cape Colony'. *Slavery & Abolition* 9, no. 3 (1 December 1988): 209–19.
Ross, R. *Status and Respectability in the Cape Colony, 1750–1870: A Tragedy of Manners*. African Studies Series 98. Cambridge: Cambridge University Press, 1999.
Scully, P. *Liberating the Family? Gender and British Slave Emancipation in the Rural Western Cape, South Africa, 1823–1853*. Social History of Africa. Portsmouth, NH: Heinemann, 1997.
Shell, R.C.-H. 'The Family and Slavery at the Cape, 1680–1808'. In *The Angry Divide: Social and Economic History of the Western Cape*, edited by W.G. James and M. Simons, 20–30. Cape Town: David Philip, 1989.
Shell, R.C.-H. *Children of Bondage: A Social History of the Slave Society at the Cape of Good Hope, 1652–1838*. Hanover: Wesleyan University Press published by University Press of New England, 1994.
Shell, R.C.-H. and P. Rama. 'Breeders or Workers? The Structure of Slave Prices in the Cape Colony, 1823–1830'. *Safundi* 8, no. 4 (2007): 413–33.

Stellenbosch University digital collections, *De Zuid-Afrikaan*, 9 April 1830–28 November 1834, 235 eds. Available online: https://digital.lib.sun.ac.za/handle/10019.2/1060.

Taylor, J.E. 'Newspaper-Brokered Slave Trade Advertisements in North America, 1704–1807'. *Journal of Slavery and Data Preservation* 2, no. 2 (2021): 36–42.

Tewari, A. 'The Reform Bill (1832) and the Abolition of Slavery (1833): A Caribbean Link'. *Proceedings of the Indian History Congress* 73 (2012): 1140–7.

Watson, R.L. *Slave Emancipation and Racial Attitudes in Nineteenth-century South Africa*. Cambridge: Cambridge University Press, 2012.

Wigston, D. 'A History of the South African Media'. In *Media History, Media and Society*, edited by P.J. Fourie, 2nd ed., 1:3–57. Media Studies. Cape Town: Juta Academic, 2008.

Worden, N. *Slavery in Dutch South Africa*. African Studies Series 44. Cambridge: Cambridge University Press, 1985.

Worden, N. 'Indian Ocean Slaves in Cape Town, 1695–1807'. *Journal of Southern African Studies* 42, no. 3 (2016): 389–408.

Appendix A: Data Collection

Today archival newspapers are digitised *en masse*.[92] This presents researchers with a huge amount of data. Electronic aids such as automated deep learning analysis tools[93] would struggle to cope with the frequent changes in the layout of *De Zuid-Afrikaan* during its formative years as a result of changing editors, different printers, and moving offices. We therefore examined all 235 editions which appeared between the newspaper's first edition in April 1830 and emancipation on 1 December 1834 manually. We read through 9,076 advertisements and analysed 1,180 that referred explicitly or implicitly to enslaved people for hire or sale.[94] We categorised these advertisements into general sales with slaves, slave-specific sales, service hiring request and service hiring offer.

Our four categories are not watertight: some advertisements fit into more than one category. Where this is the case we have chosen a main category, to avoid double counting the number of advertisements. We counted re-publications of the same advertisement towards the number of appearances.

We first used Atlas.ti, to and then constructed a separate dataset for the corresponding numbers, calculations and transcriptions. Following the first language of the newspaper, our dataset consists of all the Dutch-language advertisements extracted from the Dutch advertising section of the *Zuid-Afrikaan*. Based on checking a number of the editions to ascertain whether all advertisements were carried in both Dutch and English, we are confident that by extracting the Dutch advertisements our dataset covers most if not all advertisements for slave sales.

Appendix B: The four advertisement categories

General sale with slaves covers advertisements for public sales of goods that include enslaved people. These sales were often, although not exclusively, advertised by curators and executors of wills, with the goods being sold to the highest bidder, if they had not been privately sold beforehand. Purchases could be paid for at the sale or on credit under good security. Enslaved people are either explicitly mentioned as such in total numbers, or listed individually by their name, age, origin, type of work and, in the case of women only, their children. Very rarely, a single enslaved individual is advertised for sale among other goods, being incorporated in the description of the entire inventory and thus almost indistinguishable from furniture or utensils put up for sale.

---

[92] For example, the British Newspaper Archive, or Delpher by the Royal Library of the Netherlands. Also see: Paul Gooding, *Historic Newspapers in the Digital Age: 'Search All about It!'* (Abingdon and New York: Routledge, 2018): 14–18.

[93] For example, Layout Parser, a unified Python toolkit for deep learning based on document image analysis.

[94] Stellenbosch University digital collections (SUNDigital), De Zuid-Afrikaan (ZA), 9 April 1830–28 November 1834, 235 eds.

Slave-specific sales captures advertisements for public and private sales of enslaved people only. Unlike the general sales with slaves, these advertisements were more often submitted by the owners themselves, which allowed for more varied wording. Again, buyers could pay immediately or on credit. In these advertisements the enslaved people are commonly described in terms of their desirable characteristics. Terms like 'work boy' or 'work girl' are sometimes substituted for the word 'slave', or the individual is reduced to a job description, such as 'cook'. Details are added of the enslaved person's type of work, gender, estimated age, behaviour, any children and the reason for the sale.

Service hiring requests and *Service hiring offers* are advertisements for services to be performed either by free persons or specifically by enslaved persons. These advertisements include a wide variety of descriptions. Some requests for services require free persons to do the work; others specify enslaved individuals or apprentices. The requests are almost entirely reduced to the job description. The offers include slave-specific services and general services offerings. It is not always clear who submitted the advertisements offering slave-specific services, whether the slave owners or perhaps enslaved persons themselves. We applied the service-related categories quite broadly and included any advertisements where there was a possibility of an enslaved person being involved. For example, we included an advertisement which requested several labourers to work on arable land, but we excluded an advertisement by a housekeeper who had arrived at the Cape from England and was offering her services to a reputable family.

CHAPTER 7
DOMESTIC SERVICE IN CAPE TOWN BEFORE THE SECOND WORLD WAR

*Amy Rommelspacher**

Introduction

Approximately one million women in South Africa are today employed as domestic workers.[1] Domestic work is at the centre of debates about privilege and oppression and the legacies of apartheid and colonialism. In this chapter I argue that the employers of domestic workers and coloured women working as domestic workers have been underrepresented and misunderstood in the existing historiography. To remedy this I use new approaches to sources that have not been utilised to study domestic workers or their employees, and focus on Cape Town before the Second World War.

Ena Jansen's book, *Soos Familie* (Like Family), describes the complex relationships involved in domestic employment and created a stir about the persistent social inequality associated with the job.[2] Her research echoes observations made in other studies of female domestics in South Africa, from which the following quotations are a sample:

> The fact that even the poorest of white families might employ an African servant established an incontrovertible racial hierarchy, lessening the likelihood of solidarity in other contexts.[3]

> 'White' women in Cape Town were able to take advantage of their privileged class position to enter higher skilled and paid jobs. Their relatively well paid jobs probably allowed the employment of domestic workers to do the domestic work which was usually their responsibility.[4]

---

*Rommelspacher: Department of History, Stellenbosch University, South Africa.

[1] 'South Africa added 45,000 domestic workers to the economy last year', *Business Tech*, 12 February 2019. Available online: https://businesstech.co.za/news/lifestyle/298946/south-africa-added-45000-domestic-workers-to-the-economy-last-quarter/ (accessed 19 October 2022).

[2] E. Jansen, *Soos Familie* (Pretoria: Protea, 2015): 16.

[3] I. Berger, *Threads of Solidarity: Women in South African Industry* (Bloomington: Indiana Press, 1992): 38.

[4] E. Boddington, 'Domestic Service in Cape Town 1891–1946: An Analysis of Census Reports' (Conference on Economic Development and Racial Domination, University of the Western Cape, Paper 19, October 1984): 8.

Domestic service is often the point of entry to wage employment by newcomers to the job market, but others remain in the job all their lives. The labour itself is generally looked upon in society as inferior, servile, low in status, badly paid; those who can escape up or out, do so where possible. Conversely, it is the weakest and most socially subordinate strata who end up in the job: women, immigrants, ethnic minorities. In South Africa, the people who 'end up' in the job are African women.[5]

Although these claims have been made about domestic service in Cape Town and South Africa, little has been done to understand the extent to which they were true (or not). Understandably, most of the research into the history of domestic work in South Africa takes the perspective of the domestic worker rather than the employer. While domestic work was the most common form of employment for women in England until the Second World War, in South Africa this trend differed by race.[6] For coloured women, domestic work *was* the most common occupation in the Union before and after the Second World War. In 1936, 72 per cent of employed coloured women were domestic workers and by 1946, this was 58 per cent.[7] Although the largest sector of employment for black women was agriculture for the first half of the twentieth century, most academic attention has been on their role as domestic workers. In 1946, 56 per cent of employed black women in the Union worked in agriculture and 37 per cent as domestic servants.[8] Despite most coloured women working as domestic workers for this period, they are missing from South African historiography.

The main source for this chapter is a household survey from 1938–9 that shows who these domestic workers were and who they worked for. This Social Survey of Cape Town was headed by Professor Edward Batson (Professor of Social Science at the University of Cape Town from 1935).[9] The total initial survey, of 2,000 households, represented about 3 per cent of households in the city at the time.[10] For both employers and employees, each

---

[5]D. Gaitskell, et al., 'Class, Race and Gender: Domestic Workers in South Africa', *Review of African Political Economy* 10, nos. 27–8 (1983): 88.

[6]P. Taylor, *Women Domestic Servants 1919–1939* (London and New York: Routledge, 2007).

[7]Union of South Africa. *Union of South Africa Sixth Census, Vol 5, Occupations* (Pretoria: Government Printers, 1938): 105; *Union of South Africa. Union of South Africa Population Census, 7th May 1946, Volume V Occupations* (Pretoria: Government Printer, 1955): 105.

[8]*Union of South Africa Population Census, 7th May 1946, Volume V Occupations*, 191–3.

[9]Batson Collection, Ms, 451. Manuscripts section, Stellenbosch University Library and Information Service. Diverse items including field book, specimens in newspaper envelopes, visitors' cards. University of Cape Town Department of Social Science: Reports and Studies Issued by the Social Survey of Cape Town, Edited by Edward Batson, 'Surveying Methods', 12 March 1944. No. SS9, p. 2.

[10]Ibid. The Department of Social Science at UCT carried out the research and was funded by the Carnegie Corporation. The Carnegie Corporation was founded in 1911 and remains one of the biggest trusts in the world to this day. The benefactor of the corporation, Andrew Carnegie, was born into a poor family in Scotland in 1835. He immigrated to America and when he retired in 1901 he was one of the richest Americans. He founded a number of charitable trusts 'to better the world'. The Carnegie Corporation was involved in a number of efforts to investigate and alleviate poverty in South Africa. Most famously the corporation funded

survey card provides information on wages, homes (size, renting/bond, whether or not it was shared), family composition, occupation, birthplace of head of household and religion, among others. There is also a comments section where the respondents could elaborate on their answers. From this information I was able to investigate the characteristics of employers and employees. For instance, information relating to the age and marital status of domestic workers is useful information that cannot be seen in censuses. As Mbem and de Haas, Chapter 9, show, this information can also be used to investigate the lives of those who migrated to Cape Town from the eastern Cape, who would otherwise be 'uncharted'. I used the survey in conjunction with newspaper and magazine sources. The use of this source, in conjunction with quantitative techniques, enables an understanding of broad patterns of economic behaviour common across households which might otherwise be hidden to qualitative, anecdotal or case-based investigations. I will refer to 'domestic servants' as 'domestics' in this chapter for the sake of brevity and clarity.

I have transcribed just over 1,000 of the survey cards from the Batson Household Survey, representing over 500 coloured (565) and just under 500 white (498) households. The original survey contained 1,017 white households, 834 coloured households and 166 households classified as black or Asian.[11] Since the black households represented such a small part of the survey, only coloured and white household cards have been utilised for this study.

After the introduction, this chapter is divided into four sections. The first section provides an overview of existing assumptions about domestic workers in South African history. The second section investigates whether or not employers of domestic workers in Cape Town met these assumptions, and the third section looks at whether or not domestic workers in Cape Town met these assumptions. The final section concludes with the finding that Cape Town had low rates of employment of domestic workers in the 1930s, contradicting the claim that 'even the poorest of white families might employ an African servant'.[12]

Assumptions about domestic servants in South Africa

The quotations in the previous section epitomise the views of much of the literature on domestic workers in South Africa today. They focus on the exploitative nature of domestic service and focus on black women as domestic workers. Marxist historians

---

two inquiries into poverty in the country – one in the 1920s and 1930s and one in the 1980s. M. Bell, 'American Philanthropy, the Carnegie Corporation and Poverty in South Africa', *Journal of Southern African Studies* 26, no. 3 (2000): 483–4.

[11] E. Batson, ed., 'Surveying Methods', 12 March 1944. No. SS9: 7.

[12] Berger, *Threads of Solidarity*, 38. The term 'coloured' has derogatory connotations in some parts of the world, but in southern Africa it is the accepted and preferred name for people of mixed race. M. Adhikari, *Burdened by Race: Coloured Identities in Southern Africa* (Cape Town: University of Cape Town Press, 2013): viii–ix. In this quote the term 'African' means black, but while this may be true of domestic workers in other parts of the country, in Cape Town many women in domestic service were coloured.

were the first to study domestic workers in South African history and they did so in the 1980s when women's history was an emerging field in the country. Literature written during apartheid emphasises the subjugation of black women and literature written in the post-apartheid period has continued to focus on the impacts of oppression on black women as domestic workers. Some generalisations of the literature produced during the apartheid period include the idea that if women worked, they worked as domestic workers. A *problem* with both sets of literature is that they largely ignore two groups of women: coloured women, many of whom worked as domestic workers (especially in the Cape), and the women who employed domestic workers. Marxist historians have theorised domestic labour as 'a product of the complex operation of race, class, and gender divisions over time'[13] and their work has largely remained focused on just that – theory. In this chapter I seek to understand whether these assumptions about domestics and their employees in South African history were applicable to pre-Second World War Cape Town. My goal is to understand the reality of who employed domestics as well as those who were employed as domestics.

Jacklyn Cock describes domestic work in South Africa as 'a kaleidoscopic institution … as it has involved slaves, San, Khoikhoi, "coloureds", Indians, Europeans and Africans'.[14] She relates how domestic work underwent significant changes from the time of the arrival of Jan van Riebeeck in 1652 to 1980s apartheid South Africa.[15] In the eighteenth and nineteenth centuries, the local indigenous people provided (or were coerced into providing) domestic labour – as they were with other forms of labour. In the Cape most domestic workers were slaves until emancipation in 1834. They were then replaced by emancipated slaves or by European domestic servants, for those who could afford them. As the nineteenth century progressed, with the growth of urban areas and middle- and upper-class society at the Cape, the demand for white servants increased. Immigration schemes and a demand for labour saw over 14,000 British immigrants arrive at the Cape in the 1840s and among these were many domestic servants. Cock notes that these immigrants did not, however, want to stay in domestic service but moved on to other occupations as soon as they could.[16]

By the beginning of the twentieth century domestic work looked different in different parts of South Africa. Gaitskell et al. used census data to show that in 1911 the Cape and Natal had very different gender balances: three quarters of Natal's domestic servants were men and a quarter women, whereas at the Cape they were the reverse, three women

---

[13]Gaitskell, et al., 'Class, Race and Gender', 96. See also: J. Cock, *Maids and Madams: A Study in the Politics of Exploitation* (Johannesburg: Ravan, 1980); C. Walker, ed., *Women and Gender in Southern Africa to 1945* (Cape Town: Philip, 1990); Boddington, 'Domestic Service in Cape Town'.

[14]Cock, *Maids and Madams*, 6.

[15]The earliest evidence we have of a domestic servant at the Cape is the story of Krotoa, a Goringhaikona girl taken into service by the Van Riebeeck family as a companion and child minder. Jansen, *Soos Familie*, 16.

[16]Cock, *Maids and Madams*, 178, 182.

to one man.[17] Although domestic work has been done by a number of different races, existing literature mostly represents black women as domestic workers. Cock argues that from the 1840s to 1880s domestic work went from being a predominantly white occupation to being almost completely black.[18]

The experiences of domestic workers have also been studied anecdotally. Existing literature explains the experience as follows. Entering domestic service usually meant that Xhosa women would have to relocate, moving from their homes in the Eastern Cape to their employer's farm or to areas known as locations in the towns and cities from which they could travel to their employer's home daily. Some would live in, a practice still fairly common in South Africa today. In cities and towns this would entail a domestic worker living in their employer's home or in some kind of dwelling attached to their home or property. These women often lived alone, many of them not returning home to their families more than once a year until their retirement.[19] We do not have statistics of the ratio of domestic workers 'living in' to those who commuted daily.

Perceptions of the relationship between domestic workers and their employers in South African history vary. The extent to which the lives of these domestic workers were intertwined with those of their employers, and especially their employer's children, led to many white South Africans in the past and today referring to 'the help' as family. The image of domestic workers as part of the family has been both promoted and criticised by white scholars. Evidence for this sentiment has largely been anecdotal. Jansen offers the example of the poem 'Amakeia' by A. G. Visser (1878–1929) as encapsulating the perception of black domestic workers as fiercely loyal and protective of the white children in their care.[20]

Existing literature pictures domestic work as a form of employment that was avoided at all costs, entered into only in desperation. There was always more demand for household labour than there was supply and Iris Berger argues that women were hesitant to work in domestic service.

> African families, also fearing exploitation, were reluctant to allow their daughters and wives to enter domestic service; and black women themselves preferred more independent occupations, whether legal or illegal. For coloured women too, the demand for domestic labour generally exceeded the supply; while they predominated among domestic workers at the Cape, 'complaints are rife … of the difficulty of getting good servants'.[21]

---

[17] Gaitskell, et al., 'Class, Race and Gender', 96.

[18] Cock, *Maids and Madams*, 173–8.

[19] Jansen, *Soos Familie*, 55–6.

[20] Cited in Jansen, *Soos Familie*, 58–9. Jansen says this poem still resonates with black and white readers alike today. Cock, however, questions this, arguing instead that relationships between domestic workers and their employers were varied and often strained. Cock, *Maids and Madams*, 87.

[21] Berger, *Threads of Solidarity*, 22.

Berger states that while there were some other forms of employment for white women, this was not case for black and coloured women in the first quarter of the twentieth century. She finds that specific jobs were usually reserved for specific genders and races – although there may not always have been a formal law barring entry.[22]

Although existing literature focuses on black women as domestics, in Cape Town, most domestics in the first half of the twentieth century were coloured women. Gaitskell et al. provide a graph showing that low numbers of African women in Cape Town were counterbalanced by large numbers of coloured women.[23] This was the case until migration of black women to the city and increasing job opportunities in the manufacturing sector for coloured women shifted more black women into domestic service. In 1911, 31 per cent of all domestic workers in South Africa were black women.[24] This changed dramatically over the century and by 1970, 79 per cent of domestics in South Africa were black women.[25] Although they were in the majority before 1911, coloured women as domestic workers have received little research attention.

The 1930s saw coloured domestic workers in Cape Town organise to form the Domestic Employees' Union. Among their complaints, noted by Berger, were a 50 per cent drop in pay over the past ten years, doing double duty in two different households, long and irregular hours, and dishonest employers.[26] Other issues they raised were to do with unsanitary and inadequate accommodation, infrequent holidays and low wages.[27] Their meetings were held in District Six[28] on Wednesday evenings and the union grew out of shortages of domestic workers in the 1930s.[29] The union lasted a number of years, but by 1940 they were struggling to find enough members.

In other parts of the world the employment of domestic servants decreased dramatically with the invention of household appliances. In the United States, for instance, domestic service represented 18 per cent of the female labour force in 1930 but only 8 per cent in 1960.[30] One study finds that in the United States employing domestic workers would make people less likely to buy washing machines. Furthermore, having labour-saving appliances such as washing machines and vacuum cleaners actually

---

[22]Ibid, 23.

[23]Gaitskell, et al., 'Class, Race and Gender', 95–6.

[24]Ibid, 95; Jansen, *Soos Familie*, 67.

[25]Ibid.

[26]Berger, *Threads of Solidarity*, 119.

[27]Ibid.

[28]District Six was a residential area in the centre of Cape Town with mixed-race residents. It was proclaimed a white area in 1966 under the Group Areas Legislation during apartheid. About 55,000 people were displaced over the following two decades and the houses in the area were razed. D.M. Hart, 'Political Manipulation of Urban Space: The Razing of District Six, Cape Town', *Urban Geography* 9, no. 6 (1988): 603–28.

[29]Berger, *Threads of Solidarity*, 119.

[30]G. Bose, T. Jain and S. Walker, 'Women's Labor Force Participation and Household Technology Adoption', *UNSW Economics Working Paper* (2020): 31.

increased labour loads for women, because they were now expected to work outside the home and still do all of the domestic work.[31] South Africa is of course different from the United States in many ways and the uptake of appliances was very slow in South Africa in the twentieth century. While there is much research to be done on the use of appliances in South Africa and the relationship between appliances and the employment of domestic workers, evidence from advertisements shows that this technology was marketed at poorer households that could not afford to employ domestic workers.[32] Rebecca Ginsburg argues that in affluent white households that had appliances, domestic servants were not allowed to use them.[33] The use of appliances in South Africa deserves further research.

It is important to discuss the availability of sources in studying domestics. While writing the history of domestic servants is important, finding informative source material is a barrier. Most existing literature is based on limited qualitative sources, drawing on the experiences of small groups of domestic servants.[34] Exceptions to this are the works by Gaitskell et al. and Cock. Gaitskell et al. base their research on the censuses of 1911, 1921 and 1936, and focus only on black women as domestic servants. Cock's seminal study, *Maids and Madams*, is based on interviews with 175 domestic workers and fifty employers of domestic workers in the Eastern Cape in South Africa. The employers were predominantly white English women and the domestic workers were black Xhosa women.[35] Penelope Hetherington commented on Cock's work, saying that 'the focus is largely on the exploitation and ideology of black women under capitalism, with less attention paid to black women in pre-capitalist societies or to the white women who are the employers'.[36] Despite this being written in 1990, it still encapsulates the trend in literature today about domestic workers in South Africa.

---

[31]Ibid.

[32]R. Ginsburg, *At Home with Apartheid: The Hidden Landscapes of Domestic Service in Johannesburg* (Charlottesville: University of Virginia Press, 2011): 68.

[33]Ibid.

[34]See for instance: D. Gaitskell, '"Christian Compounds for Girls": Church Hostels for African Women in Johannesburg, 1907–1970', *Journal of Southern African Studies* 6, no. 1 (1979): 44–69; J. Yawitch, 'Black Women in South Africa: Capitalism, Employment and Reproduction: Editorial Collective of Africa Perspective' (Hons diss., University of the Witwatersrand, Johannesburg, 1980); D. Gaitskell, 'Housewives, Maids or Mothers: Some Contradictions of Domesticity for Christian Women in Johannesburg, 1903–1939', *Journal of African History* 24, no. 2 (1983): 241–56; I. van der Waag, 'Wyndhams, Parktown, 1901–1923: Domesticity and Servitude in an Early Twentieth-Century South African Household', *Journal of Family History* 32, no. 3 (2007): 259–95.

[35]Cock, *Maids and Madams*, 18.

[36]Penelope Hetherington in her historiography of South African women mistakenly understands that Cock's study was based on 800,000 Black domestic workers in South Africa as a whole. P. Hetherington, 'Women in South Africa: The Historiography in English', *International Journal of African Historical Studies* 26, no. 2 (1993): 254.

The employers of domestic workers in Cape Town before the Second World War

The employment of domestic workers is necessitated by the existence of housework. Sociologist Ann Oakley states that across cultures women who do not work fulltime or employ a domestic worker are themselves usually fulltime domestic workers.[37] Historically, at least in the past two centuries in the Western World, women have been responsible for the majority of housework, and mostly still are. If wives are unable to do this work themselves, for whatever reason, daughters and domestic workers are useful substitutes. Laundry, cooking, cleaning and childcare all need to be done by someone on a daily basis.

A 1937 *Cape Times* article is informative about the relationship between domestic workers and their employers and the domestic work that kept them busy. The late 1930s saw a big drive in South Africa to promote electrical appliances for the home as the Electricity Supply Commission (ESCOM or ESKOM as the electricity supply utility is known today) expanded its power capacity. The author of the article, Josephine Alrick, relates her experience with the 'two-compartment unit with a large enamel-lined washing section and a centrifugal or spin-dryer type of water extractor'[38] she had owned for five years:

> For the first two years I had the machine I did the laundry work myself, for a family of six, with only the assistance of my two young daughters who, I felt, might with advantage be given a little practical training in this branch of housewifery.
>
> I had previously employed a laundry woman for two or more days a week – depending on weather conditions – at 5s. a day, plus two meals and two teas. She refused even to try the new machine, and so did two or three others whom I tried, without success, to induct into my service.
>
> So, like the Little Red Hen of nursery tales fame, I did it myself, saving in wages alone, during the two years hire-purchase period, more than enough to meet the monthly instalments of £1 18s. 6d.[39]

It seems that a housewife could use a washing machine to replace a domestic. Josephine's story suggests that domestics could move in and out of employment relatively quickly. The purchase of a washing machine, and the domestic's willingness to use it, could determine whether or not she stayed employed. At first Josephine saw the washing machine as

---

[37] A. Oakley, *The Sociology of Housework* (London: Robinson, 1974): x.
[38] J. Alrick, 'My Washing Machine Is Five Years Old and Has Cost 2s. 6d. for Repairs', *Cape Times*, 26 January 1937, 8.
[39] Ibid.

something that could be used by a washerwoman but later she saw it as a replacement, with the added benefit of saving money. The anecdote suggests that the introduction of labour-saving technology like washing machines, did affect the employment of domestic workers in Cape Town.

The high numbers of coloured women working as domestics are visible in the Batson Household Survey of 1938-9. The 1936 census showed that just over two thirds (12,706) of all coloured working women in Cape Town were domestics. Of the 3,285 black women over the age of ten in Cape Town, 1,132 were domestics.[40] The next biggest group of coloured working women was sewer/sewing machinist, with 995 women listed as such.[41] In the Batson survey, most coloured women are listed as domestic servants, washerwomen or factory workers. Domestics are described only by gender, title (name of occupation) and race in the household surveys of their employers. The domestics are, however, the only individuals visible in the survey more than once, because they appear in the survey cards of their employers (although their names are not recorded) and in the survey cards of the households they were part of. In the survey cards of their own households, some of them report the name of their employer. Most domestics in white households are coloured women. Only six households list domestics of other races: one household employed Asians, two households employed white women and three employed coloured men.

Less than a third, 153 (31 per cent) of the 498 white households, employed some kind of domestic help, 45 per cent of which were live-in domestics. Three households employed a live-in domestic and a washerwoman, but it was uncommon to employ more than one domestic worker. The rest of white homes in the survey employed domestics who did not live in, listed as: 'domestic servant', 'charwoman', 'washerwoman', 'general servant', 'char and washerwoman', 'general', 'daily' or 'maid'. These are classified into the categories in Table 7.1. In the 565 coloured households in the survey, 105 individuals listed themselves as domestic workers. Only fourteen of coloured households (2 per cent) are listed as employing a domestic. These employers are referred to later in this section. An unpublished work by Kevin Elliott shows that Cape Town had a much lower rate of white homes employing domestic workers than other cities in the Union. He finds that in 1950 only 20 per cent of white homes in Cape Town employed domestic help. The figure in Durban in 1950, the city with the highest rate for the years 1950-90, was just under 75 per cent.[42]

Table 7.1 shows that just over half of white households that employed domestic workers employed daily rather than live-in domestics. Very few of the 153 households (only twelve) employed more than one domestic, with the most common combination being a 'daily' and a washerwoman. Only one household employed a cook and only one a

---

[40] Gaitskell, et al., 'Class, Race and Gender', 101.

[41] *Sixth Census of the Population of the Union of South Africa, Volume V, Occupations*, 1936, 110-11.

[42] K. Elliott, 'The Living Standards of African Female Domestic Workers in South Africa' (Unpublished manuscript, March 2019): 11.

Table 7.1 Types of domestic employees in white households.

	No. of households	Percentage
Only live-in	60	39%
Only daily	77	50%
Only washerwoman	3	2%
Only houseboy	1	1%
Live-in and washerwoman	3	2%
Live-in and cook	1	1%
Daily and washerwoman	8	5%
Total	153	100%

Source: Batson Household Survey, 1938–39.

'houseboy'. Charles van Onselen notes that, as with domestics, 'it is difficult to generalise about the duties of a "houseboy" … duties tended to vary according to the class of employer, the size and age of the family, the number of staff kept and the individual experience and attributes of the servant himself.'[43] Van Onselen finds that in 1905 and 1906 on the Witwatersrand, 'houseboys' and 'housemaids' could expect to earn about the same – a wage between £4 and £5.[44] The household employing the most servants in the survey was that of the Japanese secretary to the Japanese Consul: a cook, a nurse and a general domestic, all of whom were listed as 'Asian' and could perhaps have come to Cape Town with the family.[45] An advertisement in the *Cape Times* in 1937 shows that sometimes couples could be employed together and housed on the employers' premises: 'Cook-General and Houseboy Gardener, married couple preferred, for a modern home in Herschel-road, Claremont. Good wages and excellent quarters. References – Apply Waldorf Restaurant, St. George's Street.'[46] An example of this can also be seen in the Batson survey. I discuss this couple in the next section.

Figure 7.1 illustrates an important phenomenon. One obvious difference I found between white households that employed domestic workers and those that did not was income. Employers of domestics had an average monthly income £9 higher than the non-employers. Berger's view, that 'even the poorest of white families might employ an

---

[43]Research into the lives of 'houseboys' in Johannesburg and the Witwatersrand shows that they were often adult men. Some 'houseboys' did much the same work as domestics did, but others could also be involved specifically related to the kitchen or work outside of the house. C. van Onselen. *New Babylon New Nineveh* (Jeppestown: Jonathan Ball Publishers, 2012): 239–40.

[44]Ibid, 215–16.

[45]Batson Collection, Ms, 451. Manuscripts section, Stellenbosch University Library and Information Service. I refer to the survey cards by their reference number. The Japanese household is Card 1975.

[46]'Situations Vacant', *Cape Times*, 28 June 1937, 2.

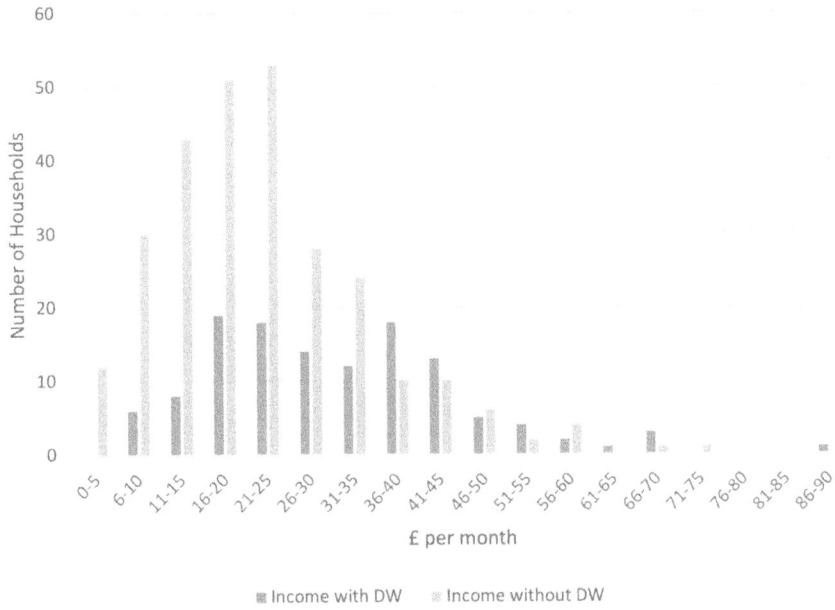

Figure 7.1 Monthly incomes of white households that did and did not employ domestic workers (n = 498).
Source: Batson Household Survey, 1938–39.

African servant' does not therefore seem to be true. I also found a number of households with higher-than-average incomes that did not list domestic workers. The Jardine family, for instance, had a total monthly income of £71 (£49 higher than the monthly average for white households), and they did not list a domestic. The head of the household, Mr Jardine, ran a café called Outspan in Maitland with two of his children – a daughter (thirty-one) and son (thirty). Two of his other children also contributed to the household income: a daughter (twenty-one) who worked as a machinist and a son (twenty-four) who worked as a French polisher. Mrs Jardine was listed as a housewife, and the couple had one school-going son. Mr and Mrs Jardine were Madeira-born and had come to Cape Town in 1899 and 1903 respectively.[47] Although this family could afford to employ a domestic worker, they did not – which seems to indicate that this was not a priority for everyone.

Conversely, I also found households with lower-than-average incomes that did employ domestic workers, though it is possible that not everyone in the household stated their income. Mr and Mrs Weatherly, for instance, were a working couple, with no children, who listed a domestic worker. Mrs Weatherly (twenty-six) worked

---

[47] Card 1372.

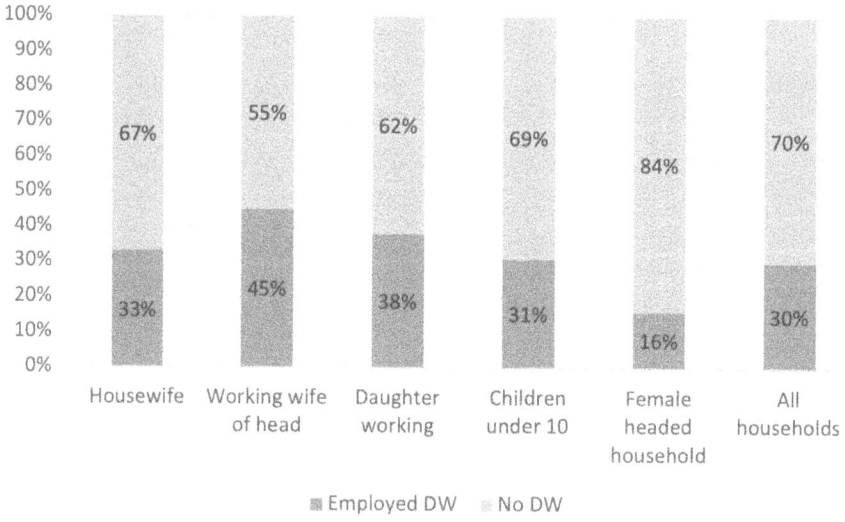

Figure 7.2 Share of different types of white households according to domestic worker employment (n = 153).
Source: Batson Household Survey, 1938/39.

as a typist and her wages were £7 per month. Mr Weatherly (thirty-one) worked as a clerk and his income was not stated in the survey – which meant that their household income appears to be £7 per month.[48] The other households with 'low' monthly incomes employing domestic workers include households headed by retired people who were no longer working and therefore no longer earning an income (or perhaps earning an income from investments). Poorer white families in the Batson surveys did not, however, hire domestics. The fact that fewer than a third of the white households in the survey reported employing a domestic further contradicts Berger's view.[49]

Another difference between white employers and non-employers was the occupation of the wife of the household head. Some clear trends can be seen in Figure 7.2. The small group of households (29 of 498) with a working wife of the household head had the highest rate of domestic worker employment. Households with children under the age of ten were less likely to employ domestic workers. Those with a working daughter were fairly likely to do so, as were the 65 per cent of households with housewives (the wife of the household head not working outside the home). Working outside the home seems to have been a strong reason for a woman to seek help with the housework. Female-headed households, which were also houses with lower incomes, were the least likely to employ a domestic worker.

---

[48]Card 1822.
[49]Berger, *Threads of Solidarity*, 38.

The employment of a domestic also seems to have freed young unmarried women living with their parents to engage in an occupation outside of the home. Young women working outside of the home, instead of staying at home and learning to be a housewife, were a concern in the media at the time.[50] But the survey shows that in Cape Town young unmarried white women's work was more valuable outside of the home. Their employment outside of the home was more beneficial for their household than being involved in domestic duties. Since it was the wealthier households that employed domestics, this could mean that young women in those households were more likely to be expected to have a job before marriage, or that those households were wealthier because the unmarried daughters worked. Otherwise, this could indicate that these young women got a job in order to pay a domestic to do the work that they would otherwise have been doing in an unpaid capacity.

Children in white households could and did help with domestic work when they were old enough. Figure 7.2 shows that households did not rely on domestic workers to a greater extent when they had children under ten. It is clear, however, that on leaving school the sons and daughters were expected to find a job, whether their family needed the income or not: the survey asked respondents to state (in the comments section) whether children were living in the home who had left school but were not working. Miss Canning (nineteen), for instance, was listed as a non-wage earner, but she clarified that she 'helps at home' and her brother (eighteen) was 'awaiting appointment to S.P.S. Battalion'.[51] It appears that daughters were expected to help in the home, while sons were not. There is not a single case, in white or coloured households, where a son was described as helping in the home. Also noted were daughters of school-going age but not attending school. A fifteen-year-old girl, for instance, was described as having 'passed Std.VI and helps at home'.[52] She was part of a family of seven living together in one house with only two bedrooms, which could have required much domestic labour. There are also indications of family members helping the domestic. An example of this is Mrs M. van Niekerk's family of seven. Her fourth sister, the only one in the household not working outside the home, cared for their sickly mother and the comment explained that she helped the domestic with housekeeping.[53]

Households with domestics were slightly more likely to have a husband and wife working than those without domestics.[54] Female headed households were less likely to employ domestics. Only 76 of the 498 white households were headed by women. As Figure 7.2 shows, 16 per cent of these employed a domestic servant of some kind. One

---

[50] A. Rommelspacher, 'The Everyday Lives of White South African Housewives: 1918–1945' (MA diss., Stellenbosch University, Stellenbosch, 2017): 93.

[51] Card 1607.

[52] Card 1685.

[53] Card 1303.

[54] Of the working women in households employing domestic workers, 22 per cent were the wife of the working head of the household, which is higher than the 18 per cent for all households.

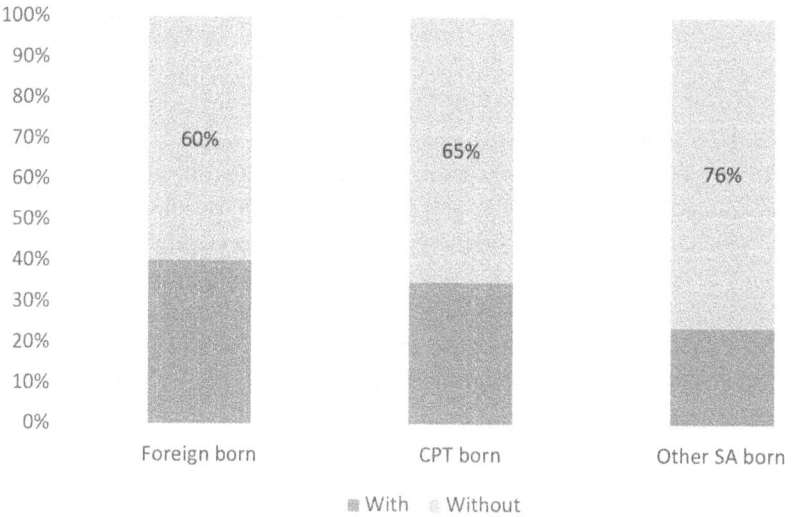

Figure 7.3 Birthplaces of white household heads with and without a domestic worker, that is the employment of domestic workers according to birthplace of white household head.
Source: Batson Household Survey, 1938–9.

example was Mrs van Niekerk's household, mentioned above. She was forty years old in 1938, unmarried, working as a teacher, and living with her widowed unemployed mother, unemployed younger sister, nephew attending university, two younger sisters who both worked as typists and an unmarried male lodger. None of the household members' incomes were stated. They employed a daily servant to clean the four-bedroom home they rented. An example of a female-headed household without a domestic worker was that of Mrs Johanna Croker, aged fifty, a divorcee who ran her own boarding house. At the time of the survey, she provided lodging for two working men (both over the age of sixty) and one non-working woman in her twenties who was married to one of the lodgers. Mrs Croker's income was not stated, but it is conceivable that she could not afford to pay a domestic servant to help with the boarding house and therefore did all the housework herself. Despite the fact that she did not employ any domestic help, she lived in a four-bedroomed house which she rented which also contained two '"servants" rooms'.[55]

I found clear differences between the households that could and could not afford to employ domestics, between the types of households that employed them, and between the employers' birthplaces. Of the 153 white households listed as employing domestic workers, only forty-eight had a household head born in Cape Town. This means that 105 (69 per cent) of these household heads had moved to Cape Town from elsewhere in South Africa or immigrated from another country. Figure 7.3 shows that immigrants

---

[55]Card 1915.

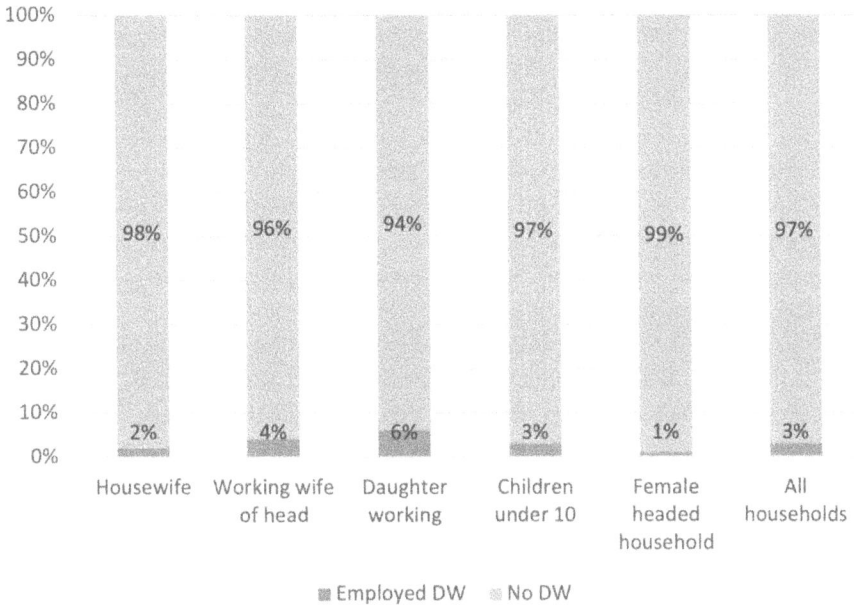

Figure 7.4 Share of different types of coloured households according to domestic worker employment.
Source: Batson Household Survey, 1938–9.

were more likely to employ domestic servants than other white households. One example is the Jurowecki household. Mr and Mrs Jurowecki had come to Cape Town from Poland in 1927. Although they employed a domestic servant once a week, their living situation seemed difficult. They did not have any children, but they shared a flat with other families. Mr Jurowecki worked as a baker and his wife was very ill. She noted that they could 'barely manage' because Mr Jurowecki had to send money home to his aged parents in Poland.[56]

The Batson survey recorded only a few coloured homes employing domestic workers. I compared their characteristics with those of the white households employing domestic workers. Of the 565 coloured households, only fourteen employed domestic workers, representing 3 per cent of coloured households – a much lower rate than that of white households. Of these fourteen, four had a working wife of the household head. Figure 7.4 shows that the trends of the types of households employing domestic workers for coloured households were similar to those of white households. Households with working daughters and working wives of the head were more likely to employ a domestic servant, just as with white households. For coloured households, unlike white

---

[56] Card 1995 (1/2).

households, having a housewife meant that a household was less likely to employ a domestic servant. More than half (55 per cent) of the domestics employed by coloured households were live-in, which is a higher rate than for white households. The other 45 per cent were daily domestic workers.

Just like the white households, the coloured households employing a domestic worker had a higher average monthly income, £22 a month as opposed to £12. The difference in income between those employing domestic workers and those that did not is similar to that of the white group, despite the big difference in average household incomes. Although the low numbers do represent a challenge, some examples may serve to illustrate the differences between white and coloured employers of domestic workers. One coloured household employed a domestic and also had a member of the household working as a domestic. In this household Mr E. Ford (thirty-five) worked as a woodchopper. His wife (thirty-three) worked as a cook. Their eldest daughter (fifteen) worked as a domestic servant and the couple had six other younger children living at home. They employed a live-in 'general servant'. The family's total monthly income was just over £7, which was lower than the average for coloured households. Mrs Ford contributed the most, bringing in just under £4 herself. This made it worthwhile for her to employ a servant to do the housework and care for the children, as most domestics earned less than £4 a month.[57]

What is clear from the analysis of the employers of domestics is that not all white households could afford to employ a domestic, which contradicts a statement made by Berger. Households with a working wife of household head and/or a working unmarried daughter of the household head were more likely to employ domestics than other households. This agrees with Boddington's statement that the employment of domestics freed white women in Cape Town to earn money outside of the home.

Domestic workers in Cape Town's coloured community before the Second World War

Of the 565 coloured households, seventy-nine had a member of the household working as a domestic worker. This section investigates whether the assumptions made about domestic workers in existing literature applies to coloured women working in Cape Town. I look at what these women did, who they worked for and what they earned. These women listed themselves as 'domestic', 'general', 'domestic servant', 'housemaid' and 'charwoman', among other terms. The survey shows that the type of work done by domestics varied and that their positions were diverse and insecure. For instance, Sara Jacobs was a widow who listed herself as 'cleaner and caretaker as well as charwoman' though she only named one employer.[58] Because of a lack of sources recording the

---

[57] Card 1500.
[58] Card 2501.

everyday lives of domestic workers and because of variation between employers and situations, it is hard to know exactly what an average workday looked like for domestic servants. An excerpt from *Die Huisvrou*[59] (The Housewife) women's magazine, which was aimed at equipping housewives in South Africa, shows the types of tasks a live-in domestic could be expected to complete in a day.

Schedule for the servant:

Work begins at 07:00 in the morning
Prepare and serve breakfast
Discuss the meals of the day with the mistress of the house
Normal housework
Prepare and dish the midday meal
Organise the children
Rest until afternoon tea/coffee
Prepare and serve supper
Free time after supper and organise the kitchen
Sleep at 21:00[60]

The comment section of the Batson survey provides real-life glimpses into nature of the arrangements domestic servants had with their employers. Mrs Williams (forty-nine), for instance, worked as a 'char and washerwoman' for 'various' employers. She was a widow and lived with her four children, the eldest of whom was fifteen. She earned £1 4s. 6d. a week and they all lived in one room of a house. They shared a kitchen with the ten other households residing in the same building. Her fifteen-year-old son sold newspapers and she worked five days a week at different houses.[61] Bickford-Smith et al. describe one domestic worker's relationship with her employers. These employers ranged from a temporary resident from Britain who treated her like a person, lending her books and allowing her baby into the house, to others, such as a 'screeching' Greek immigrant for whom she worked for over 18 hours a day, who referred to her as 'the girl'.[62] Many coloured women in the survey worked in two or more homes during the week, and the survey cards of those who employed domestics show that it was common for employers to employ domestic help once or twice a week.

---

[59] *Die Huisvrou* was a women's magazine compiled and published in Cape Town. It was in publication from 1922 to 1976. Its circulation, upon closure in 1976, was 12,000 copies a month. L. Rabe, 'Die Ontstaan en Ontwikkeling van Sarie Marais as Massatydskrif vir die Afrikaanse Vrou' (MA diss., Stellenbosch University, Stellenbosch, 1985): 8; A. Rommelspacher, 'Food, Nutrition and the Afrikaans Housewife in Die Huisvrou, 1922–1945', *Historia* 65, no. 2 (2020): 44.

[60] Rommelspacher, 'Food, Nutrition and the Afrikaans Housewife', 45.

[61] Card 1894 (9/11).

[62] V. Bickford-Smith, E. van Heyningen and N. Worden, *Cape Town in the Twentieth Century: An Illustrated Social History* (Claremont: David Philip, 1999): 194.

Some comments reveal the domestics' varied daily and weekly routines and show that how much work they did depended on who they worked for. Mrs L. Davids (thirty-one) worked as a 'domestic' and did not disclose the name of her employer. She had a husband and three children and they were in the process of buying the house they were living in at the time of the survey. She said she 'comes home daily for 2 hours in the afternoon and sleeps at home'.[63] Another domestic explained that she 'comes home each evening and on Wednesdays at 2 P.M.'.[64] Other descriptions included the daughter-in-law of the head of a household doing 'char' work one day a week.[65] Another comment reveals the life and routine of a young domestic servant who lived in. Miss K. Baxter (twenty-five) lived alone in a bedroom in a shared house when she was not working as a live-in servant for the Woodhear family in Clifton. The survey conductor wrote that she 'does not cook on the premises for she has her meals at place of work' and that she 'comes home to sleep while the employers are away on holiday, otherwise she comes home about 3 times a week'.[66] This comment shows that in Cape Town some live-in domestic servants did go home a few times a week. Because these domestics were not migrant workers, their families lived close enough to visit frequently, which is something that made live-in domestic work in Cape Town different to that of domestic work in other cities. The comments show that the domestic workers' type of work, hours of work and income varied greatly.

The demographics of the domestics in Cape Town also varied considerably. I found no distinct type but rather a broad spectrum of ages, relationships and positions in households. The household headed by John Louw, for instance, had three wage earners: Mr Louw himself, and his mother and mother-in-law, both of whom were in their fifties and worked as domestics.[67] A number of households with a member of the household working as a domestic had two wage earners – one being the male head of household and the other their daughter working as a domestic. Mrs Farquhar, a widow, worked as a washerwoman and lived with her two unmarried daughters, both of whom worked as domestics.[68] There were also men working as domestics and couples who both worked for a family. An example of the latter is Jimmy Lucas (thirty-five) and his wife (thirty-five). Jimmy was listed as a 'houseboy' and Mrs Lucas was the highest earning domestic worker in the survey, with a salary of £12 a month. Domestic work was not something done by a particular demographic of coloured women (or men) in Cape Town at this time but a form of employment open to anyone willing to engage in it and something that coloured women entered into as and when they needed employment.

---

[63] Card 1534.
[64] Card 1542.
[65] Card 1051.
[66] Card 2022 (2/2).
[67] Card 1180.
[68] Card 2081 (1/2).

Working outside the home as a domestic reduced a person's time for work in the family home. The comments section of the survey cards often states how the rest of a family would operate when someone in the household, usually a wife or daughter, was working as a domestic, and who in the household would be responsible for 'helping in the home'. One explained that the daughter of a particular domestic worker was 'too delicate to go to work so cares for household in mother's absence'.[69] Mrs Fester (fifty-three), as another example, was a widow who worked as a 'domestic servant' and 'cook' for Mrs Du Toit. She and her daughter (eighteen) both worked outside the home while her mother (eighty-three) cared for the home.[70] In some households, the wife of the head of household would stay at home as a housewife and while a daughter worked outside the home as a domestic, she would enlist the help of other, usually younger, daughters in the home. An example of this is the August household. Mr and Mrs August had ten children, all living at home. Their eldest daughter (sixteen) worked as a 'housemaid' and their next oldest daughter (fourteen) helped with the housework.[71]

Without personal testimonies or interviews with domestics and their employers (as Jacklyn Cock used later in the twentieth century) it is hard to get a clear picture of the relationships between employer and employee. However, I was able to get some idea of this by matching the cards of a domestic servant and her employer (only possible, of course, in cases where the domestic stated the employer's name). An example of this is Mrs Williams (forty-one), a domestic worker who lived with her unemployed husband and eleven-year-old son and worked as a 'charwoman'. She listed her employers as Mrs Johnson and Mrs Geldenhuis and she earned less than £1 a month (about £65 or R1350 in today's money) working for them. At the time of writing, in 2022, the minimum wage in South Africa for domestic workers was approximately R23.19 an hour or R3,7100 a month. The family's only other source of income was Mr Williams's pension of £2 a month. The Williams family rented a room which included the use of a kitchen in a home shared with five other households. The comments section mentions their difficult circumstances and Mrs Williams explained that her earnings varied according to the amount of work her employers required of her and that she 'has to work v hard to keep things together'.[72] I found a card with a Mrs Johnson that could be Mrs Williams's employers. Mrs Johnson's husband was a constable and he earned £19 a month. Mrs Johnson did not list an occupation. The couple had a two-year-old daughter at the time of the survey. They said they employed a coloured female servant to clean their rented three-bedroomed home.[73]

The varied nature of domestic work in Cape Town is also reflected in the wages domestics listed in the survey. What women could earn fluctuated wildly and depended

---

[69] Card 1219 (3/3).
[70] Card 2102.
[71] Card 1087.
[72] Card 1888 (4/5).
[73] Card 1973 (1/2).

on their employer. Mr John Stevens said that his daughter's earnings as a domestic depended on the amount of work she got. Sometimes she worked only one day in a week, at a rate of four shillings and sixpence, and sometimes she worked three days in a week at different rates because she was working more days in the week.[74] While it was often the employers who determined how much a domestic worked, one of them said her work depended on the weather: she 'does charring at Sea Point. Depends on weather, how many days per week she works'.[75] Young girls could work outside the home as domestic servants and live with their employers, but still be linked to the parent household and aid their families financially. One such case read as follows: 'Support from daughter – this is another young daughter (20) in domestic service, who sleeps in at her work. She gives No 9 [head of household] her earnings of £1-10 pm but No 9 must also clothe her out of that sum.'[76]

Coloured households with a member working as a domestic had a lower average monthly income than other coloured households, £9 as opposed to £11. I did, however, find some exceptions. Two households with a member working as a domestic earned far more than the average. One of these consisted of the head (twenty-five), who worked as a 'delivery boy', his wife (twenty-four), working as a domestic, and the head's brother (twenty-four), a labourer for ESCOM. Together they earned £22 a month.[77] The other, with four wage earners, brought in £31 a month. The highest earner was the head of the household (fifty-seven), who worked as a salesman and earned £16 a month. The other three wage earners were his son and two daughters, one of whom worked as a domestic.[78]

Domestics often contributed their wages in households where a number of members were contributing. In the 1980s Boddington noted that:

> The Cape Coloured family in urban areas very often forms an earning unit, the income of the parents and one or more of the children being pooled to meet household needs. It does not appear to be exceptional for the contributions of a mother and daughter from domestic service or the washing of clothes and similar work to be as important as those of the 'chief' wage earner, the father.[79]

The Batson survey shows that these 'earning units' were common in white households too, and that it was rare for the father to be the main wage earner in coloured households. Instead, in many cases the woman working as a domestic was also the household head, and the other wage earners in the household were their family and their children – often daughters working as domestic workers themselves.

---

[74] Card 1881 (2/3).

[75] Card 1074 (1/3).

[76] Card 1949 (2/3).

[77] Card 2843 (1/2).

[78] Card 2078.

[79] Boddington, 'Domestic Service in Cape Town', 4.

I found many examples of households where at least one member of the household was a domestic and there was a sick or invalid member of the household. Of the households with a domestic worker, 10 per cent mentioned the ill health of a member of the household: 'did not work fully owing to wife's illness',[80] 'has lung trouble, does not go to school',[81] 'too delicate to work',[82] 'too sickly to work. Waiting to go to hospital for operation, cannot work again'[83] and 'cripple from birth'.[84] The details of the women working to provide a living for their ill or infirm family members provide further insights into their lives and the way their working life affected their home life. One woman working as a 'domestic' for 'various' employers was the only wage earner in the household and a comment says her husband was 'mentally deficient since the war and for 7 years he has been out of employment because of this defect'.[85] Mrs Fontaine (thirty-five) was a widow who worked as a 'charwoman' in the Gardens area of the city headed a household made up of herself and her daughter (sixteen) who was listed as being 'Simple – unable to get work'.[86] The comment on the card also notes that although Mrs Fontaine was not a live-in domestic, she worked until after six in the evening every day. Mrs Fontaine's sister lived nearby and looked after her daughter during the day. It appears that domestic workers often worked more than five days a week, as the comment says Mrs Fontaine 'worked only 5 days last week'.[87]

The survey contains details of the coloured households' origins. Figure 7.5 shows the birth places of all coloured household heads and compares households with and without a member who worked as a domestic. The former were more likely to have been born in other parts of South Africa and moved to Cape Town. Of the households with a household head born in other parts of the country, 22 per cent had a member who was a domestic worker, as opposed to 17 per cent whose household head was born in Cape Town. This could indicate a few things. It shows that upon arriving in the city, domestic work was an easy job to obtain. It could suggest that, as others have shown, that domestic service was entered into by those most desperate for work. If given a choice, women would work as something else.[88] It could indicate that working as a domestic

---

[80]Card 1051.

[81]Card 1285 (2/3).

[82]Card 1219 (3/3).

[83]Card 1049.

[84]Card 1471 (3/3).

[85]Card 1235 (3/3).

[86]Card 2098.

[87]Card 2098.

[88]Iris Berger writes that women still chose to avoid certain jobs: 'When white and coloured women chose the mechanised routine of factory jobs over domestic service, and when black women struggled to maintain the viability of casual home-based economic activities, they were striving to assume responsibility for their own lives and for the well-being of their families in an increasingly hostile environment.' Berger, *Threads of Solidarity*, 47.

Figure 7.5 Birthplaces of coloured household heads comparing households that did and did not have someone working as a domestic help.
Source: Batson Household Survey, 1938-9.

was often something done by those who were relatively new to the city, and therefore an occupation that was easy to move into, but not one that they wanted to stay in. Coloured women born in Cape Town were probably more likely to have had more options and thus chose other occupations available to them. If the head of the household was born in Cape Town, they were more likely to have access to better jobs than those who had moved to the city more recently.

Conclusion

Existing research of domestic workers in South African history makes assumptions about domestic workers and their employers without providing substantial evidence to support the assumptions. One of the assumptions is that in the past most white households employed domestic workers in South Africa. This was not the case in Cape Town just before the Second World War. This chapter used the Batson Household Survey to investigate domestic service in Cape Town in the late 1930s and, importantly, who employed domestics. I found that only 18 per cent of the coloured households in the survey had a female member who worked as a domestic servant and only 31 per cent of the white households employed some form of domestic worker. South African literature has said little about the type of people employing domestic workers – or, in other words, who employed domestic workers. I found that white households employing domestic workers earned £9 more per month than those that did not – which shows that not everyone could afford to employ domestic help. Some coloured households also employed domestic workers and their monthly income was £12 higher than the average monthly income for coloured households. It is clear that only those with a certain income could and would employ domestic workers.

The types of domestic workers employed differed between households. A substantial 45 per cent of white households employing domestics employed live-in domestics. For both white and coloured households, I found that those with working wives of the household heads and working daughters were more likely to employ domestic workers. This confirms the idea that employing a domestic enabled women to earn money by working outside of the home. Surprisingly, households with children under the age of ten were less likely than other household types to employ a domestic. Foreign-born white household heads were most likely to employ domestic servants while those born in South Africa but outside of Cape Town were least likely to do so.

The domestics themselves occupied varying positions in their employer's homes. It is hard to generalise the experience of coloured women as domestic workers because of the extent to which their situations differed. The Batson survey shows that one woman could work for a number of employers concurrently and that the number of days they worked changed from week to week and could be affected by the needs of their employers, or even by the weather. The demographics of domestic servants also varied considerably: domestic workers included very young women living with their parents, widowed women and their daughters, older female relatives forming a household together and young single women living alone. Comparing the average monthly income of coloured households showed that those with a member working as a domestic earned less per month than those that did not have a member of the household that was a domestic worker. The birthplaces of the household heads also revealed that those born in Cape Town were less likely to have a member of the household working as a domestic servant than those born in other parts of South Africa.

This work has found evidence that some of the assumptions about domestics and their employers in South African history are applicable to Cape Town before the Second World War, while others are not. Not all white households employed domestics, but if they did, employing a domestic enabled white women to earn money by working outside of the home. White women were freed from domestic work by the employment of domestics. An assumption about domestic workers themselves is that the 'weakest and most socially subordinate strata' worked as domestics. This is confirmed in that the domestics were some of the lowest paid women in the survey and their employment was uncertain and ever-changing.

Bibliography

Adhikari, M. *Burdened by Race: Coloured Identities in Southern Africa*. Cape Town: University of Cape Town Press, 2013.

Bell, M. 'American Philanthropy, the Carnegie Corporation and Poverty in South Africa'. *Journal of Southern African Studies* 26, no. 3 (2000): 481–504.

Berger, I. *Threads of Solidarity: Women in South African Industry*. Bloomington: Indiana Press, 1992.
Bickford-Smith, V., E. van Heyningen and N. Worden. *Cape Town in the Twentieth Century: An Illustrated Social History*. Claremont: David Philip, 1999.
Boddington, E. 'Domestic Service in Cape Town, 1891–1946: An Analysis of Census Reports'. Conference on Economic Development and Racial Domination, University of the Western Cape, Paper 19, October 1984.
Bose, G., T. Jain and S. Walker, 'Women's Labor Force Participation and Household Technology Adoption'. *UNSW Economics Working Paper* (2020).
Cock, J. *Maids and Madams: A Study in the Politics of Exploitation*. Johannesburg: Ravan, 1980.
Elliott, K. 'The Living Standards of African Female Domestic Workers in South Africa'. Unpublished manuscript, March 2019.
Gaitskell, D. '"Christian Compounds for Girls": Church Hostels for African Women in Johannesburg, 1907–1970'. *Journal of Southern African Studies* 6, no. 1 (1979): 44–69.
Gaitskell, D. 'Housewives, Maids or Mothers: Some Contradictions of Domesticity for Christian Women in Johannesburg, 1903–1939'. *Journal of African History* 24, no. 2 (1983): 241–56.
Gaitskell, D., J. Kimble, M. Maconachie and E. Unterhalter. 'Class, Race and Gender: Domestic Workers in South Africa'. *Review of African Political Economy* 10, nos. 27–28 (1983): 86–108.
Ginsburg, R. *At Home with Apartheid: The Hidden Landscapes of Domestic Service in Johannesburg*. Charlottesville: University of Virginia Press, 2011.
Hart, D.M. 'Political Manipulation of Urban Space: The Razing of District Six, Cape Town'. *Urban Geography* 9, no. 6 (1988): 603–28.
Hetherington, P. 'Women in South Africa: The Historiography in English'. *International Journal of African Historical Studies* 26, no. 2 (1993): 241–69.
Jansen, E. *Soos Familie*. Pretoria: Protea, 2015.
Oakley, A. *The Sociology of Housework*. London: Robinson, 1974.
Rabe, L. 'Die Ontstaan en Ontwikkeling van Sarie Marais as Massatydskrif vir die Afrikaanse Vrou'. MA diss., Stellenbosch University, Stellenbosch, 1985.
Rommelspacher, A. 'The Everyday Lives of White South African Housewives: 1918–1945'. MA diss., Stellenbosch University, Stellenbosch, 2017.
Rommelspacher, A. 'Food, Nutrition and the Afrikaans Housewife in Die Huisvrou, 1922–1945'. *Historia* 65, no. 2 (2020): 38–60.
Taylor, P. *Women Domestic Servants, 1919–1939*. London and New York: Routledge, 2007.
Van der Waag, I. 'Wyndhams, Parktown, 1901–1923: Domesticity and Servitude in an Early Twentieth-Century South African Household'. *Journal of Family History* 32, no. 3 (2007): 259–95.
Van Onselen, C. *New Babylon, New Nineveh*. Jeppestown: Jonathan Ball Publishers, 2012.
Walker, C., ed. *Women and Gender in Southern Africa to 1945*. Cape Town: Philip, 1990.
Yawitch, J. 'Black Women in South Africa: Capitalism, Employment and Reproduction: Editorial Collective of Africa Perspective'. Hons diss., University of the Witwatersrand, Johannesburg, 1980.

Primary Sources

Alrick, J. 'My Washing Machine Is Five Years Old and Has Cost 2s. 6d. for Repairs'. *Cape Times*. 26 January 1937, 8.
Business Tech. 'South Africa Added 45,000 Domestic Workers to the Economy Last Year'. 12 February 2019. Available online: https://businesstech.co.za/news/lifestyle/298946/south-africa-added-45000-domestic-workers-to-the-economy-last-quarter (Accessed 19 October 2022).

Cape Times. 'Situations Vacant'. 28 June 1937, 2.
Stellenbosch University Library and Information Service. Batson Collection, Ms 451. Manuscripts.
Union of South Africa. *Union of South Africa Sixth Census of the Population of the Union of South Africa, Vol. 5, Occupations*. Pretoria: Government Printer, 1936.
Union of South Africa. *Union of South Africa Population Census, 7th May 1946, Vol. 5, Occupations*. Pretoria: Government Printer, 1955.

CHAPTER 8
FEMALE INVESTORS AT THE CAPE, 1892–1902
Lloyd Maphosa* and Edward Kerby**

Introduction

In 2014, an investment company founded by women, declared 'invest like a woman because money is power'.[1] Its calls for women to use financial markets to attain economic freedom are, however, not unique to the twenty-first century; the slogan also resonates with the objectives of women across many British colonies during the late Victorian period. Then and now, women are often paid less than men for the same work, face gender stereotypes or usually bear the brunt of domestic work and childcare.[2] We use newly transcribed limited liability company records to shine a light on how joint stock companies in the late nineteenth century may have provided similar opportunities to advance women towards economic freedom. Along with Chapter 7, our analysis provides insight into women's economic activity albeit in a previous era.

Limited liability, the core principle of the joint stock company, was hailed as a revolutionary technology when it was first introduced in the nineteenth century.[3] Prior to its inception, financial losses in business ventures trickled down to the personal property of business owners. To safeguard against this, it was decided to consider the persons composing a company as acting not together but as an entity. In a limited liability business partnership, the action would thus be independent of themselves.[4] When the English Joint Stock Company Act of 1844 was promulgated, business relations changed in Britain as losses in joint business arrangements were now limited to the amount each partner or shareholder contributed towards the venture.[5] This changed the nature of

---

*Maphosa: Department of History, Stellenbosch University, South Africa.
**Kerby: Department of History, Stellenbosch University, South Africa.

[1] *Ellevest: A Financial Company for Women*, 2014. Available online: www.ellevest.com (accessed 15 August 2019).

[2] K. Leaver, *The Financial Power of Your Femininity*, 2017. Available online: http://www.future women.com/wealth/financial-power-femininity (accessed 15 August 2019).

[3] J. Micklethwait and A. Wooldridge, *The Company: A Short History of a Revolutionary Idea* (New York: Modern Library, 2003).

[4] C.A. Cooke, *Corporation, Trust and Company: An Essay in Legal History* (Manchester: Manchester University Press, 1950).

[5] Micklethwait and Wooldridge, *The Company*.

the capital market, creating greater access to smaller parcels of shares with downside risks limited to the initial equity value. The practice of buying and selling shares was no longer limited to wealthy merchants, capitalists and businessmen, but could be extended to people of moderate means and those who had been deliberately excluded from most economic activities. Women featured prominently among the new investors.

During the mid-Victorian era in Britain, women were at the centre of Parliamentary debates about the morality and advisability of making limited liability available to joint stock companies. Because of their perceived vulnerability and lack of business prowess, they were viewed as victims of joint stock companies.[6] James Freshfield, solicitor to the Bank of England from 1820 to 1840, confirmed this earlier perception when he referred to 'the loss and ruin in which persons ignorant of business, particularly ladies and clergy, have been involved by attractive baits held out by speculators in the form of shares'.[7] Women were perceived to be short of funds, like the clergy, many of whom barely survived on small stipends, and, worse, lacking judgement on financial matters. The societal conclusion was that women had little experience in the financial world, and were likely to have a poor understanding of risk, with unrealistic expectations of returns.

On the contrary, Rutterford and Maltby, together with many other scholars, show that there were a substantial number of female investors in the nineteenth century, and attribute it to the development of new financial assets.[8] To support their observation, Froide shows that as early as the eighteenth century women were actively involved in money-lending markets.[9] They played a significant role in financing important industrial infrastructure, such as canal and railway companies. But in the nineteenth century, their participation in the economy became severely constricted by the 'separate spheres' culture which further entrenched gender roles.[10] They were dissuaded from participating in the financial world and allocated the role of house bearers.[11] Although there is little evidence of women investing in the Cape Colony prior to the nineteenth century, they too were actively involved in economic activities and took part in money-lending schemes. After the second British occupation in 1820, Ross argues that gentility became the norm for women.[12] From this point onwards, it was contrary to the ideal womanly image to take

---

[6]J. Rutterford and J. Maltby, '"The Widow, the Clergyman and the Reckless": Women Investors in England, 1830-1914', *Feminist Economics* 12, nos. 1-2 (2008): 111-38.

[7]Quoted in Rutterford and Maltby, 'Widow, Clergyman and Reckless', 119-20.

[8]Ibid.

[9]A. M. Froide, *Silent Partners: Women as Public Investors during Britain's Financial Revolution, 1690-1750* (Oxford: Oxford University Press, 2017).

[10]M. Freeman, R. Pearson and J. Taylor, '"A Doe in the City": Women Shareholders in Eighteenth and Early Nineteenth-Century Britain', *Accounting, Business and Financial History* 16, no. 2 (2006): 265-91.

[11]L. Davidoff and C. Hall, *Family Fortunes: Men and Women of the English Middle Class, 1780-1850* (London: Routledge, 2002).

[12]R. Ross, *Status and Respectability in the Cape Colony, 1750-1870: A Tragedy of Manners* (Cambridge: Cambridge University Press, 2004).

part in activities in the public sphere for financial gain. This paper, therefore, broadens our knowledge about Cape women by showing that not all women conformed to this ideology; our quantitative analysis reveals patterns in economic behaviour which might otherwise be hidden behind the dominant culture. They found ways to navigate the economic sphere despite being subjected to restrictive institutions, and that the capital market was a vehicle they used to attain economic freedom.

Framework and methods

Studies of the experiences of women investors in Victorian Britain were relevant to this paper, because events in Britain influenced business at the Cape – the Cape Joint Stock Company Act No. 25 of 1892 was based on the later versions of the English Companies Act of 1844 – and British culture influenced gender relations. We found Davidoff and Hall's 'separate spheres' theory a suitable framework for analysing women investors at the Cape.[13] The idea that men and women should act in separate spheres narrowed the range of activities that middle-class women in Victorian Britain could engage in, relegating them to the private sphere, where their sole duty was to nurture children and manage the household. Men on the other hand were given the public sphere, where they could work and earn salaries.[14] Within this view of society, women who engaged in waged labour put themselves at risk of transgressing the boundaries of gentility. The few who were active in the economy were overwhelmingly concentrated in four overcrowded and poorly paid occupations – governesses, seamstresses, milliners and ladies' companions.[15]

Shareholding in limited liability companies became a commonly accepted way for women to generate income. Although some scholars have cast doubt on the extent of their participation in the capital market, Green and Owens described this as 'gentlewomanly capitalism' (a play on Cain and Hopkins's 'gentlemanly capitalism'[16]). This is because women's wealth was of crucial importance to the expansion of the British state by means of investments in government securities. Many scholars have tried to explain the rapid increase of female investors in the nineteenth century, and the Women's Property Acts of 1870 and 1882 in Britain have featured prominently in this discussion because shares counted as property for separate use as equity.[17]

---

[13] Davidoff and Hall, *Family Fortunes*.

[14] E. Gordon and G. Nair, 'The Economic Role of Middle-Class Women in Victorian Glasgow', *Women's History Review* 9, no. 4 (2000): 791–814.

[15] D.R. Green and A. Owens, 'Gentlewomanly Capitalism? Spinsters, Widows, and Wealth Holding in England and Wales, c.1800–1860', *Economic History Review* 56, no. 3 (2003): 510–36.

[16] P.J. Cain and A.G. Hopkins, 'Gentlemanly Capitalism and British Expansion Overseas I: The Old Colonial System, 1688–1850', *Economic History Review* 39, no. 4 (1986): 501–25.

[17] L. Holcombe, *Wives and Property: The Reform of Married Women's Property Law* (Oxford: Oxford University Press, 1983).

The Acts played a big part in giving women financial freedom, and Freeman, Pearson and Taylor note that the growth of the railways was another possible stimulus, because it attracted more women to the city than the earlier stock ventures.[18] The railways stimulated the growth of the financial press, making information on stock and markets readily available to women. Rutterford and Maltby note that women's involvement in the securities market was influenced by their different needs and backgrounds.[19] They identify three categories of Victorian women: housewives, spinsters and widows. The first tended to speculate for capital gain. The second usually sought income from investments in order to lead a life befitting their social status, being anxious to steer clear of the degradation associated with paid work. The third on the other hand tended to hold shares as part of a family group, either as a source of income, to ensure control of the firm or to act as conduits of shares to the next generation. The spinsters were the largest group of investors, although their investment value was lower than the average for women in general.[20]

Freeman, Pearson and Taylor note the variety of women investors' occupations in eighteenth and early nineteenth-century Britain.[21] These investors were recorded, for example, as ladies, housewives, artists, servants, confectioners, butchers, housekeepers, drapers and grocers. Some, particularly widows and spinsters, were recorded as business proprietors. Financial organisations, because they generated regular and fairly high dividends, were a popular investment choice. Family shareholdings were common too. In most instances, having neither the networks nor the professional advice that were available to men, women invested where people with the same surname had invested. The societies, clubs, inns and public houses that men used to network were hostile to women.[22]

Data

When the Cape Companies Act of 1892 was promulgated, every joint stock company had to register its operations with the registrar of companies. This created an archive of 2,997 company records and more than 10,000 investors in the Western Cape Archives and Records Service (WCARS). This paper is based on records of registrations from 1892 to 1902, the end of the South African War. Political relations after this period probably had important implications for financial developments at the Cape, so registrations from 1902 to 1910, the year of the South African Union, will be material for a different study.

---

[18]Freeman, Pearson and Taylor, 'A Doe in the City'.

[19]Rutterford and Maltby, 'Widow, Clergyman and Reckless'.

[20]Green and Owens, 'Gentlewomanly Capitalism?'.

[21]Freeman, Pearson and Taylor, 'A Doe in the City'.

[22]H. Doe, 'Investment Opportunities and the Role of Business Networks for Women in the Nineteenth Century English Maritime Communities', Conference Paper: XIV International History Congress, Helsinki (2006).

From 1892 to 1902 a total of 6,883 investors in the Cape capital market were registered, 374 of them women, with investments in sixty-seven companies. We identified these women by using company shareholder lists. Green and Owens, and Rutterford and Maltby used similar records to identify women investors in Victorian Britain, with the difference that they collected data from publicly traded companies whereas we used privately traded companies.[23] Although Cape women may have invested in public companies in Britain or even the Johannesburg Stock Exchange, the Cape during the period under study did not have an active stock market. Therefore, all joint stock concerns in our archive were privately held at the time of registration. These records provide investors' name, surname, occupation, marital status, address and capital value. As mentioned in the previous section, the separate spheres theory provided an ideal context to analyse Cape women investors. For this reason, women in this study fall under the umbrella category of middle-class investors. The middle class was the largest group of investors in the capital market, injecting more capital into joint stock companies than any other group. Women made up 17 per cent of this group of investors and contributed 19 per cent of its capital.

Gendered roles at the Cape

Various suggestions have been put forward to explain the adoption of gendered roles at the Cape. One is that a move to the colonies gave men with declining rural squirearchy in Britain an opportunity to regenerate their authority, which had been threatened not only by the rise of a new manufacturing class but also by a working class that included women. Another is that in the late nineteenth century women's reproductive capacity at the Cape had become essential for establishing the settler society and building its economy. Their position, then, became influenced by new economic needs. As a result, colonial authorities established mechanisms that controlled the extent to which married white women could commit themselves to formal employment. This was specifically designed to prevent wage labour from interfering with their 'proper duties' at home.[24]

A rather common explanation is simply that the Cape, like many other colonies in the empire, adopted British culture. The early Dutch and later Afrikaner societies also prescribed specific roles for men and women. By the second British occupation of the Cape in 1820 the emphasis was on gentility, which could be acquired by various means. Ross attributes it to the Cape's education system, which, with its concern for moulding character, was instrumental in teaching children the roles they were expected to fill later in their lives.[25] Once finished with nursery school, boys and girls were taught differently.

---

[23]Green and Owens, 'Gentlewomanly Capitalism?'; Rutterford and Maltby, 'Widow, Clergyman and Reckless'.
[24]C. Walker, *Women and Resistance in South Africa* (Cape Town: David Philip, 1991).
[25]Ross, *Status and Respectability*.

Girls were not prepared for any profession, but for a life as future wives and mothers. Subjects such as domestic economy and sewing were at the centre of their curriculum, while mathematics and other scientific studies were prioritised for boys, as they were moulded to become future intellectuals, professionals and leaders.

Religion was another influence in conditioning the way individuals viewed themselves. Christian doctrine taught the roles women were expected to play in the family and society. It would be misleading to assume that all women were dissatisfied by this arrangement; some found comfort in being consumers, rather than producers like the men. Duff, in her work on the College Girls Huguenot Seminary School, shows that while some women appreciated education, they believed that it was not supposed to interfere with their domestic roles.[26] She quotes a letter in which a student emphasised that the power of an educated woman was not in her ability to lead, but her role as a 'gentle and mild' wife and mother.

Despite these restrictions on the spaces that women could navigate, some did deviate from what was expected of them, showing that despite the way they were conditioned to perceive themselves, they still possessed the same curiosity about life as men did. Such incidents increased in the mid-nineteenth century with the emergence of feminism and the idea of the 'New Woman'. Both of these new trends supported unconventional lifestyles, which were becoming more common in Europe, such as joining political organisations, riding bicycles, wearing bloomers and cutting their hair short. Commenting on the values of the New Woman in a Huguenot Seminary School annual article, Maggie Ferguson, an alumnus of the college, said the time had arrived for women to participate actively in life, and not vicariously through their husbands and fathers. She said the spirit of the age had produced 'women who begin to think, crudely no doubt, on many questions, for she is still handicapped by her long submission; but above all has made woman no longer willing to be a mere consumer, she must also be a producer'.[27]

Her remarks revealed not only how women were eager to penetrate the public sphere, but also how connected the colonies were with Britain. Letters were instrumental in maintaining this contact and keeping people abreast with what was happening in Britain. Literature was another important medium, as there was a big reading culture among the Colony's elite women. This made them susceptible to prevailing ideological influences that shaped notions of social and gender behaviour, such as public media and novels.[28]

Women's voices at the Cape seldom made it into the public sphere. To highlight these social changes we use the example of Olive Schreiner an outspoken writer who influenced feminist ideology not only at the Cape but also abroad in the mid-nineteenth century. Her first novel, *The Story of An African Farm*, published in 1883, drew a lot of attention

---

[26]S.E. Duff, 'From New Women to College Girls at the Huguenot Seminary and College, 1895–1910', *Historia* 51, no. 1 (2006): 1–27.

[27]Ibid, 17.

[28]N. Erlank, 'Letters Home: The Experiences and Perceptions of Middle Class British Women at the Cape, 1820–1850' (MA diss., University of Cape Town, Cape Town, 1995).

from colonial society.[29] Many women welcomed this book as it fed into their imagination through female characters who occupied male positions in the story. Although some of her most revered works were posthumously published, they were drafted and set in the context of the late-nineteenth century when our study peaks. Therefore, the stories she shared in them shed light on growing feminist perceptions in the Cape Colony between 1870 and 1911. For instance, through the female character Bertie, her novel *From Man to Man, or Perhaps Only* suggested that modern civilisation had robbed middle-class women of their share in social labour, even in the sphere of child-rearing.[30] Mental and physical inactivity caused individual and social decline and degeneration. In one of her short writings, she praised women by stating that 'You and such as you are the mothers of the South African nation of the future, and the shaping of that future lies in your hands'.[31]

In 1872, after working as a governess, Schreiner joined her brother in Du Toit's Pan in search of wealth. It was there that she drafted her first novels. Despite the harsh realities of 'separate spheres' in the Colony, she believed that women had the capacity to change their fortunes. These beliefs were reinforced by her experience as a teacher at the Fouchés farm at Klein Ganna Hoek Farm, Cradock, in 1876. During those years she read John Stuart Mill's *Logic*, a revolutionary piece that discussed possibilities for women's existential independence, and how investment opportunities in joint stock companies could free them from socio-economic restraints.[32]

Although her work did not directly comment on investment in these companies, her strong message about women as future leaders of South Africa shows that John Stuart Mill's work resonated with her. Moreover, her interest in the diamond trade confirmed Sharpe's assertion that women did not just fall victim to capitalism.[33] They too sought out the financial opportunities that came along with it. Her experiences mirrored those of other women. There were many of them who explored these avenues in silence and often their experiences were either not recorded, or the letters that they wrote were lost. Our quantitative analysis is thus revealing of these women's stories.

By 1902 media platforms such as the *Imperial Colonist* openly campaigned for the employment of women in various sectors of the Colony. Its first issue after the South African War advertised employment opportunities for women in sectors previously dominated by men, and prospects for vocational education. The jobs it listed for women were in the agricultural industries, education and the health sector.[34] This may have helped to build new identities among women who were inspired by the desire for economic freedom.

---

[29] O. Schreiner, *The Story of An African Farm* (1883; Oxford: Oxford University Press, 2008).

[30] O. Schreiner, *From Man to Man or Perhaps Only* (London: Fisher Unwin, 1926).

[31] A. Snaith, *Modernist Voyages: Colonial Women Writers in London, 1890–1945* (Cambridge: Cambridge University Press, 2014).

[32] Ibid.

[33] P. Sharpe, *Adapting to Capitalism: Women in the English Economy, 1700–1850* (London: Macmillan, 1996).

[34] J. Bush, '"The Right Sort of Woman": Female Emigrants and Emigration to the British Empire, 1890–1910', *Women's History Review* 3, no. 3 (1994): 385–409.

Despite all these influences that were preparing women in the Colony to become investors, access to securities during the period of our study was bound to be more difficult in the Colony than in Britain. British company promoters in the mid-nineteenth century designed mechanisms to educate women about financial markets.[35] The Cape did not have these, and this was a major handicap because dealing in company shares was dependent on information that could only be accessed in the public sphere. With the strong limits that were placed on women in the Colony, women had to devise new ways to obtain this information without overstepping their boundaries. The following section discusses how this was made possible.

Navigating the public sphere through the private space

The strategies women developed to navigate the public sphere during this period were not specifically tailored to help them access the equity securities market but more broadly to seek purpose and recognition in the economy. These efforts created foundations that were vital for women's participation in the capital market.

The earliest strategies by Cape women to navigate the public sphere can be traced to two British societies: the Female Middle-Class Society (FMCS) created in 1862, and the British Women's Emigration Society (BWES) founded in 1880. The FMCS campaigned for the protection and enhancement of the rights of working-class women. Formed at the height of feminism in Britain, this society encouraged young women to seek formal employment. It further shielded single and ambitious women from male prejudices about marriage and assisted women to make their own choices. The BWES on the other hand helped young women to emigrate to the colonies. Many mid-Victorian emigrants were seeking paid work to help them attain freedom and self-fulfilment.[36] Between 1884 and 1914 this society provided such assistance to about 20,000 women, of whom 2,705 went to the Cape between 1901 and 1906. The result was that during this period there was a generation of women determined to break the barriers to their participation in the economy. The South African Colonisation Society (SACS), formed in 1902, was an offshoot of those two societies,[37] continuing the campaign for the economic emancipation of women.

Evangelical societies were another strategy women used to navigate the public sphere. Following the French and American Revolutions, evangelical Christianity became increasingly popular in Britain. Fears of social dislocation scourged the British crown and forced it to seek ways of prohibiting societal moral decay. The solution was a resurgence of evangelicalism, with philanthropy at the core of its ethos. In times of

---

[35] D.R. Green, et al., 'Men, Women, and Money: An Introduction', in *Men, Women, and Money: Perspectives on Gender, Wealth, and Investment, 1850–1930*, eds. Green, et al. (Oxford: Oxford University Press, 2011): 1–30.

[36] Bush, 'Right Sort of Woman'.

[37] Ibid.

economic distress and social uncertainty, Christian faith, through self-discipline and self-sacrifice, offered a haven to preserve the soul. This often took several forms of charity, such as financial assistance, food, clothing and/or moral support to the underprivileged. This presented opportunities for women to participate actively in the economy, because they were placed at the helm of these operations due to their roles as moral guardians in the micro-family.[38]

In addition, charity work was generally socially acceptable for women. As a result, many women flocked to these societies. This was partly because they provided a legitimate occupation for middle-class women. Erlank says that religious convictions were not always the reason why women were fond of these organisations. There were underlying social and economic imperatives. This included power and authority over other women, and financial necessity.[39]

With the growth of philanthropic activities, administration duties escalated. For instance, women raised money for these activities through subscriptions, donations and bazaars. These proceedings had to be monitored, and the solution was to equip members with skills such as bookkeeping, secretarial work and sewing.[40] This immediately challenged the perceptions about women in the Colony, as they were paid for some of the duties they carried out. Moreover, regular contact with the poor meant that they spent much of their time in public. This allowed them to step into different worlds and to interact with a variety of people.

Apart from meeting new people, members of these societies met regularly for various activities such as sewing.[41] Networks were created in this process, which in turn enhanced the transmission of information among women. For instance, the Ladies' Benevolent Society at the Cape was heavily involved in sewing programmes from the 1820s. It was one of the earliest female-led organised volunteer philanthropic work societies in the Colony. Women may have not been welcome in the coffee shops and public houses, but through such organisations they could acquire information that would have otherwise been limited to men. It is not far-fetched to argue that it was by means of such spaces that ideas to challenge gender stereotyping manifested through women's movements in the nineteenth century.[42] For instance, in 1924 the Ladies Benevolent Society went on to establish a multi-racial school for girls (the School of Industry).

Such activities made it possible for Cape women to navigate their way into the securities market. In the absence of stock markets and structures to educate women on how to manage their investments, word of mouth was very important. They came from different backgrounds, and some were privy to vital information that they shared with their peers.

---

[38] F. Prochaska, *The Voluntary Impulse: Philanthropy in Modern Britain* (London: Faber & Faber, 1988).
[39] Ibid.
[40] Ibid.
[41] Ibid.
[42] Erlank, 'Letters Home'.

Quantitative History and Uncharted People

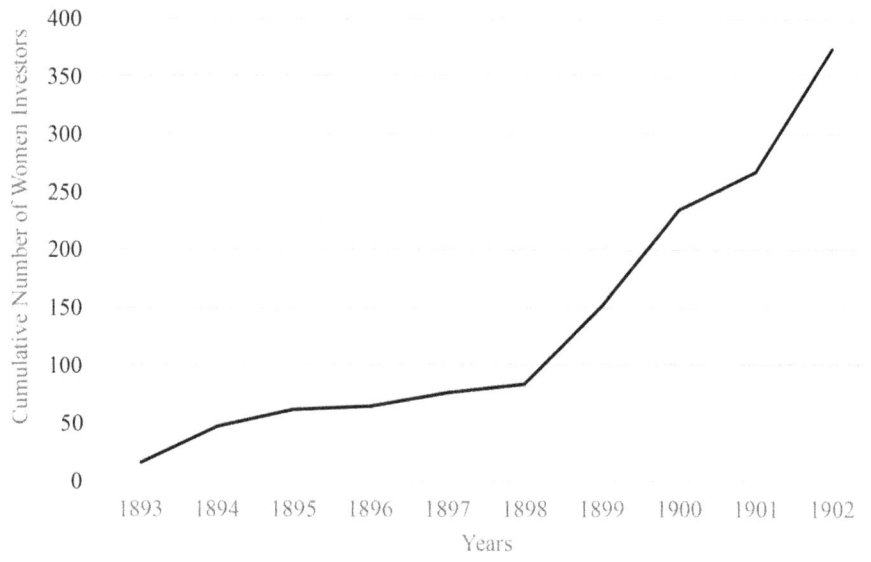

Figure 8.1 Cumulative number of women investors in the Cape capital market, 1892–1902.
Source: WCARS, LC 1 – LC 467, 1892–1902.

Women investors at the Cape 1892–1902

As a first step towards understanding women's involvement in the capital market at the Cape we looked at where the money they invested came from. As we have already noted, very few of them had full-time employment. The most common source of income was inheritance from parents.[43] Some young women in the Colony were so wealthy they were almost regarded as property themselves, because they brought their wealth into a marriage.

We then looked at the annual growth of the number of women investors in the capital market. Figure 8.1 shows that they had a very slow start in participating in the capital market. The first women investors were recorded in 1893. Their numbers rose substantially on the eve of the South African War in 1899, and the highest number for the period 1892–1902, 28 per cent of the total, was in 1902, after the war.[44]

Two possible explanations for these steep increases may have been the proliferation of feminist ideas on economic control, but also the uncertain outcomes of the war and the pursuant effect on inheritance. As regards the former, Bush's work has shown that there

---

[43]W. Dooling, 'The Making of a Colonial Elite: Poverty, Family and Landed Stability in the Cape Colony, c.1750–1834', *Journal of Southern African Studies* 31, no. 1 (2005): 147–62.
[44]WCARS, LC 1 – LC 467, 1892–1902.

Female Investors at the Cape, 1892–1902

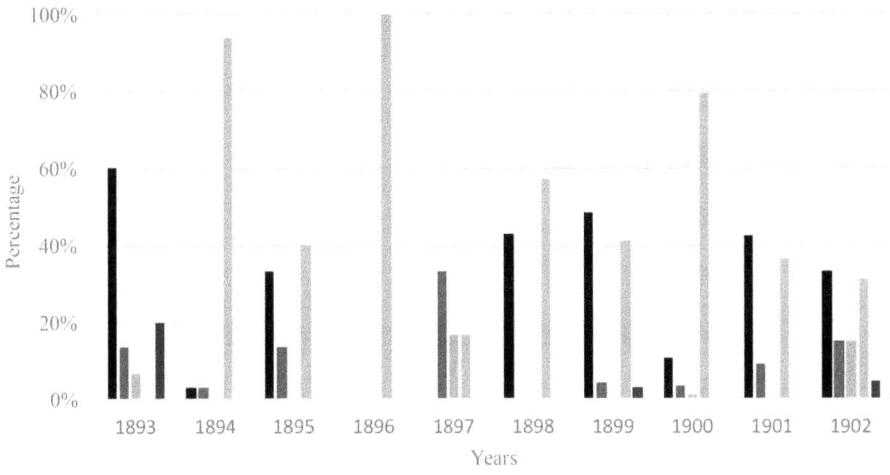

Figure 8.2 Annual distribution of women investors at the Cape, 1892–1902.
Source: WCARS, LC 1 – LC 467, 1892–1902.

was a rapid increase in the number of women's societies in the Colony during this period, and this, together with the impact in 1902 of publications like the *Imperial Colonist*, may have inspired women to explore and exercise economic freedom in various ways, which may have included investing in joint stock companies.[45] As regards the latter, the likelihood that many women were going to be widows after the war was high. The war, and the escalating turmoil between the British colonists and the Dutch republics, may have influenced women to start thinking about a possible future alone. Securities in joint stock companies were a practical safety net to help women raise their children if their spouses died in the war.[46]

Appendices 1 and 2 show that 50 per cent of women investors from 1892 to 1902 came from the western region of the Cape. They contributed 63 per cent of the total capital invested by women during this period. On the other hand, 29 per cent of women came from the eastern region of the colony and contributed 21 per cent of the total capital. Women from the northern region, together with those from Europe and neighbouring territories, constituted less than 10 per cent of women investors and contributed less than 10 per cent of the capital. Figure 8.2 sheds more light on this by showing the annual geographic distribution of women in the Cape capital market.[47]

Given the 1895 boom in mining shares, we expected to find that women investors from the northern region would constitute a large proportion of the capital market in that year, but in fact their numbers dropped between 1893 and 1897. This may have

---

[45]Bush, 'Right Sort of Woman'.
[46]WCARS, LC 1 – LC 467, 1892–1902.
[47]WCARS, LC 1 – LC 467, 1892–1902.

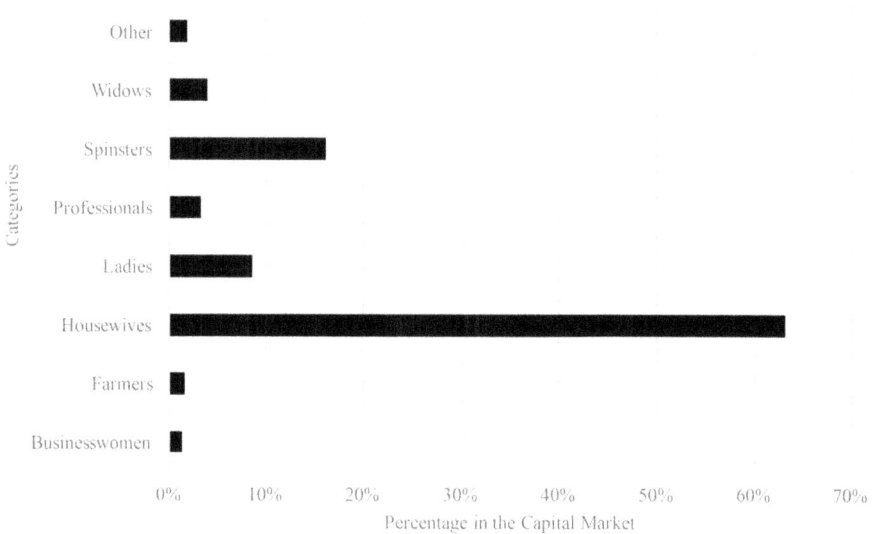

Figure 8.3 Profile of Cape female investors, 1892–1902.
Source: WCARS, LC 1 – LC 467, 1892–1902.

been because this was largely a mining region and the number of women would be small.[48] It may also have been because during this time only foreign women, mostly British, really invested in the mining sector. Local women investors shied away from mining companies and explored securities in companies involved in other sectors of the economy. They only started investing in mining companies in 1902.

Although women constituted only 7 per cent of the investors in the Cape capital market, importantly they were as diverse as the women investors in Britain. The only difference was that, whereas share ownership in the British capital market came mostly from widows and spinsters, at the Cape it largely came from housewives. In contrast to what one would have expected, this was not in any way due to the 1870 and 1882 Married Women's Property Acts, because there is no evidence of these laws in the Cape Colony. Using occupational information provided by women in the shareholders lists, we classified Cape women investors into seven main categories (Figure 8.3).[49] Housewives made up 63 per cent of this group, possibly because there were far fewer women than

---

[48] A.E. van der Merwe, et al., 'The Origins of the Late Nineteenth-Century Migrant Diamond Miners Uncovered in a Salvage Excavation in Kimberley, South Africa', *South African Archaeological Bulletin* 64, no. 192 (2010): 175–84.

[49] Although the titles housewife, spinster, widow and lady cannot be easily classified as occupations, women at the Cape, as well as Britain in the mid-Victorian era, listed these them as their occupations.

men at the Cape, whereas in Britain women outnumbered men by nearly 10 per cent in the manufacturing and port cities of Manchester, Leeds, Bristol and Liverpool.[50] This may have greatly influenced the profile of female investors, as many of them were obliged to get married. They were likely to marry at a young age, and few of them lived for any length of time as unmarried women. A remark in a letter written by a Mrs Emma Rutherford, a Cape resident in the nineteenth century, epitomises the importance of marriage in the Colony: she wrote that 'no greater calamity can befall us than that … our daughters [are] not given in marriage'.[51]

The Victorian idealisation of the role of the housewife may be another reason why the Cape capital market had few women investors who were professionals, farmers or businesswomen. All the investments that were made by female farmers and business owners were in companies where their spouses (who were also farmers) were either directors or shareholders. These were unlike the cases of the women who were professionals, who had evidence of income.[52]

'Ladies', although occupying a higher status, were no different from housewives when it came to investments, because they too were married women. They made up only 9 per cent of our sample, making them the third largest group. Their small number at the Cape, when compared to the British capital market, can be attributed to the fact that there were not many members of the titled aristocracy at the Cape.

Spinsters and widows, on the other hand, were the only investors in this group who had the privilege of being able to hold property independently. This, together with favourable inheritance laws for unmarried women in the Colony, made it highly likely that they were among the few who were wealthy enough to speculate in the capital market. For instance, as early as the mid-eighteenth century, the Roman Dutch inheritance laws allowed widows to inherit the wealth of their spouses. Von Fintel, Du Plessis and Jansen show that some of this wealth was used to invest in productive assets.[53] It is therefore possible that in the nineteenth century this law enabled women with inheritance to direct some of their wealth into the capital market. This may be why spinsters are the second largest group in our sample, but widows do not seem to have been affected in the same way, as they had little representation in the Cape capital market. In Britain the fact that few widows invested was sometimes attributed to the financial burdens widows faced after the death of their spouses.[54] This caused them to become frugal with the wealth they inherited. While this may be the reason why there are few widows in our sample of women investors at the Cape, it is important to consider that, given the

---

[50] Green and Owens, 'Gentlewomanly Capitalism?'.

[51] Quoted in Ross, *Status and Respectability*, 90.

[52] WCARS, LC 1 – LC 467, 1892–1902.

[53] D. von Fintel, S. du Plessis and A. Jensen, 'The Wealth of Cape Colony Widows: Inheritance Laws and Investment Responses Following Male Death in the 17th and 18th Centuries', *Economic History of Developing Regions* 28, no. 1 (2013): 87–108.

[54] Ibid.

shortage of women, widowhood was likely to be short-lived in the Colony. In his work on wealth distribution in the Colony during the seventeenth and eighteenth centuries, Shell notes that:

> Settler women came to occupy a commanding social position, both because of their scarcity, and because of the particular system of partible inheritance at the Cape, and their scarcity in the short run empowered them to maintain their dominant position over the long term ... there was at the Cape what E.S. Morgan ... had termed 'widowarchy'. Some Cape widows remarried as many as three times, and in remarrying they acted as the conduits of large fortunes.[55]

They were, therefore, constantly sought after by men. There were numerous cases of widows who did not struggle to find new partners after their husbands died, and in some instances, they married men who were much younger than they were. The case of Maarten Melck and Anna Margareth Hop is a good example of this phenomenon. In 1752 Melck married the widow of his late employer Johan Giebler who owned Elsenburg farm. Having been a man of moderate means, after this marriage he owned vast tracts of land.[56] We therefore argue that this tendency in Cape society contributed to the low number of widows in the capital market.

In terms of value, our sample of women investors contributed 7 per cent of the capital that financed Cape joint stock companies. In addition, the amount of capital contributed by each group was disproportionate to their size. For instance, ladies contributing much more than one would expect from their smaller numbers (Figure 8.3). Table 8.1 sheds more light on the capital value of the shares our sample held in the capital market.

In fact, ladies invested the largest and most varied amounts of capital. Of the other categories, professionals and housewives had the largest mean capital values, which means that their individual investments were on average greater than those made by most other women with lower mean capital values. Other indicators of this difference are the median and maximum value of investment and the standard deviation. Categories with lower capital value means also had lower medians, except in the case of businesswomen. The reason why businesswomen had a high median is that they were the smallest group in our sample: there were only five of them, and on average this group's capital value was within the range of its median.

The maximum capital values and their standard deviations shed more light in this regard, as they show that, even with a higher median, businesswomen made the least valuable investments in the women's category. Their capital value was not as varied as that of the three leading investor categories in our sample. A larger standard deviation

---

[55]C.H. Shell, 'An Early Colonial Landed Gentry: Land and Wealth in the Cape Colony, 1682–1731', *Journal of Historical Geography* 9, no. 3 (1983): 270.

[56]D.W. Kruger and C.J. Beyers, *Suid Afrikaanse Biografiese Woordeboek I* (Pretoria: Raad vir Geesteswetenskaplike Navorsing, 1977).

Table 8.1 Descriptive statistics of the capital value contributions for women investors at the Cape, 1892–1902. Values in British Pounds.

Descriptive statistics	Business women	Farmers	Housewives	Ladies	Professionals	Spinsters	Widows	Other
Mean	288.4	56.6	577.6	2412.6	866.8	202.4	310	426.4
Median	231	50	100	500	100	50	50	50
Maximum	600	100	48,125	18,200	9500	3234	2800	2400
Minimum	1	20	1	5	10	1	1	25
Standard deviation	298.9	36.1	3310.2	4513.6	2719.5	546	713.8	878.20

Source: WCARS, LC 1 – LC 467, 1892–1902.

for the housewives, 'ladies' and professionals categories suggests that their capital value was very broadly spread from their average value. This is confirmed by the maximum capital value of each of these three groups. The largest single investment was in the housewives category, by Mrs Courteney Thompson, who invested £48,125 in the *Mining Plants Company Limited* in 1902.[57] There were other large investments in the housewives' category, such as £15,000 invested by Mrs Mary Coghlan in a mining company in Kimberley.[58] The investment of such large sums of money in joint stock companies contradicts the stereotype of women as risk-averse investors. There were clearly some women, although few, who invested as dauntlessly as their male counterparts.

As noted above, women engaged in the securities market because they wanted economic freedom. The forces that pushed them to the securities market were varied. Erlank reveals some of the frustrations Cape women experienced in the mid-nineteenth century.[59] Using letters written by various women, she shows that, as early as the 1850s, women shared their unfortunate experiences with their close friends and relatives. In most cases the misfortunes involved financial difficulties. One letter details how a woman left her husband in Grahamstown in pursuit of employment opportunities in Graaff-Reinet and Colesberg. In letters to her relatives, she writes with a heavy heart of how the man she married had failed to meet the conventional expectations of a husband. She says that he lacked the basic instinct for taking care of his wife and children.

Although this could befall any woman, it was bound to be disastrous for a housewife who had not inherited wealth to cushion her in times of crisis. This could also explain why the housewives' share value was the lowest in the top four categories in our sample of female investors. The letters in Erlank provide some psychosocial insight to how Cape

---

[57] WCARS, LC 456, The Mining Plants Company Limited, 1902.
[58] WCARS LC 402, The Central Diamond Mining Company (Leicester Mine) Limited, 1902.
[59] Erlank, 'Letters Home'.

women thought about money in the mid-nineteenth century.[60] In her study, Erlank refers to Mrs Philips, co-founder of the Ladies' Benevolent Society, who in her letters advised women to be useful and dutiful. Her study shows that some women sought alternative sources of income because of what Mrs Philips described as 'foolish choices of a husband'.[61]

Women also sought alternative sources of income to keep up appearances. Mrs Maclear who was married to Sir Thomas Maclear, an astronomer living at Observatory, wrote about the challenges of maintaining a specific lifestyle on her husband's meagre salary.[62] Suicide often followed the shame of going bankrupt. Social pressure and the need to maintain a certain standard of living in a fiercely competitive society led people to live beyond their means. Cape society was a small world and secrets could not be kept. Social indiscretions would quickly become public knowledge. The end of any social standing in the community was always a possibility.[63]

In addition, like most colonial societies, the Cape developed certain cultures that evolved around material goods. Mitchell says the consumption of specific material goods at the Cape had become a way in which individuals attempted to either affirm or re-affirm their identity.[64] Material goods had become status symbols that were associated with certain segments or groups of society. However, most women could not keep up with these trends, and the need to find alternative sources of income was a serious concern.

Like their counterparts in Britain, women at the Cape also had networks in the capital market. We noted earlier that these networks had their roots in the social activities that women engaged in prior to the passing of the 1892 Companies Act. Smith-Rosenberg suggests that these activities were an outcome of the culture of separate spheres.[65] In her collection of essays on women in Victorian America, she argues that gender-role differentiation within society caused the emotional segregation of men and women. This resulted in women spending most of their time in female company, causing a specifically female world to develop, a world built around a generic and unselfconscious pattern of single-sex or homosocial networks.[66] We can perhaps see an instance of this in the case of Mrs Elizabeth McCartney and Mrs Selina Betteridge, who were shareholders in the Kimberley Co-operative Society Company and also immediate neighbours, as we discovered from the residential addresses they provided in the list of shareholders.[67] It is perhaps not far-fetched to suggest that these women had an established relationship prior

---

[60]Ibid.

[61]Ibid, 67–8.

[62]C.H. Rautenbach, *Suid-Afrikaanse Biografiese Woordeboek* (Cape Town: Plurabelle Books, 1968).

[63]Erlank, 'Letters Home'.

[64]L.J. Mitchell, *Belongings: Poverty, Family and Identity in Colonial South Africa* (New York: Columbia University Press, 2009).

[65]C. Smith-Rosenberg, *Disorderly Conduct: Visions of Gender in Victorian America* (Oxford: Oxford University Press, 1986).

[66]Ibid.

[67]WCARS, LC C428, The Kimberley Co-operative Society Ltd, 1902.

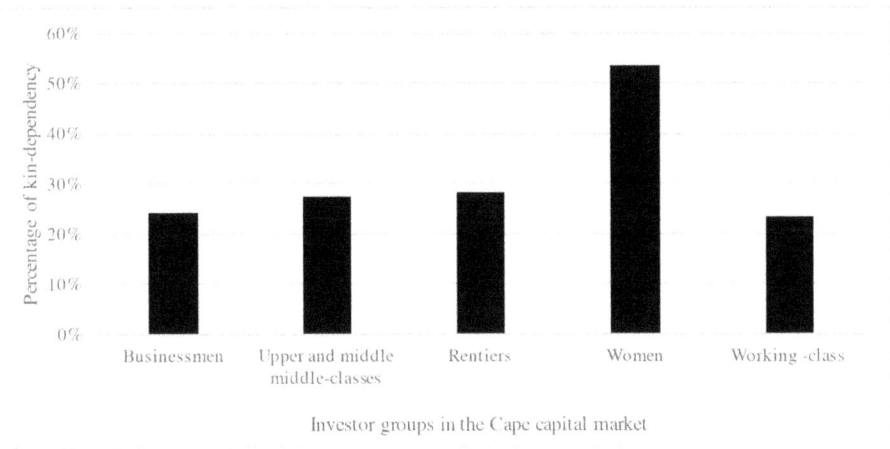

Figure 8.4 Kin-dependency among Cape women investors in the capital market, 1892–1902.
Source: WCARS, LC 1 – LC 467, 1892–1902.

to their investing in this company. We found similar evidence of networks at the Cape among the few women who operated in the public sphere. For instance, Dr Clement and Dr Fismer, medical practitioners from Cape Town, invested in the same company, the South African Fisheries.[68]

What was interesting about these four women was that they appeared to have been part of a much broader network that included men. For example, Mrs Betteridge's husband was an investor in the same company. Dr Clement and Dr Fismer were also part of a network consisting of several medical practitioners (Doctors Anderson, Beck, Clement, Fismer, Impey, Thompson and Marius). Men were valuable sources of information, especially considering the limited effort made in the Cape to educate women about the securities market. It is possible that Mrs Betteridge had access to information about investing via her husband, and shared this with her friend. Doe notes that in the absence of stock exchanges and very few professional brokers, word of mouth was an important source of information.[69] At the Cape, men were at the centre of this network. Mary Ward in the Cape Peninsula Lighting Company was another example of this trend. She was part of a network that included four male investors in the middle-class category who all originated from London.[70] This explains why the middle-class in our sample contained the largest number of women who invested in companies where people with their surnames and shared residential addresses also invested, as shown in figure 8.4.

Our findings suggest that women relied on men for information about the securities market. Sometimes they were in female networks, but often they invested in companies

---

[68] WCARS, LC C249, The South African Fisheries Ltd, 1898.

[69] Doe, 'Investment Opportunities'.

[70] WCARS, LC C309, The Cape Peninsula Lighting Company, 1900.

together with their male counterparts. In some instances, they were in a family network, as in the case of Miss Anna Ansley, who invested in a company with four men who shared her surname and lived at the same address.[71] Spinsters were particularly inclined to invest in companies in which their relatives also held shares. About 72 per cent of the investments made by this group in our sample were in companies together with their relatives, mostly male, as shareholders. In the case of widows, 60 per cent of their investments were kin-dependent, for housewives it was 50 per cent and for ladies 38 per cent, which suggests that these last were the most independent investors.[72]

Men also featured prominently in these arrangements. Usually when a man and woman owned shares jointly, the man was likely to hold control over them.[73] This also brings to light the possibility that in family business arrangements, women were simply used to retain control of the company by their male relatives, or to obtain majority seats. Our sample, on the contrary, shows the opposite. A. J. Coleman and Company was a good example of this. Mrs Wilhelmina Coleman, Alfred Coleman's wife, owned large amounts of shares.[74] This meant that there was a very slim chance of business partners instigating a take-over by means of majority share ownership. This was also the case with Ginsberg and Company[75] and the Ingerid Steamship Company[76] where shareholdings were dominated by family members.

Nevertheless, women's reliance on men for information on the securities market was not necessarily a weakness, but a form of adaptation to capitalism. There were numerous cases where women invested more than their male connections did. For instance, both Mrs Mary Coghlan and Mrs J. Croghan invested more than their husbands (by a large margin) in the Central Diamond Mining Company.[77] The same was true of Mrs Maria van der Merwe, who had more shares than her husband in the Lourens River Estates Company.[78] Investing in companies together with their male relatives seems to have bolstered their confidence, as Figure 8.5 suggests.

The largest sum of capital provided by women in our sample was invested in companies where women were related to some of the shareholders. Housewives are an excellent example of this, with 50 per cent of their investments being kin-dependent and 50 per cent independent. Figure 8.5 shows the extent to which they invested along with their relatives, which may have given them confidence. There were some independent investments, but most of them of lower value than those made by housewives. Spinsters,

---

[71] WCARS, LC 302, The African Mutual Trust and Assurance Company Ltd, 1900.
[72] WCARS, LC 1 – LC 467, 1892–1902.
[73] Freeman, Pearson and Taylor, 'A Doe in the City'.
[74] WCARS, LC 313, A. J. Coleman and Co. Ltd, 1900.
[75] WCARS, LC 319, The Ginsberg and Company Ltd, 1900.
[76] WCARS, LC 322, The Ingerid Steamship Company Ltd, 1900.
[77] WCARS, LC 402, The Central Diamond Mining Company (Leicester Mine) Ltd, 1902.
[78] WCARS, LC 441, The Lourens River Estates Ltd, 1902.

Female Investors at the Cape, 1892–1902

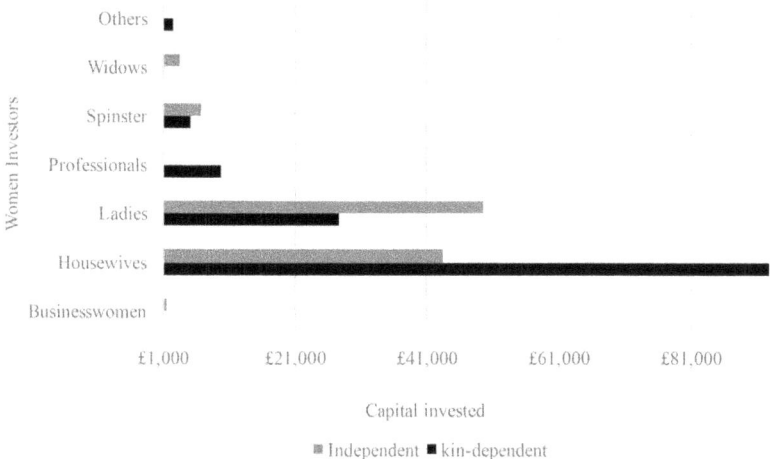

Figure 8.5 The influence of kin-dependency on the distribution of women's capital value, 1892–1902.
Source: WCARS, LC 1 – LC 467, 1892–1902.

widows and ladies in particular, invested more independently. The social class to which the ladies belonged was on the whole better educated. This meant that they were likely to be intellectually capable of independently assessing which companies they wanted to invest in, and were possibly less afraid to take risks.[79]

The women in our sample invested not only in a variety of ways but also in a variety of companies and sectors. Figure 8.6 shows these sectors. Financial organisations were the most favoured destination for women's capital. Housewives and ladies dominated this sector, although their preferences differed somewhat. For example, housewives invested in both insurance and trust companies, but ladies only in insurance companies. More housewives than the other groups invested in the insurance sector, and the amount they invested in this sector was twice the amount they invested in trust companies. A possible explanation for this is related to the concept of networks and kin-dependent investments. It was common in these financial organisations to find investors that were neighbours and shared the same surname or status. For example, the Colonial Marine Assurance and Trust Company was made up of 'ladies' and 'gentlemen'.[80]

The findings from our sample suggest that ladies and rentiers seldom invested in small family businesses, unless the business belonged to their families. In addition to financial organisations, much of their capital went into the real estate sector. This is perhaps a choice that was informed by their spouses. Professionals also seemed uninterested in small organisations. They were among the many that invested in financial organisations

---

[79] WCARS, LC 1 – LC 467, 1892–1902.
[80] WCARS, LC C53, The Colonial Marine and Assurance Company Ltd, 1894.

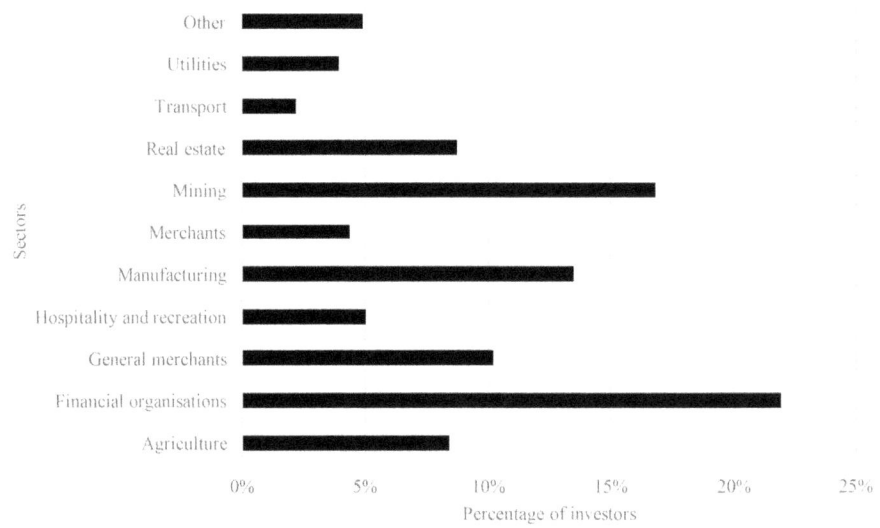

Figure 8.6 Industries financed by women, 1892–1902.
Source: WCARS, LC 1–LC 467.

and mining companies. Widows, on the other hand, did not seem to have a clearly defined preference, although they do not seem to have been keen to invest beyond their environment. Our findings suggest that only spinsters and housewives speculated in companies that operated beyond their region. The utilities were another sector that seems to have attracted women rapidly in our sample between 1899 and 1902. The potential for high returns in this sector was high, because its services were relatively new in most areas of the Colony. However, despite such good prospects, in our sample housewives constituted 95 per cent of the women investors in that sector.[81]

Although women made up only 17 per cent of middle-class investors, their contribution was noticeable in four specific sectors: finance, mining, manufacturing and 'other' – a sector made up of various less common economic sectors (laundry, fishing and stationary companies). Table 8.2 shows that they were the second largest providers of capital in the mining sector within the subgroups of the middle-class. This was an astonishing finding considering that only 12 per cent of investors in the women's category held shares in mining companies. This can only be attributed to the few women discussed above who injected large sums of capital into the sector. Further, it is important to note that over 90 per cent of investments in the mining sector in the women category came from housewives.

---

[81] WCARS, LC 1 – LC 467, 1892–1902.

Table 8.2 The financial contribution of women in the middle-class category, 1892–1902.

Sector	Upper Middle-class	Middle Middle-class	Women	Working-class
Agriculture	20%	47%	13%	20%
Financial organisations	30%	40%	30%	1%
General merchants	5%	68%	8%	19%
Hospitality	31%	55%	11%	3%
Manufacturing	16%	51%	32%	1%
Merchants	52%	43%	4%	1%
Mining	13%	50%	34%	3%
Real estate	20%	70%	8%	2%
Transport	86%	6%	8%	1%
Utilities	17%	72%	5%	3%
Other	16%	50%	31%	3%

Source: WCARS, LC 1 – LC 467.

The presence of women was also felt in the financial sector. Here, as in the mining sector, they were also the second largest providers of capital, with the difference that here it was ladies who provided the largest sum of capital, followed by housewives and spinsters. Verhoef explains that these companies may have offered stable and regular returns on investments and avenue of investment to small investors.[82] Manufacturing was the third sector to which women made a substantial financial contribution during this period, followed by the 'other' sector. Our findings show that, despite being excluded from most economic activities, women made important contributions to the growth of joint stock companies in the Colony. What is also important is that the emergence of joint stock companies in the Colony provided them with alternative sources of income, which could have otherwise been difficult to find.

Conclusion

Throughout the Victorian era women investors in Britain and those in the British colonial territories lived subject to a set of social rules prescribed by the separate spheres ideology. On a practical level this meant that they could not operate in the public sphere, as they were designated the role of taking care of the family. However, in the mid-1800s there was a rising sentiment among women that supported economic freedom.

---

[82] G. Verhoef, 'Investing in Enterprise: Women Entrepreneurs in Colonial "South Africa"', in *Female Entrepreneurs in the Long Nineteenth Century: A Global Perspective*, ed. J. Aston and C. Bishop (Cham: Palgrave Macmillan, 2020): 57–83.

Faced with limited employment opportunities, the securities market became a practical solution for them in that it afforded them the opportunity to generate an income. This paper has outlined how this happened and some of the reasons why women held shares at the Cape. Like the women who invested in British capital markets, Cape women investors were diverse, comprising of spinsters, widows, housewives and professionals. Although they shared a few traits, they had visible differences. For instance, it seems that housewives and professionals invested comfortably in companies alongside their male relatives, but ladies, spinsters and widows seemed to do the opposite.

This paper has also shown who women investors were at the Cape, and how they navigated the capital market. It contributes to existing studies on women in colonial South Africa, particularly their role in the economy. There is potential for further studies, especially considering that women seemed to have gained momentum in the capital market during the last decade of the nineteenth century at the Cape. An extended study beyond 1902 might reveal to what extent women played a role in financing companies, not only in colonial South Africa, but in southern Africa as a whole.

Bibliography

Bush, J. '"The Right Sort of Woman": Female Emigrants and Emigration to the British Empire, 1890–1910'. *Women's History Review* 3, no. 3 (1994): 385–409.

Cain, P.J. and A.G. Hopkins. 'Gentlemanly Capitalism and British Expansion I: The Old Colonial System, 1688–1850'. *Economic History Review* 39, no. 4 (1986): 501–25.

Cooke, C.A. *Corporation, Trust and Company: An Essay in Legal History*. Manchester: Manchester University Press, 1950.

Davidoff, L. and C. Hall. *Family Fortunes: Men and Women of the English Middle Class, 1780–1850*. London: Routledge, 2002.

Doe, H. 'Investment Opportunities and the Role of Business Networks for Women in the Nineteenth Century English Maritime Communities'. Conference Paper, XIV International History Congress in Helsinki, 2006: 1–15. Available online: https://www.academia.edu/3238589/Investment_opportunities_and_the_role_of_business_networks_for_women_in_nineteenth_century_English_maritime_communities (Accessed 3 March 2018).

Dooling, W. 'The Making of a Colonial Elite: Poverty, Family and Landed Stability in the Cape Colony, c.1750–1834'. *Journal of Southern African Studies* 31, no. 1 (2005): 147–62.

Duff, S.E. 'From New Women to College Girls at the Huguenot Seminary and College, 1895–1910'. *Historia* 51, no. 1 (2006): 1–27.

Ellevest: A Financial Company for Women, by Women. Available online: www.ellevest.com (Accessed 15 August 2019).

Erlank, N. 'Letters Home: The Experiences and Perceptions of Middle Class British Women at the Cape, 1820–1850'. MA diss., University of Cape Town, Cape Town, 1995.

Freeman, M., R. Pearson and J. Taylor. '"A Doe in the City": Women Shareholders in Eighteenth and Early Nineteenth-Century Britain'. *Accounting, Business and Financial History* 16, no. 2 (2006): 265–91.

Froide, A.M. *Silent Partners: Women as Public Investors during Britain's Financial Revolution, 1690–1750*. Oxford: Oxford University Press, 2017.

Gordon, E. and G. Nair. 'The Economic Role of Middle-Class Women in Victorian Glasgow'. *Women's History Review* 9, no. 4 (2000): 791–814.

Green, D.R. and A. Owens. 'Gentlewomanly Capitalism? Spinsters, Widows, and Wealth Holding in England and Wales, c.1800–1860'. *Economic History Review* 56, no. 3 (2003): 510–36.

Green, D.R., A. Owens, J. Maltby and J. Rutterford. 'Men, Women, and Money: An Introduction'. In *Men, Women, and Money: Perspectives on Gender, Wealth, and Investment 1850–1930*, edited by D.R. Green, A. Owens, J. Maltby and J. Rutterford, 1–30. Oxford: Oxford University Press, 2011.

Holcombe, L. *Wives and Property: The Reform of Married Women's Property Law*. Oxford: Oxford University Press, 1983.

Kruger, D.W. and C.J. Beyers. *Suid Afrikaanse Biografiese Woordeboek I*. Pretoria: Raad vir Geesteswetenskaplike Navorsing, 1977.

Leaver, K. *The Financial Power of Your Femininity*. 2017. Available online: http://www.futurewomen.com/wealth/financial-power-femininity (Accessed 15 August 2019).

Micklethwait, J. and A. Wooldridge. *The Company: A Short History of a Revolutionary Idea*. New York: Modern Library, 2003.

Mitchell, L.J. *Belongings: Poverty, Family and Identity in Colonial South Africa*. New York: Columbia University Press, 2009.

Prochaska, F. *The Voluntary Impulse: Philanthropy in Modern Britain*. London: Faber and Faber, 1988.

Rautenbach, C. H. *Suid-Afrikaanse Biografiese Woordeboek*. Cape Town: Plurabelle Books, 1968.

Ross, R. *Status and Respectability in the Cape Colony 1750–1870: A Tragedy of Manners*. Cambridge: Cambridge University Press, 2004.

Rutterford, J. and J. Maltby. '"The Widow, the Clergyman and the Reckless": Women Investors in England, 1830–1914'. *Feminist Economics* 12, no. 1–2 (2008): 111–38.

Schreiner, O. *The Story of an African Farm*. 1883; repr. Oxford: Oxford University Press, 2008.

Schreiner, O. *From Man to Man or Perhaps Only*. London: Fisher Unwin, 1926.

Sharpe, P. *Adapting to Capitalism: Women in the English Economy, 1700–1850*. London: Macmillan, 1996.

Shell, C.H. 'An Early Colonial Landed Gentry: Land and Wealth in the Cape Colony 1682–1731'. *Journal of Historical Geography* 9, no. 3 (1983): 265–86.

Smith-Rosenberg, C. *Disorderly Conduct: Visions of Gender in Victorian America*. Oxford: Oxford University Press, 1986.

Snaith, A. *Modernist Voyages: Colonial Women Writers in London, 1890–1945*. Cambridge: Cambridge University Press, 2014.

Van Der Merwe, A. E., I. Ribot, D. Morris, M. Steyn and G.J.R. Maat. 'The Origins of Late Nineteenth-Century Migrant Diamond Miners Uncovered in a Salvage Excavation in Kimberley, South Africa'. *South African Archaeological Bulletin* 65, no. 192 (2010): 175–84.

Verhoef, G. 'Investing in Enterprise: Women Entrepreneurs in Colonial "South Africa"'. In *Female Entrepreneurs in the Long Nineteenth Century*, edited by J. Aston and C. Bishop, 57–83. Cham: Palgrave Macmillan, 2020.

Von Fintel, D., S. Du Plessis and A. Jensen. 'The Wealth of Cape Colony Widows: Inheritance Laws and Investment Responses Following Male Death in the 17th and 18th Centuries'. *Economic History of Developing Regions* 28, no. 1 (2013): 87–108.

Walker, C. *Women and Resistance in South Africa*. Cape Town: David Philip, 1991.

Quantitative History and Uncharted People

Appendix 1

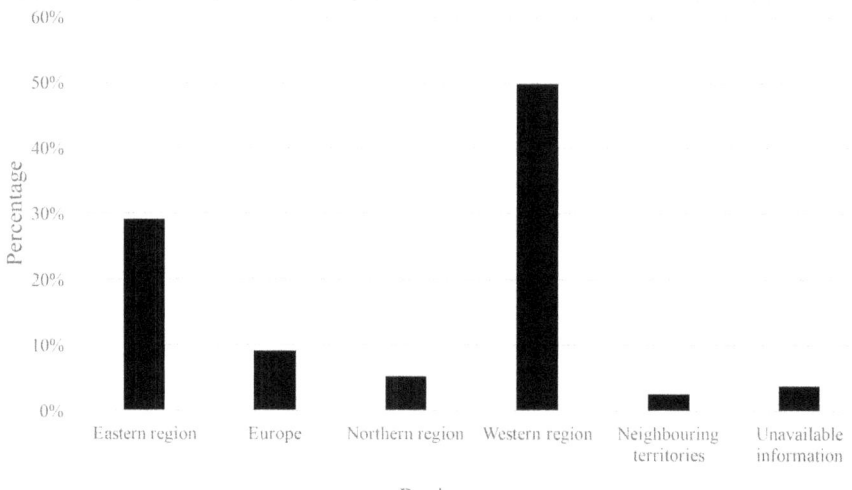

Figure 8.7 Women investors per region at the Cape, 1892–1902.
Source: WCARS, LC 1 – LC 467.

Appendix 2

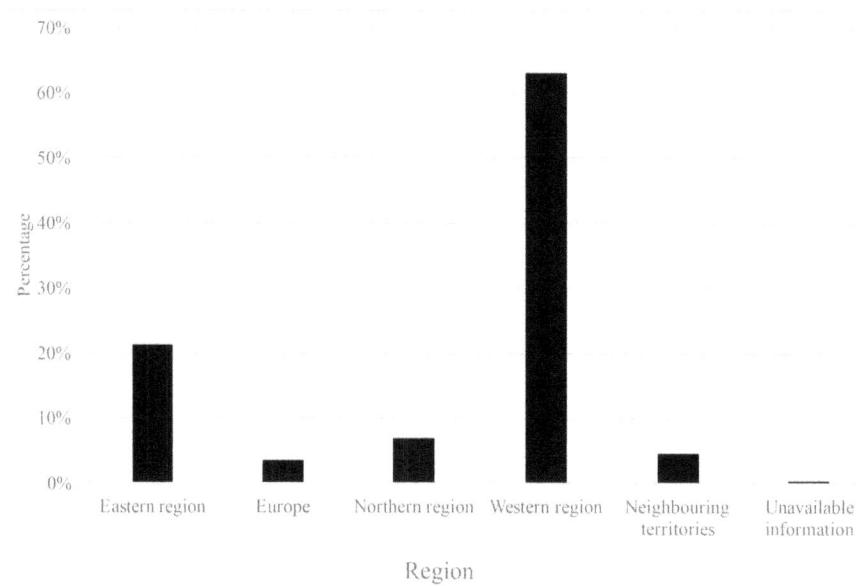

Figure 8.8 Capital value of women's investments in the Cape capital market broken down in regions, 1892–1902.
Source: WCARS, LC 1 – LC 467.

CHAPTER 9
BLACK AFRICANS IN CAPE TOWN, 1890-1939
Nobungcwele Mbem* and Michiel de Haas**

Introduction

In the late nineteenth and early twentieth century many black Africans,[1] willingly or unwillingly, gravitated towards South Africa's emerging cities. Most of these migrants were involved in mining, various forms of low-skilled labour, and, less commonly, domestic service. The mines of Kimberley and the Transvaal attracted black Africans from various parts of southern Africa.[2] The labour forces of the factories and farms of Durban and the harbour of Port Elizabeth consisted mostly of black Africans of various ethnicities from the nearby rural homelands.[3] As black Africans were not permitted to own land in the cities, this rendered their presence in the urban areas temporary and often resulted in circulatory systems of migration, aspects of South African migration that are extensively covered in the historiography.[4] Cape Town's commercial economy, even though dominated by white and coloured workers, attracted black African migrants

---

*Mbem: Department of History, Stellenbosch University, South Africa

**De Haas: Economic and Environmental History Group, Wageningen University, the Netherlands

[1] We use the term 'black' in this chapter to mean only black people and not, as in Cape Colony and South African historiography, to mean the group disenfranchised by apartheid, which includes coloured, Indian and Asian people as well as black.

[2] See Teresa K. Connor, 'Ambiguous Repositories: Archives, Traders and the Recruitment of Mineworkers in the Eastern Cape: 1900-1946', *South African Historical Journal* 72, no. 1 (2020): 98-124; David Yudelman and Alan Jeeves, 'New Labour Frontiers for Old Black Migrants to the South African Gold Mines, 1920-85', *Journal of Southern African Studies* 13, no. 1 (1986): 101-24 and Robert Vicat Turrell and Turrell Robert Vicat, *Capital and Labour on the Kimberley Diamond Fields, 1871-1890*, vol. 54 (Cambridge: Cambridge University Press, 1987).

[3] Alan Jeeves, 'Sugar and Gold in the Making of the South African Labour System the Crisis of Supply on the Zululand Sugar Estates 1906-1939', *South African Journal of Economic History* 7, no. 2 (1992): 7-33 & Gary Baines, 'The Control and Administration of Port Elizabeth's African Population, c. 1834-1923' (1989); R.F. Callebert, *Livelihood Strategies of Dock Workers in Durban, c. 1900-1959* (PhD Thesis, Queen's University (Canada), Department of History, 2011).

[4] William Beinart and Peter Delius, 'The Historical Context and Legacy of the Natives Land Act of 1913', *Journal of Southern African Studies* 40, no. 4 (2014): 667-88; Wayne Dooling, "Cape Town Knows, but She Forgets": Segregation and the Making of a Housing Crisis during the First Half of the 20th Century', *Journal of Southern African Studies* 44, no. 6 (2018): 1057-76; Wayne Dooling, 'Poverty and Respectability in Early Twentieth-century Cape Town', *The Journal of African History* 59, no. 3 (2018): 411-35.

as well. Most arrived in Cape Town at a mature age, became semi-permanently settled and returned to their rural homelands at retirement age. This does not match the general circulatory pattern of black mobility in South Africa.

This chapter studies black African migrants who arrived in Cape Town from around 1890 to the 1930s. These were not the 'pioneers' but the 'early adopters', preceding the much larger influx in the second half of the twentieth century, during and after apartheid.[5] We look particularly at household composition, gendered experiences and employment to see how these marginalised people in Cape Town took advantage of opportunities and overcame constraints. We argue that black migrants from the Transkeian Territories and the Ciskei who chose Cape Town over other migrant destinations traded the risk of a more precarious lifestyle for potential higher wage earnings and more freedom in their decisions about family life, work and residence.

The chapter helps to complete the picture of South Africa's black migration history, in two ways. Firstly, black African migrants are often discussed as a *category*, subjected to the policy decisions of a powerful and discriminatory state apparatus. South African migration historiography has often analysed black African mobility in relation to migration policy, town planning and urban governance; rarely do the migrants themselves surface as individuals with diverse experiences, preferences and choices. Rather than their agency and individuality, it has stressed their *commonality* and *uniformity* as subjects to be governed.[6] By taking individuals as the focal point, this chapter diverges from this tendency.

Secondly, the chapter adds to our knowledge about migratory moves of black Africans to Cape Town before apartheid, when the city had a small black population which had often travelled long distances, and whose migration and settlement was less controlled and more diverse than in the mining compounds of the Transvaal. This migration to Cape Town was particularly notable for the tension between the migrants' agency and the precariousness of their situation. The chapter illustrates this by tracing their histories of migration and family formation, experiences, work and livelihoods in the late interwar period. Understanding more about these 'early adopter' migrants could illuminate migration research today. Some consequences of internal migration, such as the stepwise gravity flow characterising recent migration, have origins in institutions and strategies of

---

[5] On the concepts of 'pioneer' and 'early adopter' migrants within broader 'migration transition' theory, see Hein De Haas, 'The Internal Dynamics of Migration Processes: A Theoretical Inquiry', *Journal of Ethnic and Migration Studies* 36, no. 10 (2010): 1599, 1607–9.

[6] See, for cases related to migration to Cape Town: Barry Kinkead-Weekes, 'Africans in Cape Town: State Policy and Popular Resistance, 1936–73' (PhD thesis, University of Cape Town, Faculty of Arts, Department of History, 1992); Maynard W. Swanson, 'The Sanitation Syndrome: Bubonic Plague and Urban Native Policy in the Cape Colony, 1900–1909', *The Journal of African History* 18, no. 3 (1977): 387–410; Muchaparara Musemwa, 'Aspects of the Social and Political History of Langa Township, Cape Town, 1927–1948' (Master's thesis, University of Cape Town, 1993) and Dooling, 'Cape Town Knows, but She Forgets': 1057–76. A major exception is the life histories collected by Belina Bozzoli and Mmantho Nkotsoe. See B. Bozzoli and M. Nkotsoe, *Women of Phokeng: Consciousness Life Strategy and Migrancy in South Africa, 1900–1983* (Johannesburg: Ravan, 1991); Callebert, *Livelihood Strategies of Dock Workers in Durban*.

the period we examine.⁷ Most black African residents of Cape Town today are isiXhosa speakers.⁸ Most have links with the former Transkei and Ciskei rural homelands. Moving from an agricultural to a commercial economy leads to changes in household composition and survival strategies, and this is still true of migrants to Cape Town today.⁹

Our key source of information for this effort of historical reconstruction of agency and precarity is – perhaps counterintuitively – largely quantitative. We used microdata from 101 African households recorded in the Social Surveys of Cape Town 1938 and 1939, a rich sample of black African residents drawn from the metropolitan area's black communities, almost all of whom had migrated to Cape Town in the preceding decades. These surveys provide detailed information on the work and income, current and previous residence, and age and family of 159 people, and cover a total of 300 individuals.[10] We had to exercise some caution because of biases arising from the nature of the sample. Nevertheless, the dataset yielded valuable information for writing the stories of previously 'unaccounted' Cape Town residents in the 1930s and enriching our understanding of their experiences, the difficulties they faced, and their aspirations.

Historical background

With the mineralisation and industrialisation of South Africa's economy in the late nineteenth and early twentieth century, large flows of black African migrants converged on the cities. Most were temporary and often circular sojourners, but became more permanent settlers. Within the broader landscape of South Africa's migration histories, Cape Town is a peculiar case. Whereas most black African migration in South Africa was state-directed and controlled by labour recruiting agencies, the migrants who moved to Cape Town from rural homelands did so on their own account. Up to the era of our study, moreover, they made up less than 5 per cent of the city's mainly white and coloured population. In this section we look at how early twentieth century Cape Town became a receiving region for growing numbers of black migrants, despite the precariousness of residency and employment for many of the newcomers, who nonetheless chose this destination deliberately.[11]

---

[7]Simon Bekker, 'Migration from South Africa's Rural Sending Areas: Changing Intentions and Changing Destinations', *Migration to South Africa within International Migration Trends* (2006).

[8]Robert Mongwe, 'The Importance of Language Identities to Black Residents in Cape Town and Johannesburg', *Reflections on Identity in Four African Cities* (2006): 171–88.

[9]Bekker, 'Migration from South Africa's Rural Sending Areas'.

[10]We also looked at other variables, such as religion and education, which remain to be analysed elsewhere.

[11]See, for this point, especially the work of William Beinart. William Beinart and Colin Bundy, *Hidden Struggles in Rural South Africa: Politics & Popular Movements in the Transkei & Eastern Cape, 1890-1930* (Berkeley: University of California Press, 1987); William Beinart, 'Beyond "Homelands": Some Ideas about the History of African Rural Areas in South Africa', *South African Historical Journal* 64, no. 1 (2012): 5–21; William Beinart, 'A Century of Migrancy from Mpondoland', *African Studies* 73, no. 3 (2014): 387–409; Beinart and Delius, 'The Historical Context and Legacy of the Natives Land Act of 1913', 667–88.

Table 9.1 Black African population of Cape Town, 1865–1939.

Census year	Black Africans in 'CT proper'	Share of total CT pop.	Black Africans in 'greater CT'	% of total 'greater CT' pop.	% of Black Africans outside 'CT proper'
1865	274	1.0%	707	1.8%	61.2%
1875	173	0.5%	202	0.5%	14.4%
1891	623	1.2%	781	1.0%	20.2%
1904	2,147	2.8%	7,492	4.3%	71.3%
1911	964	1.4%	2,088	1.3%	53.8%
1921	4,468	2.4%	8,691	4.1%	48.6%
1926	11,565	5.4%	n/a	n/a	n/a
1936	13,034	4.4%	14,160	4.1%	8.0%
1938	n/a	n/a	15,788	5,2%	n/a
1939	n/a	n/a	18,500	5,9%	n/a

Source: SS1 – Series of reports and studies issued by the Social Survey of Cape Town: The Growth Population (1942), Kinkead-Weekes, Barry. 'Africans in Cape Town: State Policy and Popular Resistance, 1936–73': 31 and Worden, Nigel, Elizabeth Van Heyningen, and Vivian Bickford-Smith. Cape Town: the making of a city: an illustrated social history. Uitgeverij Verloren (1998):71, Fast, Hildegarde Helene. 'Pondoks, houses, and hostels: a history of Nyanga 1946–1970, with a special focus on housing.' PhD thesis., University of Cape Town, Faculty of Arts, Department of History (1995): 32.

Table 9.1 shows the enumerated size and share of the black African population in Cape Town from 1865 to 1939. It illustrates a number of stylised facts, each of which we address further in the historical narrative below. First, the black presence in Cape Town has deep roots, going back at least to the mid-nineteenth century, even though population numbers and shares remained very small until a sustained take-off in the second quarter of the twentieth century. Second, the size and share of Cape Town's black African population did not expand in a linear fashion, but dipped significantly between 1904 and 1921. Third, a large proportion of Cape Town's black Africans did not live in the city proper but in the surrounding areas, especially during the first quarter of the twentieth century, when the black population of 'greater Cape Town' was more than double that of 'Cape Town proper'. As the borders of 'Cape Town proper' were not stable over time but shifted outward, population-size comparisons over time are more accurately made with reference to 'greater Cape Town'.[12]

---

[12] Cape Town's growth is discussed in the 'Growth of Population Report'. This report was part of a series of reports on the Social Surveys of Cape Town funded by the Carnegie Corporation, found at Batson Collection, Ms, 451. Manuscripts section, Stellenbosch University Library and Information Service. University of Cape Town Department of Social Science: Reports and Studies Issued by the Social Survey of Cape Town, Edited by Edward Batson, 'Growth of Population', May 1941, no. SS1.

In the early twentieth century, the Transkeian Territories comprised the major sending region of South Africa's black migrants, and have often been referred to as South Africa's 'labour reserve'.[13] The agricultural economy of these territories was disrupted by the nineteenth-century frontier wars, disasters such as the 1856–7 cattle killings and 1890s rinderpest, and the promulgation of the Natives Land Act of 1913.[14] The decline of the agricultural economy weakened the economic position of black African traders and merchants, leading many to seek wage incomes. Many heads of households who were unable to pay hut taxes were pushed to explore alternative means of earning an income such as selling their labour.[15] Wage earnings, in turn, not only affected the livelihoods of the migrants themselves but also contributed to socio-economic changes in the rural homelands which further spurred migration.[16]

The Transvaal mines were the largest receiving region of Transkeian Territories labour migrants. In 1912, 26 per cent of all South-Africa-sourced migrant labour in the Rand mines came from these territories (Mozambique contributed 48 per cent).[17] The Transvaal mines had a great appetite for cheap unskilled labour and used labour brokers for recruitment. Monopsonistic brokers such as the Native Recruiting Corporation (NRC) and the Witwatersrand Native Labour Association (WNLA) were instrumental in controlling the direction of labour migrancy.[18] Taking advantage of the pass laws, the WNLA enforced restrictions which limited the choice of jobs for black African migrants outside of the mining sector.[19] The Transvaal mines attracted an estimated 15,000 black

---

[13]William Beinart, *Political Economy of Pondoland, 1860–1930* (Cambridge: Cambridge University Press, 2011): 35–6. We use the term 'labour reserve' with caution because it is commonly used by historians to describe lands and communities occupied by black African people, and to an extent black African governance structure. The term may seem harmless because most of the systems and archives we consulted are colonial, but we find it problematic because it reduces the rural black African communities to sources of labour. One way to bring out the narratives of an unaccounted people is to discourage the use of such terms.

[14]Beinart and Delius, 'The Historical Context and Legacy of the Natives Land Act', 667–88; Roger Southall, *South Africa's Transkei: The Political Economy of an 'Independent' Bantustan* (London: Pearson Education, 1982); Jeffrey. B. Peires, *The Dead Will Arise: Nongqawuse and the Great Xhosa Cattle-Killing Movement of 1856–1857* (Johannesburg: Ravan, 1989) & Nomalanga Mkhize, 'In Search of Native Dissidence: RT Kawa's Mfecane Historiography in Ibali lamaMfengu, (1929)', *International Journal of African Renaissance Studies – Multi-, Inter- and Transdisciplinarity* 13, no. 2 (2018): 92–111.

[15]Southall, *South Africa's Transkei*, 67–73.

[16]See, Gordon Pirie, 'Railways and Labour Migration to the Rand Mines: Constraints and Significance', *Journal of Southern African Studies* 19, no. 4 (1993): 713–30; Kombo. J. Moyana, 'The Political Economy of the Migrant Labour System: Implications for Agricultural Growth and Rural Development in Southern Africa', *Africa Development / Afrique et Développement* 1, no. 1 (1976): 34–41; Bank, Leslie, 'City Slums, Rural Homesteads: Migrant Culture, Displaced Urbanism and the Citizenship of the Serviced House', *Journal of Southern African Studies* 41, no. 5 (2015): 1067–81.

[17]Pirie, 'Railways and Labour Migration to the Rand Mines'.

[18]Jeeves, 'Sugar and Gold in the making of the South African Labour System: The Crisis of Supply on the Zululand Sugar Estates, 1906–1939'. Based on a paper presented to the Seventh Biennial Conference of the Economic History Society of Southern Africa, Pietermaritzburg, July 1992.

[19]Sheila Van der Horst, *Native Labour in South Africa* (London: Oxford University Press, 1942): 158 & 164.

African migrants from across southern Africa in 1890, with the flow swelling rapidly to 318,000 by 1936 through WNLA and NRC recruitment.[20]

Despite its distance from the mining towns, Cape Town was indirectly affected by the mines' migrant labour system, not only because migrants to both regions came from the same sending region, but also because of the railway connecting the mines to Cape Town's harbour.[21] Because of the ease with which information and people could travel between the mines and the harbour, we should expect that labour markets and wages were integrated and that at least some of the migrants considered both destinations as alternatives. At the same time, Cape Town had distinct characteristics as a migrant destination, some of which it shared with emerging urban destinations in the Transvaal. Unlike migration to the mines, labour migration to Cape Town was self-organised and self-funded and did not offer a predetermined, time-restricted place of residence as arranged through a recruitment process. Cape Town's growing manufacturing industries relied on white and coloured labour and employed black Africans only to fill labour shortages. Others found work in the informal sector,[22] which was insecure because the jobs were mostly casual and seldom based on a contract.[23] Furthermore, the casual jobs were mostly for men.

The South African War (1899–1901) boosted black African migration to Cape Town. During the war, the Transvaal mines were shut down and the migrant labour system put on hold. The migrants were diverted to military work, for example in the Cape ports, which attracted tens of thousands of Transkeian and Ciskeian migrants.[24] War-time wages in Cape Town were comparatively favourable. From 1899 to 1902 the Cape ports paid workers four shillings per day (about £6 a month); a substantial premium over the pre-war monthly Transvaal mine wages of £2 to £3 in 1895 and £2 10s 0d to £2 14s 0d in 1899. As a consequence of the slow performance of the mines during and after the war, the WNLA reduced wages from a fixed monthly amount of £2 10s 0d in 1901 to a minimum of £1 10s 0d and maximum of £1 15s 0d in 1903, despite the increasing cost of living.[25] After the war, military work ceased at the Cape ports and the mines resumed operations. However, the mines struggled to reach pre-war numbers of unskilled migrant

---

[20]J.S. Harington, N.D. McGlashan and E.Z. Chelkowska, 'A Century of Migrant Labour in the Gold Mines of South Africa', *The Journal of the Southern African Institute of Mining and Metallurgy* 104, no. 2 (2004): 66.

[21]A. Rommelspacher, '"Too Delicate to Work"? Women and Work in Cape Town 1938–1939', Unpublished doctoral thesis chapter. Pirie, 'Railways and Labour Migration to the Rand Mines': 713–30; Gordon Pirie, 'African Township Railways and the South African State, 1902–1963', *Journal of Historical Geography* 13, no. 3 (1987): 283–95.

[22]Rommelspacher, 'Too Delicate to Work'; Goldin, 'The Coloured Labour Preference Policy, Co-option and Contradiction', *Collected Seminar Papers. Institute of Commonwealth Studies* 33 (1984): 108–20.

[23]Batson Collection, Ms, 451. 'A Socio-Economic Classification of Occupations in Cape Town', November 1946, no. SS8.

[24]Van der Horst, *Native Labour in South Africa*, 162. William Beinart and Colin Bundy, 'Introduction: "Away in the Locations"', in *Hidden Struggles in Rural South Africa*, ed. William Beinart and Colin Bundy (Johannesburg: Ravan, 2017): 20.

[25]Van der Horst, *Native Labour in South Africa*, 164 & 166.

labourers.[26] In 1903 only half of the 90,000 black African migrants working on the mines in 1899 had returned to work, owing to the lower wages and the risky nature of the work.[27] Wages in the Cape harbours declined but remained more competitive than those offered on the Transvaal mines.[28] Between March 1901 and November 1903, only 9,725 black African migrant workers were transported by railway to the Transvaal mines.[29] Between June 1903 and June 1904 nearly 10,000 workers were given passes to work in Cape Town.[30]

With migrant numbers in Cape Town growing, the colonial administrators established townships as an entry point for black Africans and to monitor their movements.[31] The Dock Native Location was established at the Cape Town docks in 1884 as the city's first settlement for black Africans. At its peak in 1900–1 it accommodated 10,000 people.[32] In a 1901 report, the Cape Town Office of the Commissioner of Public Works for Native Location Uitvlugt (later renamed Ndabeni) identified three kinds of black African resident: temporary, migratory and permanently settled. Most were migratory and would typically move between the rural homelands and their job in the city.[33] Although the numbers were said to be small, the Commission noted that the numbers of permanent black African residents were already increasing, hence the need to locate them far from white residential communities.[34] Spurred on by an outbreak of bubonic plague, approximately 7,000 of them (including 500 women) were resettled in 1902 in Ndabeni.[35] The much larger number of black residents in greater Cape Town than in Cape Town proper (Table 9.1) reflects the importance of Ndabeni location as a residential area in 1904. A highly skewed sex ratio (thirteen men for every woman) testifies to its migratory and male-dominated community.[36]

---

[26]Harington, McGlashan and Chelkowska, 'A Century of Migrant Labour in the Gold Mines', 66.

[27]Pirie, 'Railways and Labour Migration to the Rand Mines', 717.

[28]William Beinart, 'Jamani – Cape Workers in German South West Africa, 1904–12', in *Hidden Struggles in Rural South Africa*, ed. William Beinart and Colin Bundy (Johannesburg: Ravan, 2017): 168.

[29]Pirie, 'Railways and Labour Migration to the Rand Mines', 717.

[30]Beinart, 'Jamani – Cape Workers', 168.

[31]Dooling, '"Cape Town Knows, but She Forgets"', 1057–76.

[32]Swanson, 'The Sanitation Syndrome', 387–410.

[33]Cape Archives Depot, Cape Town. Department of Native Affairs. NA 457, Commission of Native Location for Cape Town Report: To Honourable Thomas Lynedoch Graham, K. C., M. L. C, Colonial Secretary of the Colony of the Cape of Good Hope, 1901.

[34]Goldin, 'The Coloured Labour Preference Policy', 108–20. A similar development took place in the Transvaal, where growing numbers of black residents were located in townships such as Klipspruit in Johannesburg. Susan Parnell, 'Race, Power and Urban Control: Johannesburg's Inner City Slum-yards, 1910–1923', *Journal of Southern African Studies* 29, no. 3 (2003): 615–37.

[35]J.E. Holloway, R.W. Anderson, et al., Report of Native Economic Commission, 1930–1932. Part III, 'Natives in Urban Areas', 64. Available online: http://hdl.handle.net/10500/5028; and see, Swanson, 'The Sanitation Syndrome', 387–410.

[36]Black African sex ratios in other African cities at the time tended to be much lower. See, for example, Felix Meier zu Selhausen, 'Urban Migration in East and West Africa: Contrasts and Transformations', in *Migration in Africa: Shifting Patterns of Mobility, 19th to 21st Centuries*, ed. Michiel de Haas and Ewout Frankema (Abingdon and Routledge, New York: Routledge, forthcoming in 2022): 281–307.

Cape Town's manufacturing sector employed skilled and semi-skilled whites, many of whom were immigrants from Britain and Australia. Semi-skilled and 'unskilled' black Africans operated the largely informal urban service sector. In 1904, Cape Town was hit by a recession which resulted in large-scale job losses.[37] Many white immigrants left and most black Africans lacked the skills to replace them. The recession hit Cape Town's black African population hard as jobs were scarce in both the informal and domestic sectors.[38] The cost of living was high, and most Ndabeni residents had zero to low incomes. Difficulties in sustaining livelihoods were compounded by restrictions on livestock ownership and a ban on owning a business licence or operating a shop.[39] These conditions resulted in numerous residents returning to their rural homelands, and a substantial decline in the number and share of black Africans in Cape Town in between the census years 1904 and 1921 (Table 9.1).

With Cape Town's economy in crisis, a new opportunity for its black African residents arose when German South West Africa (GSWA) began recruiting workers to support the German military efforts to root out Herero and Nama resistance against colonial rule (1904–7) and to build GSWA's railroad network. In the peak years, the number of South African migrants working in GSWA reached around 10,000, which equalled the number employed in the largest Cape ports.[40] GSWA recruitment resulted in a stepwise migration pattern, in which Cape Town – Ndabeni in particular – served as the receiving region for self-funded migrants from parts of the Ciskei and Transkeian Territories and the sending region (i.e. recruitment ground) for GSWA. Black African migrants were offered competitive wages of £5 per month, which included free transport, food and clothes. In comparison, wages in the mines had increased only to an average of £3 between 1903 and the 1910s.[41] Recruitment from Cape Town to GSWA was facilitated through labour brokers, who often reneged on promises and failed to pay labourers their full wages at the end of their assignment. Labour recruitment to GSWA was discontinued in 1912, partly because of poor working conditions and maltreatment of workers, as well as resurging labour demand on the Transvaal mines.

During the 1910s, now that it was part of the Union of South Africa, Cape Town's economy recovered from the post-South African War depression of 1903–9. Later, the demand for exports as a consequence of the First World War boosted the Cape's industrial sector.[42] The factories that sprang up – supported by laws such as the Civilised Labour

---

[37]C. Simkins and E. van Heyningen, 'Fertility, Mortality, and Migration in the Cape Colony, 1891–1904', *The International Journal of African Historical Studies* 22, no. 1 (1989): 85–6; Martin Nicol, 'A History of Garment and Tailoring Workers in Cape Town, 1900–1939' (PhD thesis, University of Cape Town, Faculty of Commerce, School of Economics, 1984): 68–70.

[38]Goldin, 'The Coloured Labour Preference Policy', 108–20.

[39]Cape Archives Depot, NA 457.

[40]Beinart. "Jamani" – Cape Workers', 168.

[41]Ibid, 169–70.

[42]Nicol, 'A History of Garment and Tailoring Workers in Cape Town', 71.

Policy of the 1920s – employed a large number of coloured women and some coloured men. Employment opportunities in the manufacturing and informal sector arose for black Africans as well, attracting more migrants which in turn triggered petitions from white and coloured ratepayers pressuring the city council for segregated living. The claim was that an increase in black African presence in the central city depreciated the value of property and was a security threat. Despite the hostile response, new arrivals increased resulting in overpopulation and poor sanitation in black residential and squatter areas.[43]

The Natives Urban Area Act of 1923, which aimed to firmly establish segregationist urban residential spaces, linked black presence in Cape Town to employment and regulated black mobility through 'influx controls'. In line with this Act, a plan was made to resettle Ndabeni's residents in a new township, which became known as Langa.[44] Like Ndabeni, Langa, completed in 1927, was built to accommodate the increasing labour demands for informal and unskilled work in the city, and the growing black African population. Conditions in Langa were designed to be slightly better than those in Ndabeni. Poor white labourers were hired to build the houses in Langa, but the 'civilised' wage rates offered to them by the government to address the 'poor white problem' made this labour expensive so rent was increased to recover costs.[45] However, protesting black African residents managed to negotiate rental reduction three times.[46] Resettlement took place during 1927–8 and Langa took over from Ndabeni as Cape Town's main 'bridgehead' community for newly arriving migrants.

Already in 1901 the Commission of Native Location had noticed that black women were increasingly migrating to Cape Town, contributing to the growth of a settled black population. The point was again stressed by the Native Economic Commission (1930–2).[47] Some degree of permanency was beneficial to employers, ensuring a consistent supply of labour with the skills they required. Unlike the corrugated structures of Ndabeni, which were mostly intended for one person, Langa had married quarters set aside for couples and families, even though the majority of the accommodation was designed as a temporary arrangement for single occupancy.[48] Langa also had sections of unlisted barracks which were often occupied by people undocumented in the official books.[49] Langa is particularly important for this chapter since it was the neighbourhood hosting the largest number of the black households in the Batson survey.

---

[43] Kinkead-Weekes, 'Africans in Cape Town', 13–26.

[44] Holloway, Anderson, et al., Report of Native Economic Commission, 5.

[45] Hildegarde Helene Fast, 'Pondoks, Houses, and Hostels: A History of Nyanga 1946–1970, with a Special Focus on Housing' (PhD thesis., University of Cape Town, Faculty of Arts, Department of History, 1995): 31–4.

[46] Holloway; Anderson, et al., Report of Native Economic Commission.

[47] Cape Archives Depot, NA 457; Holloway, Anderson, et al., Report of Native Economic Commission, 64.

[48] Dooling, 'Poverty and Respectability', 417; Sipokazi Shambu, *Social History, Public History and the Politics of Memory in Re-making 'Ndabeni's' Pasts* (Master's thesis, University of the Western Cape, 2010).

[49] Batson Collection, Ms, 451. 'Distribution of Households', May 1944, No. SS25, 8.

Quantitative History and Uncharted People

Economic prospects in the Cape, already challenging for most black Africans, worsened with the Great Depression of 1929–34, which brought economic decline to economic sectors outside the gold mine value chain.[50] Meanwhile, the deteriorating environmental conditions in the Ciskei and other parts of the Transkei in the early 1930s forced many black Africans to abandon the rural agricultural economy for urban wage earnings as a household survival strategy.[51] As a result the number of recorded (Table 9.1) and unrecorded black Africans residing in and around Cape Town increased sharply.[52] The 1937 Natives Law Amendment Act acknowledged some black Africans as permanently provided that they complied with the pass laws and could prove continuous residence or Cape Town as a birthplace.[53]

Although the city council had made attempts in 1926 to enforce 'seek-work permits', it struggled to enforce compliance. This resulted in the promulgation of the more restrictive Proclamation 105 in 1939, which restricted the entry of new arrivals without *"firm offer of employment"*. Failure to comply was a criminal offence.[54] Proclamation 105 coincided with the start of the Second World War, which generated new employment opportunities for black Africans, as had been the case with earlier war-time episodes.[55] Pass laws compliance was suspended in 1941–3 due to high demand for black African labour and the city council's inability to provide sufficient formal housing.[56] After the war, the construction of Nyanga, beginning in 1945, definitively entrenched a policy of segregationist residence.

Social surveys of Cape Town by Professor Edward Batson

The Batson social surveys of Cape Town were conducted from October 1938 to April 1939. The records are stored in Stellenbosch University's special collections library and were recently transcribed and digitised. They are a useful source for understanding migration to and residence in Cape Town before apartheid.[57] The surveys were part of

---

[50] Nicoli Nattrass and Jeremy Seekings, 'The Economy and Poverty in the Twentieth Century in South Africa'. Centre for Social Science Research, University of Cape Town. CSSR Working Paper No.276 (2010): 7–8; Barry Eichengreen, 'Gold and South Africa's Great Depression', *Economic History of Developing Regions* 36, no. 2 (2021): 175–93.

[51] Charles Hilliard Feinstein, *An Economic History of South Africa: Conquest, Discrimination, and Development* (Cambridge: Cambridge University Press, 2005): 72.

[52] Kinkead-Weekes, 'Africans in Cape Town', 28 & 31 –26.

[53] Fast, 'Pondoks, Houses, and Hostels', 35.

[54] Kinkead-Weekes, 'Africans in Cape Town', 32, 38.

[55] Ibid, 32 and Fast, 'Pondoks, Houses, and Hostels', 35, 41.

[56] Ibid, 42.

[57] The Social Surveys for Cape Town were transcribed by Nobungcwele Mbem as part of her doctoral thesis research project. These surveys were accessed at the Stellenbosch University Library Special Collections. The transcription was made possible through the Biography of an Uncharted People project based at Stellenbosch University funded by the Mellon Foundation.

a project headed by sociologist Professor Edward Batson from the University of Cape Town that investigated the standard of living and incidence of poverty in white, coloured and black households in Cape Town.[58] The survey used the methods of Professor A. L. Bowley of the University of London, who conducted a similar project in England in 1913 in Merseyside, New London and Bristol. To apply these methods to Cape Town, Batson made some adjustments to account for socio-cultural and administrative-institutional differences.[59] Some of the problems he encountered were language barriers, an ethnically mixed and illiterate population, lack of comprehensive and accurate maps, and lack of sufficiently trained staff.[60]

Batson collected data for a randomised sample of Cape Town's full population of about 59,000 private households. Just over 3 per cent of all households were visited for the project.[61] Close to 2,000 surveys were conducted, with 1,980 yielding analysable results.[62] Of these, only 101 (about 5 per cent) were black households, comprising a total of 300 residents, corresponding to about 2 per cent of Cape Town's black African population, and 3 per cent of black African households.[63] The households surveyed were located across greater Cape Town, with concentrations in the city proper, Woodstock, Langa, Athlone and Kensington (see Figure 9.1). Households in the informal settlements or single quarters (barracks) of the southern parts of Cape Town, where in fact the majority of black residents lived, were not included.[64]

Measuring living standards, the prime objective of Batson's project, is complicated because of fundamental differences in diverse cultures' and communities' ideas of quality of life and what they value and why.[65] In Cape Town the measurement was complicated further because it was white officials and surveyors who did the measuring, using racial hierarchies and a 'Western template' as the desired standard. The Native Economic Commission's 1930-2 report, founded on the premise that black Africans are 'lesser' humans until assimilated to European standards, emphasised the need to urbanise and westernise them:

> In the original Native economy the variety of articles of consumption was limited. [...] The European, and civilised races generally, have opened up new avenues of enjoyment for those who had more than was necessary to satisfy the purely

---

[58] The Poverty Datum Line was an estimate of the income needed to survive or to attain the 'minimum essentials for health and decency'. See, Batson Collection, Ms, 451. 'Poverty Datum Line', May 1941, No. SS3, 1.

[59] Batson Collection, Ms, 451. 'Surveying Methods', May 1941, No. SS9, 1 & 3.

[60] Ibid, 3.

[61] Ibid, 3 & Batson Collection, Ms, 451. 'Distribution of Households', May 1944, No. SS25, 1.

[62] Ibid, Appendix A.

[63] For the population, see Table 9.1. The 'Distribution of Households' report estimated the number of black residents in private households in Cape Town as 3,100. Ibid., 1.

[64] Ibid, 8.

[65] Amartya Sen, 'The Living Standard', *Oxford Economic Papers* 36 (1984): 3-4.

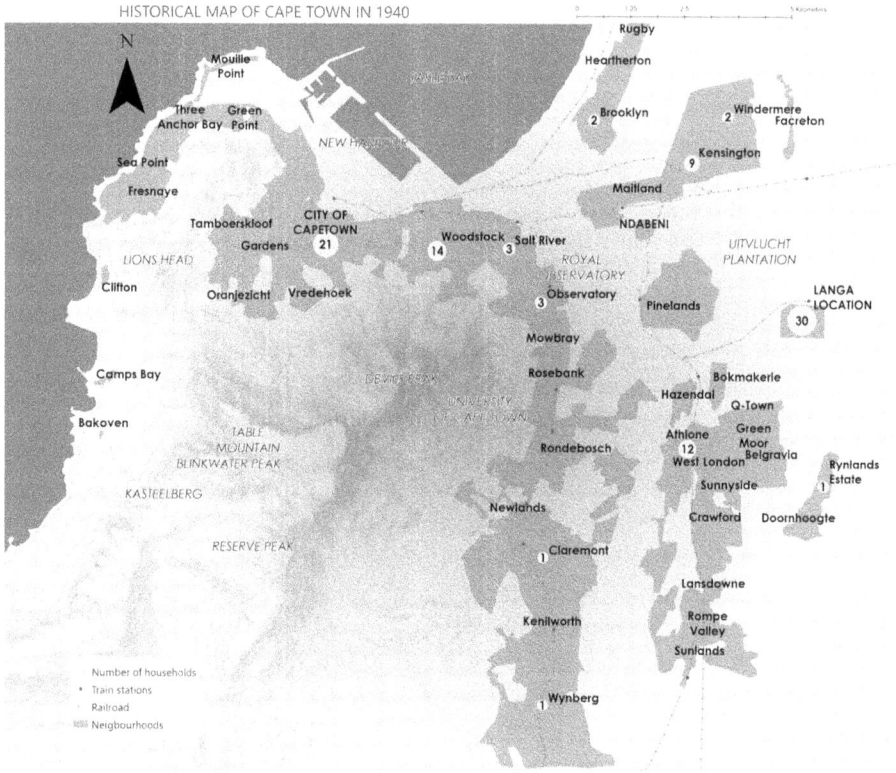

Figure 9.1 Location of surveyed households.
Source: Created by Zina Janssen, based on a map from c. 1940 from National Geo-Spatial Information (Trig Survey), and made available by Adrian Frith. (https://htonl.dev.openstreetmap.org/50k-ct/#10/-34.0000/18.5000/c1940).
Note: we were able to link 97 households (out of 101) to a neighbourhood.

physiological requirements, by the introduction of conventional necessaries. [...] The urbanised Natives have followed Europeans in this. Instead of continuing on a standard in which the limits of personal expenditure for necessaries were determined by physical capacity, they have adopted the more diversified standard of living of the Europeans. This is a 'higher' standard because it is more diversified, and therefore free of the monotony of eating merely to live; it is also higher because it is based on, and gives scope for, a higher development of the arts.[66]

Batson's Social Surveys of Cape Town were similarly based on methods developed in western contexts, with little sensitivity to issues of racially segregationist spatial planning and its relation to poverty and respectability, the importance of which has been stressed

---

[66] Holloway, Anderson, et al., Report of Native Economic Commission, 78.

Table 9.2 Categories of household members, sorted by frequency.

HH members	No.	No. per HH	Av. age	Earners	Share earning
Head	101	1.00	38	98	97%
Wife	58	0.57	33	16	28%
Daughter	51	0.50	8	3	6%
Son	50	0.50	8	4	8%
Lodger	12	0.12	28	8	67%
Nephew	6	0.06	21	3	50%
Niece	5	0.05	16	0	0%
Granddaughter	3	0.03	1	0	0%
Grandson	3	0.03	1	0	0%
Brother	2	0.02	23	1	50%
Sister	2	0.02	41	1	50%
Stepson	2	0.02	21	1	50%
Cousin	1	0.01	21	1	100%
Mother	1	0.01	62	0	0%
Sister-law	1	0.01	24	0	0%
Stepdaughter	1	0.01	13	0	0%
Wife of lodger	1	0.01	21	0	0%
TOTAL	**300**	**2.97**	**25**	**136**	**45%**

Source: Batson Social Survey.
Note: The final column shows the share of individuals in each category of household members who is an income earner.

in earlier scholarship.[67] Moreover, surveyor comments reveal that residents were often hesitant to share information, especially about their incomes, which at least some probably underreported.

The questionnaire Batson used aimed to elicit as much detailed information as possible about the head of the household, often the primary wage earner. Information was also gathered about other wage earners and members of the household, categorised according to their relationship to the head. Name, age, sex, occupation, address, wages, mode of transport, next-of-kin, rent, birthplace and year of migration of household heads and wives were recorded. Less information was collected about other household members. The number of the household head's children who were not in Cape Town was also mentioned. Table 9.2 shows the relationship of the household members to the head. All the households were recorded as having at least one wage earner, frequently

---

[67] Dooling, 'Poverty and Respectability', 411–35.

the household head. The smallest households contained one person (27 per cent of all households) and the largest eight, the average household size being 2.95 and the median two. The average number of people per room was 2.01 and the median two. The density of occupation varied from six people sharing a single room to one person having two rooms to their own.

The resultant dataset is rich and diverse and gave us many insights into the lives and decisions of black Africans in Cape Town. However, it is clearly not fully representative. Firstly, it represents the population of black *residents* in Cape Town (and only those in formal houses), but not the population of black *migrants* – those who migrated to Cape Town at some point in their life. Migrants who stayed only briefly were less likely to appear in the survey and are thus underrepresented. Since migration was the object of our study, we must take sample selection bias (survivorship bias) into account and not overstate the importance of long-term settlement relative to more temporary and circular forms of migration, which largely remain outside our purview. Secondly, the sample represents migrants at a particular stage in their lives and cannot give us any idea how long they typically stayed in Cape Town. The length of stay of household heads and their wives is recorded, but not of other household members. It is likely that those who stayed the longest in Cape Town would also be household heads, about whom the survey provides a lot more information. We cannot know the survey respondents' future plans, particularly the more recently arrived younger ones, who may have either stayed long beyond the survey date or instead have left soon after. Most older people would have returned to their home regions, so those who decided to stay in Cape Town into old age (and are thus observed in the Batson survey) may have had specific reasons for doing so.[68] These caveats do not prevent meaningful analysis of the sample, but should be borne in mind.

Migration, marriage and family formation strategies

In what follows, we explore key life course events of Cape Town's black African residents. In particular, we look at *patterns* and *variation* in individuals' timing of migration to Cape Town in relation to marriage and family formation strategies. We also explore the extent to which Cape Town's residents retained their links with the sending regions. Jointly, these explorations offer important clues about the residents' migratory decision-making and the permanency of their stay.

---

[68]Notably, however, we do not observe a correlation between the length of stay (or age) of household heads and wives, their living costs (rent) and their earnings. We found null results in bivariate and multivariate regressions with these variables (and after controlling for sex). Space does not allow us to report these results here.

Black Africans in Cape Town, 1890–1939

Migration histories

As a first step, we are interested to find out to what extent Cape Town's late-1930s residents can be classified as migrants. This proves to be overwhelmingly the case. Of the household heads and wives with a known migration history, ninety-four heads (97.9 per cent) and fifty-four wives (93.0 per cent) reported that they arrived in Cape Town at some point during their life. Only two heads and four wives were born in Cape Town (between 1889 and 1911). Figure 9.2 ranks the heads and wives with a known migration history by age, showing how many years they had lived in Cape Town at the time of the survey.

As is common with urban migration, by far the majority of migrants had arrived at working age. Fourteen household heads (15.1 per cent of all migrant heads) and ten wives (20.4 per cent of all migrant wives) arrived before their twentieth birthday. Only six household heads (6.5 per cent) and four wives (8.2 per cent) arrived after the age of forty. The average age of arrival was 28.3 for household heads and 26.2 for wives, and the corresponding medians were 28 and 25. Importantly, we only know when they arrived

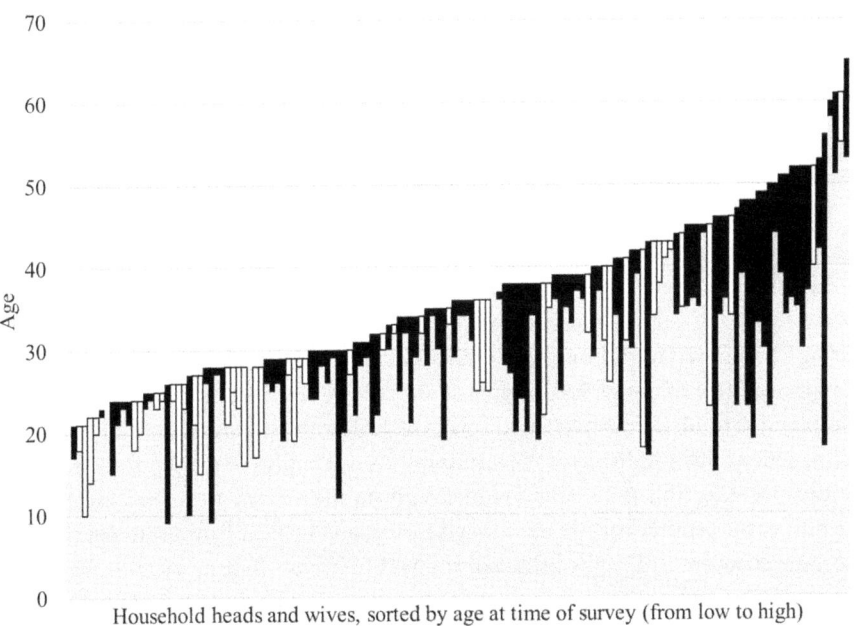

Figure 9.2 Migration histories of migrant household heads and wives.
Source: Authors' calculations, based on data from the Batson Survey.
Note: Two non-migrant household heads and four non-migrant wives are excluded from the graph.

233

Table 9.3 Duration of current residence in Cape Town at time of survey, by age cohort.

Age	Frequency	Av. no. of years
20–29	43	5.49
30–39	51	6.96
40–49	32	12.97
50–59	11	17.55
60–69	5	7.50
ALL	142	8.65

Source: Batson Social Survey.

for their *current* stay. Some may have lived in Cape Town or other migration destinations at earlier periods in their lives. These would be either *circular* migrants, if they alternated between Cape Town and one particular place, or *stepwise* migrants, if they moved to a new place each time. The Batson survey does not provide any direct evidence on this issue, although references to some family members of Cape Town residents having moved on to Johannesburg testify to the incidence of stepwise migration.[69] The fact that older residents (at the time of the survey) had arrived, on average, at an older age than the younger ones,[70] may imply that they had some unrecorded earlier migratory experience (to Cape Town or a different destination) before their current stay in Cape Town, but it can also be attributed to increasing migration over the half century preceding the survey, affecting all age groups.

Table 9.3 shows the lengths of residents' current stay in Cape Town, broken down by age cohort. The average for all 142 household heads and wives of various ages at the time of the survey is almost nine years. Because long-stayers were more likely to have been picked up by the survey, and because residents were observed at some unknown point during (as opposed to at the end of) their stay in Cape Town, the figures cannot be taken as representative of the typical lengths of stay. However, they do indicate some pattern of prolonged residence among Cape Town's migratory black population. Another clue to permanency (albeit indirect) is the strikingly even sex ratio of the figures: only 1.3 men for each woman. This is a marked reduction from the extremely skewed ratio of 13:1 at the turn of the century that we mentioned earlier, and in clear contrast to the situation of the more transient migrants contracted from six to twenty-four months on the Transvaal mines. Again, caution is warranted when interpreting these figures, which capture Cape Town's household heads, and exclude other household members and those in informal settlements, whose presence was likely more transient.

---

[69] As does the migration to German South West Africa in an earlier period, discussed above.

[70] The average (median) age of arrival of those above forty was 33.8 (34) and 25.3 (25) for those below forty.

Migration strategies

The ability to reside with, or even seek out, a spouse is an important factor determining migrants' decision to settle at their destination. Most of the male household heads observed in the Batson Survey were married (eighty-four men or 85.8 per cent of the sample). For eighty of these the wife's place of residence is recorded: about two-thirds (fifty-three) were in Cape Town. The large share of married residents indicates a fairly settled urban population (in line with the markedly balanced sex ratio), especially when placed in contrast to the Transvaal's transient migrant population. We can only speculate about the various reasons why the remaining wives (twenty-seven) were not in Cape Town. Some couples may have been *de facto* divorced, others pursued multi-sited livelihood strategies, with the wife occupying a rural home. A surveyor reported on a remarkable case of a couple who had moved to Cape Town in 1927, after having been married for as much as twenty-nine years. After two years in Cape Town, the wife, now fifty-two years old, 'went back home', and had since 'always' been coming and going. All the while, the husband, sixty-five-year-old Simon Makana[71] had plenty of reason to remain in Cape Town. He was a construction worker, presumably with considerable skill and experience, living in Cape Town with his son aged nineteen and daughter aged nine, who were attending the local St Cyprian school. Two other children, probably adults, lived elsewhere. Three of his children had died. Simon sent regular and sizeable remittances 'home'.

The Batson survey recorded only five female household heads living without a husband in Cape Town. Four reported to be married and one was a widow. That few women lived independently in Cape Town was, at least for a large part, an outcome of government policy. A black African woman would be granted a certificate to live in the city only to join her spouse or, if she was unmarried, to visit her father, who had to provide proof he had been working in the city for a minimum of two years.[72] While such policies strongly restricted independent female mobility, the Batson survey provides some evidence of women circumventing these limitations. For example, in one case, a husband left Cape Town for Johannesburg around 1928. For eleven years, his wife occupied the two-room dwelling in the married quarters of Langa until when, in 1939, her brother, George Makwenkwe, who had been living in Cape Town since 1927, got married to his newly arrived bride and could move in.

How did men and women time their marriage and migration? The survey records the year of marriage and arrival dates of male heads and their wives for forty-six couples resident in Cape Town. Figure 9.3 shows how many years before or after their marriage the respective spouses moved to Cape Town. It also indicates the years during which they were separated because one spouse migrated to Cape Town while the other stayed

---

[71] We use the names recorded in the survey, some of which may have been misspelt.
[72] Holloway, Anderson, et al., Report of Native Economic Commission, 1930–1932. Part IV, 'General'. Available online: http://hdl.handle.net/10500/5028.

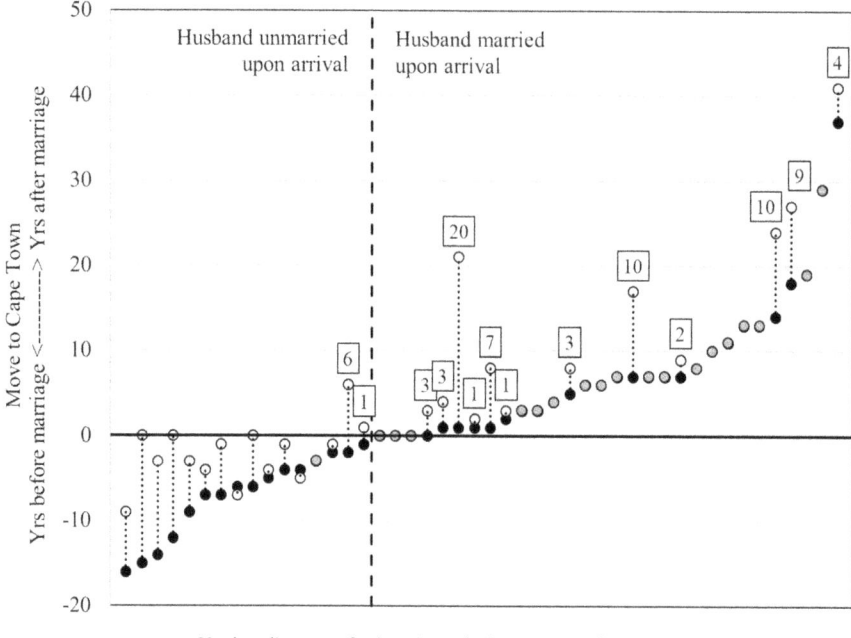

Figure 9.3 Year of migration relative to marriage (sorted by male year of migration relative to marriage), years of separation during marriage (if any) indicated.
Sources: *Authors' calculations, based on data from the Batson Survey.*
Notes: Of the fourteen married men who did not live with their wives in Cape Town and who are not included in this figure, eight (57.1 per cent) had married before and six (42.9 per cent) after arrival, shares that are comparable to those whose wives were present at the time of the survey. Of the wives who lived without a husband, all three had been married upon arrival in Cape Town.

behind. The right-hand side of the panel shows the majority of twenty-six men who were married upon arrival (56.5 per cent) and the four who married in the year they arrived (8.7 per cent). Unsurprisingly, in none of these cases were the prospective wives already living in Cape Town. Of the twenty-six couples who had married before either party migrated, fifteen (57.7 per cent) arrived together (or at least in the same year), while eleven (42.3 per cent) did not. In the latter cases, the time it took for the wife to follow her husband to Cape Town was on average 6.4 years. In one extreme case, W. Nqoweni, aged twenty-two, and his bride, aged seventeen had gotten married in 1913, presumably in Kentani (close to Butterworth), where they were both born. In the next year, W. migrated to Cape Town, while his wife followed only in 1934: twenty years later.

The fact that spouses were spatially separated for prolonged intervals suggests that migrants retained strong ties with the sending regions. Notably, a majority of ten out of fourteen wives (71.4 per cent) who followed their husbands to Cape Town hailed from the same home region. This suggests that the couple knew each other and that the marriage was consolidated before the husband migrated, initially by himself, to Cape Town.[73]

The left-hand side of the panel shows the minority of sixteen men (34.8 per cent) who migrated to Cape Town before marriage. In the majority of cases, unmarried men arrived in Cape Town many years before their future brides (4.9 years earlier, on average), possibly saving for bridewealth before making a marriage proposal in their home regions. Surprisingly, in most cases, prospective wives arrived in Cape Town several years before their actual marriage took place (a time gap of 2.1 years on average). Only in three cases (18.8 per cent) did brides arrive in the year of marriage. Given the restrictions on the mobility of non-married women, we might hypothesise that the (stated) intention of their migration was to reside with their future husbands, with whom they already had formed a union, albeit not ordained by the church, in their joint sending region. In two remarkable cases, prospective wives arrived before their future husbands, possibly to set up a home.

One striking observation, however, is that of the eleven women who married their current husband after first arriving in Cape Town, only three (27.3 per cent) stated the same home region as their husbands, a much lower share than for the twenty-five out of thirty-five women (71.4 per cent) who had married before or upon arriving in Cape Town. Similarly, of the sixteen men who married their current wife after first arriving in Cape Town, only six (37.5 per cent) came from the same home region, compared to twenty-two out of thirty (73.3 per cent) of those who had married before or upon arrival.[74] That the majority of those who married after arriving in Cape Town found partners from a different home region suggests that at least some spouses met in Cape Town itself, that is, that a 'marriage market' existed in Cape Town. However, our exceedingly small sample does not lend itself to definitive conclusions, and future research, for example using marriage registers, will elucidate Cape Town's marriage dynamics further.

Child-rearing strategies

The information about the number of children and whether they were present in Cape Town can tell us to what extent couples pursued an urban 'nuclear family' strategy or continued to rely on extended families in sending regions. The average number of children reported by household heads was 2.45, of whom 0.91 were present in Cape Town, 0.90 away, and 0.65 deceased (which corresponds to a child mortality rate of 26.7 per cent). In the remainder, we only consider the living children.

The timing of marriage mattered for child-rearing strategies. The average number of living children reported by male household heads (whether their wives were present in

---

[73]Sometimes these home regions are defined broadly as 'Transkei'.

[74]We have more observations for men, because for seven women the year of migration is unknown.

Cape Town or not) who were already married when they came to Cape Town was 3.35, of whom more were away (an average of 2.12, or 63.2 per cent) than present (1.24, or 36.8 per cent). The shares were reverse in the case of those who married in Cape Town: an average of 1.62, of whom fewer were away (0.38, or 23.8 per cent) than present (1.23, or 76.2 per cent). Whether the wife was present in Cape Town or not also mattered greatly for child-rearing strategies. Among male households heads whose wife was present in Cape Town, the majority of their average total number of 2.45 children were present (1.43, or 58.5 per cent), while the reverse was true for the average total number of 1.30 children of household heads whose wife was not present (0.19, or 14.3 per cent). If we combine information about the timing of marriage and presence of wives, we find, as expected, that the largest share of children present was among those married in Cape Town and with the wife present (82.9 per cent), followed by those who married before migrating and with the wife present (46.5 per cent), those who married in Cape Town but with the wife absent (42.9 per cent) and, lastly those married before migrating and with the wife absent (7.1 per cent).

This difference suggests that couples whose marriages were sealed in Cape Town were more likely to rear their children in the urban setting, especially if the wife was present. Those who had married in the sending regions were more likely to raise their children long-distance, possibly with the help of extended families. However, it should be borne in mind that the men who married before coming to Cape Town were on average older than those who married after (43.3 years as opposed to 36.3), which means that the observed difference in child-rearing strategies may also be explained, at least partly, by the fact that their children were older and therefore less dependent on their parents.

Remittances

Remittances are an important indication of continued contact between Cape Town residents and their home regions. Unfortunately, evidence on remittances from the Batson Survey is incidental and anecdotal. In ten cases mention is made in the surveyor comments of remittances being sent by Cape Town residents to family members living in the sending regions, typically a wife and/or children. Among those who remitted income was Stuart Boromane, a sixty-year-old self-employed man who had arrived in Cape Town recently, in 1937, and lived alone in Langa's 'special quarters'.[75] His first wife had died during the 1918 flu pandemic and he had remarried in 1923. He had six children, of whom two had died and four were living elsewhere. Through his business, Stuart made on average 10 shillings per week, with his highest earnings reaching 12 shillings per week. He had just begun to send remittances, totalling £1 between January and May of the year the survey was conducted, about 7.7 per cent of his income for this period.

---

[75]'Special quarters' were reserved for single men who escaped living in the barracks because they could afford higher rental costs of the single compounds. See Musemwa, 'Aspects of the Social and Political History of Langa Township', 36.

In some cases, the amounts appear to have been quite substantial. For example, Gideon Fouqjo, an unmarried resident of Langa reported sending on average £2 per month to his father's sister in Port Elizabeth, corresponding to 31 per cent of his reported income. John Mdeni, a resident of Langa's 'special quarters' reported sending £1 10s 0d to his wife and two living children in Umtata District per month, 38 per cent of his reported income. In most other reported cases, remittances took up some 10 per cent of reported income. In one further case, the respondent, Joseph Nqewu, who was living with his wife and one child in Langa's married quarters, indicated that he would like to send remittances home to his six children but was unable to afford it.

Living conditions, work and livelihoods

In this section we analyse the living conditions and livelihood strategies of Cape Town's black African residents, teasing out clues about the ways in which they navigated opportunities and obstacles in an urban setting. We also draw a comparison with earnings of migrant workers in the Transvaal mines.

Earnings and occupations

Households had an average of 1.4 wage earners and a median of 1. Each household had at least one person bringing in income, including the female-headed households. The largest number of wage earners in one household, located in central Cape Town, was five, which is also the total number of members of that household. All five were unmarried males between the ages of twenty-six and thirty-six, of whom three were employed full-time and two part-time. The five men shared the £4 monthly rent. Included in the rent were municipal rates and water but the premises did not have electricity or gas. The surveyor mentioned that he had failed three times to find someone at the household before 6 pm. This household was an exceptional case, however, as most addresses were occupied by one or multiple households formed around a family, sometimes hosting one or more lodgers who paid rent to the household head (see Table 9.2).

The average household earnings reported were £1 16s 0d per week, of which £1 7s 0d (75 per cent) was earned by the head, and 9s (25 per cent) by other members of the household. £1 13s 5d (93 per cent) came from wage income and the remaining 2s 7d (7 per cent) from other activities which were predominantly done by women, such as providing meals, brewing beer or hosting lodgers. Some households also had access to a garden for self-provisioning. For example, dock labourer Moulley Qubuka and his unemployed wife, both aged sixty-one, lived in Langa's married quarters where they had access to a garden where they kept fowls and grew vegetables.

The Batson survey reports occupations for almost all earners. Unfortunately, the categories used to describe occupations are sometimes rather crude, with many workers simply listed as 'labourers', while for others a much more specific description is given. Figure 9.4 shows the frequency of occupations, based on our own occupational

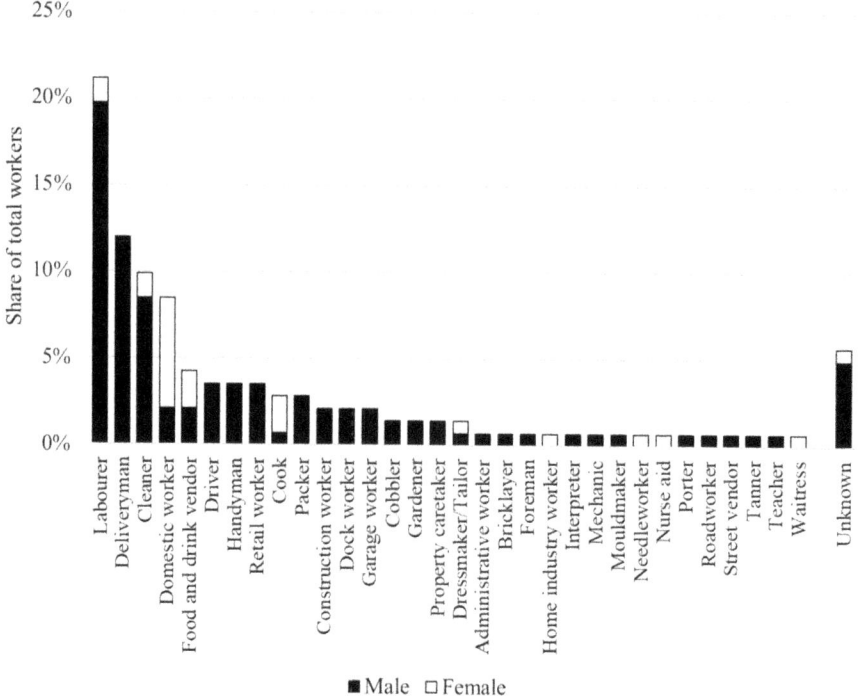

Figure 9.4 Occupations observed in the Batson survey and their frequency.
Sources: *Authors' calculations, based on data from the Batson Survey.*
Note: Those without an occupation are excluded from the graph.

classification that is just slightly more aggregated than the descriptions given in the survey. Although the four most frequent occupations (labourer, deliveryman, cleaner and domestic worker) account for over half of all workers, we find a reasonable amount of occupational diversity in the remainder of the sample, including tailors, a bricklayer, an interpreter and a teacher. Women were mostly employed as domestic workers and cooks, but we also find a waitress, a nurse aid and a dressmaker.

The weekly wage for workers in the sample was on average £1 4s 2d, with an average of £1 7s 2d for men and 10s 5d for women. Figure 9.5 shows earnings by occupation and sex. Unsurprisingly, the more precisely defined and hence more specialised occupations, such as cobbler, teacher, mechanic or foreman yielded higher wages. We can clearly see that working women, mostly engaged in the lower-earning occupations to the left of the graph, earned less than men, even within the same occupations (37 per cent of the men's incomes, on average). Even women who headed a household struggled to bring in income. The stories of Jane Bangazi aged fifty and L. Nkomyahlaba aged thirty-nine illustrate this pattern. Both were married but did not live with their husbands. Jane lived a few houses away from her estranged husband, whom she had married in 1918, but who

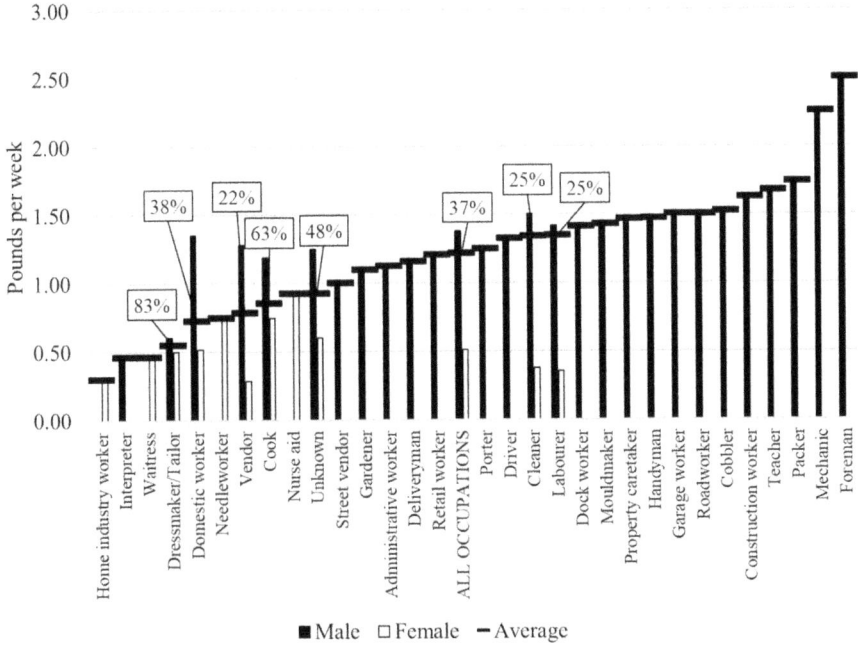

Figure 9.5 Earnings per occupation: average and by gender.
Sources: *Authors' calculations, based on data from the Batson Survey.*
Note: Female share of male wage indicated if both were available.

now lived with his second wife, who had arrived in Cape Town in 1937. Jane's occupation was described as 'home industry' by the surveyor, according to whom she struggled to make ends meet without her husband's support, 'doing odd jobs, selling beer, and getting presents from men'. L. Nkomyahlaba's husband had moved back to the Transkei four months before the interview and did not support her. She told the surveyor that she borrowed money for rent and food. The surveyor added that she 'undoubtedly sells beer' and suspected that she lived intermittently with a man.

Living costs

Housing facilities were basic. None of the households had gas and only 18 per cent had electricity. Some workers incurred commuting costs. Transport costs for all workers, added up to an average of 10d per week per worker (3.4 per cent of income). Those who used transport paid an average of 2s 4d per week (8.9 per cent of their income). Feeding a household was expensive. Batson calculated that the cost of the minimum adult male equivalent food basket for a week (at what he defined as the poverty line) was 7s 3d. If we assume that each worker supported 2.5 adult male equivalents, the weekly food costs add up to £1 1s 9d, which represents a striking 90 per cent of a worker's average income. In the next subsection, however, we re-assess Batson's cost calculation, and find it too high in comparative perspective to serve as a realistic benchmark of food costs.

As Figure 9.6 shows, rent costs were substantial but appear to have been reasonable as a proportion of income, in most cases. On average, households paid £1 11s 0d rent per month, or 7s 2d per week, corresponding to 20 per cent of total household income. The female-headed household of widow Esther Emmett is a clear outlier, apparently paying more than 100 per cent of its income on rent. Esther arrived in Cape Town in 1935 from Queenstown at age forty-three and lived with her domestic worker daughter, aged twenty-one, the only wage earner. It may be that this household supplemented the wages from domestic work with income from the illegal selling of homebrewed beer. The surveyor expressed concerns about the accuracy of the information given:

> Kitchen-dining room 'questionable' house. Daughter gave information. Mother only spoke native language. The daughter said there were several joining native men about and another young girl. I asked how they could pay 2 pounds per month rent when she only earns 25 shillings. She replied angrily 'well we do and it's no business of yours'.

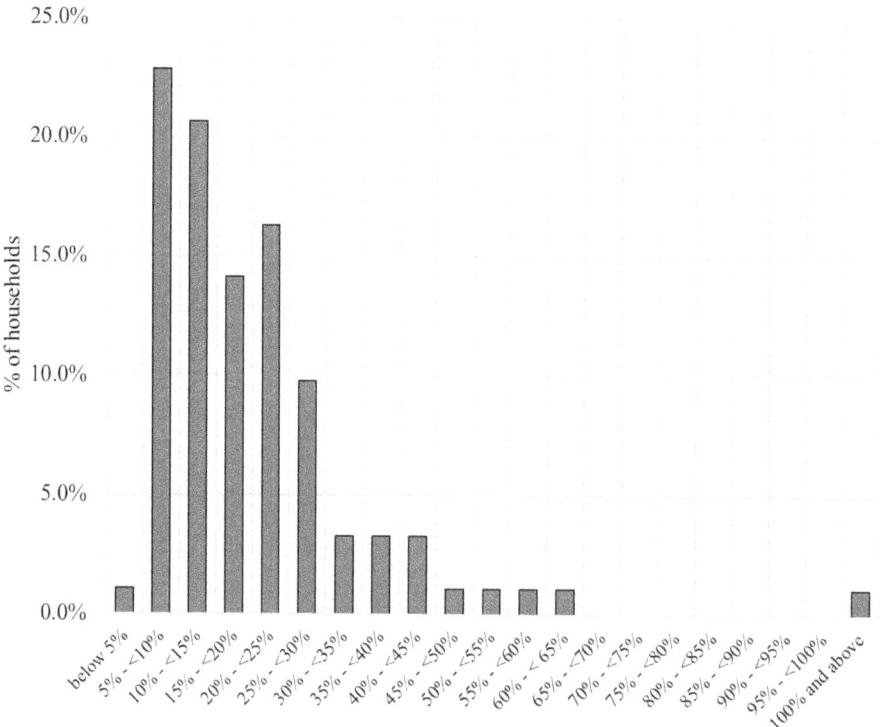

Figure 9.6 Distribution of rent as percentage of household income.
Sources: *Authors' calculations, based on data from the Batson Survey.*

Comparison of Cape Town and Transvaal living standards

Incomes in Cape Town can be interpreted more meaningfully if we compare them to wages on the Transvaal mines, which were between £34 and £35 per year in the late 1930s.[76] The median male worker in Cape Town earned £77 11s 5d and those classified as 'labourer' earned on average £73 6s 5d. Since Cape Town did not provide free accommodation and transport, we should subtract 25 per cent of this annual wage (based on the above living cost calculations) to make a proper comparison. This leaves us with average net earnings of £54 19s 10d for Cape Town's 'labourers': 57 per cent more than their counterparts on the mines.

However, for an accurate comparison we also need to take into account that mineworkers received rations as part of their pay, and that most Cape Town labourers had to support family members living with them, which was not the case for mineworkers, whose family members were able to generate income and self-provision in their rural homes. When we take these factors into account, the wage gap in favour of Cape Town shrinks considerably. If we assume that each worker had to feed 2.5 'adult male equivalents' (for example: himself, a wife and one child aged ten) at the poverty line established by Batson, this would require £56 11s 0d, which would consume the entire annual wage (before clothing, fuel and other basic necessities are even included). It should be noted, though, that Batson put his poverty line at a rather high level, in terms of the food's caloric content (3400 calories per day per adult male equivalent), and especially variety (which is unlikely to reflect the rations given to mineworkers). This helps us realise that many of Cape Town's black residents were unable to attain living standards that Batson considered appropriate at the time, but it obscures the comparison with mineworkers.

If instead we follow the (much lower) minimum food intake at the poverty line that is more commonly defined in the historical 'real wage' literature (and more likely to correspond with the value of actual mining rations), the comparison becomes more favourable for Cape Town's workers. This poverty line is based on a 'barebones survival basket' consisting mainly of the cheapest staple (rice, in this case), alongside several non-food items.[77] The annual cost of the food component of this basket in Cape Town

---

[76] Dácil Juif and Ewout Frankema, 'From Coercion to Compensation: Institutional Responses to Labour Scarcity in the Central African Copperbelt', *Journal of Institutional Economics* 14, no. 2 (2018): 313–43.

[77] For this calculation, we used three 'per capita' baskets of 2100 calories each, adapted from Michiel De Haas, 'Measuring Rural Welfare in Colonial Africa: Did Uganda's Smallholders Thrive?' *The Economic History Review* 70, no. 2 (2017): 605–31. For further information about this approach see Robert C. Allen, 'The High Wage Economy and the Industrial Revolution: A Restatement', *The Economic History Review* 68, no. 1 (2015): 1–22. For an earlier application to South Africa, see Pim De Zwart, 'South African Living Standards in Global Perspective, 1835–1910', *Economic History of Developing Regions* 26, no. 1 (2011): 49–74. For the seminal contribution on British colonial Africa, see Ewout Frankema and Marlous Van Waijenburg, 'Structural Impediments to African Growth? New Evidence from Real Wages in British Africa, 1880–1965', *The Journal of Economic History* 72, no. 4 (2012): 895–926.

in 1938–9 was a mere £8 18s 7d for three persons per year.[78] Subtracting this amount leaves the Cape Town worker with a wage premium of 32 per cent over his mineworker counterpart.

The precise wage gap is contingent on the assumptions underlying the calculation, which can be debated. Nevertheless, a broad picture does emerge of the average Cape Town worker enjoying an income slightly but not spectacularly above that of a Transvaal mineworker. However, we should also consider the fact that wages and living costs in Cape Town were quite variable, probably varying as much over time as they did within this cross-sectional sample.

Conclusion

Our inquiry into Cape Town's black African migrant residents focused on a comparatively understudied period, which nevertheless marks a crucial era of transition: well after the initial 'early adopters', highly migratory and mostly male, had come to Cape Town in the nineteenth and early twentieth century, and just before the emergence of a much larger and more stabilised black African population from the mid-twentieth century onwards under apartheid. Our effort at bottom-up historical reconstruction gives us some tantalising glimpses of black African lives within the greater Cape Town area in the late 1930s. While the fact that only current residents were included in the Batson survey limited our ability to investigate migratory dynamics fully, it has become clear that by this time Cape Town's black Africans had put down strong roots in the city itself, and that the formation of a stable community of settlers was well underway.

We find a population consisting almost entirely of migrants: people who had moved to Cape Town at some point in their lives. Ndabeni's population around the turn of the twentieth century had been overwhelmingly male, which testifies to its migratory character. But the population that Batson and his surveyors found in the late 1930s was quite settled. Household heads and their wives had been present in Cape Town for nine years on average at the time of the survey, and those over fifty years old twice as long. The sex ratio was much more balanced than it had been only a few decades earlier. Most of the male household heads in Cape Town were married, and most of them lived with their wife and children in the city. Some may even have met their future wives in Cape Town. While their presence in Cape Town was consolidated, black residents also retained close ties with their homelands. We observed cases where spouses were separated for long periods of time, or where wives and children were absent, especially when people had been married before coming to Cape Town. Remittances appear to have been common.

---

[78]This is the cost of three baskets of 2100 calories, each containing 440 lbs of rice, 6.6 lbs of meat, 6.6 lbs of vegetable fat and 4.4 lbs of sugar per year each. Using mealie meal (490 lbs) pushes up the cost of the basket to £12 18s 7d, and leaves the Cape Town worker with an advantage of 20 per cent. Prices from Batson Collection, Ms, 451, 'The Poverty Datum Line', May 1941, No. SS3, 6.

Most of the households were formed around a family, with groups of cohabiting single male migrants being a small minority. They were heavily dependent on wage incomes, and all households, including those headed by women, had at least one wage earner. Despite limited opportunities in Cape Town's labour market, we found some occupational variation, but most who reported an occupation were men and were simply described as 'labourer'. Women also worked, but their incomes tended to be substantially below those of men, even in the same occupation. Some households were able to supplement their wage incomes through gifts, cooking and brewing, maintaining a garden and subletting to new arrivals. This testifies to their willingness and ability to consolidate their urban livelihoods and establish a more stable presence in town.[79]

According to Batson's own cost of living estimates, Cape Town's workers were barely able to sustain a minimum level of consumption. However, his basket was informed by assumptions about a 'respectable' lifestyle modelled on white consumption standards, which did not necessarily reflect the preferences and aspirations of Cape Town's black residents. If we set aside Batson's basket and place Cape Town's wages in a comparative perspective, we find that they contrasted favourably with those of contract labourers in the Transvaal mines. The main difference was that the city afforded more freedom to choose one's employer and type of work, and more opportunities for permanency of urban living and the family life that comes with it. Despite the many restrictions imposed by segregationist policies, such processes of individual decision-making similarly informed succeeding generations of urban migrants and residents, whose choices and aspirations deserve more attention in South Africa's historiography.

Bibliography

Archive Materials

Batson Collection, Ms, 451. Manuscripts section, Stellenbosch University Library and Information Service. University of Cape Town Department of Social Science: Reports and Studies Issued by the Social Survey of Cape Town, Edited by Edward Batson, "Growth of Population", May 1941, No. SS1.

Batson Collection, Ms, 451. Manuscripts section, Stellenbosch University Library and Information Service. University of Cape Town Department of Social Science: Reports and Studies Issued by the Social Survey of Cape Town, Edited by Edward Batson, "The Poverty Datum Line", May 1941, No. SS3.

Batson Collection, Ms, 451. Manuscripts section, Stellenbosch University Library and Information Service. University of Cape Town Department of Social Science: Reports and Studies Issued by the Social Survey of Cape Town, Edited by Edward Batson, "Surveying Methods", May 1941, No. SS9.

---

[79] For a similar argument about Cape Town today, see Leslie Bank, 'Living Together, Moving Apart: Homemade Agendas, Identity Politics and Urban-rural Linkages in the Eastern Cape, South Africa", *Journal of Contemporary African Studies* 19, no. 1 (2001): 130.

Batson Collection, Ms, 451. Manuscripts section, Stellenbosch University Library and Information Service. University of Cape Town Department of Social Science: Reports and Studies Issued by the Social Survey of Cape Town, Edited by Edward Batson, "Distribution of Households", May 1944, No. SS25.

Batson Collection, Ms, 451. Manuscripts section, Stellenbosch University Library and Information Service. University of Cape Town Department of Social Science: Reports and Studies Issued by the Social Survey of Cape Town, Edited by Edward Batson, "A Socio-Economic Classification of Occupations in Cape Town", November 1946, No. SS8.

Cape Archives Depot, Cape Town. Department of Native Affairs. NA 457, Report: To Honourable Thomas Lynedoch Graham, K. C., M. L. C, Colonial Secretary of the Colony of the Cape of Good Hope, 1901.

Holloway, J.E., R.W. Anderson, et al. Report of Native Economic Commission, 1930–1932. Available online: http://hdl.handle.net/10500/5028

Theses and Dissertations

Callebert, R.F. *Livelihood Strategies of Dock Workers in Durban, c. 1900–1959*. PhD Thesis, Queen's University (Canada), Department of History, 2011.

Fast, H. H. *Pondoks, Houses, and Hostels: A History of Nyanga 1946–1970, With a Special Focus on Housing*. PhD Thesis., University of Cape Town, Faculty of Arts, Department of History, 1995.

Kinkead-Weekes, B. *Africans in Cape Town: State Policy and Popular Resistance, 1936–73*. PhD Thesis., University of Cape Town, Faculty of Arts, Department of History, 1992.

Musemwa, M. *Aspects of the Social and Political History of Langa Township, Cape Town, 1927–1948*. Master's thesis, University of Cape Town, 1993.

Nicol, M. *A History of Garment and Tailoring Workers in Cape Town, 1900–1939*. PhD Thesis., University of Cape Town, Faculty of Commerce, School of Economics, 1984.

Rommelspacher, A. "'Too delicate to work"?: Women and Work in Cape Town 1938–1939'. Unpublished doctoral thesis chapter.

Shambu, S. *Social History, Public History and the Politics of Memory in Re-making 'Ndabeni's' Pasts*. Master's Thesis submitted at the University of the Western Cape, 2010.

Books

Beinart, W. *Political Economy of Pondoland, 1860–1930*. Cambridge: Cambridge University Press, 2011.

Beinart, W. and C. Bundy. *Hidden Struggles in Rural South Africa: Politics & Popular Movements in the Transkei & Eastern Cape, 1890–1930*. (No. 40). Berkeley and Los Angeles, California: University of California Press, 1987.

Bozzoli, B. and M. Nkotsoe. *Women of Phokeng: Consciousness Life Strategy and Migrancy in South Africa, 1900–1983*. Johannesburg: Raven, 1991.

Feinstein, C.H. *An Economic History of South Africa: Conquest, Discrimination, and Development*. Cambridge: Cambridge University Press, 2005.

Peires, J.B. *The Dead Will Arise: Nongqawuse and the Great Xhosa Cattle-Killing Movement of 1856–1857*. Johannesburg: Ravan Press, 1989.

Southall, R. *South Africa's Transkei: The Political Economy of an Independent Bantustan*. London: Heinemann, 1982.

Turrell, R.V. and T.R. Vicat. *Capital and Labour on the Kimberley Diamond Fields, 1871–1890*. Vol. 54. Cambridge: Cambridge University Press, 1987.

Van der Horst, S. *Native Labour in South Africa*. London: Oxford University Press, 1942.
Worden, N., E. Van Heyningen and V. Bickford-Smith. *Cape Town: The Making of a City: An Illustrated Social History*. The Netherlands: Uitgeverij Verloren, 1998.

Journal Articles and Book Chapters

Allen, Robert C. 'The High Wage Economy and the Industrial Revolution: A Restatement'. *The Economic History Review* 68, no. 1 (2015): 1–22.

Baines, Gary. 'The Control and Administration of Port Elizabeth's African Population, c. 1834–1923', 1989.

Bank, L. 'Living Together, Moving Apart: Home-made Agendas, Identity Politics and Urban-rural Linkages in the Eastern Cape, South Africa'. *Journal of Contemporary African Studies* 19, no. 1 (2001): 129–47.

Bank, L. 'City Slums, Rural Homesteads: Migrant Culture, Displaced Urbanism and the Citizenship of the Serviced House'. *Journal of Southern African Studies* 41, no. 5 (2015): 1067–81.

Beinart, W. 'Beyond 'Homelands': Some Ideas about the History of African Rural Areas in South Africa'. *South African Historical Journal* 64, no. 1 (2012): 5–21.

Beinart, W. 'A Century of Migrancy from Mpondoland'. *African Studies* 73, no. 3 (2014): 387–409.

Beinart, W. and P. Delius. 'The Historical Context and Legacy of the Natives Land Act of 1913'. *Journal of Southern African Studies* 40, no. 4 (2014): 667–88.

Bekker, S. 'Migration from South Africa's Rural Sending Areas: Changing Intentions and Changing Destinations'. *Migration to South Africa within International Migration Trends* 25, no. 20 (2006): 59–76.

Coetzer, N. 'Langa Township in the 1920s – An (Extra)Ordinary Garden Suburb'. *South African Journal of Art History* 24, no. 1 (2009): 1–19.

Comaroff, J.L. and J. Comaroff. 'The Madman and the Migrant: Work and Labor in the Historical Consciousness of a South African People'. *American Ethnologist* 14, no.2 (1987): 191–209.

Connor, T.K. 'Ambiguous Repositories: Archives, Traders and the Recruitment of Mineworkers in the Eastern Cape: 1900–1946'. *South African Historical Journal* 72, no. 1 (2020): 98–124.

De Haas, H. 'The Internal Dynamics of Migration Processes: A Theoretical Inquiry'. *Journal of Ethnic and Migration Studies* 36, no. 10 (2010): 1587–617.

De Haas, M. 'Measuring Rural Welfare in Colonial Africa: Did Uganda's Smallholders Thrive?'. *The Economic History Review* 70, no. 2 (2017): 605–31.

De Zwart, P. 'South African Living Standards in Global Perspective, 1835–1910'. *Economic History of Developing Regions* 26, no. 1 (2011): 49–74.

Dooling, W. '"Cape Town Knows, but She Forgets": Segregation and the Making of a Housing Crisis during the First Half of the 20th Century'. *Journal of Southern African Studies* 44, no. 6 (2018): 1057–76.

Dooling, W. 'Poverty and Respectability in Early Twentieth-century Cape Town'. *The Journal of African History* 59, no. 3 (2018): 411–35.

Eichengreen, B. 'Gold and South Africa's Great Depression'. *Economic History of Developing Regions* 36, no. 2 (2021): 175–93.

Frankema, E. and M. Van Waijenburg. 'Structural Impediments to African Growth? New Evidence from Real Wages in British Africa, 1880–1965'. *The Journal of Economic History* 72, no. 4 (2012): 895–926.

Goldin, I. 'The Coloured Labour Preference Policy, Co-option and Contradiction'. *Collected Seminar Papers. Institute of Commonwealth Studies* 33 (1984): 108–20.

Harington, J.S., N.D. McGlashan and E.Z. Chelkowska. 'A Century of Migrant Labour in the Gold Mines of South Africa.' *The Journal of the Southern African Institute of Mining and Metallurgy* 104, no. 2 (2004): 65–71.

Jeeves, A. 'Sugar and Gold in the Making of the South African Labour System the Crisis of Supply on the Zululand Sugar Estates 1906–1939'. *South African Journal of Economic History* 7, no. 2 (1992): 7–33

Juif, D. and E. Frankema. 'From Coercion to Compensation: Institutional Responses to Labour Scarcity in the Central African Copperbelt'. *Journal of Institutional Economics* 14, no. 2 (2018): 313–43.

Meier zu Selhausen, F. 'Urban Migration in East and West Africa: Contrasts and Transformations'. In *Migration in Africa: Shifting Patterns of Mobility, 19th to 21st Centuries*, edited by Michiel de Haas and Ewout Frankema, 281–307. New York: Routledge, forthcoming in 2022.

Mkhize, N. 'In Search of Native Dissidence: RT Kawa's Mfecane Historiography in Ibali lamaMfengu, (1929)'. *International Journal of African Renaissance Studies – Multi-, Inter- and Transdisciplinarity* 13, no. 2 (2018): 92–111.

Mongwe, R. 'The Importance of Language Identities to Black Residents in Cape Town and Johannesburg'. *Reflections on Identity in Four African Cities* (2006): 171–88.

Moyana, K.J. 'The Political Economy of the Migrant Labour System: Implications for Agricultural Growth and Rural Development in Southern Africa'. *Africa Development / Afrique Developpement* 1, no. 1 (1976): 34–41.

Nasson, B. 'Why They Fought: Black Cape Colonists and Imperial Wars, 1899–1918'. *The International Journal of African Historical Studies* 37, no. 1 (2004): 55–70.

Nattrass, N. and J. Seekings. 'The Economy and Poverty in the Twentieth Century in South Africa'. Centre for Social Science Research, University of Cape Town. CSSR Working Paper No. 276, 2010.

Parnell, S. 'Race, Power and Urban Control: Johannesburg's Inner City Slum-yards, 1910–1923'. *Journal of Southern African Studies* 29, no. 3 (2003): 615–37.

Pirie, G. 'African Township Railways and the South African State, 1902–1963'. *Journal of Historical Geography* 13, no. 3 (1987): 283–95.

Pirie, G. 'Railways and Labour Migration to the Rand Mines: Constraints and Significance'. *Journal of Southern African Studies* 19, no. 4 (1993): 713–30.

Sen, A. 'The Living Standard'. *Oxford Economic Papers* 36 (1984): 74–90.

Simkins, C. and E. van Heyningen. 'Fertility, Mortality, and Migration in the Cape Colony, 1891–1904'. *The International Journal of African Historical Studies* 22, no. 1 (1989): 79–111.

Swanson, W.M. 'The Sanitation Syndrome: Bubonic Plague and Urban Native Policy in the Cape Colony, 1900–1909'. *Journal of African History* 18, no. 3 (1977): 387–410.

Yudelman, D. and A. Jeeves. 'New Labour Frontiers for Old: Black Migrants to the South African Gold Mines, 1920–85'. *Journal of Southern African Studies* 13, no. 1 (1986): 101–24.

CHAPTER 10
POLITICAL INNOVATION IN AFRICAN NATIONALIST ORGANISATIONS, 1880-90
Jonathan Schoots*

Introduction

The 1880s saw an explosion of new African political organisations across the eastern region of the Cape Colony, ushering in a period of rapid innovation in African politics. The resulting transformation of institutions, ideas and action laid the foundation for African nationalism. In this chapter I examine this 'proto-nationalist' movement and how it was able to create new visions of political identity and new forms of political action as African nationalism emerged.

To do so, I turn to quantitative techniques of network analysis – which make visible the invisible social structures created by social relationships – and combine this with an in-depth examination of the innovative ideas and actions of emerging African political organisations. This approach shows one way that quantitative methods can partner with and complement qualitative approaches attentive to culture, understanding and meaning making. Mapping the social network reveals broad patterns of social and political connections which shape the possibilities for innovation. This pattern is then revealed in action through a close examination of how innovation worked itself out in key African political organisations.

I focus on how the social network of political leaders and organisations between 1870 and 1890 facilitated this process of innovation. Proto-nationalist organisations were connected to each other through shared members. I use network analysis techniques to map the way these connections linked local movements across the eastern Cape into an increasingly interconnected larger movement. This chapter examines two broad processes of innovation in these emerging political organisations, which I call 'repertoire transposition' and 'repertoire syncretisation'.

The first type, repertoire transposition, can be seen in a closely connected core of *abantu basesikolweni* ('school people') organisations which united those from missionary-educated as well as more urban African communities. These organisations took up colonial political models and reshaped them into innovative forms of action in African-only political contexts. The second type, repertoire syncretisation, can be seen

---

*Schoots: Department of Economics, Stellenbosch University, South Africa.

in a group of *isizwe* ('ethnic' or 'national') organisations which foregrounded the interests of communities based in local *isizwe* identities. These organisations drew together rural traditional leaders and missionary-educated leaders and syncretised colonial and rural political forms to create new ideas and strategies of action.

To examine these two forms of innovation in practice, I turn to case studies of three key organisations, the Independent Order of True Templars, *Imbumba Yama Nyama*, and the Thembu Association. I draw on the work of historians (notably Odendaal 2013) to contextualise these three organisations and then turn to primary source analysis, looking at newspaper articles and government petitions to reveal their innovative political vision expressed in their own words. I thus combined a 'zoomed out' analysis of the political structure with a 'zoomed in' analysis of the voices of African political actors to show how structural and relational connections shaped a wave of African proto-nationalism. In doing so I examine the social processes which enabled innovation, and contribute both to the history of nascent African nationalism in South Africa and to broader social science research on the dynamics of political innovation and transformation.

Research design

The theoretical and methodological approach taken in this chapter is network analysis. This approach shows how emerging proto-nationalist ideas, vision and strategy were shaped not just by a single organisation or individual leader but by the connections made in a broader community. I follow a tradition of historical network analysis in the social sciences,[1] and draw inspiration from André Odendaal's historical work on early African nationalism in the Eastern Cape. Since the 1980s Odendaal has made much use of the 'network' metaphor in his analysis. Where his contemporaries focused on the role of class,[2] or studied biographies of important leaders,[3] Odendaal emphasised

---

[1] P. Bearman, *Relations into Rhetorics: Local Elite Social Structure in Norfolk, England, 1540–1640* (New Brunswick: Rutgers University Press, 2005); J.F. Padgett and C.K. Ansell, 'Robust Action and the Rise of the Medici, 1400–1434', *American Journal of Sociology* 98, no. 6 (1993): 1259–319; R. Gould, *Insurgent Identities: Class, Community, and Protest in Paris from 1848 to the Commune* (Chicago: University of Chicago Press, 1995); R. Gould, 'Patron-Client Ties, State Centralization, and the Whiskey Rebellion', *American Journal of Sociology* 102, no. 2 (1996): 400–29; C. K. Ansell, 'Symbolic Networks: The Realignment of the French Working Class, 1887–1894', *American Journal of Sociology* 103, no. 2 (1997): 359–90; H. Hillmann, 'Mediation in Multiple Networks: Elite Mobilization before the English Civil War', *American Sociological Review* 73, no. 3 (2008): 426–54; J.F. Padgett and W.W. Powell, *The Emergence of Organizations and Markets* (Princeton: Princeton University Press, 2012).

[2] C. Bundy, *The Rise and Fall of the South African Peasantry* (Berkeley: University of California Press, 1979); W. Beinart and C. Bundy, *Hidden Struggles in Rural South Africa: Politics and Popular Movements in the Transkei & Eastern Cape, 1890–1930* (Berkeley: University of California Press, 1987).

[3] D. Williams, *Umfundisi: A Biography of Tiyo Soga, 1829–1871* (Lovedale, South Africa: Lovedale Press, 1978); S. Marks, *The Ambiguities of Dependence in South Africa: Class, Nationalism, and the State in Twentieth-Century Natal* (Baltimore: Johns Hopkins University Press, 1986).

the organisational precursors of the African National Congress and highlighted the connections between leaders and organisations.[4]

This chapter builds on the network metaphor: here I formalise the idea of 'networks' by systematically gathering data on the connections between people and organisations, and then drawing on a set of network analysis methods to visualise and analyse such social connections.

Data and methods

In order to examine social and political links of the proto-nationalist movement I created a database of membership of the first African political organisations of the Eastern Cape between 1870 and 1890, with the support of two research assistants Bathobele Mcilongo and Siphenkosi Hlangu.[5] I created a list of Eastern Cape African political organisations up to 1890 drawn from Odendaal's work,[6] including key mission schools and newspapers which played an important role in this political development. I used the names of these organisations, and aliases, synonyms and related keywords, to find news articles by or about these organisations between 1870 and 1890 through a keyword search of newspapers, primarily the newspapers *Isigidimi sama-Xosa* (The Xhosa Messenger) and *Imvo Zabantsundu* (Black Opinion), supplemented by other colonial newspapers.[7] This yielded in total a sample of 293 newspaper articles.

From the newspaper articles that named members of organisations I created a database of organisational membership. This newspaper source is best at making visible influential members of organisations: those who are named often held official leadership positions, had been appointed to committees and delegations, or had chaired or actively participated in a meeting. While some ordinary members are mentioned in newspaper articles, many remain invisible. The emphasis on leading figures is a bias in my sample. Yet because we see the most influential members it strengthens my assumption that organisations that share members may have influenced each other's political ideas and

---

[4] A. Odendaal, *The Founders: The Origins of the ANC and the Struggle for Democracy in South Africa* (Kentucky: University Press of Kentucky, 2013). See also: A. Odendaal, 'African Political Mobilisation in the Eastern Cape, 1880-1910' (PhD diss., University of Cambridge, Cambridge, 1983); A. Odendaal, *Vukani Bantu! The Beginnings of Black Protest Politics to 1910* (Cape Town: Philip, 1984); A. Odendaal, '"Even White Boys Call Us 'Boy'!": Early Black Organisational Politics in Port Elizabeth', *Kronos* 20 (1993): 3–16.

[5] The research assistances worked with me in coding both isiXhosa and English newspaper articles. This involved capturing all members mentioned, their organizational role and additional article metadata. We also created short English summaries of all coded articles which supported my later qualitative analysis. Both research assistants are first language isiXhosa speakers, and I am proficient in reading isiXhosa.

[6] Odendaal, *The Founders*, chs 3–14.

[7] In addition to *Isigidimi sama-Xosa* and *Imvo Zabantsundu*, we also searched the *Afrikaanse Patriot*, *Cape Mercantile Advertiser*, *Eastern Province Herald*, *Friend of the Free State and Bloemfontein Journal*, *Natal Witness*, *Port Elizabeth Telegraph* and *Eastern Province Standard* and South

practice. These leading members would have a greater impact on the organisations they participated in and thus be more likely to be able to transmit ideas and strategies from one organisation to another than ordinary members.

The membership coding gave me a dataset of 865 links between members and organisations, including some duplication when individuals were mentioned in several newspaper articles. I supplemented this dataset with the organisation leaders that Odendaal identified using information from letters, government documents and reports, mission school archives and Xhosa newspapers.[8] This yielded 262 links between members and organisations. Most of these links are also captured in the newspaper articles I coded, but Odendaal's text was my primary source for membership of the Lovedale and Healdtown mission schools and for participation in the newspaper *Isigidimi*. This resulted in a combined dataset of 1,127 links between members and organisations. With duplication removed, this became a dataset of 604 unique nodes (nineteen organisations and 585 individuals, 463 of whom were members of only one organisation) and 784 unique links. I included only the 122 individuals who held membership in two or more organisations, thus focusing on how these organisations were linked through co-membership. The analysis was thus undertaken on a network that has 140 nodes, eighteen organisations[9] and 122 members, which was connected by 321 links. Table 10.1 reports these organisations, including the full name and English translation alongside the shortened labels used throughout the paper. Here I also report the founding date, total number of members captured from newspaper reports and the number of members who make links to at least one other organisation, and are thus included in the analysis.

To bring this network formalisation to life, I link this network analysis with case studies of the three key organisations, the Independent Order of True Templars, *Imbumba Yama Nyama*, and the Thembu Association. Here I track their political visions, beliefs and practices and show how they were shaped by the social structure revealed in the network analysis. These case studies were based on my close textual analysis of primary sources: the newspaper articles mentioned above, particularly from *Isigidimi sama-Xosa* and *Imvo Zabantsundu*, and African petitions to the Cape Parliament between 1880 and 1890.[10] Petitions, as Dimitruk and Lemon show, (Chapter 11), can be used to understand

---

[8] Odendaal, *The Founders*, chs 3–14.

[9] I excluded organizations that listed no members, and also the *Intlangansio ye Teachers* (Teachers Association) because only one of its members was listed.

[10] The newspaper articles were collected from Readex's African Newspapers, Series 1 and Series 2. Access to articles is available by subscription (see https://www.readex.com/products/african-newspapers-series-1-and-2-1800-1925.) The petitions were collected from the Western Cape Provincial Archives and Records in Cape Town (WCARS), Petitions to the House of Assembly (WCARS, HA). The collection and analysis of key African petitions was supported by the digitised list and summaries of all petitions to the Cape Parliament between 1875 and 1895, created and graciously shared with me by Kara Dimitruk. Dimitruk and Lemon, Chapter 11, examine a dataset of petitions presented to the House and show how patterns in petitioning changed over time.

Political Innovation in African Nationalist Organisations, 1880–90

Table 10.1 Organisations and members included in the analysis.

Label	Full Name	English name/translation	Founded	Members	Linkers
EBS	Ethiopian Benefit Society		1877	18	16
Eliliso_Lomzi	Imbumba Eliliso Lomzi Yabantsundu	Union of Native Vigilance Associations	1887	107	35
ETNAS	Emigrant Thembuland Native Agricultural Society		1876	30	16
Healdtown	Healdtown		1855	24	19
Imbumba	Imbumba Yama Nyama		1882	89	33
Int_Fundisi	Intlanganiso yaba Fundisi	Ministers' association	1884	38	5
Intla_Ngqika	Intlanganiso Ye Nqubelo Pambili Yama Ngqika	Association for the Advancement of the Ngqika	1885	14	9
IOTT	Independent Order of True Templars		1879	103	27
Isigidimi	Isigidimi sama-Xosa		1870	18	11
Lovedale	Lovedale		1824	37	25
Many_Zabant	Manyano nge Mvo Zabantsundu	Union for Native opinion	1887	26	7
NEA	Native Educational Association		1880	137	56
SANA	South African Native Association		1882	6	6
Thembu_A	Thembu Association		1882	24	11
TMIA	Transkei Mutural Improvement Association		1884	37	13
TTA	Transkeian Teachers Association		1882	18	14
Umanyano	Umanyano lwase Batenjini	Thembuland Union	1886	58	21

changing political expression among various nineteenth-century Cape society groups and organisations. I also draw on secondary source histories of Odendaal, Mills and Beinart and Bundy to detail these organisations' practices and situate them in their historical context.[11]

---

[11] Odendaal, *The Founders*; W.G. Mills, 'The Roots of African Nationalism in the Cape Colony: Temperance, 1866–1898', *International Journal of African Historical Studies* 13, no. 2 (1980); Beinart and Bundy, *Hidden Struggles*.

Theoretical framework

When participating in politics, people most often draw on familiar and well-established 'scripts' of political ideas and action.[12] Scholars call this repeated use of a limited set of strategies and concepts a 'repertoire' and highlight how such repertoires can be stable over time. Jansen notes the effects of this repetition in politics:

> Because they tend to be reproduced with minimal modification, such repertoires come to stabilise the meanings of those practices through which politically opposed groups routinely interact, and thus to circumscribe what is strategically 'thinkable.' In this way, they play a role in constituting the political culture of a given time and place.[13]

Identifying such stability has been insightful for scholars studying waves of protest in historical periods.[14] Yet stability has always raised the question of its inverse: transformation. Given these patterns of stability, how do such a wide range of political forms emerge across time and space?[15] In other words, how do repertoires transform? This question has been the subject of research for two decades.[16] This chapter contributes to the field by examining how political ideas and strategies were transformed in the early African nationalist movement in South Africa. This chapter builds on existing theory to develop two conceptual models which explain the innovation seen in this case which can generalise to other contexts of political transformation.

---

[12] R.S. Jansen, *Revolutionizing Repertoires* (Chicago: University of Chicago Press, 2017); C. Tilly, *From Mobilization to Revolution* (Reading, MA: Addison-Wesley, 1978); P.H. Mooney and S.A. Hunt, 'A Repertoire of Interpretations: Master Frames and Ideological Continuity in U.S. Agrarian Mobilization', *Sociological Quarterly* 37, no. 1 (1996): 177–97; D.A. Snow and R.D. Benford, 'Master Frames and Cycles of Protest', in *Frontiers in Social Movement Theory*, ed. A.D. Morris and C.M. Mueller (New Haven: Yale University Press, 1992).

[13] Jansen, *Revolutionizing Repertoires*, 323.

[14] Tilly, *Mobilization to Revolution*; C. Tilly, *The Contentious French* (Cambridge, MA: Harvard University Press, 1986); J.G. Ennis, 'Fields of Action: Structure in Movement' Tactical Repertoires', *Sociological Forum* 2, no. 3 (1987): 520–33; S.G. Tarrow, *Democracy and Disorder: Protest and Politics in Italy, 1965-1975* (Oxford: Clarendon Press, 1989); S.G. Tarrow, 'Cycles of Collective Action: Between Moments of Madness and the Repertoire of Contention', *Social Science History* 17, no. 2 (1993): 281–307; M. Traugott, 'Barricades as Repertoire: Continuities and Discontinuities in the History of French Contention', *Social Science History* 17, no. 2 (1993): 309–23; Snow and Benford, 'Master Frames'.

[15] Tilly, *Mobilization to Revolution*.

[16] See, for example: E.S. Clemens, *The People's Lobby: Organizational Innovation and the Rise of Interest Group Politics in the United States, 1890-1925* (Chicago: University of Chicago, 1997); A.G. Walder, 'Political Sociology and Social Movements', *Annual Review of Sociology* 35, no. 1 (2009): 393–412; Padgett and Powell, *Emergence of Organizations and Markets*; R.S. Jansen, 'Situated Political Innovation: Explaining the Historical Emergence of New Modes of Political Practice', *Theory and Society* 45, no. 4 (2016): 319–60; Jansen, *Revolutionizing Repertoires*.

Repertoire transposition

My first model of innovation, repertoire transposition, shows how existing repertoires can be transformed when applied in new contexts. When actors bring repertoires of organisation, understanding or action from one domain to a significantly different domain they must transform them to fit this new context. At times this process of adaption can transform the pre-existing practices to such an extent that it yields new forms of political practice. These innovations become truly transformative when they feedback to the mainstream system of politics and result in altering mainstream practice. Two examples of such repertoire transposition are shown in Clemens's *The People's Lobby* and Padgett and Powell's study of 'transposition and refunctionality'.[17]

Clemens shows how interest group politics emerged historically in the United States. Agrarian, labour and women's groups pioneered new organisational forms: they took up existing corporate lobbying practices and transformed them to create interest group lobbies. In doing so they enabled a fundamental shift in political organising from party-based organisation to interest group mobilisation. Clemens's analysis of repertoire transformation focuses on the adoption and transformation of organisational repertoires. She shows how challenger groups adopted the organisational forms, or repertoires, of dominant groups. Yet, instead of simply reproducing the organisational practice of these dominant groups, the application of these organisational repertoires in new contexts resulted in an adaption and transformation of practices which produced new political scripts. This transformation gave rise to new forms of popular politics focused on specific interests or policy demands instead of the party, class, language or religion based political communities of the past.[18]

A similar analysis of organisational transformation is expressed in Padgett and Powell's concept of transposition and refunctionality: 'the movement of a relational practice from one domain to another and its reuse for a different function or purpose in the new domain'.[19] Examining the birth of the partnership system in Renaissance Florence, Padgett shows how domestic Florentine bankers were transposed into international trading systems.[20] The bankers combined their own master-apprentice system with the dominant patrilineal family system of international politics to create the new organisational form of the partnership system. This created innovations in financial practices including current accounts, credit and double-entry bookkeeping which transformed both Florentine and European international finance. Further, the innovation fed back into Florentine social practices, refiguring marriage as a form of elite inter-family partnership formation.[21]

---

[17] Clemens, *People's Lobby*; Padgett and Powell, *Emergence of Organizations and Markets,* chs 1 and 6.
[18] Clemens, *People's Lobby*.
[19] Padgett and Powell, *Emergence of Organizations and Markets,* 12.
[20] Ibid, ch 6.
[21] Ibid, 172–3.

Thus, as Clemens and Padgett and Powell show, novelty is possible when an existing repertoire is transposed to a new context, where it can offer 'a new purpose for an old tool'[22] and in doing so bring transformation.

Repertoire syncretisation

My second model, repertoire syncretisation, shows how innovation can be produced by the intersecting of two or more existing repertoires. Swidler argued that in 'unsettled times' people turn to their available cultural toolkits in order to generate political action and ideological positions.[23] Repertoire syncretisation becomes possible when *multiple* repertoires are brought together as people from different political backgrounds are connected in new shared contexts. These contexts allow elements from different political cultures and practices to be combined and can yield new syncretic forms of political action, organisation and ideas.

My repertoire syncretisation model builds on studies which have shown how transformed social relations can yield new political identities,[24] and new political symbols.[25] My model goes a step further; it shows how new social connections bring together previously separate repertoires and enable them to interact in a way which can produce innovative possibilities. It thus focuses on the transformation that becomes possible when previously separated elements are united to create new syncretic political practices.

The organisational patterns of emerging proto-nationalist politics

I turn now to explain how political innovation and repertoire transformation were enabled and shaped by the structure of political connections in emerging African political organisations in the eastern Cape Colony between 1870 and 1890.

I first show the connections between these organisations that created a network which connected local political movements into an increasingly interlinked 'proto-nationalist' movement. Using network analysis techniques, I map the way organisations were connected through co-membership – political activists often being members of more than one organisation. In the terminology of network analysis: individuals and organisations are the 'nodes' of this network, and the membership links between them are the 'ties' which connect them together. Examining this network reveals how people and organisations were connected through memberships in the multiple organisations of the nascent African nationalist movement.

---

[22] Ibid, 12.
[23] A. Swidler, 'Culture in Action: Symbols and Strategies', *American Sociological Review* 51, no. 2 (1986): 273–86.
[24] Bearman, *Relations into Rhetorics*.
[25] Ansell, 'Symbolic Networks'.

These networks shaped the way people and organisations shared ideas and political imagination.[26] As isiXhosa-speaking communities created new political organisations they drew on and transformed political knowledge available in their social networks. Studying the structure of these social networks offers insight into how these young organisations took up the political knowledge of their communities and transformed it into new forms of politics which would ground African nationalist vision and practice.

Mapping the political network

Figures 10.1a and 10.1b visualise the social networks of African political organisations up to 1890. The former shows the ties between organisations and members and the latter presents the same data, but now showing only the organisations to simplify and clarify the visualisation. Organisations are shown by icons which represent their primary area of activity (Political, Civic, Education, and News). Members are shown as small circles. Members who were ordained church reverends or ministers are shown in dark grey, and Chiefs or headmen are shown in medium grey with a dark boarder. The named members are those who linked at least four organisations and thus were the most important political mediators.

These figures represent 'social distance' as two-dimensional 'spatial distance'. This is done by applying a force-directed layout approach to the network.[27] When organisations share many members, they are 'pulled' together by the connecting ties as though these ties were springs. The strength of each tie is weighted by membership frequency in Figure 10.1a and by the number of shared members in Figure 10.1b,[28]

---

[26]Network scholars have long shown how social connections facilitate the flow of ideas and forms of action. See, for example: M.S. Granovetter, 'The Strength of Weak Ties', *American Journal of Sociology* 78, no. 6 (1973): 1360–80; R.V. Gould and R.M. Fernandez, 'Structures of Mediation: A Formal Approach to Brokerage in Transaction Networks', *Sociological Methodology* 19 (1989): 89–126; R.S. Burt, 'Structural Holes and Good Ideas', *American Journal of Sociology* 110, no. 2 (2004): 349–99; R.S. Burt, *Structural Holes: The Social Structure of Competition* (1992; repr., Cambridge, MA: Harvard University Press, 2009); M.L. Small, *Unanticipated Gains: Origins of Network Inequality in Everyday Life* (Oxford: Oxford University Press, 2009); K. Stovel and L. Shaw, 'Brokerage', *Annual Review of Sociology*, 38, no. 1 (2012): 139–58.

[27]Here I apply ForceAtlas 2 (Jacomy et al. 2014), a 'force-directed' algorithm, to lay out the network. This algorithm uses the 'spring embedding' or 'force directed' approach developed by Kamada and Kawai (1989) and Fruchterman and Rheingold (1991) but with its own modifications. Edges attract their nodes with a force modelled on springs ($F_a = -K \cdot d$), and nodes repel each other with a force modelled on charged particles ($F_r = K/d^2$). These forces converge on a balanced state. Attraction and repulsion formulae are modified for visual clarity. See M. Jacomy, et al., 'ForceAtlas2, A Continuous Graph Layout Algorithm for Handy Network Visualization Designed for Gephi Software', M.R. Muldoon ed, *PLoS ONE* 9, no. 6 (2014): 1–12 for details. T. Kamada and S. Kawai, 'An Algorithm for Drawing General Undirected Graphs', *Information Processing Letters* 31, no. 1 (1989): 9; T.M.J. Fruchterman and E.M. Reingold, 'Graph Drawing by Force-Directed Placement', *Software: Practice and Experience* 21, no. 11 (1991): 1129–64.

[28]For Figure 10.1a, the weight is the number of unique newspaper articles that mention the person as a member of the organization. The analysis assumes that frequent mentions imply more organizational authority and influence, represented as stronger ties. Organizational membership listed in Odendaal *The Founders* adds an additional weight of 1. For visual clarity these weights are not shown in the figure but still inform the layout.

Quantitative History and Uncharted People

Figure 10.1a[29] Whole network overview – organisations and members.

For Figure 10.1b, the strength of the tie is the number of shared members and does not include the weight of the members' tie. This approach helps to mitigate the differences in frequency of reporting on different organizations. The results remain similar when the ties are weighted by the strength of the members' ties.

[29] Organisations are shown as large icons and members as small circles. The shading of a node represents an organisation's or member's primary area of operation. The named members (the most important political mediators) are those who linked at least four organisations.

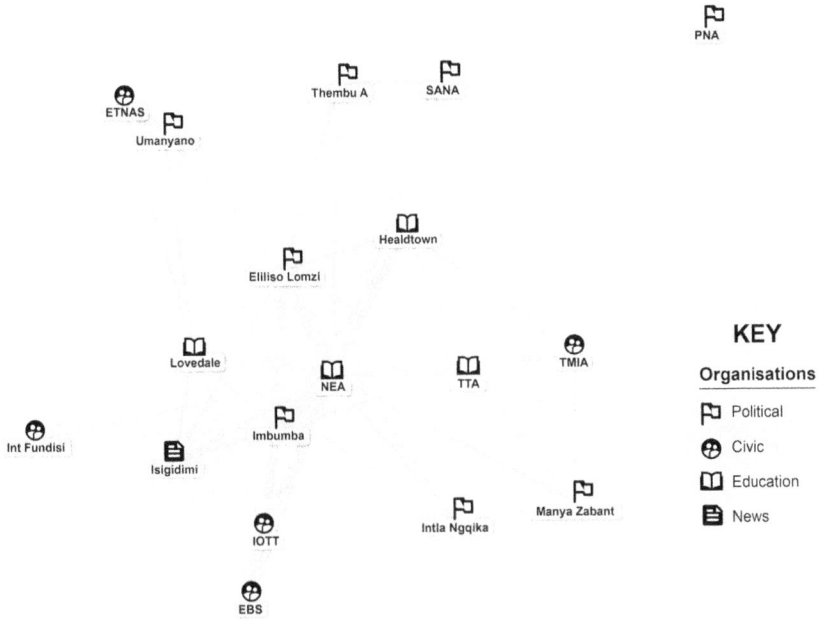

Figure 10.1b Whole network overview – organisations only.

visualised by the thickness of the connecting line. In this layout approach, members or organisations that share many social connections are positioned close together and those with fewer connections are positioned further apart. This method also reveals the social structure of a broader community: members and organisations at the periphery of the network map are less socially connected to the wider community than those positioned towards its centre. I validated my map by redrawing it using a multidimensional scaling approach. This yielded an almost identical layout with equivalent organisational clusters and distances.[30]

This network visualisation of the social structure created through connections between proto-nationalist organisations reveals an important core-periphery pattern. Figure 10.1a has a closely connected central core that includes the NEA, *Imbumba yama Nyama*, the newspaper *Isigidimi* and the Lovedale School, with peripheral clusters radiating out from it.

---

[30]Multi-dimensional scaling attempts to preserve some defined 'distances' between all nodes. It represents these distances in two-dimensional space as accurately as possible. To calculate these distances, I defined the 'similarity' of organizations by calculating each organization's correlation on membership using the Pearson correlation coefficients for the adjacency matrix of Organisations by Members. I then used the Euclidean distance approach to identify the 'distance' between organizations whose similarity is defined by this correlation. I used metric multidimensional scaling in my analysis. I did this analysis using the Scikit-learn package sklearn.manifold.MDS in Python.

In the following I describe various closely connected sub-groups or 'communities' within the network. To find these I applied community detection analysis, using an algorithm developed by Blondel et al. which identifies communities that are densely connected internally and sparsely connected to other communities.[31] This approach makes visible underlying closely connected sub-communities in the network. Figure 10.2a presents the results of this community detection approach[32] run on the two-mode network. Here communities are visualised by giving their nodes the same shape symbol. Figure 10.2b shows these communities in the network showing only organisations. I validated these communities by comparing the results from a hierarchical cluster analysis,[33] which produced almost identical communities.[34]

Social connections and cleavages

Taken together, the network map (Figures 10.1a & b) and the community detection (Figures 10.2a & b) show a closely connected central community (shown by the cross shapes) which is linked to five peripheral sub-communities. Examining these communities reveals the social connections and cleavages in the first decade of proto-nationalist political organising. We see two major types of cleavage in this network: first between mission-educated African political communities and rural

---

[31] This difference in the density of connections (between or within communities) is called modularity. Blondel et al.'s algorithm (2008) tests whether modularity increases if each node is reassigned to the community of each of its neighbouring nodes. This is repeated until a local maximum is reached. V.D. Blondel, et al., 'Fast Unfolding of Communities in Large Networks', *Journal of Statistical Mechanics: Theory and Experiment* 10 (2008): 1–12.

[32] For details, see Blondel, et al., 'Fast Unfolding of Communities'; R. Lambiotte, et al., 'Geographical Dispersal of Mobile Communication Networks', *Physica A: Statistical Mechanics and Its Applications* 387, no. 21 (2008): 1–12. I used the 'modularity' tool in the Gephi software package.

[33] Hierarchical clustering is a method for grouping a set of elements such that those in a common group are more similar to each other than other groups on some defined measure of similarity. I used agglomerative clustering (bottom up) which iteratively combines the most similar clusters to reduce the number of clusters at each level of iteration – producing a hierarchy of clusters. I group organizations based on their similarity in membership composition. I used the weighted adjacency matrix of Organisations by Members to calculate similarly between organizations. To decide which groups are combined, Hierarchical clustering applies a metric to find the smallest distance between any two clusters. I calculate this distance using Euclidean distance $\sqrt{\Sigma_i (a_i - b_i)^2}$ and I compared three linkage methods: 1. Single (minimum) linkage (the minimum distance among all data points in the two clusters: $(min\{d(a,b): a \in A, b \in B\})$), 2. unweighted average linkage clustering (the average distance of each datapoint in two clusters: $\frac{1}{|A|\cdot|B|} \Sigma_{x \in A} \Sigma_{y \in B} d(x,y)$), and 3. weighted average linkage clustering ($d_{(i \cup j),k} = \frac{d_{i,k} + d_{j,k}}{2}$). My analysis compared the dendrogram outputs of these three linkage methods. I did this analysis using the Scipy package scipy.cluster.hierarchy for Python.

[34] Healdtown is grouped with the star rather than the triangle cluster, and with the minimum or single-linkage method the rectangle and cross clusters are joined into one 'educated elite' cluster.

Political Innovation in African Nationalist Organisations, 1880–90

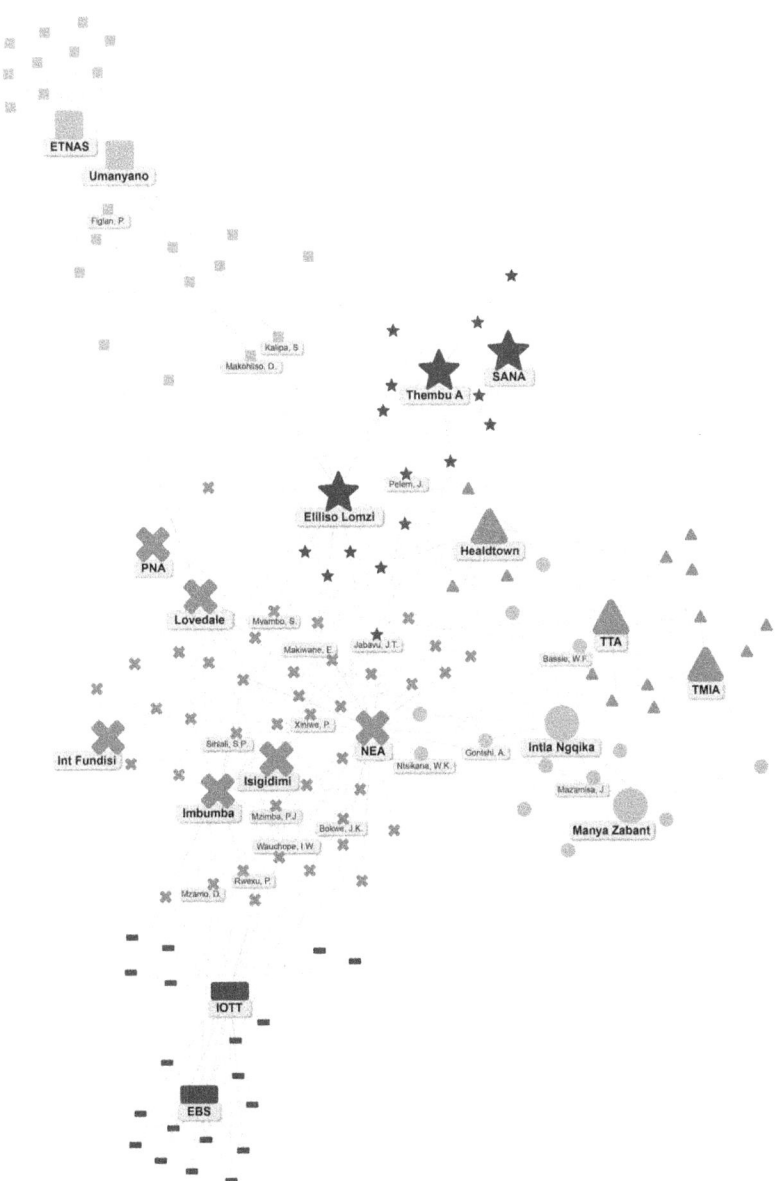

Figure 10.2a Community detection – organisations and members.

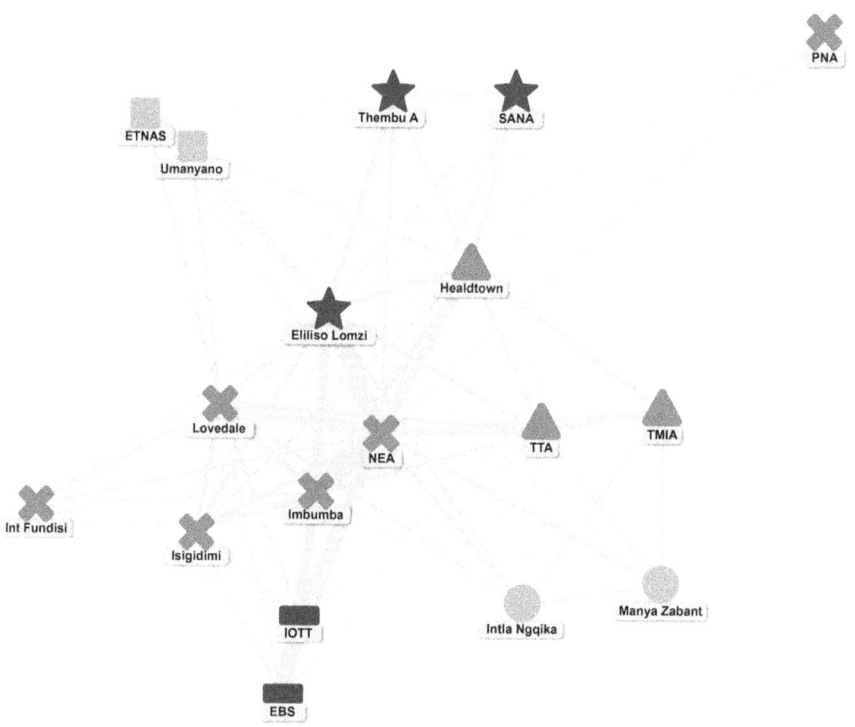

Figure 10.2b Community detection – organisations only.

political communities, and second between different *isizwe* communities located in different regions of the more rural area beyond the Kei river (the Transkei region).

To give spatial context to this discussion, see the map of the Eastern Cape area (Figure 10.3), which shows important towns and other towns named through this paper, as well as the relevant territorial divisions of the Transkei region.

First, I consider the emerging politics of mission-educated African communities. The clusters marked by the cross and triangle shapes show the connections and political influence of the two leading mission schools of the Eastern Cape: Lovedale (cross), founded in 1824, and Healdtown (triangle), founded in 1850. They were the elite pinnacle of African mission education,[35] and it was here that many upcoming political leaders received their education and their first exposure to political ideas and practice. Connected to Lovedale we see the isiXhosa newspaper *Isigidimi sama-Xosa*. Founded

---

[35]D. Atwell, *Rewriting Modernity: Studies in Black South African Literary History* (Pietermaritzburg: KwaZulu-Natal University Press, 2005): 27.

by missionaries in 1870, with African editorship from 1876,[36] this was the first enduring African language newspaper in southern Africa and it created a new public sphere for African politics, fostering debate through the 1870s and offering an important platform for political organisations in the 1880s.[37] In this same cross cluster we see two influential African-only political organisations which fostered the first African interest-group politics. One is the Native Educational Association (NEA), also called *Umanyano nge Mfundo*, founded in 1880 as an organisation for African teachers. In its early days it focused on teachers' issues, but engaged increasingly in political activity over time. While it remained politically cautious, as it developed it broadened its political scope and became a hub which united many of the most prominent mission-educated political leaders. In this broader political role it engaged in a wide range of political issues as it sought to support the interest of African peoples.[38] The second is *Imbumba yama Nyama* (*Imbumba* in the rest of the chapter). Founded in 1882, it was the first explicitly political African organisation in the Eastern Cape. I will return to discuss this organisation in detail, as it shows how mission-educated communities created new forms of politics in the earliest African-only political organisations. In the triangle cluster we see the Healdtown mission school. We also see the organisations in the Transkei which were led by Healdtown graduates: the Transkei Teachers Association (TTA), which was founded in 1882 and, like the NEA, brought local teachers together, and the Transkei (or Butterworth) Mutual Improvement Association (TMIA), founded in Butterworth in 1884, which coordinated local self-help efforts.[39]

At a slightly earlier date than these came some more urban political organisations, also founded by African mission-educated political leaders. These are shown in the rectangle cluster at the bottom of the figures. The Ethiopian Benefit society (EBS) was an early self-help organisation, founded by Africans in Port Elizabeth in 1877, which collected money for mutual aid and funeral costs,[40] and was a forerunner of a mutual aid form of organisation which would flourish through the 1880s. Many members of the EBS were also important leaders in the Independent Order of True Templars (IOTT) – a widely influential and politically impactful temperance organisation promoting abstinence from alcohol, which I will return to below.

The remaining three clusters are organisations which emerged from rural political struggles in the more deeply rural region beyond the Kei river, called the Transkei. These organisations were led by chiefs and headmen. In the Glen Grey area of Thembuland (star cluster), the South African Native Association (SANA), comprised primarily of mission-educated Africans, was created in 1882. It worked closely with the Thembu Association

---

[36] L. Switzer and D. Switzer, *The Black Press in South Africa and Lesotho: A Descriptive Bibliographic Guide to African, Coloured, and Indian Newspapers, Newsletters, and Magazines, 1836–1976* (Boston: Hall, 1979): 45–6.

[37] Odendaal, *The Founders*, ch 6.

[38] Ibid.

[39] Ibid, ch 9.

[40] Odendaal, 'Even White Boys Call Us "Boy"!', 9.

Quantitative History and Uncharted People

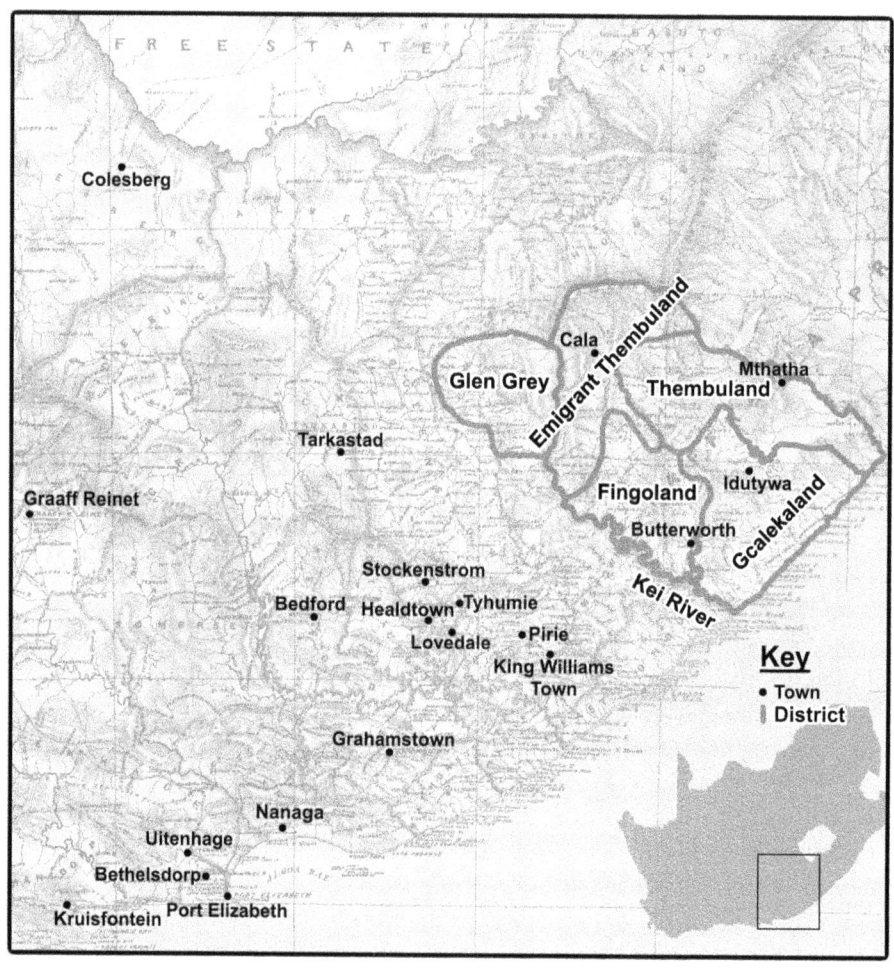

Figure 10.3 Map of the Eastern Frontier of the Cape Colony and adjacent territories.

(founded in the same year), where mission-educated leaders, Thembu rural farmers, and chiefs and headmen united in a struggle against land expropriation– a political development which I describe in detail below.[41] On the top left, in the square cluster, we see the organisations in Emigrant Thembuland, including the Emigrant Thembuland Native Association (ETNAS) founded in 1876, which united relatively elite African 'moderniser' farmers. Later some of its leaders joined *Umanyano lwase Batenjini* (*Umanyano* in the figures), which served as the political wing of ETNAS from its formation in 1886.[42] On the lower right the circle cluster shows two Transkei organisations that united chiefs and

---

[41]Odendaal, *The Founders*, ch 8.
[42]Ibid.

headmen of the Ngqika and Mfengu with mission-educated leaders to advocate for their political group based on *isizwe* identities. *Intlanganiso Ye Nqubelo Pambili Yama Ngqika* (*Intla_Ngqika*), founded in 1885, and *Manyano nge Mvo Zabantsundu* (*Manya_Zabant*) founded in 1887, represented Ngqika and Mfengu interests respectively.[43, 44]

Broad patterns of political communities

These analyses help to identify two broad structural patterns emerging in these organisations: One set of organisations was made up of educational, religious and self-help organisations and are shown in the cross, triangle, and rectangle clusters. These organisations were headed by missionary-educated elite leaders, including many ordained African ministers, who received advanced educations at schools including Lovedale and Healdtown. Considered spatially (see Figure 10.3), these organisations were based at important mission schools, and in more urban towns in the region South and East of the Kei river (or the Ciskei) which had been brought under colonial influence sooner than the Transkei region.

The second set of organisations, shown as stars, squares, and circles, explicitly marked their *isizwe* identification in their names. These organisations were located in the more rural areas such as around or North of the Kei river (the Transkei region – see Figure 10.3), geographically further away from colonial influence, and had a number of mission-educated leaders who partnered with the chiefs and headmen who had political authority in these areas.

The different positions of these two groups of organisations in the social structure (as revealed in the network maps) had an important impact on the kinds of politics these organisations engaged in and the political imagination they developed. In the following analysis I refer to the first set of organisations as *abantu basesikolweni* ('school people') organisations and the second as *isizwe* ('ethnic' or 'national') organisations.

The *abantu basesikolweni* organisations were first modelled on missionary and colonial organisations and at first reproduced many of their values. The political and cultural authorities in these organisations were missionary-educated elite – African ministers and teachers. They drew membership largely from Africans educated at mission schools. They operated primarily in communities which were more closely connected to the colonial economic, political and social world: around established mission stations and/or more urban communities, such as Port Elisabeth or Butterworth. These organisations often began pursuing missionary values of education, Christianity, and 'progress', uplifting and developing African communities. Yet, this missionary and colonial starting

---

[43] Ibid, ch 9.

[44] Map adapted from the 1878 'Map of the Eastern Frontier of the Cape Colony and adjacent territory', created by H. Malthouse. Accessed from University of Cape Town Libraries, South Africa, digital collections. Available online: https://digitalcollections.lib.uct.ac.za/collection/islandora-19613. Marked districts of Transkei and Glen Grey are drawn from Bergh and Visagie 1985, p.63 and p.65 respectively. J.S. Bergh and J.C. Visagie, *The Eastern Cape Frontier Zone, 1660–1980: A Cartographic Guide for Historical Research* (Durban: Butterworths, 1985).

point was transformed to emphasise *abantsundu* ('black' or 'African') interests, shifting the vision of political action in the process.

The *isizwe* organisations linked chiefs and headmen with missionary-educated leaders. They drew their membership from more rural communities who had largely not received mission education, and at times had actively rejected colonial culture.[45] These organisations emerged to engage a range of local issues as communities united to challenge land dispossession, provide ethnically based mutual aid, or advance agricultural interests. These organisations brought together the political and cultural authority of the chiefs and headmen, the interests of the rural and often non-Christian peasantry, and the adeptness in colonial politics of the mission-educated leaders.

Dynamics of political innovation in early African political organisations

These two organisational forms created two types of political innovation and transformation which shaped emerging African politics. Innovation happened primarily through repertoire transposition in the *abantu basesikolweni* organisations and repertoire syncretisation in the *isizwe* organisations. To demonstrate how the structure of social relationships created different opportunities for innovation, we now look at three case studies: The Independent Order of True Templars, *Imbumba yama Nyama* and the Thembu Association.

Transforming colonial political forms – Repertoire transposition

Repertoire transposition best describes the form of innovation created by the *abantu basesikolweni* organisations emerging from missionary school networks (the cross, triangle, and rectangle clusters in Figure 10.2). My case studies of two organisations, the Independent Order of True Templars and *Imbumba yama Nyama*, illustrate the dynamics of this form of innovation.

The Independent Order of True Templars

The Independent Order of True Templars (IOTT)[46] with branches first founded in Port Elizabeth in 1875[47] and Lovedale in 1876[48] (see locations in Figure 10.3), grew out of the Independent Order of Good Templars – a global movement of temperance organisations

---

[45]See: J.P. de Wet, 'Passive Resistance to Western Capitalism in Rural South Africa: From "Abantu Babomvu" to "AmaZiyoni"', *Journal for the Study of Religion* 21, no. 2 (2008): 33–61.

[46]Studied in depth by Mills, 'Roots of African Nationalism'.

[47]Odendaal, *The Founders*.

[48]Mills, 'Roots of African Nationalism'.

founded by prohibitionists in the United States in 1851 that spread to Britain in 1868 and then across the British Empire and across the globe.[49] Faced by the colonists' resistance to the inclusion of black people in their societies, in 1879 Henry Kayers of the London Missionary Society and John Geard of Lovedale founded the IOTT as a separate interracial society. Kayers and Geard applied the same organisational form as the Independent Order of Good Templars, 'a highly elaborated example of American fraternal societies of a semi-masonic type'. Herewith local 'temples' (branches) were linked together into regional 'Grand Temples' all under the umbrella of a 'Right Worthy True Temple'.[50] The pageantry of this semi-masonic form shaped the everyday practice of the organisation, and it used grand titles for leading members (such as the 'Right Worthy True Templar' or 'Right Worthy Sentinel')[51] and secret passwords (circulated in Xhosa, English and Dutch).[52]

The IOTT grew rapidly in the Eastern Cape. In 1883 the annual meeting reported a membership of over 3,500 members, constituting forty-two Temples in the midlands and frontier districts, and fifteen in the diamond fields and the Orange Free State.[53] The organisation's popularity endured, and in 1898 an article in *Imvo Zabantsundu* reported that the 'Eastern Grand Temple' was made up of over forty Temples and more than 5,000 members.[54]

As Africans participated in and co-opted this imported organisational form, they drew lessons for their own political practice, and brought new emphasis to the already existing prohibition goals. I highlight three key shifts. First, the IOTT offered one of the earliest venues where African leaders could learn the leadership practices of a multi-branched and territory-wide organisation. African leaders, particularly the African clergy, including figures like Daniel Mzamo, John Knox Bokwe, Pambani Jeremiah Mzimba and Isaac Williams Wauchope, held major leadership positions in the IOTT from its early days[55] and had de facto control over the organisation from the 1890s.[56] Figure 10.4 shows the members of the IOTT who were also linked to other African political organisations. As is clear, many IOTT leaders (especially those marked with

---

[49]Ibid.

[50]Ibid, 206.

[51]'Independent Order of True Templars' *Port Elizabeth Telegraph and Eastern Province Standard*, 31 March 1883, 3.

[52]Mills, 'Roots of African Nationalism', 206.

[53]'Independent Order of True Templars', *Port Elizabeth Telegraph and Eastern Province Standard*, 31 March 1883, 3. The IOTT's fifth annual meeting had thirty-four delegates from across the Eastern Cape region, including Richmond, Graaff-Reinet, Tarkastad, Bedford, Stockenstroom, Chumie [Tyhumie], Lovedale, King William's Town, Pirie, Uitenhage, Bethelsdorp, Kruis Fontein, Strand Fontein, Nanaga, Port Elizabeth and Graham's Town (see Figure 10.3).

[54]Mills, 'Roots of African Nationalism', 206.

[55]See reports in *Isigidimi sama-Xosa*, 1 February 1880, 5; *Port Elizabeth Telegraph and Eastern Province Standard*, 31 March 1883, 3; *Isigidimi sama-Xosa*, 1 May 1883, 3; *Port Elizabeth Telegraph and Eastern Province Standard*, 28 June 1887, 3.

[56]Mills, 'Roots of African Nationalism', 208.

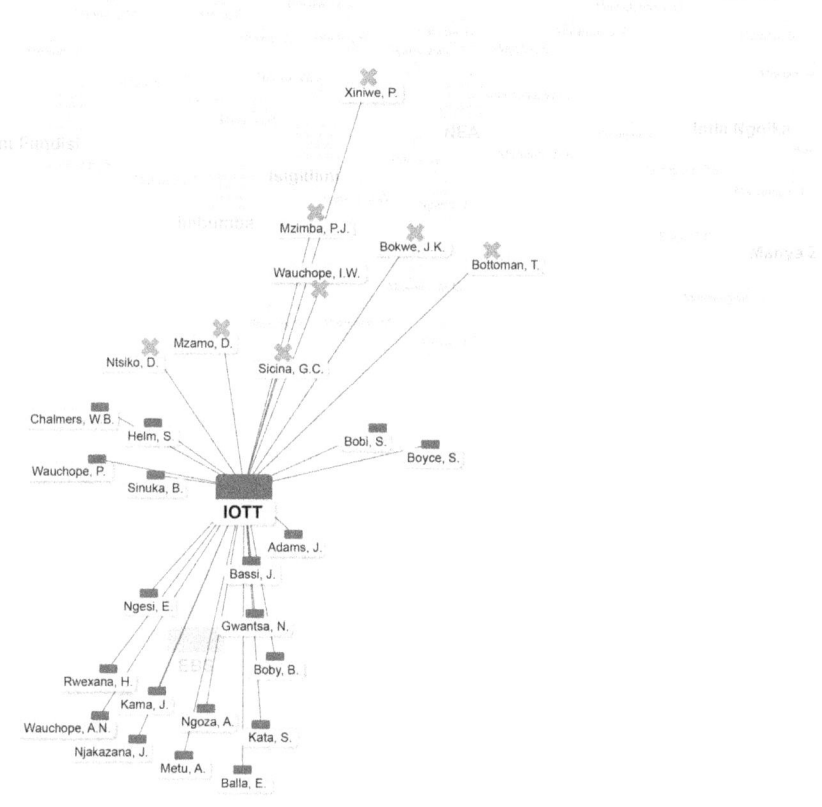

Figure 10.4 IOTT with members who linked to other organisations.

crosses) were also leaders in the first African-only political organisations, including *Imbumba* to which I will return. Thus, the political experience gained here offered an organisational model which was replicated in later African political organisations.

Second, participation in this temperance movement developed a social and political commitment to racial and ethnic identities. The explicit racial exclusion from the Independent Order of Good Templars fostered a racial identity among IOTT members, including as *abantsundu* (black people). In addition, *isizwe* identities were brought to the fore in the struggle against alcohol: imported colonial liquor was seen as destroying African *izizwe* (nations)[57] and the writings of Templar leaders like Pambani Mzimba[58]

---

[57] For example in an article written in 1875 W.W. Gqoba argues '*kutshabalala izizwe … yotywala bomlungu*' ('the white man's liquor is destroying whole nations'). W.W. Gqoba, *Isizwe Esinembali: Xhosa Histories and Poetry (1873–1888)*, ed. J. Opland, W. Kuse and P. Maseko (Kwa-Zulu Natal: University of KwaZulu-Natal Press, 2015): 52.

[58] See for example: P. Mzimba, 'Ingxelo Yabatunywa Base Lovedale', *Isigidimi sama-Xosa*, 1 May 1883, 3.

and Isaac Wauchope,[59] framed the struggle against alcohol as a struggle for the wellbeing of Xhosa and Mfengu communities.[60] This commitment to winning gains for African communities was an ideological focus across the emerging political organisations.

And third, participation in the IOTT offered African leaders an early model of collective political action which engaged the colonial legislature with the aim of transforming laws pertaining to Africans. The IOTT went beyond only focusing on personal pietism: it aimed to perfect society by eliminating social evils – a task for political action.[61] The imported model had this political activism baked in: in both the United States and Britain, Good Templar organisations lobbied government for prohibition laws. The IOTT followed this same strategy including 'petitions to parliament (almost annually), representations before parliamentary commissions, and legal actions opposing the issuing or renewal of canteen licenses'.[62] This anti-liquor petitioning was an important precursor to later petition politics, which I return to in the discussion below of the Thembu Association.

In summary then, although the IOTT took up a temperance model which came from overseas, this model was transformed through African participation. African activists learned new political repertoires even as they centred new racial and ethnic identities in the existing prohibition politics. These leaders learned strategies for leading a large, multi-branch and territorially wide organisation. They were exposed to a vision of societal transformation which could in part be achieved by directly lobbying the colonial state for support and legal reform, and they developed both *abantsundu* identity (against racist exclusion) and *isizwe* identities as they focused on the ills facing the Xhosa and Mfengu *izizwe* ('nations').

The IOTT thus illustrates an early form of African uptake of colonial political models. In this organisation, African leaders were at first incorporated into a structure headed by white missionaries in its early years and which used political practices developed overseas. The organisation shows the clear transposition of colonial political models to African political communities, but only limited avenues for African political control, which limited innovation. Yet this African engagement with colonial political forms laid the groundwork for new African-led organisations which resulted in more radical transformation and innovation.

---

[59] See for example I.W. Wauchope, 'Intlanganiso Enkulu Yabazili Benene e-Rini', *Isigidimi sama-Xosa*, 1 May 1883, 3.

[60] Note that Xhosa and Mfengu groups were repeatedly relocated into different 'tribal reserves' as the colonial state expanded. Figure 10.3 shows divisions in the Transkei: the Mfengu area of 'Fingoland' and the Xhosa of 'Gcalekaland'. Similar reservations were also created in the Ciskei area.

[61] Mills, 'Roots of African Nationalism'.

[62] Ibid, 211.

Imbumba yama Nyama

An example of the next step in this political development can be seen in the organisation *Imbumba yama Nyama*,[63] my second case study. Emerging from a tradition of debates held in *Isigidimi*, and then from the ground-breaking yet largely apolitical NEA, *Imbumba* was the first political organisation to explicitly articulate political interests based on an African and pan-racial identity. This political identity is made clear in a newspaper article reporting on the organisation's inaugural meeting. *Imbumba* aimed to be an '*intlanganiso yomanyano lwaba ntsundu base South Africa*' ('association for the unity of the black people of South Africa'), with a pan-racial vision of unity: '*Zonke izinto zelungelo laba ntsundu ziya kuxoxwa ezintlanganisweni zolu manyano, eziya kumiswa kwindawo ngengawo kulo lonke eli laba ntsundu ukuba kunokwenzeka*' ('All affairs of black people will be discussed at the meetings of this union, which will be held at various places in all the black areas if possible.').[64]

The organisation's instigator and first president, Simon Peter Sihlali, intended that the organisation would cure the illness of disunity and unite '*usapo lwase Africa*' ('the family of Africa') and Isaac Wauchope, the first Chairman, envisaged that '*lembumba mayihlanganise imihlambi eyalanayo. Kubunjwe um Xosa ne Mfengu nom Tshaka nom Sutu*' ('this *Imbumba* should unite diverse flocks. A Xhosa and a Mfengu and a Zulu and a Sotho should be bound together').[65]

This African-centric, pan-racial political vision emerged from a growing public sphere made up for the first time almost exclusively of missionary-educated Africans no longer under missionary authority. The members of this public sphere had been trained in the colonial and missionary world and exposed to its political repertoires, and in this African-only social context they drew from these repertoires and in doing so transformed them to suit their own context and needs, producing new ideological positions in the process. In *Isigidimi*, published from 1870, Africans began to discuss and debate their political context. The teacher-focused NEA discussed above offered the first organisational form to extend this space to a physical Africans-only organisation, but in its early days it remained focused on education issues. The IOTT represented African political engagement with the Cape government, yet still under missionary guidance. *Imbumba* grew out of both the tradition of social and political engagement of the IOTT and the African-only intellectual spaces of *Isigidimi* and the NEA. Growing in political assertiveness, *Imbumba* was the first full-blown African-only political organisation to emerge from the mission-educated community.

This trajectory of political development is visible in the network map. *Imbumba*'s close social proximity to *Isigidimi* and the NEA (Figure 10.1a) shows that these

---

[63] Studied in depth by Odendaal, *The Founders*, ch 7.

[64] 'Imbumba Yomfo ka Gaba', *Isigidimi sama-Xosa*, 1 November 1882, 4–5. The translation is from Wauchope, *Isaac Williams Wauchope*, item 3.2: 174.

[65] 'Imbumba Yomfo ka Gaba', *Isigidimi sama-Xosa*, 1 November 1882, 4.

Political Innovation in African Nationalist Organisations, 1880–90

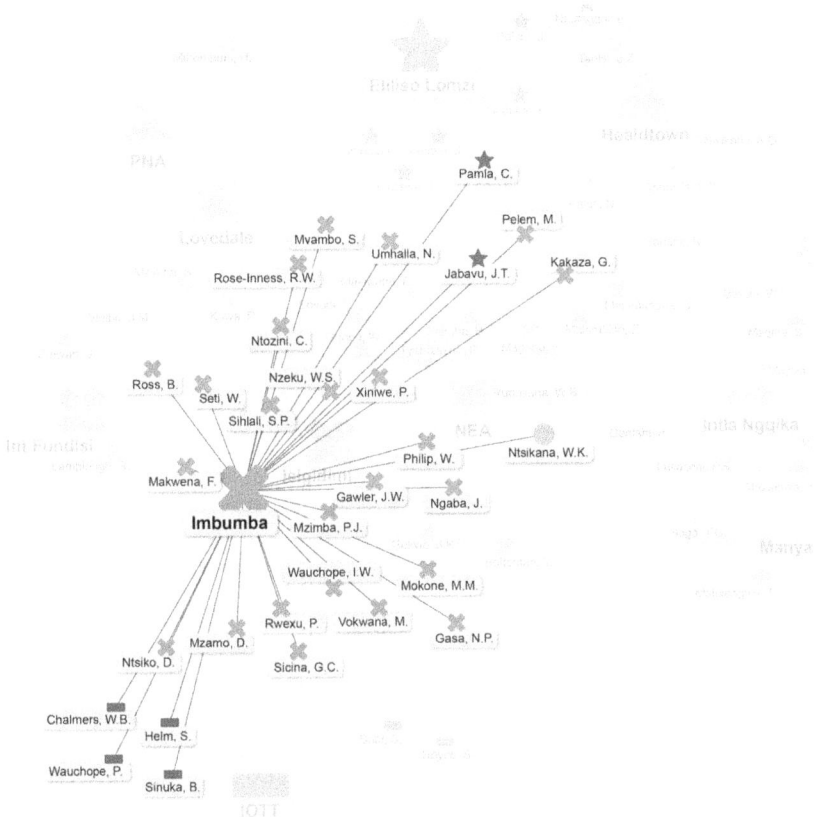

Figure 10.5 *Imbumba* with members who linked to other organisations.

organisations shared many members. It is also clear that many members of the IOTT and the Ethiopian Benefit Society were important leaders in *Imbumba* (Figures 10.1a and 10.3). Indeed, as Odendaal has shown, in the early 1880s, *Imbumba* built its organisational branches in the same urban areas which were the core of the IOTT's urban organising.[66] The overlap of members and areas of organising show that IOTT offered a scaffold for *Imbumba's* political growth. Figure 10.5 shows these linking members.

Imbumba was thus an early hub of missionary-educated Africans which explicitly set its sights on political engagement. As such, it drew on other political strategies and organisational forms, including missionary, temperance and colonial interest group organisations and the white farmer organisation the Afrikaner Bond. But as an African-only organisation it transformed the ideological and symbolic framework of these colonial organisations to create perhaps the earliest political organisation explicitly fighting for black (*abantsundu*) interests in South Africa.

---

[66]Odendaal, *The Founders*, 71.

This familiarity with colonial political models also had an impact on political practice. *Imbumba* both participated in local urban politics, with three branches located in the urban towns of Port Elizabeth, Graaff-Reinet and Colesberg (see Figure 10.3), and also brought a range of broader African issues to the Cape government. At the local level, the Port Elizabeth *Imbumba* branch worked directly within colonial political institutions to assert African interests. Activities that *Imbumba* undertook included bringing African dissatisfaction with municipal laws before the town council, opposing licences for canteens near African areas (note the alignment with IOTT), opposing the town council's attempts to remove the largest African settlement further away from Port Elizabeth (thus opposing segregation), seeking to establish a Native Management Board and working to register African voters.[67] Its broader level of engagement with Cape politics can be seen in its first annual congress, where delegates from the three branches (Port Elizabeth, Graaff-Reinet and Colesberg) formed committees to tackle a range of issues including the registration of voters, the political and educational needs of urban African settlements, and passed 'several resolutions for submission to parliament' which included a request 'that the franchise qualifications should not be raised in order to deny the vote to blacks'.[68]

In *Imbumba* we see how the repertoires and practices of colonial style political organisations were transformed to generate new political identities as they were 'transposed' into African-only contexts. Its African leaders, educated in mission schools and engaged in political projects like the temperance movement, adhered to many of the political values and visions of their colonial counterparts. They reproduced many missionary values, including supporting African education and the isiXhosa press and opposing the sale of alcohol. Their political projects were strongly connected to local urban struggles within the colonial legal framework (such as engaging in local municipality council politics) and also set its sights on the Cape colony's legal framework as it met with government officials,[69] and aimed to challenge and influence the Cape parliament's laws.[70] In so doing, *Imbumba* reproduced colonial-style political repertoires. Yet the fundamental underlying shift seen in this organisation was the rise and assertion of a shared black identity to unite Africans and defend their interests. From its basis in missionary-educated and urban communities, the organisation envisaged a pan-racial form of politics which aimed to overcome ethnic divisions among Africans. It looked beyond the identity divisions which remained powerful and salient for more rural political communities, and was an early political voice defending an *abantsundu* identity which would grow in power and prominence throughout the 1880s.

The earliest vision of 'African' or 'black' political interests was pioneered by organisations like *Imbumba* which, instead of fighting the colonial system with military

---

[67] Ibid, 72.
[68] Ibid, 73.
[69] *Isigidimi sama-Xosa*, 1 May 1883, 1.
[70] *Isigidimi sama-Xosa*, 1 November 1883, 4.

resistance which would now be crushed by imperial might,[71] adopted the political repertoire of the colonial system. Yet in doing so they were not simply conforming to the colonial political vision. Instead, organisations like *Imbumba* were able to transform the vision and goals of these political systems, putting the old tools to work in new ways. As they did so, they increasingly understood their own political project as an *abantsundu* project: their work was to unite Africans and to fight for their interests. In *Imbumba*, the IOTT, and other organisations emerging from mission school networks we see a repertoire transposition which transformed colonial and missionary organisational forms. The individuals in this part of the network were teachers, pastors and journalists deeply involved in the schools and newspapers founded by missionaries. Yet it was in uniting to confront increasingly racist government policies that these people created a new vision and basis for political action: the earliest organisational foundations for *African* interest politics.

New possibilities by combining political resources – Repertoire syncretisation

In the *isizwe* organisations which appear on the periphery of the network (star, square, and circle clusters in Figure 10.2) we see a different pattern of political innovation and transformation – that of repertoire syncretisation. These organisations brought together a variety of members: the chiefs and headmen who held traditional authority, the missionary-educated elite, and the rural African communities comprised primarily of subsistence farmers. The uniting of these groups produced new political imagination which merged elements of the repertoires of the various members and the social contexts they came from, and it also yielded new forms of politics which would not have been possible without the diverse repertoires and resources which were combined in these organisations.

As previously noted, these communities came from more rural regions, around or North of the Kei River that served as a colonial border (the Transkei – 'beyond the Kei'). This region had a colonial history markedly different from the Ciskei region ('before the Kei') to the south and west of the Kei River which was the centre of *abantu basesikolweni* organising we have followed until now (see Figure 10.3). Long-running military conflict, white settler farmers, and small but growing urban centres marked the colonisation of the Ciskei region. By contrast, the Transkei region remained unannexed (although influenced by colonial power) until 1872. Instead, the colonial government treated different parts of this area as separate geographic units. It engaged, negotiated, and interfered with the local power-structures of these territories in order to promote African leaders who would be loyal to the Cape government. What began

---

[71] As in the Bambatha uprising of 1906. S. Marks, *Reluctant Rebellion: The 1906–8 Disturbances in Natal* (Oxford: Clarendon Press, 1970).

with colonial conquests and the capture of land for colonial allies culminated between 1872 and 1895 in the annexation of the territories known as Fingoland, Gcalekaland, Thembuland, Emigrant Thembuland, East Griqualand, Pondoland and those peopled by the Mpondmise, Bhaca, Hlubi and Sotho (see Figure 10.3).[72] Under Cape rule this region was named the Transkeian Territories.[73]

Even when the area was annexed, prominent African political leaders, lineages and local identities continued to shape politics. Colonial authorities cultivated patron-client relationships with allied African leaders, giving them land taken from communities who rebelled, and often an income as well. Yet these leaders and their communities still most often understood the legitimacy of their leadership as based on their royal or ethnic political legitimacy.

This colonial and political history shaped the development of political identity, strategy and action in the region, leading to unique forms of political innovation. As Beinart and Bundy argue:

> Although the imposition of taxes, colonial laws, and colonial institutions defined the political issues that confronted rural Africans, they do not alone explain patterns of alliance and conflict. Political thinking and behaviour grew out of what were still real and self-conscious local communities, with their own internal dynamics.[74]

Beinart and Bundy's keen analysis of Transkei politics between 1890 and 1930 holds true for the *isizwe* organisations of the 1880s examined in this chapter. They identify four broad social, economic and political classes which shaped the politics of the period: the 'educated elite', mission school graduates who held secure salaried jobs and had influence in church leadership, which supported their agricultural production; the 'traditional leaders', hereditary chiefs and headmen, who retained their authority to 'conduct traditional court cases, collect tributary fees and dues, and to exercise considerable authority over the distribution of land' and were increasingly involved in the colonial administrative system, as local authorities under a colonial magistrate; the 'old loyal communities', mostly Christian peasants or workers in small towns, who had received land and economic opportunities for their loyalty to the Cape government, but were slowly being pushed into unskilled migrant labour; and the 'traditionalist followers', the largest group in most districts, who rejected Christianity and 'the assimilationist ideas that accompanied it' and 'displayed a cautious and selective traditionalism', balancing a focus on land and livestock with some forms of migrant and wage labour.[75] This last group would join in 'alliances with Christian or radical Africanist groups when there

---

[72]C. Saunders, 'The Annexation of the Transkeian Territories (1872–1895), with Special Reference to British and Cape Policy' (PhD diss., University of Oxford, Oxford, 1972); Beinart and Bundy, *Hidden Struggles*, 5.

[73]Ibid, 6.

[74]Ibid, 7.

[75]Ibid, 11–12.

were appropriate targets to fight', but were mobilised primarily around 'ethnic or localised associations or behind their chosen branch of the royal family'.[76]

These social groups, which I refer to below as the 'mission-educated elite', 'traditional leaders', 'loyalists' and 'traditionalist followers', created a context for political organising distinct from that of the *abantu basesikolweni* politics discussed previously. *Abantu basesikolweni* organisations emerged in mission school communities and urban areas which were more powerfully influenced by colonial culture and rule. In contrast, *isizwe* organisations emerged in regions more distant from colonial culture and shorter under colonial rule (see the districts marked in Figure 10.3). Here new alliances between the traditional leaders and the educated elite, aiming to mobilise large rural communities, created novel forms of demand making and collective action in the early proto-nationalist movement – a form of innovation which I call 'repertoire syncretisation'.

The Thembu Association

The Thembu Association, my third case study, exemplifies this repertoire syncretisation which can also be seen in other *isizwe* organisations. In what follows I draw on newspaper reports and petitions to the Cape parliament to explore the political form this organisation developed. I support these primary sources by drawing on Odendaal's analysis of the Thembu Association and the South African Native Association (SANA), which were both formed in the Glen Grey district of Thembuland in 1882 (see Figure 10.3).[77]

SANA was made up of missionary-educated teachers and leaders from Healdtown, such as David Malasi, Richard Kawa and James Pelem. It repeated much of the same pattern seen in the political organisations of missionary-educated leaders discussed above, and indeed SANA explicitly linked itself to both the NEA and *Imbumba* and sought closer association with them. But in Glen Grey this missionary-educated organisational form did not have the same political base that it had elsewhere and by 1884 SANA had merged into the Thembu Association. The Thembu Association, also founded in 1882, emerged from a political movement engaged in land struggles between the approximately 20,000 strong Thembu community who lived in the district and the colonial settlers who were pressuring the colonial government to give them more land.[78] In the process of mobilising to resist land dispossession, the Thembu Association united the leadership and political resources and acumen of the educated elite and the traditional leaders. It also mobilised mass support from the loyalists and the traditionalist followers to create a new form of mass mobilisation to engage the Cape government. From 1883, the Thembu Association organised delegations to the government and mass

---

[76]Ibid.
[77]Odendaal, *The Founders*, ch 8.
[78]Ibid, 77.

Figure 10.6 Thembu Association (left) and South African Native Association (right) with members who linked to other organisations.

meetings (including one of 600 people and another of 1,000) to assert Thembu land rights in the face of settler expansion. Odendaal highlights the way the co-operation between the traditional leaders and the mission-educated elite 'succeeded in establishing a popular base for political action'.[79] Figure 10.6 visualises the members who linked the Thembu Association and SANA.

An example of the kind of politics created by this alliance of the mission-educated elite and the traditional leaders can be seen in a petition the leaders of the Thembu Association sent to the government in 1886.[80] It shows how new forms of political action drew these two groups together. Presented to the Cape parliament on 16 April 1886, the petition is remarkable for two reasons: its huge number of signatories and its synthesis of the political strategies of mission-educated elites and traditional leaders. Where petitions received by the Cape parliament usually carried tens or at most hundreds of signatures, this one had 2,138 – a clear break from the norm and an early appearance of mass petitioning politics. The language of the petition shows a remarkable synthesis of the logic of political claim making, combining the logic of the mission-educated elite and the traditional leaders into a syncretic composite which made the best of the claiming power of both.

Petitions were a colonial mode of engagement with the government that these two groups had begun experimenting with in the late 1870s and 1880s. One early use of

---

[79] Ibid, 79.

[80] Western Cape Archives and Records Services, Petitions to the House of Assembly (henceforth WCARS, HA) 799, no. 11.

petitions by the mission-educated elite was in the IOTT temperance movement discussed above. Among those who headed petitions for the prohibition of liquor sales to Africans were James Dwane, an influential African minister, and a pioneer of the Ethiopian Church movement, together with African members of the Mount Coke Wesleyan Methodist Church in 1884; Isaac William Wauchope, together with IOTT members in 1885; Walter B. Rubusana, together with Peelton inhabitants in 1886, and Pambani J. Mzimba, together with Africans living in Victoria East in 1887.[81] These petitions, headed by pre-eminent African political and religious leaders, were just four of a huge number of petitions (at least seventy-nine between 1883 and 1887) to prohibit the sale of liquor to Africans. These petitions were submitted by missionaries, African communities and colonist communities beginning from 1883 and continuing through the rest of the century.[82] From this base, the mission-educated elite expanded the petition form to engage in other political issues, especially to oppose African voter disenfranchisement.[83]

The petition records show that some traditional leaders had also begun to use petitions to engage directly with the Cape government instead of working through the magistrates of their area. Some of the earliest petitions came from the Basotho paramount chief Letsie, in 1877, 1878 and twice in 1880,[84] showing that this direct petitioning by African chiefs was not unheard of. However, between 1877 and 1886 when the Thembu Association petition was sent, only eleven petitions mention chiefs or headmen, and came from five different chiefs.[85] The use of petition politics by traditional leaders was still fairly rare.

The 1886 petition from the Thembu Association was thus a political strategy little used before this date. After this, mass petitioning became a political form that African communities increasingly used to make demands on the government. In this case, the creation and presentation of a petition with over 2,000 signatures was made possible by combining the political skills and resources of both the traditional leaders and the mission-educated elite. Chiefs and headmen could mobilise mass support from their rural communities, and the mission-educated elite could protest and appeal in the language of colonial politics.

---

[81]WCARS, HA 793, no. 183; 798, no. 240; 800, no. 70; and 804, no. 76, respectively.

[82]'Abstract of Petitions', *Votes & Proceedings of the House of Assembly*, various volumes (1854–1909), Stellenbosch University Library. See also Dimitruk and Lemon (this volume).

[83]For example P. J. Mzimba (WCARS, HA 804, no 73) and J. T. Jabavu (WCARS, HA 804, no. 114) led inhabitants from Victoria East and King William's Town respectively in petitions against the Parliamentary Registration Bill in 1887.

[84]Petitions from chief Letsie: WCARS, HA 774, no. 27; 11; 778, no. 15; 778, no. 16, respectively.

[85]Chief Letsie (see previous footnote); Darala, Mantanzima, Gecelo and Stockwe, Emigrant Thembuland chiefs in 1880 (WCARS, HA 779, no. 109); Chief Seyesi Siwani in 1882 (WCARS, HA 784, no. 2; 784, no. 6), Johannes Tshatshu (a.k.a. Jan or Dyani Tzatzoe) Chief of the Amantinde in 1883 (WCARS, HA 789, no. 267); Jonathan Molapo, son of Molapo, Chief of the Leribe in 1882 and 1883 (WCARS, HA 784, no. 7; 791, no. 28); and Kosana, Chief of the Amavundhlu in 1883 (WCARS, HA 790, no. 350).

This syncretisation of political repertoires is visible in the language of the petition itself. The careful legal and historical argument developed in the petition shows that the mission-educated elite had mastered the elaborate governmental style and could use arguments from the government's own documents to support the petition's claim. We also see three political strategies from the repertoire of traditional leaders: the strong *isizwe* political identity of the Thembu people, the mass mobilisation of the community through the rural political hierarchy of chiefs and headmen, and an expectation that loyalty to the government should be met with colonial protection.

The petition syncretises these repertoires to build a legal argument that the Thembu people had been given the territory of the Glen Grey District in 1852 by the Governor of Cape of Good Hope and his appointed agent, and that they had entered into no agreement to exchange this territory for another. The petition recounts government offers to exchange the Glen Grey territory for territory beyond the colonial border. It goes into detail to defend the claim that no relocation was agreed on. It notes that the first two proposals (1864 and 1865) were rejected and

> after this our Tembu chiefs, three of them minor chiefs, applied for leave to move into the vacant country, and permission was granted ... but this was a special arrangement entered into with a fragment of the tribe and acceded to by the Government with the full knowledge that his proposals had not been accepted by the Tembu tribe.

Furthermore, they argue, the terms of this proposal could not have been honoured because 'more than one half of the country originally offered by Sir Philip Wodehouse to the Tembu in exchange for the locations was by Sir Philip's directions filled up with Fingoes [Mfengu] shewing conclusively that the then Government admitted the failure of their proposed exchange'. The legal basis of this argument is made clear, as the petition asserts that 'your petitioners will be prepared to prove all these statements by evidence at the bar of your Honorable House'.

Establishing that the Thembu retained the original rights to the Glen Grey district, the petition then argues that this territory, allotted in 1852 by the government, had been 'very considerably reduced in extent' by the seizure of the lands of the Chief Gangubelle, by the land given to the Indwe and Imvani railway project,[86] and by the 300 families who had been forcibly relocated to Qumbu and nearly as many 'forced to leave their homes to be located elsewhere'.

The petition lays the blame for these removals squarely on the shoulders of the most powerful colonial officials of the region, not shying away from explicit accusations:

> [T]he proceedings of Mr. Frost [the Member of Parliament] and Mr. Jenner the Resident Magistrate in connection with these removals complied with the

---

[86] Noted in the petition as twelve farms. Odendaal says this was '25,000 morgen of land, about a tenth of the district'. Odendaal, *The Founders*, 77.

assertions of Mr. De Wet [the Government Secretary of Native Affairs] at his interview with the Queens Town Council and Chamber of Commerce have caused great uneasiness to your petitioners and have created a feeling that your petitioners may be driven from their homes and rendered incapable of acquiring and holding lands.

Quoting the government's own documents in support, the petition argues that the legal title to the Glen Grey territory held by the Thembu should be vested in a Thembu Board of Trustees. It says that 'in or about the year 1881', the Governor of the Colony had appointed a commission which recommended 'that these locations should continue to be reserved for native occupation; and that this reservation should be reserved by means of Folk or Forest Deeds issued for that purpose in favor of Boards of Trustees who shall hold and administer these lands for and on behalf of the natives in occupation of the same'.

This argument in place, the petition concludes with three requests: that key figures be summoned to the House of Assembly for an inquiry into the history of the proposed and actual removals of Thembu from the area, supported by documents which the House should request from the Civil commissioner of Queenstown and the Resident Magistrate of Glen Grey; that the territory currently occupied by Thembu should be vested in Trustees, as recommended by the government's own report; and that the government should provide other relief as the House of Assembly deemed fit.

This document illustrates a syncretic form of political demand making which emerged as the political repertoires of the mission-educated elites and the traditional leaders merged to create new possibilities. The influence of the mission-educated elite is clearly visible in the careful adherence to the form and language of government petitions; in the deployment of a clear legal framework setting forth the history of governmental decrees and agreements, to be supported by documentary evidence and legal argument before the House if needs be; and in the quoting of the government's own documents to support the petitioners' arguments. The political skill of the mission-educated elite was the ability to use the language and the political and legal tools of the colonial regime to serve their own ends.

This strategy is something we have already seen in the repertoire transposition model of political innovation discussed above. But in the Thembu Association we see it combined with the political power which the traditional leaders brought to the table. We can see their political strategy in three ways in the petition. First, the appeal that the Thembus were 'well-disposed natives' who the government wanted to situate in land taken from the Gcaleka Xhosa, builds on the logic of mutual political interdependence. Here we see the logic of rural colonial governance: rural leaders loyal to the government received support because the colonial state depended on them to have any governance power in regions further away from the centre of colonial power. Pointing out that the government itself had sought out the 'well-disposed' Thembu, the petition reminds the government of its need for African allies, and invokes the spectre of the alternative: a possible repeat of the uprisings in Thembuland in 1880–1. Those had been forged out of political discontent, led by rural leaders who did not see a reason to be 'well disposed' to the Cape government.

Second, where the organisations led by the mission-educated elite had built an increasingly *abantsundu* political identity, here instead we see the political community conceptualised along *isizwe* lines: the political unit is clearly articulated as the Thembu people. This Thembu identity overcomes any internal political divisions of the area, and at the same time limits the claimed rights to a community unified by a Thembu identification, drawn from both a precolonial Thembu political identity and by the colonial concept of the Thembu as a legitimate 'tribe' which could make collective demands. Thus, the petition is not made on behalf of the followers of any chief or headman, and indeed internal political divisions (such as the 'three minor chiefs' who took up the offer for relocation) are dismissed as illegitimate political units. Instead, the petition appeals to the whole 'Thembu tribe', asserting that agreements were made, and can only be renegotiated, with this whole community. This Thembu identity offered a common unity for the thousands of signatories, and demonstrates the importance of *isizwe* political identity in shaping the rural political imagination and demands. The mission-educated elite developed a common *abantsundu* identity as they confronted the 'white vs black' political cleavage created by racist colonial institutions. The *isizwe* identity seen here emerged from a different political cleavage. The petition shows that the group interests of the Thembu are still seen as competing with both the colonial settlers who wanted Thembuland territory and the Gcaleka Xhosa whose land was taken and the Mfengu who were given half of that territory. Here the reality of ethnic political communities and the colonial recognition of 'tribal' groups made *isizwe* political identity a powerful shared identity for collective mobilisation.

And third, the petition demonstrates the political power of the traditional leaders through their ability to mobilise their large support base. The more than 2,000 signatures show that these leaders can effectively coordinate political resistance. Further, the petition document emphasises the relative power of individual leaders, as each signatory added the name of the headman of their area, showing just how many people each leader could mobilise. The petition thus implicitly invokes the claim of all mass movements, a threat that was ever present in the minds of the settlers: We outnumber you; don't forget to play nice.

Each of these different political repertoires and logics had a power of their own and in the previous decade had won gains for the traditional leaders negotiating with expanding colonial influence in the Transkei or for *abantu basesikolweni* organisations. Yet, separately, each political form was losing ground in the Glen Grey region in the 1880s. In the Thembu Association we see a merger of these two political repertoires to generate new political imagination and political action. Here the mode of legal challenge and skilled engagement with colonial political institutions was linked to the capacity for rural mobilisation that had once enabled anti-colonial uprisings. This yielded new forms of action, such as the mass petition politics seen in this example above, and it also yielded new political imagination – asserting the legal and political rights of an *isizwe* community, pushing the government to use its institutional power to pursue legal justice for the Thembu community, and envisioning formalised legal land rights, not for the individual property holder, but for the community as a whole, held in trust not only by the chief or headman who remained in the good graces of government leaders, but held in trust as a formal and legal affirmation of the land rights of a community.

My case study of the Thembu Association reveals a pattern which can be seen more widely. Other organisations, such as *Umanyano Batenjini*, *Manyano nge Mvo Zabantsundu*, and *Intlanganiso Ye Nqubelo Pambili Yama Ngqika*, also linked the skills and strategies of the mission-educated elite with traditional leaders. In a similar fashion they mobilised rural communities around *isizwe* identities to develop new forms of political engagement with the Cape government to defend the interests and well-being of their own *isizwe* group, including movements focused on farming, property development, infrastructure development and mutual aid.[87] These different organisations all generated new forms of political engagement by drawing together existing repertoires and syncretising them in order to create new political opportunities to make gains for their local communities. In doing so they developed new political subjectivities for their local communities, reiterating political identities based on pre-colonial and colonial 'ethnic' political groups, yet at the same time directing this unity to make demands on the government for rights and support by selectively incorporating colonial political forms.

Conclusion

This chapter examined the social networks and innovative political strategies of proto-nationalist political movements in the Eastern Cape. I have used a network analysis approach to show the patterns of social and political connections in emerging African nationalist politics and have argued that this structure of social relationships shaped the kinds of political innovation which were possible.

In the *abantu basesikolweni* organisations we see innovation through *repertoire transposition* – the innovation which occurs by shifting strategies and ideas from one context to another. In these organisations made up of mostly missionary-educated African members anchored in established mission stations and more urban areas largely in the Ciskei region south and west of the Kei River (see Figure 10.3), we see the rise of the first African political interest organisations. I have looked in detail at the Independent Order of True Templars and *Imbumba yama Nyama* to show how such political innovation occurred. These organisations took up the strategies of colonial politics and transformed them into tools to serve African interests, creating an early pan-racial political vision of *abantsundu* ('black' or 'African') identity in the process.

In the *isizwe* organisations we see innovation through *repertoire syncretisation* – innovation which emerges by creatively combining ideas and strategies from different political traditions. In these organisations which emerged in more rural contexts, like the

---

[87]See Odendaal, *The Founders*, chs 8 and 9, for more.

Transkei region North and East of the Kei River (Figure 10.3), we see traditional leaders who developed new alliances with mission-educated leaders, creating organisations which could both mobilise rural communities and make new demands on the colonial state, asserting *isizwe* ('national' or 'ethnic') political identities and forging new forms of mass political mobilisation in the process. To show these dynamics of innovation I have examined the political ideas and action of the Thembu Association.

These innovative forms of politics would ultimately be welded into a growing African nationalist movement. Later these *abantu basesikolweni* and *isizwe* organisations united. Diverse forms of innovation converged and cleavages were overcome as consolidated political organisations like the *Imbumba Eliliso Lomzi Yabantsundu* (Union of Native Vigilance Associations) drew local movements together into a united front against the 1887 laws which sought to disenfranchise Africans.

The innovation studied in this chapter was an early, yet profoundly influential, first step in forging many of the core identities, issues and strategies which would guide the growing African Nationalist movement. Here I have used quantitative approaches to reveal the historically new structure of social relations which emerged in this period of colonisation. To flesh out how these social relations shaped African political creativity and innovation I have drawn on case studies and qualitative analysis.

This study thus makes two broad contributions: It deepens our understanding of the social and political history of early African nationalism in South Africa, and it offers a theoretical model of two different modes of innovation which may shed light on the social dynamics of political innovation more broadly. Here, the dynamics brought to light under the conditions of colonialism in South Africa can reveal lessons for both the closely connected histories of other African and anti-colonial nationalisms, as well as for the social scientific analysis of innovation in political movements across the globe.

Bibliography

Ansell, C.K. 'Symbolic Networks: The Realignment of the French Working Class, 1887–1894'. *American Journal of Sociology* 103, no. 2 (1997): 359–90.
Atwell, D. *Rewriting Modernity: Studies in Black South African Literary History*. Pietermaritzburg: KwaZulu-Natal University Press, 2005.
Bearman, P. *Relations into Rhetorics: Local Elite Social Structure in Norfolk, England, 1540–1640*. New Brunswick: Rutgers University Press, 1993.
Beinart, W. and C. Bundy. *Hidden Struggles in Rural South Africa: Politics & Popular Movements in the Transkei & Eastern Cape, 1890–1930*. Berkeley: University of California Press, 1987.
Bergh, J.S. and J.C. Visagie. *The Eastern Cape Frontier Zone, 1660–1980: 1660–1980; a Cartographic Guide for Historical Research*. Durban: Butterworths, 1985.
Blondel, V.D., J. Guillaume, R. Lambiotte and E. Lefebvre. 'Fast Unfolding of Communities in Large Networks'. *Journal of Statistical Mechanics: Theory and Experiment* 10 (2008): 1–12.
Bundy, C. *The Rise and Fall of the South African Peasantry*. Berkeley: University of California Press, 1979.
Burt, R.S. 'Structural Holes and Good Ideas'. *American Journal of Sociology* 110, no. 2 (2004): 349–99.

Burt, R.S. *Structural Holes: The Social Structure of Competition.* 1992. Reprint. Cambridge, US: Harvard University Press, 2009.
Clemens, E.S. *The People's Lobby: Organizational Innovation and the Rise of Interest Group Politics in the United States, 1890-1925.* Berkeley: University of Chicago Press, 1997.
De Wet, P. 'Passive Resistance to Western Capitalism in Rural South Africa: From "Abantu Babomvu" to "AmaZiyoni"'. *Journal for the Study of Religion* 21, no. 2 (2008): 33–61.
Ennis, J.G. 'Fields of Action: Structure in Movements' Tactical Repertoires'. *Sociological Forum* 2, no. 3 (1987): 520–33.
Fruchterman, T.M.J. and E.M. Reingold. 'Graph Drawing by Force-Directed Placement'. *Software: Practice and Experience* 21, no. 11 (1991): 1129–64.
Gould, R.V. *Insurgent Identities: Class, Community, and Protest in Paris from 1848 to the Commune.* Chicago: University of Chicago Press, 1995.
Gould, R.V. 'Patron-Client Ties, State Centralization, and the Whiskey Rebellion'. *American Journal of Sociology* 102, no. 2 (1996): 400–29.
Gould, R.V. and R.M. Fernandez. 'Structures of Mediation: A Formal Approach to Brokerage in Transaction Networks'. *Sociological Methodology* 19 (1989): 89–126.
Gqoba, W.W. *Isizwe Esinembali: Xhosa Histories and Poetry (1873-1888)*, edited and translated by J. Opland, W. Kuse and P. Maseko. KwaZulu-Natal: University of KwaZulu-Natal Press, 2015.
Granovetter, M.S. 'The Strength of Weak Ties'. *American Journal of Sociology* 78, no. 6 (1973): 1360–80.
Hillmann, H. 'Mediation in Multiple Networks: Elite Mobilization before the English Civil War'. *American Sociological Review* 73, no. 3 (2008): 426–54.
Jacomy, M., T. Venturini, S. Heymann and M. Bastian. 'ForceAtlas2, a Continuous Graph Layout Algorithm for Handy Network Visualization Designed for the Gephi Software'. *PLoS ONE* 9, no. 6 (2014): 1–12.
Jansen, R.S. 'Situated Political Innovation: Explaining the Historical Emergence of New Modes of Political Practice'. *Theory and Society* 45, no. 4 (2016): 319–60.
Jansen, R.S. *Revolutionizing Repertoires.* Chicago: University of Chicago Press, 2017.
Kamada, T. and S. Kawai. 'An Algorithm for Drawing General Undirected Graphs'. *Information Processing Letters* 31 (1): 9.
Lambiotte, R., V.D. Blondel, C. de Kerchove, E. Huens, C. Prieur, Z. Smoreda and P. Van Dooren. 'Geographical Dispersal of Mobile Communication Networks'. *Physica A: Statistical Mechanics and Its Applications* 387, no. 21 (2008): 5317–25.
Marks, S. *Reluctant Rebellion: The 1906-8 Disturbances in Natal.* Oxford: Clarendon Press, 1970.
Marks, S. *The Ambiguities of Dependence in South Africa: Class, Nationalism, and the State in Twentieth-Century Natal.* Baltimore: Johns Hopkins University Press, 1986.
Mills, W.G. 'The Roots of African Nationalism in the Cape Colony: Temperance, 1866-1898'. *International Journal of African Historical Studies* 13, no. 2 (1980): 197–213.
Mooney, P.H., and S.A. Hunt. 'A Repertoire of Interpretations: Master Frames and Ideological Continuity in U.S. Agrarian Mobilization'. *Sociological Quarterly* 37, no. 1 (1996): 177–97.
Odendaal, A. 'African Political Mobilisation in the Eastern Cape. 1880-1910'. PhD diss., University of Cambridge, Cambridge, 1983.
Odendaal, A. *Vukani Bantu! The Beginnings of Black Protest Politics to 1910.* Cape Town: Philip, 1984.
Odendaal, A. '"Even White Boys Call Us "Boy"!" Early Black Organisational Politics in Port Elizabeth'. *Kronos* 20 (1993): 3–16.
Odendaal, A. *The Founders: The Origins of the ANC and the Struggle for Democracy in South Africa.* Kentucky: The University Press of Kentucky, 2013.
Padgett, J.F. and C.K. Ansell. 'Robust Action and the Rise of the Medici, 1400-1434'. *American Journal of Sociology* 98, no. 6 (1993): 1259–319.

Padgett, J.F. and W.W. Powell. *The Emergence of Organizations and Markets*. Princeton: Princeton University Press, 2012.
Saunders, C.C. 'The Annexation of the Transkeian Territories (1872–1895), with Special Reference to British and Cape Policy'. PhD diss., University of Oxford, Oxford, 1972.
Small, M.L. *Unanticipated Gains: Origins of Network Inequality in Everyday Life*. Oxford: Oxford University Press, 2009.
Snow, D.A. and R.D. Benford. 'Master Frames and Cycles of Protest'. In *Frontiers in Social Movement Theory*, edited by A.D. Morris and C. McClurg Mueller, 133-55. New Haven: Yale University Press, 1992.
Stovel, K. and L. Shaw. 'Brokerage'. *Annual Review of Sociology* 38, no. 1 (2012): 139–58.
Swidler, A. 'Culture in Action: Symbols and Strategies'. *American Sociological Review* 51, no. 2 (1986): 273–86.
Switzer, L. and D. Switzer. *The Black Press in South Africa and Lesotho: A Descriptive Bibliographic Guide to African, Coloured, and Indian Newspapers, Newsletters, and Magazines, 1836-1976*. Boston: Hall, 1979.
Tarrow, S.G. *Democracy and Disorder: Protest and Politics in Italy, 1965–1975*. Oxford: Clarendon Press, 1989.
Tarrow, S.G. 'Cycles of Collective Action: Between Moments of Madness and the Repertoire of Contention'. *Social Science History* 17, no. 2 (1993): 281–307.
Tilly, C. *From Mobilization to Revolution*. Reading, US: Addison-Wesley, 1978.
Tilly, C. *The Contentious French*. Cambridge, US: Harvard University Press, 1986.
Traugott, M. 'Barricades as Repertoire: Continuities and Discontinuities in the History of French Contention'. *Social Science History* 17, no. 2 (1993): 309–23.
Walder, A.G. 'Political Sociology and Social Movements'. *Annual Review of Sociology* 35, no. 1 (2009): 393–412.
Wauchope, I. W. *Isaac Williams Wauchope: Selected Writings 1874–1916*, edited and translated by J. Opland and A. Nyamende. Cape Town: Van Riebeeck Society, 2008.
Williams, D. *Umfundisi: A Biography of Tiyo Soga, 1829–1871*. Lovedale, South Africa: Lovedale Press, 1978.

Primary Sources

Mzimba, P. 'Ingxelo Yabantunywa Base Lovedale'. *Isigidimi sama-Xosa*. 1 May 1883, 3.
Isigidimi sama-Xosa. 1 February 1880, 5.
Isigidimi sama-Xosa. 1 November 1883, 4.
Isigidimi sama-Xosa. 'Imbumba Yomfo ka Gaba'. 1 November 1882, 4–5.
Isigidimi sama-Xosa. 1 May 1883, 1.
Isigidimi sama-Xosa. 1 May 1883, 3.
Port Elizabeth Telegraph and Eastern Province Standard. 31 March 1883, 3.
Port Elizabeth Telegraph and Eastern Province Standard. 'Independent Order of True Templars'. 31 March 1883, 3.
Port Elizabeth Telegraph and Eastern Province Standard. 28 June 1887, 3.
Western Cape Archives and Records Services. Petitions to the House of Assembly. Various items.
Stellenbosch University. 'Abstract of Petitions'. *Votes & Proceedings of the House of Assembly*. Various volumes, 1854–1909.
Wauchope, I.W. 'Intlanganiso Enkulu Yabazili Benene e-Rini'. *Isigidimi sama-Xosa*. 1 May 1883, 3.

CHAPTER 11
PETITIONS TO THE CAPE PARLIAMENT, 1854-1909
Kara Dimitruk* and Kelsey Lemon**

Introduction

Universal political participation is a central element of modern democracies. Voting is one way to participate, another is lobbying via petitioning. We look at petitions to the Cape Parliament to gain a novel perspective on political voice and organisation in the Cape Colony from the mid-nineteenth to the early twentieth century. Much research has been done on the disenfranchisement of the larger part of the Cape's population, the development of national political parties and specific issues like temperance.[1] Less attention has been paid to the efforts of groups of citizens, enfranchised or not, to lobby the government and influence policies via petitions.

Our quantitative analysis of all petitions submitted to the House of Assembly between 1854 and 1909 offers a new measure of political voice and activity, which in turn makes visible general patterns in political participation and connections across issues at the Cape that have not been recognised.[2] This approach therefore also adds new perspective on the existing historiography, which we discuss further below. Petitions, a somewhat neglected source material, can give us a better understanding of political voice in the past.[3] They enable us to look at 'ordinary people as historical

---

†We thank Sasha McGhee, Cailin McRae, Munashe Chideya, Vuyiswa Dlamini and Sarah Schab for excellent research assistance. We are also grateful to our colleagues in the Democracy and Disenfranchisement research group at LEAP for helpful comments and feedback.

*Dimitruk: Department of Economics, Swarthmore College, US and Department of Economics, Stellenbosch University, South Africa.

**Lemon: Department of History, Stellenbosch University, South Africa.

[1] See: R. Davenport, *The Afrikaner Bond: The History of South African Political Party, 1880-1911* (Cape Town: Oxford University Press, 1966); S. Trapido, 'African Divisional Politics in the Cape Colony, 1884-1910'. *Journal of African History* 9, no. 1 (1968): 79-98; W.G. Mills, 'Cape Smoke: Alcohol Issues in the Cape Colony in the Nineteenth Century', *Contemporary Drug Problems* 12, no. 2 (1985): 221-48; H. Giliomee, 'Western Cape Farmers and the Beginnings of Afrikaner Nationalism, 1870-1915', *Journal of Southern African Studies* 14, no. 1 (1987): 38-63; F. Nyika and J. Fourie, 'Black Disenfranchisement in the Cape Colony, c.1887-1900: Challenging the Numbers'. *Journal of Southern African Studies* 46, no. 3 (2020): 455-69.

[2] Christopher (2018) examines petitions submitted from South Africa to the British Parliament. A.J. Christopher, 'South African Petitions to the House of Commons, 1833-1914: Grievances, Protests, Advice and Information'. *Historia* 63, no. 1 (2018): 1-23.

[3] R. Huzzey and H. Miller, 'Petitions, Parliament and Political Culture: Petitioning the House of Commons, 1780-1918', *Past & Present* 248, no. 1 (2020): 123-64.

actors'.[4] They are a useful source for quantitative analysis because they often have detailed descriptions of complaints, giving us a window on historical socioeconomic and political problems. Details such as language and signatures can be used to examine political organisation.

We document patterns in types of petitions, types of petitioners and their geographic distribution during the consolidation of an independent state in South Africa: from the beginning of Representative Government in 1854, through the years of Responsible Government after 1872, up to the creation of the Union of South Africa in 1910. We find there was a distinct shift in the quantity and nature of petitions from the 1880s. From 1856 to 1879, Parliament saw an average of 100 petitions each session, and never more than 200. After 1880, Parliament received an average of 250 petitions, with three sessions each receiving over 400 petitions. The increase was due to a shift in petitioned issues, from those about local matters, like transport needs and the creation of local government authorities, to general socioeconomic issues like temperance. The Abstracts show that petitions were sent from both urban and rural areas across the Cape. There is spatial variation across issues, however. Those on social issues tended to come from urban areas, such as Port Elizabeth, and those on economic issues from rural-interior regions.

Lastly, we draw on other archival material to examine the motivations for lobbying on labour issues and temperance. Labour and temperance have a rich historiography, but there is little quantitative work and virtually no work relating their organisation to strategies for petitioning the Cape Parliament. Coercive labour laws and the temperance movement are also thought to have been connected, most obviously through the *dop* or 'tot' system.[5] This system – whereby labourers were paid partly in alcohol – is considered

---

[4] A. Würgler, 'Voices from Among the "Silent Masses": Humble Petitions and Social Conflicts in Early Modern Central Europe', *International Review of Social History* 46, no. 9 (2001): 11–34.

[5] The importance of alcohol and labour institutions to the history of South Africa is well represented in the literature. See, for instance: C. van Onselen, 'Randlords and Rotgut, 1886–1903', *History Workshop* 2 (1976): 33–89; C. Crush and C. Ambler, 'Alcohol in Southern African Labor History', in *Liquor and Labor in Southern Africa*, ed. C. Crush and C. Ambler (Athens, US: Ohio University Press, 1992); A. Cobley, 'Liquor and Leadership: Temperance, Drunkenness and the African Petty Bourgeoisie in South Africa', *South African Historical Journal* 31 (1994): 128–48; P. La Hausse, *Brewers, Beerhalls, and Boycotts: A History of Liquor in South Africa* (Johannesburg: Ravan Press, 1998); A.K. Mager, '"White Liquor Hits Black Livers": Meanings of Excessive Liquor Consumption in South Africa in the Second Half of the Twentieth Century', *Social Science and Medicine* 59, no. 4 (2004): 735–51; A.K. Mager, *Beer, Sociability, and Masculinity in South Africa* (Cape Town: University of Cape Town Press, 2010); G. Williams, 'Slaves, Workers, and Wine: The "Dop System" in the History of the Cape Wine Industry, 1658–1894', *Journal of Southern African Studies* 42, no. 5 (2016): 893–909. On labour, see C. Bundy, 'The Emergence and Decline of a South African Peasantry', *African Affairs* 71, no. 285 (1972): 369–88; P. Scully, 'Criminality and Conflict in Rural Stellenbosch, South Africa: 1870–1900', *Journal of African History* 30, no. 2 (1989): 289–300; C.H. Feinstein, *An Economic History of South Africa: Conquest, Discrimination, and Development* (Cambridge: Cambridge University Press, 2005). Similarly, organizational aspects of the international temperance campaign have been studied for organizations like the Women's Christian Temperance Union (WCTU); see I. Tyrrell, *Woman's World/Woman's Empire: The Woman's Christian Temperance Union in International Perspective, 1880–1930* (Chapel Hill: University of North Carolina Press, 2010). Some of the classic works on labour coercion in the nineteenth century are Scully, 'Criminality and Conflict', Bundy, 'Emergence and Decline', Feinstein, *Economic History*, and R. Ross, 'Emancipations and the Economy of the Cape Colony', *Slavery & Abolition* 14, no. 1 (1993): 131–48.

a central part of coercive labour practices. Drunkenness was a criminal offence and could be prosecuted by white farmers. The threat of prosecution could coerce labourers to stay on farms; conviction could result in fines that would increase dependence on wage work. Payment in kind with alcohol may have also bolstered farmers' notions of their labourers' psychological and economic dependence.[6] The *dop* system angered temperance activists. They argued that it increased demand for drink and created a culture of drunkenness, which they linked to indolence, degradation and criminality. They called for total prohibition of the system, but this was economically impractical given the effectiveness of the *dop* system in attracting and regulating labour.[7]

We use labour and temperance petitions to provide a quantitative investigation of political organisation in two ways. First, we provide descriptive evidence that labour and temperance petitions tended to be submitted in sessions when Parliament worked on legislation regarding those issues. We also find that citizens, via petitions, shaped policy formation in the Cape. For example, liquor regulations tended to be more successful when temperance petitions were submitted. Second, we draw on a sample of 450 full-text labour and temperance petitions to provide a more detailed examination of the organisation of petitioners and their motivations. Patterns in the format of the petitions, the petitioners' names and signatures, the language used and the petitioners' geographic location provide evidence of close-knit communities who sought changes to the labour system and promoted temperance.[8] These patterns, along with the increase in the number of petitions and the shift to national issues in the 1880s, suggest that these communities became connected to broader, Colony-wide campaigns largely from the 1880s.

The new dataset and more quantitative analysis allow us to support and qualify existing work on political and economic change in the Cape, and on the labour laws and the temperance movement. The change in the quantity and nature of petitions from the 1880s onwards is consistent with the commercialisation of the economy after the discovery of diamonds in 1867.[9] It also coincides with expansion and devolution of power from Britain. For example, the local government held more power and policy-making authority with the advent of Responsible Government in 1872, after which citizens sought to influence this authority and the direction of its policies.[10] In our last section, we integrate petitions more fully into the existing literature on labour and temperance. One substantial finding is both labour and temperance petitioners were concerned about the reliability of labour but suggested different legislative solutions to the problem. The reliability of labour is generally only discussed by the literature on

---

[6]Scully, 'Criminality and Conflict'.

[7]P. Scully, 'Liquor and Labour in the Western Cape, 1870–1900', in *Liquor and Labor in Southern Africa*, ed. C. Crush and C. Ambler (Athens, US: Ohio University Press, 1992).

[8]By formatting, we mean petitions had exactly, or nearly so, the same text.

[9]A. Gwaindepi, 'State Building in the Colonial Era: Public Revenue, Expenditure and Borrowing Patters in the Cape Colony, 1820–1910' (PhD diss., Stellenbosch University, Stellenbosch, 2018); Feinstein, *Economic History*.

[10]Giliomee, 'Western Cape Farmers'.

labour laws. Therefore, our work suggests the petitions are useful not only for further subject-specific work, but also for revealing links across seemingly disparate issues.

More broadly, our quantitative approach contributes to understanding petitioning in the nineteenth century. This was an important period in the transition to more modern democratic structures and practices, albeit in a non-linear fashion, particularly in Europe and North America.[11] While we also find evidence of petitioning by marginalised communities, as described by Huzzey and Miller (2020) for the British House of Commons, in the Cape petitioning was done mainly by the politically dominant white minority. The Cape petitions can thus be used to understand some of the topics and issues, like temperance, important to marginalised communities, such as black African and coloured petitioners, but they offer only a limited view of the scope of those communities' political activity. As Chapter 10 shows, petitions, when combined with other sources, can provide a more complete picture of black Africans' non-electoral political activity in the eastern Cape during the late nineteenth century, for instance.

With respect to political organisation, we can also better place the Cape in an international context with our quantitative approach. To the best of our knowledge, for example, we provide the first evidence outside of Britain and the Atlantic world of mass organisation to submit petitions.[12] Our evidence from the Cape suggests Colony-wide petitioning campaigns were related to national and international social and political movements, like temperance and the development of national political parties, that sought to influence the direction and shape of laws. We propose that these Colony-wide efforts were in part spurred by commercialisation and facilitated by the lower costs of communication after the discovery of diamonds, mentioned above. Though we find evidence of Colony-wide campaigns, the scale of Cape petitioning was smaller than that of European and North American countries. One of our estimates suggests that *at most* 7 per cent of the population submitted a petition during the most active petitioning year from 1854 to 1909.[13] During these fifty-five years, 11,441 petitions were submitted in the Cape. In contrast, nearly 82,000 public petitions were submitted to the British House of Commons during the five years from 1849 to 1854 alone. From 1789 to 1865, the US Congress received 145,892 petitions.[14]

---

[11] H. Miller, 'Introduction: The Transformation of Petitioning in the Long Nineteenth Century (1780–1914)', *Social Science History* 43, no. 3 (2019): 409–29.

[12] Ibid.

[13] If we assume there were 100 signatures on each petition (the average from our samples) and the most active year saw 400 petitions, then at most 40,000 people signed a petition each year (assuming no one signed two separate petitions). There were about 565,000 people in the Colony in 1865 and therefore at most 7 per cent of the population petitioned. This is probably an upper bound estimate because the population grew after the discovery of diamonds, and we find little evidence of more signatures on temperance or labour petitions over time.

[14] Miller, 'Introduction', 413.

Background on petitioning

Petitioning has long been a part of the political process in South Africa. The earliest recorded petition was in 1657, at the time of the first Dutch settlers at the Cape.[15] We can thus assume that by the second half of the nineteenth century people were aware of their right to petition. Petitioners were not limited to petitioning the House of Assembly; they could also send petitions to the Legislative Council (upper house of parliament) or individual parliamentarians, for instance. We study petitioning to the House of Assembly specifically and assume that much of the same process applied to petitions sent elsewhere.

As stipulated in a parliamentary manual, to be accepted by the House of Assembly, petitions had to have a clear style and use the conventional format. They had to be handwritten (printed petitions were accepted later) and display at least one original signature. All signatures attached to the petition had to be original and could not be copied. Illiterate petitioners could attach their 'mark' to the petition alongside two witness signatures. Any petitions in a language other than English had to be accompanied by a certified translation by the member presenting it or a sworn translator.[16] In our sample of petitions, we find all petitions were either submitted in English or Dutch.

The text of a petition had to be 'couched in respectful and temperate terms' and be free of disrespectful language or offensive imputations against the authority involved.[17] In the text of our petitions, the language is formally polite: a petition typically 'humbly showeth' or a petitioner 'duty bound will ever pray'. Primarily, petitions had to include a supplication or 'prayer' – a plea for redress, a call for intervention or an appeal for a request to be granted. Petitions in the style of 'a declaration, an address of thanks, or a remonstrance only' were not considered petitions and would not have been accepted.[18]

Petitioners could mail a petition to any member of the House for free.[19] If the member agreed to present the petition, he needed to check that it contained no irregularities and conformed to the right standards. The petition would then be transmitted to the Clerk of the House at least a day before Parliament's next sitting. The Clerk thereafter submitted the petition to the Speaker of the House, who either approved the petition for presentation or rejected it. The petition was then formally presented to the House by the assenting member who had attached his signature to it. Since members of the House could not be compelled to present a petition, we assume a member would

---

[15]R. Kilpin, *The Parliament of the Cape* (London: Longmans, Green & Co., 1938): 11.

[16]E.M.O. Clough, *The South African Parliamentary Manual* (London: Whittaker & Co., 1909): 242.

[17]Ibid, 242. The Cape was not unique in this regard. See for example: D. Zaret, 'Petitions and the "Invention" of Public Opinion in the English Revolution', *American Journal of Sociology* 101, no. 6 (1996): 1497–555.

[18]Clough, *Parliamentary Manual*, 243.

[19]Unfortunately, the parliamentary manual does not explain how the postal system took in and delivered petitions. In general, petitions were presented to Parliament in the absence of the petitioners, but exceptions were made for those who could prove that their individual rights or interests were 'peculiarly affected by any bill'. Clough, *Parliamentary Manual*, 244.

associate himself with a petition only if he approved of its message or if it was politically advantageous. He would present the petition by indicating the number and identities of the petitioners and by reading out the request. He would then refer the petition to the relevant Select Committee if applicable.[20] The petition would be summarised and entered in the 'Abstracts of Petitions' in the *Votes & Proceedings*.

If a petition did not meet these standards, it could be rejected and would need to be resubmitted.[21] These standards and costs of submitting a petition, which may not have been intuitive or widely known at the time, influenced the process of petitioning. For example, the international Women's Christian Temperance Union (WCTU) taught its members how to petition and distributed ready-made petitions to its member unions.[22] Parliamentary agents or middlemen could be employed to assist in petition submission.[23] Training, ready-made petitions and the involvement of specialists are understandable given that most signatories to the petition were likely illiterate.

In general, however, there has been less work on how individuals or groups generated petitions and then obtained the tens- or even hundreds of signatures that often attended them. We use a sample of petitions on agricultural labour issues (coercive labour laws) and temperance to discuss the possible role of organisations like the WCTU and Afrikaner Bond in the process of petitioning. We speculate about the processes behind the mobilisation to petition and how petitioners obtained signatures in support.

Data

Our main source of data is the 'Abstracts of Petitions', which appear at the beginning of the *Votes & Proceedings of the House of Assembly*. Two supplementary sources are the House of Assembly's 'Proceedings on Bills' and petitions, which we use later in our investigation of the petitioners' organisation on labour issues and the temperance movement.[24]

The Abstracts served as an index to petitions submitted to Parliament in a legislative session. They are organised in a proto-spreadsheet with the headings 'petition number', 'when presented', 'name of member presenting', 'names or description of petitioners',

---

[20]Ibid, 245.

[21]For example, in 1890 a petition was 'returned as informal' (no. 186, Abstract of Petitions, *Votes and Proceedings* 1890).

[22]J. McKinnon, 'Women's Christian Temperance Union: Aspects of Early Feminism in the Cape, 1889 to 1930' (MA diss., University of South Africa, Pretoria, 1995): 58–9; WCTU, 'Printed Minutes of the Annual Conventions, 1891–1899' (Western Cape Archives and Records Services, A1696, vol. 2/2, 1898).

[23]Clough, *Parliamentary Manual*, 243.

[24]Most of the *Votes and Proceedings*, which have the 'Abstracts' and 'Proceedings on Bills', are found in Stellenbosch University Library. The full collection is available at the Western Cape Archives and Records (WCARs). The actual petitions are currently kept in the House of Assembly (HA) volumes in WCARs. All archival petitions referred to here are locatable in the WCARs. We omit WCARs from petition citations for simplicity.

'place', 'number of signatures', 'prayer' (a short description of the requests of the petitioners) and 'remarks'. The 'number of signatures' field is not always completed. We use the 'names or description of petitioners', 'place' and 'prayer' fields in our approach to classifying petitions.

From 1854 to 1909, 11,441 petitions were submitted to the House of Assembly. Figure 11.1 shows the evolution in the number of petitions submitted to the lower house (the House of Assembly) and upper house (the Legislative Council) during this period. The average number of petitions submitted to the House of Assembly is stable at about 100 per session from 1854 to 1880. After 1880, there is an average of 250 petitions with peaks of about 400 and 500 petitions in 1883 and 1895. Below, we show that the growth was due to an increase in petitions about national, rather than local, social and economic issues.

The petitions requested changes to, among other things, labour laws, company law, property rights to land and the tax system. Petitions were submitted from rural and urban areas, from the frontier districts, and from the economic centres of Cape Town and Port Elizabeth. There was a wide variety of petitioners: descendants of Dutch and English colonists, black Africans, coloured residents, political groups, mechanics, farmers, social groups like the Women's Christian Temperance Union and many others.

Our approach categorises the types of petitions and petitioners and georeferences petitions that had geographical information to document new facts about lobbying across the Colony.

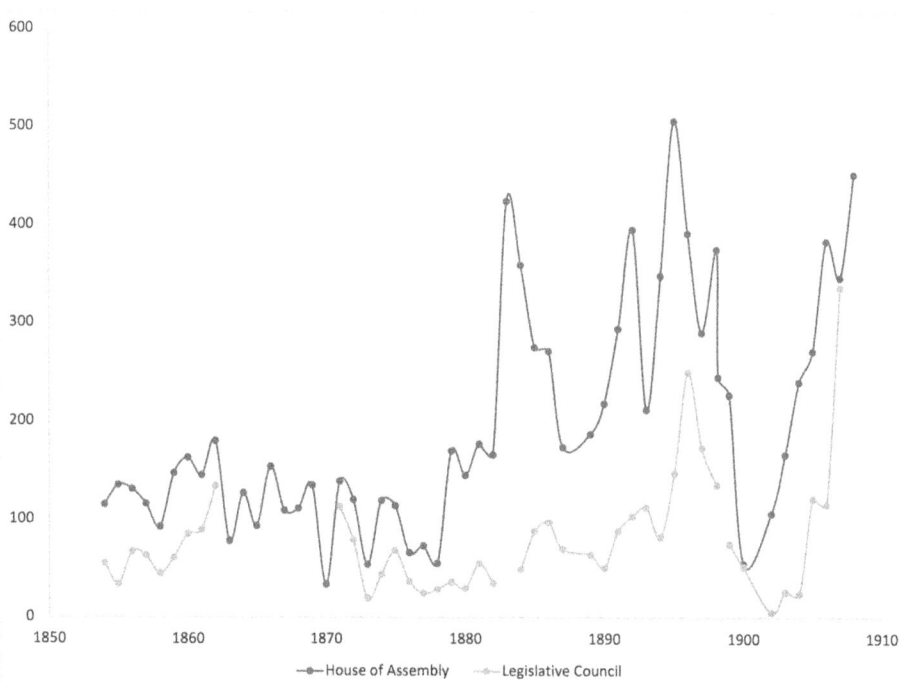

Figure 11.1 Petitions submitted to the Cape Parliament, 1854–1909.

Classifying petition types

First, we classify the petitions according to the issues they raised in the 'prayer'. Those with a single issue are easy to classify. For example, a prayer in an 1888 petition by C. A. Mostert and some other inhabitants of Namaqualand 'In favour of the construction of a line of Telegraph from Port Nolloth, via O'okiep, to Clanwilliam' is easily classified as 'transport – telegraph'.[25]

Others, however, are less straightforward because they presented multiple issues or could fit into several categories. One with multiple issues is an 1882 petition by G. Jordaan and other inhabitants of Somerset East 'On the subject of the use of the Dutch Language in Parliament, the Repeal of the Immigration Act, the Freedom of the Colony of all Responsibility with regard to Basutoland, the Raising of the Franchise, and the Publication of a Dutch Code of Laws'.[26] One that could fit into several categories is a 1908 petition by J. L. Burke and others, requesting that 'any proposal to survey and sub-divide Boesmansland [in Namaqualand] may be postponed until boreholes have been sunk and water found in sufficient quantities on all surveyed farms there'.[27] This petition could be classified as land rights, water infrastructure or agriculture.

The first step in our approach is to expand the petitions that had several issues. This increases our 11,441 petitions to a dataset of 12,203 petition-issues, a fairly small increase because most petitions were about a single issue.

The second step is to classify the issues. We read each issue and developed a classification scheme with two levels: scope of the issue (national, local or individual) and type of issue. Both levels are mutually exclusive categories. There are eleven types: social, such as temperance, and education; transport and infrastructure; economic, such as agriculture, labour and manufacturing; government; taxation and trade; land rights; law and order; company and finance; territory; church and religion; and personal, which is mostly about pensions or individual compensation. For multi-layered issues, we choose a primary type for each, for the sake of simplicity. For example, the petition on surveying and sub-dividing land for a borehole in Namaqualand is classified as 'land rights'.

Lastly, given the importance of race in South Africa, we code an indicator equal to 1 (and 0 otherwise) if the petition explicitly mentioned race. For example, petitions for the prohibition of alcohol frequently mention that the policy will target black Africans: 'That the House may not consent to any legislation which will result in giving opportunities for further degradation by means of intoxicants, of the aboriginal people of South Africa'.[28]

---

[25] No. 14, 'Abstract of Petitions', *Votes and Proceedings* 1888.

[26] No. 35, 'Abstract of Petitions', *Votes and Proceedings* 1882.

[27] No. 347, 'Abstract of Petitions', *Votes and Proceedings* 1908.

[28] No. 119, 'Abstract of Petitions', *Votes and Proceedings* 1907.

Petitioner characteristics

We use the 'description of petitioners' field to code petitioner characteristics. These characteristics are not mutually exclusive. The Abstracts mostly describe petitioners as 'inhabitants' or 'rate-payers' of a specific area or division. Zaeske argues that the use of identifiers like 'inhabitants' or 'residents' instead of 'citizens' or 'rate-payers' was strategic.[29] Using the more general term meant that a petition did not have to specify that some signatories were enfranchised citizens and others were not. The franchise was based on gender and income or property holdings, not race, so a petition was likely to use the term 'inhabitants' or 'residents' when women or lower-income, often black or coloured, petitioners signed.

Some 'descriptions of petitioners' record an affiliation to an organisation, such as the WCTU, the Afrikaner Bond, or the local government. We extract this additional information from the petitioner field and then code an indicator equal to 1 for four types of organisations: local government (for example, divisional council, town/municipal council or mayor), church (for example, Bishop, mission, synod, clergy), Afrikaner Bond or Farmers' Protection Association,[30] and WCTU. These are the only types of organisations found.

To infer the gender of petitioners, we rely on petitioner descriptions that give a specific 'presenting petitioner' or first signatory, who was probably the leader or main organiser of the petition, as done by Lemon.[31] For example, in 1907, 'Margaret J. Russell and others, inhabitants' petitioned for the repeal of the Contagious Diseases Act.[32] In some cases third-person singular pronouns give the gender, as in M. J. Hicken's petition 'That the House take *her* case into consideration and grant *her* relief'.[33] The number of petitioners we classify as 'female' will likely be an underestimate. First, petitioners commonly used only their first initial and surname to identify themselves, so we may miss women also using this norm. Though it seems that women were more likely than men to use their first name. Second, as discussed in the last section, we find female signatures among those presented by a male and in petitions from 'inhabitants' (see Table 11.5).

We also use the petitioner description from the Abstracts to code the petitioners' race. For example, petitioners are described as 'natives of British India', 'African' and 'coloured'. We use the term 'black African' generally as an identifier, given that some race terms used in the actual petitions are no longer acceptable. The patterns gleaned from the Abstracts will likely be an understatement of the racial and ethnic composition of

---

[29] S. Zaeske, 'Signatures of Citizenship: The Rhetoric of Women's Antislavery Petitions', *Quarterly Journal of Speech* 88, no. 2 (2002): 147–68.

[30] As we discuss in the last section, the Farmers' Protection Association was the precursor to the Afrikaner Bond political party.

[31] K. Lemon, '"No Sex in Citizenship": Investigating Women's Petitions to the Cape Parliament, 1873–1902' (BA Hons diss., Stellenbosch University, Stellenbosch, 2019).

[32] No. 193, 'Abstract of Petitions', *Votes and Proceedings* 1907.

[33] No. 241, 'Abstract of Petitions', *Votes and Proceedings* 1895.

the petitioners. Many 'inhabitants' who signed a petition are not described in detail. We look more closely at petitioner types in the final section, using the full texts and sets of signatures of a selection of petitions. We discuss this source further on.

Geography

We identify the geography of petitions using the 'place' field. The 'place' is often a district or a town or municipality in a district. We match place names to coordinates available on Google Maps. For the 174 petitions that have several places we used the first-mentioned place. For places that only name a district, we use coordinates for the prominent town in the district, which often has the same name. For example, Stellenbosch town is in Stellenbosch district. For towns mentioned in only a few petitions, we used the largest town in the district. For example, in 1906 a teacher from a high school in Franschhoek petitioned the government to consider allowing breaks in his service (presumably for the purpose of his pension).[34] There are only a handful of petitions from Franschhoek. Franschhoek is in the district of Paarl, so we used Paarl, the district's largest town. We did not classify petitions hailing from 'the Colony' or 'the frontier districts' or places outside the Colony, such as Natal, Basutoland (now Lesotho) or places in England.[35] There were also approximately 120 places that we could not locate. This approach will skew figures towards showing a few main towns as petitioning centres in each division. This gives us broadly accurate patterns of petitioning across the colony but will be less informative about the geography of petitioning within a district.

Labour and temperance bills and petitions

In later sections, we look at petitions on labour laws and labour issues (such as immigration) and petitions connected to the temperance movement. The descriptions of the petitioners' requests in the 'prayer' recorded in the Abstracts enabled us to positively identify petition-issues related to labour and the temperance movement. In the expanded dataset, there are 460 labour petition-issues (about 4 per cent of all petition-issues) and 975 temperance petition-issues (about 8 per cent of all petition-issues).

Further on we examine whether labour and temperance petitions were submitted when Parliament worked on policy for the respective bills. We collect data on all bills the House of Assembly worked on from the 'Proceedings on Bills' section of the *Votes & Proceedings* from 1854 to 1900.[36] Using each bill's short title, we code an

---

[34]No. 100, 'Abstract of Petitions', *Votes and Proceedings* 1906.

[35]Interest groups in England petitioned the Cape Government to amend the Ocean Mail Contract, so that mail from the Cape Colony would enter Britain via Plymouth and not Southampton.

[36]There were no Proceedings on Bills in the Abstracts in 1855. We end in 1900 and not 1909 because the data was originally collected for a different purpose. We do not think the results presented below are sensitive to the sample period because few labour and temperance bills were worked on after 1900. Bills could be introduced to either House but had to be approved by both houses before becoming law. We ignore bills introduced to the Legislative Council but did not make it to the House of Assembly. In our analysis, we assume that petitions were submitted to the House of Assembly if it was working on a labour bill, or a bill related to temperance.

indicator equal to 1 if a bill was related to a labour law (Pass, Masters & Servants, Location, Squatting, Vagrancy) and 0 otherwise, and an indicator equal to 1 if the bill sought to place restrictions on the sale or distribution of alcohol and 0 otherwise.[37] We also code whether the bill was passed by Parliament and therefore became a law. From 1854 to 1900, the House of Assembly worked on 2,196 bills: 2 per cent on labour laws and 1 per cent related to temperance.

In our final section we examine the political organisation of and the motivations for petitions on labour laws and the temperance movement using the full text and signatures of the original petitions. The Abstracts, as mentioned earlier, served as an index to the original, physical petitions. We therefore use the Abstracts to construct a sample of original petitions from WCARs, which gives us the full request and all signatures.[38] There are 450 original petitions in our archival sample. For labour petitions, we collect most identified in the Abstracts. There are 300 labour petitions in our archival sample, which are most of the 460 petition-issues identified in the Abstracts. For temperance, we collect all temperance-related petitions, whether for or against, in two-year sequences in ten-year intervals (1855 and 1866, 1865 and 1866, 1875 and 1876, 1885 and 1886, 1895 and 1896, 1905 and 1906). There are 150 temperance petitions in the sample. Most (87 per cent) were pro-temperance.

We code three pieces of information from both types of petitions: language of the petition (Dutch or English), whether the petition has the same format as another petition (i.e. exact same or nearly so text), and the number of signatures. For a selected subset of petitions, we also code information on the signatures (for example, place of residence, race or ethnicity). Some petitions record residence next to a signature. We use names as a source of information on gender, race, and ethnicity.

Patterns in the types of petitions

We document new facts about the distribution of types of petitions, their evolution over time and distribution across space. The patterns point to two main conclusions. First, we find a significant shift in the overall character of petitions, from local issues like transport and the creation of government authorities towards general social and economic issues, like temperance, from the 1880s. Second, we find that women and a variety of racial and ethnic groups were not well-represented in the Abstracts, relative to the total number

---

[37]We rely on the historical literature to identify bills related to temperance. These are bills related to liquor licensing (i.e. with short titles including 'Liquor Licensing'). We exclude excise bills (which regulated taxes on beer or other types of alcohol) since these are less overtly connected to temperance in the literature and pro-temperance petitions more commonly suggested changes in the liquor licence to promote temperance.

[38]The Abstracts record a petition number (petitions are numbered based on their order of introduction to the House of Assembly) and the original petitions are generally organised by petition number. A few petitions are out of order or have a different number from the one in the 'Abstracts'. We went through all the petitions in the volume to find the correct original petition.

of petitions and the sizes of these groups, which is why we use the sample of full-text petitions in our analysis in the final section.

Panel A of Table 11.1 shows that most petition-issues (51 per cent) were about general, Colony-wide concerns. Local issues made up 30 per cent of all petition-issues and individual issues 19 per cent. Panel B shows that the most common type of petition-issue was about social concerns, such as education, alcohol restrictions (temperance) and public health (in particular, contagious diseases). The percentage columns show that most petitions about social issues (92 per cent) were also general in scope. The second most common type of petition-issue, at about 16 per cent, was about transport or

Table 11.1 Types of Petitions, 1854–1909.

	N	Share of petition-issues	% of which are individual	% of which are local	% of which are general
Panel A: Scope					
Individual	12,203	18.9%			
Local	12,203	29			
General	12,203	51.7			
Panel B: Type					
Social	12,203	20%	1.7%	5.9%	92.2%
Transport and infrastructure	12,203	15.8	0	93.4	6.5
Personal	12,203	14.8	99.5	0.4	0
Economic	12,203	13.7	0.6	12.1	87.3
Government	12,203	11.2	1.4	46.7	49.5
Taxation and trade	12,203	7.3	0.1	1.5	98.3
Land rights	12,203	7	50.6	35.3	13.9
Law and order	12,203	4.9	1.3	52.3	46.3
Company and finance	12,203	2.2	1.5	35.2	63.2
Territory	12,203	1.7	0	0.4	99.5
Church and religion	12,203	1.6	0	21.4	78.6
Ambiguous	12,203	0.2	10.7	14.2	75
Panel C: Petitions about race					
Mentions race	12,203	6%	0.89%	9%	90%

Source: 'Abstract of Petitions' *Votes & Proceedings of the House of Assembly, 1854–1909*.
Notes: N is the number of petition-issues in the expanded petition dataset. Panels A and B are mutually exclusive categories. Panels B and C also report the share of petition type by scope. For example, of the 2,441 social petitions (20% x 12,203), 1.7 per cent were personal, 6 per cent were local and 92 per cent were general.

infrastructure concerns (roads, railways, bridges, the telegraph). In contrast to the social issues, petitions about transport and infrastructure (93 per cent) were largely local in their scope. Petitioners were not asking the government to build a Colony-wide railway network; they wanted local lines given the government had decided to build a railway network.

Three other types (personal, economic and government) together made up at least 10 per cent of petition-issues. Personal petitions were largely submitted by government officials seeking appointment and individuals seeking redress or compensation (for example, after the Border Wars). Petitions on economic issues were about agriculture (for example, the passing of the Scab Acts), labour (the passing of labour laws or immigration issues) and manufacturing or mining.[39] Economic petitions were largely general in scope (87 per cent). Petitions about government issues, in which we included petitions about politics and the constitution, made up about 11 per cent of all petition-issues. These were fairly evenly split between local concerns (such as creating new fiscal divisions or electoral divisions) and general concerns (such as constitutional issues like the use of Dutch in Parliament, courts and schools).

Patterns in time and geography

Because of their quantitative importance, we document patterns across time and space in petitions on social, economic, government and transport and infrastructure issues. Figures 11.2(a) and (b) show that there were significant changes in the types of petitions submitted to Parliament over time, reflecting the changing economy and politics in the Cape Colony. From 1854 to about 1880, Parliament mostly saw petitions about transport and government (which were largely local in nature). After 1880, social and economic petitions grew dramatically. After 1889, Parliament regularly saw over 100 petitions per year on social and economic concerns. This, we argue, was in part related to local communities becoming connected to Colony-wide campaigns. As we show in the final section, one indication of this is that diverse geographic communities used the same format in their petitions after 1880. We also explore how organisations like the WCTU and the Afrikaner Bond helped to connect these local communities.

Figure 11.3(a)–(c) shows the geographic distribution of petitions. Figure 11.3(a) shows that most petitions came from Cape Town and its suburbs, but there were also large numbers from Port Elizabeth, East London and Kimberley, and a fair number from larger towns of the rural-interior Eastern Cape like Queenstown and King Williams Town. Figures 11.3(b) and (c) show that the types of petitions were not uniform across space. Port cities like Cape Town, Port Elizabeth and East London were most concerned

---

[39] Scab Acts sought to prevent the spread of scab, which is an allergic reaction that ruins sheep's wool caused by a mite. The acts implemented compulsory veterinary hygiene certifications and required 'dipping' sheep to treat for mites.

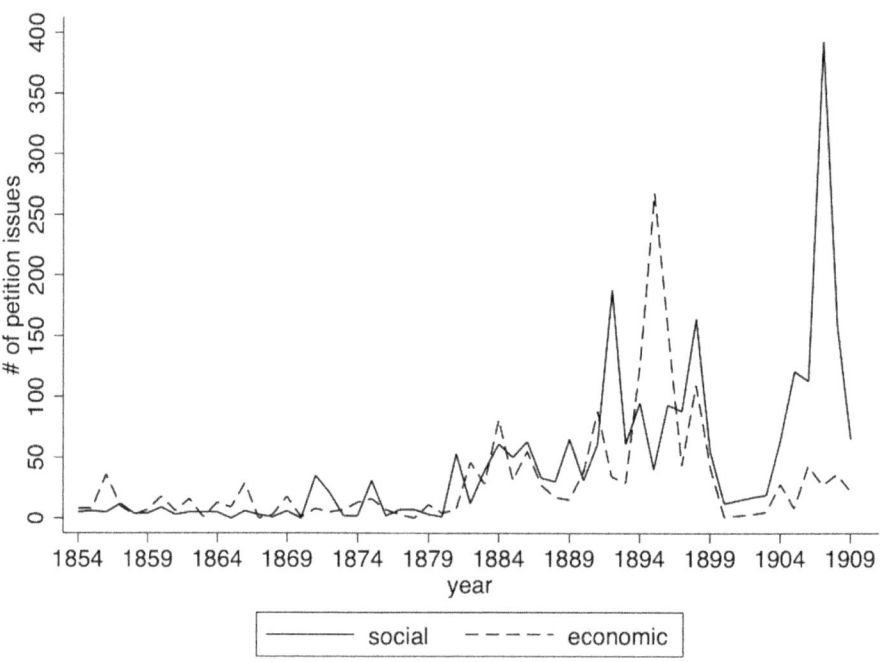

Figure 11.2a Social and economic petitions, 1854–1909.

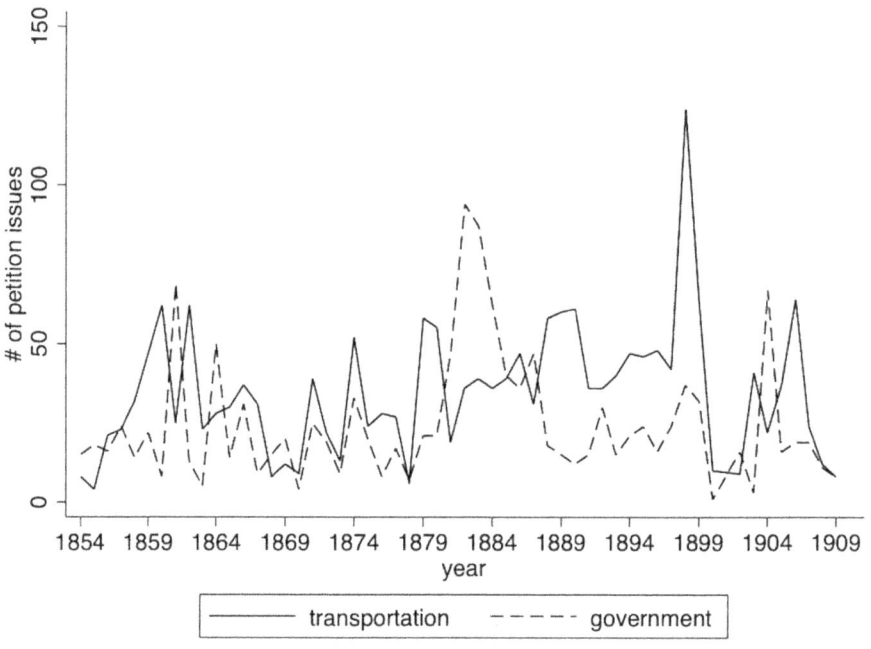

Figure 11.2b Transport and government petitions, 1854–1909.

Petitions to the Cape Parliament, 1854–1909

Figure 11.3a Number of petition-issues.

Figure 11.3b Social petitions.

Quantitative History and Uncharted People

Figure 11.3c Economic petitions.

with social issues, particularly contagious diseases, and temperance, whereas economic petitions were largely a rural phenomenon, with the main concerns being labour laws and the Scab Acts.

Patterns in types of petitioners

The Abstracts reveal a variety of petitioners voiced concerns to Parliament. Our approach allows us to draw out as much detail as possible from the brief Abstracts. Table 11.2 shows that about 7 per cent of all petition-issues were led by a female petitioner and 2 per cent by someone explicitly identified by race or ethnicity. Many petition-issues, 22 per cent, were affiliated with a larger organisation such a municipal government, church or social group (rather than being described only as inhabitants, residents or taxpayers). Where there is racial, ethnic and religious information (234 petition-issues total), 75 per cent of petitioners are identified as black African and 18 per cent as coloured, Malay, Khoisan, Muslim or British Indian. A few describe the signatories as 'black and Coloured inhabitants'. A small number are described as Chinese, or European, such as Italian or Scottish. In the petitions from organisations, local government officials were prominent, as were church congregations and ministers. A small number of petitioners are explicitly associated with the Afrikaner Bond and Farmers' Protection Associations and the WCTU. Many of the signatories on temperance petitions are white, coloured and black women.

Table 11.2 Types of petitioners.

	N	share
Female	12,203	7.3%
Race, ethnicity, religion	12,203	1.98
Black	234	75.2
Coloured, Malay, Muslim, British Indian, Khoe	234	18.8
Chinese	234	0.8
European	234	5
Organisations	12,203	22.2
Government	2714	25.4
Church	2714	22.3
Afrikaner Bond or Farmers' Protection Association	2714	4.3
WCTU	2714	7.9
# of petitioners	2907	100.72 average

Source: 'Abstract of Petitions' *Votes & Proceedings of the House of Assembly, 1854–1909*.
Notes: # of petitioners is taken from the reported 'number of petitioners' field in the Abstracts.

The Abstracts only sporadically record the number of signatories. The 2,907 that did this have an average of 100 signatures per petition-issue – a minimum of two and a maximum of 5,300. For the subset of petitions on temperance and labour laws, we further document the variation in the number of petitioners across issues in the last section.

Petitions and law making

One important question is whether lobbying was connected to the law-making process. Here we present evidence that petitions were submitted at times when Parliament was working on legislation. We use our dataset to see whether petitions on labour and temperance issues were correlated with Parliament's work on laws in these areas. We also provide qualitative evidence, drawn in part from the historiography, that petitions affected law-making.

Table 11.3 reports the results from a time series bivariate regression analysis. The results in Columns (1) to (5) are different measures of Parliament's work on labour laws. For example, the outcome in Column (1) is an indicator equal to 1 if Parliament worked on at least one labour bill in a year and 0 otherwise. The outcome in Column (2) is an indicator equal to 1 if Parliament worked on at least one Masters & Servants bill in a year

Table 11.3 Correlation between labour laws, temperance laws and petitions.

Outcome:	(1) Labour bill	(2) m&s bill	(3) v&s bill	(4) Location bill	(5) Pass bill	(6) Temperance bill	(7) Share liquor success
Labour petition	0.275 (0.192)						
m&s petition		0.417*** (0.132)					
v&s petition			-0.030 (0.124)				
Location petition				0.267* (0.143)			
Pass petition					0.054 (0.102)		
Temperance petition						0.499*** (0.148)	0.288** (0.121)
N	46	46	46	46	46	46	46
ymean	0.739	0.370	0.196	0.326	0.130	0.435	0.207

Notes: Each column reports the estimated coefficient from a bivariate regression where the outcome is a measure of the types of bills submitted to the House of Assembly in a year and the variable of interest is a measure of petitioning. There are forty-six years in which Parliament worked on legislation. Columns (1) to (6) use different indicators for whether a particular type of bill was introduced (e.g. Column (1): =1 if at least one labour bill was introduced and 0 otherwise). The outcome in Column (7) is the share of liquor (temperance) bills in a year that were successful (passed by parliament). The variables of interest are all indicators equal to 1 if at least one type of petition was introduced in a year and 0 otherwise. m&s – 'Masters & Servants' petition or law; v&s – 'Vagrancy and Squatting' petition or law.

and 0 otherwise. The outcome in Column (7) is the share of temperance bills that were successful (i.e. passed by Parliament) in a year.

There is a positive relationship, though imprecisely estimated, between the number of labour bills introduced and labour petitions (Column 1). Columns (2) to (5) suggest this effect is driven by differences across types of labour laws. There is a strong positive relationship between Masters & Servants bills and petitions, and between 'Native Location' bills and petitions.[40] There is no correlation between Vagrancy and Squatting and Pass bills and petitions, perhaps because our dataset contains only a small number of petitions on these bills and because Parliament worked on amendments to them only a few times, much less than on the Masters & Servants laws. Temperance petitions are significantly correlated with the number of temperance bills and the share of temperance bills that were passed (Columns 6 and 7). There is no correlation between labour petitions and passage of labour laws, so we omit this result for brevity.

Narrative evidence complements the quantitative results and illustrates how petitioning influenced Parliament's legislative work. Parliament's passing of labour laws in response to petitioners was uneven. Farmers became dissatisfied with the laws when their labour demands increased as the economy commercialised after the discovery of diamonds and when their sheep or cattle were at risk of theft.[41] The laws were part of the Cape's criminal code, which made breaking them a criminal offence, punishable by a fine or imprisonment. Successful amendments to the laws changed the types of infractions considered criminal, the punishments and the authorities who could administer them. Many petitions complained about the distance from the farms to the courts, where they had to go to enforce Masters & Servants contracts. Recent evidence suggests that Parliament adapted the court system in response to these petitions.[42] It did not, however, approve amendments to the Masters & Servants law that would allow the use of corporal punishment, which was a frequent request in petitions. As shown in Dimitruk, debates in the House of Assembly suggest that politicians were concerned about the legality of the proposed changes. In considering whether to authorise corporal punishment, Cecil Rhodes, member of the House of Assembly, said the key issue was whether the Cape Parliament 'could empower the magistrate to inflict corporal punishment'. He suggested looking at Masters & Servants laws in the British colonies of Natal and India. If a precedent for such a course could be found in other colonies, it would strengthen Parliament's argument.[43]

---

[40] Native locations were by law dense settlements 'occupied by any of the native races [...] situate[d] on private property not being in the bona fide and continuous employment of the owner of such land' (Native Locations, Act no. 8 of 1876). Different Location acts altered the exact density requirements. Native locations had their own governance structures and institutions. Specific taxes on inhabitants in native locations are thought to have been important for forcing residents to seek wage work on white owned farms. Feinstein, *Economic History*.

[41] F. Wilson, 'Farming, 1866–1966', in *Oxford History of South Africa, Vol II*, ed. M. Wilson and L. Thompson (Oxford: Oxford University Press, 1971); Bundy, 'The Emergence and Decline'; Scully, 'Criminality and Conflict'; L. van Sittert, 'Holding the Line: The Rural Enclosure Movement in the Cape Colony, c.1865–1910', *Journal of African History* 43, no. 1 (2002): 95–118; L. van Sittert, 'Writing on Skin: The Entangled Embodied Histories of Black Labour and Livestock Registration in the Cape Colony, c.1860–1909', *Kronos* 40 (2014): 74–98; G.M. Swiegers, 'Britain and the Labour Question in South Africa: The Interaction of State, Capital, Labour and Colonial Power, 1867–1910' (PhD diss., University of the Free State, Bloemfontein, 2014); K. Dimitruk, 'Before Apartheid: Labor Markets, Political Parties, and Labor Institutions in 19th Century South Africa', mimeo (2021).

[42] Ibid.

[43] *Debates*, House of Assembly, 1890, 125.

Petitions for temperance also influenced parliament's legislative work. The temperance movement aimed to restrict the sale of alcohol. Until the 1880s, the sale of liquor and licensing of liquor outlets had been regulated primarily at the divisional level under Ordinance 9 of 1851.[44] As with the labour laws, Bradlow suggests that dissatisfaction with the operation of Ordinance 9 built up over time. In response to this dissatisfaction and the emergence of the temperance campaign, the government began to reconsider its licensing regulations. One result was the passing of the Liquor Licensing Act in 1883. The new Act in part regulated the sale of alcohol to black Africans by delegating authority to the governor to decide on the granting of liquor licences in 'native locations'.[45] Also included in the Act was a provision for 'local option', which meant that any new application could be rejected if Parliament received a petition against the licence signed by 50 per cent of the registered voters in an area.[46] Temperance petitions from 1885 frequently comment on the beneficial yet insufficient operation of the 1883 Act. The petitioners asked either for the Act to be extended to include more proclaimed areas, or to completely prohibit the sale or gift of intoxicating liquors to black Africans. This shows how petitioners responded in real time to work being done in Parliament. Later, petitioners would write in support of a bill introduced by Member of Parliament and prominent temperance activist, James Rose Innes. The bill commonly known as the Innes Bill was passed in 1898.[47]

The questions of labour and temperance were resolved in different, though not independent, ways. By 1898 the government had implemented restrictions on black Africans' purchase of alcohol. The *dop* system continued to be used for coloured labourers. Communities continued pushing for further regulation of alcohol after 1898.[48] The labour laws were generally in place until the late twentieth century. Masters & Servants law, for example, was repealed in 1974. Perhaps one of the most significant changes during the late nineteenth century was the development of the court system so the laws could be more effectively administered and enforced.[49]

The organisation and motivation of petitioners

The information from the Abstracts gives us an overall picture of lobbying campaigns in favour of labour laws and temperance. Patterns in the language, format, signatures and places of residence from the actual petitions suggest petitioners were close-knit

---

[44] E. Bradlow, 'Drunkenness at the Cape of Good Hope in the 1870s: A Case Study of a Colonial Ruling Class and Its Philosophy', *Kleio* 30, no. 1 (1998): 11–27; Mills, 'Cape Smoke'.

[45] Bradlow, 'Drunkenness'.

[46] Mills, 'Cape Smoke'.

[47] McKinnon, 'Women's Christian Temperance Union'; P. Nugent, 'The Temperance Movement and Wine Farmers at the Cape: Collective Action, Racial Discourse, and Legislative Reform, c.1890–1965', *Journal of African History* 52, no. 3 (2011): 341–63.

[48] Scully, 'Liquor and Labour'.

[49] A. Sachs, *Justice in South Africa* (Berkeley: University of California Press, 1973); Dimitruk, 'Before apartheid'.

Table 11.4 Language, number of signatures and format.

	Labour		Temperance	
	Share or average	Min, max	Share or average	Min, max
Share Dutch	44%	(0, 1)	4%	(0, 1)
Same format	43%	(0, 1)	66%	(0, 1)
# signatures	85	(1, 2642)	93	(1, 3676)
# of petitions in sample	300		150	

Source: Authors' sample of labour and temperance petitions. Full petitions available at WCARS.

communities who sought changes to the labour system and promoted temperance. They became connected to broader, Colony-wide campaigns largely from the 1880s. We look at these two types of petitions in detail here and discuss how their stated motivations relate to the literature.

Table 11.4 compares three aspects of the 300 labour law petitions and 150 temperance petitions in our sample. First, labour petitions were more likely than temperance petitions to be submitted in Dutch: 44 per cent compared to only 4 per cent. Second, temperance petitions were more likely than labour petitions to have the same format as another petition on the same issue in the same session: 66 per cent compared to 43 per cent. Last, the two types of petitions had a similar average number of signatures, eighty-five signatures on labour and ninety-six on temperance. The distributions of the number of signatures for both types are left skewed: most petitions had fewer than 100 signatures, though some ran into the thousands. Our finding that temperance petitions were more consistently organised (in terms of format) and labour petitions more likely to be written in Dutch is consistent with the literature, which we discuss further below. In the following sections we present findings related to the organisation of petitions in our sample and discuss their stated motivations. Figure 11.4 shows the districts we refer to in this section.

Labour petitions

Comparing the earlier labour petitions with those after the 1880s suggests that petitioners continued to be close-knit geographically and were often related. For the entire period of our study, a typical labour petition often has clusters of signatures with the same surnames, and petitions with more detailed residential information often suggest that petitioners lived in the same neighbourhoods. It is possible that surnames become less clustered over time, suggesting a change in petitioning practices or in the underlying communities, but it is beyond the scope of our study to investigate this further.

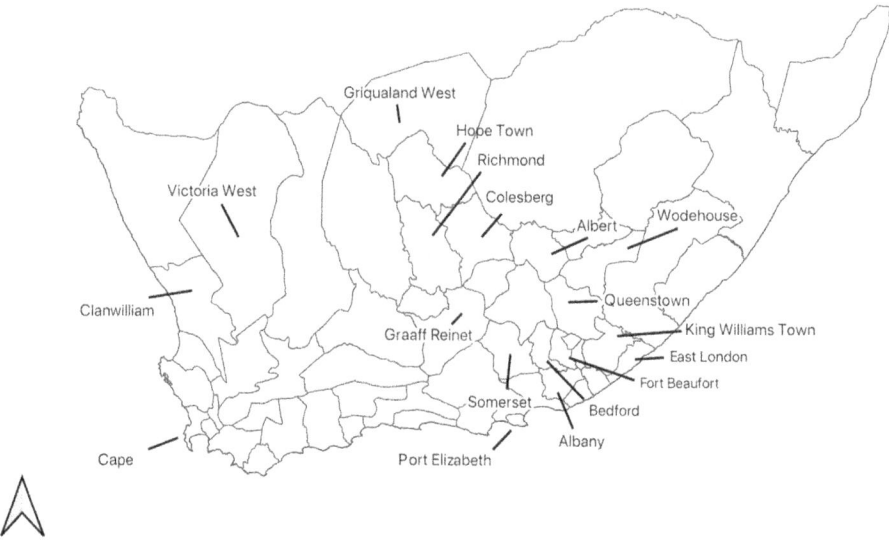

Figure 11.4 British Cape Colony, 1879 District Borders.

The first page of signatures in a petition from eighty-six 'Inhabitants of Colesberg' to amend the Masters & Servants law in 1856 shows clustering of surnames.[50] Of the twenty-eight signatures in total, eight are clustered (six 'Du Plessis' in sequence and two 'Venter' in sequence) and thirteen have the same surname as at least one other person on the page.[51] Similar patterns are found in petitions in the 1880s. In 1881, for example, 284 petitioners from Wodehouse called for an amendment to the Masters & Servants and Pass laws, changes to the boundary of the Cape, and called for the use of Dutch in the government and courts of law. There are nine signatures on the first page and two clusters of families: four 'Greylings' signed in sequence and two 'Bloms'. The Greylings are listed as living at Andover, Aloteran and Wayhill and both Bloms at Counivel. It seems likely that these are farm names. The last Greyling and petitioner LSV Kruger are shown as living at the same place, Wayhill.[52] Table 11.5 shows the signatures on the first pages of these two labour petitions. It looks as though a canvasser may have collected signatures from farmers, or perhaps the signatures were collected at a meeting where farmers were sitting next to their kin or acquaintances. The evidence from temperance petitions described in the next section suggests that canvassers were involved, which would indicate a different type of organising to lobby Parliament. In contrast, the Abstracts sometimes describe

---

[50] There are variations in the spelling of surnames (e.g. Du Plusie and Duplesie as shown in Table 11.5). We assume they are the same surname.

[51] HA 753 (1856), no. 35.

[52] HA 780 (1881), no. 167.

Table 11.5 Examples from the first page of signatures in four petitions.

Labour petitions		Temperance	
(1)	(2)	(3)	(4)
HA 753 (1856), no. 35	HA 780 (1881), no. 167	HA 851 (1905), no. 110	HA 771 (1875), no. 102
CI Du Plusie	GS Strijton [?], Havalao	Mrs G G Ward	EY Brabant, Captain
CT duplesie	A Syreyleny [?], Buikeshell	Miss F McEwan	John Miller, Cabinet maker
PT Du Plesie	OA Greyling, Andover	Mrs SJ Howse, 28 Gladstone Ave	RH Colg
PTT du Plesie	JK Greyling, Aloteran	Mrs HS Howse, 28 Gladstone Ave	H Mack, Carpenter
WA Du Plesie	JH Greyling, Aloteran	Mrs AH Webber, 22 Gladstone Ave	I Hees, Carpenter
DC Du Pliesie	MJ Greyling, Wayhill	Mrs G Trent, 35 Gladstone Ave	William Paddock, Carpenter
TL Pretorius	LSV Kruger, Wayhill	L Colin, 35 Warren St	Michael Paddock, Painter
Jan Van de Merwe	BJ Blom, Counivel	I MacRitchie, 33 Warren St	Jessie Soga, Groom
TST Venter	L Blom, Counivel		Mrs Barns
SN Venter			David Brown, Shoemaker
TD Voster			Agnes Prowers
MM Venter			William G. Goodall, Tinsmith
IC Pretorius			Joseph Clizela, Painter
SO Voster			C Musgrove, Carpenter
A Van Wyk			Ellen Musgrove
MS Havinga			PM Ryan, Trader
JS van der Merwe			A Burton, Trader
WJ Du Pliesies			Elizabeth Wild
EA Havenga			John Ryan, Tailor
illegible			David Williams, Tailor
JD van der Merwe			W Burton, Tailor
Gert Jakobus Potgieter			C Dilley, Tailor
J Koetzee			W Wingham, Tailor
DJ Venter			Lydia Davantier
JP vd Walt			

Source: Authors' sample of labour and temperance petitions. Full petitions available at WCARS.

farmers or petitions originating from a meeting. For example, 'M.J. Potgieter, Chairman of Meeting of Farmers at Graaff-Reinet' was responsible for submitting a petition to amend the Masters & Servants law in 1888.

Petitions early in the sample appear to be coordinated more at the district level. For example, in 1856 there were seven petitions to amend the Masters & Servants law. All had the same format, and all came from 'landed proprietors' in Colesberg. We see similar patterns in three petitions from Albert in 1859, two from Queenstown in 1860 and three from Cradock in 1864. This type of lobbying did not disappear in the 1880s or 1890s. For example, five 1884 petitions sought to prohibit squatting or locations on private farms. All have the same format, and all were from communities in Somerset East. Again, we see similar patterns in petitions in the 1890s. The first twenty names on petitions from Colesberg in 1856 and Somerset East in 1884 are all different, suggesting that different communities in the district were coordinated in one petition. Residential information for each signatory, as found in the 1881 petition in the previous paragraph, is unfortunately missing from many petitions.

Petitions submitted later in the sample suggest more national coordination of farming communities in the interior. Petitions in a series in 1866 have the same format but are more geographically diverse than petitions in the 1850s and early 1860s. They were submitted not from just one district but from a cluster of districts in the eastern interior: Colesberg, Hope Town, Albany, Bedford and Queenstown. They all sought revision to the Masters & Servants and Pass laws because of concerns about pastoral farming and hiring labourers in rural areas. The Masters & Servants Act in operation was unsuitable 'for the punishment of careless and negligent herdsmen'. The laws also required farmers to travel to the resident magistrate to sign contracts with workers, which led to 'losses and inconveniences'. Petitioners complained about sheep being stolen because of the inadequacy of pass and citizenship certificates and the 'customs of dancing and the buying and selling of wives'.[53] Van Sittert also observes a connection between sheep theft and vagrancy laws.[54] As we discuss further in the next section, petitioners promoting temperance also complained about the state of the labour market and the unreliability of labour but argued that this was due to drunkenness. These petitions and the political organisation during this period deserve further research because they appear to pre-date the Farmers' Protection movement, which eventually became the Afrikaner Bond in the Western Cape.[55]

A set of petitions in 1884 appears to be related to national coordination among farming communities across the Cape to lobby Parliament to amend the Masters & Servants Law. They specifically sought to allow corporal punishment in lieu of fines for employees convicted of breaking the law. Ten petitions were submitted with the same format. In contrast to the 1866 series that complained of theft, these petitions

---

[53] HA 764 (1866), no. 46.
[54] Van Sittert, 'Holding the Line'; Van Sittert, 'Writing on Skin'.
[55] Giliomee, 'Western Cape Farmers'.

complained that 'Agriculture and Stock-farming interests' suffered greatly because of the distance to the local courts. They also hailed from more diverse districts across the interior than the 1866 series: Griqualand West, Clanwilliam, Richmond, Albert, Hope Town, Queenstown, Victoria West, Fort Beaufort and Albany. Clusters of surnames can be found in each of these petitions.

The shift towards national coordination of petitions was probably linked to the development of the national Afrikaner Bond. Amending the Masters & Servants laws and promoting the Dutch language were part of the farmers' original concerns and these came to national prominence as suggested in the Bond's main founding documents.[56] Labour petitions were not only more likely to be submitted in Dutch than temperance petitions (shown in Table 11.4), but they were also increasingly submitted in Dutch.[57] Petitions from 1881 addressing labour issues called for the use of Dutch in Parliament, courts of law and the government.[58] Some petitioners during the 1884 session were also explicitly coordinated by the Afrikaner Bond. Representatives from the Afrikaner Bond branch in Alexandria submitted two petitions for a more stringent Pass Law and sought reforms to the Masters & Servants law to allow corporal punishment. It seems likely that the national effort was also aided by the lower costs of communication due to the diffusion of the railways and the telegraph.[59]

Temperance petitions

Clusters of temperance petitions with identical formats, submitted sequentially but emanating from geographically diverse regions and from racially diverse petitioners, can be seen from the 1870s onwards. These findings both bolster claims made in the existing literature and provide novel insights into the organisation of the temperance campaign. Temperance petitions indicate the involvement of close-knit communities as well as Colony-wide cooperation. The petitions reveal a rich set of social ties between petitioners and a cross-organisational network of pro-temperance activists. Petitioners seem to have been connected by the social organisations they subscribed to, churches they attended and communities in which they lived. We look at petitions with the same format and compare petitioner, geographic and signature information to investigate organisational aspects of the temperance campaign.

There was a clear emergence of coordinated petitioning campaigns. As mentioned, petitions with identical formats were more common in the temperance than the labour sample. Temperance petitions from the 1850s and 1860s, however, do not seem to have

---

[56] M.A.S. Grundlingh, 'The Parliament of the Cape of Good Hope, with Special Reference to Party Politics, 1872 to 1910' (PhD diss., Stellenbosch University, Stellenbosch, 1945): Appendices A-E, 436–46.

[57] Dimitruk, 'Before apartheid'.

[58] For example, HA (1882), nos. 32, 35, 50, 57, 58, 59, 60, and 62.

[59] A. Herranz-Loncán and J. Fourie, '"For the Public Benefit?": Railways in the British Cape Colony', *European Review of Economic History* 22, no. 1 (2018): 73–100.

coordinated formats. This could be because the temperance organisations which would go onto attract thousands of followers only appeared in the Colony after 1870.[60]

Clusters of identically worded petitions tend to appear yearly and were commonly presented in sequence on the same day or over several days, implying a level of coordination. For instance, petitions 88, 98, 99, 100, 101 and 102 all share the same formatting and were presented between 28 May and 2 June 1875.[61] Similarly, a group of seven petitions, all from Port Elizabeth and with the same format, were presented by the same member of Parliament, Mr. Jones, with six being presented on 29 May and three on 19 June 1896.[62]

In general, it can be said that temperance petitions were urban in origin. For instance, all six of the consistently formatted 1875 petitions were sent from major urban centres in the eastern part of the Colony.[63] The same can be said of twelve uniformly formatted petitions from 1886 which also came from these centres.[64] The best example of geographic diversity across petitions with the same format can be seen in 1905 and 1906.[65] In both years, places as distant as Kimberley, East London, Grahamstown, Somerset East, Graaff-Reinet and Woodstock and Sea Point (two suburbs of Cape Town) were listed in the Abstracts with the petitions using the same basic text.

Where more fine-grained residential information is provided, we see localised connections between signatories, with many living in one neighbourhood or even on the same street. For instance, in a 1905 petition from G. G. Ward and 'the women of Gladstone, Kimberley', several signatories list the same street as their address. The streets Warren, Hull and Innes feature prominently, with forty-four of seventy-four signatories listed as residing there (twenty-five of them in Warren Street). This provides insight into the signature collecting process. Signatories on the same street seem to have signed in sequence, suggesting that a canvasser moved along a street and knocked on each door. For instance, one sequence of signatures lists 24, 22, 18, 16 and 14 Hull Street in succession. Table 11.5, Column (3) shows a sample of signatures from a page in this petition. This petition also shows how these localised connections between signatories were linked to Colony-wide networks. The Kimberley petition used the same basic text

---

[60]Crush and Ambler, 'Alcohol in Southern African Labor History'. As mentioned, 87 per cent of the sampled temperance petitions were in favour of temperance. Petitions we identify as against temperance were typically opposed to liquor licence fee increases or licence regulations. Some argued that changes to the liquor licensing laws were not an effective deterrent and rather prejudicial against the 'respectable and influential dealers', leaving them 'at the mercy of unprincipled and vicious individuals' (HA 771 (1875), no. 30).

[61]HA 771 (1875).

[62]HA 830 & 831 (1896), nos. 208, 210–14, 302, 305–6.

[63]HA 771 (1875), nos. 88, 98–102.

[64]HA 800–802 (1886), nos. 105, 112, 129, 139, 152, 156, 172, 206, 208, 224, 229, 258.

[65]HA 850–852 (1905), nos. 19, 28, 29, 41, 60, 82, 95, 110, 117, 118, 129–132, 135, 141, 171, 209–17, 249–51; HA 853–855 (1906), nos. 65, 75, 76, 78, 96, 108, 110, 119, 122, 135, 139, 185, 193, 209, 216–18, 222–4, 227, 238, 242, 246, 249.

and format as all thirty temperance petitions presented that year, save for one. The use of the same petition text implies connections between this community on Hull, Warren and Innes Street of Kimberley to others in Uitenhage, Queenstown and Sea Point. The kind of people who signed these petitions identified diversely as women, church leaders and congregants, and members of the WCTU.

In contrast to the labour petitions, which were signed mostly by people with Dutch surnames and who were presumably mostly men, the signatures on temperance petitions show evidence of more diversity in gender and race across many petitions and sometimes within a single petition. Reflecting their organisational affiliations, petitions for temperance in 1886 hailed from Peelton mission station (signed for example by Walter Rubusana, Bombo Herman, Haron Bakaco and Richard Payi) and 'petitioners from the Independent Order of Good Templars' (signed for example by William Duvey, Thomas Green, Thos. R Clark and Thomas Delaney).[66] As Bradlow has shown, the temperance campaign had roots in the white, English-speaking elite.[67] Nugent notes how the Englishness of organisations like the WCTU and the South African Temperance Alliance worked against the temperance cause, particularly in Dutch Reformed Church circles, where it was associated with 'Anglophone domination'.[68] This can be seen in the paucity of Dutch-language temperance petitions and the preponderance of English-origin surnames. Individual petitions tend to be signed by people of the same race or ethnicity, which is consistent with the WCTU and the Independent Order of Good Templars having parallel, segregated organisations for coloured and black African members, such as the Independent Order of the True Templars.[69] Though separated in signing specific petitions, the communities coordinated with one another. We find petitions from separate racial groups had the same format.[70] Similarly, the WCTU is recorded as communicating with the reverend of a black African church on petitioning for the Innes Liquor Bill.[71]

Nevertheless, there are examples of diverse communities signing a single petition. Signatures on a temperance petition from inhabitants of King Williams Town (see Column (4) of Table 11.5) show that petitioners of both genders, and different races, such as John Miller and Jessie Soga, lobbied together.[72] Petitioners' occupations were also diverse. A petition from 'citizens, agriculturalists, and others residing in Uitenhage and

---

[66] HA 800 (1886), no. 70 and no. 112, respectively.

[67] Bradlow, 'Drunkenness'.

[68] Nugent, 'Temperance Movement', 346.

[69] W. G. Mills, 'The Roots of African Nationalism in the Cape Colony: Temperance, 1866–1898', *International Journal of African Historical Studies* 13, no. 2 (1980): 205.

[70] HA 850 (1906), no. 19 from Catherine Wither and other inhabitants of Somerset East and no. 28 from J. Nikolaad and others coloured inhabitants of Uitenhage.

[71] WCTU, 'Minutes of Annual Conventions'.

[72] HA 711 (1875), no. 102. Notably, all these signatures appear to have industrial or urban professions, such as shoe-maker, carpenter and cabinet maker.

its vicinity' in 1875 was signed by, among others, John Winch (Butcher), James Webb (Gardener), Isane Jaftha (Labourer), January Jocbets (Labourer), Christine Scheepers (Blacksmith), Bont Karal (Evangelist), Jonas Hoha (Teacher), Kankani (Labourer), James Mhloklela (Woolwasher) and Ibrahim (Painter).[73] These patterns suggest that it could be worthwhile documenting petition signatories' gender, racial and occupational diversity across issues and examining how they evolved over time.

The content of the temperance petitions is useful in both supporting the existing literature and providing novel insights into the movement. Pro-temperance petitions were commonly of three kinds: general requests for prohibition, calls for specific restrictions related to liquor licences and the 'local option', or responses to work being done in Parliament (such as with the 1883 Liquor Act or the Innes Bill). Petitioners relied on the same justifications in favour of temperance. These tended to be repeated throughout the period studied. For the most part, temperance has been presented in the literature as an economically impractical system based on moral prescription. In many ways this is reflected in the temperance petitions. Liquor is described as 'pernicious', 'demoralising' and inimical to progress, morality and civilisation.[74]

Crush and Ambler have shown how ideas about the ruinous nature of alcohol, when combined with upper-class European notions of excess and pseudo-scientific theories about race, led to the belief that black Africans were uniquely vulnerable to the lure of alcohol.[75] For this reason, most petitions focus on temperance for black Africans. Of the 150 petitions sampled, 112 included a specific request for prohibition for black Africans. This did not mean that black Africans were not themselves in favour of temperance. For many pro-temperance black Africans, prohibition held the promise of a more equal society,[76] and the resuscitation of a people mired in war and damaged by the 'cattle killing' of 1856–7.[77] Schoots demonstrates and expands on this phenomenon in Chapter 10.

The literature has portrayed the temperance movement primarily as a moral crusade. However, some petitioners presented economic arguments in favour of temperance, largely in reference to black African consumption.[78] Many petitions linked drunkenness and criminality, saying things like: 'Drunkenness is at the bottom of much of the stock stealing, and most of the crimes committed by our people'.[79] Although they are not explicit about the economic consequences of such crimes, such as fines or imprisonment

---

[73] HA 771 (1875), no. 99.

[74] HA 800 (1886), no. 105; HA 796 (1885), no. 1; HA 800 (1886), no. 70.

[75] Crush and Ambler, 'Alcohol in Southern African Labor History'.

[76] Mills, 'Roots of African Nationalism'.

[77] Mills, 'Cape Smoke'.

[78] These petitions were submitted by a variety of petitioners; from those who did not overtly identify themselves (either by race or gender), such as 'inhabitants of the town of Beaufort West' (HA 752 (1855), no. 115), to members of the WCTU, the Independent Order of Good Templars and the Independent Order of True Templars, and those who identified themselves as black African.

[79] HA 834 (1897), no. 227.

resulting in lost income, it would be logical to assume this is what they meant. Some petitioners linked drunkenness and poverty, arguing that licensed canteens, 'keep the people habitually poor by swallowing up their earnings'.[80]

Drunkenness was also associated with idleness and a lack of agricultural industriousness. One 1886 petition, whose format was much repeated, explained how petitioners' renewed sobriety due to the 1883 Act had encouraged them to till their lands 'which before were neglected'.[81] For employers, drunkenness was said to create an unreliable and insolent workforce.[82] This offers an interesting counterpoint to the labour petitions which also complained of an unreliable workforce, although for different reasons, as noted above. Labour and temperance petitions suggested different legislative solutions to this problem.

Still other petitions described widespread drunkenness as a burden on the state. One petition said that 'what might have been a useful part of the State becomes an expensive burden to it, a disgrace to their own class, an annoyance and a source of loss to their employers, and replenishers of our hospitals, jails and convict stations'.[83] Drunkenness, they argued, further contributed to uprisings, rebellions and war, which were an additional cost to the state.[84]

Conclusion

We use a new dataset of 11,441 petitions submitted to the Cape Parliament to study political voice from 1854 to 1909. We find a significant shift after 1880 from petitions about local concerns, like transport and local government bodies, to petitions about national concerns. Using petitions on labour and temperance issues, we provide evidence that petitions were directly related to Parliament's legislative work. The impact of petitions on the successful passing of bills is, however, unclear since the passing of laws at the Cape came under other influences, including the British colonial laws.

Our detailed examination of a sample of 450 original petitions on labour and temperance also gives an idea of the political organisation of the period. We find evidence of a degree of organisation. Specifically, clusters of geographically dispersed communities became connected in Colony-wide campaigns largely from the 1880s. This coincides with the development of the Afrikaner Bond and the international temperance movement. Future research might profitably investigate their communication methods and organisational strategies. It would be interesting, for example, to know how much political organisation entailed a 'top-down' approach initiated by temperance

---

[80]HA 796 (1885), no. 1.
[81]HA 800 (1886), no. 70.
[82]HA 801 (1886), no. 196.
[83]HA 798 (1885), no. 213.
[84]HA 801 (1886), no. 196.

organisations or the Afrikaner Bond and how much stemmed from community meetings or other gatherings of local groups.

Last, we find that both labour and temperance petitioners were concerned about the reliability of labour. In addition to different legislative solutions, the way in which labour and temperance petitions speak about the issues is distinct. Their rhetoric betrays different sentiments and views about labour as it related to race. Petitioners in 1891 sought a compulsory Masters & Servants law for people and their children so that the Colony would be 'greatly relieved from an idle and dishonest class'.[85] A set of petitions from evidently black African and white communities in 1896 sought prohibition of liquor for black Africans because it was 'ruining their health, morals and capabilities as citizens' and asked Parliament to pass temperance laws on 'Christian and economic grounds'.[86] Future work could use text analysis tools to provide a more complete picture of sentiment across different types of petitions.

Bibliography

Bradlow, E. 'Drunkenness at the Cape of Good Hope in the 1870s: A Case Study of a Colonial Ruling Class and Its Philosophy'. *Kleio* 30, no. 1 (1998): 11–27.

Bundy, C. 'The Emergence and Decline of a South African Peasantry'. *African Affairs* 71, no. 285 (1972): 369–88.

Christopher, A.J. 'South African Petitions to the House of Commons, 1833–1914: Grievances, Protests, Advice and Information'. *Historia* 63, no. 1 (2018): 1–23.

Clough, E.M.O. *The South African Parliamentary Manual*. London: Whittaker & Co., 1909.

Cobley, A. 'Liquor and Leadership: Temperance, Drunkenness and the African Petty Bourgeoisie in South Africa'. *South African Historical Journal* 31 (1994): 128–48.

Crush, C. and C. Ambler. 'Alcohol in Southern African Labor History'. In *Liquor and Labor in Southern Africa*, edited by C. Crush and C. Ambler, 1–55. Athens, US: Ohio University Press, 1992.

Davenport, T.R.H. *The Afrikaner Bond: The History of a South African Political Party, 1880–1911*. Cape Town: Oxford University Press, 1966.

Dimitruk, K. 'Before Apartheid: Labor Markets, Political Parties, and Labor Institutions in 19th Century South Africa'. *Mimeo* (2021).

Feinstein, C.H. *An Economic History of South Africa: Conquest, Discrimination, and Development*. Cambridge: Cambridge University Press, 2005.

Giliomee, H. 'Western Cape Farmers and the Beginnings of Afrikaner Nationalism, 1870–1915'. *Journal of South African Studies* 14, no. 1 (1987): 38–63.

Grundlingh, M.A.S. 'The Parliament of the Cape of Good Hope, With Special Reference to Party politics, 1872 to 1910'. PhD diss., Stellenbosch University, Stellenbosch, 1945.

Gwaindepi, A. 'State Building in the Colonial Era: Public Revenue, Expenditure and Borrowing Patterns in the Cape Colony, 1820–1910'. PhD diss., Stellenbosch University, Stellenbosch, 2018.

---

[85] HA 813 (1891), no. 131.

[86] HA 830 (1896), nos. 208, 210.

Herranz-Loncán, A. and J. Fourie. '"For the Public Benefit?" Railways in the British Cape Colony'. *European Review of Economic History* 22, no. 1 (2018): 73–100.

Huzzey, R. and H. Miller. 'Petitions, Parliament and Political Culture: Petitioning the House of Commons, 1780–1918'. *Past & Present* 248, no. 1 (2020): 123–64.

Kilpin, R. *The Parliament of the Cape*. London: Longmans, Green & Co., 1938.

La Hausse, P. *Brewers, Beerhalls, and Boycotts: A History of Liquor in South Africa*. Johannesburg: Ravan, 1998.

Lemon, K. '"No Sex in Citizenship": Investigating Women's Petitions to the Cape Parliament, 1873–1902'. BA Hons diss., Stellenbosch University, Stellenbosch, 2019.

Mager, A.K. '"White Liquor Hits Black Livers": Meanings of Excessive Liquor Consumption in South Africa in the Second Half of the Twentieth Century'. *Social Science and Medicine* 59, no. 4 (2004): 735–51.

Mager, A.K. *Beer, Sociability, and Masculinity in South Africa*. Cape Town: UCT Press, 2010.

McCracken, J.L. *The Cape Parliament, 1854–1910*. Oxford: Oxford University Press, 1967.

McKinnon, J. 'Women's Christian Temperance Union: Aspects of Early Feminism in the Cape, 1889 to 1930'. MA diss., University of South Africa, Pretoria, 1995.

Miller, H. 'Introduction: The Transformation of Petitioning in the Long Nineteenth Century (1780–1914)'. *Social Science History* 43, no. 3 (2019): 409–29.

Mills, W.G. 'The Roots of African Nationalism in the Cape Colony: Temperance, 1866–1898'. *International Journal of African Historical Studies* 13, no. 2 (1980): 197–213.

Mills, W.G. 'Cape Smoke: Alcohol Issues in the Cape Colony in the Nineteenth Century'. *Contemporary Drug Problems* 12, no. 2 (1985): 221–48.

Nugent, P. 'The Temperance Movement and Wine Farmers at the Cape: Collective Action, Racial Discourse, and Legislative Reform, c. 1890–1965'. *Journal of African History* 52, no. 3 (2011): 341–63.

Nyika, F. and J. Fourie. 'Black Disenfranchisement in the Cape Colony, c.1887–1900: Challenging the Numbers'. *Journal of Southern African Studies* 46, no. 3 (2020): 455–69.

Ross, R. 'Emancipations and the Economy of the Cape Colony'. *Slavery & Abolition* 14, no. 1 (1993): 131–48.

Sachs, A. *Justice in South Africa*. Berkeley: University of California Press, 1973.

Scully, P. 'Criminality and Conflict in Rural Stellenbosch, South Africa, 1870–1900'. *Journal of African History* 30, no. 2 (1989): 289–300.

Scully, P. 'Liquor and Labour in the Western Cape, 1870–1900'. In *Liquor and Labor in Southern Africa*, edited by C. Crush and C. Ambler, 56–77. Athens, US: Ohio University Press, 1992.

Swiegers, G.M. 'Britain and the Labour Question in South Africa: The Interaction of State, Capital, Labour and Colonial Power, 1867–1910'. PhD diss., University of the Free State, 2014.

Trapido, S. 'African Divisional Politics in the Cape Colony, 1884–1910'. *Journal of African History* 9, no. 1 (1968): 79–98.

Tyrrell, I. *Woman's World/Woman's Empire: The Woman's Christian Temperance Union in International Perspective, 1880–1930*. Chapel Hill: University of North Carolina Press, 2010.

Van Onselen, C. 'Randlords and Rotgut, 1886–1903'. *History Workshop* 2 (1976): 33–89.

Van Sittert, L. 'Holding the Line: The Rural Enclosure Movement in the Cape Colony, c. 1865–1910'. *Journal of African History* 43, no. 1 (2002): 95–118.

Van Sittert, L. 'Writing on Skin: The Entangled Embodied Histories of Black Labour and Livestock Registration in the Cape Colony, c. 1860–1909'. *Kronos* 40 (2014): 74–98.

Williams, G. 'Slaves, Workers, and Wine: The "Dop System" in the History of the Cape Wine Industry, 1658–1894'. *Journal of Southern African Studies* 42, no. 5 (2016): 893–909.

Wilson, F. 'Farming, 1866–1966'. In *The Oxford History of South Africa: Volume II*, edited by M. Wilson and L. Thompson. Oxford: Oxford University Press, 1971.

Würgler, A. 'Voices from among the "Silent Masses": Humble Petitions and Social Conflicts in Early Modern Central Europe'. *International Review of Social History* 46, no. 9 (2001): 11–34.

Zaeske, S. 'Signatures of Citizenship: The Rhetoric of Women's Antislavery Petitions'. *Quarterly Journal of Speech* 88, no. 2 (2002): 147–68.

Zaret, D. 'Petitions and the "Invention" of Public Opinion in the English Revolution'. *American Journal of Sociology* 101, no. 6 (1996): 1497–55.

Primary Sources

'Abstract of Petitions', *Votes & Proceedings of the House of Assembly*, various volumes (1854–1909), Stellenbosch University Library.

'Abstract of Petitions', *Votes & Proceedings of the Legislative Council*, various volumes (1854–1909), Stellenbosch University Library.

Debates, House of Assembly, various volumes, Stellenbosch University Library.

HA, 753–855 (various volumes): Petitions of the House of Assembly (1854–1909), Western Cape Archives and Records Services.

'Proceedings on Bills', *Votes & Proceedings of the House of Assembly*, various volumes (1854–1909), Stellenbosch University Library.

WCTU (Women's Christian Temperance Union). 1898. A1696. Vol 2/2. Printed Minutes of the Annual Conventions, 1891–1899. Western Cape Archives and Records Services.

CHAPTER 12
DEATH DURING THE INFLUENZA OF 1918
Jonathan Jayes* and Johan Fourie**

Introduction

The 'Spanish flu' of 1918 was the most severe epidemic in South African history. Estimates of the actual death toll vary. An official estimate published only a few years afterwards arrived at a figure of 139,471 deaths. Howard Phillips, in his magisterial history of the 1918 influenza in South Africa, backwardly projected the Quarterly Abstract of Union Statistics of 1920. He estimated that between 450,000 and 520,000 people were 'missing' from the census, and thus that a fairer estimate of the deaths would be between 250,000 and 300,000, or 6 per cent of the population.[1] This would make South Africa one of the most badly affected countries globally. Much of what we know about the deaths from the 1918 influenza in South Africa comes from officially published statistics, such as the Influenza Epidemic Commission – or backward projections like those done by Phillips. We used a new source, individual-level death certificates, to reassess these estimates and to investigate social and demographic factors that could explain differences in influenza mortality across the Cape Province. Our findings indicate that the Influenza Epidemic Commission underestimated the number of deaths in six of the fifteen districts in our sample, with a systematic undercounting of deaths in districts with smaller populations. This indicates an underestimation of the number of deaths across the country by the Commission by an order of magnitude.

We were able to do this because of the recent transcription of just over 40,000 death certificates across fifteen Cape Province districts for the years 1915–20. These individual-level records include a wealth of biographical information about each deceased individual that enabled us to tease out the mortality rates by gender, race and occupational category. They open up many new avenues for research, but they also introduce new questions

---

†We thank Kara Dimitruk, Kate Ekama, Kelsey Lemon and Laura Richardson for research assistance and for Dan de Kadt for sharing data. This research was made possible by a South African National Research Foundation postgraduate bursary, a Vice-Rector (Research) Institutional Covid-19 grant, and the Andrew W. Mellon Foundation 'Biography of an Uncharted People' project.
*Jayes: Department of Economic History, Lund University, Sweden and Department of Economics, Stellenbosch University, South Africa.
**Fourie: Department of Economics, Stellenbosch University, South Africa.
[1] H. Phillips, 'Black October: the impact of the Spanish influenza epidemic of 1918 on South Africa' (PhD diss., University of Cape Town, Cape Town, 1984).

about sample selection and bias. Because we can compare death certificates before, during and after the pandemic, we believe we can provide a more reliable account than hitherto. We also used natural language processing to reveal differences in methods of recording statistics that could, if unadjusted, introduce errors into the results. Our findings shed new light on the incidence of the influenza at the Cape, revealing trends that deserve more attention in future.

We believe this is important, for two reasons. First, new methods now allow historians to use innovative sources, like death certificates, to discover new facts about the past. By calculating the average duration of an illness, for example, we can show that what was previously thought about the Spanish flu – that it was a disease with a relatively short disease duration – seems to be false: instead of a 'three-day illness', the average illness duration for those who died (and hence appear in our dataset) was two weeks.[2]

But secondly, we can use the new facts to help us understand the present. For example, our findings about the 1918 influenza could shed light on the Covid-19 pandemic.[3] When Covid-19 arrived in South Africa in March 2020, policymakers responded in various ways. The most obvious was to ask epidemiologists to attempt to estimate what might happen, but as can be expected, there was much debate about the correct response. This is because there was at that stage too little information available to populate the epidemiologists' models. An alternative approach, and, as Barry Eichengreen explains, one that policymakers used to make sense of the Great Recession of 2009, is to look at history.[4] Such an analogical approach, however, requires accurate information about past pandemics. We have some very good accounts of the 1918 influenza, but our statistical knowledge of how the disease spread, the demographic and social correlates of the disease, and which public responses were successful, remains limited. Those questions are what motivated our study.

1918 pandemic mortality in South Africa

The 1918 influenza was the largest pandemic of the twentieth century. Precise estimates of deaths are unavailable, owing to poor administrative systems in many countries and the speed with which the virus killed. Killingray and Phillips suggest that between 50 and 100 million died globally, reflecting the uncertainty that persists.[5]

---

[2]Average duration 15.7 days, a median of 10 days, and a modal value of 9 days for those who died of Spanish influenza

[3]In April 2020, the 'Biography of an Uncharted People' team was contracted by the South African Presidency to undertake a report on the Spanish flu. The report was submitted in May 2020.

[4]B. Eichengreen, *Hall of Mirrors: The Great Depression, the Great Recession, and the Uses-and Misuses-of History* (Oxford: Oxford University Press, 2015).

[5]D. Killingray and H. Phillips, eds., *The Spanish Influenza Pandemic of 1918–19: New Perspectives* (London: Routledge, 2011).

South Africa had one of the highest mortality rates. This was unexpected. An early variant of the flu had arrived via Durban in early 1918, reaching the gold mines of the Transvaal.⁶ At first there were several cases, but excess mortality rates were generally unaffected and fears about a possible pandemic were soon put to bed. One journalist said that since such a very large number of people had been affected, the fact there had been only one death could be considered 'reassuring'.⁷ Just days earlier, however, a more virulent variant had arrived in Cape Town with the soldiers returning from the trenches of the First World War. It rapidly spread along the Cape railroads, bringing death and despair to distant parts of the Cape Province. It is the mortality effect of this second variant that we study in this chapter.

Despite the high death toll in South Africa, little scholarly interest was shown for several decades. Phillips notes that prior to his own study, 'extensive documentation' from unpublished evidence in the report of the government-appointed Influenza Epidemic Commission had lain on the shelves of the Library of Parliament unexamined.⁸

In 2018, to investigate the causes and consequences of the 1918 flu in South Africa, the 'Biography of an Uncharted People' project at Stellenbosch University began to transcribe Cape Province death certificates. When Covid-19 struck in March 2020 and interest in the 1918 flu returned, the Biography team was fortunate to have new historical evidence to report. Two avenues of research particularly interested us. First, we wanted to assess how far inequality in access to healthcare services could explain pandemic mortality. This was in response to concerns at the time that unequal access to healthcare would affect Covid-19 mortality. Using transcribed records of just over 40,000 death certificates and a novel proxy for access to healthcare, we found that access to healthcare fell during the pandemic period and that this was especially true for black and coloured households. The 1918 flu, we found, exacerbated existing health inequalities.

Second, we wanted to identify the correlates of pandemic mortality. To do this, a team of economists used district-level statistics obtained from South African censuses to correlate pre-pandemic district characteristics with official mortality figures. The resulting article reports that factors such as the black and coloured share of the population, the population density and railway access were correlated with pandemic mortality.⁹ The authors noted, however, that individual-level information would produce a much richer set of mortality correlates and be more likely to reveal the true level of mortality across districts. This chapter shows how information from the death certificates helped in this regard.

---

⁶L. Spinney, *Pale Rider: The Spanish Flu of 1918 and How It Changed the World* (New York: Public Affairs, 2017).

⁷Phillips, 'Black October', 11.

⁸Ibid, 9.

⁹D. De Kadt, et al., 'The causes and consequences of the 1918 influenza in South Africa.' Stellenbosch Working Paper Series, No. WP 12/2020 (Department of Economics: Stellenbosch University, 2021).

The death certificates and data extraction

To investigate the extent of excess mortality during the influenza months of October 1918 to February 1919, and to identify correlates of excess mortality, we transcribed just over 40,000 'Forms of Information of a Death of Individuals', or death certificates, across fifteen districts of the Cape Province between 1915 and 1920. The death certificates were recorded and preserved in accordance with Act No. 7 of 1894 of the Cape Colony, which required all deaths in the Cape Colony (the Cape Province after 1910) to be recorded. Death registrations were initially sparse, but by 1915 a large proportion of deaths would have been recorded. There were exceptions, as could be expected, in rural areas and notably during the chaotic period of the pandemic, particularly in 'black October', the deadliest pandemic month, when many deaths simply went unrecorded.

The death certificates have been digitised by FamilySearch.org and are freely available online. A small team of retired historians and librarians transcribed each one manually.[10] We created a template record of a death certificate in Microsoft Excel and the transcribers entered the information from the digitised online records, each row representing one deceased individual. The entries are largely chronological, although not all deaths were registered immediately. Deaths during December, for example, were often registered in January. Our sample covered six years, from 1915 to 1920. The years prior to the pandemic serve as a baseline against which to compare excess mortality during the pandemic.

The certificates contain demographic information about the deceased and the informant, and the cause of death and other details. Most often the informant was a family member. Demographic information helps us identify the correlates of mortality. Race is one important factor. Figure 12.1 shows the death certificate of Liza Goxo as an example. She was forty-five years old when she died on 24 October 1918. She was born in the Cape Province and was unmarried. The informant, Stofile Goxo, presumably a father, uncle or brother, reported her race as 'Pondo'. She died of influenza after an illness of nine days.

Health in the early twentieth century Cape was closely correlated to race, but there was little consistency in how race was recorded. Often the term used was what we today would call ethnicity, such as 'Pondo' or 'Fingo'. And there were many ethnicities. Of the 419 different ethnicities recorded on the certificates, more than 200 appear only once. To turn the unique ethnic labels into race categories, we used a machine-learning model that classified the 419 different ethnicities to three groups. Table 12.1 shows the distribution by race; 45 per cent black, 39 per cent coloured and 16 per cent white.[11]

---

[10] We thank Elizabeth Baldwin, Chris de Wit, Martie du Toit, Kate Ekama, Anneen Fourie, Hans Heese and Gustav Hendrich for valuable research assistance.

[11] See https://github.com/j-jayes/spanish-flu. The model was trained on manually labelled data for 15,000 observations and then used to predict race in the case of the remaining 25,000 observations. The model achieved 99.8 per cent accuracy on unseen testing data and could be useful in other contexts. For this purpose, the exact code is included in the Appendix, and data and scripts are available on GitHub.

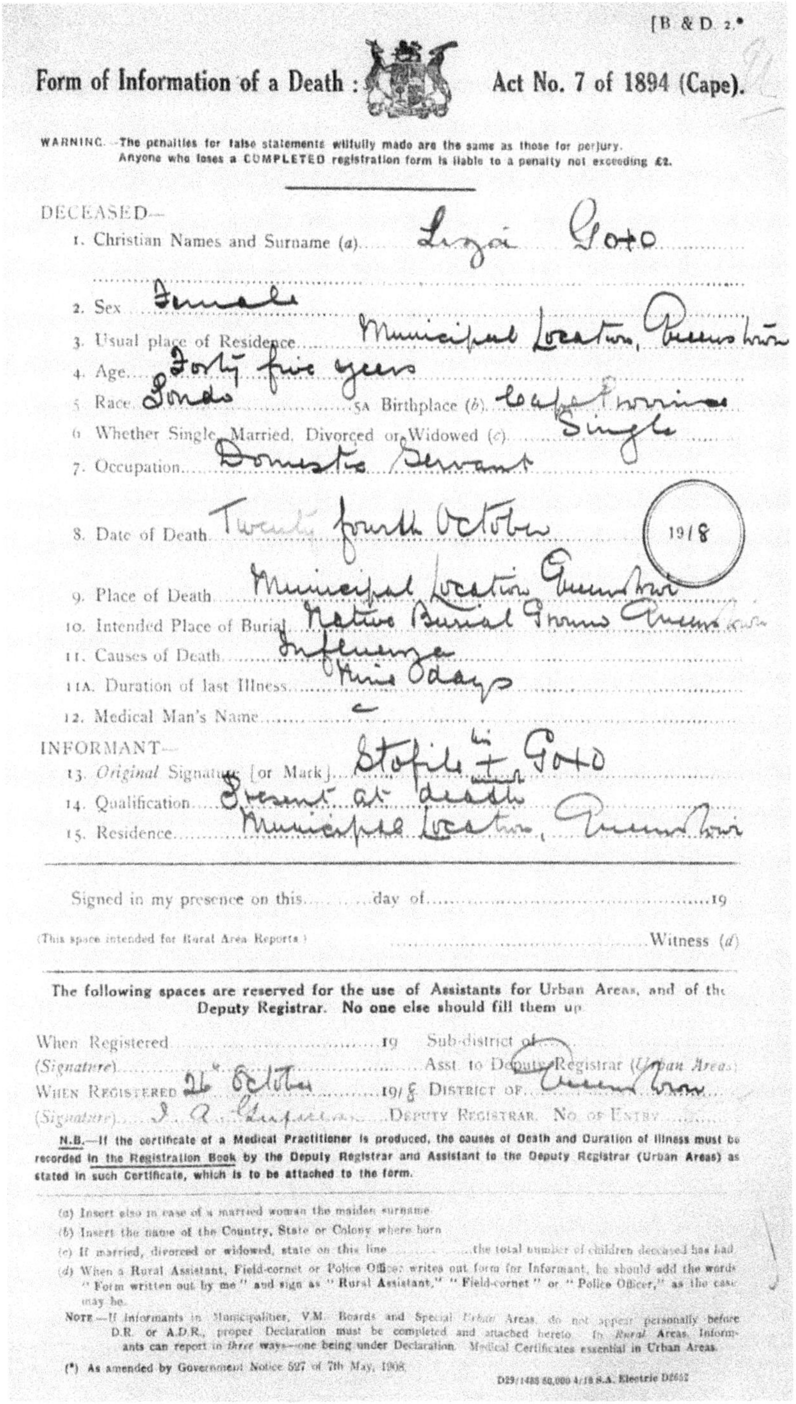

[B. & D. 2.*

Form of Information of a Death : Act No. 7 of 1894 (Cape).

WARNING.—The penalties for false statements wilfully made are the same as those for perjury.
Anyone who loses a COMPLETED registration form is liable to a penalty not exceeding £2.

DECEASED—
1. Christian Names and Surname (*a*) Lizai Goxo
2. Sex Female
3. Usual place of Residence Municipal Location, Queenstown
4. Age Forty five years
5. Race Tondo 5A Birthplace (*b*) Cape Province
6. Whether Single, Married, Divorced or Widowed (*c*) Single
7. Occupation Domestic Servant
8. Date of Death Twenty fourth October 1918
9. Place of Death Municipal Location Queenstown
10. Intended Place of Burial Native Burial Ground Queenstown
11. Causes of Death Influenza
11A. Duration of last Illness Nine Odays
12. Medical Man's Name —

INFORMANT—
13. *Original* Signature [or Mark] Stofile his + mark Goxo
14. Qualification Present at death
15. Residence Municipal Location, Queenstown

Signed in my presence on this .... day of 19

(This space intended for Rural Area Reports.) .... Witness (*d*)

The following spaces are reserved for the use of Assistants for Urban Areas, and of the Deputy Registrar. No one else should fill them up.

When Registered .... 19 Sub-district of ....
(*Signature*) .... Asst. to Deputy Registrar (*Urban Areas*)
When Registered 26 October 1918 District of Queenstown
(*Signature*) J. A. .... Deputy Registrar. No. of Entry ....

N.B.—If the certificate of a Medical Practitioner is produced, the causes of Death and Duration of Illness must be recorded in the Registration Book by the Deputy Registrar and Assistant to the Deputy Registrar (Urban Areas) as stated in such Certificate, which is to be attached to the form.

(*a*) Insert also in case of a married woman the maiden surname.
(*b*) Insert the name of the Country, State or Colony where born.
(*c*) If married, divorced or widowed, state on this line .... the total number of children deceased has had.
(*d*) When a Rural Assistant, Field-cornet or Police Officer writes out form for Informant, he should add the words "Form written out by me" and sign as "Rural Assistant," "Field-cornet" or "Police Officer," as the case may be.

NOTE.—If Informants in Municipalities, V.M. Boards and Special *Urban* Areas, do not appear personally before D.R. or A.D.R., proper Declaration must be completed and attached hereto. In *Rural* Areas, Informants can report in *three* ways—one being under Declaration. Medical Certificates essential in Urban Areas.

(*) As amended by Government Notice 527 of 7th May, 1908.

D29/1488 60,000 4/18 S.A. Electric D2652

Figure 12.1 Form of information of the death of Liza Goxo.
Source: Civil Deaths 1895–1972 database with images National Archives Pretoria (1918).

For our study, the date and cause of death and demographic information about the deceased were of particular interest. Most fields were recorded consistently but there were some inconsistencies in the cause of death and duration of last illness. These are discussed in detail in Fourie and Jayes.[12] Where a doctor had tended to the deceased and completed a certificate, the certificate would include the pertinent information from the medical practitioner's certificate. In the absence of such a certificate, the informant could provide this information, if known. The text on the death certificate below the input fields reads:

> N.B. – If the certificate of a Medical Practitioner is produced, the causes of Death and Duration of Illness must be recorded in the Registration Book by the Deputy Registrar and Assistant to the Deputy Registrar as stated in such certificate, which is to be attached to the form.

From Figure 12.1, it would appear that no doctor attended to Liza Goxo before her death, as the line for 'Medical Man's Name' is left blank. Her death was during 'black October'.

Table 12.1 shows the distribution of death certificates by town, sex, race and age. It also includes our literacy proxy and the duration of illness. The common name for the flu was *driedag-siekte* ('three-day sickness'), but we found that the median duration of last illness was ten days, with an interquartile range of between seven and thirty days. Using other measures of central tendency, we find a mean duration 15.7 days, and a modal value of nine days. We note also that for pandemic deaths the median age in years of the deceased was twenty, nearly double the twelve years in our entire sample, and four times the median age of other recorded deaths (five years). This matches the findings of Phillips and Fourie and Jayes that young adults in South Africa were particularly hard hit by the flu.[13]

We expected that the pandemic would have exacerbated differences in reporting by district. Some deaths might not have been registered at all. Phillips notes that 'even under normal conditions in 1918, the South African government lacked the means to record every death in the country'.[14] This was clear from the wide variation in the infant and child mortality rates we calculated from the death certificates prior to the pandemic. There would also probably be differences in the quality of the records. Queenstown, the district where Liza Goxo lived, was mostly rural. Phillips notes that the legislation that stipulated the recording of deaths, the 1894 Births and Deaths Registration Act, 'in theory applied to all inhabitants, but in practice was largely a dead letter in predominantly black rural areas'.[15] The instructions on the death certificates below the

---

[12] J. Fourie and J. Jayes, 'Health Inequality and the 1918 Influenza in South Africa', *World Development* 141 (2021): 105407.

[13] Phillips, 'Black October'; Fourie and Jayes, 'Health Inequality'.

[14] Phillips, 'Black October', 288.

[15] Ibid.

Table 12.1 Descriptive statistics of sample from fifteen districts.

Variable	Overall, N = 40,087[1]	Flu death, N = 15,376[1]	Other death, N = 24,711[1]
Town			
Cradock	2,698 (6.7%)	1,119 (7.3%)	1,579 (6.4%)
Elliot	1,185 (3.0%)	611 (4.0%)	574 (2.3%)
Fraserburg	1,246 (3.1%)	362 (2.4%)	884 (3.6%)
Komga	2,250 (5.6%)	1,342 (8.7%)	908 (3.7%)
Kuruman	1,476 (3.7%)	593 (3.9%)	883 (3.6%)
Mafeking	2,296 (5.7%)	921 (6.0%)	1,375 (5.6%)
Oudtshoorn	5,894 (15%)	1,855 (12%)	4,039 (16%)
Paarl	5,051 (13%)	1,718 (11%)	3,333 (13%)
Peddie	2,520 (6.3%)	1,145 (7.4%)	1,375 (5.6%)
Queenstown	6,226 (16%)	2,135 (14%)	4,091 (17%)
Riversdale	1,219 (3.0%)	374 (2.4%)	845 (3.4%)
Sea Point	324 (0.8%)	45 (0.3%)	279 (1.1%)
Stellenbosch	3,835 (9.6%)	1,438 (9.4%)	2,397 (9.7%)
Stockenstrom	2,487 (6.2%)	1,126 (7.3%)	1,361 (5.5%)
Vryburg	1,380 (3.4%)	592 (3.9%)	788 (3.2%)
Sex			
Female	20,000 (50%)	7,968 (52%)	12,032 (49%)
Male	20,087 (50%)	7,408 (48%)	12,679 (51%)
Race			
Black	18,034 (45%)	8,049 (52%)	9,985 (40%)
Coloured	15,508 (39%)	5,738 (37%)	9,770 (40%)
White	6,545 (16%)	1,589 (10%)	4,956 (20%)
Literacy proxy			
No	23,448 (58%)	9,709 (63%)	13,739 (56%)
Yes	16,639 (42%)	5,667 (37%)	10,972 (44%)
Age in years	12 (1, 40)	20 (2, 34)	5 (1, 47)
Missing	769	205	564
Duration of illness in days	14 (7, 30)	10 (7, 30)	14 (6, 30)
Missing	2,672	573	2,099

[1] n (%); median (IQR)

Source: Authors' analysis of Civil Deaths 1895–1972 database with images National Archives Pretoria (1918).

input fields, sensibly, make allowances for the difficulty of recording deaths in some areas, especially rural areas. Informants in municipalities and special urban areas who did not appear personally before the District Registrar had to complete and attach 'a proper Declaration'. In rural areas, informants could report in three ways, one being by declaration. Medical certificates were essential in urban areas. Evidently, government officials at the time accounted for the difficulty in recording deaths in rural areas by reducing the requirements.

Figure 12.2 shows the official mortality rates in the fifteen districts of the Cape Province that our study covered.

Liza Goxo's location in the rural Eastern Cape could have made it hard for her to access medical care and affected the quality of the information on her death certificate. To account for differences between areas, we chose geographically and demographically diverse districts of the Cape Province, from Sea Point in Cape Town to Komga in the east, Mafeking in the north-east and Kuruman in the north.

Another way we controlled for selection biases was by using individual-level information. Because we had details for each deceased individual, we could control for characteristics that might be related to selection. When comparing pre-pandemic with

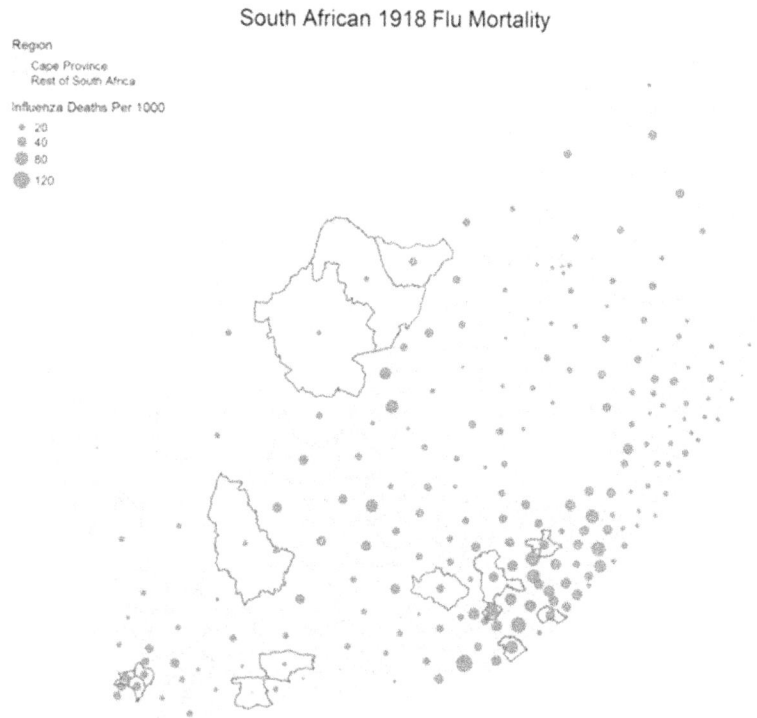

Figure 12.2 Map of 1918 flu mortality across South Africa.

pandemic mortality rates, for example, instead of having to assume that under-reporting did not exist, we were able to use the individual-level information to make the less onerous assumption that the level of under-reporting remained constant within each district. In other words, comparing mortality rates in a district prior to the pandemic with rates in the same district during the pandemic overcomes the problem of underreporting if we assume the levels of underreporting were constant within each district. This is an important extension of our analysis over previous work.

We recognise, however, that biases remain. Where the pandemic caused official recording services to be disrupted or, in the extreme case, to cease, deaths were likely to be seriously undercounted. Although the Influenza Epidemic Commission had hoped to account for this in their statistics, it is not entirely clear how this was done. Although our estimates are likely to be conservative given the missing deaths, we use alternative methods to account for pandemic deaths that may not have been registered as such. We believe this is a more transparent attempt at reconciling the recorded and actual death toll.

Counting the dead

We first show that the pandemic increased the mortality figures dramatically. Figure 12.3 is a heatmap that shows the frequency of deaths in each of the fifteen districts whose death certificates we transcribed. October 1918 is clearly an outlier, with much higher frequencies than any other month between 1915 and 1920. Note also the large variation between districts: the 'hotter' districts mostly reflect their size.

Figure 12.4 provides a better way to show the crude death rate, defined as the total number of deaths during a given time interval divided by the population of interest. There are two things to note. First, the pandemic arrived in districts at different times. In those close to Cape Town, where the soldiers disembarked soon after they were released from quarantine at port, and along the railway line they took to Kimberley, the virus spread rapidly. As can be seen from Figure 12.4, the spikes in these towns were sudden and extreme. This corroborates the evidence from De Kadt et al. which finds proximity to the railway as one correlate of pandemic mortality.[16] Second, the rate of death, and probably the spread of the disease, differed between districts. The figure corroborates the finding by Phillips that the virus abated rapidly after the peak in October.[17] Only in Oudtshoorn and Komga do the effects of the flu appear to have lingered, with elevated mortality rates into December of 1918.

Of course, not all deaths during the pandemic period were as a result of influenza. Because each death certificate records the cause of death, it should be straightforward to

---

[16] De Kadt, et al., 'Causes and Consequences'.
[17] Phillips, 'Black October'.

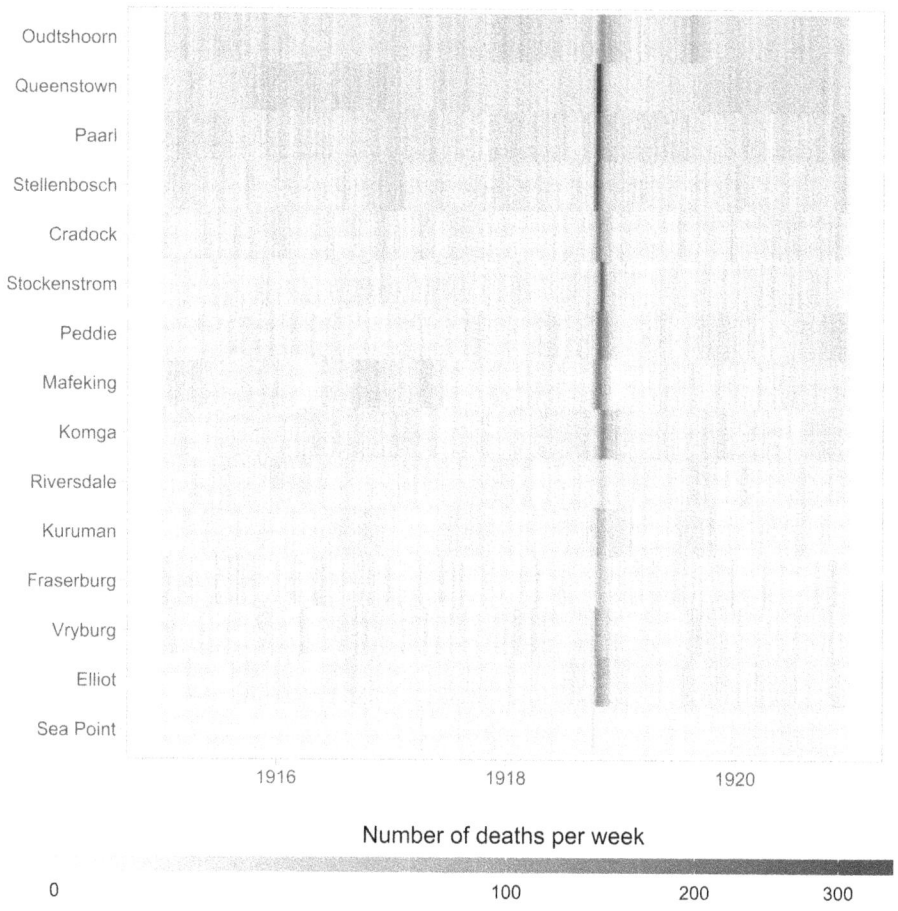

Figure 12.3 Heatmap of deaths per week across fifteen districts, 1915–1920.
Source: Authors' analysis of Civil Deaths 1895–1972 database with images National Archives Pretoria (1918).

calculate the number of pandemic deaths. In reality, however, despite the standardised template of the death certificates, there are numerous reasons why pandemic deaths might be under-recorded. First, as news of the disease probably travelled across the country slower than the disease itself, as explained by Arthi and Parman in an international context, those who reported to the registrar the cause of death may not have known that the deaths at the beginning of the pandemic were due to the Spanish flu.[18] Second, there is probably some selection bias, by location within a district, in the provision of a cause of death. As noted earlier, informants reporting deaths in rural areas were not required to have a certificate from a medical practitioner, who would have investigated the death

---

[18] V. Arthi and J. Parman, 'Disease, Downturns, and Wellbeing: Economic History and the Long-run Impacts of Covid-19', *Explorations in Economic History* 79 (2021): 101381.

Death during the Influenza of 1918

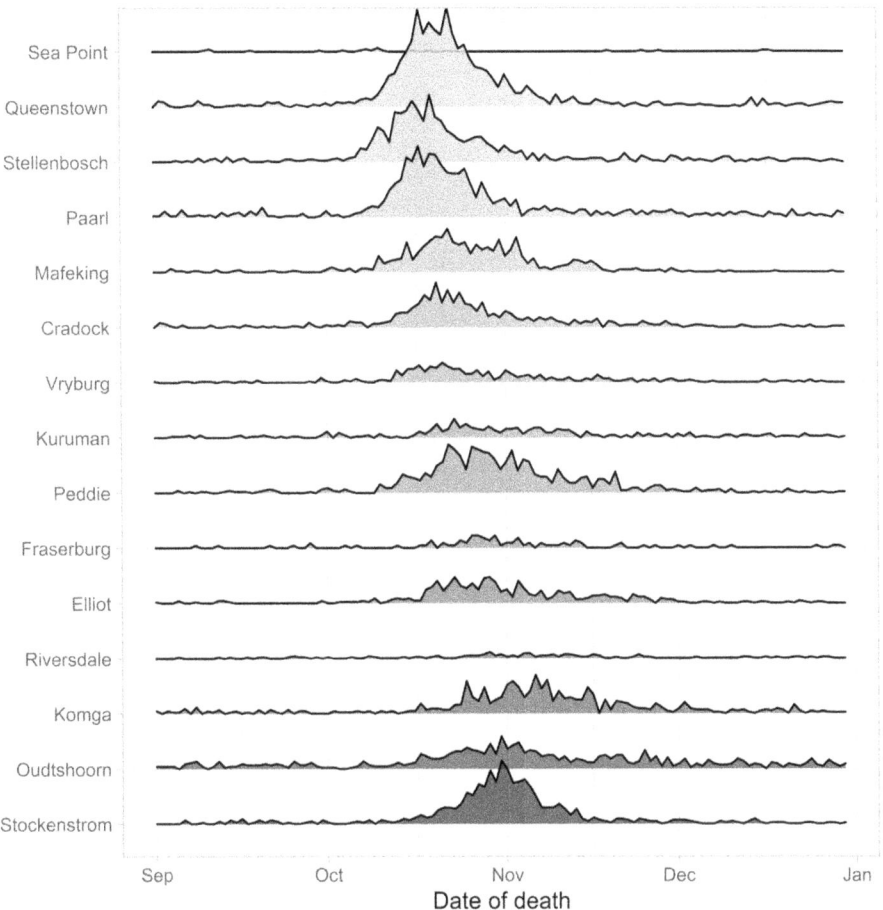

Figure 12.4 Number of deaths in district by day during pandemic peak, Sep-Dec 1918.
Source: Authors' analysis of Civil Deaths 1895–1972 database with images National Archives Pretoria (1918).

and recorded its cause. Urban districts are therefore more likely to record cause of death accurately. Third, there are idiosyncratic discrepancies in the reporting of the disease by district. Contrast, for instance, the labelling of deaths in Cradock and Paarl. Figure 12.5 shows that most of the deaths in Cradock (a rural district) during the pandemic were labelled 'Spanish flu', but fewer than half of those in Paarl.

To avoid complications, it was tempting to simply count the number of deaths in each district during the pandemic period and conclude that they were caused by the Spanish flu. But there are good reasons not to do this. Districts with different population sizes would have expected different numbers of deaths in the absence of the pandemic. Whether a population was older or younger would influence the susceptibility to influenza (and other diseases). Lumping all deaths together as pandemic deaths could also hide important comorbidity trends.

Quantitative History and Uncharted People

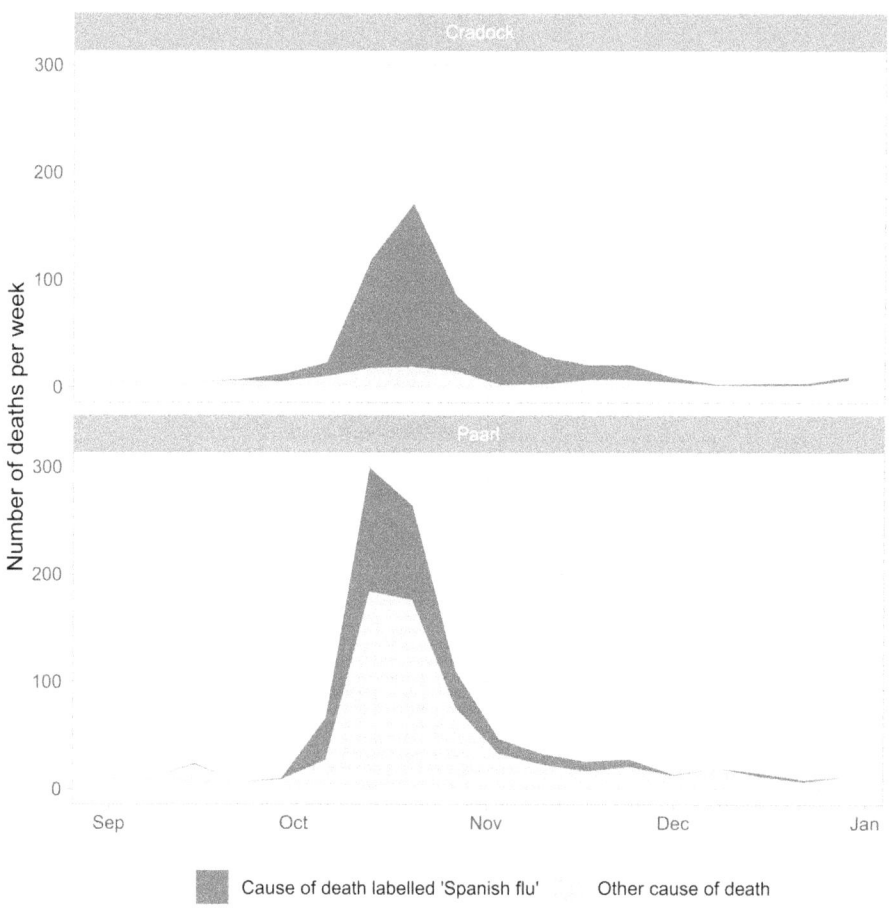

Figure 12.5 Density plot comparing causes of death during the pandemic in Cradock and Paarl.
Source: Authors' analysis of Civil Deaths 1895–1972 database with images National Archives Pretoria (1918).

Table 12.2 provides a breakdown of the most common causes of death in Cradock and Paarl. In Paarl, most cases were simply labelled 'Influenza', in contrast to 'Spanish Influenza' in Cradock. It would obviously be wrong to include only cases labelled 'Spanish Influenza'.

An alternative set of methods for quantifying excess mortality uses history as a guide. A baseline is calculated of the number of deaths we could expect to occur in each district during the pandemic period in the absence of the pandemic. This baseline is then subtracted from the observed values to calculate excess mortality, or the number of deaths in addition to those we would expect without the pandemic. We used three methods of this kind (SAMRC, Acuña-Soto et al. and a combination of three regression models), using the mortality figures for 1915, 1916 and 1917, the three years preceding the pandemic, as a guide.

Table 12.2 Comparison of common causes of death in Cradock and Paarl during the pandemic.

Cause of death	Number in Cradock	Cause of death	Number in Paarl
Spanish influenza	444	Influenza	367
Flu	21	Spanish influenza	247
Influenza	20	Pneumonia	35
Bronchitis	10	Spanish influenza, pneumonia	17
Broncho pneumonia	7	Convulsions	16
Convulsions	6	Spaanse Griep	15
Teething	5	Spanish influenza (pneumonia)	15
Diarrhoea	3	Bronchitis	14
Old age	3	Broncho pneumonia	13
Consumption	2	Gastroenteritis	12
Inflammation of lungs	2	Spanish flu	12
Pneumonia	2	A) Spanish influenza B) Pneumonia	11

Source: Authors' analysis of Civil Deaths 1895–1972 database with images National Archives Pretoria (1918).

We first used the method laid out by the South African Medical Research Council (SAMRC) in Dorrington et al.[19] We calculated the average number of deaths per month in each district during October, November and December (the pandemic months in 1918) in those three years, as a baseline. The SAMRC defines excess mortality as 'the number of all-cause deaths in the last week less the number that might have been expected to have occurred'.[20] We widened the bandwidth from one week to one month because of the coarseness of the data at district level. The resulting smoother estimates had less noise and appeared reasonable. We then subtracted this expected number of deaths from the observed number during the pandemic to calculate excess mortality during the three months of the pandemic peak in 1918.

The advantage of this method is that it captures the seasonal variation in mortality, as shown in Figure 12.6, which displays the death rates for 1915, 1916, 1917, 1919 and 1920, calculated from the death certificates for those years. It is interesting to note that the smoothed line shows a peak in mortality in the third quarter of the five non-pandemic years. This contrasts with the seasonal pattern in South Africa today where mortality usually peaks during mid-winter.

---

[19] R. Dorrington, et al., 'Predicted Numbers of Deaths by Epi-week for South Africa in 2020 and 2021 (Burden of Disease Research Unit: South African Medical Research Council, 2021).
[20] Dorrington, et al., 'Predicted Numbers of Deaths', 2.

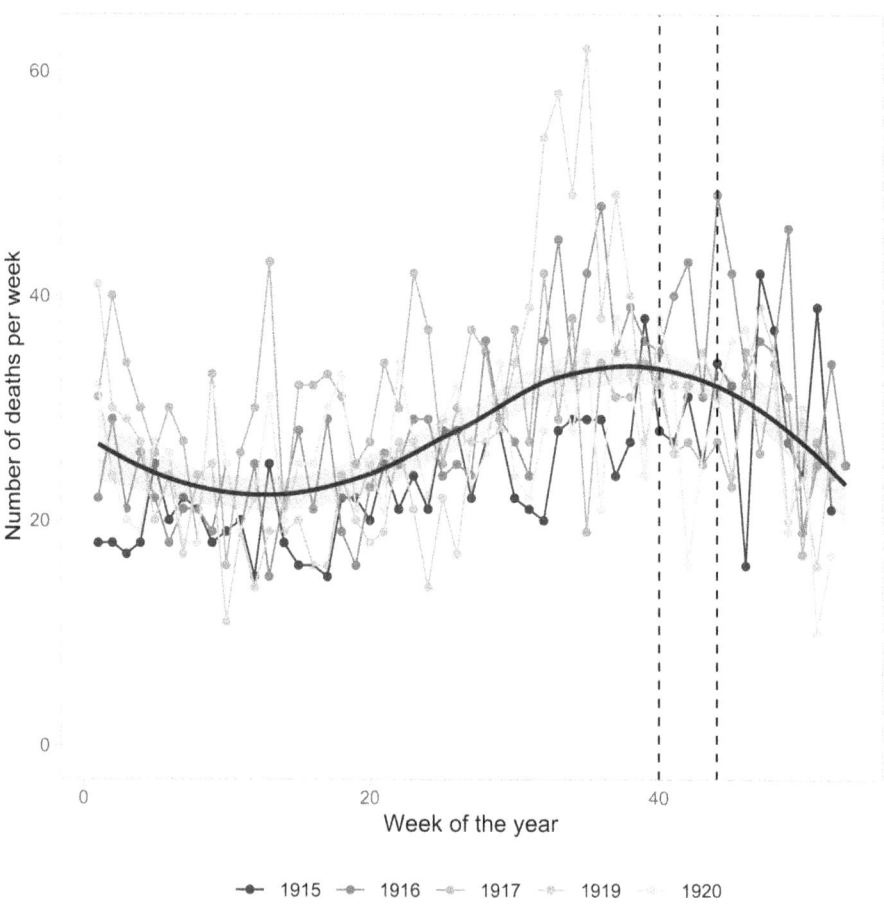

Figure 12.6 Mortality by week across districts, excluding 1918.
Source: Authors' analysis of Civil Deaths 1895–1972 database with images National Archives Pretoria (1918).
Note: Dotted lines indicate pandemic period from October to November.

This first method produced the estimates of excess mortality shown in Table 12.3. Here it is evident that, while the largest number of deaths occurred in Queenstown and Paarl, the districts of Peddie and Elliot saw more than ten times as many deaths as they had in October, November and December in the three years preceding the pandemic. Proportionally, Peddie and Elliot were worse hit than Queenstown and Paarl, despite their lower absolute numbers of deaths during the pandemic.

Our second method was taken from Acuña-Soto et al.[21] They define excess mortality as 'deaths observed during the pandemic years minus the average death counts in the

---

[21] R. Acuña-Soto, et al., 'Influenza and Pneumonia Mortality in 66 Large Cities in the United States in Years Surrounding the 1918 Pandemic', *PLoS ONE* 6, no. 8 (2011): 494–506.

Table 12.3 Excess mortality based on SAMRC method.

District	Pre-pandemic mean	Pandemic period	Excess mortality	Percent excess mortality
Queenstown	266	1,211	945	355%
Paarl	187	951	764	409%
Peddie	75	831	756	1 008%
Stellenbosch	157	816	659	420%
Stockenstrom	90	708	618	687%
Oudtshoorn	245	646	401	164%
Mafeking	101	627	526	521%
Komga	73	593	520	712%
Cradock	110	551	441	401%
Elliot	33	432	399	1 209%
Vryburg	58	300	242	417%
Kuruman	64	276	212	331%
Fraserburg	55	152	97	176%
Riversdale	55	84	29	53%
Sea Point	14	17	3	21%

Source: Authors' analysis of Civil Deaths 1895–1972 database with images National Archives Pretoria (1918).

pre-pandemic years'.[22] They had access to seven years of data preceding the pandemic. For the three preceding years available to us, we calculated a simple average of the number of deaths per year in each district and subtracted the number of deaths in 1918. Table 12.4 shows the mortality by district from 1915 to 1917, and the average across these three years following the Acuña-Soto et al. method. Although the absolute size of the excess mortality differs using this method, the ranking is largely the same, with Peddie and Elliot experiencing the largest excess mortality.

Figure 12.7 shows the excess mortality based on this second method. It is important to note that, although there is a positive correlation between mean mortality from 1915 to 1917 and mortality in 1918, the relationship is not perfect. Cradock, for example, has a higher mean mortality than Peddie between 1915 and 1917, but Peddie's 1918 mortality rate is much higher than Cradock's.

For our third method we used three regression models to extrapolate the mortality rate we would expect in each district if the historical trends from 1915 to 1917 continued. The first was a linear model with only an intercept, similar to the averaging procedure

---

[22]Ibid, 23.

Table 12.4 Excess mortality based on Acuña-Soto, Viboud and Chowell method.

District	1915	1916	1917	'15-'17 Average	1918	Excess mortality	Percent excess mortality
Peddie	266	264	270	267	1,048	781	293%
Queenstown	843	1,083	849	925	1,701	776	84%
Paarl	731	715	755	734	1,474	740	101%
Stockenstrom	264	331	335	310	942	632	204%
Stellenbosch	503	556	604	554	1,165	611	110%
Oudtshoorn	816	768	1,019	868	1,413	545	63%
Komga	241	338	301	293	823	530	181%
Mafeking	344	382	344	357	781	424	119%
Elliot	97	143	104	115	525	410	357%
Cradock	378	400	382	387	757	370	96%
Vryburg	198	214	187	200	453	253	126%
Kuruman	182	247	194	208	424	216	104%
Fraserburg	244	230	192	222	260	38	17%
Riversdale	199	203	204	202	213	11	5%
Sea Point	19	43	70	44	54	10	23%

Source: Authors' analysis of Civil Deaths 1895–1972 database with images National Archives Pretoria (1918).

in the Acuña-Soto et al. method described above. We averaged the number of deaths per year in the three years prior to 1918 as a guide for the average number of deaths per district.

Next, we used a simple linear regression. This accounts, for instance, for population growth and consequent linear increases in the number of registered deaths per district per year that we would expect with a larger population. The linear trend from this second regression model is shown in Figure 12.8, alongside a line of equality. Figure 12.8 shows that all districts with a higher predicted mortality in 1918, based on the linear trend, had a higher actual mortality in 1918 than would be expected if the linear trend continued. The actual mortality for districts with larger populations prior to the pandemic was not only higher than the linear trend predicted; the discrepancy was much bigger than for districts with smaller populations. For example, Queenstown saw 82 per cent more deaths in 1918 than the linear trend predicted, while Fraserburg saw 53 per cent more deaths. This finding contrasts with the work by Acuña-Soto et al. which found that smaller cities saw greater excess mortality than larger ones in the United States.[23]

---

[23] Ibid.

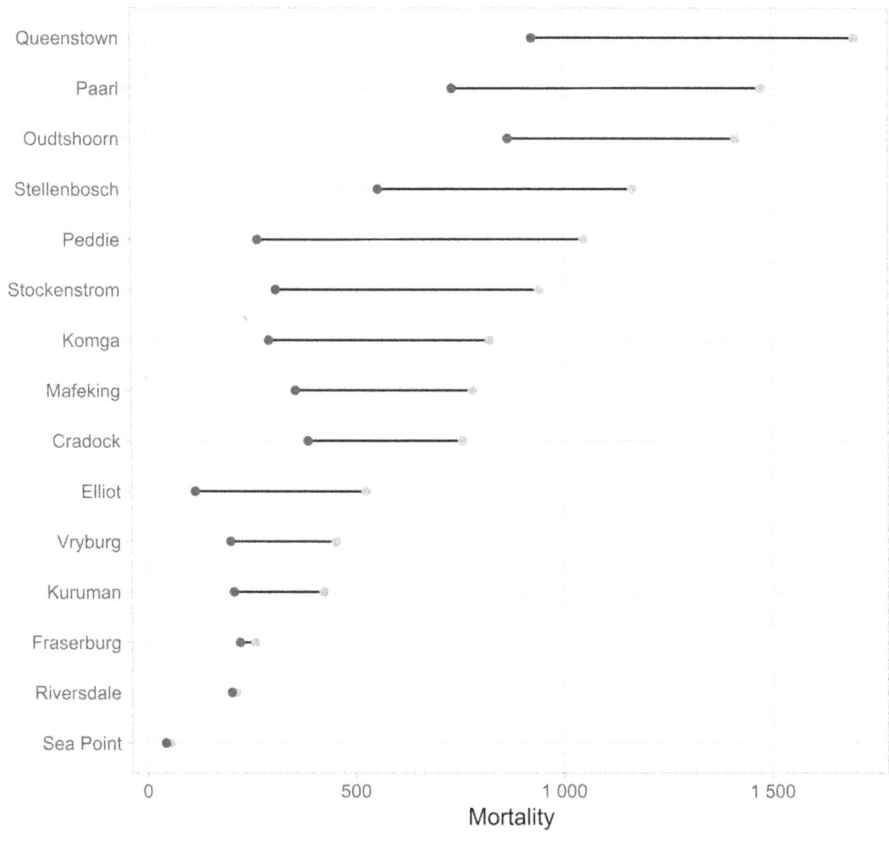

Figure 12.7 Excess mortality based on methodology by Acuña-Soto et al.
Source: Authors' analysis of Civil Deaths 1895–1972 database with images National Archives Pretoria (1918).
Note: Length of line represents absolute excess mortality.

Finally, we used a regression model created by Serfling to account for the seasonality of respiratory diseases like flu and influenza. Serfling's method uses cyclic regression to model the weekly proportion of deaths from pneumonia and influenza and to define an epidemic threshold and accounts for seasonal variation.[24]

Figure 12.9 shows the mean and predicted ranges of expected mortality based on the three methods, and the actual pandemic mortality. The districts with larger populations also have a larger range in the mortality predictions based on these methods; in other words, the predictions vary more widely for the larger districts. Oudtshoorn has the

---

[24] R.E. Serfling, 'Methods for Current Statistical Analysis of Excess Pneumonia-influenza Deaths', *Public Health Reports* 78, no. 6 (1963): 644–54.

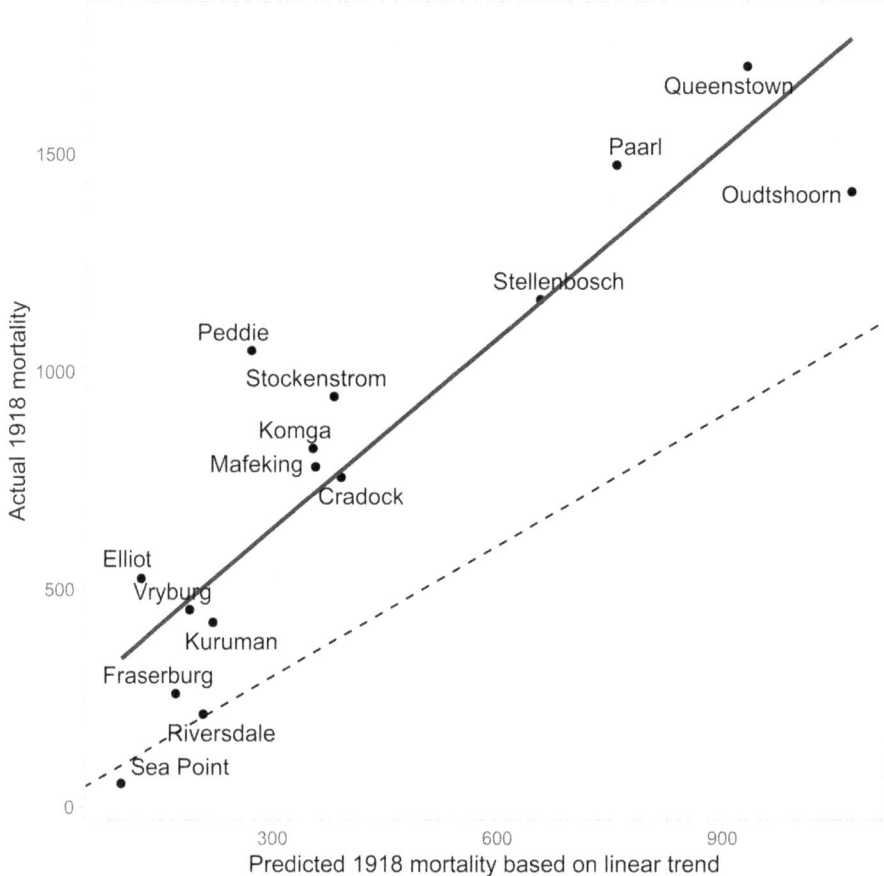

Figure 12.8 Linear trend for predicted and excess mortality.
Source: Authors' analysis of Civil Deaths 1895–1972 database with images National Archives Pretoria (1918).
Note: Dotted line is line of equality and solid line is line of best fit.

largest range, followed by Paarl and Queenstown. Again, Peddie and Elliot have the highest excess mortality, as can be seen by the gap between the estimates for the predicted and actual mortality.

In Table 12.5 we show the excess mortality based on a combination of the three regression methods. The estimates of excess mortality are similar in magnitude to those produced by the Acuña-Soto et al. method. The excess mortality percentages are lower than those produced by the SAMRC method (because that method uses a lower denominator in calculating the percentages).

In Figure 12.10 we compare the ranking of each district in terms of percentage excess mortality, calculated using each of our three methods. Elliot, with an excess mortality ranging from 357 per cent to 1,209 per cent depending on the method used, has the highest percentage excess mortality across all three methods, and Peddie the second

Death during the Influenza of 1918

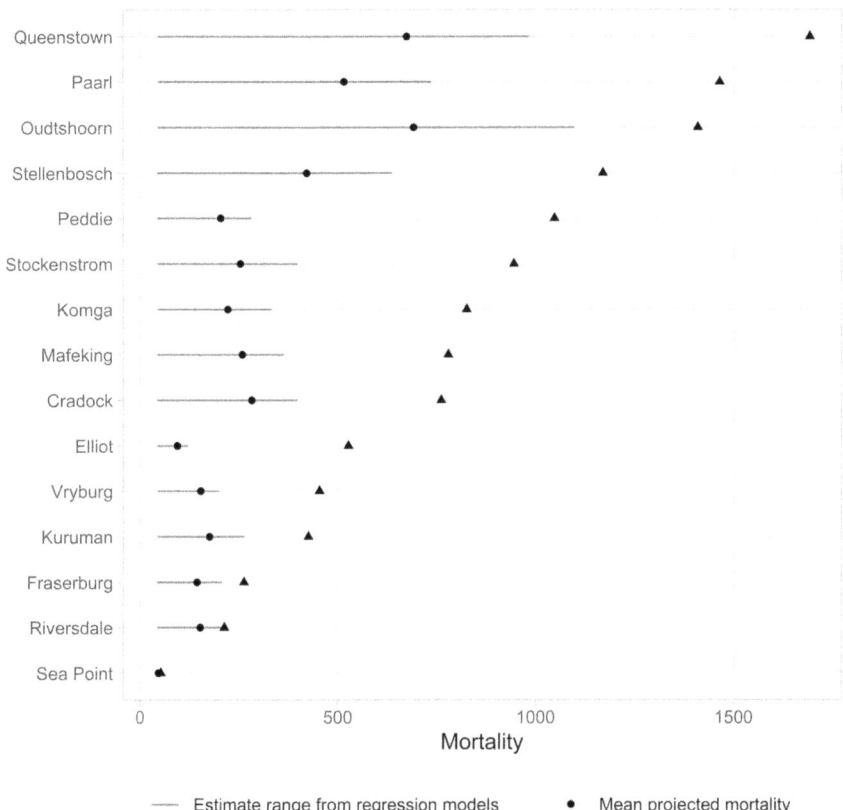

Figure 12.9 Excess mortality based on ensembled regression methods
Source: Authors' analysis of Civil Deaths 1895–1972 database with images National Archives Pretoria (1918).

Table 12.5 Excess mortality based on ensembled regression methods.

District	Observed deaths	Projected deaths	Excess mortality	Percentage excess mortality
Queenstown	1,693	886	807	91%
Paarl	1,465	675	790	117%
Peddie	1,048	259	789	305%
Stockenstrom	946	325	621	191%
Stellenbosch	1,170	550	620	113%
Komga	827	283	544	192%
Oudtshoorn	1,410	910	500	55%
Mafeking	781	332	449	135%
Elliot	527	112	415	371%

Quantitative History and Uncharted People

District	Observed deaths	Projected deaths	Excess mortality	Percentage excess mortality
Cradock	763	364	399	110%
Vryburg	455	191	264	138%
Kuruman	427	220	207	94%
Fraserburg	264	178	86	48%
Riversdale	214	189	25	13%
Sea Point	54	51	3	6%

Source: Authors' analysis of Civil Deaths 1895–1972 database with images National Archives Pretoria (1918).

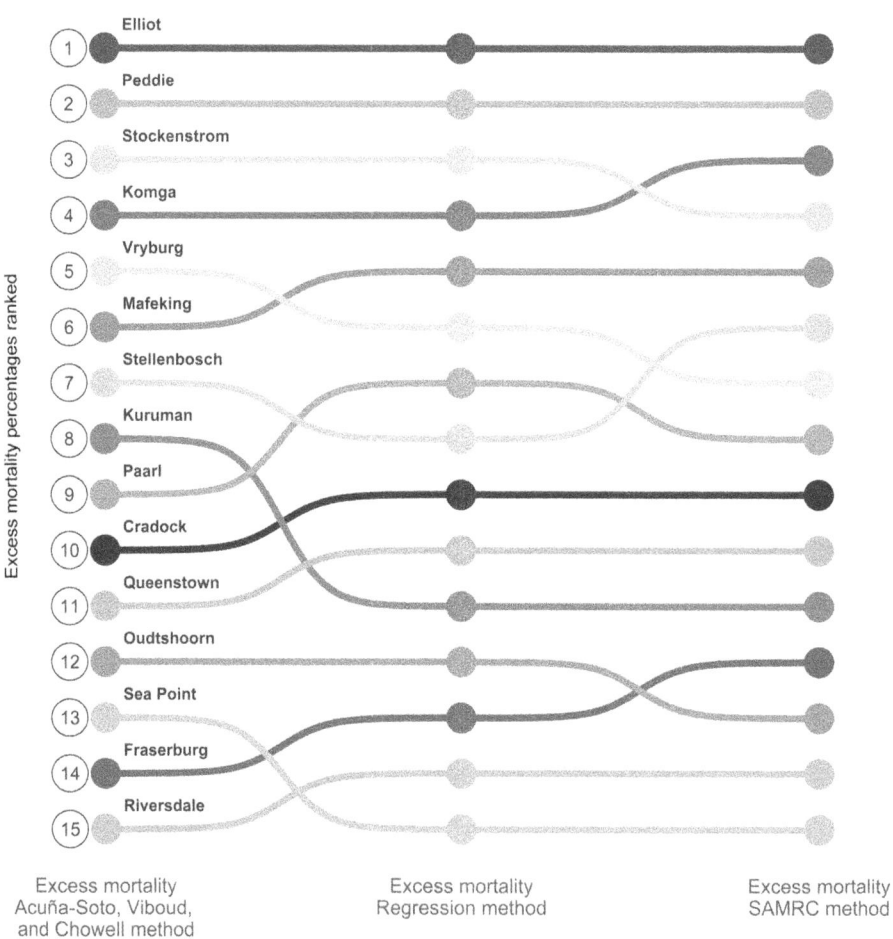

Figure 12.10 Bump chart of district ranking across our three methods or calculating excess morality.
Source: Authors' analysis of Civil Deaths 1895–1972 database with images National Archives Pretoria (1918).

highest, again irrespective of method. Stockenstroom and Komga switch positions between third and fourth when we move from the Acuña-Soto et al. method to the regression and SAMRC methods. The takeaway is that while there is some movement across the rankings, by and large there is congruency in the ranking of districts by excess mortality.

Counting deaths from respiratory illnesses

By estimating excess mortality using three different methods based on individual-level data, and finding congruence between these methods, we were able to produce a reliable estimate of the death toll from the pandemic in our fifteen districts that we could compare with previously published official reports. We were also able to compare our excess mortality figures against mortality figures based on the rich individual-level data from the death certificates – specifically, the deaths that include a respiratory illness in the 'cause of death' field on the death certificate.

To quantify the number of deaths caused by respiratory illnesses we used a simple natural language processing approach, correlating words that are used together in the cause of death field. This method helped to reduce the variation caused by the use of different languages, delays in information reaching certain towns and inconsistent spelling. We wanted to ensure that we classified deaths caused by respiratory diseases during the pandemic as deaths due to the pandemic. Figure 12.11 shows a network plot of words that are frequently used together in the cause of death field, throughout the period 1915–20. The clusters include words that are some of the most highly correlated (with a correlation score above a threshold of 0.15).

We note that *Spaanse griep*, the Afrikaans for 'Spanish flu', is prominent in the network plot. Other clusters include the terms 'epidemic', 'influenza' and 'Spanish', as well as 'inflammation' and 'lungs'. To find all the terms that were indicative of respiratory diseases, we took these clusters, filtered for terms that clearly represented respiratory diseases, and then classified any death during the pandemic period that included these terms, or any of their highly correlated terms, in the cause of death field as a death due to the pandemic. Looking back to Table 12.2 which illustrated the classification problem at hand, this method classifies deaths reported only as caused by 'influenza' as pandemic deaths, as well as those including the terms 'pneumonia' and *Spaanse griep* during the pandemic period. However, other terms that appear in Table 12.2, for example 'old age', 'convulsions' and 'teething' are not classified as pandemic deaths.

To contextualise our estimates, we compared our combined excess mortality figures for each district and the number of deaths we recorded as caused by respiratory diseases with the official figures from the Influenza Epidemic Commission used by Phillips.[25] Figure 12.12 compares the absolute number of deaths in each district from the three sources we have discussed. The black bars indicate the number of deaths cited in Phillips. The light grey bars indicate the respiratory deaths identified using text analysis. The dark

---

[25] Phillips, 'Black October'.

Quantitative History and Uncharted People

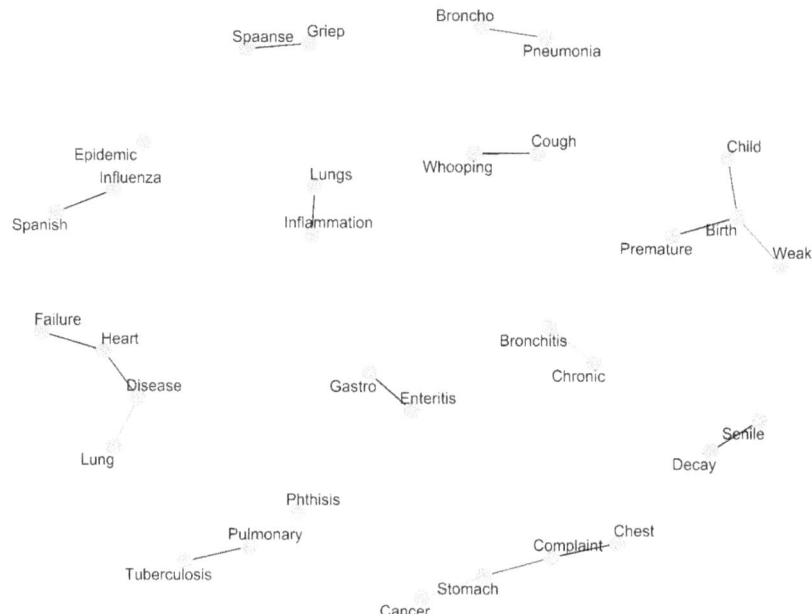

Figure 12.11 Correlation between terms used in cause of death.
Source: Authors' analysis of Civil Deaths 1895–1972 database with images National Archives Pretoria (1918).
Note: darker lines between nodes indicate stronger correlations.

grey bars sandwiched between these indicate the numbers of excess deaths by district, as calculated using our combination of methods described above.

We observe that in the districts with larger populations the estimates of the Influenza Epidemic Commission cited in Phillips are larger than both the number of respiratory deaths and the mean excess mortality we calculated with our three methods. In contrast, in the smaller districts, such as Oudtshoorn, Elliot and Kuruman, the numbers of deaths from respiratory illness recorded during the pandemic are larger than the estimates cited in Phillips. This could indicate undercounting on the part of the Influenza Epidemic Commission in the smaller districts. In the larger districts, two factors could explain the discrepancy between the Commission's estimates and ours calculated from the death certificates. One, which we mentioned earlier, and which Phillips thought was the case, is significant under-recording of deaths in the large districts. Capacity constraints could be the reason: the death toll may have been so severe that families either did not have the resources to visit towns to record deaths or that commissioners themselves fell ill and the recording of deaths ceased temporarily.[26] The other is that the Influenza Epidemic Commission overestimated excess mortality in the larger districts, notably in places like Queenstown, Peddie and Mafeking that had large black populations where information about the mortality rate may have been less reliable.

---

[26] The latter explanation seems unlikely, as we did not find evidence in the records that death registrations temporarily ceased.

Death during the Influenza of 1918

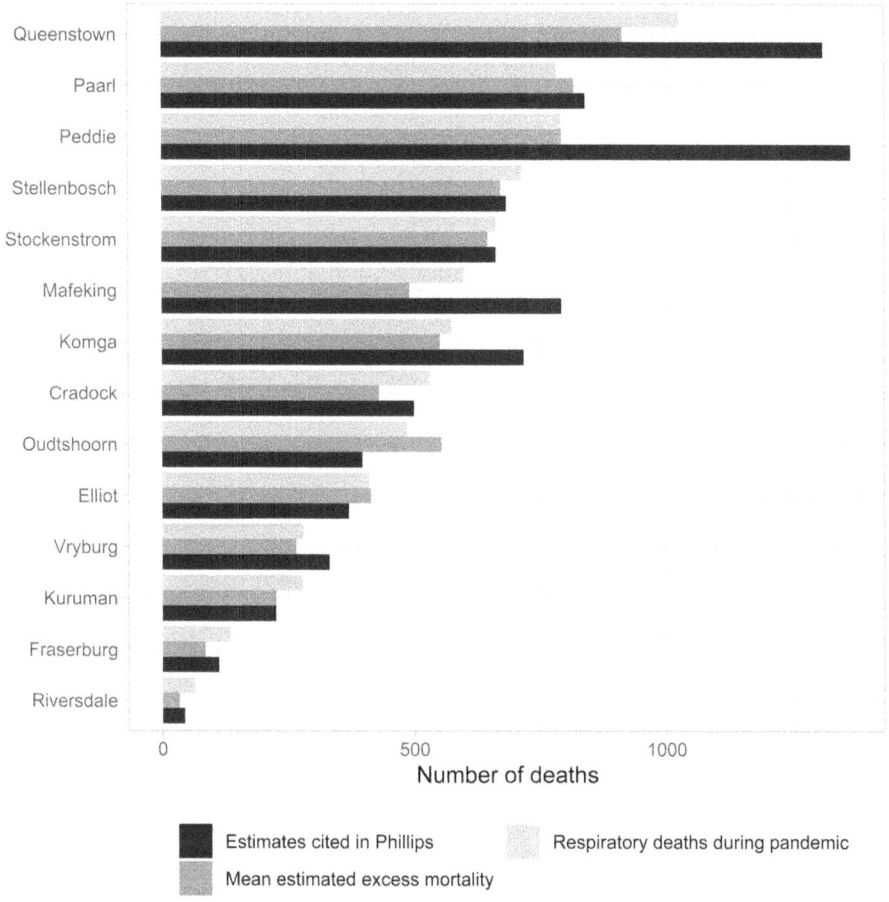

Figure 12.12 Comparison of excess mortality estimates, respiratory deaths and government estimates.
Source: Authors' analysis of Civil Deaths 1895–1972 database with images National Archives Pretoria (1918).

In the remainder of the chapter we discuss our findings about mortality and calculations of the mortality rates based on our estimates of respiratory deaths; estimates, we believe, that most accurately reflect pandemic deaths.

Correlates of mortality

Pandemic mortality was not randomly distributed. Our aim in what follows is to identify factors that might be predictive of pandemic mortality. This is not only of historical value; an understanding of the factors that predict pandemic mortality could help to set policy priorities in future pandemic episodes.

Quantitative History and Uncharted People

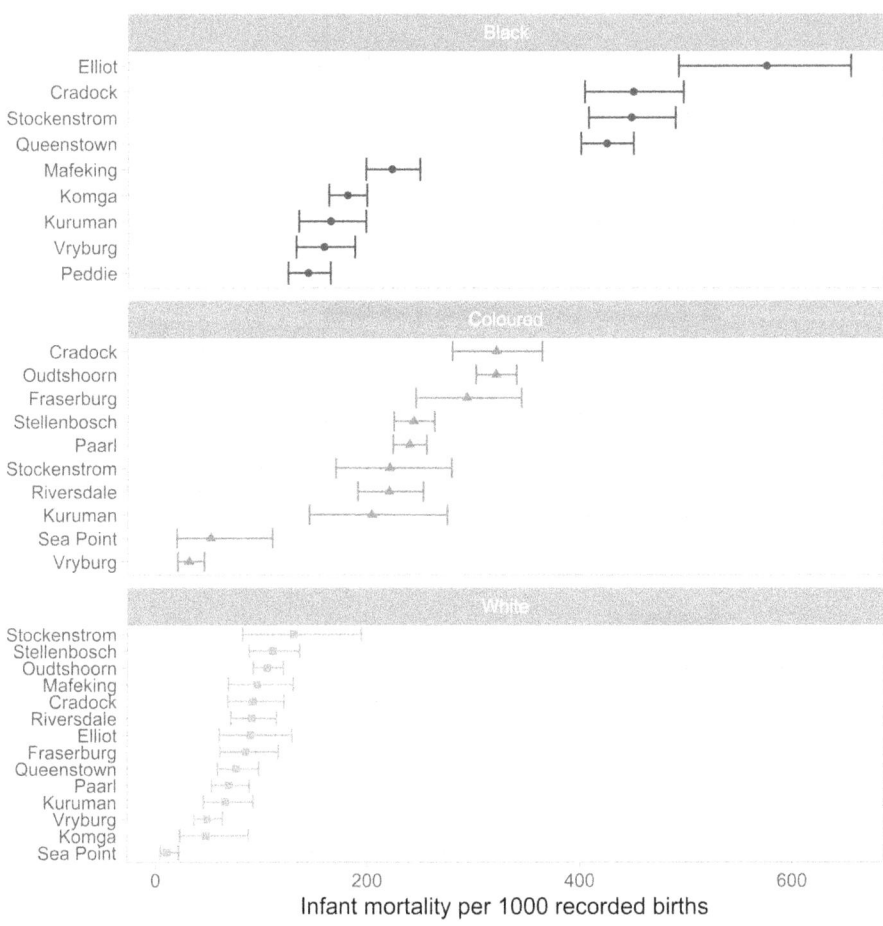

Figure 12.13 Infant mortality per 1000 children, with confidence band.
Source: Authors' analysis of Civil Deaths 1895–1972 database with images National Archives Pretoria (1918).

Our hypothesis was that communities with poorer health outcomes before a pandemic were likely to experience higher levels of mortality during the 1918 influenza. We tested two measures of pre-existing health in the fifteen districts which constitute the sample. The first uses infant and child mortality statistics as a proxy for the level of existing health and healthcare in a district. The second assesses mortality from influenza and pneumonia prior to the pandemic to gauge levels of health in different communities.

Infant and child mortality

We began with a proxy for pre-existing health in a district by calculating the infant mortality rate prior to the pandemic in each district. We divided the recorded infant deaths between January 1915 and December 1917 by the population of infants in each district as recorded in the Statistics of Population: Vital and Health Statistics of 1916.[27] We extrapolated the full population of infants for all three years by multiplying the 1916 figure by three. This could be criticised as unrepresentative of births in the two previous and following years, but it is the best data available and not an unreasonable assumption to work with.

Figure 12.13 shows the number of deaths per 1,000 births by race in each district between 1915 and 1917. Here infants are classified as less than one year old, to be comparable with the number of births per year reported in the statistics. There is heterogeneity in infant mortality by race and district, such that this may be correlated with pandemic mortality rates. While the infant mortality rates may appear very high,

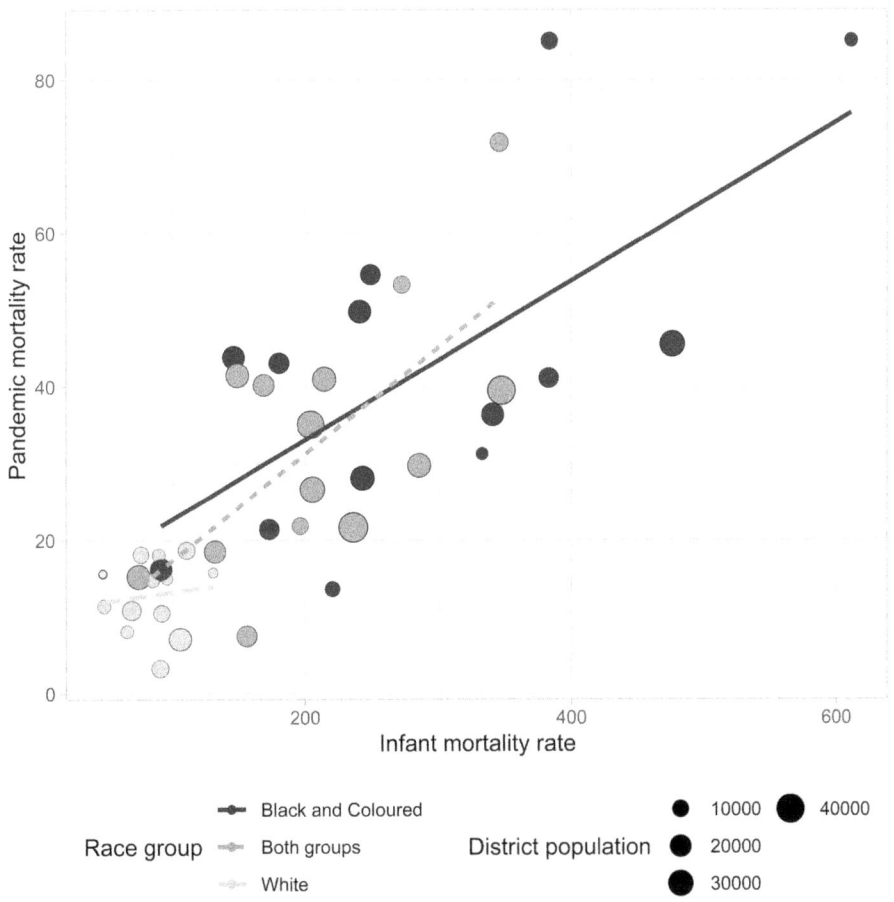

Figure 12.14 Scatterplot and linear fit of infant and pandemic mortality by district.
Source: Authors' analysis of Civil Deaths 1895–1972 database with images National Archives Pretoria (1918).

[27]Statistics of Population, Vital and Health Statistics of 1916 (Government of South Africa, 1916).

Quantitative History and Uncharted People

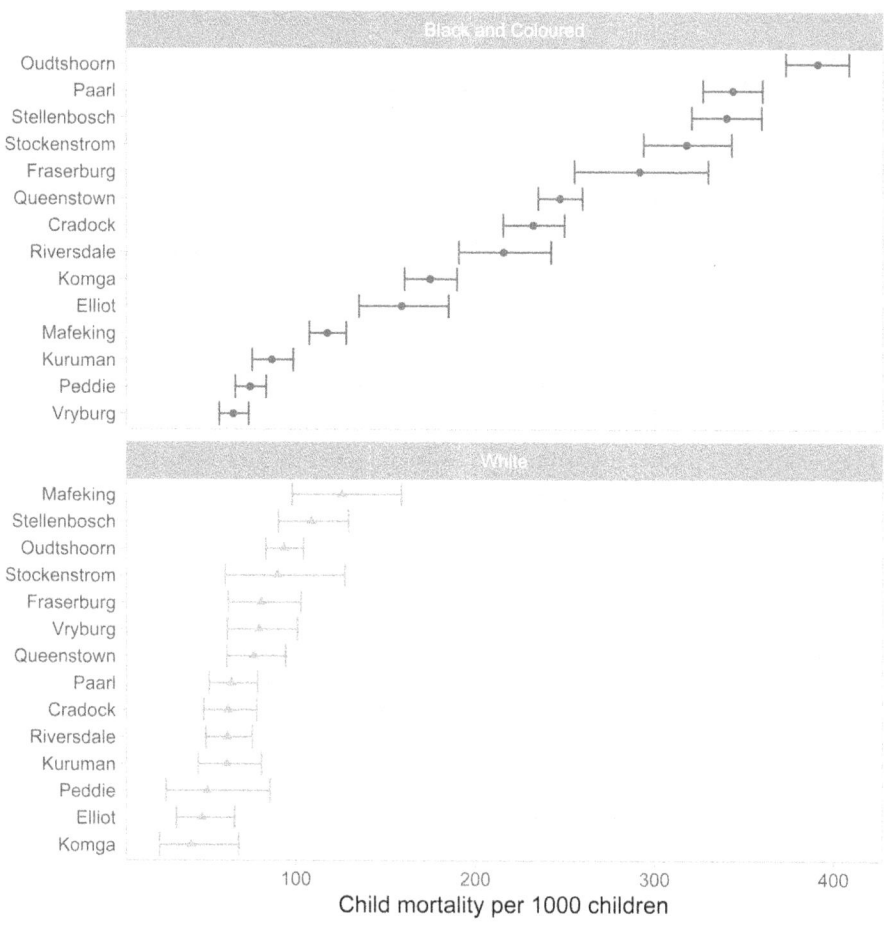

Figure 12.15 Child mortality per 1000 children by race.
Source: Authors' analysis of Civil Deaths 1895–1972 database with images National Archives Pretoria (1918).

it is possible that there is under-reporting in the number of births by district, though the death of a child is so tragic that it is rarely unrecorded. Even if births were under-recorded, these estimates serve as a proxy for levels of health in a community which we can correlate with mortality rates during the pandemic.

Figure 12.14 shows the relationship between infant mortality rates (detailed above) and pandemic mortality rates, calculated by dividing the number of respiratory deaths from the death certificates by the population of individuals by race in each district from the 1911 census (in the case of black and coloured individuals) and the 1918 census (in the case of white individuals, conducted just prior to the pandemic). The aggregation of black and coloured mortality rates is a function of the denominator (population) reported in the census in aggregate. Figure 12.15 shows a strong linear correlation between infant

Table 12.6 Association between infant mortality and pandemic mortality.

	Pandemic mortality rate					
	(1)			(2)		
Variable	N	Beta[1]	SE[2a]	N	Beta[1]	SE[2a]
Constant	14	0.00	0.010	28	0.04***	0.005
Infant mortality rate	14	0.14**	0.046	28	0.02	0.012
Race				28		
Black and Coloured					—	—
White					-0.03***	0.006

[1]*$p<0.1$; **$p<0.05$; ***$p<0.01$
[2]SE = Standard Error
[a]Heteroskedastic SE's from Sandwich package

mortality rates and pandemic mortality rates across districts for black and coloured individuals, and across groups. The slope of the linear fit is lower for white residents (the lighter dashed line) of fourteen districts.[28] This implies that there is a weaker association between infant mortality and pandemic mortality for the white population than for the black and coloured population.

Table 12.6 shows the relationship between infant mortality rates and pandemic mortality rates by district. Before we controlled for race we found a strong positive correlation between the two rates across districts, with a 5 per cent significance level and a slope coefficient of 0.139, but no significant correlation after we accounted for race. This means that among the entire population, we find that districts with higher infant mortality prior to the pandemic, indicating poorer pre-existing health conditions, also have higher mortality during the pandemic.[29]

In a similar way, we assessed the correlation between child mortality and pandemic mortality. We calculated child mortality as the number of children under five years of age, recorded in the death certificates, who died prior to the pandemic, divided by the population below five years of age from the 1911 census for black and coloured individuals and the 1918 census for white individuals. The results are shown in Figure 12.16.

Figure 12.15 shows that the child mortality rates varied widely across districts, and that, on average, child mortality was lower for white populations than for black and coloured populations. This heterogeneity in child mortality, as a proxy for the levels of

---

[28] We could not include Sea Point because that district was reported together with the figures from Cape Town in both censuses.

[29] In conducting these tests, we assume that there is no correlation between the two variables: infant mortality and pandemic mortality. A statistically significant result means that we can reject the hypothesis that there is no relationship between the two in favour of the alternative that there is indeed a correlation between infant mortality and pandemic mortality. A 5 per cent significance level means we will make a type 1 error, or erroneously reject the null hypothesis, about one in every twenty times.

Table 12.7 Association between child mortality and pandemic mortality by district.

	Pandemic mortality rate					
	(1)			(2)		
Variable	N	Beta[1]	SE[2a]	N	Beta[1]	SE[2a]
Constant	14	0.02	0.011	28	0.03***	0.009
Child mortality rate	14	0.09	0.058	28	0.07*	0.038
Race				28		
Black and Coloured					—	—
White					-0.02**	0.008

[1]*p<0.1; **p<0.05; ***p<0.01
[2]SE = Standard Error
[a]Heteroskedastic SE's from Sandwich package

pre-existing healthcare in a district, may explain in part the mortality rates by district during the pandemic.

Table 12.7 shows the statistical relationship between child mortality prior to the pandemic and the mortality rate in a district during the pandemic. After accounting for race, we found that child mortality was correlated with pandemic mortality at the 10 per cent level, with a slope coefficient of 0.066. This means that districts with higher rates of child mortality prior to the pandemic also had higher mortality during the pandemic.

The takeaway from this section on infant and child mortality is that pre-existing health conditions in a district mattered for mortality rates during the pandemic, and that in the case of child mortality these conditions mattered even beyond the difference in mortality rates by race.

Influenza and pneumonia mortality

Acuña-Soto et al. showed how influenza and pneumonia mortality prior to the pandemic was predictive of mortality rates during the pandemic in sixty-six large cities in the United States.[30] We use their method here to see if the same was true in the Cape Province. We first calculated the pre-pandemic mortality rates by district from influenza and from pneumonia, and from both. Figure 12.16 shows that while the lines separated by race are lower, there is still a strong correlation between pre-existing influenza and pneumonia mortality rates and the pandemic mortality rate in each district. The strongest correlation appears to be in the aggregated sample.

---

[30] Acuña-Soto, et al., 'Influenza and Pneumonia Mortality'.

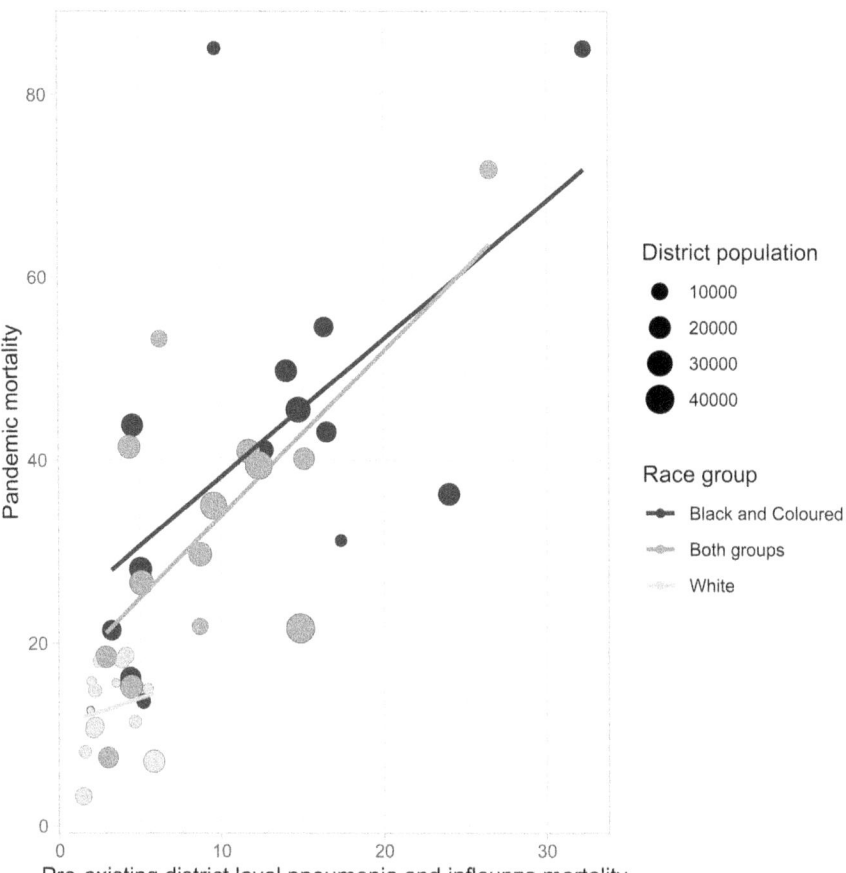

Figure 12.16 Scatterplot and linear fit of pneumonia mortality and pandemic mortality by district.
Source: Authors' analysis of Civil Deaths 1895–1972 database with images National Archives Pretoria (1918).

Table 12.8 shows that, after controlling for race, mortality rates from influenza, pneumonia and both conditions are highly correlated with mortality rates during the pandemic, at the 5 per cent level and below. The combination is significantly correlated with pandemic mortality rates at the 1 per cent level.

The conclusion is that the districts with high mortality from these respiratory conditions prior to the pandemic saw higher mortality during the pandemic than districts with lower mortality from these conditions. In other words, pre-existing respiratory health appears important in determining mortality from the flu. Note that this result could not have been obtained by just studying aggregate health statistics, reported at the district level in censuses. Respiratory illnesses are not recorded separately in censuses. It is this additional precision that shows the benefits of using individual-level records.

Table 12.8 Association between pneumonia and influenza mortality prior to the pandemic and pandemic mortality.

	Pandemic mortality rate								
	(1)			(2)			(3)		
Variable	N	Beta[1]	SE[2a]	N	Beta[1]	SE[2a]	N	Beta[1]	SE[2]
Constant	26	0.03***	0.006	28	0.03***	0.006	28	0.02***	0.007
Influenza mortality	26	3.2**	1.44						
Pneumonia mortality				28	1.4**	0.511			
Pneumonia and influenza mortality							28	1.5***	0.431
Race	26			28			28		
Black and Coloured		—	—		—	—		—	—
White		-0.02***	0.007		-0.02***	0.007		-0.02**	0.007

[1]*$p<0.1$; **$p<0.05$; ***$p<0.01$

[2]SE = Standard Error

[a]Heteroskedastic SE's from Sandwich package

Government response[31]

This was a period that saw little or no government intervention, though eventually some measures similar to those used in the Covid-19 pandemic were implemented. The individual death certificates not only provided evidence on the early spread and severity of the deaths from the disease; they also helped us to test how effective the various forms of government response were. Before explaining how we did this, we first consider the steps taken by the local and national government.

Phillips argues that the South African government's response to the Spanish flu was insufficient.[32] Attendees at a meeting in the Pretoria Town Hall on 4 November 1918 expressed their 'disappointment and disgust' at the government's 'lack of sense of responsibility in regard to the present loss of life throughout the Union'.[33] In the absence of a national Ministry of Health, and with little guidance from the central government, responses to the flu crisis were organised at municipal level. Some municipalities were better equipped than others. The attendees at the Pretoria meeting were particularly concerned that the absence of central government intervention was having a disproportionate effect on black citizens who lived outside the municipal areas.

---

[31]This section is largely the result of research and written work by Kelsey Lemon, Kate Ekama and Kara Dimitruk.

[32]H. Phillips, *Epidemics: The Story of South Africa's Five Most Lethal Human Diseases*. (Athens, US: Ohio University Press, 2012).

[33]'Nothing Doing on Saturday', *Rand Daily Mail*, 4 November 1918, 5.

Town Councils and Boards of Health put ad hoc measures in place to try to curb the spread of the virus, to look after the poor, ill and dying, and to bury the dead. Municipalities closed schools, limited transport and sought to improve medical responses. Phillips says the interventions, or lack thereof, had a disproportionate racial impact.[34] Knowledge about the scale and scope of the policies implemented and whether they mitigated the spread of the Spanish flu or left groups unprotected is currently limited, but using newspaper evidence we can provide an initial documentation of the variety and timing of local health measures. Ideally, we should construct a detailed non-pharmaceutical intervention (NPI) series for each of the towns in our sample to investigate whether and how public interventions influenced the Spanish flu spread and mortality across South Africa, similar to the series constructed by Markel et al. for the United States.[35] We leave that for future researchers.

We collected notices and reports of NPIs undertaken by Town Councils and Health Boards from three daily newspapers, the *Rand Daily Mail, Eastern Province Herald* and *Mafeking Mail and Protectorate Guardian*. Each paper focused on its own geographical area but also reported on measures undertaken elsewhere in the Union (receiving information through a Reuters telegram). We collected all items referring to government policies in these three papers for one week during the outbreak of the flu (14–18 October 1918) and for one week towards the end of the epidemic (1–9 November 1918).

Examples of social and spatial distancing measures that were implemented and lifted at different times are shown in Figures 12.17 and 12.18. The timeline in Figure 12.17 shows that local and provincial governments across towns in South Africa, from Heilbron to Cape Town, implemented a variety of NPIs to mitigate the mortality effects of the epidemic and provide medical support and economic relief. This suggests that towns in our sample would have taken similar action. Figure 12.17 shows that local governments implemented some NPIs and economic policies that are similar to the policies adopted by the South African government in 2020: the closure of schools, churches and centres of entertainment, cancellation of civic and organised labour meetings, restrictions on movement or immigration, limitations on retailers and libraries' operating hours and changes to the healthcare system.

Various other policies were also implemented. Economic measures were considered in a number of localities. Mafeking and Port Elizabeth, for example, created local relief funds to help the poor and suffering during the crisis. Authorities in Beaufort West sought help to continue running a soup kitchen, an effort which became increasingly difficult as the number of cases was constantly increasing, while helpers were diminishing. Local governments also sought to improve medical support by calling for volunteer nurses, turning churches and town halls into hospitals, and improving the ambulance services.

---

[34] Phillips, 'Black October'; Phillips, *Epidemics*.

[35] H. Markel, et al., 'Nonpharmaceutical Interventions Implemented by US Cities during the 1918–1919 Influenza Pandemic', *Journal of the American Medical Association* 298, no. 6 (2007).

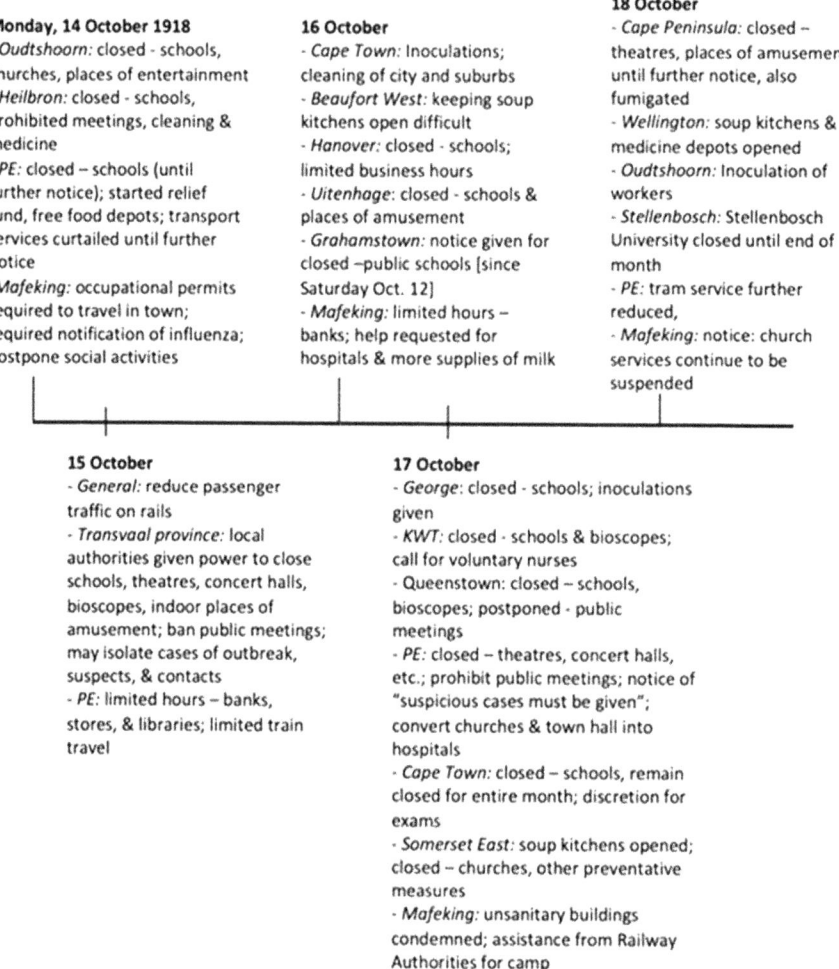

Figure 12.17 Sketch of local government policies adopted during 'outbreak' week, 14 October to 18 October 1918.

Sources: Rand Daily Mail, 14 October to 18 October 1918; Eastern Province Herald, 14 October to 18 October 1918; Mafeking Mail and Protectorate Guardian, 14 October to 18 October 1918.

Notes: Timeline shows a sketch of the types of policies adopted or continued to be implemented 14 October to 18 October 1918. If a specific town is named, policy implemented by the municipal government (Town Council). PE: Port Elizabeth, KWT: King Williams Town.

Figure 12.18 shows how measures were lifted during a week towards the end of the outbreak. Newspapers reported discussions by municipalities about lifting NPIs and noted when an NPI was lifted. For example, in Mafeking on 1 November 1918, Town Council members were concerned about the premature lifting of NPIs because they thought this would lead to a resurgence of infections. They recognised the trade-off that

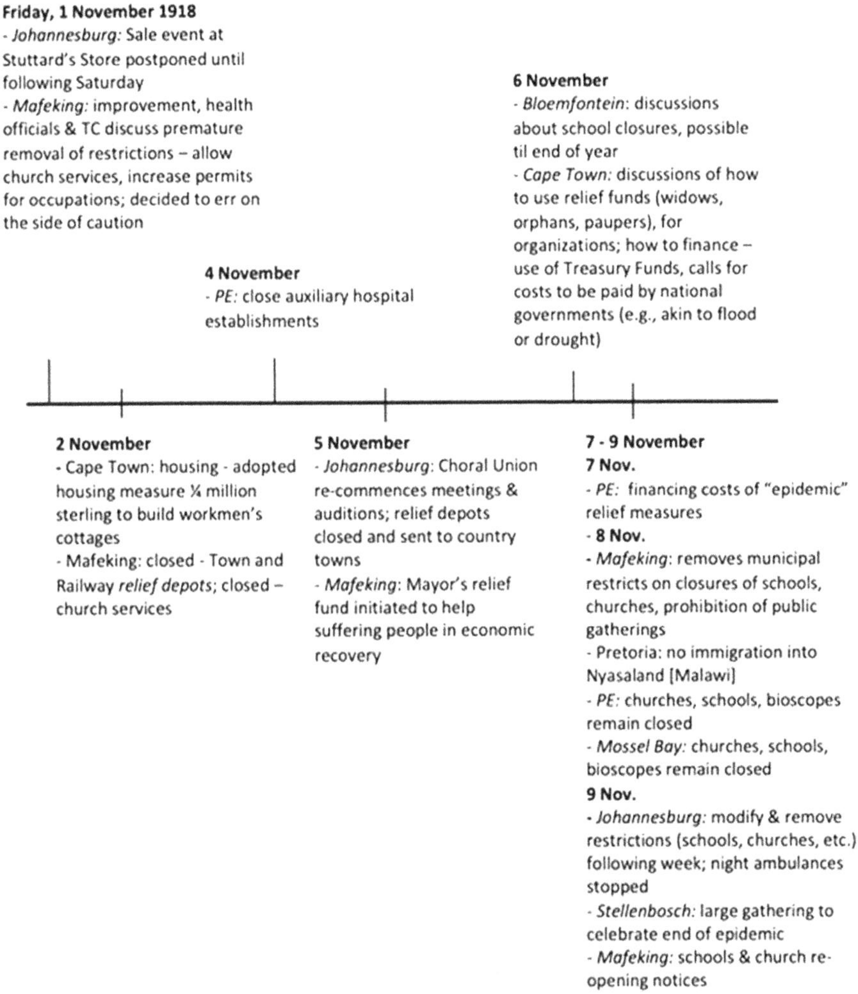

Friday, 1 November 1918
- *Johannesburg:* Sale event at Stuttard's Store postponed until following Saturday
- *Mafeking:* improvement, health officials & TC discuss premature removal of restrictions – allow church services, increase permits for occupations; decided to err on the side of caution

4 November
- *PE:* close auxiliary hospital establishments

6 November
- *Bloemfontein:* discussions about school closures, possible til end of year
- *Cape Town:* discussions of how to use relief funds (widows, orphans, paupers), for organizations; how to finance – use of Treasury Funds, calls for costs to be paid by national governments (e.g., akin to flood or drought)

2 November
- Cape Town: housing - adopted housing measure ¼ million sterling to build workmen's cottages
- Mafeking: closed - Town and Railway *relief depots*; closed – church services

5 November
- *Johannesburg:* Choral Union re-commences meetings & auditions; relief depots closed and sent to country towns
- *Mafeking:* Mayor's relief fund initiated to help suffering people in economic recovery

7 - 9 November
7 Nov.
- *PE:* financing costs of "epidemic" relief measures
8 Nov.
- *Mafeking:* removes municipal restricts on closures of schools, churches, prohibition of public gatherings
- *Pretoria:* no immigration into Nyasaland [Malawi]
- *PE:* churches, schools, bioscopes remain closed
- *Mossel Bay:* churches, schools, bioscopes remain closed
9 Nov.
- *Johannesburg:* modify & remove restrictions (schools, churches, etc.) following week; night ambulances stopped
- *Stellenbosch:* large gathering to celebrate end of epidemic
- *Mafeking:* schools & church re-opening notices

Figure 12.18 Sketch of local government policies removed towards the end of the epidemic, 1 November to 9 November 1918.
Sources: Rand Daily Mail, 1 November to 9 November 1918; Eastern Province Herald, 1 November to 9 November 1918; Mafeking Mail and Protectorate Guardian, 1 November to 9 November 1918.
Notes: Timeline shows a sketch of the types of policies discontinued or discussion of discontinuance, 1 November to 9 November 1918. If a specific town is named, policy implemented by the municipal government (Town Councils). PE: Port Elizabeth, KWT: King Williams Town.

is echoed today: continuation of strict NPIs caused hardships. After receiving further evidence that the epidemic had slowed sufficiently, they decided to lift restrictions on schools, churches and entertainment centres later that week (on 8 November).

A key policy discussion, that we know little about, concerned the public financing of emergency measures. The newspapers all report that municipalities were worried they would not be reimbursed by the central government for losses due to the emergency measures. In Circular No. 17, the central government said they were prepared to assist municipalities financially only 'to the extent of refunding one-half of the expenditure which the Public Health Department is satisfied was reasonable and necessarily incurred in carrying out measures approved by it'.[36] Municipalities argued that the epidemic was similar to a national disaster, such as a flood or drought, and thus the central government should cover all costs incurred by municipalities. The Mafeking Town Council, for example, considered that 'any action on which they decided should be taken in conjunction with the other Municipalities'.[37] With regard to Circular No 17, it was of the opinion that the epidemic 'was nothing but a national disaster' and the government 'should bear the whole of the expenses the Town had incurred'.[38] It is thus instructive for policymakers today to know how the financing of the costs of emergency relief undertaken by municipalities during the Spanish flu was resolved and whether it had economic and political consequences in subsequent years.[39]

Conclusion

When Covid-19 arrived in South Africa in March 2020, policymakers were keen to understand the likely predictors of pandemic mortality. Although the Spanish flu had been studied extensively, the factors most likely to predict influenza deaths were poorly understood. We used more than 40,000 death certificates, first to calculate excess mortality and second to identify the factors that are predictive of pandemic mortality. We found that excess mortality in conjunction with deaths recorded as caused by respiratory illnesses provided a more reasonable and more expansive quantification of the number of South Africans who died during the 1918 pandemic.

Our study could be extended in several directions. First, and most obviously, we could add more districts to the analysis. The considerable variation across districts would help improve the precision of our estimates. Including more districts would also allow us to identify the districts that are outliers, at either the top or the bottom. Case studies of those outliers might point to the influence of non-pharmaceutical interventions at the local level, offering lessons that could help policymakers today. Another extension of our study would be to match the deceased individuals in the death certificates to the same individuals in other records, for example as spouses in the marriage records or as parents in baptism records. This would allow for a greater number of predictors, perhaps based on early life conditions like age at marriage or fertility rate.

---

[36]'Mafeking Town Council', *Mafeking Mail and Protectorate Guardian*, 2 December 1918, 3.
[37]Ibid.
[38]Ibid.
[39]De Kadt, et al., 'Causes and Consequences'.

The application of a large dataset like the early twentieth-century death certificates to previously neglected questions shows, more generally, the benefits of quantitative social science history. Without the advent of stronger computing power, new and freely available software (and an active online community that adds additional functionality) and generous financial support for the transcription of archival records, this study would not have been possible. As more historical administrative datasets are transcribed, and linked, the possibilities become endless for testing new hypotheses and revealing unsuspected trends, to help us understand and explain the world.

Bibliography

Acuña-Soto, R., C. Viboud and G. Chowell. 'Influenza and Pneumonia Mortality in 66 Large Cities in the United States in Years Surrounding the 1918 Pandemic'. *PLoS ONE* 6, no. 8 (2011): e23467.

Arthi, V. and J. Parman. 'Disease, Downturns, and Wellbeing: Economic History and the Long-run Impacts of COVID-19'. *Explorations in Economic History* 79 (2021).

De Kadt, D., J. Fourie, J. Greyling, E. Murard and J. Norling. The Causes and Consequences of the 1918 Influenza in South Africa'. Stellenbosch Working Paper Series No. WP12/2020. Department of Economics, Stellenbosch University, 2021.

Dorrington, R., D. Bradshaw, R. Laubscher, P. Groenewald and T. Moultrie. 'Predicted Numbers of Deaths by Epi-week for South Africa in 2020 and 2021'. Burden of Disease Research Unit: South African Medical Research Council, 2021, 1–11.

Eichengreen, B. *Hall of Mirrors: The Great Depression, the Great Recession, and the Uses-and Misuses-of History*. Oxford: Oxford University Press, 2015.

Fourie, J. and J. Jayes. 'Health Inequality and the 1918 Influenza in South Africa'. *World Development* 141 (2021): 105407.

Killingray, D. and H. Phillips, ed. *The Spanish Influenza Pandemic of 1918–19: New Perspectives*. London: Routledge, 2011.

Markel, H., H.B. Lipman, J.A. Navarro, A. Sloan, J.R. Michalsen, A.M. Stern and M.S. Cetron. 'Nonpharmaceutical Interventions Implemented by US Cities during the 1918–1919 Influenza Pandemic'. *Journal of the American Medical Association* 298, no. 6 (2007): 644–54.

Phillips, H. 'Black October: The Impact of the Spanish Influenza Epidemic of 1918 on South Africa'. PhD diss., University of Cape Town, Cape Town, 1984.

Phillips, H. *Epidemics: The Story of South Africa's Five Most Lethal Human Diseases*. Athens, US: Ohio University Press, 2012.

Serfling, R.E. 'Methods for Current Statistical Analysis of Excess Pneumonia-influenza Deaths'. *Public Health Reports* 78, no. 6 (1963): 494–506.

Spinney, L. *Pale Rider: The Spanish Flu of 1918 and How It Changed the World*. New York: Public Affairs, 2017.

Primary sources

Census of the Union of South Africa 1911 (Government Printer, Pretoria, 1913).
Civil Deaths 1895–1972 database with images, National Archives Pretoria (1918)

Quantitative History and Uncharted People

'South Africa, Cape Province, Civil Deaths, 1895–1972.' Database with images. FamilySearch. Available online: http://FamilySearch.org: 9 April 2020 (Department of the Interior, Registrar of Births, Marriages, and Deaths. National Archives, Pretoria).

Statistics of Population, Vital and Health Statistics of 1916 (Government of South Africa, 1916) Accessed in Stellenbosch University Library.

Rand Daily Mail, *Eastern Province Herald* and *Mafeking Mail and Protectorate Guardian*. Various items, 14 to 18 October 1918 and 1 to 9 November 1918.

CHAPTER 13
QUANTITATIVE HISTORY IN PRACTICE
Johan Fourie

In this book we have shown how quantitative approaches can help to tell the stories of people who were left out of the history books. By using methods like regression analysis, network analysis and text analysis, and simple statistical concepts like means and medians, we have demonstrated that numbers are not antithetical to writing histories 'from below'. Now that large datasets of administrative records are available and accessible, the curious scholar can answer old questions in new ways and dig up new facts that invite further research. This is exciting.

Yet the potential of such approaches can only be realised if the next generation of historians is exposed to them. Although several forces are pushing against such an education, new technologies may help. Stellenbosch University's Biography of an Uncharted People project has created resources to help nurture these skills. Quantitative approaches to history should be part and parcel of any historian's training today.

This is even more true in a country like South Africa where the prejudice of a previous regime has left sharp divisions within the education system. We see historical privilege or disadvantage reflected in students' varying ability to work with quantitative tools. The resources we make available as part of the Biography project, and those available elsewhere, are designed to remove handicaps and produce young scholars skilled in the complementary use of quantitative approaches. This, we hope, will empower a new generation to write more complete and inclusive histories.

Teaching quantitative techniques to history students

With a few exceptions, quantitative history is not on the curriculum of most history departments. This was not always the case. Around 40 per cent of American history programmes in the early 1980s offered some form of quantitative training.[1] Two textbooks appeared in the early 1970s: Dollar and Jensen's *Historian's Guide to Statistics* and Floud's *An Introduction to Quantitative Methods for Historians*.[2] It is primarily the

---

[1] A. Bogue, *Clio and the Bitch Goddess: Quantification in American Political History* (Beverley Hills: Sage Publications, 1983).

[2] C. M. Dollar and R. J. Jensen, *Historian's Guide to Statistics: Quantitative Analysis and Historical Research* (New York: Holt, Reinhart, and Winston, 1971); R. Floud, *An Introduction to Quantitative Methods for Historians* (London: Methuen, 1979).

latter that has proved popular: at the time of writing, it had run into fourteen editions.[3] By the early 1990s, three more books had appeared: Haskins and Jeffrey's *Understanding Quantitative History* (1990), Jarausch and Hardy's *Quantitative Methods for Historians* (1991) and Darcy and Rohrs's *A Guide to Quantitative History* (1995).[4] Another wave arrived in the early 2000s, with Hudson's *History by Numbers* (2000) and Feinstein and Thomas's *Making History Count* (2002).[5]

But quantitative history teaching was on the decline. Where it remained, it had become part of a much broader curriculum for 'digital history' or the 'digital humanities'. As Crymble explains in *Technology and the Historian*, the opening of mass-digitised archives during the early twentieth century 'would revolutionise access to primary sources' and shift the emphasis from quantification to reading and analysing digital texts.[6] The title of Cohen and Rosenzweig's widely prescribed 2005 book, *Digital History: A Guide to Gathering, Preserving, and Presenting the Past on the Web*, suggests a shift in emphasis away from quantification towards digitisation and, in particular, coding. Computational history had displaced quantitative history.

Since *Making History Count*, only one book on quantitative methods for historians has appeared, Lemercier and Zalc's wonderfully accessible *Quantitative Methods in the Humanities*.[7] Yet its reach has been limited. In a summary article, Lemercier and Zalc note that 'quantification in history has not yet recovered from past excesses: in many circles, it still has a bad reputation or is considered extinct'.[8]

There are both demand-side and supply-side reasons for the lack of quantitative training. According to Lemercier and Zalc, young historians 'probably have no incentive to learn non-standard quantification methods; many journals and hiring committees value standard methods above all'.[9] In short, students are not rewarded for mastering these methods, nor are faculty expected to use these methods in their publications. In *Technology and the Historian*, Crymble describes an interaction with a PhD student of African history in the United States. The student asks (on Twitter) how she can be expected to teach herself topics as diverse as textual analysis, statistics and data visualisation, when 'my committee doesn't count this work until it's in a neat little narrative with bow on top'.[10]

---

[3] A. Crymble, *Technology and the Historian: Transformations in the Digital Age* (Urbana: University of Illinois Press, 2021).

[4] L. Haskins and K. Jeffrey, *Understanding Quantitative History* (Cambridge, US: MIT Press, 1990).

[5] P. Hudson, *History by Numbers: An Introduction to Quantitative Approaches* (London: Bloomsbury, 2000).

[6] Crymble, *Technology and the Historian*, 122.

[7] C. Lemercier and C. Zalc, *Quantitative Methods in the Humanities: An Introduction* (Charlottesville: University of Virginia Press, 2019).

[8] C. Lemercier and C. Zalc, 'Back to the Sources: Practicing and Teaching Quantitative History in the 2020s', *Capitalism: A Journal of History and Economics* 2, no. 2 (2021): 473–508.

[9] Ibid.

[10] Crymble, *Technology and the Historian*, 108.

Of course, not all historical research can be quantitative, nor should it be, but surely it need not all be exclusively qualitative? Floud answered this fifty years ago: 'Quantitative questions complement qualitative questions, and quantitative evidence complements qualitative evidence; neither can replace the other, and neither can pretend to comprehend the whole of historical study.'[11]

One major challenge, however, and one that has not received the attention it deserves, is on the supply side: many history students fear numbers, a fear often exacerbated by not having done mathematics in high school. Students often choose the humanities precisely because of their poor performance in high school mathematics and perceived inability to cope with the subject. The consequence is that few first-year history students have either the competence or the willingness to master quantitative tools.

Take the first-year cohort of history students at Stellenbosch University in South Africa. Of the 410 first-year students in the 2022 class, almost 60 per cent had not done high school mathematics.[12] Of the 40 per cent who had done it, only 3 per cent (5 of the 169) achieved an A (80 per cent or above) in matric, the final year of school in South Africa. Of the whole class, then, only 1 per cent had achieved an A in mathematics in high school.

This low level of mathematics achievement in a history class is not only a matter of concern as regards our difficulty in teaching students to use quantitative tools; it affects achievement in other subjects. We have found that mathematics predicts performance in first-year history.[13]

Table 13.1 shows the first and second semester average history grades for each high-school mathematics performance category.[14] The average grade achieved by the students who entered a history course without having done mathematics in high school was 57 per cent in 2021. Those with an above 80 per cent grade in mathematics achieved an average of 77 per cent – a 20 percentage point difference. The discrepancy is even larger for the second semester, where we see a 24 percentage point difference. The finding that achievement in mathematics is so predictive of achievement in history shows that the logical thinking you learn by doing mathematics is a basic skill needed for doing well in history and supports our argument that numbers and words should be seen as complements rather than substitutes.

Much of this can be explained by a history of underinvestment in the formerly black schooling system and the inability of the post-apartheid government to improve those schools' performance.[15] In other words, the students who did poorly in history may

---

[11]Floud, *Introduction to Quantitative Methods for Historians*, 3.

[12]I include only students who wrote the NSC matriculation exams and exclude students who repeat the subject, and only students who did 'Mathematics' in high school and not 'Mathematical Literacy'. I thank Loumarie Kistner of the Unit for Information Governance at Stellenbosch University for her support in accessing these statistics.

[13]At the time of writing, grades for 2022 were not yet available.

[14]75 per cent and above is rated A in South African universities.

[15]N. Spaull, 'Poverty & Privilege: Primary School Inequality in South Africa', *International Journal of Educational Development* 33, no. 5 (2013): 436–47.

Quantitative History and Uncharted People

Table 13.1 First-year history grades by high-school mathematics grade, 2018–21.

Mathematics grade in high school	2018	2019	2020	2021
	\multicolumn{4}{c}{Grade in history 114 (first semester)}			
<60	60.1	62.5	62.2	60.0
60–69	65.7	65.1	67.7	67.9
70–79	63.4	69.6	71.0	69.4
80+	75.9	71.4	73.8	77.0
Without	57.8	56.5	60.5	57.0
Total	60.5	60.9	62.6	60.0
	\multicolumn{4}{c}{Grade in history 144 (second semester)}			
<60	59.2	55.9	57.2	56.0
60–69	63.9	60.9	63.4	61.9
70–79	65.6	60.9	60.3	61.3
80+	66.3	68.2	70.5	74.3
Without	58.1	54.2	54.4	50.1
Total	60.0	56.6	56.6	54.1
Grand total	60.2	58.9	59.6	57.0

Source: Unit for Information Governance, Stellenbosch University.

have had bad teaching generally, not only in mathematics. But history is not destiny. Indeed, Lemercier and Zalc are explicit about not mistaking quantitative history for mathematics: 'It is possible to understand quantification, learn the necessary skills, and develop an appetite for quantitative methods without being good at mathematics. We have to address math anxiety, not reinforce it.'[16]

The good news is that rapid technological advances now make it much easier to allay this anxiety. The democratisation of tools for doing transcription and analysis is now in full swing. Many tools are available for transcription. Transkribus is an AI-powered, handwritten text recognition tool, available, as the website states, 'from any place, any time, and in any language'.[17] The economist Melissa Dell offers a free deep-learning toolkit for document image analysis.[18] FamilySearch, a global repository of genealogical records operated by the Church of Jesus Christ of Latter-day Saints, has invested in OCR (optical character recognition) techniques to make its vast collection of digitised handwritten documents searchable. For printed rather than handwritten text, software

---

[16] Lemercier and Zalc, 'Back to the Sources', 484.

[17] See https://readcoop.eu/transkribus/.

[18] Z. Shen, et al., 'LayoutParser: A Unified Toolkit for Deep Learning Based Document Image Analysis', in *International Conference on Document Analysis and Recognition*, ed. Josep Lladós, Daniel Lopresti and Seiichi Uchida (Cham: Springer, 2021): 131–46.

like Adobe Acrobat Pro DC, OmniPage Ultimate or Abbyy FineReader now deliver high-quality transcriptions fast. OCR apps that are available on a smartphone, such as Google Keep, Text Fairy, CamScanner, Office Lens or OCR Quickly, do a decent job of turning archival photos into text.

Data analysis tools have also never been more accessible. Some, like the R software environment or QGIS mapping tool, are available for free. Almost all students have a Microsoft package with Excel installed on their computers. Online support services, from free YouTube tutorials to more advanced courses on DataCamp, Udemy or Stack Overflow, give even the most innumerate university student access to training options. And AI platforms, like ChatGPT, will expand access further.

Such tools are also changing the way historians work with historical records. Most software packages allow users to run code on top of a dataset. This enables researchers to transcribe the original and then standardise the information using code that captures all changes to the initially transcribed source. This improves transparency by enabling researchers to go back to earlier versions. This is very different from the first era of quantification when changes were often non-reversible.

But there is another way in which such tools will be helpful to the historian and, consequently, to the humanities and the social sciences. Historians and archivists do not have privileged access to the past; for much of the twentieth century, economists, political scientists and other social scientists expanded their reach into the historian's domain.[19] Access to new tools and online datasets has accelerated this process. The list now includes data scientists, geneticists, climatologists, linguists and scholars from other more distant fields.[20]

This is both a threat and an opportunity. It is a threat because if they fail to engage with the digital revolution historians may risk becoming irrelevant. Others have made the same point, as Ruggles does here:

> There are new historical longitudinal data sets from China, Europe, and the United States; administrative records from Norway and Sweden; and local historical censuses from across Europe. Historians can exploit vast new archives of historical GIS data from around the world, as well as climate data spanning hundreds of years. The next frontier is text: virtually the entire contents of the world's archives and libraries are being transformed into machine-readable form. We do not yet

---

[19] R. Burke and Q. Skinner, eds., *History in the Humanities and Social Sciences* (Cambridge: Cambridge University Press, 2022).

[20] This can be seen for example in new work on the history of the Bantu expansion: A. Semo, et al., 'Along the Indian Ocean Coast: Genomic Variation in Mozambique Provides New Insights into the Bantu Expansion', *Molecular Biology and Evolution* 37, no. 2 (2020): 406–16; D. Seidensticker, et al., 'Population Collapse in Congo Rainforest from 400 CE Urges Reassessment of the Bantu Expansion', *Science Advances* 7, no. 7 (2021): eabd8352; M. González-Santos, et al., 'Exploring the Relationships between Genetic, Linguistic and Geographic Distances in Bantu-speaking Populations', *American Journal of Biological Anthropology* 179, no. 1 (2022): 104–17.

really know how to capitalise on the computerisation of the entire historical record, but it is certain to involve counting at some level. *Other social sciences are already exploiting all these sources; if historians do not get on board, we will become irrelevant.*[21]

There is some evidence that the risk of irrelevance is real. Consider how students vote with their feet. In the United States, as digital historian Benjamin Schmidt notes, the number of history degrees awarded in the United States has fallen by half in the past fifteen years.[22] Schmidt shows that fewer tenure-track jobs are available in history. The only subfields to have shown an increase in job advertisements are those containing the words 'black/African American', 'methodological' (notably 'digital history') and 'interdisciplinary'.[23]

But the interest from other scholars is also an opportunity. History is, by its very nature, interdisciplinary. Historians are well placed to be facilitators and synthesizers of debates across fields. One obvious benefit is the availability of more historical evidence that is epistemologically distinct. Evidence from independent, unrelated disciplines can converge on a conclusion, a process that is termed 'consilience'. McCormick describes this as: 'a convergence in parallel but independent investigations that result in deductions that are much more robust than any investigation would be able to produce on its own'.[24] In short, a diversity of methods can lead to a better understanding of the past.

Historians' interdisciplinarity offers a further opportunity, one that few historians, at least in South Africa, have taken advantage of. It makes them uniquely positioned, as I've argued elsewhere, to tackle the big, bold research questions of our time. This is because history is one of the few disciplines that can accommodate – and actually thrive on – audacious projects. Operating at the intersections of the social sciences, and thus well positioned to tackle the big research questions about human and societal behaviour, the historian is the ideal unifier, bringing together the best of those sciences to work on major issues that affect us all.[25]

The aim of introducing history students to quantitative approaches, then, is to make their work and their skills more relevant, to expand the nature and scope of the questions they seek to answer, and to broaden the range of their interactions across the sciences and beyond the academy. The following section offers some practical ways to do this.

---

[21] S. Ruggles, 'The Revival of Quantification: Reflections on Old New Histories', *Social Science History* 45, no. 1 (2021): 21. Emphasis added.

[22] Schmidt used IPEDS data for his analysis. His results were posted on Twitter: https://twitter.com/benmschmidt/status/1562212497272279041.

[23] Schmidt reported the decline in tenure-track jobs, taken from H-net job listings, in this Twitter thread: https://twitter.com/benmschmidt/status/1564612348350005259.

[24] M. McCormick, 'History's Changing Climate: Climate Science, Genomics, and The Emerging Consilient Approach to Interdisciplinary History', *Journal of Interdisciplinary History* 42, no. 2 (2011): 251–73.

[25] J. Fourie, et al., 'Making South African Historians Count', *Historia* 66, no. 1 (2021): 4.

Moving forward: some practical steps, and some obstacles to overcome

If historians are serious about nurturing a new generation that has the gumption to borrow approaches from other disciplines, we need to consider a more organised attempt at establishing quantitative history courses within history curricula, in South Africa and elsewhere. As Lemercier and Zalc emphasise, such courses 'would ideally be part of any history curriculum – not an option for the sole use of students interested in economic (or demographic) questions, and not a course taught by non-historians'.[26]

At Stellenbosch University, as part of the Biography of an Uncharted People project, second-year tutorials in a course on 'A history of wealth and poverty' were adapted to include simple quantitative exercises, such as using Microsoft Excel to calculate and interpret means and medians or reading papers that use regression analysis. In the graduate course on 'Methodologies in History', students are introduced to a variety of quantitative techniques, such as network analysis and ordinary least square regressions.

To facilitate greater adoption of quantitative history approaches, the eleven chapters in this book and the introduction have each been turned into an undergraduate lecture with accompanying questions. The lectures, tutorials and datasets are freely available on the project website: unchartedpeople.org. This is in addition to the many other teaching materials we use, such as Lemercier and Zalc's excellent textbook.

Introducing quantitative history courses at the undergraduate and graduate level is an important first step, but it cannot be the only one. An openness to such methods is of critical importance. Sadly, students are rarely encouraged to move beyond the permit of their supervisors' interests and toolkit. Given that most history faculty at South African universities were trained in South Africa, or at least at departments within the purview of prevailing disciplinary approaches, there is little incentive to 'rock the boat'. New positions are seldom advertised to expand methodological diversity but rather to strengthen existing specialities.

There are ways to cure these habits. Innovative recruitment strategies – like encouraging dual appointments, in History and Political Science, or History and Economics, or History and Geography – could not only expose students to new approaches in the classroom but also spur interdisciplinary research collaboration across departments and faculties. Private and public donors, an increasingly important component of university funding and recruitment, could insist on funding such interdisciplinary research chairs.

It is not just history departments and their curricula that need attention. Historical societies, I believe, can help too, even if only by encouraging more interdisciplinary work in their journals. The American Historical Association has done much to encourage digital history practices, including hosting workshops during its annual conferences. More can be done to expose scholars from other parts of the world to these exciting developments.

---

[26] Lemercier and Zalc, 'Back to the Sources', 474.

Ultimately, quantitative history of the kind on display in this book relies on access to large quantities of administrative documents. These are often preserved in government archives or, more recently, in government departments. Digital access to these sources is essential if historians are to extract the full value from them. This is easier said than done. Archives are cautious about opening their sources to digitisation and transcription. The experience of the Biography project is telling. The Western Cape Archives and Records Service has an abundance of administrative records, but full digitisation of these records is not allowed. Researchers are forced to spend countless hours commuting to Cape Town, increasing the costs (and the frustrations) of research unnecessarily. Interactions with officials in government departments can be equally frustrating. This is, fortunately, not the case everywhere. Archivists and government bureaucrats who see the mutual benefits of digitisation – which allows the application of OCR techniques, for example – can make the life of the quantitative historian much easier.

One legitimate fear archivists and government bureaucrats may have, and one that has further constrained access to administrative datasets, is legislation that protects personal information. In South Africa, the Protection of Personal Information Act, promulgated in July 2020, has created concerns about personal liability if information deemed protected under the Act is provided to researchers. Many government employees are simply denying any new request for access. As a result, large administrative series could remain locked away and ultimately be lost. The decisions of university ethics committees, even if well-intentioned, can be equally pernicious. This just reinforces the need for collaboration. Historians must partner with archivists, copyright experts and OCR specialists (who may come from diverse backgrounds, including engineering, applied mathematics and computer science) to ensure that digitisation and transcription adheres to all legal requirements and that concerns about privacy are addressed.

A final hurdle for the quantitative historian is funding. Whatever the method, the digitisation and transcription of large historical administrative series are expensive. The Biography of an Uncharted People project has spent almost half its budget on transcription, making use of a team of retired librarians and historians to maintain a high level of quality. (Earlier attempts at using student transcribers were less successful.) In specific cases where the data allowed, researchers also made use of OCR techniques.

Through the Biography project, the Andrew W. Mellon Foundation has been an important partner in promoting quantitative history in South Africa. The same is true for digital history, several digitisation projects having been sponsored through a large Mellon Foundation grant to Wits University. The fear is that as these projects come to an end, the teaching and training of the new methods will wither as well. That cannot be allowed to happen.

The way to cultivate a welcoming adoption of quantitative tools is to introduce them into the classroom. We hope that this book's thirteen chapters and the additional teaching material, tutorials and test questions will encourage more departments to introduce quantitative history approaches in their undergraduate and graduate courses.

Research is ultimately the consequence of teaching. Here we fall back on the experience of Lemercier and Zalc:

> Teaching quantification also means learning from one another in class – especially when teaching is centered on the idea that any source can be quantified. A class in quantitative methods is then a great opportunity to discover diverse sources and questions and discuss their mutual adjustment. This opportunity is open not only to historians, but also to economists, quantitative sociologists, digital humanists, and anyone who routinely uses formal methods, as long as the latter are willing to learn about the constitution of data.[27]

In South Africa and elsewhere, teaching quantitative methods to history students will not only equip them with skills that are increasingly in demand in the private and public sectors, allowing them to communicate beyond their disciplinary enclave, but it will also allow them to ask new questions of the past, or find innovative ways to answer existing questions. Teaching quantitative methods should be seen as an investment in the future of history as a discipline. Those who resist it will regrettably be left behind.

Bibliography

Bogue, A. *Clio and the Bitch Goddess: Quantification in American Political History*. Beverley Hills: Sage Publications, 1983.

Burke, R. and Skinner, Q. eds. *History in the Humanities and Social Sciences*. Cambridge: Cambridge University Press, 2022.

Crymble, A. *Technology and the Historian: Transformations in the Digital Age*. Urbana: University of Illinois Press, 2021.

Dollar, C.M. and R.J. Jensen. *Historian's Guide to Statistics: Quantitative Analysis and Historical Research*. New York: Holt, Reinhart, and Winston, 1971.

Floud, R. *An Introduction to Quantitative Methods for Historians*. London: Methuen, 1979.

Fourie, J., F. Ballim, G. Groenewald, J. Upton, T. Nyamunda and J. Parle. 'Making South African Historians Count'. *Historia* 66, no. 1 (2021): 2–38.

González-Santos, M., F. Montinaro, R. Grollemund, D. Marnetto, M. Atadzhanov, C.A. May and N. Mabunda. 'Exploring the Relationships between Genetic, Linguistic and Geographic Distances in Bantu-speaking Populations'. *American Journal of Biological Anthropology* 179, no. 1 (2022): 104–17.

Haskins, P. and K. Jeffrey. *Understanding Quantitative History*. Cambridge, US: MIT Press, 1990.

Hudson, P. *History by Numbers: An Introduction to Quantitative Approaches*. London: Bloomsbury, 2000.

Lemercier, C. and C. Zalc. *Quantitative Methods in the Humanities: An Introduction*. Charlottesville: University of Virginia Press, 2019.

Lemercier, C. and C. Zalc. 'Back to the Sources: Practicing and Teaching Quantification History in the 2020s'. *Capitalism: A Journal of History and Economics* 2, no. 2 (2021): 473–508.

---

[27]Ibid, 503.

McCormick, M. 'History's Changing Climate: Climate Science, Genomics, and the Emerging Consilient Approach to Interdisciplinary History'. *Journal of Interdisciplinary History* 42, no. 2 (2011): 251–73.

Ruggles, S. 'The Revival of Quantification: Reflections on Old New Histories'. *Social Science History* 45, no. 1 (2021): 1–25.

Seidensticker, D., W. Hubau, D. Vershuren, C.F. Lima, P. de Maret, C.M. Schlebusch and K. Bostoen. 'Population Collapse in Congo Rainforest from 400 CE Urges Reassessment of the Bantu Expansion'. *Science Advances* 7, no. 7 (2021): eabd8352.

Semo, A., M.G. Vidal, C.F. Lima, B. Alard, S. Oliveira, J. Almeida and A. Prista, 'Along the Indian Ocean Coast: Genomic Variation in Mozambique Provides New Insights into the Bantu Expansion'. *Molecular Biology and Evolution* 37, no. 2 (2020): 406–16.

Shen, Z., R. Zhang, M. Dell, B.C.G. Lee, J. Carlson and W. Li. 'Layout Parser: A Unified Toolkit for Deep Learning Based on Document Image Analysis'. In *International Conference on Document Analysis and Recognition*, 131–46. Cham: Springer, 2021.

Spaull, N. 'Poverty & Privilege: Primary School Inequality in South Africa'. *International Journal of Educational Development* 33, no. 5 (2013): 436–47.

INDEX

abantsundu (black people) 266, 268–9, 271–3, 280–1
abantu basesikolweni (school people) organisations 249, 265–6, 273, 275, 280–2
Abstracts 295–6, 295 n.38, 300–1
Acuña-Soto, R. 330–4, 337, 344
advertisements 139–41, 145–6, 163–4, 167
  Cape Times 133, 176, 178
  characteristics 157–60, 167–8
  De Zuid-Afrikaan (newspaper) 27, 139, 141–54, 143 n.20, 156–8, 162–4, 167
  slave-specific sale 146, 149–51, 154–8, 160, 163, 167–8
  trends 146–54
Afrikaner Bond 271, 290, 293, 297, 300, 308–9, 313–14
Alrick, J. 176
Ambler, C. 312
Anderson, S. 82
Andrew W. Mellon Foundation 25, 360
Anglican Church 16, 33, 38–9, 42 n.36
Anglican marriage registers 24, 117, 119, 124–9, 132, 135–6
An Introduction to Quantitative Methods for Historians (Floud) 353
Annales school 2, 9
appearance 120–3
Arthi, V. 326
artisanal quantification 8, 119

Bank, A. 148, 150–1, 159
baptism 16, 25–6, 33, 39–40, 42, 50–1, 55, 60, 62
Basque family system 94
Batson, E. 170, 228–32, 243–5
  earnings and occupations 239–41
  living costs 241–2
Batson Household Survey 171, 177–8, 180, 183, 185, 188, 190–1, 227, 232, 234–5, 238–40, 244
Bauman, Z. 12
Becker, G. S. 99
Beinart, W. 253, 274
Berger, I. 174, 178–80, 184, 189 n.88
Bickford-Smith, V. 185
Bigsten, A. 95
Biography project 11, 353, 360
Births and Deaths Registration Act 322

black Africans 219–21
  history 221–8
  population 222, 226–7, 229, 244
  resident 225–6
  sex ratios 225 n.36
black population 68, 81, 85–6, 220, 222, 227, 234, 338
Blondel, V. D. 260, 260 n.31
Boddington, E. 188
Bolt, J. 95
Boniface, C. E. 141, 146, 163
Botha, W. C. 156, 156 n.61
Bowker, G. C. 118, 123
Bowley, A. L. 229
Bradlow, E. 304, 311
Braudel, F. 3
Breckenridge, K. 15–16
Brettell, C. B. 105
bridal pregnancy 16, 26, 33, 35–6, 39–42, 44–56, 61–2
brideprice 80, 82–3, 86
British Women's Emigration Society (BWES) 202
Bundy, C. 253, 274
Burke, J. L. 292
Burke, P. 2
Burman, S. 36, 43, 45
Burns, C. 34
Butterworth 236, 263

The Cambridge Group for the History of Population and Social Structure 4
Cape Colony 13, 16–18, 23, 27, 60, 63–8, 71, 91, 95–6, 98–9, 101, 139, 141, 157, 163, 196, 201, 206, 249, 256, 264, 272, 297, 306
Cape of Good Hope Literary Gazette 141 n.11
Cape population 71, 74, 76, 85, 146
Cape Province 16–18, 63, 66–8, 71, 317, 319–20, 324, 344
Cape slavery 18
capital value 199, 208–9, 213, 218
Carnegie Corporation 170 n.10
Carr, E. H. 12
Carstens, P. 99
child mortality 237, 322, 340–44
child-rearing strategies 201, 237–8
Chowell, G. 330–4, 337, 344
Christopher, A. J. 285 n.2

Index

Cilliers, J. 24
Civilised Labour Policy (1920s) 226–7
Clark, S. 84
cleavages 260–5
Clemens, E. S. 255–6
cliometricians 3, 18
Cock, J. 172–3, 175
Coleman, A. J. 212
Colonial Marine Assurance and Trust Company 213
coloured households 125, 177, 181, 183–4, 188–91, 319
Coloured Joint Council 45
Commission of Native Location (1901) 227
community acceptance 120–4, 131–2
community detection 260–2
Conrad, A. H. 2
consilience 358
conventional pregnancy 44
Covid-19 pandemic 318–19, 345, 350
    in Cradock and Paarl 327–31
    death certificates and data extraction 320–5
    government response 345–50
    mortality in South Africa 318–19
    number of deaths 325–37
    respiratory illnesses 337–9, 345, 350
Crush, C. 312
Crymble, A. 8, 354

death certificates 317–26, 329, 337, 341–3, 345, 350
dehumanising 14
de Jager, A. W. J. 134
De Kadt, D. 325
Dell, M. 356
Derrida, J. 5
Die Huisvrou (The Housewife, women's magazine) 185, 185 n.59
Digital History (Cohen and Rosenzweig) 354
Dimitruk, K. 17, 303
discrimination 11, 15, 45, 51, 63–4, 70, 83–4
District Six 39, 42, 52, 174, 174 n.28
Dock Native Location 225
Dollar, C. M. 353
domestic servants 171–5
domestic service 170–4, 188–90, 219
domestic trade 144–5, 149, 163
domestic work 26, 169–70, 172–3, 175–6, 181, 186–7, 189, 191, 195, 242
Dönges, E. 120
Dooling, W. 151
dop system 286–7, 304
drunkenness 287, 308, 312–13
Dunstun, M. 134
Du Plessis, Sophia 17, 207

Du Plessis, Stan 17
Dutch Reformed Church 16–17, 38, 55, 311
Dwane, J. 277

economic history 2–4, 23–5, 27, 92
economic petitions 297
ego-documents 55
Eichengreen, B. 3, 318
Ekama, K. 25
Electricity Supply Commission 176
Elliott, K. 177, 334
Ellison, G. T. H. 118–19
Elphick, R. 18
Emigrant Thembuland Native Association (ETNAS) 264
Engerman, S. 3
Erasmus, Y. 118–19
Erlank, N. 203, 209–10
Esterhuyze, J. C. 146
Ethiopian Benefit society (EBS) 263
Evans, R. J. 11

Farley, R. 94
female investors 196–7, 206–7, 209
Female Middle-Class Society (FMCS) 202
Findlay, J. 99
First World War 24, 226, 319
Floud, R. 6–7, 353
Fogel, R. 2–3
ForceAtlas 2 257 n.27
Foucault, M. 5, 14
Fourie, J. 24–5, 95
frérèche 94
Fruchterman, T. M. J. 257 n.27

Gaitskell, D. 175
Geard, J. 267
gendered roles 199–202
general sale with slaves 167
geographic information systems (GIS) 8, 357
German South West Africa (GSWA) 226
Giliomee, H. 18
Goldberg, D. 132
Government Gazette 142
Great Depression 228
Great Recession 318
Group Areas Act 131

Hammel, E. A. 105
Healdtown 260 n.34
Heese, H. 18
Hetherington, P. 175, 175 n.36
Hicken, M. J. 293
hierarchical clustering 260 n.33
Hillbom, E. 95

Index

Hindus, M. 54
Historia 19–21
Historian's Guide to Statistics (Dollar and Jensen) 353
Hoernlé, A. W. 99
Horrell, M. 136
household. *See* Khoe household
House of Assembly 120, 279, 285, 289–91, 294, 294 n.36, 295, 303
human nature 12
Huzzey, R. 288

Imbumba Yama Nyama 250, 252, 260, 263, 266, 270–3, 281
immigration 149, 172, 294, 297, 347
Imperial Colonist 201, 205
Imvo Zabantsundu (black Opinion) 251–2, 267
Independent Order of Good Templars 266–8, 311
Independent Order of True Templars (IOTT) 250, 252, 263, 266–9, 267 n.53, 281
Industrial Colour Bar (1956) 130
infant mortality 64, 81, 84, 340–44, 343 n.29
Influenza Epidemic Commission 317, 319, 325, 337–8
influenza mortality 317, 344–6
Ingalls, W. 82–3
Innes Bill 304, 311–12
Innes, J. R. 304, 310
Innes Liquor Bill 311
Intlanganiso Ye Nqubelo Pambili Yama Ngqika (Intla_Ngqika) 265
Inwood, K. 24
Isigidimi sama-Xosa (The Xhosa Messenger) 251–2, 260, 262, 270
isiXhosa 221, 257, 262, 272
isizwe organisations 250, 262, 265–6, 268–9, 273–5, 278, 280–2

Jansen, E. 169, 173 n.20, 254
Jaro-Winkler string distance 60, 60 n.68
Jenkins, K. 10
Jensen, A. 207
Jensen, R. J. 353
Job Reservation Act of 1957 130
Jordaan, G. 292
Joubert, G. J. 146
Journal of African History (JAH) 20–1
Journal of Southern African Studies (JSAS) 20–1

Kamada, T. 257 n.27
KaNgwane, B. 13
Kawai, S. 257 n.27
Kayers, H. 267
Khoe household 91–112
Kimberley mines 79, 209, 219, 310–11, 325

kin-dependency 211–13
Klasen, S. 83
Kok, J. 35
Kuznets, S. 91–2

labour
  demands 151, 226–7, 303
  law 286–8, 290–1, 294–5, 297, 300–5
  market 37, 71, 94, 136, 149, 153, 224, 245, 308
  petitions 305–9
  reliability 287, 314
  reserve 223, 223 n.13
  and the temperance movement 294–5
Labrousse, E. 2
Ladies Benevolent Society 203, 210
land-to-labour ratio 64, 80
Laslett, P. 7, 105
law-making process 301–4
Leewner, J. C. 146
Legislative Council 289, 291, 294 n.36
Lemercier, C. 5, 9, 119, 354, 356, 359, 361
Lemon, K. 293
Levi, G. 9
liquor licensing 295 n.37
Liquor Licensing Act (1883) 304
Liza Goxo, death certificate of 320–4
Louw, J. 186

Mafeking 324, 338, 347, 350
Magnuson, D. L. 4, 22–3
Maids and Madams (Cock) 175
Making History Count (Feinstein and Thomas) 354
Manyano nge Mvo Zabantsundu 265
Marco-Gracia, F. 25
Mariotti, M. 24
Markel, H. 347
marriage 4, 7, 9, 16, 24–6, 33, 35, 38–9, 41–7, 51–6, 60–1, 74, 76, 80, 82–3, 86, 92, 109, 117, 119, 124–9, 135–6, 207–8, 235–8
Martin, D. 119
Mason, J. E. 144, 149
Masters and Servants law 301, 303–4, 306, 308–9, 314
mathematics grade 355–6
McCormick, M. 358
Meyer, J. R. 2
migration 232
  histories 233–4
  marriage and 235–7
  strategies 235–7
Miller, H. 288
Mills, W. G. 253
Mitchell, L. J. 140
Morgan, E. S. 208
mortality
  excess 63, 69, 71, 86, 319–20, 328–39, 350

365

Index

infant and child 64, 74, 81, 84, 86, 237, 322, 340–44
influenza and pneumonia 317, 344–6
on SAMRC method 330–1
in South Africa 318–19, 324
Morton, B. 105–6
Mostert, C. A. 292
Mpeta, B. 24
Mzimba, P. 268, 277

Native Economic Commission (1930–2) 227
Native Educational Association (NEA) 259–60, 263, 270, 275
native locations 303–4, 303 n.40
Native Recruiting Corporation (NRC) 223–4
Natives Law Amendment Act (1937) 228
Natives Urban Area Act (1923) 227
Naude, M. 36, 43
Ndabeni 225–7, 244
Neethling, M. C. A. 156–7, 159
network analysis 249–52, 256–60
Niger-Congo group 80–2, 85
non-pharmaceutical intervention (NPI) 347–8
North, D. C. 2
nuclear family 93, 237
Nugent, P. 311
numeracy 74
Nyika, F. 24

Oakley, A. 176
Odendaal, A. 250–3, 271, 275–6
Omotoso, K. 133
opgaafrolle 17, 25, 98
optical character recognition (OCR) 8, 356–7, 360

Padgett, J. F. 255–6
pandemic mortality 318–19, 325, 333, 339, 341–6, 343 n.29, 350. *See also* Covid-19 pandemic
Parman, J. 326
Paulse, M. 53 n.59
The People's Lobby (Clemens) 255
petitioners
  characteristics 293–4
  organisation and motivation 304–13
  types 300–1
petitions/petitioning 277, 288–90, 294, 303, 305, 309, 311
  geography of 294
  labour and temperance bills and 294–5, 304
  and law making 301–4
  personal 297
  time and geography 297–300
  types 292, 295–301
Phillips, H. 317–19, 322, 325, 337–8, 346
Piketty, T. 109–10

pneumonia 337
pneumonia mortality 344–6
policymakers 318, 350
political communities 265–6, 269, 272, 280
political innovation 266–74, 279, 281–2
population growth 36, 38, 332
Population Registration Act 16, 39 n.35, 117–18, 120–1, 127
Port Elizabeth 219, 239, 263, 266, 272, 286, 291, 297, 310, 347
Posel, D. 118–19
Potgieter, M. J. 308
Poverty Datum Line 229 n.58
Powell, W. W. 255–6
pregnancy 33, 35–6, 39, 41–56, 61–2, 78–9
Proceedings on Bills 290, 294, 294 n.36
Prohibition of Mixed Marriages Act (1949) 127
Protection of Personal Information Act 360
proto-nationalist movement 251, 275
proto-nationalist politics 256–7
public sphere 197, 200, 202–4, 211, 215, 263, 270

quantification 3–9, 14–15, 18–19, 21–3, 119, 350, 354, 356–8, 361
quantitative history 353–61
  rise of 2–6
  in South Africa 15–25
Quantitative Methods in the Humanities (Lemercier and Zalc) 354
quantitative techniques 2, 23, 117, 171, 249, 353–9

Rabe, L. 142 n.14
racial
  classification and reclassification 120–4, 129–32
  discrimination 11, 45, 51
Rand Daily Mail 121–2, 127–9, 134
random forest model 60
Reay, B. 61 n.70
record linkage 60, 60 n.68
Reddy, T. 121
regression 22, 22 n.78, 46–50, 61–2, 72–7, 334–6
  Ordinary Least Squares (OLS) 71–3, 75–6, 108–9
Reingold, E. M. 257 n.27
remarriage 46
remittances 238–9
repertoire syncretisation and transposition 249–50, 255–6, 266–75, 279, 281
Rettaroli, R. 78
Rive, R. 39, 133–4
Robinson, J. H. 3
Romano, S. 37 n.25
Rosenberg, A. 12
Rosenthal, C. 8
Ross, R. 18, 153 n.48
Ruggles, S. 4, 6, 22–3, 357

Index

Sampson, A. 133
Scab Acts 297, 297 n.39, 300
Scalone, F. 78
Schlesinger, A. Jr. 7–8
Schmidt, B. 358
screeching 185
Second World War 6, 24, 169–70, 172, 176–91, 228
Sellars, E. 14–15
Sen, A. 63
Serfling, R. E. 333
service hiring requests 146, 151, 153, 167–8
sex ratios 25, 63–72, 74–83, 85–6, 234
Shell, R. 18, 140, 149–50
Sihlali, S. P. 270
Simiand, F. 2
simple linear regression 71, 77, 332
Skinner, G. W. 92–3
Slabbert, F. v. Z. 135
Smith, D. S. 54
Smith-Rosenberg, C. 210
social connections 256, 259–65
social distance 257
social history 2, 4, 10, 27
Social Science History Association 4
Social Surveys of Cape Town 228–32, 228 n.57
Soos Familie (Jansen) 169
South African Colonisation Society (SACS) 202
South African Commercial Advertiser 141 n.11, 142–3, 143 n.17, 145, 163–4
South African Historical Journal (SAHJ) 21
South African Medical Research Council (SAMRC) 329, 331, 334, 337
South African Native Association (SANA) 263, 275
South African War 36, 198, 201, 204, 224, 226
Spanish flu 15–16, 26, 317–18, 326–7, 337, 346–7, 350
Star, S. L. 118, 123
Stoler, A. L. 13
Stone, L. 5
sub-Saharan Africa 63–4, 68–71, 80, 82, 84, 86
Sunday baptism 50–1, 62
Suzman, A. 118
Swellendam 96–7. *See also* Khoe household
Swidler, A. 256

Taylor, J. E. 141, 163
Technology and the Historian (Crymble) 354
temperance movement 268–9, 272, 277, 286–7, 290, 294–5, 304, 312–13
temperance petitions 287, 294–5, 300, 303–5, 309–14
Thembu Association 250, 252, 263–4, 266, 269, 275–82
Thompson, E. P. 5, 10
Transkei 220, 223, 226, 262–5, 273–4, 280, 282

Transkei Mutual Improvement Association (TMIA) 263
Transkei Teachers Association (TTA) 263
transposition and refunctionality (Padgett and Powell) 255
Transvaal mines 219–20, 223–5, 225 n.34, 226, 234–5, 239, 243–5, 319

Umanyano nge Mfundo. See Native Educational Association (NEA)

Valentine, S. 132–5
Van Bavel, J. 42
Van der Spuy, P. 45
Van der Walt, R. 134–5
Van Duin, P. 18
Van Onselen, C. 19, 178
Van Sittert, L. 308
Van Wyk, J. W. A. 122–3
Vereenigde Oostindische Compagnie (VOC) 17–18
Viboud, C. 330–4, 337, 344
Viljoen, R. 97–8, 101
Visser, A. G. 173
Von Fintel, D. 95, 207
Votes and Proceedings 290 n.24

Ward, G. G. 310
Watson, G. 123
Watson, R. 143 n.17
Wauchope, I. W. 269–70, 277
Weekend Argus 135
Western Cape Archives and Records Services (WCARS) 98, 198, 290 n.24, 295
The White Cross League 38
white households 26, 171, 175, 177–84, 188, 190–1
Williams, W. M. 35
Witwatersrand Native Labour Association (WNLA) 223–4
Wodehouse, P. 278, 306
women 51, 169
    capital value 208–9, 213, 218
    financial contribution of 215
    investors 197–9, 204–16, 218
Women's Christian Temperance Union (WCTU) 290, 311
Women's Property Acts 197, 206
Worden, N. 18
Wright, R. E. 99

Yanagisako, S. J. 105

Zaeske, S. 293
Zalc, C. 5, 9, 119, 354, 356, 359, 361
Zuid-Afrikaan. See advertisements, *De Zuid-Afrikaan* (newspaper)

www.ingramcontent.com/pod-product-compliance
Ingram Content Group UK Ltd.
Pitfield, Milton Keynes, MK11 3LW, UK
UKHW020132240225
455489UK00004B/38